BRITISH DOCUMENTS ON THE END OF EMPIRE

General Editor S R Ashton
Project Chairman D A Low

Series B Volume 3

Malaya

Editor
A J STOCKWELL

Part III
THE ALLIANCE ROUTE
TO INDEPENDENCE
1953–1957

Published for the Institute of Commonwealth Studies
in the University of London

LONDON : HMSO

ISBN 0 11 290542 0

British Library Cataloguing in Publication Data

A CIP catalogue record for this book
is available from the British Library

Write to PC11C, Standing Order Service, HMSO Books, PO Box 276,
LONDON SW8 5DT quoting classification reference 040 30 017 to
order future volumes from the British Documents on the End of
Empire project.

Published by HMSO and available from:

HMSO Publications Centre
(Mail, fax and telephone orders only)
PO Box 276, London, SW8 5DT
Telephone orders 0171 873 9090
General enquiries 0171 873 0011
(queuing system in operation for both numbers)
Fax orders 0171 873 8200

HMSO Bookshops
49 High Holborn, London, WC1V 6HB
(counter service only)
0171 873 0011   Fax 0171 831 1326
68–69 Bull Street, Birmingham, B4 6AD
0121 236 9696   Fax 0121 236 9699
33 Wine Street, Bristol, BS1 2BQ
0117 9264306   Fax 0117 9294515
9–21 Princess Street, Manchester, M60 8AS
0161 834 7201   Fax 0161 833 0634
16 Arthur Street, Belfast, BT1 4GD
01232 238451   Fax 01232 235401
71 Lothian Road, Edinburgh, EH3 9AZ
0131 228 4181   Fax 0131 229 2734
The HMSO Oriel Bookshop
The Friary, Cardiff CF1 4AA
01222 395548   Fax 01222 384347

HMSO's Accredited Agents
(see Yellow Pages)

and through good booksellers

Printed in the United Kingdom by HMSO
Dd299903   C7   7/95

Contents

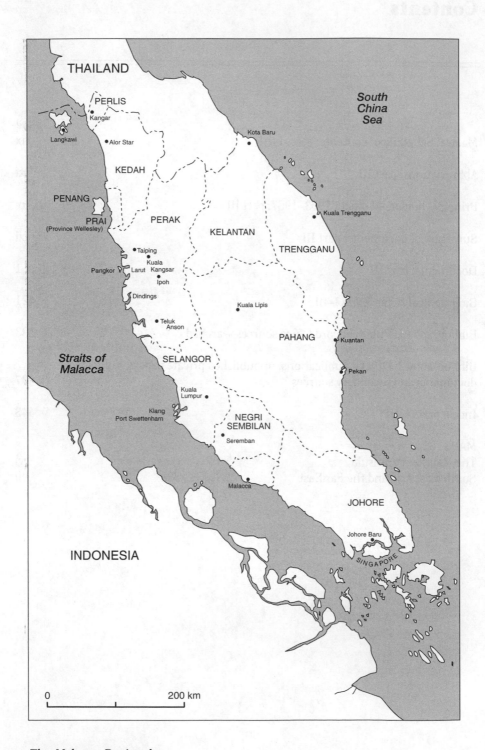

The Malayan Peninsula

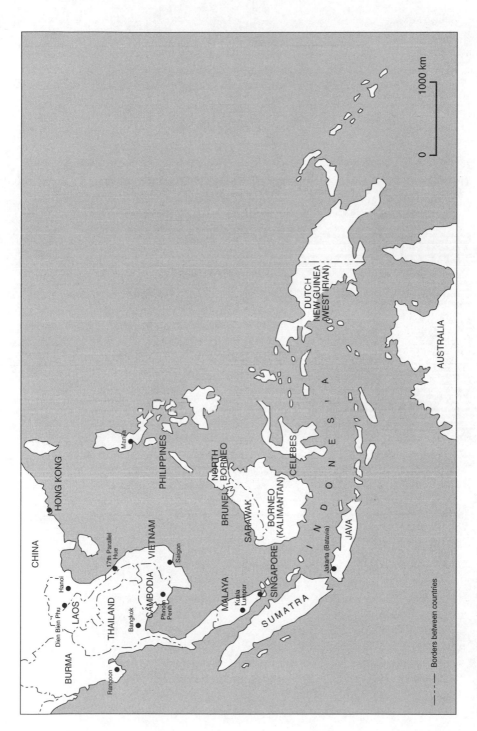

South-East Asia and the Far East

Malaya

Schedule of Contents: Parts I–III

Abbreviations: Part III

ADO	assistant district officer
AEI	Associated Electrical Industries
AMCJA	All Malayan Council of Joint Action
ANZAM	Australia, New Zealand and Malaya
AOC	air officer commanding
BBC	British Broadcasting Corporation
BDCC(FE)	British Defence Co-ordinating Committee (Far East)
BDEEP	British Documents on the End of Empire Project
BMA	British Military Administration
CAB	Cabinet
CH	Companion of Honour
CIGS	chief of the imperial general staff
CMG	Companion of the Order of St Michael and St George
CO	Colonial Office
Comm-gen	commissioner-general
Con	Conservative (Party)
COS	Chiefs of Staff
CPC	Colonial Policy Committee
CPO	chief police officer
CRO	Commonwealth Relations Office
Dept	Department
DO	Dominions Office
ECAFE	Economic Commission for Asia and the Far East
FCO	Foreign and Commonwealth Office
FEAF	Far Eastern Air Force
FMS	Federated Malay States
FO	Foreign Office

GCVO	Grand Cross of the Royal Victorian Order
GHQ	general headquarters
GOC	general officer commanding
GOC-in-C	general officer commanding in chief
gov	governor
gov-gen	governor-general
HH	His Highness
HMG	Her Majesty's Government
HMOCS	Her Majesty's Oversea Civil Service
H of C Debs	House of Commons Debates
H of L Debs	House of Lords Debates
IBRD	International Bank for Reconstruction and Development (World Bank)
IF	Imperial and Foreign (Division, Treasury)
IMP	Independence of Malaya Party
IRA	Irish Republican Army
JCC	Joint Co-ordination Committee
KBE	Knight Commander Order of the British Empire
KCB	Knight Commander of the Bath
KCIE	Knight Commander of the Order of the Indian Empire
KCMG	Knight Commander of the Order of St Michael and St George
KG	Knight of the Order of the Garter
KL	Kuala Lumpur
KMT	Kuomintang
Kt	Knighthood
Lab	Labour (Party)
MAS	Malay Administrative Service
MCA	Malayan Chinese Association
MCP	Malayan Communist Party
MCS	Malayan Civil Service
memo	memorandum
MIC	Malayan Indian Congress
MNLA	Malay National Liberation Army

MNP	Malay Nationalist Party
MP	member of parliament
MPAJA	Malayan Peoples' Anti-Japanese Army
MPU	Malayan Planning Unit
MRLA	Malayan Races' Liberation Army
MTUC	Malayan Trades Union Congress
NATO	North Atlantic Treaty Organisation
OAG	officer administering the government
OCF	Overseas Commonwealth Forces
OCPD	officer commanding police district
PM	prime minister
PMIP	Pan-Malayan Islamic Party
PUTERA	Pusat Tenaga Raayat (lit. centre of people's strength: Malay movement for justice)
RAF	Royal Air Force
RN	Royal Navy
RPC	Rubber Producers' Council
SACSEA	Supreme Allied Command(er) South-East Asia
SCA	senior civil affairs (officer)/secretary for Chinese affairs
SEATO	South-East Asia Treaty Organisation
S of S	secretary of state
SUNFED	Special United Nations Fund for Economic Development
TECSAM	The European Civil Servants' Association of Malaya
Tel	telegram
UK	United Kingdom
UMNO	United Malays National Organisation
UPAM	United Planters' Association of Malaya
UN(O)	United Nations (Organisation)
US(A)	United States (of America)

Principal Holders of Offices 1953–1957: Part III

UNITED KINGDOM

1. *Ministers*

(a) *Conservative governments (Sept 1953 to Aug 1957)*[1]

Prime minister	Sir Winston Churchill (26 Oct 1951) Sir Anthony Eden (6 Apr 1955) Mr M H Macmillan (13 Jan 1957)
S of S colonies	Mr O Lyttelton (28 Oct 1951) Mr A T Lennox-Boyd (28 July 1954)
Chancellor of Exchequer	Mr R A Butler (28 Oct 1951) Mr M H Macmillan (20 Dec 1955) Mr P Thorneycroft (13 Jan 1957)
S of S foreign affairs	Mr R A Eden (KG 20 Oct 1954) (28 Oct 1951) Mr M H Macmillan (7 Apr 1955) Mr J Selwyn Lloyd (20 Dec 1955)
Lord president of the Council	Marquess of Salisbury (24 Nov 1952) Earl of Home (29 Mar 1957)
Minister of defence	Earl Alexander (1 Mar 1952) Mr M H Macmillan (18 Oct 1954) Mr J Selwyn Lloyd (7 Apr 1955) Sir Walter Monckton (20 Dec 1955) Mr A H Head (18 Oct 1956) Mr D E Duncan-Sandys (13 Jan 1957)
S of S Commonwealth relations	Viscount Swinton (24 Nov 1952) Earl of Home (7 Apr 1955)

---

[1] Of the junior ministers mentioned in part III of this volume, the Marquess of Reading was parliamentary under-secretary of state, FO (31 Oct 1951 – 11 Nov 1953), and minister of state (11 Nov 1953 – 17 Jan 1957); Mr J D Profumo was parliamentary under-secretary of state, CO (19 Jan 1957 – 1 Dec 1958).

(b) *Cabinet Committees*

Colonial Policy Committee

The Committee sat from Oct 1955. Prime minister (chair), S of S Colonies, S of S foreign affairs, S of S Commonwealth relations, minister of defence.

2. *Civil servants*

(a) *Secretary to the Cabinet*   Sir Norman Brook (1947–1962)

(b) *Colonial Office*

Permanent under-secretary of state	Sir Thomas Lloyd (1947–1956) Sir John Macpherson (1956–1959)
Deputy under-secretary of state	Sir Charles Jeffries (1947–1956) ⎱ joint Sir Hilton Poynton (1948–1959) ⎰ Sir John Martin (1956–1965) ⎱ joint
Assistant under-secretary of state, with superintending responsibility for South-East Asian Department, Far Eastern Department from 1954	J J Paskin (1948–1954) Sir John Martin (1954–1956) E Melville (1956–1957)
Assistant secretary, head of South-East Asian Department, Far Eastern Department from 1954	J D Higham (1948–1953) A M MacKintosh (1953–1956) J B Johnston (1956–1957)

(c) *Foreign Office*

Permanent under-secretary of state	Sir William Strang (1949–1953) Sir Ivone Kirkpatrick (1953–1957)

(d) *Defence*

Permanent under-secretary of state	Sir Harold Parker (1948–1956) Sir Richard Powell (1956–1960)

SOUTH-EAST ASIA

British territories in South-East Asia

Commissioner-general	Mr M J MacDonald (1948–1955) Sir Robert Scott (1955–1959)

MALAYA

(a) *Federation of Malaya*

High commissioner	Sir Gerald Templer (7 Feb 1952) Sir David MacGillivray (31 May 1954)

Deputy high commissioner	Sir David MacGillivray (1952–1954)
Chief secretary and officer administering the government	(Sir) David Watherston (1952–1957)

(b) *Federal Executive Council (from Aug 1955)*

(i) *Appointments in order of precedence after the 1955 elections*

President	Sir David MacGillivray
Chief minister and minister for home affairs	Tunku Abdul Rahman
Chief secretary	Sir David Watherston
Minister for transport	Col H S Lee
Attorney-general	J P Hogan
Financial secretary	E Himsworth
Minister for natural resources	Dr Ismail bin Dato Abdul Rahman
Minister for economic affairs	O A Spencer
Secretary for defence	A H P Humphrey
Minister for education	Dato Abdul Razak bin Hussein
Minister for health and social welfare	Leong Yow Koh
Minister for labour	V T Sambanthan
Minister for local government, housing and town planning	Suleiman bin Dato Abdul Rahman
Minister for agriculture	Abdul Aziz bin Ishak
Minister for works	Sardon bin Haji Jubir
Minister for posts and telecommunications	Ong Yoke Lin

(ii) *Appointments on the eve of independence in 1957*

President	Sir David MacGillivray

Chief minister, minister for home affairs and minister for internal defence and security	Tunku Abdul Rahman
Chief secretary	Sir David Watherston
Minister of finance	Col H S Lee
Attorney-general	T V A Brodie
Minister for commerce and industry	Dr Ismail bin Dato Abdul Rahman
Minister for education	Dato Abdul Razak bin Hussein
Minister for health and social welfare	Leong Yew Koh
Minister for labour	V T Sambanthan
Minister for natural resources and local government	Suleiman bin Dato Abdul Rahman
Minister for agriculture	Abdul Aziz bin Ishak
Minister for works, posts and telecommunications	Sardon bin Haji Jubir
Minister for transport	Ong Yoke Lin

(c) *Rulers of Malay States*[2]

Johore	HH Ibrahim (1873–1959) Accession 7 Sept 1895
Pahang	HH Abu Bakar (1904–1974) Accession 23 June 1932
Negri Sembilan	HH Abdul Rahman (1895–1959) Accession 3 Aug 1933
Selangor	HH Alam Shah (1898–1960) Accession 4 Apr 1938
Perak	HH Yussuf (1890–1963) Accession 31 Mar 1948

---

[2] Rulers are listed in order of seniority, not with their full titles but with the name by which they are normally referred to.

Kedah   HH Badlishah (1894–1958)
                                       Accession 15 May 1943 (position
                                       confirmed by British in 1945)

Perlis   HH Syed Putra (b 1920)
                                       Accession 4 Dec 1945

Kelantan   HH Ibrahim (1897–1960)
                                       Accession 21 June 1944 (position
                                       confirmed by British in 1945)

Trengganu   HH Ismail (b 1907)
                                       Accession 16 Dec 1945

SINGAPORE

Governor   (Sir) John Nicoll (21 Apr 1952)
                                       Sir Robert Black (30 June 1955)

Chief minister   Mr D S Marshall (Apr 1955)
                                       Lim Yew Hock (June 1956)

Colonial secretary, chief   W L Blythe (1950–1953)
   secretary from 1955   W A C Goode (1953–1957)

Summary of Documents: Part III

Chapter 9
Planning federal elections, Sept 1953 – July 1954

Chapter 10
Taking stock: regional security, Malayanisation
and the first MCP peace offer, July 1954 – July 1955

Chapter 11
Alliance ascendancy: electoral victory and Baling talks, July–Dec 1955

Chapter 12
The London conference and the Reid Commission,
Jan 1956 – Feb 1957

Chapter 13
Achievement of independence within the Commonwealth, Feb–Aug 1957

304 CO 1022/86, no 66   28 Sept 1953
[Member system]: inward telegram no 990 from Sir G Templer to Mr
Lyttelton on the appointment of members from UMNO and MCA

As you are aware, there has been greatly increased political activity during the last
two months, and UMNO-M.C.A. alliance has shown its strength in the country by
winning seats at local council elections as far apart as Alor Star and Seremban.[1]
There has been a recent re-affirmation at UMNO annual conference of the Alliance's
demand for elections to the Legislative Council in 1954.[2] There is reason to believe,
however, that the Alliance would not in any case expect elections to take place before
the very end of 1954 at the earliest and in certain circumstances, if it could be done
without losing face, might even be prepared to relegate the demand to a less
prominent place in their political programme.

2. I have been increasingly conscious of the fact, both in the Executive Council
and in the Legislative Council that no members of the Government belong to either
branch of the Election Alliance and that Alliance is under-represented in the
Legislative Council. I have decided therefore that the time is ripe to appoint as
Members of the Government one of the leaders of UMNO and one of the leaders of
M.C.A. This can be done without amendment of the Federation Agreement by:—

(a) Creating new appointment of Member for Local Government, Housing and
Town Planning. This has been contemplated for some time. Seat amongst
Government Members on the Legislative Council can be found by not appointing
Acting Secretary for Chinese Affairs to the Council while Gray[3] is acting as Chief
Secretary.
(b) Discontinuing arrangement under which General Manager of Railways also
carries out duties of Member for Railways and Ports. Sanders[4] is prepared to
relinquish the latter appointment to an Asian and to stay on as General Manager of
Railways for another six months before retirement.

3. As these proposals might have produced serious reactions among IMP
Committee of National Conference Group, I discussed them with Onn before
approaching any member of the Alliance, and he expressed himself as completely in
agreement. He was also ready to relinquish Local Government to the new member
from his Portfolio as Member for Home Affairs.

4. I have now invited H.S. Lee to be a Member and he has accepted. Tunku Abdul
Rahman prefers not to accept himself and, with his agreement, I have invited Dr.
Ismail, who possesses more administrative ability. He too has accepted.

5. Following rearranged portfolios are involved and will take effect from 1st
November:—

---

[1] Established as an *ad hoc* pact to defeat the IMP in the Kuala Lumpur municipal elections in Feb 1952,
the Alliance, despite severe tensions between UMNO and MCA, went on to contest further local and
municipal elections later in 1952, in 1953, and in every succeeding year to independence.
[2] At UMNO's general assembly at Alor Star (Kedah) in Sept.
[3] D Gray joined the MCS in 1930, became secretary for Chinese affairs in 1951 and was acting chief
secretary of the Federation on occasions thereafter.
[4] J Sanders worked in FMS railways before the war, became general manager of Malayan railways in 1946
and was member for railways and ports, 1951–1953.

(a) Dato Nik Kamil to move from Lands, Mines and Communications to new Portofolio of Local Government Housing and Town Planning;
(b) Dr. Ismail to take over Nik Kamil's present Portfolio;
(c) Lee to take over Railways and Ports.
(d) Carey loses Housing and Town Planning but remains Member for Works.

I intend to inform the Executive Council of the new appointments on 29th September and to issue press communiqué (see my immediately following telegram) in time for morning papers on 1st October.
6. Only changes involved in the Executive Council will be:—

(a) Dr. Ismail will be appointed an Official Member. A vacant seat is available.
(b) H.S. Lee will remain on the Council as an Official instead of an Unofficial Member.

Dato Bukit Gantang has indicated that he does not wish to be re-appointed when his present term expires on 1st October, and I am not replacing him.
7. Further changes in Member appointments may be necessary on 1st February when appointments of present Members of the Legislative Council expire, but these will depend largely on political developments during the next four months and on experience of running a "coalition" Government. I intend, in any case, to replace Tunku Yaacob[5] as Member for Agriculture, where he has achieved little. It will be another Malay. I shall also appoint an Asian as Member for Industrial and Social Relations in place of Duckworth.[6]
8. I am also considering making certain changes in the Legislative Council on 1st February. No amendment of the Federation Agreement will be involved, nor will there be any change in race or functional distribution of the fifty unofficial seats. But I hope it will be possible slightly to increase the relative proportions of adherents of the Alliance to accord with their weight in the country. In my speech to the Council at the Budget meeting at the end of November I intend to announce that fresh appointments to the Legislative Council will be for a period of twelve months from 1st February. Actual names of persons appointed could not, of course, be announced until later, probably in January.

---

[5] Tunku Yaacob, son of the late Sultan Abdul Hamid of Kedah and half-brother of Tunku Abdul Rahman, was keeper of the rulers' seals 1950–1951 and 1954–1955, member for agriculture 1951–53 and chairman of the public service commission 1955–1958.
[6] F V Duckworth joined the MCS in 1925, was member for industrial and social relations in 1953 and appointed British resident of Selangor in 1954.

305 T 220/285, ff 57–69   3 Nov 1953
[Financial difficulties of the Federation]: letter from H T Bourdillon[1] to A E Drake[2] putting the case for Treasury assistance   [Extract]

In the course of discussions at the Treasury on the 21st July it was agreed that a letter should be sent by my Secretary of State to the Chancellor explaining the

---

[1] Bourdillion was now head of the CO's Finance Department.
[2] A E Drake was in the Indian Civil Service, 1930–1947, entered the Treasury, 1947, assistant secretary, 1950–1957.

serious financial position of the Federation with the prospect of heavy deficits in 1953 and 1954. Meanwhile my Secretary of State made the Cabinet aware of the position at the 46th Meeting on the 28th July, when he stated that the 1954 deficit might well cost the United Kingdom Exchequer about £18 million.[3] The Chancellor confirmed that he was making allowances for this contingency (along with Kenya's needs). On the 30th July my Secretary of State wrote to the Chancellor enclosing a statement on the financial situation as then seen and asking that the High Commissioner should be at liberty to tell his Executive Council and Finance Committee that Her Majesty's Government would come to the Federation's aid in 1954.[4] The Chancellor in this letter of the 5th August agreed, and the terms of a statement which, at the Deputy High Commissioner's request, could be made public were settled as set out in MacKintosh's letter to you of the 7th August. No figure was given in the statement for the amount of aid promised, which was to be worked out in consultation with the Federation Government. It was understood that the Federation Government were seeking all possible economies in expenditure and increases in revenue and that Her Majesty's Government would give the assistance which was necessary so that, in accordance with previous public undertakings, the Federation's plans for Defence and Development should not be retarded in 1954.

2. We have recently discussed at the Treasury, with MacGillivray's help, the extent to which the financial position set out in the July memorandum has changed. The Federation has already taken measures to ensure that, despite all difficulties, the Revised Estimate of Expenditure in 1953 would be as realistic as possible. . . .[5]

8. In spite, therefore, of all the efforts which have been made on the Revenue side there is no doubt that the Federation Government is genuinely faced with the problem of meeting a deficit in 1954 of at least $233 million, or $18 million more than the July Estimate of $215. As we have shown even this estimate is based on figures for rubber prices which have since been falsified.

9. The disposable surplus balance which it is estimated will be available to the Federation is no more than $222 million. This is made up of:—

		$ million
	Cash at the Bank	35
	Investments (excluding the Electricity Undertaking)	273
	Advances Redeemed from Loans	63
		371
LESS	An overdraft of with the Joint Colonial Fund,	97
	A minimum Cash Balance of	35
	The Balance of the 1949 Loan	8
	Liabilities for the early 1954 Payment	9
		149
	BALANCE	222

The crux of the problem before us is, of course, simply how far the disposable surplus balance should be run down and to what extent the assistance of Her Majesty's Government should be made available to avoid running it down completely.

[3] See part I of this volume, 302, note.   [4] See *ibid*, 302.
[5] The rest of para 2 and paras 3–7 contain statistical details demonstrating attempts to make the estimates for 1954 'as realistic as possible' by way of savings on expenditure and a review of revenue.

10.   In our discussion I think it was agreed that we could not look at the year 1954 in isolation. We can ignore neither the contributions which the Federation Government and Her Majesty's Government have made to the cost of the Emergency in the past, nor the Liabilities which they face for the future. On the Federation side there has been a treble sacrifice. The Emergency has imposed delay, with cumulative effect, on the programme of rehabilitation and development to which the Malayan people could naturally have looked forward after the ravages of the Japanese occupation. Then a large part of the Revenue Surpluses which might otherwise have been devoted to this work have been applied to the cost of the Emergency and will not be available to meet the cost of the delayed works in the development programme now that there is labour and material available again. Finally, new money which might also have been available for development has been mortgaged in the form of the $100 million 1953 Security Loan—to meeting a part of the 1953 deficit. It is against this background that Her Majesty's Government was asked to give an assurance of assistance to enable the plans for Defence and Development to go on, but in announcing that such an assurance had been received, we did not neglect to acknowledge the great financial help which the Federation had received from Her Majesty's Government since the Liberation for such purposes as the rehabilitation of war damage, schemes made under the Colonial Development and Welfare Acts and Emergency measures.

11.   Before finally determining the amount of assistance for which we think it is reasonable for the Federation to look to Her Majesty's Government we have considered whether there is any other source from which assistance might be got. There is, in our view, a strong case for a contribution being made by the Government of Singapore and, as you are aware, we have put the matter to the Governor of Singapore with the suggestion that a contribution of $50 million should be made. We now understand from him that a contribution is possible (though by no means certain) but that anything more than $25 million is out of the question. Taking account of this possible relief there is still $208 million to be found and we feel justified in proposing that Her Majesty's Government should provide $100 million (£11.7 million), or approximately half the remaining deficit.

12.   We realize that on the figures on which we have been working this would leave the Federation with a balance of realizable assets amounting to $114 million. Obviously this is a proposal which requires justification, but we feel that even on purely financial grounds we could not suggest that Malaya should eat into the balance to any greater extent. We fully recognise that this reserve would be over and above the cash balance of $35 million already allowed for in calculating the available surplus balance, but that amount represents only a day to day working balance. The reserve would be needed to meet any of a number of different contingencies. For instance the experience of the past few years has shown that where there is an Emergency to be dealt with there is inevitably a considerable amount of additional expenditure to be authorised in the course of the year for which supplementary provision becomes necessary. I have already referred to the likelihood that supplementary provisions may exceed savings. There may also be further commitments in respect of the strategic stock-pile. Clearly a balance in excess of the minimum cash requirement must be retained to meet any such unforeseen expenditure, particularly when we bear in mind that the Federation is already meeting its short term requirements by Treasury bills to the full extent to which the local market for these

bills can be relied upon. Finally, I have already pointed out that the rubber price has even now fallen well below the figure on which the Estimates are based. We are warned, moreover, that while the long-term prospects of rubber are not considered desperate there may well be a period next year when the price of rubber will be below even the present levels. With this possibility ahead, a liquid reserve of about two months' expenditure is certainly no more than a minimum.

13. The matter cannot, however, be looked at purely as one of arithmetical calculation. Over recent years the people of the Federation have carried a tremendous burden in fighting the Emergency. Up to the end of this year direct expenditure on the Emergency by the Federation Government has amounted to over £80 million. The true deficit in 1953, if we take into account the absorption of the Revotes Reserve and the $100 million Security Loan, is now estimated at no less than $231 million. The Federation has, it is true, been fortunate in having the revenues to meet these commitments, but they have been met, as pointed out in paragraph 10 above, at the cost of development. Even so, they have only been met with the aid of a large local loan which has transferred to posterity a part of the burden of this entirely unproductive expenditure. Finally, there have been the recent taxation increases to which I have referred. This is a very fine record and we feel that Malaya now has a right to expect prompt and adequate help from Her Majesty's Government. The Federation is reaching a crucial stage in political development. A Federal Committee is examining the introduction of elections to the Federal Legislative Council, and at the same time State committees are preparing plans for State elections. Government is thus implementing its undertaking to go ahead with constitutional advance as soon as the pressure of the Emergency permits. The successful handling of these delicate issues is of vital importance, since the prospects of avoiding communal strife in the future will be greatly improved if the basic Malay/Chinese communal problem can be dealt with satisfactorily at this stage. Britain's standing in Malaya is at present high, and our ability to influence developments in this field is probably as great as it ever will be. There is moreover a widespread feeling that the Emergency has been well handled during the last year or two. On the other side of the picture there is increasing alarm about economic prospects as a result of the fall in rubber and tin prices. Equally important, there is a dawning realisation that the Emergency, so far from coming to a rapid end, is entering a new and very difficult phase. It is not difficult to see what a crucial effect on morale Her Majesty's Government's attitude in financial matters can exercise at such a time.

14. These political facts are not adduced in order to bolster up financial arguments which are not considered strong enough in themselves. I should repeat that we regard the case as fully made out on purely financial grounds. The political background is, however, of fundamental importance and in our view it makes the financial arguments unanswerable. I very much hope, therefore, that you will be able to let us have an early and favourable reply to our request. As we told you at our meeting, the last day on which a decision could be communicated to the Federation by telegram would be November 18th, so I hope you will find it possible to let us have a reply some days before then. If in the meanwhile you would like to follow up the suggestion which you made to us that MacGillivray should come over for a further talk with the Treasury, we should of course be only too happy to arrange this.

15. Before closing this letter there are two further points to which I should like to refer:—

(a) At our meeting you expressed alarm at the Federation's apparent inability even to meet its normal recurrent committments [sic], quite apart from the Emergency. The problem of meeting future recurrent commitments is undoubtedly a serious one, and this is fully recognised by the Federation Government. I think we were able to show you, however, that it is possible to take too gloomy a view of the position by regarding the "Emergency" head of expenditure in the Estimates as representing the sum total of expenditure on the Emergency. That is not in fact the case. There is a good deal of expenditure elsewhere in the Estimates which is in fact occasioned by the Emergency and which will cease or diminish when the Emergency comes to an end.

(b) I have now received Collier's[6] letter of the 30th October about the Tin Buffer Stock scheme. We are most grateful for the Chancellor's readiness in principle to assist, and we quite appreciate the Treasury's insistence on looking at the matter against the background of the Federation's need for financial assistance in general. Our position, however, will be clear to you from what I have already said. We regard the proposed Emergency assistance in 1954 as sufficient only to maintain the Federation's liquid balances at an essential minimum, even assuming the additional contribution of $25 million from Singapore. In the circumstances we have no alternative but to ask for the full assistance towards the Buffer Stock, which is of course purely a matter of temporary accommodation, as an additional measure. We shall be writing to you further about the Buffer Stock in a separate letter.

16. In conclusion I should just like to emphasize that we do realise that the request which we are putting to the Treasury is a very big one compared with previous requests for Malaya or with the normal run of requests which come to you from the Colonial Office. I am sure you will realise that we would have limited ourselves to a smaller sum if we had felt at all justified in doing so particularly in view of the present budgetary position of the United Kingdom which has been so forcibly brought to the Secretary of State's attention by the Chancellor.

---

[6] A J Collier was then a principal in the Treasury.

306 T 220/285, ff 79–82, 101, 106–107   9–17 Nov 1953
[Treasury assistance to Malaya]: minutes by Sir A Johnston,[1] Sir H Brittain,[2] Mr Boyd-Carpenter,[3] and Mr Butler

Sir Herbert Brittain
Mr. Drake's minute of 6th November sets out the position regarding the application received from the Colonial Office for financial assistance to Malaya in the coming calender year and recommends that we should make an offer of £3,000,000 against the £11,700,000 recommended by the Colonial Office.

Mr. Drake and I saw Sir Donald MacGillivray, the Assistant High Commissioner of the Federation of Malaya, this morning. I said that, as Mr. Drake had examined in

---

[1] Third secretary at the Treasury, 1951–1958.
[2] Second secretary at the Treasury, 1953–1957.
[3] Conservative MP and financial secretary at the Treasury, 1951–1954.

detail with him the level of taxation and of expenditure in Malaya and was reasonably satisfied with what they were doing, there was no need to go over that ground again this morning, but that we did want to hear what he had to say on the suggestion that, instead of H.M.G. being expected to pay £11.7m.[4] in order to keep their reserve at about $150m., the reserve should be allowed to run down to about $70–75m. and we should only give $3m. It would, of course, be understood that, if unforeseen contingencies arose, we should promptly and sympathetically consider a request for further assistance. I pointed out that it was difficult to ask H.M.G., which had already helped Malaya very substantially in recent years, to provide a large sum in order that Malaya might keep its reserves at a desirable level. In view of H.M.G's heavy financial commitments elsewhere, we felt that we could only reasonably be asked to assist when the Malayan reserves were reaching danger level. Moreover, Malaya in the past had tended to under-estimate her revenue and to over-estimate her expenditure, and it would be difficult to justify to Parliament the payment of a large sum if it seemed, through under- and over-estimating, that quite substantial reserves remained at the end of 1954.

Sir Donald MacGillivray did not dissent from the view that, on strictly financial grounds, Malaya could get along with a reserve of, say, $75m. The minimum day-to-day working balance was about $35m. and a further $40m. would enable them to deal with the kind of crisis which might arise, always on the understanding that H.M.G. would act promptly if serious difficulties arose. He disputed, however, the view that there were likely to be funds available from cautious budgeting in 1953 and 1954. This year and next year's budgets were being prepared on the assumption that rubber fetched 65 cents. a lb., whereas it was reasonably clear that they would be lucky if in 1954 and 1955 the price did not fall below the present level of 55 cents. Admittedly, thereafter it might rise, but there would be some loss of revenue from the export duty on rubber in 1953, a full year's loss of revenue from the same source in 1954 and 1955, and considerable loss on income tax (payable 12 months in arrears) towards the end of 1954, 1955 and 1956. His main objection to a small grant from H.M.G. of £3m. ($25m.) was that, as a result of the statements that had been made, the people of Malaya assumed that fairly substantial assistance would be given by H.M.G. He would rather see no assistance given and Malaya left to run out her reserves beyond the danger point, than a sum given which would be regarded as derisory and which would forfeit a great deal of the goodwill towards this country. There would be a general feeling that the emergency had cost Malaya a great deal and that she should be allowed to have a reserve of rather more than $100m. (in addition to the working balance of $35m.) which would be available for reconstruction work, either in a depression or when the present emergency had been dealt with and rehabilitation and reconstruction were in full swing. The furthest that he felt able to go was to suggest that, instead of making a payment of £11.7m. ($100m.) H.M.G. might offer to give some unspecified amount which would ensure that the reserve, other than the working balance, never fell below $100m.

I did not find Sir Donald MacGillivray's exposition convincing. If these are real reserves, then they will presumably remain unspent and are not to be regarded as a "nest-egg" for reconstruction work. Moreover, it is not clear who are the public in Malaya who follow with such closeness the size of the reserve held by the

---

[4] See 305, para 11.

Government of Malaya. It is relatively small in amount in relation to the size of the total budget and it is being substantially run down this year without any of the catastrophic effects on public opinion which Sir Donald MacGillivray portrayed. My impression was that he was unwilling to give anything away and no doubt was not empowered to do so.

We discussed briefly the position after 1954. Sir Donald MacGillivray said that he hoped that expenditure on the emergency would gradually fall. He thought, for example, that the emergency police expenditure might come down from $100m. in 1954 to $70m. in 1955 and progressively thereafter. Other emergency expenditure would also fall. The outlook is, therefore, not too bad for the years after 1954, particularly if the price of rubber begins to rise again as some seem to think it will.

Mr. Drake and I feel that the case for allowing the Malayan reserves to fall to about $75m. is sound and that the political difficulties to which Sir Donald MacGillivray referred can be met by the way in which the assistance afforded by H.M.G. is presented. It could be said that we were prepared to ensure that the reserves did not fall below $75m., and that we were making a payment of £3m. ($25m.) as an initial[5] sum to secure this object. The aim would be to represent H.M.G. as standing behind the Government of Malaya and giving over the money as the need arises.

(I.F. Division have discovered that there is a payment due to the Federation of Malaya from the old Straits Settlements funds which may add as much as $26m. to Malayan reserves.[6] Sir Donald MacGillivray did not mentioned this until taxed with it and said that he was not entirely satisfied that the money would in fact represent a net addition to the reserves. We are looking into it to try and get a firm answer. But it is perhaps not unfair to say that the way in which the matter arose and was dealt with by Sir Donald MacGillivray illustrates a tendency to try and keep a little in hand, while coming to H.M.G. for assistance on the ground of financial difficulties.)

A.J.
9.11.53

The Government of Malaya have now revised the figures that were previously given to us about their estimated revenue in 1954; and they believe that, if the price of rubber does not increase, their revenue in that year will drop by $30m. This means that, if we are to maintain Malaya's liquid reserves at $70–75m. at the end of 1954, we shall have to give them next year at least $50m. (approximately £6m.) instead of $25m. (£3m.) as previously proposed and approved by the Chancellor of the Exchequer.

If we give £6m., I suggest that, as the sum is a substantial one and requires no apology, we might be a little more chary about giving any definite guarantee that we shall see that Malaya's reserves are maintained at $70–75m. Although Malaya has a record of financial caution and economy, [to] guarantee that we shall ensure that their reserves will stand at a certain figure is not exactly an incentive to economy and it might be enough if we said that, in giving £6m., we had in mind that we should not wish to see the reserves of Malaya, by the end of 1954, falling below $70–75m. I doubt whether it would be wise to attempt to give the grant in two parts, the second

---

[5] Brittain minuted in the margin here: 'I think we might try to avoid the word "initial" at this stage'.
[6] Brittain minuted in the margin here: 'Later information shows that there is nothing in this point—so *no* windfall'.

part depending on what actually had happened in the course of 1954. We shall have to put a figure in our Estimates and it looks as though that will have to be £6m.

A.J.
12.11.53

I am sorry that the Chancellor has to be troubled with this again.

In view of the revised estimates I do not see how we can now recommend less than £6mns, to be accompanied by the explanation at X above.[7]

H.B.
12.11.53

Discuss rapidly in office.

R.A.B.
14.11.53

Chancellor of the Exchequer
1. I do not see why even if the calculations of the Malayan Government are reliable there is anything particularly sacred about keeping their liquid reserves at $70 million to $75 million. Confidence can surely be maintained by indicating that H.M.G. is behind them.

2. For that reason while I agree with Sir A. Johnston that on the new figures it is necessary to go beyond the £3 million originally recommended, I think we shall do enough if we make it £5 million.

3. Apart from saving a million pounds this may have its value in other similar cases, e.g. Kenya, since however different the circumstances are different suppliants are apt to compare our generosity with one as with the other.

4. I would therefore recommend £5 million.

J.A.B-C.
16.11.53

A final word morning. We may as well be hung for a sheep £6 as a lamb £5.

R.A.B.
16.11.53

I will now agree to £6m.

R.A.B
17.11.53

---

[7] ie that part of the second para of Johnston's minute of 12 Nov which reads: 'we should not wish to see the reserves of Malaya, by the end of 1954, falling below $70–75m'.

307   CO 1022/86, no 87   10 Nov 1953
'Committee on federal elections in Malaya': CO note of a meeting with Sir G Templer and Sir D MacGillivray on 9 Nov

[The full committee met for the first time on 17 Aug and approved the composition of a working party which conferred five times in the period to 23 Oct when the committee held its second meeting and approved a progress report from the working party.]

Points arising from the work of this Committee were discussed at a meeting between Sir T. Lloyd, Sir G. Templer, Sir D. MacGillivray, Mr. Paskin, Mr. Watt[1] and Mr. Jerrom on the 9th November, 1953.

Sir Donald MacGillivray explained that the Working Party appointed by the Committee had recently submitted its first report and that the Committee might soon be reaching the stage of decision on several matters of political importance. If there was to be any attempt to influence the Committee's recommendations it must be made now.

The points discussed were:—

1. *The eligibility of civil servants for election to the Legislative Council*

The Working Party had reached no final conclusion but might do so in the near future. It was pointed out that most of the few educated Malays in the country were civil servants, and it could be argued that it should be made easy for them to take part in politics in order that the Malays might be represented by men of ability. On the other hand *Sir D. MacGillivray* felt that the number of senior civil servants who would wish to enter politics would be small, and that more important considerations were to establish from the outset the separation of the civil service from politics and to maintain its efficiency.

It was agreed that for the first (partly elected) Legislative Council only, some special provision would be desirable. It was suggested that civil servants who were elected to Legislative Council should be allowed to retire with the pension they had earned. Candidates would be given leave without pay from the date of nomination until the result of the elections was known. This rule would apply to civil servants of all grades; the desirability of differentiation between grades on the lines of the Masterman Report (which governs the political activities of civil servants in the U.K.) could be considered after the first Council.[2]

2. *Literacy qualifications for voters*

Sir Donald MacGillivray explained that the Working Party had decided against literacy qualifications for voters, but if the Secretary of State thought it desirable it might be possible to reopen the issue. It was pointed out that the only Colonial territories with such qualifications at present were Mauritius and Tonga, that public opinion would oppose the introduction of such a qualification for reasons of national prestige, that the Malays might oppose it on the ground that it favoured the Chinese, and that tests would be difficult to organise.

It was agreed that no attempt should be made to impose a literacy qualification.

3. *Literacy qualifications for candidates*

The Working Party recommend that candidates should be required to read and write Malay or English, that there should be no tests, and that if a member's qualifications are challenged it should be left for the Legislative Council itself to decide. It was pointed out that this could lead to political controversy in individual cases. In the Gold Coast if a member is challenged on these, as on other, grounds the decision is

---

[1] I B Watt, principal at the CO 1946–1956; working in the CO's general department in the 1950s, Watt became an expert in comparative constitutions.

[2] The secretary of state later agreed to accept this device provided that it was the unanimous recommendation of the working party.

left to the Courts, and in Kenya to the Governor in Council. The meeting could see no reason why a suitable test should not be devised and taken by candidates at the nomination stage, and this suggestion might be put to the Working Party. It was considered undesirable to make Legislative Council itself the arbiter in any challenged election.

4. *System of voting*

The Working Party had considered several possible systems of voting but had not yet made up its mind. *Sir D. MacGillivray* thought that simple majority voting in single member constituencies would be dangerous, e.g. in Selangor Chinese might gain nearly all the seats and large Malay minorities might consider themselves disfranchised. For this reason he had given some consideration to proportional representation. Admittedly this could lead to proliferation of parties, but this might be no bad thing in Malaya, for only a coalition could form a Government, and any coalition would probably include representatives of the principal communities.

After further discussion it was agreed that proportional representation would probably be too complex a system for use at present. But there was clearly a case to consider some half-way house between simple majority voting and proportional representation. It was suggested that the limited vote with, say, three member constituencies and two votes for each elector (which could not be given to the same candidate) might offer advantages.[3] This system of voting is intended to favour minorities by enabling them to concentrate on one candidate. *Sir Thomas Lloyd* emphasised that any system of this sort would have to be applied throughout the Federation. *Sir D. MacGillivray* thought that it would be possible to divide the country into three member constituencies but this might involve cutting across State boundaries. It was agreed that the first step must be to examine the possibility of such a system. Meanwhile the Colonial Office would consider whether there would be any political objection to this system if it proved practicable.

5. *Ex-officio members*

The Working Party had recommended that there should be only three *ex-officio* members (the Chief Secretary, Attorney-General and Financial Secretary) in Legislative and Executive Councils. Mr. Hogan had reported that there would be difficulty in securing agreement to additional seats for the Member of [for] Economic Affairs and the Secretary for Defence. *Sir G. Templer* and *Sir D. MacGillivray* felt that in view of the High Commissioner's special responsibility in matters of defence we should press for the inclusion of the Secretary for Defence in both Executive and Legislative Councils. It was pointed out that in addition to the *ex-officio* members there would be ten or more Ministers. If precedence was a difficulty it might be overcome by working on length of tenure in office for all Members other than the Chief Secretary.

It was agreed that every effort should be made to bring the Commitee to recommend a fourth *ex-officio* seat for the Secretary for Defence.

---

[3] After the meeting on 9 Nov an official at the Home Office informed MacGillivray and CO officials that the limited vote had been operated in Birmingham and twelve other constituencies between 1867 and 1885 and had appeared to be reasonably successful in achieving its object, ie ensuring representation for any substantial minority. On 25 Nov Paskin referred Templer, who had returned to Malaya, to J H Humphreys, *Proportional representation*, 1911 (CO 1022/86, no 88) and see 310, note 3.

6. *Boundary commission to delimit constituencies*
The Working Party drew attention to the need for an obviously impartial boundary commission with a chairman from outside Malaya. It was suggested that this appointment might be a matter of urgency, but it was later agreed that the system of voting and nature of constituencies under (4) above would have to be considered further before arrangements for a boundary commission were dealt with.

308   CO 1022/98, no 21   16 Nov 1953

[Appointment of next high commissioner]: minute no PM(53)18 by Mr Lyttelton to Sir W Churchill recommending that Sir D MacGillivray succeed Sir G Templer on 1 June 1954

[This recommendation arose from a meeting between Lloyd and Templer at the CO on 5 Nov. Templer himself considered that the stage had been reached in the emergency when reversion to a civilian high commissioner would be justified and also desirable on political grounds. At the same time he believed that 'the way should be kept open for the re-appointment of a military High Commissioner if there should be a serious deterioration in the internal security situation', such as might be provoked by a French collapse in Indo-China (see CO 1022/98, no 17).]

Prime Minister
Sir Gerald Templer has established for himself in Malaya and in the minds of all her races a position never before enjoyed by anyone. His name there, to use a well worn phrase, is one to conjure with and no one more than yourself will know what that means.

The period for which Templer was seconded from the Army expires in February next but there are strong reasons why he should remain a little longer. He himself advocates this course and he can be spared for a short time by the Army.

On the military side the picture in Malaya is better than we dared hope for but I am satisfied that it would pay a handsome dividend if he could be left in charge of operations for another few months.

On the civil side there is no doubt that the public must be carefully prepared for the change. I believe that he should be given time both to carry the military campaign a stage further and to build up public confidence in the regime which would succeed him.

The position has been fully discussed with the Secretary of State for War and the C.I.G.S. who are prepared to agree that he should stay on in Malaya until the 1st of June and should then come on leave before taking up his appointment as Commander, Northern Army Group in Western Europe in October 1954.[1]

My suggestions are thus:—

(a) Sir G. Templer should be succeeded as High Commissioner by the present Deputy High Commissioner Sir Donald MacGillivray. The post of Deputy High Commissioner would not be filled.
(b) The G.O.C. Malaya should become Director of Operations with wider powers of operational command than those enjoyed by General Briggs, and with the right to

---

[1] This appointment was later cancelled and, after carrying out an investigation into security throughout the colonial empire, Templer became CIGS in Sept 1955.

report to the C.I.G.S. in the unlikely event of any difference of opinion with the High Commissioner on a matter affecting the conduct of operations.[2] The C.I.G.S. could then take the matter up with me. I understand that there is likely to be a change of G.O.C. in April, but I am satisfied that the man in view would be very suitable for this assignment.[3]

Sir Donald MacGillivray is 47 and has had a distinguished career in the Colonial Service. He was appointed a cadet in Tanganyika in 1925 and having there reached the rank of Under-Secretary, he was transferred to Jamaica as Colonial Secretary in 1947. In 1952 he was specially selected to serve under Sir Gerald Templer as Civil Deputy High Commissioner in the Federation of Malaya.

Templer and MacGillivray have worked toether in the closest harmony for all these two critical years. Templer has the greatest confidence in him and we are both satisfied that he is completely fitted to take over the heavy responsibilities which will fall upon his shoulders. During the past two years he has fully established himself in the confidence of the Service and of the public in Malaya.

In order that Templer may have full opportunity to accustom the public to the impending changes, I suggest that they should be announced, including Templer's appointment, in December. I consider it essential that the public in Malaya should be given these five months in which to accustom themselves to the change. Templer himself will use this period to see that the new regime starts with the full support of all races. I also consider it important that it could be said that The Queen herself has approved the appointment of Sir Donald McGillivray. If therefore you agree, I propose to submit this appointment to Her Majesty before she leaves this country.[4]

The Secretary of State for War has seen this minute in draft and is in agreement with it.[5]

---

[2] It was agreed not to disclose this arrangement in order 'to avoid any derogation, in the eyes of the public from the overall authority of the High Commissioner'.

[3] Lt General Sir Geoffrey Bourne (GOC, Malaya, 1954–1956) replaced Sir Hugh Stockwell (GOC, Malaya, 1952–1954) in Apr 1956.

[4] The Queen and the Duke of Edinburgh were about to depart on a six-month tour of the empire and Commonwealth.

[5] Churchill replied to Lyttelton the same day: 'Are you sure that MacGillivray can fill the gap?' MacGillivray's name was submitted to the palace on 31 Dec, only after he had been interviewed by the prime minister on 18 Dec.

309   CO 1022/85, no 36   18 Nov 1953

[Protection of Malayan students from undesirable influences]: minutes by R L Baxter[1] and T C Jerrom on discussions with Sir G Templer and Sir D MacGillivray on 11 and 14 Nov

[Following their visit to Malaya in Aug 1952 (see part II of this volume, 272), Victor Purcell and Francis Carnell had separately published on Malayan problems. Purcell was particularly critical of Templer's regime: his attack on the 'police state' would culminate in 1954 with the appearance of *Malaya: communist or free?* Templer complained to Lyttelton: 'It seems that Purcell, largely in order to vent his personal spite against me,

---

[1] Assistant principal, CO, 1950–1955.

may be infusing poison into successive batches of students from Malaya, and into any other students who come his way. This strikes me as fundamentally evil and I hope you will have the matter thoroughly investigated.' CO 1022/85, no 35.]

The protection of Malayan students from undesirable influences and the influence of the Press on Malayan politics were discussed at a meeting with General Sir Gerald Templer on the 11th November. Sir Charles Jeffries, Mr. Paskin, Mr. Carstairs,[2] Mr. E.R. Edmonds,[3] Mr. Jerrom and Mr. Baxter were present.

2. *General Templer* distinguished between the influence of Communism and that of Dr. Purcell, Mr. Carnell and their supporters. To take Dr. Purcell and his friends first, they were of the opinion that now that the pressure of the Emergency was slackening the only way to hold the Malayan communities together was to unite them in common opposition to the British. This was a most pernicious doctrine. There was no racial hatred in Malaya at present; many of the British Civil Servants were respected and liked; and almost everybody, both Malay, and Chinese and Indian, agreed for their different reasons in wanting the British civil servants and the British High Commissioner to remain in Malaya for many years to come. To introduce racial dissension would benefit nobody except the Communists. *General Templer* believed that Dr. Purcell was insinuating his views into the minds of students at Cambridge (such as Mr. Blacking,[4] who had recently had to be dismissed from his probationary appointment as Assistant Adviser on Aborigines), and that Mr. Carnell was doing the same thing at Oxford.

3. *General Templer* went on to discuss the efforts of the Communists themselves to subvert Malayan students in England. He was relieved that they appeared to have gained no foothold at the Malayan Teachers' College at Kirkby. But he was disturbed at the election of Mr. John Eber[5] as Secretary to the Malayan Forum in London. He hoped that the Malayan Students Section under Mr. Hicks[6] would be able to take steps to counteract this dangerous development. One thing that might be done was to warn all students on their arrival of the approaches they might expect from the Communists; this could be done for all students and not merely those from Malaya. *Mr. Carstairs* thought that if this pre-indoctrination was to achieve its purpose it had better be given before the students left their own country. *General Templer* agreed.

4. *General Templer* went on to describe the measures that are being taken to protect Malayan students at Al Azhar University in Cairo, who were particularly liable to dangerous influences because of their miserable living conditions. He said that he was trying to persuade the Rulers to establish a religious university in Malaya. This would reduce the number of Malayan students in Cairo to manageable proportions; and it would then be possible to accommodate the greater part of them in a government hostel, for which a lease was already being negotiated.

5. *General Templer* then raised the wider question of the influence of the Press

---

[2] C Y Carstairs was director, Information Services, CO, 1951–1953, and assistant under-secretary of state, 1953–62.

[3] E R Edmonds, assistant secretary, CO, 1947–1961.

[4] John Blacking was dismissed after two weeks in the job because he disagreed with the government's method of winning over the aborigines.

[5] John Eber had been detained in 1951 and exiled to London in 1953 where he became secretary of the Colonial Freedom Movement.

[6] E C Hicks had entered the Malayan educational service in 1921 and had been acting principal of the Sultan Idris Training College in 1938.

on the political development of Malaya. He deplored the influence of the "Singapore Standard",[7] with its doctrinaire left-wing views. What the country needed was a newspaper that would preach the gospel of decent Liberalism and good government. It was a pity too that Malayan affairs received such biased treatment in "The Times", though he was glad to see that most other newspapers, including the "Manchester Guardian", were now treating them more impartially. *Mr. Carstairs* said that he would try to interest Mr. Vernon Bartlett of the "News Chronicle" in a visit to Malaya.[8] He also promised that if the Federation would keep us provided with up-to-date material on social and political developments in Malaya, Information Department would take a positive line to influence British journalists in the right direction. *General Templer* said that he would welcome a visit by Mr. Bartlett. He went on to mentioned that Han Sin Yin (?),[9] author of "A Many Splendoured Thing", had written a book about life in the new villages. Unfortunately this was based on the authoress's own experience of two particularly bad villages and General Templer felt that it might give a most misleading impression to people outside Malaya. *Mr. Carstairs* said that it might be possible to do something to counteract this by judicious publicity when the book is issued.

R.L.B.

18.11.53

I had a further word with Sir D. MacGillivray about this on the 14th November.

Dr. Purcell
Sir D. MacGillivray had a long talk with Dr. Purcell at Cambridge last week. I think it is fair to say that he does not go nearly so far as Sir G. Templer in condemning Dr. Purcell, although he does feel that Purcell's somewhat unbalanced advocacy of the Chinese case is doing harm. I reminded Sir D. MacGillivray that the Federation Government had undertaken to make available to Dr. Purcell, as a member of the Colonial Labour Advisory Committee, information about wage rates and industrial conditions in Malaya. Sir Donald MacGillivray thought that this was quite right. He appreciated that there was really nothing that we could do to divert Dr. Purcell from his present courses, and he expressed the opinion that Dr. Purcell was now so openly biased that many people suspected his judgment, e.g. the B.B.C mentioned to Sir D. MacGillivray that Dr. Purcell (apparently a very good and keen broadcaster) was constantly asking them for radio times, but they felt that he was not sufficiently impartial to be given exceptional facilities.

We left it on the basis that we in the Colonial Office would watch for any evidence that Dr. Purcell's activities were in fact having a serious effect, and what we would take any opportunity that offered to talk to Dr. Purcell about his Malayan publicity operations.

---

[7] Formerly edited by T H Tan who became secretary of the MCA in 1953 and later secretary of the Alliance.
[8] Vernon Bartlett, journalist and broadcaster; MP (Independent Progressive) 1930–1950; on the staff of the *News Chronicle* (London), 1934–1954; political commentator for the *Straits Times* (Singapore), 1954–1961; SE Asia correspondent for the *Manchester Guardian*, 1954–1961; publications included *Report from Malaya*, 1954.
[9] Han Suyin's *A many splendid thing* (London, 1952) carried an introduction by Malcolm MacDonald. Her *And the rain my drink* was set in the Malayan emergency and, though written in 1952–1953, was not published until 1956.

Malayan students in the U.K.

Sir D. MacGillivray is not particularly concerned at John Eber's appointment as Secretary of the Malayan Forum; he feels that the best course may be to let this ride and try to ensure as far as possible that the activities of the Forum remain open to our inspection, e.g. by allowing them to continue to meet at Malaya Hall. I told him that we were at present making enquiries and would consult Raja Sir Uda before taking any action.

On the more general question of undesirable influences on Malayan students in London, I mentioned to Sir D. MacGillivray that we had been intending for some time to take action to become better informed about the students' affairs, but that we had deferred this until Mr. Hicks had taken over the students' unit. I said that we were very anxious not to appear to intrude in matters which were properly Raja Sir Uda's responsibility, but that Sir G. Templer's strong views of the Secretary of State's personal interest would make it necessary for us to take a more prominent part in these things than we had done in the past. Sir D. MacGillivray fully appreciates this and agreed with my suggestion that we should discuss the whole matter with Raja Sir Uda and Mr. Hicks and try to work out a system which would satisfy Sir G. Templer.

T.C.J.

18.11.53

310 CO 1022/86, no 93   8 Dec 1953

[Committee on federal elections]: inward savingram no 2018/53 from Sir G Templer to Mr Lyttelton on developments since 23 Oct

The Working Party has held four further meetings since the 23rd October[1] and copies of the minutes are attached for information.[2] As anticipated in paragraph 4 of my savingram No. 1845/53, some of the more controversial issues have been under discussion in these meetings of the Working Party and it seems unlikely that all difference of opinion on these issues can be eliminated, though it has been possible in most instances to narrow the viewpoints to two clear streams of thought which, if not entirely satisfactory, is probably as much as can reasonably be expected in the circumstances.

2. Members have on the whole shown an encouraging desire gradually to moderate the hitherto accepted principle of representation on communal lines though it is generally felt that it will be necessary, until political parties have become more firmly established and communal considerations play a lesser part in the lives of the people, to make limited provision for seats to be reserved for certain substantial though small communities which are unlikely to find effective representation through the electoral process. The Working Party accordingly propose to recommend that nominated seats should be reserved for the Eurasian and Ceylonese communities and the aboriginal peoples only. This recommendation would exclude any provision for separate representation for such communities as Indians, Pakistanis, Europeans and Indonesians, though some of these may find a place in the nominated seats reserved for commercial interests.

3. The Working Party have also reached unanimous agreement on the extent to

---

[1] See 307, note.   [2] Not printed.

which provision should be made for "scheduled" interests which comprise integral and important aspects of the economic life of the country. Particulars of this are recorded in paragraph 5 on pages 23 and 24 of the minutes which are attached. In this connection, it will be noted from paragraph 11 on page 28 of the minutes that the Working Party does not consider that any seats should be specially reserved in the legislature for labour since labour could fairly expect to obtain adequate representation through the electoral process. This may be questioned on the grounds that a labour party is unlikely to gain a foothold without the active and positive support of the trade union movement and that a strong current of opinion in the trade unions thinks, not without good reason, that the time is not yet ripe for them to participate in politics. On the other hand, the labour vote is too substantial to be ignored by the major parties.

4. The two major controversial issues at the moment are the precise number of seats in the legislature which should be filled by elected members and whether Government servants should be permitted to stand as candidates for election. The record of the discussion on the first of these two matters is contained in paragraph 8 onwards on page 27 and it will be seen that the difference of opinion in regard to the number of elected members is not great. The I.M.P. members of the Working Party and some independents comprising in all a majority, favour not more than 42 in a council of 88 members whilst the Alliance advocate an elected majority of 57 in a council of 93, emphasising that a proportion of less than 3/5 would place the elected members in too weak a position, having regard to the fact that they are unlikely to belong entirely to one party. The I.M.P. proposals incorporate a "nominated reserve" of 10 seats which would be filled by appointments made by the High Commissioner for the purpose of safeguarding the special position of the Malays and the legitimate interests of other communities as stated in Clause 19 of the Federation of Malaya Agreement. The Alliance are not, however, prepared to concede the inclusion of any further nominated members other than those for the scheduled interests and racial minorities, on which the current proposals differ somewhat from their own original proposals which they say they only agreed to modify with some reluctance. In this connection, it is interesting to note that some of the leading members of U.M.N.O. which is the largest organised party of Malays, argue that the Malays do not wish to be accorded any special treatment and that during the years that this policy had been adopted by the Government it had failed in its purpose of helping the Malays to attain equality with other races and, instead, it had tended to place them in an inferior position and make them more dependent on outside assistance. The other group of members in the Working Party contend, however, that it would be most unfortunate if the Malays found themselves outnumbered in the legislature and that during the interim period at least it would be necessary to provide some safeguard of the kind suggested. With so predominantly a Malay electorate this argument seems to rest on a somewhat insubstantial basis.

5. Neither of the two main currents of opinion is disposed to further compromise at the moment. Though it might be possible at a cost in time and effort to bring the two sides somewhat closer together, having succeeded in crystallising a variety of opinions into two clear cut proposals embodying a considerable measure of common ground, it is thought that further pressure for a compromise at this juncture would hardly be justified. When the Report as a whole comes to be considered by the High Commissioner in consultation with the Rulers and ultimately by the Secretary of

State, the measure of choice that lies between the two proposals as they stand at present may not prove unwelcome on this particular issue. To narrow this choice or to press the parties into some reluctantly accepted compromise might prove unsatisfactory if the Rulers, the High Commissioner and the Secretary of State should ultimately find the compromise unacceptable or the field of choice too narrow.

6. The record of the discussion on the other matter, that which concerns the position of Government servants, is shown on pages 34, 36 and 37 of the minutes which are attached. It will be seen that the Alliance advocate the granting of a concession to enable Government servants to stand as candidates and, if successful, to be granted no pay leave and to take their places in the legislature for one term only whilst still retaining their position mutatis mutandis in the public service. The arguments in favour of and those against this proposal are shown in the record and the matter will certainly come up for further discussion when the Working Party is preparing its final report to the full Committee, if not before. There is no doubt that the proposal to exclude Government officers from sitting as elected members is regarded by U.M.N.O. as an unnecessarily severe and sudden alteration in the present policy which has conceded to Government officials the right to sit and vote as unofficials whilst continuing to hold and function in their civil service offices. They recognise that this cannot be applied "in toto" to elected members but they feel that the interests of the Malay community will be damaged if for a period of four years the modified proposal they have put forward fails to find acceptance.

7. The interim report on the Constituency Delineation Commission has been prepared and is awaiting the approval of members of the Committee. The report does not deal with the final terms of reference as these cannot be decided at this stage of the Committee's deliberations though an indication of the Commission's task is given on page 29 of the minutes. The purpose in submitting the report now is to initiate the preliminary arrangements to secure the services of the Chairman, who will come from the United Kingdom, and the two members. A copy of this report will be forwarded to you shortly with a formal request for assistance in finding a suitable person to be chairman of the Commission.

8. The Committee is making reasonably good progress with the difficult tasks assigned to it and there are indications that its full report will be submitted in the early part of the new year. I am replying separately to your personal telegram No. 136[3] and will keep you informed of the progress made by the Committee.

---

[3] See 307, note 3. As regards the suggestion of the limited vote, it was reported that the working committee preferred single member constituencies and the simple majority vote (CO 1022/86, No 94).

311 CO 1022/245, no 24   12 Dec 1953
'The cold war in South-East Asia': inward saving telegram no 64 from Mr M J MacDonald to FO on the commissioner-general's conference, 9–12 Dec

The Conference reviewed the recent developments of the situation in South-East Asia in the cold war.

2. The Communists lost the first phase of their campaign to win South-East Asia

when they failed between 1945 and 1948 to capture by "peaceful" means the Nationalist movement in any country except Indo-China. They are now similarly losing the second phase, i.e. the shooting war everywhere except in Indo-China. In the Philippines and Malaya the campaign had gone hard for them, while in Burma the rebels are no longer an organised threat to the Government. In Siam they have never grasped the initiative. In Indonesia the only Communist attempt to start an armed insurrection was promptly suppressed.

3. The only place where the Communists still have a chance of winning the shooting war is Indo-China. A Communist success there would adversely affect the situation in Siam and would help the Communists to put fresh energy into armed action in Burma and Malaya.[1] Nevertheless, the change of command in Indo-China and French reinforcements have arrested the earlier decline. If the French pursue their present policies energetically, and provided the Chinese Communists do not intervene with aircraft or manpower, there is hope that in time a military ascendancy may be achieved which would enable the French and Vietnamese to establish political ascendancy. They can then either negotiate from strength or continue the military campaign until victory has been won, according to the circumstances and prospects prevailing at the time. Even if these policies are successful, a considerable period must elapse before Vietnamese forces can protect Vietnamese independence with very substantially reduced French aid.

4. A third phase of Communist strategy may be beginning with more emphasis on political and economic factors.[2] The recent Soviet move towards the exchange of manufactured goods for Burmese rice may well be an opening move in this game. The effectiveness of Communist action in this phase depends to a great extent on whether economic prosperity and standards of living are maintained. If they were to fail, the Communists would have a fertile ground for their activities.

South-East Asian cooperation

5. The conference considered means of furthering cooperation and mutual knowledge amongst the countries of South-East Asia and their leaders. This hardly exists at present.

6. Meetings between the leaders, together with working level contacts, either for general liaison or for specific purposes (following the example of the Thai/Malayan frontier arrangements)[3] would lead to a greater sense of interdependence and ultimately to a degree of effective political and defence co-operation in the region.

7. A good beginning might be to bring the members of the Government of Siam to meet separately the Laotian and Vietnamese rulers and political leaders. It would, of course, be necessary to act in concert and full agreement with the French. Another possibility which would be welcome would be a meeting between Burmese and Indonesian leaders.

Korean negotiations

8. The conference recognized that the maintenance of Western forces in Korea and Japan is a deterrent to Chinese Communist aggression in the South. From this point of view a continuation of uncertainty in North-East Asia is helpful to

---

[1] See 301, note.
[2] See part II of this volume, 284.   [3] Concluded in 1949 and extended in 1952.

South-East Asia, though the Conference fully recognized the many disadvantages of the lack of a settlement in Korea.

9. Foreign Office please pass to Colonial Office and Commonwealth Relations Office.

312 CO 1022/298, ff 38–39   15 Jan 1954
[State elections]: minute by T C Jerrom commenting on confused planning

[The work of the federal elections committee seemed to command the attention of British officials and Malayan politicians in the second half of 1953 and over-shadow earlier concern with planning state and settlement elections. The result was that by the start of 1954 the long-term relationship between federal and state governments (and their respective legislatures) had yet to be determined.]

It was suggested on these and other papers as long ago as the Autumn of 1952 that the Federation Government would be well advised to consider its future policy on constitutional development, both in the Federal and State fields, with the object of assessing its most important aims and deciding how they could best be approached. For several reasons no review of this sort was ever carried out, and as a result there is as far as I know no sort of "blueprint" to serve as a guide to future policy. Instead a great deal of work has been done on the ground, and the policy is being evolved during this work. This method of procedure has obvious drawbacks, and I must confess that to my mind the position on State elections disclosed in these papers is confused and unsatisfactory. I think we can only hope that the policy proposals for Federal elections will be sufficiently clear early in February to enable the Government to give proper consideration to the difficult questions involved in State elections when the Joint Committee meets on February 10th (paragraph 5 of (51)).

2. When Mr. Hogan was here in the Summer I think he hoped that it might be possible to secure general agreement on Federal elections in a year or two's time, probably with an elected majority in the Federal Legislature, and on State/Settlement elections either before or after the Federal elections but with elected minorities. I imagine that the reasoning behind this was largely that our general aim should be, while maintaining the Federal form of Government (as we are of course bound to do), to work gradually towards a stronger unitary State; it was felt that this process would be better served by the introduction of democracy at the centre before it reached the States. But if Penang is determined to have an elected majority in its Council (paragraph 6 of (51)) it does seem probable that there will be very strong pressure for elected majorities in most if not all of the States, and possibly in Malacca.

3. Some of the issues involved in this are difficult or impossible to assess in London, and I think the most important thing at the moment will be for Sir D. MacGillivray to see these papers (preferably after dealing with the papers on Federal Elections) and to indicate his own views on the more important points involved.

4. I do not want to raise details at this stage, but on the franchise I am inclined to wonder (as in the case of Federal elections) whether the balance is not tilted against citizens of the U.K. and Colonies. In the Settlements all Federal citizens are to have

the franchise subject to a short residential qualification. But in the States citizens of the U.K. and Colonies can only qualify as Federal citizens or subjects of the Ruler. As in the case of Federal elections it may be that the building up of Federal citizenship towards a Malayan nationality is the key factor in this decision; and I should have thought that in this case it would be politically undesirable to raise the issue.

313   CO 1030/309, no 23   1 Apr 1954

[Federal elections]: telegram from Tunku Abdul Rahman and Tan Cheng Lock to Mr Lyttelton protesting against the recommendations and requesting a meeting in London with the secretary of state

[The Federal Elections Committee reported on 21 Jan 1954 (see M J Hogan, *Report of the Committee appointed to examine the question of elections to the Federal Legislative Council*, Council Paper no 20 of 1954, Federation of Malaya). UMNO and MCA leaders had formed a minority on the committee and, because their ideas had not been incorporated within the majority report, they called another session of the 'national convention' on 14 Feb (see part II of this volume, 298). This meeting produced petitions to the high commissioner and Malay rulers demanding, amongst other things, a minimum of a three-fifths elected majority on the legislative council. Lyttelton would respond to each of these points after his meeting with the Alliance delegation in May (see 319). Meanwhile, since elections involved fundamental constitutional change, the first priority of the British was to secure the approval of the conference of rulers; an agreement was announced on 29 Mar, although its details were not published until 28 Apr. It consisted of a series of compromises between majority and minority reports. The most contentious issue was the proportion of elected members; while the majority favoured 44 out of 100, the minority demanded 60 out of 100. The rulers' conference finally accepted 52 out of 99. The rulers' decision was bitterly criticised by the Alliance which tried to enter into direct negotiations with the secretary of state.]

We are aggrieved that Their Highnesses the Rulers did not make public the decision on the subject of Federal elections reached at their Conference on 27th March 1954. The citizens of the Federation of Malaya and subjects of Their Highnesses are entitled to know this decision which is of vital importance and which will materially affect the structure of Malayan political and social life. Three petitions amongst many others had been sent by the United Malays National Organisation and the Malayan Chinese Association to Their Highnesses praying for acceptance of the recommendations contained in the Alliance petitions copies of which had been sent to you and duly acknowledged. No reply to these three petitions has been received from Their Highnesses while Their Highnesses' decision has been conveyed to you for assent by Her Majesty's Government.

The Rendel Commission[1] recommendations, presumably accepted by the Singapore Government, were published in detail for public comment before submission to you, whereas the terms of the agreement reached between Their Highnesses and the High Commissioner have not been so published. Thereby Her Majesty's Government would be making a decision without being acquainted with the full views and sentiments of the peoples of the Federation of Malaya as represented by their political parties on the agreement reached between Their Highnesses and the High Commissioner.

---

[1] Appointed in 1953 to review the constitution of Singapore.

Representatives of the United Malays National Organisation participated in the deliberations on the Constitution in 1946 and 1947 which culminated in the establishment of the Federation of Malaya. Now that the United Malays National Organisation and the Malayan Chinese Association have formed an Alliance, enjoying popular support as evidenced by the success of the Alliance in elections held thus far, the Alliance has not been asked to take part in the discussion of this vital matter by Their Highnesses. It is felt that the least the Alliance had expected was to have been given the opportunity to comment on the details of the agreement reached between Their Highnesses and the High Commissioner before submission to you. We fear that if this course of action is continued it will embarrass the Rulers in their Relations with their subjects as happened in the MacMichael incident.

In the circumstances, a delegation from the United Malays National Organisation and the Malayan Chinese Association requests an interview with you before Her Majesty's Government makes any decision. The delegation will fly to London on receipt of your reply.

314 CO 1030/309, no 23   13 Apr 1954
[Alliance delegation to London]: letter from D Gray[1] to Tunku Abdul Rahman and Tan Cheng Lock containing the text of Mr Lyttelton's reply to the Alliance leaders

I am directed by His Excellency the High Commissioner to refer to the telegram[2] handed by you to the Deputy High Commissioner on the 1st April for transmission to the Secretary of State for the Colonies requesting the Secretary of State to receive a delegation from the United Malays National Organisation and the Malayan Chinese Association, and to inform you that the Secretary of State is unable to accede to this request and has desired His Excellency to convey this reply to you in the following terms:—

"The UMNO/MCA Alliance message to me reveals a number of misunderstandings. First, the equivalent in the Federation of the Rendel Commission Report is not agreement between the High Commissioner and the Conference of Rulers but the Report of the Federal Elections Committee. The recommendations made by that Committee were also published in detail and there was full opportunity for public comment before their consideration in the Conference of Rulers.[3] Second, the terms of the Federation Agreement clearly require the High Commissioner to consult the Conference of Rulers before making recommendations to me on matters of this kind and, for obvious reasons almost universally accepted, such consultations must have necessarily taken place in private between the only parties (i.e., the High Commissioner and Their Highnesses the Rulers) who at that stage had any standing in the matter. Third, the result of these consultations is transmission to me not of "decisions" for assent by Her Majesty's Government but of agreed proposals for consideration by Her Majesty's Government. It then becomes my duty to

---

[1] Acting chief secretary, Federation of Malaya.   [2] See 313.   [3]See *ibid*, note.

consider these proposals and, in due course, to convey to the High Commissioner and the Conference of Rulers the views of Her Majesty's Government upon them.

2. The representatives of the UMNO/MCA Alliance have had the fullest opportunities to participate in making recommendations on all questions connected with the introduction of Federal Elections and they have rightly made the fullest use of those opportunities. The UMNO/MCA Alliance was represented on the Federal Elections Committee and in addition had every freedom to submit representations to the Committee. Their representatives on the Committee did in fact formulate proposals which, together with their supporting arguments, are fully reflected in the minority recommendations of the Committee's Report, and it is these same views and arguments which have been reiterated in the petitions to the High Commissioner and the Rulers. Copies of these petitions have been forwarded to me and are being taken into account in the formulation by Her Majesty's Government of their views upon all the matters in question. I have therefore no doubt that I am fully seized of the views of all parties and sections of opinion in the Federation and I see no occasion for further intervention by any of them in the discussions and exchange of views between the High Commissioner, Their Highnesses the Rulers and myself leading to the agreed conclusions necessary for the amendment of the Federation Agreement.

3. The whole ground has already been fully covered in the usual well established manner in the Federation without intervention from outside and I do not think it would serve any useful purpose if, after the long and thorough process of consultation and deliberation which has already taken place, I were now to throw the whole matter back into the melting pot by agreeing to receive the delegation from the UMNO/MCA Alliance or any other quarter—and, of course, if I were to agree to receive the delegation from the Alliance, I should also have to give time and opportunity to others if they too wanted to send delegations. Moreover, I am naturally anxious that the constitutional machinery established by the Federation Agreement should work as smoothly and effectively as possible. As I see it, on occasions such as this, once every opportunity has, as now, been given to all parties and sections of opinion in the Federation to make known their views, that machinery will not in fact function smoothly and effectively except by direct consultation restricted to Their Highnesses the Rulers and Her Majesty's Government, whose agreement—and whose agreement alone—is constitutionally required for the introduction of legislation to amend the Federation Agreement."[4]

---

[4] Lyttelton's reply, which was sent against the advice of Templer and MacGillivray, did not deter the Alliance delegation from seeking a meeting with the secretary of state in London.

315 CO 1030/309, no 20   20 Apr 1954
[Alliance delegation to London]: letter from Lord Ogmore[1] to Mr
Lyttelton

I have been approached on behalf of the U.M.N.O.-M.C.A. Alliance to request you to
receive a Deputation, led probably by Tunku Abdul Rahman Putra and Dato Sir Tan
Cheng Lock. They have also sent me copies of the telegram from themselves to you
and the reply that you caused to be sent to it.[2]

I strongly urge you to receive the Deputation from the U.M.N.O.-M.C.A. Alliance
in order that they can, in a constitutional manner, put before you their views.

I believe that it is always a mistake, if I may say so, for a Secretary of State to refuse
to meet an important Delegation from the Colonies and always causes much
resentment. In this particular case much harm will be done unless you do receive
them.

As you possibly know, I have been in touch with Malayan matters for the last 24
years and am personally acquainted with most of the leading figures in Malaya.

---

[1] Lord Ogmore, formerly D Rees-Williams, had known Tunku Abdul Rahman since his time in Penang
during the 1930s.
[2] See 313 and 314.

316 CO 1030/309, no 25   22 Apr 1954
[Alliance delegation to London]: letter (reply) from Mr Lyttelton to
Lord Ogmore

Thank you for your letter of the 20th April[1] asking me to receive a deputation from
the UMNO-MCA Alliance.

I cannot receive a deputation for the reasons I have already explained in the
message of which the Alliance have informed you (and of which I am enclosing a
copy in case you have not seen the full text).[2] I should, however, be very willing to
meet the persons you name, so long as it is understood that this is informal and that
I cannot at this stage enter into discussion of the Constitutional proposals with
them.

As you may know, I am leaving for Uganda on the 26th April and today is my last
day in London before I go. I understand that in any case Dato Sir Cheng Lock Tan is
travelling by sea and will not have arrived by Monday. I expect to be back about the
10th May, and would be willing to see him and Tunku Abdul Rahman together any
time after that date, on the understanding I have indicated above.

---

[1] See 315   [2] See 314.

317 CO 1030/309, no 27   **22 Apr 1954**

[Alliance delegation to London]: inward telegram no 316 from Sir G
Templer to Mr Lyttelton

My telegram No. 304.

Visit of Alliance Representatives to London.

Tunku Abdul Rahman and T.H. Tan are due to arrive London this afternoon by
B.O.A.C. Flight BA. 705/698. Sir Cheng Lock Tan has provisionally booked a sea
passage from Singapore and will leave about about 5th May.

2. Particulars of Tan are: aged about 40, born Singapore, educated Raffles College
Singapore, was reporter and later editor of Singapore Standard, became paid
executive Secretary of M.C.A. about 12 months ago and more recently Secretary of
Alliance.

3. In view of this visit to the United Kingdom you will no doubt wish to be aware
of what transpired at meeting convened by the Alliance leaders in Malacca last
Sunday 18th. It was an emergency meeting of U.M.N.O. General Assembly and was
well attended. Among 1,500 persons present there were nearly 100 delegates from
U.M.N.O. Branches in the Federation. The M.C.A. sent a small delegation of
members from its Malacca Branch, headed by Sir Cheng Lock Tan, the President.

4. The purpose of the meeting was to pass a number of resolutions reaffirming
U.M.N.O.'s primary objective to secure independence for Malaya, and advocating
measures to introduce a fully elected Legislative Council, including sending of a
delegation to the United Kingdom to hold discussions with Her Majesty's Government, and Parliamentary and other influential sources, so as to press for U.M.N.O.
demands and make them known in the United Kingdom and elsewhere, particularly
United States of America. The resolutions were passed by a two thirds majority. The
meeting had been preceded by a private meeting of the Alliance leaders held on 14th
to consider steps to be taken after your refusal to accede to Alliance request to receive
a delegation. At this private meeting a demand was put forward for a fully (omission
?elected legislature) as against a three fifths (omission ?elected majority among)
members of Council which owed its origin to the left wing elements led by Saadon
bin Haji Zubir, who is Vice President of U.M.N.O. Youth League.

5. The meeting on the 18th was largely dominated by left wing elements who,
however, did not apparently succeed in stirring up the strong anti-British feelings on
which they had counted in order to carry through the resolution more convincingly.
There were nevertheless, some potentially dangerous and irresponsible outbursts
advocating active measures to secure political freedom and references to drastic
action that should be taken in the event of the Delegation's mission proving
unsuccessful. These were, however, tempered by moderating influence of the Vice
President, Dr. Ismail, the Member for Natural Resources, whose plea to postpone
Delegation's visit until after publication of White Paper on the elections failed in the
event to find support. Tunku Abdul Rahman nominated Dr. Ismail as his successor as
President during his absence, and appealed to U.M.N.O. members to remain calm
and restrained until his return and to avoid doing anything which might prejudice
U.M.N.O. cause. Probably most significant feature of the meeting was the unity of
purpose it apparently stimulated among left and right wing elements in U.M.N.O.
and consequent preponderant swing to the left of U.M.N.O. as a whole.

It is possible that once in London they will, directly or indirectly, renew their application for an interview with you on the subject of Federal elections. It is also likely that at some stage, but probably not until after Cheng Lock Tan arrives in London, they will ask to see you on subjects such as Federal Citizenship, the Education Ordinance, the Immigration Ordinance and (corrupt group) for entry of non Malays into M.C.S. There would, I think, be much criticism here if you were not to give them an opportunity to make representations on such matters and I hope you will feel able to do so, at the same time making it quite clear you are not prepared to discuss the elections issue. Your attitude towards any request for an interview might appropriately be made known publicly by arranging for a Question to be asked in Parliament. If a reply is made after publication of despatches on 28th April, its terms might, I suggest be on the following lines:—

> *Begins.* "Whilst I shall be ready to receive representatives of U.M.N.O. and M.C.A. who are now in the United Kingdom and to have a general exchange of views on Malayan affairs, I must reiterate the decision conveyed in Malaya to the Presidents of both Organisations on 14th April that I cannot accede to their request to open discussions on the subject of elections to the Federal Legislative Council. These bodies were represented on the Committee which drew up proposals for the introduction of elections to the Council and their views were clearly reflected in the report of that Committee and were again expressed in petitions addressed to their Highnesses the Rulers of the Malay States and the High Commissioner, copies of which were sent to me.
>
> The introduction of these elections involves the amendment of the Federation Agreement and this legislative change requires the prior consent of Her Majesty and the Rulers. Before reaching conclusions contained in my despatch of 20th April to the High Commissioner, I was quite satisfied that I had been fully informed of views of the Organisations, parties and other interests whose representatives served on the Elections Committee and that it would have been improper to re-open in London with two of these Organisations discussions on these matters after the long and thorough process of consultation and deliberations which had already taken place in the Federation.
>
> If, therefore, the representatives of U.M.N.O. and M.C.A. wish to see me, I shall be very ready to grant their request on the understanding that discussions on the elections cannot be reopened." *Ends.*

318   CO 1030/309, no 53   15 May 1954
[Alliance delegation to London]: outward telegram no 62 from Mr Lyttelton to Sir G Templer on his talks with Tunku Abdul Rahman, T H Tan and Dato Abdul Razak

[On 21 Apr Tunku Abdul Rahman and T H Tan left Singapore for London by air. They were joined in London by Dato Abdul Razak who flew in from New York but Tan Cheng Lock remained in Malaya. While they awaited the secretary of state's return from Uganda, the Malayan leaders spoke with Ogmore and MPs from all parties, but particularly with Labour members. Lyttelton was back at Westminster to answer questions on Malaya on 12 May and he received the Alliance delegation on 14 May.]

My Regent telegram No. 60.

Alliance delegation.

Nearly all talking was done by Rahman, whose so-called arguments are no doubt well-worn and well-known to you. They were mainly:—

(a) That so small elected majority was unacceptable to mass of people, who demanded at least three-fifths. Alliance leaders could not resist them on this because if they did they would be thrown over and replaced by extremists. For so few seats the people would not think it worth-while supporting elections, and vast expense of fighting them would be waste of money to political parties.

(b) No party could hope to win more than seventy per cent of seats. On present figures that would mean unworkably small majority and winning party could therefore have no hope of governing with confidence. They would be in impossible position if they always had to rely for majority upon substantial help from non-elected elements in Council.

(c) Moreover, Opposition would have too few seats to function effectively and debates would thus lack reality.

(d) They were not asking for so large a number of elected seats as would ensure that winning party would in all circumstances enjoy over-all majority. Matter was one of degree only and their request introduced no new principle.

(e) They had nothing to gain personally in all this as all three of them had sacrificed security and good positions to take part in politics. Rahman himself would be happy if only it were possible to go back to old days of wholly nominated Council but this was ruled out by the will of the people.

(f) Rahman even suggested that, if Rulers objected to any increase in number of elected seats, you should overrule their objections by tendering them formal advice.

2. Main lines of my reply were:—

(a) I rubbed home argument that it was no sort of leadership tamely to obey all the demands of your followers. I also pointed out that the flood of people registering for State elections in Johore (where elected members will be in no stronger position than is proposed Federally) did not support their contention that proposed Federal elected majority was too small to ensure the people's interest in elections.

(b) I pointed out that majority party would in forming government automatically enjoy the additional support of the three *ex-officio* and two other official members of Council; that they would very likely have some permanent support from among the other non-elected members; and that, if their policies were reasonable, they would almost certainly enjoy the support of many more of those other members. I felt sure that if the Alliance were majority party their policies would be reasonable, and their present argument did them injustice by implying that their conduct of business would involve rash experiments on such a scale that they would be unable to carry with them any members outside their own ranks. I emphasised that decision to overrule majority recommendation of Federal Elections Committee and to take unprecedented step of introducing elected majority on occasion of first elections ever to be held was a very bold one, justified only by maturity and responsibility which the Malayan peoples had shewn in the past. That being so, I was fully satisfied that in this important experimental stage of advance towards self-government the checks and balance provided by proposed allocation of seats between elected and non-elected members, and by the kind of nominated members who would sit in the Council, were entirely necessary and desirable.

(c) I pointed out that they could not at one and the same time argue that majority party required more seats in order to govern satisfactorily and that the elected Opposition should be stronger. The two arguments were not compatible and the point was not in any case really relevant to their main contention.

(d) I said that even in matters of degree there was nearly always a breaking point and that I was absolutely certain myself that any attempt now to increase the size of the elected majority would throw right back into the melting pot the whole agreement which had so far been reached, and that the entire process of consultation would have to begin again, with the certainty of much delay in introducing elections and with other possible consequences which could not be calculated at this stage. I repeated this several times as strongly as I could. Without explicit reference to Conference of Rulers I also stressed that I was not in a position on my own to agree to anything that they asked, as might have been the case in some territories. Finally I stated in the most categorical terms my own conviction that to go back on present arrangements would do grievous harm to the best interests of the country and that if Alliance continued to press for a three-fifths elected majority they would precipitate a very damaging crisis and would be regarded by all reasonable people as pursuing a thoroughly irresponsible course. I had already heard of their threat of mass resignation but they did not mention it to me; nor did they make any suggestion of a Royal Commission.

(e) I said that I fully recognised that there was nothing personal in their demands.

(f) I told them that the terms of the Federation Agreement put this right out of the question. My legal advice is that there is an unresolved doubt about the relationship between the proviso in Clause 6 (1) and Clause 8 of the Federation Agreement, and that it cannot be said with certainty on purely legal grounds that the proviso over-rides Clause 8; but I am quite clear that if question about this had to be answered it would be necessary to take the line that in view of the proviso it would not be proper for the High Commissioner to tender formal advice on matters involving amendment of the Agreement. I should prefer to avoid making such a statement in view of fact that it might tie our hands on some future occasion when we found it necessary to allow ourselves greater latitude.

3.   You should know that delegation has been having talks with Opposition here.[1] Ogmore came to see me on Thursday and said that he and Griffiths believed Alliance would be satisfied if they could be given all the seats in the nominated reserve. He claimed that this could be done within the terms of our exchange of despatches. That is clearly not so and I do not think that anything can be done on those lines.[2] I understand in any case that this proposal has already been made to you and that you have rejected it.

4.   My impression of the delegation is that they are three worried little men and on the evidence of their attitude when with me I should doubt whether they will in

---

[1] eg Stanley Awbery, Fenner Brockway, James Griffiths, W T Proctor, and R W Sorensen.
[2] See 320.

fact press their opposition to the present proposals by the extreme measures which they have threatened. On the other hand they seem to have gone much further when talking to Griffiths and Ogmore and have certainly left them with the firm impression that they are quite determined to carry out their threat of resignation if they don't get what they want. I am quite determined not to budge at all from our present position but I think that it might ease the situation greatly if we could open to the Alliance some emergency exit from the position in which they have put themselves, and I am very anxious if possible to find some such expedient. My first hasty thought was that I might tell them that if the new constitution did work really well during the first year I would welcome the appointment of a fresh commission to consider what further changes, if any, could be made at any time between then and the end of the four-year period. On reflection, however, I think that this will not do, partly because it would virtually commit us to giving them what they want at the end of a year and partly because that might make it look as though the face-saving were being done by us rather than by them. Another idea which I entertained but rejected was to suggest reducing the period of the new Legislature from four to three years. One suggestion which I think may be practicable, however, is that I should repeat my belief that the arrangement now proposed is right and that if the majority party pursue sound policies they will have no difficulty in obtaining all the non-elected support that they need, but go on to add that it is our intention that the majority party should be able to function effectively in government and that if it were found in practice that their ability to do so was being consistently frustrated by unreasonable obstructiveness I would consider what steps could be taken to remedy the situation. It might also help if the Alliance could be told that there will not in fact be any multiple-member constituencies. This presumably could be done only if you could tell Merthyr[3] that, should his Commission already have come to that conclusion, it would help you to have his agreement to make it public at once.

5.   Most grateful for your comments on all this, particularly on my tentative ideas about emergency exits, and for any other suggestions that you can make to that end.

6.   I ought to write to delegation not later than Tuesday and therefore feel bound to ask you for a reply to this telegram by Monday mid-day. As the contents of my letter would almost certainly leak in any case I think that I must write in terms suitable for publication, and I may even decide to release the letter myself.[4]

---

[3] Lord Merthyr, a lawyer, chaired a three-man commission appointed by the high commissioner to divide Malaya into election districts of approximately equal population with some 'weightage' for area. See *Report of the Constituency Delineation Commission*, Council Paper no 36 of 1954, Federation of Malaya.
[4] See 319 and Tunku Abdul Rahman's reply at 321. Both letters were published at the time.

319   CO 1030/310, no 56   18 May 1954
[Alliance delegation to London]: letter from Mr Lyttelton to Tunku Abdul Rahman

I was glad last week to have an opportunity to meet your colleagues and yourself as representatives of the United Malay National Organisation and the Malayan Chinese Association, and to have at first hand a full account of your views upon certain of the present proposals for the introduction of elections to the Federal Legislative Council.

I undertook to give your views my careful consideration and to write to you about them before you left London on your return to Malaya on Thursday next, the 20th May. I am sure that our discussion was valuable in enabling us to understand each other's point of view; and looking back upon it I am encouraged by the reflection that, as I think you will agree from what follows, there is between us no essential disagreement upon principle and little even upon practical issues.

Your party has raised six points of criticism against the proposals of the Federal Elections Committee. I deal with them in detail below but it may be convenient for me first to summarise the present position in regard to each:—

(a) your desire that Government servants should not be debarred from standing for election to the Legislative Council has been met to the greatest extent possible without eroding the vital principle of the impartiality of the civil servant in relation to politics;

(b) your desire that there should be a simple majority vote in all constituencies has been met in full;

(c) for the logical and practical reasons given below it is not possible to depart from the general practice in modern States that only citizens enjoy the right to vote;

(d) your desire that nominated members of the Legislative Council should be eligible for Ministerial office has also been met in full;

(e) there is no difference between us in our anxiety that the first Federal elections should be held as soon as possible: it is a practical impossibility to hold them before the end of this year but they will be held as early as possible next year; and

(f) above all, your desire that the majority party in the Legislative Council should be able to function effectively in government will be fully satisfied by my assurance that, if it were prevented from doing so by deliberate obstructiveness, I should at once ask the High Commissioner to consider with the Conference of Rulers how the situation might be remedied, and that I should be prepared, if necessary, to agree to amendment of the Federation Agreement in order to apply a suitable remedy.

Our discussion last week turned almost entirely upon your request that at least three-fifths of the new Legislative Council should be elected members—and you clearly regard this as much the most important of your counter-proposals—but before coming to that I should like to deal with the other five points. First, you have asked that Government servants should not be debarred from standing for election to the Council. I am convinced, however, that the decision which we have taken is the right one. This is one of those issues of principle upon which it is scarcely possible to compromise and I am sure that the majority of the Federal Elections Committee were right in coming to the conclusion that: "It is of paramount importance at this juncture to establish firmly and irrefutably that the roles of the politician and the civil servant are separate and distinct and should be kept entirely apart." On the other hand, Their Highnesses the Rulers, the High Commissioner and I myself fully recognised the difficulties that might arise from this decision in finding a sufficient number of candidates of the necessary calibre and experience in public affairs to enter the Legislative Council as elected members, and we therefore gave very close attention to your arguments on the subject. As a result it was decided to modify the majority recommendations of the Federal Elections Committee by two substantial concessions which in my view very largely meet your wishes without endangering the fundamental principle involved. These are, first, that Government servants in the junior grades will before polling day be allowed to take one month's leave without pay in order to stand as candidates; and, second, that, for the first elections only, Government servants in the senior grades who have reached the age of 46 on nomination day will be allowed to retire with the pension or gratuity which they have earned so far. To go further than this would involve the risk of grave damage to the status and efficiency of the Federation's civil service, upon which so heavily depends the success of its advance towards self-government and its stability when that has been achieved. Experience in the United Kingdom and elsewhere has long and clearly demonstrated the importance to the political leaders of a nation of being able to rely with complete confidence upon the integrity and impartiality as well as upon the ability of their senior civil servants; and I am sure that in years to come the peoples of Malaya will look back with gratitude to those who at this decisive stage were sufficiently far-sighted to stand firmly by this vital principle.

Second, you have asked that there should be a simple majority vote in all constituencies, whether multiple-member or single-member. I am able to tell you that on this your wishes will be met, for I have learned from the High Commissioner that the Constituency Delineation Commission does not intend to recommend the establishment of any constituency with more than two members, and that there will therefore be no provision for a limited vote.

Third, you have asked that, in addition to Federal citizens and subjects of the Rulers, certain other persons should be given the right to vote. Adoption of this proposal would run counter to the general practice in modern States, which is to restrict the franchise to citizens of the State. I need not elaborate the powerful logical justification for this almost universal practice, but I may, perhaps, add my personal opinion that adherence to it is indispensable to the aim which we all share of building up an united Malayan nation conscious and proud of its claim to that title. I realise that the problem of citizenship is complicated but I have no doubt that the high privilege of the right to vote in the Federation should be reserved to its citizens.

Fourth, as you know, it has been decided to go beyond the majority of the Federal Elections Committee and to provide that nominated members of the Legislative Council should not be precluded from Ministerial office as holders of portfolios in the Executive Council. Here again your wishes have been met.

Fifth, I am satisfied after thorough examination of all the problems involved that it is in fact simply impossible to complete the legislative, administrative and other arrangements for the first elections in time for them to be held before the end of this year. I can, however, assure you with equal confidence that no effort will be spared to hold the elections at the earliest practicable date in 1955. There is thus no difference between us on this issue: we are just bound by the limits of practical possibility.

I come now to your request that at least three-fifths of the new Legislative Council should be elected members. You put it to me that the matter was one only of degree and not of principle since you were not asking for so large a number of elected seats as to ensure that the party which won the elections would in all circumstances enjoy a clear majority in the Council. You put forward two arguments in support of this contention. First, you said that if the majority of elected members were no more than was at present intended, the people would not think it worth while participating fully in the elections; and, second, you said that, as no party could hope to win more than seventy per cent of the seats, the present proposals would allow the victorious party too small a majority for it to function effectively in government, since it could not always be sure of the substantial support from non-elected members of the Council upon which it would have to rely to secure approval of its policies.

I fully appreciate the sincerity of these apprehensions but I believe that, when you have been able to reflect upon what I am now about to say, you will recognise that you need have no anxiety upon either of these counts, and that, as the responsible leaders of your party, you will be able so to persuade your supporters. There is already convincing evidence of the readiness of the peoples of Malaya to play their part in elections without insisting upon an elected majority larger than that at present contemplated. It seems to me significant that registration for the State elections in Johore is going forward enthusiastically despite the fact that the elected members of the State Legislature will not be in a majority at all. I believe that the Federal elections will command the same enthusiasm without need on that account for any increase in the proposed majority of elected members.

Moreover, there is in my view every likelihood that the victorious party in the Federal elections will be able to rely on such stable support in the Legislative Council as will enable it to take part with real confidence in the government of the country. For one thing, in becoming the Government party it will automatically secure the support of the three *ex officio* members of the Legislative Council and also of the two other official members charged with the duties of Secretary for Defence and Member for Economic Affairs. Again, it seems clear that if, for example, your party commanded a majority of the elected members of the Council they would be regularly supported by a number of the nominated members, since it is a reasonable expectation that these will include some Councillors who are already members of the party. Finally, I am sure that, whatever party may win the elections it will set itself with a high sense of purpose to pursue sober and progressive policies; and if it does I have no doubt that it will enjoy the dependable support of a large number of the other nominated members. To think otherwise is to imply that the majority party might pursue such unreasonable experiments or so mishandle the conduct of public business that it was unable to carry with it any members of the Council outside its own ranks. I do not believe that your own or any other party would follow a course so prejudicial to the true interests of the Federation. On the contrary, it is because of the evidence of maturity and responsibility which the political leaders in the Federation have hitherto shown that it has been possible to go further than the majority recommendation of the Federal Elections Committee on this subject and to take the quite exceptional step of introducing a majority of elected members on the occasion of the first elections ever to be held in the country.

At the same time, it must be recognised that that is a bold and adventurous step, a token not of timidity or distrust but of appreciation of past achievement and faith in future progress. But, with the welfare of the Malayan peoples as our only touchstone in these matters, it would be wrong for us to pass beyond what is bold into what would be reckless; and I am bound to express my conviction that, at this important experimental stage in the advance towards self-government, the checks and balances provided by the proposed allocation of seats between elected and nominated members, and by the quality of the nominated members who are likely to sit in the Council, are both necessary and desirable. I have already expressed my confidence that whatever party may win the elections will, in helping to govern the country, itself be governed only by the best interests of the country, and that any party so disposed will have no difficulty in carrying with it a solid and regular majority of the Legislative Council: but when elections are being introduced for the first time, when all the political parties are still comparatively young and have as yet had insufficient opportunity to prove themselves fully in the arduous business of government, and when the Federation is passing through a period during which that business will, because of the emergency and of financial stringency, constitute a formidable burden of responsibility, it would to my mind be unwise to let our ambitions, however reasonable, involve us in the risk of irremediable mistakes. I am certain that this would be the view of all the thinking people in the Federation who sincerely combine a desire for political progress with a jealous interest in the country's stability and welfare.

It will be clear from what I have said that it is our firm intention that the majority party in the Legislative Council should be able to function effectively in government, and that I have every confidence that it will not from any quarter meet with unreasonable opposition in trying to do so. I should, however, like to reinforce this by giving you my assurance that, if it were found in practice that the ability of the majority party to function effectively in government was being frustrated by a deliberately obstructive minority, I should at once ask the High Commissioner to consider with the Conference of Rulers what steps should be taken to remedy the situation—and that, in order to give effect to such a remedy, I should be prepared, if necessary, to agree to further amendment of the Federation Agreement without waiting until the end of the four-year period for which the present proposals provide. I think that you will agree that this important fresh assurance finally removes any anxiety which you may hitherto have felt upon the whole question.

In my personal opinion the Federal Elections Committee was as representative and authoritative a body as could have been constituted (in the circumstances of the Federation today;) and its achievement in reaching unanimity on many of the issues involved, some of them highly controversial, and in narrowing down to negligible proportions its differences on many others, seems to me very impressive. I realise that in your view the representation of your party upon the Committee was inadequate, but in matters of this kind none of us can ever hope to have all his desires entirely satisfied and I believe that the composition of the Committee was as just a cross section of all shades of opinion and of all legitimate interests in the Federation as was possible if it were to remain of manageable size. Moreover, I think that I have shown in this letter that the decisions which have now finally been taken upon the Committee's recommendations, while necessarily a compromise, have reduced to a very narrow compass the points of disagreement between the main sections of opinion in the Federation, including your party. The appointment and procedure of the Committee provided ample opportunity for individuals and organisations in the Federation to ensure that full account was taken of their views in the formulation of recommendations upon the important issues which the Committee was charged to consider. Your party rightly took full advantage of these opportunities, both through its representatives upon the Committee and by making its views known in other ways; and you again naturally and rightly made known your views upon the Committee's recommendations when its report was released for the consideration of public opinion. Thereafter, in accordance with the terms of the

Federation Agreement, there followed prolonged and meticulous consultation upon the Committee's recommendations between the Conference of Rulers, the High Commissioner and myself on behalf of Her Majesty[.] Under the constitution of the Federation only these, and all of these, were at that stage properly concerned in reaching the agreement without which no decisions could be taken. I myself was not then and am not now in a position unilatorly [sic] to reach decisions or to vary them.

The decisions taken as a result of these consultations, and since published in a Legislative Council paper, are thus the outcome of a most careful and exhaustive process of investigation, debate and deliberation at all levels and over the widest possible field. Even in matters of degree there is always a breaking point and I am sure that you will agree that it would be a tragedy to stand uncompromisingly upon differences involving no question of principle and in reality not even any significant question of degree. I believe that this would do grievous harm to the best interests of the Federation and I am confident that you will agree with me—as, I have no doubt, will all reasonable opinion in the Federation and this country alike—that our sense of responsibility requires us to avoid a damaging crisis of this kind. Let us not cast away the true substance of our common aims and agreement for a shadow which has no body behind it.

320 CO 1030/310, no 65   22 May 1954

[Federal elections and Alliance demands]: letter from Mr Lyttelton to Lord Ogmore on the use of reserved seats

I gave very careful thought to the suggestion which you put to me last week as a possible means of inducing the U.M.N.O./M.C.A. "Alliance" to withdraw their demand for an increase up to three-fifths in the number of elected members in the Federal Legislative Council in the Federation of Malaya. The idea was that the High Commissioner should use the seven seats in the "nominated reserve" to strengthen the majority of whatever party won the first elections.

The Federal Elections Committee recommended a rather larger nominated reserve of ten members and gave as their reason the desirability "of giving a voice in the Council to any important element which had not found adequate representation through the electoral process". They added that this also would be helpful to the High Commissioner "for the purpose of facilitating the discharge of the special responsibilities imposed on him by Clause 19 of the Federation Agreement and his other special responsibilities". In his despatch to me about the report of the Federal Elections Committee the High Commissioner said that the Rulers and he endorsed this proposal since it would enable the High Commissioner "to give a voice in the Council to any major element which does not secure adequate representation through either the electoral or nominating processes". They expressed the view, however, that the size of the nominated reserve should be reduced to seven. I accepted this recommendation and even if I wanted to vary it I could not do so entirely on my own responsibility but should have to refer it back for reconsideration by the High Commissioner and the Conference of Rulers, who would, I think, be unlikely to agree.

It seems to me, therefore, that the High Commissioner could not undertake to use these nominated seats primarily and automatically to increase the majority of the party or parties commanding major support amongst the elected members. It may well be, however, that in filling these seats for the purposes indicated in paragraph 31 of the Elections Committee's Report the High Commissioner would inform the majority leader of his intentions and take into account any views that that leader might express, since one of the responsibilities which the High Commissioner will have in mind is the creation of an efficient government and he may think that the representation of the interests concerned would be more effectively achieved by members likely to find themselves in harmony with majority opinion and to be in a position to support and guide it. For your personal information, the High Commissioner proposes to mention the matter on these lines to his Executive Council (including Rahman) on Tuesday.

I saw the Alliance delegation last Friday and now enclose for your private and personal information a copy of the letter which I have written to them in reply to their representations. I have told the delegation that I propose to make it public in due course but that I will not do so until they have returned to the Federation and been able to acquaint their colleagues of it.

What I have said to them seems to me to demonstrate that the decisions which have already been taken together with my assurances about how it is intended to put them into practice, leave very little margin indeed between what we propose and the Alliance want. The margin that remains is, I believe, indispensable and I do not think that the Alliance now have any grounds for persisting in further opposition to the agreed proposals. If you and Griffiths would like to come and have a word with me about all this I should be very glad to see you.

I am writing a similar letter to Griffiths.[1]

---

[1] James Griffiths, secretary of state for the colonies in the previous Labour government.

321 CO 1030/310, no 91   25 May 1954
[Federal elections and Alliance demands]: inward telegram (reply) from Tunku Abdul Rahman to Mr Lyttelton

[Readers may find it helpful to consult 322 in advance of this document.]

I refer to your letter of the 18th May[1] and to my acknowledgement of the 20th May. The Alliance has now had the opportunity of discussing the contents of your letter, and I am to send you this further reply in the following terms: while we appreciate that you have accepted several of our recommendations, you have rejected the most fundamental of our recommendations, which is that three-fifths of the future members of the Federal Legislative Council should be elected. Having accepted the principle of elected majority, Her Majesty's Government in our humble opinion should have made the application of that principle effective. Instead Her Majesty's Government insists that 52 elected to 46 appointed will give the victorious party at the election sufficient majority to run the government.

---

[1] See 319.

The Alliance begs to differ, for we consider that this majority of six is insufficient to enable the victorious party to have a working majority in the Council to form a stable government.

With such a small majority of elected members, the party in power will be subject to the whims and fancies of the nominated members, because our experience has shown that there are elements who are opposed to real democratic progress.

While appreciating your assurance that in the event of the future government being frustrated because of deliberately obstructive minorities, you would ask the High Commissioner to consider with the Conference of Rulers what steps should be taken to remedy the situation, we beg to point out that this assurance is of no real value because such action will then have to be taken in any case. No responsible party will willingly form a government in these circumstances.

Finally, I am to inform you that the Alliance held a meeting at Kuala Lumpur last night and adopted a resolution.[2] The resolution was handed this morning by the Alliance delegation consisting of myself, Hon. Col. H. S. Lee, (Member for Transport) and Hon. Ismail Abdul Rahman (Member for Natural Resources), and Hon. Mr. Leong Yew Koh,[3] to the High Commissioner who will no doubt communicate with you and their Highnesses the Rulers as the parties concerned.

---

[2] See 322.   [3] Secretary-general of the MCA.

322   CO 1030/310, no 72   26 May 1954
[Federal elections and Alliance demands]: inward telegram no 418 from Sir G Templer to Mr Lyttelton on the Alliance resolution of 24 May

Federal Elections.

Four Members of the Alliance (Rahman, Lee, Ismail and Leong Yew Koh) called on me yesterday morning and presented me with the following resolution which had been adopted at the Alliance meeting the previous evening.

"That the White Paper to introduce national elections in the Federation of Malaya is not acceptable to the Alliance and, therefore, the Alliance strongly opposes its implementation by the Federation Government.

In order to get an unbiased assessment of the country's progress towards self-Government, the Alliance requests that a special independent commission, consisting entirely of members from outside Malaya, be sent immediately to the Federation with the concurrence of Her Majesty and Their Highnesses to report on constitutional reforms in the Federation. The Alliance believes the appointment of such a commission will have the support of all who believe in democracy.

Fully realising its responsibilities towards the people and the country, the Alliance will continue to give its fullest co-operation to the Government in all respects, particularly with a view to bringing the emergency to an early end, if this request is acceded to. On the other hand, if the authorities insist on implementation of the White Paper, the Alliance with great regret will have no choice but to withdraw all its members from participation in the Government".

2.   They stated that this resolution was by the way of being the Alliance's reply to

your letter of 18th May to Rahman[1] and I undertook to convey it to you. Rahman said he would also send a reply to your letter. The "Straits Times" this morning contains text of that reply which I understand he telegraphed direct to you last night.[2]

3. After they had presented the resolution to me we had some discussion. It became clear that the Alliance is not going to shift its ground. They are determined to resign if the White Paper is implemented. Their present intention is that all Alliance party members shall resign from the Federal Executive and Legislative Councils, State Councils, Municipal and Town Councils (but not from Local Councils since they did not contest these as a political party) and will not participate in Federal Elections. The resignations would take place as soon as the order paper for the meeting of the Legislative Council of 23rd June is in their hands (about 15th June).

4. They explained that what they meant by "constitutional reform in the Federation" was reform of the whole framework of the Federation Agreement and not merely amendments of the agreement to provide for Federal elections; this would cover the relationship between the Federal and State Governments and I think they probably also include in their minds the constitutional position of the Rulers. Rahman added, however, and Lee agreed, that their main concern was the appointment of a commission, and that provided this was done they would be content with a more limited field of enquiry.

5. I told them that it was my firm intention to go ahead with consideration of the Bill in the Executive Council that afternoon and to publish it at once so as to make it possible to introduce it at the meeting of the Legislative Council on 23rd June. I explained that the question of the appointment of a commission to examine the whole field of constitutional reform was one to be considered by you and the Rulers; that if such a commission should be agreed to, a considerable period of time must elapse before it could be appointed and complete its work, and before any decisions could be taken upon its recommendations; after that there would no doubt be protracted negotiations in the Rulers' Conference and elsewhere. If therefore, the present election proposals were not proceeded with meantime, Federal elections would inevitably be postponed for a long period, perhaps until the end of 1956. They said they were quite prepared to accept this and that the delay would be preferable to proceeding with the present proposals. I suggested that if the appointment of a commission to go into the wider issues of constitutional reform should be agreed to they should then accept the present election proposals as an interim arrangement, but they rejected this idea on the grounds that political parties cannot afford to fight two elections within a short period. Rahman said that the Federal elections would cost U.M.N.O. $250,000 a time.

6. They offered an absolute guarantee that they would accept the findings of such a commission and that even if those findings contained a recommendation for a very small elected majority they would nonetheless accept that and contest the elections.

7. They stated that they would not expect to be consulted about the composition of the commission but they would hope to be shown the names. They seemed to have some idea that the members of the commission should be chosen from various countries in the Commonwealth and not merely from the United Kingdom.[3]

---

[1] See 319.   [2] See 321.
[3] This is the first reference to an independent Commonwealth commission which would take shape in 1956 as the Reid Commission.

8. Throughout the talks they kept harking back to the fact that unless they adopted a determined attitude in the matter of the White Paper they would lose half their followers and that U.M.N.O., and maybe M.C.A. as well, would get into the wrong hands. It is clear that they are being led by extremist element in U.M.N.O. and that they are prepared to go a long way with that element in order to avoid a break-up of the Alliance and within U.M.N.O. itself.

9. I asked them whether they would consider deletion of the last sentence of their resolution since this was in effect a threat which might be interpreted to mean that they would not help to bring the emergency to an early end and in my opinion would have a bad effect with the Rulers when Their Highnesses came to consider the request for a commission. They said they had discussed this sentence for a very long time and were now unable to alter it in any way as they thought it was better to come out into the open and not attempt to conceal anything.

10. In the Executive Council in the afternoon the three Alliance members stated that they strongly opposed the Federation of Malaya Agreement (Amendment) Bill and that they would not take part in any discussion on it. They remained silent during the subsequent discussion of the Bill but did not say anything about resignation.

11. I will let you have my considered views on the position at the end of this week after it has been possible to gauge public reaction to the publication of your letter to Rahman, and to this latest move by the Alliance. Although it was agreed with the Alliance yesterday that the contents of their resolution would not at present be divulged to the public, the "Straits Times" today stated that the Alliance had demanded 'a Royal Commission to review immediately the question of the Federal Elections' and that otherwise 'they would boycott the Government' and resign from all Councils. The request for a commission to undertake a complete review of the Federation Agreement will appear to be a very reasonable one to many people since there are unacceptable parts in the Agreement which are clearly in need of change e.g. (corrupt group ?reasonable) working of financial arrangements between the Federal and State Governments; moreover it is likely to have the support of the Indian community who have begun to realise that the Federal Elections arrangement approved in the White Paper will not operate to their advantage, and also of labour groups who have throughout asked for one hundred per cent Elected Council. The rejection of the request out of hand would therefore be ill received by many and would strengthen the position of the Alliance. But the proposal is likely to be bitterly opposed by the Rulers and Party Negara.[4] It is difficult to gauge what support the Alliance is likely to receive in a campaign of boycott and whether it could develop into one of widespread civil disobedience, and although many including (those) unacceptable to the present Alliance adherents would undoubtedly rally behind the Rulers on this issue, possibility of support for the Alliance being considerable cannot be ignored.

12. The proposal now made by the Alliance is obviously one which must be put before the Rulers. If it should be put to them at once for decision as a matter of urgency, the reply would almost certainly be 'no' and the Alliance would then carry out their threat of resignation and boycott. I have some reason to believe that rejection of suggestion mentioned at the end of paragraph 5 above was not a

---

4 See part II of this volume, 298, note 5.

considered and final one. There may therefore be just a chance that the Alliance will refrain from resignation and/or boycotting the elections and be content merely to absent themselves from the Legislative Council when the Bill is taken on 23rd June, if a reply should be sent to them before the date of issue of Legislative Council Order day to the following effect. That suggestion that there should be a review of the whole constitution of the Federation raises big issues and will require careful and deliberate consideration; you are therefore asking the High Commissioner[5] to discuss it with the Conference of Rulers at their next meeting. You might add that if a commission should be appointed to undertake such a review its report could not be expected for some time and that when it was received it might well be desirable that the view of the Legislative Council of the time should be obtained on its recommendations before decisions were taken by Her Majesty's Government and the Rulers and obviously it would be of advantage if that Legislative Council should be one containing elected element and not the present one hundred per cent nominated Council. This, however, is merely my first thought and I will telegraph again later. Meantime, since Rahman's published letter to you of yesterday states that I will no doubt communicate with you and the Rulers 'as parties concerned', I think that I must now send the Keeper of the Ruler's [Rulers'] Seal a copy of the resolution merely saying that this was handed to me yesterday and that I will communicate later with Their Highnesses on the subject.

---

[5] ie by that time the office would be held by MacGillivray not Templer.

323   CO 1030/310, no 73   28 May 1954
[Federal elections and Alliance demands]: outward telegram (reply) no 74 from Sir J Martin to Sir G Templer

Your secret telegram No. 418.[1]
    Federal Elections.
    We are most grateful for this full account of developments and your preliminary views upon them. We do not propose to refer to the Secretary of State until we have the further considered observations which you promise: but meanwhile you may care to have our first reactions at official level.
    2. It seems to us essential that we should now go ahead with elections on the basis already agreed. We think that it is quite out of the question to accept the Alliance demand in its present form i.e. involving postponement of elections pending enquiry by a Commission. As you warned them, postponement would be a long one; one example of causes of delay is that in spite of urgency it took 7 months to get together the East Africa Royal Commission.[2] The Secretary of State has so far stood firm on decisions already taken and made it clear that in his view they are right, that to go further would be wrong and that there is virtually no substance in the Alliance criticisms of them. He has also already gone publicly on record as believing that until elections have been held it is impossible to judge the claims of any one party to

---

[1] See 322.
[2] Appointed, under the chairmanship of Sir Hugh Dow, to examine the land problem and to recommend measures to improve the standard of living, see *East Africa Royal Commission, 1953–55: Report* (Cmd 9475, 1955).

support of public opinion in Federation on these issues and the only proper way to test the validity of such claims is at the polls. To accept Alliance proposal as it stands would in appearance and in fact be complete capitulation to them (and that is, at second remove, to their extremists).

3. There may be a case for appointment of a Commission to review Federation agreement, including such matters as financial relations between State Governments and Government of Federation; but there would be great advantage in associating the new Legislative Council with such matters as the settling of terms of reference of any such Commission as well the implementation of its findings.

4. We recognise of course that refusal of their demand may strengthen Alliance and that the implications of boycott may be serious. There may also be an element of public opinion here which will think it unreasonable to refuse an enquiry. An alternative which occurs to us would be to tell Alliance that as soon as elections are over you would appoint select committee of new Legislative Council, with membership based on relative strength of parties in Council, to consider and make recommendations about Alliance proposal. It would be for consideration whether this committee should contain any non-elected members and whether you could even go so far as to say that a majority party in Council would be given overall majority on committee; but we have not thought out this idea in detail.

324 CO 1030/193, no 1   29 May 1954
[MacDonald's role in Britain's regional policy]: letter from Mr M J MacDonald to Sir T Lloyd. *Minutes* by Sir J Martin, Sir T Lloyd, A M MacKintosh and J B Johnston[1]

[Anglo-Alliance confrontation over federal elections acquired added piquancy from its coincidence with the French defeat at Dien Bien Phu. By this time it was accepted in government circles that the collapse of French Indo-China might have a 'domino' effect throughout South-East Asia, and one aspect of Malayan security was the contingency plan to seal off the peninsula by advancing to the Kra isthmus in the event of a communist take-over in Thailand (see Part II of this volume, 231). On the other hand, the government was wary of appearing belligerent, and, when in Apr a Vietminh victory at Dien Bien Phu seemed inevitable, ministers were not persuaded by the argument of John Foster Dulles (US secretary of state) that the consequent threat to Malaya warranted British assistance to France (see CAB 129/68, C(54)155, 27 Apr 1954, reproduced in BDEEP series A, vol 3, D Goldsworthy, ed, *The Conservative government and the end of empire 1951–1957*, part I, 61). Instead, an international conference on Indo-China (held from May to July and co-chaired by Eden and Molotov) negotiated French withdrawal from, and the partition of, Vietnam. It was against this background that the CO and FO would review the role of MacDonald (see 335, 338 and 348).]

I enclose a copy of a personal letter[2] which I am sending to Ivone Kirkpatrick[3] to-day. You will see my reference in it to the Joint Co-ordination Committee.

No doubt you see my series of Savingrams about the progress of the Joint Co-ordination Committee,[4] so you will know that I anticipate that the Committee will be ready to proceed to discussion of its all-important third Term of Reference[5] in

---

[1] Principal private secretary to the secretary of state, 1953–1956.   [2] Not printed.
[3] Sir Ivone Kirkpatrick, permanent under-secretary, FO, 1953–1957.
[4] See part II of this volume, 300.
[5] ie to consider constitutional changes involved in closer association of British dependencies.

three or four months' time. I do not feel that we should delay the discussion any longer than we can help; so I should be back in Singapore after my holiday by, say, September.

One reason why I have been trying to press ahead is that at present my term of office here only runs until the end of this year. It is therefore desirable that the J.C.C. should have made a lot of progress in its examination of its third Term of Reference by then, otherwise it may have to continue without its Chairman. Of course, if I were going to continue here next year, then this reason for hurry would disappear. I do not know what the Government's intention may be about terminating or extending my period. As far as I am concerned, I should be quite ready to stay here for as long as may be necessary to finish this extremely important work of getting Singapore and the Federation into closer political association.

I believe that, if my British colleagues and I, with our Asian fellow members, can feel free to get ahead with the work of the Joint Co-ordination Committee at a convenient pace, we might be able to produce agreed proposals for a more closely associated Federation and Singapore sometime during the next eighteen months. Moreover, I think that there is a reasonable prospect that—assuming things go well between the Federation and Singapore members of the J.C.C.—we can devise a Constitution in which the three Borneo Territories would be willing to join in due course. As you perhaps know from my letter to Mackintosh of April 15, I propose to broach this problem again with Abell and Turnbull[6] when the three of us meet in October. It may take more than eighteen months to get the Borneo leaders to agree to our proposals, and I do not think that we should feel cramped or limited at present by trying to work too strictly to a time table. It is so important that the five territories in South-East Asia should be brought together in some workable scheme that the negotiators here should be given reasonable time and room for manoeuvre.

As I say, if I can be of any use in these matters, I would gladly stay here and play my part. I meant to discuss this with you in London next week; but now that I am stuck here for a while longer, I had better put it down in this personal and private letter to you, so that you know my attitude. The only reason why I mention it now is that it does have some bearing on the question of when I should take my leave.

Minutes on 324

Sir T. Lloyd
In the attached letter Mr. Malcolm MacDonald raises the question of a possible further extension of his appointment (already extended up to the end of 1954) in the interests of the work of the Joint Co-ordination Committee, of which he is chairman.

It would have been convenient to discuss with the Foreign Office, who may be considered to have a greater interest than we have in the continued existence of the appointment, before submitting this to the Secretary of State, but all the higher authorities concerned in the Foreign Office are away at Geneva and you may prefer to show it to him without awaiting an opportunity for inter-departmental consultation.

In proposing to the Prime Minister the present extension (in October last) Mr. Eden referred to the decision in the previous year that we could not then withdraw

---

[6] Sir Roland Turnbull, governor of North Borneo, 1954–1960.

Mr. MacDonald without damage to our interests and to the general position in South East Asia and continued:—

> "The reasons of foreign policy for which we decided to ask him to stay on this year still hold good. The situation in South East Asia is still uncertain and MacDonald's removal would be taken to mean that our interest in the area was lessening."

There can be little doubt that the case for retaining Mr. MacDonald in Singapore on these grounds is at the least no weaker now than last autumn. (The value of extending the appointment in this connection probably depends more on the personality of Mr. MacDonald and the contacts he has established than on the existence of the post of Commissioner General as such.)

In supporting the Foreign Secretary's recommendation to the Prime Minister, Mr. Lyttelton based himself on the importance of retaining Mr. MacDonald's guidance of the Joint Co-ordination Committee:—

> "During the last year or two the Federation of Malaya and Singapore have tended to drift apart, and early this year this tendency had become so hampering to the two Administrations that the High Commissioner and the Governor decided that some fresh attempt must be made to reverse it. After informal discussion between representative teams of officials and influential unofficials from both territories, a "Joint Co-ordination Committee" was set up under Malcolm MacDonald's chairmanship to consider ways and means of keeping the two Administrations in step.
>
> Discussion with the High Commissioner and Governor satisfied me that the setting up of this Committee might be made the means of progress towards our objective of re-uniting the two territories politically. I accordingly instructed MacDonald to do his best to guide the Committee towards a recommendation in favour of some sort of political association between the two territories. If the Committee does that, as it may within the next month or two, delicate negotiations will follow about the form which such closer political associations [sic] should take and it would be a great help if MacDonald were in charge of these negotiations; otherwise the momentum would almost certainly have been lost long before any successor could create for himself the position of influence with the Asiatic leaders in Malaya which MacDonald has achieved.
>
> It is impossible to say how long this process of negotiations would take but it might well be the best part of a year and I therefore regard it as important that MacDonald's term of office should be extended for sufficiently long to ensure his remaining in Malaya until the end of 1954."

The Joint Consultative Committee has now completed its discussions on the first two parts of its terms of reference and is engaged on drafting an interim report on these, *viz.*

> "To consider:—
>
> (i) those subjects on which
>
>   (a) there must be consultation and co-ordination,

(b) there must be consultation and, if possible, co-ordination
on policy and, where appropriate, administration between the Governments
of Singapore and the Federation of Malaya;
(ii) (a) the existing means of achieving that consultation and co-ordination
and their effectiveness;
(b) means in addition to or in substitution of those already existing by
which consultation and co-ordination, wherever necessary or desirable,
can be achieved within the terms of the existing Constitutions of the two
territories."

The report will be ready in three or four months time. After which the Committee
can get on to their third term of reference, *viz.*

"To consider:—

(iii) means (if any) by which co-ordination could be more effectively achieved
by modifications of the existing Constitutions, without prejudice to the
positions of Their Highnesses the Malay Rulers and of the Malay States in the
existing Constitution of the Federation of Malaya."

The political leaders both in the Federation and in Singapore may be expected to be
largely engaged in the next year in the preliminaries of establishing the respective
new constitutional arrangements. Mr. MacDonald is probably optimistic in suggesting that there is any prospect of substantial progress towards the production of
agreed proposals for constitutional machinery for the closer association of the
Federation and Singapore in as short a time as the next 18 months. It is, however,
important that such progress as is possible in this field should be made and that the
impetus should not be entirely lost. Sir Donald MacGillivray in conversation with me
before his return from leave earlier this year indicated that he attached much
importance to Mr. MacDonald being allowed to continue to guide these efforts
towards closer association.

  I need not refer to the criticisms in some quarters of the way in which Mr.
MacDonald conducts his relations with the Asian community or to the difficulties
which inevitably arise *vis-à-vis* the Governor of Singapore on account of the presence
of two such high authorities in a single island. I feel sure that on balance Mr.
MacDonald is making a valuable contribution to the consolidation of the bloc of
British territories in Malaya and Borneo and that his removal at this stage would
involve a serious setback in the promising work of the Joint Co-ordination Committee.
  As indicated above, however, the primary interest in Mr. MacDonald's appointment
  is a Foreign Office interest and perhaps the Secretary of State would authorise us
X to discuss with that Department, as soon as this can be arranged, their views on
  the desirability of recommending to the Prime Minister a further extension. If
  there is to be an extension, it would be convenient to arrange it fairly soon on
account of the effect on Mr. MacDonald's leave plans and the programme of work of
the Co-ordination Committee, and also because the appointment of Economic
Adviser to the Commissioner General is very shortly falling vacant and we must know
whether we are to select a successor.

                                                                    J.M.M.
                                                                    4.6.54

Secretary of State

The general reasons of policy stated last year by Mr. Eden certainly point to a further extension of Mr. MacDonald's term. But any extension should, I think, be conditional upon his taking, as soon as the situation in South East Asia permits that, an even longer period of leave than he has hitherto contemplated. Also it would, I suggest, be well before you definitely commit yourself on this to have an opinion from General Templer about the prospects of real progress towards closer association of the Federation and Singapore. Mr. MacDonald's idea that agreed proposals to that end might be produced at the end of next year is to my mind quite unrealistic.

None of these considerations need, I think, prevent official discussions with the Foreign Office at the official level as suggested at X in Sir John Martin's minute. Those discussions should not in any way commit you. May we have authority to start these discussions.[7]

T.I.K.L.
9.6.54

Sir J. Martin
Sir T. Lloyd

In his minute of the 9th June Sir T. Lloyd suggested to the Secretary of State that he might, in connection with the question of Mr. MacDonald's future, seek an opinion from General Templer about the prospects of real progress towards closer association between the Federation and Singapore. When I met General Templer on Thursday I threw a fly over him about this and is first re-action was that he did not want in any way to be used as a sounding board in matters of this kind. He had then, however, just come off an aeroplane and had a session with the press, and I think that he might after all a little later agree to help us in the matter. Perhaps the best way of dealing with it would be for Sir T. Lloyd to raise the question with General Templer, when, as I imagine, he has him in for a talk.

A.M.M.
19.6.54

Sir T. Lloyd

The S of S today sounded Sir G Templer on this. General Templer's view was that it was "just not on the tapis", to use the S of S's words. He is very doubtful whether any real progress can be made. I understand Genl. Templer will be in touch with you tomorrow, so there may be a chance that he would elaborate on this if you felt it desirable.

J.B.J.
22.6.54

Mr. MacKintosh

I spoke to General Templer about this yesterday and his reaction was, if anything, even more emphatic than that which Mr. Johnston has recorded. He said that it was "plain nonsense" to think that the Federation would be willing to combine politically with Singapore round about, or even for some while after, the time when the

---

[7] The secretary of state agreed to discussions taking place without commitment.

constitutional arrangements in that island had taken the new form recently approved.

T.I.K.L.
24.6.54

325   CO 1030/310, no 80   2 June 1954

[Federal elections and Alliance boycott]: inward telegram (reply) no 437 from Sir D MacGillivray to Mr Lyttelton

Your telegram Personal No. 74.[1]
    Federal Elections.
    I agree entirely with the view expressed by Martin in the second paragraph, that we should now go ahead with the elections on the basis already agreed. Not to do so would be interpreted to mean that we accepted that there was substance in the Alliance's contention that arrangements proposed are unworkable and would encourage the Alliance in their present intransigeant attitude and lead them on to demand further concessions; and we would undoubtedly run into difficulties at the same time with the Rulers and the Party Negara.
    2. It is too early to judge the amount of support which will be given to the Alliance for their plan of resignation and boycott, but there are indications in the last few days that it may not be very considerable except on the part of the U.M.N.O. extremists and they may perhaps lose some of their adherents if they decide to go through with it. However, it will be difficult for them to maintain face if they do not now at least resign, although in doing so they may risk dissension within the ranks, both from the U.M.N.O. and the M.C.A. and possibly even a break-up of the Alliance with it. It might, in the end, prove best if the Alliance were to break up and later reform without the extreme U.M.N.O. element which is now pulling them wherever it wants. M.C.A. is planning to hold meeting on the 13th June; it is probable that resolution calling for resignations will pass, although it may well be that some M.C.A. members will not obey that resolution. There are also indications that a few U.M.N.O. members may not be prepared to resign from the Legislative Council and the Councils of State. For instance, the three U.M.N.O. Mentri Besar could not do so and will be obliged, as the Presidents of their State Councils, to support the Bill in the Legislative Council on the 23rd June, since not to support it would surely be regarded as disloyalty to the Rulers' Conference. Moreover, if the Alliance goes through with the resignations and policy of boycott they will be placed in a difficult position when it comes to the State Elections in Johore next October. The U.M.N.O. members in the Council of State (including Saadon Zubir, leader of the U.M.N.O. Youth) voted in the Council of State in favour of arrangements there being adopted providing for elected minority, and they cannot very well now justify the boycott of those elections as a protest against these arrangements. Moreover, if the M.C.A. and the U.M.N.O. should boycott the State Elections, Chinese in Johore may not be prepared to forgo their chance on the Council of State and would possibly elect Chinese candidates, although these would not be under M.C.A. party ticket.

---

[1] See 323.

3. With these considerations in mind, I feel that Alliance will recognise the weaknesses in their position once they realise that we propose to stand firm and to pursue our intention to take the Bill at the meeting on 23rd June and to go ahead with our plan for the Federal Elections. The chances of bringing them to more reasonable frame of mind are therefore likely to be greater if it is clearly indicated that we are not prepared to reconsider the provisions of the White Paper on Federal Elections.

4. I still think, however, that it would be unwise to turn down flat the proposal for Commission. Whilst the tentative suggestion made in Martin's last paragraph has very real attraction, it carries implications which would not be acceptable to the Rulers at the present time and suggestion could certainly not be put to the Alliance unless conference of Rulers had agreed to doing so. Moreover, although the High Commissioner could, of course, appoint committee consisting of members of the Legislative Council, he could not himself appoint special committee of Legislative Council on a motion introduced at the High Commissioner's direction or of its own initiative to resolve to appoint such a committee to make recommendations for consideration of conference of Rulers and Her Majesty's Government.

5. I think it just possible that Rulers would agree to early appointment of Working Party representative of the present Federal Government and of the State Governments to consider certain of the provisions of the Federal Agreement, especially those concerning financial relations, with view to the Report of the Working Party being put before the newly-elected Legislative Council for debate and comment before decisions were taken thereon by the Rulers and Advisers. Debate in newly-elected Legislative Council of report of such Working Party would give opportunity for expression of views on issues not strictly covered by the terms of reference of the Working Party (e.g. on constitutional position of the Rulers themselves) and this might then persuade Their Highnesses to agree to some widening of the field for further enquiries.

6. I am, however, sure that it would prejudice the chance of getting acceptance by the Rulers of a proposal to appoint such Working Party if any hint were to be made of it in reply which must now go to the Alliance. I recommend, therefore, that this reply should merely be in the sense that proposal that there should be appointed from outside Malaya, Commission to examine the whole constitution raises wide issues and is one which cannot be considered by you unilaterally; that you are, therefore, asking the High Commissioner to discuss this proposal with Their Highnesses the Rulers at their next conference; but that meantime you see no reason for any postponement of the programme designed to give effect, at the earliest practicable moment, to the proposals which have already been decided upon for the introduction of elections to the Federal Legislative Council.

7. You will see from the last paragraph of General Templer's telegram No. 418[2] that he thought that perhaps this reply might go on to suggest the advantage of having an elected element in the Legislative Council when the proposals which the Commission might make, should a Commission be appointed, were ready for debate. On reconsideration, however, I (feel omitted) this puts the point too bluntly and also might alienate the Rulers by implying that you favour the idea of a Commission and that there is a real prospect of its being appointed. The point to bring home to the

---

[2] See 322.

Alliance is the fact that in staying out of the Council, they are staying out of the body which is likely to have arbitrary influence on further constitutional changes. (In so doing, I would like to stress the consultative capacity of the Council and its share in formulation of proposals for decision of Her Majesty's Government and the Rulers rather than the role conferred on it by Clause 6(1) of the Federation Agreement, which I would hope to see altered before long). I suggest, therefore, that your reply might include something on the following lines:—

"Legislative Council has an established place in the consideration of constitutional changes and is appropriately the consultative body for voicing representative opinion on any proposals for further constitutional development. I think it desirable that the Government proceed without delay to the incorporation of a substantial number of Elected Members in the Legislative Council, so that their representative views may have consideration when any further changes in the Federation Agreement are contemplated. I am satisfied, therefore, that nothing would be gained by now delaying the introduction of Federal Elections".

8. Delay in your reply to Alliance resolution is all to the good since it is giving opportunity for moderate elements in the Alliance and public opinion to exercise their influence before irrevocable decision taken by the Alliance. I suggest that your reply (? should be omitted) timed to reach me about 8th June.

9. First 6 paragraphs of this were in draft before Templer left;[3] he asked me to tell you that he was in entire agreement with them.

---

[3] Despite the constitutional controversy, Tunku Abdul Rahman played his part as host at the Legislative Council's farewell party for the Templers on 30 May, the eve of their departure from Malaya. Sir Gerald and Lady Templer were seen off at the airport by the Sultan of Selangor and representatives of all the other Malay rulers, the Mentris Besar, all leading politicians (including Dato Onn, Tunku Abdul Rahman and H S Lee), members of the Executive Council, and all the service chiefs.

326 CO 1030/310, no 91   11 June 1954
'Constitutional reforms in Federation of Malaya': CO press release containing the text of Mr Lyttelton's letter to Tunku Abdul Rahman on the Alliance's request for an independent commission

[Lyttelton's letter was delivered to Tunku Abdul Rahman on 10 June and released the following day for publication simultaneously in Britain, Malaya and Singapore.]

The Secretary of State for the Colonies, Mr. Oliver Lyttelton, has replied to the resolution passed by the United Malays National Organisation and the Malayan Chinese Association Alliance in which they requested that a special independent commission consisting entirely of members from outside Malaya be sent immediately to the Federation with the concurrence of Her Majesty the Queen and Their Highnesses the Rulers to report on constitutional reforms in the Federation.

The Secretary of State's reply is as follows:—

Thank you for your letter of the 20th May and your telegram of the 25th May (see Appendix I)[1] in reply to my letter of the 18th May.[2]

I have since given very careful thought to the resolution (see Appendix II)[3] adopted by the Alliance at its meeting on the 24th May and forwarded to me by the High Commissioner, proposing the appointment of a special independent Commission composed of members from outside Malaya to report upon constitutional reform in the Federation.

This proposal raises wide issues and is not one which I can properly consider or decide upon unilaterally. I have therefore asked the High Commissioner to discuss it with Their Highnesses the Rulers at their next Conference. Meanwhile, I see no reason for any postponement of the programme designed to give effect as soon as possible to the proposals already decided upon for the introduction of elections to the Federal Legislative Council. On the contrary, I feel bound to repeat three arguments which appear to me to provide conclusive reasons for adhering to those proposals. First, in all the circumstances of the Federation today those proposals seem to me to be in themselves thoroughly sound. Second, I am completely satisfied that any attempt to go back upon them now would lead to confusion or worse and would do grave harm to the best interests of the Federation as a whole. Third, while I fully recognise the feelings of the Alliance about the matter, I think that you tend to overlook two important points. As I have said before, the present proposals meet nearly all your wishes—and I frankly consider it incumbent upon you to co-operate in making a success of them, thus demonstrating that readiness for reasonable compromise which is so essential in these matters. Moreover, it must be recognised that other important sections of opinion in the Federation differ from you and that the degree of support given by public opinion to one view rather than another cannot be clearly determined until the first Federal elections have been held.

There is also one further point of major importance which in my opinion must be given its due weight. The Legislative Council has an established and important place in the consideration of constitutional change and is the appropriate consultative body for voicing representative opinion upon any proposals for further constitutional development. This makes it very desirable that a substantial number of elected members should without delay be incorporated in the Legislative Council so that their representative views may have consideration when any further changes in the Federation Agreement are contemplated.

I understand that in presenting your resolution to the High Commissioner the Alliance delegation told him that they recognised that it would be a considerable time before a report could be made by an independent Commission, and decisions taken upon its recommendations, but that the Alliance was content that Federal elections should nevertheless be postponed to allow for this. Previously, however, the Alliance has held the view that elections should take place not later than November of this year, and in my letter of the 18th May I assured you that, although I was satisfied that that was not a practical possibility, no effort would be spared to hold the elections at the earliest practicable date in 1955. For the reasons given in this letter I adhere to that view and remain satisfied that nothing would now be gained by delaying the introduction of Federal elections, and that there is no justification for doing so.

---

[1] See 321.   [2] See 319.   [3] See 322.

327   CO 1030/310, no 92   14 June 1954

[Federal elections and Alliance boycott]: inward telegram no 465 from
D Gray to Sir J Martin

[MacGillivray met Alliance leaders for the first time as high commissioner on 11 June, the day after the delivery of Lyttelton's message (see 326). Since deadlock continued, the Alliance convened an emergency session on 13 June to decide on common action.]

High Commissioner's telegram No. 454 to Secretary of State.

Federal Elections.

Letter conveying text of Secretary of State's message to Rahman was delivered 10th June.[1] The M.C.A. general committee held their meeting yesterday morning and decided to support earlier decision of U.M.N.O. to withdraw its representatives from participation of [sic] Councils of the Government at various levels. Joint meeting of U.M.N.O. and M.C.A. officials was held afterwards to consider Secretary of State's reply delivered 10th, statement was later issued to the Council. Copies of the statement will be sent you by bag Wednesday but meantime you may wish gist of it. Firstly, because of Secretary of State's refusal to accede to the Alliance request for the White Paper on the elections to be set aside and for the immediate appointment of special independent commission to enquire into constitutional reforms, Alliance announced decision to withdraw all Unofficial Members from active participation in Governments in the Federation. Secondly, Councils affected are those at Federal, State and Settlement, municipal and town levels. Action Committee has been appointed to implement this decision. Thirdly, Alliance regrets taking this step but feels it is left with no alternative since it has already demonstrated its readiness to compromise the modifying of its original request for $\frac{3}{5}$ to $\frac{3}{5}$ of the new Council to consist of Elected Members. Fourthly, White Paper proposals are unsatisfactory in spite of Secretary of State's assurance that remedial steps will be taken if these proposals cannot work satisfactorily. Fifthly, opportunity is taken of thanking the people whose votes have returned the Alliance candidates to nearly 85 per cent of seats so far contested and confidence is expressed in the Alliance being able to count on similar support in its fight for Parliamentary Democracy and proper representation of the people and thus enable the will of the people (?to) prevail.

2.   I am sending this telegram in the absence of the High Commissioner who is on tour in North.

---

[1] See 326.

328 CO 1030/310, no 109   23 June 1954

[Federal elections and Alliance boycott]: inward telegram no 496 from Sir D MacGillivray to Mr Lyttelton on the use of reserved seats. *Minute* by Sir J Martin

Your telegram Personal No.84.[1]

This question is embarrassing at the present time. I have had in mind the possibility that the proposal to consult with leader of the majority party in regard to the five reserved seats might, at the right time, provide a nucleus of agreement, but I am sure that that time has not yet arrived and feel that public discussion of it at this juncture would only minimise our chances of using it successfully later on. The feeling between parties is very high at the moment and there is likely to be little chance of agreement for some weeks. A statement was made in the Executive Council on 25th May on the lines indicated in your letters to Ogmore[2] and Griffiths (see my telegram No.405), but there has as yet been no discussion of the point in public, nor has it been raised again by the Alliance. One other reason why public discussion of this question would be embarrassing is that there has, as yet, been no opportunity for consultation with the Conference of Rulers in regard to it.

2. In the circumstances it would, I think, be best if Proctor could be persuaded to withdraw his embarrassing question. If, however, the question stands, I suggest reply should merely be on the lines that you hope it is appreciated that you and the Rulers have already gone long way to meet the Alliance's point of view, and that you had hoped that the Alliance would have been able to accept the assurances already given; that as regards the seven Nominated reserved seats, it had already been agreed unanimously in the Federal Elections Committee that two should be filled by Officials discharging the functions of Secretary for Defence and Member for Economic Affairs, and that the remaining five are being created for the purpose explained in paragraph 31 of the report of that Committee and on page 2 of the White Paper. I should prefer that it should be left at that, but if you think you must go further I suggest you go on precisely as set out in passage for your reply to Ogmore (and) Griffiths quoted in your telegram Personal No.66. To announce that I would definitely act on the lines there would, I think, be using prematurely card which cannot win the trick now but which may do so if played later on, and it would certainly be resented by the Rulers and many who are loyally standing by them in their present crisis. The Rulers and Party Negara and their supporters are very strongly of the opinion that firm stand necessary if the Alliance is to be made to see reason, and that any further concessions can only lead to further demands.

3. You may like to know that only eight of the seventeen Chinese in the Legislative Council have resigned, some of them most reluctantly. The remaining nine are in their seats in the Council this morning; most of them members of the M.C.A., although not in the Council as nominees of the M.C.A. This is a deplorable

---

[1] This requested advice on a parliamentary question put down by the Labour MP, W T Proctor, asking about the possibility of a compromise based on the use of reserved seats in the new legislative council, the essence of which was that the high commissioner should consult with the leader of the majority party before making nominations. See *H of C Debs*, vol 529, cols 418–423, 23 June 1954.
[2] See 320.

campaign amounting to intimidation by H.S. Lee with all the power of the Guilds and Associated Chinese Chamber of Commerce and Chinese Chamber of Mines behind him.

Minute on 328

Mr. Proctor telephoned today to say that Dato Abdul Razak had told him that if the Secretary of State's reply to the question about consulting the leader of the majority party regarding the filling of the nominated reserve seats could have been "Yes", this would have enabled the Alliance to accept the situation and call off the boycott. He suggested that I should also inform Sir Donald MacGillivray (though without mentioning Dato Abdul Razak's name). I have passed the information on to the High Commissioner for what it is worth.

The Secretary of State should perhaps see in case Mr. Proctor speaks to him.

J.M.M.
24.6.54

329 CO 1030/65, no 1   25 June 1954
[Independent constitutional commission]: letter from Sir J Martin to Sir D MacGillivray on CO reactions to the proposal

I thought it might be worth while to let you have our views upon the suggestion (which you are due to put to the Conference of Rulers on the 15th July) for an independent Commission from outside Malaya to examine the constitution. The Secretary of State has seen and approved the terms of this letter.

Although the Alliance took the initiative in making this suggestion[1] we think that on its merits there is much to be said for it. The Federation Agreement has now been in operation for six years and this would be a good occasion (and one which, we think, could reasonably be justified on general grounds) for a review of the whole Agreement in the light of that experience of its working. We particularly have in mind three difficulties.

The first relates to the position of the Rulers, who at present have the power to veto any changes in the Agreement[2] and therefore any changes in the constitution. With the growth of the elected element in the Federal and State Governments the exercise of such a veto appears to us to accord less and less with the political realities. We therefore think that there is a case for examining the powers of the Rulers under the Agreement in the hope that a way may be found of avoiding the sort of difficulty with which we have been faced over, for example, the question of an elected majority in the new Legislative Council.

Secondly, there are the difficulties over the allocation of revenue between the Federal Government and the State Governments. (We have been interested to see a proof of Himsworth's forthcoming paper on this.)[3]

---

[1] See 322.

[2] Clause 6 of the Federation Agreement of 1948 gave the Malay rulers power to veto any constitutional amendment.

[3] E Himsworth, financial secretary, Federation of Malaya, 1952–1955.

Finally, although much has already been done to meet the wishes of the Chinese over citizenship, we are inclined to think that we may before long have to go further still.

Admittedly it will not be easy to compose a Commission for this purpose but we think that, if carefully and successfully chosen, it could do a useful job in examining these and other problems arising out of the Federation Agreement and in offering upon the constitution as a whole impartial views of such weight as to obtain general acceptance.

Apart from the merits of the case for such a Commission—which, as you see, we consider to be strong—we think that it might prove helpful if it could be announced after their meeting on the 15th July that the Rulers had agreed to the appointment of a Commission. It might indeed be a decisive factor in inducing the Alliance first to contest the elections and thereafter to co-operate in working the new constitution.

I should add that, while we think that most (perhaps all) of the members of any Commission would have to be found from outside the Federation, we should prefer not to have a *Royal* Commission. The practice of non-payment of members of such Commissions and the method of their appointment are apt to complicate the business of launching an enquiry.

It will, I hope, help you now to have this expression of our thinking at this stage and to know that the Secretary of State is on the whole in favour of the proposal, which has been pressed upon him and was not of his invention. We in our turn should be interested and grateful to learn your views on the matter.

330   CO 1030/311, no 123   25 June 1954
[Federal elections and the Alliance boycott]: letter from Sir D MacGillivray to Sir J Martin on recent political developments

Things have been moving very fast on the Federal Elections issue, and as I have at the same time been endeavouring to keep to my arranged programme for first visits to all the States and Settlements before the middle of July, I have not, I fear, kept you very regularly posted of late with our thoughts on this problem. The salient events have, of course, been reported by official telegrams.

2.   The Action Committee of the M.C.A., working through the Associated Chinese Chambers of Commerce, the Chinese Chamber of Mines, and the many powerful Chinese Guilds which they can control, has been able to exert great pressure on other Chinese leaders and on the Chinese community generally. Even so, they have in some cases had to resort to misrepresentation of the position and to methods of intimidation to get their members to toe the line; and even then a few, notably those from the Settlement of Penang (who are proud that not a single one of their representatives in the Legislative Council has resigned), have "revolted" and refused to abide by the M.C.A. instruction.

3.   As an example of misrepresentation, I enclose[1] for comparison:—

(a) A note of the record of my interview with Tunku Abdul Rahman, H.S. Lee and Ismail on Friday, 11th June, and,

---

[1] None of the five enclosures to which MacGillivray refers has been printed here.

(b) a letter from the S.C.A. Johore giving Dato Wan Shee Fun's[2] account of what was said at the Alliance Conference in Kuala Lumpur on Sunday, 13th June.[3]

Dato Wan's account of what was actually said at that Conference may be a bit garbled, but it should, I think, be regarded as sufficiently accurate to indicate a certain amount of dishonesty in representation of the position to the Conference; for example, no mention whatever was made of the seven nominated reserved seats in the course of my interview with the Alliance leaders on 11th June, whereas the whole purpose of that interview—to let the Alliance know that it was my intention that the Bill should be taken through its first two stages only on 23rd June—was apparently never mentioned at the Alliance Conference two days later. The Alliance leaders knew perfectly well that it was not true that the Secretary of State had stated that he would persuade the High Commissioner to consult the Malay Rulers to agree to a proposal that the nominees of these seven seats should be nominated after consultation with the Alliance, but they were aware of the explanation of this point which had been given by the High Commissioner in Executive Council on 25th May, since they were present at that Council meeting and of course received a copy of the minutes wherein that explanation was fully recorded.

4. I might mention a further instance of what amounts to dishonesty on H.S. Lee's part. The prepared text of his speech last Sunday to the Chinese guilds included the following passage:—

"It was stated in the Straits Times of 19th June, 1954, that the three Bills on the elections to be introduced in the Federal Legislative Council on 23rd June, 1954, would not have their third reading and therefore would not be passed during the June meeting. If this is true it is much harder to understand why the Government must insist on the introduction of these three Bills at all in June in view of the fact that the High Commissioner has been asked by the Secretary of State to consult the Rulers on the matter of the appointment of a special independent commission."

Herein he indicates that the Alliance had no knowledge of the intention to take the Bill to its second reading only. This despite the fact that I had asked the Alliance leaders to come and see me on 11th June, two days before the final decision to resign, specifically to inform them that the Bill would only be taken through its first two stages, giving them the reasons for this decision and urging them to remain in the Council in order at least to debate the principles of the Bill.

5. Another instance of misrepresentation can be found in the attempt by the Associated Chinese Chambers of Commerce and the Chinese Chamber of Mines to obtain the resignations of the Chinese Legislative Councillors who represent commercial and mining interests. The position is that these Councillors are appointed by the High Commissioner after seeking nomination from the Chambers concerned, since this is the only convenient way of obtaining members likely to be acceptable to the mining industry and to commerce. The two organisations, however, tried to make out that these Councillors were their representatives on the

---

[2] Wan (more usually Wong) Shee Fun was a Johore state councillor, president of the Johore Chinese Chamber of Commerce and a Johore representative on the Central Working Committee of the MCA.
[3] For MacGillivray's interview on 11 June and the Alliance conference on 13 June, see 327.

Legislative Council and that they could withdraw them. Woo Kah Lim did, in fact, resign, although most reluctantly, and possibly under misapprehension as to the true position. On the other hand, Koh Sin Hock first sought a clarification of his position from the Chief Secretary, and on receipt of it refused to resign. I enclose copies of the Chambers' letters and of the reply which I have had sent to them.

6. All these recent acts of the Alliance leaders have strengthened my suspicion that some of them have never been desirous of a settlement and have for some time been intent on a trial of strength and are certainly ready to put party advantage before the best interests of the country. The advice given in London by the Gold Coast Judge to Tunku Abdul Rahman that he should seek independence through the doors of the prison rather than through the doors of the Colonial Office strengthens the point of view which had for some months already been forming in his mind.[4] The mutual distrust between Onn and H.S. Lee, which has been getting deeper ever since the M.C.A. broke with I.M.P. in the early part of 1952, and which now amounts to intense personal dislike is, I fear, another contributory factor to this desire to fight the matter out. There are others, however, among the Alliance leaders, Dr. Ismail for one, who have I think genuinely wanted to reach an understanding, but have never seen their way clearly to it. The U.M.N.O. leaders have ever been reminded by their rank and file of the resolution taken in Alor Star that they would resign if elections were not held in 1954,[5] and have felt that they must somehow honour this pledge to which the extremists in their party have consistently held them. We do know that these leaders are endeavouring to prevent any disturbance and that U.M.N.O. instructions are to conduct their campaign in an orderly and constitutional manner; but at a lower level there is the U.M.N.O. Youth and other extreme Malay elements who certainly would be the instruments of disorder if they were given half a chance. So far there has been no disturbance except at an U.M.N.O. meeting at Mersing in Johore, after which some anti-British posters were found posted up in the town; processions to present petitions to the Sultans are being organised, but there is every indication that these will be as orderly as those which were held at the time of the protests against the Malayan Union.

7. The methods which the Alliance have been using of late savour somewhat of dictatorship, and could hardly be described as methods worthy of persons whose ostensible aim is democratic self-government; they are a sad augury for the future if the Alliance should sweep into power. In the first place, there was the threat contained in their resolution of 24th May that "the Alliance will continue to give its fullest co-operation to the Government in all respects, particularly with a view to bringing the Emergency to an early end if this request is acceded to", but that "if the authorities insist on the implementation of the White Paper, the Alliance, with great regret, will have no choice but to withdraw all its members from participation in the

---

[4] Having read MacGillivray's letter on 2 July, R L Baxter minuted in the margin at this point: 'W[est] A[frica] Dept. can't tell me who this Judge can have been'. Apparently it was Mr Justice W B Van Lare (chairman of the Gold Coast's Commission of Inquiry into Representational and Electoral Reform) who told the Tunku at a private party in London: 'The way to self-government is not through the Colonial Office: it is usually through the prison gate'. Tunku Abdul Rahman Putra, *Looking back* (Kuala Lumpur, 1977) p 33; Harry Miller, *Prince and premier* (London, 1959) pp 148–149; see also BDEEP series B, vol I, R Rathbone, ed, *Ghana*, part I, pp lx, lxii, lxxvi n 94.
[5] UMNO General Assembly, Sept 1953.

Government".[6] In other words, that they wouldn't even give support to bring the Emergency to an end, and they have carried out this threat to the extent of withdrawing their members even from the War Executive Committees.

Then there is the fact that the Executive Committees of these organisations took the decision to resign without any consultation with their State and Settlement Branches and without convening any general meeting. This action has led to a good deal of criticism on the part of their branches, and may result in some of the M.C.A. branches breaking away from their central organisation.

8. I have already quoted in my telegram No. 500 of 24th June, from the speech which H.S. Lee made to the representatives of the Chinese public organisations and guilds in Selangor on 21st June. This is a fairly extreme instance of the methods of intimidation being employed to get the Chinese community to withdraw all co-operation from Government and thereby to bring pressure to bear upon the Government to accede to the Alliance demands.

9. We have not yet got full information of the extent of resignations at State and Settlement and Municipal and Town Council levels, but it seems that the majority of U.M.N.O./M.C.A. members are bowing to party discipline, albeit reluctantly. In Kedah two M.C.A. members, and in Perak one M.C.A. member, have refused to resign from their State Councils, and there have also been instances of U.M.N.O. members also defying the edict of their organisation. One of them, Tuan Haji Mohamed Esa bin Kulop Mat Shah from Perak, announced at once to the press that—"My first duty is to be loyal to my Ruler and State as I was appointed by the Sultan to represent Kuala Kangsar in the State Council and Town Board".

10. It is difficult as yet to say just what will happen in the Municipal and Town Councils. The Alliance intention apparently is to order all their nominated members to resign; these can of course be replaced by others who have never owed, or who no longer owe, allegiance to the Alliance. The Alliance elected members will take one of two courses. Either they will resign, in which case, according to law, by-elections must be held within 30 days; they would then stand again and if they got in again would immediately resign once more. They got in last year on a platform of "we will serve the people"; they couldn't use that platform again, and if they adopt these tactics they may give some advantage to their opponents who could then say that they offered themselves as candidates in order to serve the people's interests, whereas the Alliance candidates were standing merely to serve their own political ends. It is therefore more likely that the elected members will merely refuse to turn up at meetings, or, in order that their seats should not be declared vacant, turn up at every third meeting and then say nothing or merely obstruct business. But even in Councils where all the elected members are Alliance members it will still be possible to get a quorum without them, and business can be carried on. This is all extremely deplorable at a time when we are doing all in our power to demonstrate to the people of this country the value of democratic institutions. If the people see that their leaders are making a farce of the newly established Local Councils, Town Councils and Municipalities, and are using these Councils merely as pawns in a political game instead of as training grounds for public service, they will begin to question the value of institutions on this pattern and wonder whether Communist forms do not after all offer something of greater value. It is especially sad to see this happening after the

---

[6] See 322.

extremely promising start which the Town Councils and Local Councils have made.

11. "Utusan Melayu",[7] the U.M.N.O. organ, announced that—"Forms which only require the signatures of members and the filling in of dates have been sent to U.M.N.O. members on the Education Advisory Boards, including the Boards for the Malay Girls' College, the Trade School and the Technical College. Forms have also been distributed among U.M.N.O. members on the Rate and Assessment Boards, District War Committees, District Rubber Licencing Boards, Hospital and Prison Visiting Boards." Whether there have actually been resignations as yet from Hospital and Prison Visiting Boards I do not know, but it is confirmed that there have been resignations from bodies such as the Cinematograph Advisory Committee. There has been a good deal of criticism of the Alliance for taking their campaign of non-participation into these fields of voluntary service and for not limiting it to bodies of a political nature.

12. As I said in my telegram No. 496,[8] I feel that there is little chance of reaching agreement for some weeks at least. Indeed, it may be that the time will arrive after the Rulers' Conference on 15th July; on the other hand, we may have to wait until after the Legislative Council meeting on 18th August, when the Bill has been put through its final stages. It may be easier to get [Party] Negara and the other opponents of the Alliance to agree to a concession to the Alliance once the Bill has become law and present suspicion that H.M.G. may press the Rulers to go back on the Bill has thereby been removed; and it may be that the Alliance would be more prepared to come to terms once they realised that there is no longer any chance of their obtaining their demand for a three-fifths majority. It is possible, however, that we can find a way for agreement at the time of the Rulers' Conference. It is too early as yet to judge when the right moment will be, but I am sure we must not try to rush it, but wait for the right moment and then seize it. Our biggest danger at present seems to lie in the Labour Members of Parliament, whose interference merely encourages a more and more intransigent attitude on the part of the Alliance. I do not believe we should ever have reached the present pass if it had not been for the encouragement given to the Alliance delegation in London by the Labour M.P.s;[9] and articles such as that which appeared in the "Times" of 23rd June and which is commented upon in the enclosed editorial in today's "Singapore Standard" merely strengthen this intransigence. I hope you will do anything you can to prevent any more efforts to force the pace from London.

13. As regards the proposal of the Alliance that there should be a special independent commission consisting entirely of members from outside Malaya to report on constitutional reforms in the Federation, I am quite certain from talks I have had with many Malays that the Rulers will never accept examination of the Agreement by an independent body from outside Malaya. Such a proposal is not only anathema to the Rulers themselves, but also to the majority of the Malays, including many of the U.M.N.O. members. While I was in Perlis last week, the head of the local U.M.N.O. branch told me that his branch had held a meeting and had authorised him to send a telegram to Tunku Abdul Rahman saying that while the Perlis branch was

---

[7] Pledged to serve race, religion and country, *Utusan Melayu* had supported the MNP in the late 1940s and remained independent of UMNO control until 1961 when the newspaper was taken over by a group of party leaders.

[8] See 328.   [9] See 318, note and note 1, and 328, note 1.

with him all the way on the elections issue, they were not with him on any step further, and that what they meant by this was that they would have nothing to do with the proposal for an outside commission. It is, of course, well known that Cheng-lock Tan has been pressing for a Royal Commission ever since the Malayan Union was surplanted [sic] by the Federation Agreement,[10] and that the present proposal emanates from the M.C.A. side of the Alliance; and it is suspected that the design of the M.C.A. is to replace the Agreement with something much more akin to the Malayan Union and as favourable to Chinese hopes and aspirations as that Union was. The Rulers are therefore hardly likely to accept a proposal which they know is contrary to the wishes of the bulk of their Malay subjects. I have, however, in recent conversations with the Sultan of Kedah, the Raja of Perlis, Dato Onn, Bukit Gantang, the Mentri Besar Johore, and others, urged the unwisdom of the Rulers' Conference coming out with a flat "no" after their meeting of 15th July, and the great desirability of their indicating recognition of the need for review and revision of at least parts of the Federal Agreement. I have pressed them to agree at least to the issue of some statement showing appreciation of the need for constant review of the Agreement as circumstances change and for early examination of those parts which have already shown themselves to be outworn and in need of replacement. I hope I shall get them to agree to the issue of a statement which will show that they are prepared for an early examination to be undertaken of the Agreement or of parts of it, though rejecting the idea that such examination is best undertaken by an independent commission from outside Malaya. I doubt if I will get them at this meeting to go beyond that and agreement that the manner in which this examination should be tackled (with a view to recommendations eventually being placed before the partly elected new Legislative Council) should be considered at the following meeting of their Conference; that is to say, subsequent to the August meeting of the Legislative Council and the final enactment of the Elections Bill.

14. The debate on the second reading of the Bill went off well. Hogan spoke very well but Onn was, as usual, intemperate and tried to score points which will only annoy his opponents. I am having the record of Onn's and Hogan's speeches sent to you by savingram.

15. Unless the horizon clears more quickly than I anticipate, I fear I will have to postpone my visit to London until the early autumn. Would the last fortnight of September suit you?

P.S. It seems that the present intention of the Alliance is to contest with vigour the Town Council elections in Perak in August and the State elections in Johore in October—and not to decide for the present whether to contest the Federal elections next year.

---

[10] See part I of this volume, 131–134.

331 CO 1030/311, no 118   26 June 1954

[Alliance boycott and the rulers]: circular letter from Sir D Mac-
Gillivray to British advisers to the Malay rulers recommending that
they allow UMNO to hold protest demonstrations

[As at the height of the Malayan Union crisis, UMNO leaders were anxious to win over the
rulers; as in 1946, there was also considerable mistrust between princes and politicians in
1954. On 1 July Tunku Abdul Rahman and Tan Cheng Lock led an Alliance deputation in
an audience with Sultan Ibrahim of Johore, while a crowd of loyalist Malays gathered
outside, reminiscent of the demonstration outside the Station Hotel, Kuala Lumpur, on 1
Apr 1946.]

The Chief Secretary has written to the Mentri Besar in regard to applications by
UMNO to hold processions, the purpose of which would be to present petitions to the
Rulers in regard to the Federal Elections issue. I enclose a copy of the Chief
Secretary's letter,[1] and understand that at the time of the agitations against the
Malayan Union similar processions were organised by UMNO and that they were in all
cases decently conducted and entirely orderly. You will note from the enclosed that
Tunku Abdul Rahman has already given an assurance that the processions now
contemplated would be conducted in a completely orderly manner. Having regard to
this assurance and the fact that the responsible leaders of UMNO are completely
associating themselves with these processions, I feel that it would be a great mistake
to withhold permission subject, of course, to the usual conditions, unless there are
local reasons to believe that the processions are likely to cause a breach of the peace.

You will see that UMNO is being told that they should first make application for
approval in principle to hold any particular procession, to the CPO concerned; the
CPOs are being instructed that on receipt of such applications they should consult
with the Mentri Besar before approval is given in principle, and that once this
approval is given then all details and conditions can be determined between the local
UMNO leaders and the OCPD.

Before giving his approval, I assume that the Mentri Besar will make sure that His
Highness is prepared to receive a petition and will find out whether His Highness will
himself receive a delegation. My own strong view is that Their Highnesses would be
extremely unwise to refuse to receive a petition and would be well advised to agree to
accept the petition at the hands of a delegation if this should be desired by the
petitioners. If Their Highnesses do not do this they will come under very heavy fire,
and may estrange themselves still further from their subjects, who after all have a
perfect right to petition them on any matter.

There is a real danger that the present issue will be thought by the bulk of the
people of the Malayan countryside, as well as by popular opinion outside Malaya, to
be one between the British Government and the people of Malaya; indeed, Tunku
Abdul Rahman and others are already endeavouring to present it as one of the British
Government denying to the people of Malaya a perfectly legitimate demand for a
reasonable step forward towards self-government. The local danger of the creation of
such an impression lies in the opportunities which will then present themselves to
extremist elements to work up anti-British feeling. The visit of the Alliance

---
[1] Not printed.

delegation to London and the rather too prominent part which the Secretary of State has been forced to play in this matter, a prominence which is being kept alive by the keen but, I think, misguided interest which Labour M.P.s are giving to the matter, have much helped the Alliance to create this impression.[2] We here know it to be a false one and that the issue is essentially one of a difference of opinion between the Alliance on the one side and the Rulers and other influential and more conservative groups in their States on the other—a difference of opinion as to the pace at which it is safe to go towards self-government. It seems to me that the processions which UMNO now propose to hold are likely to help bring the issue back into its proper perspective as one between the Rulers and their supporters on the one hand and another section of their subjects on the other.

The Alliance is also trying to stress that the struggle is one for a three-fifths elected majority, a demand which receives considerable support and sympathy both inside and outside Malaya and which they can count to play on with some success. Their latest demand, however, was for an independent commission from outside Malaya to examine the whole constitution. This is not, I think, a popular demand among Malays generally, and is suspected by them as one designed by the MCA to bring about a return to something more akin to Malayan Union. It would seem, therefore, that UMNO is now trying to play this latest demand down and to play up the request for a three-fifths majority. It would, I think, be of advantage to us, however, at the present time, if the demand for an independent commission from outside Malaya to examine the whole constitution could be brought into focus, and the demand for a three-fifths majority relegated more to the background. I suggest, therefore, that Their Highnesses might put themselves into a stronger position if they were to receive UMNO delegations in their States, and, when doing so, try to turn attention to this demand for a commission from outside Malaya, and to seek advice from the delegation as to the attitude which they should take towards this demand, reminding the delegation that the subject is one which must be discussed at the Rulers' Conference on 15th July; at the same time, it would be as well for Their Highnesses to indicate that they propose to stand firm on the immediate Federal Elections issue, and that there can be no question of postponing the implementation of the decisions already taken on that issue until there has been a comprehensive review of the whole Federation Agreement. I hope you can get this suggestion across in any conversations you may have with the Ruler and the Mentri Besar in regard to any application for a procession.

There is one matter which I should like you to stress in conversation with political leaders, District Officers and others who are able to influence public opinion, and that is the deplorable effect on the people's attitude towards the value of democratic institutions of the present action of the Alliance leaders in calling upon their members to resign not only from Federal and State Councils but also from Local Government bodies and Committees on which they have been giving voluntary

---

[2] MacGillivray sent a copy of this letter to the CO and, in his reply of 30 June, Martin commented: 'I need not say that I entirely agree with your remark in the fourth paragraph about the rather too prominent part which the Secretary of State has been forced to play, in a way which suggests that the dispute is one between the Malayan people and the British Government. It is of course difficult to correct this impression by statements here without the risk of appearing to suggest that an enlightened Secretary of State is being held back by stick-in-the-mud Rulers—a picture which might, I suppose, well be resented by the Rulers themselves and others in Malaya.' (CO 1030/311, no 119).

public service. We had made an excellent start with our Local Councils and Town Councils in demonstrating through them how representatives of the people can participate in the work of Government. Now the Alliance leaders are undermining much of the confidence which was built up in these new instruments of democratic Government by using them as pawns in a game of politics rather than as training grounds in public service. If public opinion could see their action in this light, then perhaps the Alliance will be deterred from going further and making a complete farce of democratic forms of Government by resigning from Town Councils merely in order to stand again so as to resign once more. If they do that, then surely many people will ask themselves whether perhaps other forms of Government offered by the Communists may not be preferable to democratic ones.

332   CO 1030/65, no 3   2 July 1954

[Alliance boycott and the position of the rulers]: letter from Sir D MacGillivray to Sir J Martin on constitutional problems and ways of easing the current deadlock. *Enclosure:* draft letter from Sir D MacGillivray to Tunku Abdul Rahman

Your Secret & Personal letter SEA 36/1/01 of the 25th June[1] crossed my DHC/19/6 of the same date,[2] in the 13th paragraph of which I commented on the proposal that there should be an independent Commission to report on constitutional reform in the Federation. I now attach a copy of the paper[3] which I am circulating to the Rulers for consideration at the Conference. There is, I think, likely to be some opposition even to the proposal contained in this paper. I also attach a copy of the draft of the Press Release[4] which I am sending to the Rulers before they meet on the 14th July, should they agree to the line of approach I have suggested to them.

2.   There is a good deal of resentment on the part of some of the Rulers and their advisers about the present behaviour of the Alliance and, quite apart from other reasons, the proposal that there should be an examination of the Constitution by a Commission from outside Malaya will be strongly resisted at the present time, if only on the grounds that it is a proposal put forward by the Alliance. Their present attitude is one of "no concessions" to the Alliance. If I were to press strongly now for acceptance of the Alliance's demand, I might even prejudice my own position with the Rulers and their supporters, and certainly would not get anywhere.

3.   There is one consideration we should have in mind about the proposal for a Commission from outside of Malaya and that is that, if this proposal were to be accepted in principle, there would no doubt be a demand from certain quarters in Malaya, a demand which it might be difficult to resist, for the Commission to contain members from Commonwealth countries such as India, Pakistan and Ceylon and perhaps even from the Gold Coast. Such a Commission would not, I think, be a satisfactory one from our point of view.

4.   I agree with you that Clause 6 of the Agreement[5] requires some amendment

---

[1] See 329.   [2] See 330.   [3] Apart from draft letter, enclosures not printed.
[4] A postscript (in addition to that printed here) dated 3 July 1954 stated: 'Since this letter was signed developments have made the proposed press release . . . out of date, & it is not therefore enclosed.'
[5] Federation Agreement of 1948, see 329, note 2.

but it will be very difficult to persuade the Rulers to give up their power of veto. They do, after all, act, not on their own, but after consultation with their advisers; and they have always been anxious to follow the majority view and to give heed to public opinion. It was largely because a substantial majority of the Federal Elections Committee was in favour of a nominated majority in the Legislative Council that the Rulers resisted so long the pressure which the High Commissioner had brought to bear on them to accept an elected majority. Their strongest argument was that they would be on dangerous ground once they departed from the advice tendered to them by their advisers, many of whom were among those who had signed the Majority Report of the Committee and who were the same advisers who had stood by them at the time of the struggle against the Malayan Union. I would like to discuss Clause 6 with you when I see you. The present arrangement is obviously unsatisfactory and will be the more so when there is an elected Legislative Council.

5. Secondly, you mentioned the difficulty of allotment of revenue between the Federal Government and the State Governments and you mentioned Himsworth's Report. To my mind what is required is a re-examination of the whole relationship of the Federal Government to the State and Settlement Governments, not only in the financial field, but in the Executive Council and Legislative Council fields as well, with a view to a change which will achieve a much more clear cut division of functions. The machine creaks a bit now, but we rub along well enough because we are able to compose our differences at the official level; but the position will be very difficult when there are elected Governments with perhaps one political party in power in the Federal Government and another in some of the State Governments. There would then be constant friction and obstructionism so long as present constitutional arrangements remained unchanged. This is a wide subject which is also best left for discussion when I see you.

6. Finally you mentioned the wishes of the Chinese over citizenship. *Jus soli* must come sooner or later and the sooner the better, since I am sure that we shall never make real progress towards racial harmony until the Malays are ready to accept it. I have it in mind to discuss this with the Malay leaders, both [Party] Negara and UMNO, when the present row is over and the climate is more favourable, and see how far I am likely to get in obtaining their agreement before tackling the Rulers. If we could get *jus soli* accepted before registration of electors for Federal Elections, the effect on the Chinese would be splendid. I have not much hope, however, of succeeding in this, but I propose to have a go at it.

7. In your Confidential letter to me of the 24th June you have told me that Proctor had informed you that, if, as regards the five reserved seats, the Secretary of State's reply to the request that he should instruct me to consult with the leaders of the Majority Party had been "yes", Ogmore and he were satisfied from their discussions with the Alliance people that this would have enabled them to accept the situation and call off the boycott.[6] I am certainly not satisfied that this would have been so. It is true that H.S. Lee is now anxious to reach a settlement on these lines, but it is by no means certain that he can carry Tunku Abdul Rahman with him and it is very possible that, if the card had been played in that way by the Secretary of State, it would have been taken by the Alliance, that it would not have satisfied Rahman and that the game would have gone on. I happen to know that Rahman has stated that he

---

[6] See 328, minute by Martin.

is prepared to use Labour M.P.s, but is not prepared to be tied by their advice.

8. I propose to give the undertaking that, in giving effect to the intention of paragraph 31 of the Federal Elections Committee Report, I will "consult" with the leader of the majority party before making appointments to these five seats, but I will not give this undertaking until I am certain that, in return for this statement, both sides of the Alliance will undertake to co-operate with the constitutional arrangements set out in the White Paper and embodied in the Bill. I am assuming that the Secretary of State will agree to this. There have been feelers from H.S. Lee during the last two days, and, although I have not yet seen him myself, I have indicated that I am prepared to discuss the position with a view to reaching an understanding within the framework of the White Paper and the Bill, and it is possible that I shall now meet him, Tunku Abdul Rahman and Ismail tomorrow night.

9. Meantime, I have seen the remaining Asian members of the Executive Council at their request (Lee Tiang Keng[7] only being absent) and I enclose a record of my conversation with them. This conversation has, I think, cleared the way for further discussions with the Alliance without making Party Negara unduly suspicious of them. At least Party Negara cannot now say that they were unaware of my intention to reach agreement within the confines of the White Paper if this should prove possible.

10. I attach a draft of a letter which I would be prepared to send to Tunku Abdul Rahman provided that in preliminary conversations the Alliance leaders undertake to reply to it to the effect that, in the light of the further explanation given in this letter, they are prepared to co-operate in the establishment of new constitutional arrangements and to give their support to the Legislative measures designed to give effect to the proposals contained in the White Paper.

It would, of course, be a part of this agreement that I would reappoint the resigned members to the Legislative Council on the understanding that they would give the Bill their support when it comes up at Committee stage and third reading in August.

The Alliance may seek to make it a part of the bargain that I should invite them back into Executive Council, as well as Legislative Council; if so, I shall have first to give consideration to the effect of this on Party Negara.

11. It may be that I will reach agreement with them on this basis before the Rulers' Conference. If so, I doubt if it would be wise to withhold announcement of it until after the Conference; there would be too great a risk that the Alliance would have second thoughts about it; moreover, the longer the present situation goes on, the greater the chance of disorder. I should have to tell the Rulers, however, of the terms of any agreement reached before an announcement was made so that they would have sufficient time to make up their own minds as to what to do about the Alliance members who have resigned from the State and Settlement Councils. I hope that an announcement of agreement on this elections issue before the Rulers' Conference would not embarrass the Secretary of State, having regard to the answers given by him to Proctor's question[8] and by Munster to Ogmore's question in the Lords yesterday.[9] The question of a Commission from outside Malaya would, of

---

[7] Dr Lee Tiang Keng (born in Burma and medical practitioner in Penang) was president of the Penang branch of the MCA, 1949–1951, and member for health on the Federal Executive Council, 1951–1955.
[8] See 328, note 1.
[9] See *H of L Debs*, vol 188, cols 93–95, 29 June 1954. Lord Munster was parliamentary under-secretary of state for the colonies, 1951–1954.

course, be left over for discussion at the Rulers' Conference and would be the subject of an announcement immediately thereafter.

12. The Alliance has been plugging away at their demand for a three-fifths majority and at today's entirely orderly procession of 2000 people at Johore Bahru to present a petition to the Ruler, there were banners publicising this demand. It could therefore be represented that the Alliance will be eating fairly humble pie if they now consent to support the Bill as it stands, merely on the grounds of the further explanations given by me. They themselves will of course endeavour, through their Press (Singapore Standard and Utusan Melayu) and in their public speeches, to represent my letter as a great concession to them and an Alliance victory.

13. I am sure that, having regard to the broad issues involved, it is right to make this concession and to invite them back into the Legislative Council, if they indicate that they are now prepared to support the Bill. But at the same time I have no doubt that my action in so doing will be stigmatised by many as one of weakness. Some of the Europeans here, as well as members of Party Negara, feel strongly that there should be no concessions whatever to the Alliance.

14. I enclose also copies of the papers which are being put to the Rulers' Conference in regard to:—

(a) the residential qualification for a votor,
(b) the report of the Constituency Delineation Commission.[10]

P.S. Since dictating this letter, I have seen your telegram 506 giving me the text of the Secretary of State's replies to Proctor's question and Griffiths' supplementary. I now see that the Secretary of State did use the word "consult", saying that "the leaders will be consulted". This is not generally known here and I think the card, not having been fully exposed here (or perhaps one should regard it as having been tabled but not played) can still be played in July. The Straits Times have been most co-operative and have given no prominence to these questions and answers. I enclose the Malay Mail version of them which was the only text I had of them until I received your telegram.

Enclosure to 332

You, Col. H.S. Lee and Dr. Ismail have asked me for a further clarification of the manner in which I believe the new Constitutional arrangements arising from the proposed alterations to the Federal Agreement will operate, more particularly the manner in which a Government based on the majority of the elected members may expect to secure the adoption of its policy in the Legislative Council.

In response to this request, I would like to give you a fuller indication of how I think the new constitutional arrangements following upon the introduction of elections, will operate.

I would, at the outset, emphasise the cardinal importance which I attach to the establishment of a continuing harmony between the executive authority and the Legislative Council, so that the Government may expect to find in the Legislative Council consistent support for its policies. I have no doubt that on assuming office, a

---

[10] See 318, note 3.

Government based on the majority of the elected members will receive support in Council, not only from the 3 ex officio and 2 nominated officials, but from a substantial number of the appointed members. A point which may not have been fully appreciated is that, in effect, the 52 directly elected members will not be the only members in the Council who will owe their position to electoral support. Apart from the 11 State and Settlement representatives, no less than nineteen other appointed members will owe their position to the fact that they have been selected or elected by representative institutions, such as the Rubber Producers' Council, the Trade Unions as well as Mining and Commercial interests. Elected as they are in this way, these members might indeed be more appropriately referred to as "representative members" rather than "appointed members".

From amongst these I feel sure that a substantial measure of support for any reasonable Government policy will be forthcoming and I expect that some will also be obtained from those appointed by me to represent Malay commercial interests and agriculture (as well as from amongst the representatives of the racial minorities).

In addition, there will be the nominated members to whom reference is made in paragraph 31 of the Elections Committee Report. These members will be in a somewhat unique position as they are not to be appointed by me until the election is over, and the appointments are to be made in the light of the results of that election. Apart from the officials whom all are agreed should fill two of these seats, the primary purpose of these members is to give a voice in the Council to any important element which had not found adequate representation in the Council through the electoral process. In giving effect to this purpose, it would clearly be inappropriate for me to send into Council representatives who would be antagonistic to the majority of the elected members, indeed this might well be regarded as an attempt to thwart or frustrate the wishes of the electorate as expressed at the polls, and to be inconsistent with the promotion of that harmony and close identity between the legislature as a whole and the executive which the Elections Committee unanimously indicated in paragraph 106 of their Report should be a constant aim of the High Commissioner. Clearly, the purpose of these seats as well as the basic intention of the whole constitution will be more readily and appropriately achieved by filling these seats with representatives chosen for the purposes indicated in paragraph 31 of the Report who are not likely to find themselves out of harmony with major political opinion in the Council as reflected amongst the elected members, and consequently less able to inform and guide that opinion effectively. It is therefore my intention to consult with the leader of the majority amongst the elected members before making appointments to these seats.

I hope that with this fuller explanation, you will find yourselves able to cooperate in the establishment of the new constitutional arrangements and to give your support to the Legislative measures which will give effect to the proposals contained in Federal Council Paper No. 21 of 1954.[11]

---

[11] M J Hogan (chairman), *Report of the Committee Appointed to Examine the Question of Elections to the Federal Legislative Council*.

333   CO 1030/311, no 125   3 July 1954
[Federal elections and Alliance boycott]: inward telegram no 523 from
Sir D MacGillivray to Mr Lyttelton proposing concessions to the
Alliance as regards nomination of reserved seats

[Hogan (attorney-general) and Gray (acting chief secretary) having prepared the ground,
MacGillivray and Alliance leaders reached agreement in principle on board HMS *Alert* on
2 July, before the high commissioner embarked for a brief tour of the east-coast states.
After further consultations—the British with other parties, the Alliance leaders with their
members—both sides were ready for a formal exchange of letters on 6–7 July (see 334).
On 7 July the Alliance called off their boycott.]

Your telegram No. 511.
   Elections.
   As you know, I have for some time felt that at the appropriate moment, settlement
with the Alliance could be reached by an understanding in regard to the manner of
appointing "nominated reserve". Members (corrupt gp.)[1] have been apprehensive of
the attitude of the party Negara and, to some extent, the Rulers towards this and, at
the same time, felt doubt as to whether it would in fact satisfy the U.M.N.O. element
in the Alliance. Recent developments here and questioning in Parliament have
convinced me that the opportunity should be taken now, if it is to prove effective.
   2. Suitable occasion occurred Tuesday to discuss present position with the
remaining Asian Member of the Executive Council; I followed this up by a further
talk with Onn yesterday.
   3   It was apparent from this that, while some Members of the party Negara would
still be strongly opposed to any concession made for the purpose of reaching
accommodation with the Alliance, others, including Onn, were unlikely to oppose
such accommodation provided that it did not involve any amendment to the Bill or
departure from terms of the White Paper. Onn did not demur from the suggestion
that I should reach understanding which involved undertaking from me to "consult"
in regard to appointment of "nominated reserve" and a restoration of Alliance to its
seats in the Legislative Council on their undertaking to co-operate in the establishment of new Constitution.
   4. I also saw yesterday the Sultan of Selangor and the Mentri Besar of Johore,
who were immediately available and established that they would not oppose a
settlement within the confines of the Bill.
   5. Having cleared the way to this extent I arranged to meet Rahman, Lee and
Ismail yesterday evening on board H.M.S. "ALERT" before leaving on a visit to the
east coast States, the Attorney General, who had made preliminary soundings with
them in Johore Bahru, being present. After considerable discussion the Alliance
leaders indicated that, subject to arrangement of their own "round table" which they
anticipated would be forthcoming, they were prepared to come to an understanding
on the basis of consultation in regard to "nominated reserve" statements, provided
that the status quo in Malaya was fully restored. By this they meant that I should not
only invite the Alliance members to resume the seats on the Legislative Council but
also on the Executive Council, with offer of membership to Lee and Ismail, but

---

[1] ie phrase garbled in transmission.

should also use my good offices to persuade the State Governments to re-appoint Alliance members who had resigned. I felt it necessary in order to secure agreement to accept this in regard to Federal Legislative Council and Executive Council, but of course indicated that I could give no guarantee in regard to State Councils.

6. Outcome was that:—

(i)   U.M.N.O. would consult its Executive on the 4th and the Alliance round table would consider the matter on Monday 5th.

(ii) If acceptance agreed by the Alliance round table I would then address letter to Rahman giving undertaking to consult and requesting in return their support for new constitutional arrangements.

(iii) They would then reply accepting the assurance and undertaking to co-operate in establishing the new arrangements, but would make it clear that this did not derogate from their request for a Commission to examine other features of the Federation Agreement. Their letter would go on to indicate their willingness to co-operate with the Government as before.

(iv) I would then reply that, having regard to their statement of willingness to co-operate full status quo would now be restored and that to this end I would invite the Alliance to resume their seats on the Federal Legislative Council and Executive Council.

(v)   This exchange cannot be completed before Tuesday morning and thereafter I should wish to have 24 hours before publication so as to enable me to inform the Rulers. The earliest possible time for publication of the exchange of letters would be Wednesday.

7. Alliance leaders and Onn attach much importance to the principle that any understanding of this kind should be reached and announced in Malaya rather than in London and, indeed, Onn's reactions are likely to be coloured by this consideration. I urge therefore [that] if Ogmore cannot be persuaded to postpone the answer to the Question until after Wednesday then reply should merely be to the effect that this is a (?gp. omitted matter) which is under consideration in Malaya.[2]

8. Whilst I feel that this solution is right and that the opportunity to adopt it should not be lost, I am apprehensive as to the reaction of the party Negara and to a lesser extent that of the Rulers. I feel that the Party Negara will resent the restoration of Alliance members to the Executive Council and any pressure that I may bring to bear for their restoration in the States. It may be that they will carry their resentment so far as to submit their own resignations, but that is a risk which must, I think, be taken.

---

[2] Lord Ogmore had given notice of a parliamentary question to be put on 5 July on the possibility of using the seven nominated seats to break the deadlock.

334   CO 1030/311, no 130   7 July 1954

[Agreement with the Alliance on federal elections]: inward telegram
no 531 from Sir D MacGillivray to Mr Lyttelton transmitting his
exchange of letters with Tunku Abdul Rahman

[The text of MacGillivray's letter of 6 July may be compared with his draft at 332,
enclosure. The letters were published, see *Straits Times*, 8 July 1954.]

My immediately preceding telegram.
    Federal Elections.
    Following is text of my letter of 6th July to Tunku Abdul Rahman.
    Begins. "As a result of my recent discussions with you, Colonel H.S. Lee and Dr.
Ismail, I am writing to clarify the course I intend to pursue when appointing
"nominated reserve" members, to whom reference is made in paragraph 31 of the
Election Committee Report.
    These members are not to be appointed by me until the election is completed and
the appointments are to be made in the light of the result of that election. Apart from
officials, whom all are agreed should fill two of these seats, the primary purpose of
these members is to give a voice in the Council to any important element which had
not found adequate representation in the Council through the electoral process. In
giving effect to this purpose it would, I believe, be inappropriate for me to send these
representatives into the Council to oppose the policy of the majority among the
elected members; indeed this might well be regarded as thwarting or frustrating the
wishes of the electors as expressed at the polls and as being inconsistent with
promotion of that harmony and close identity between the Legislature as a whole and
the Executive, which the Elections Committee unanimously indicated in paragraph
106 of their Report should be the constant aim of the High Commissioner. The
purpose of these seats, as well as basic intention of the Constitution, will, I believe,
be more readily and appropriately achieved by filling these seats with representatives
chosen for purposes indicated in paragraph 31 of the Report, who are not likely to
find themselves out of harmony with major political opinion in the Council as
reflected among the elected members, and consequently less able to inform and
guide that opinion effectively.
    It is therefore my intention to consult with the leader or leaders of [the] majority
among the elected members before making appointments to these seats.
    I hope that with this statement of intention, you will find yourself able to
co-operate in the establishment of the new constitutional arrangements and to give
your support to legislative measures which will give effect to proposals contained in
Federal Council Paper No.21 of 1954." *Ends.*
    2. Following is text of Tunku Abdul Rahman's reply dated 6th July to my letter.
    Begins. "I have to thank you for your communication in regard to the course
which you intend to pursue on introduction of elections in appointing "nominated
reserve" members, which I have communicated to my colleagues.
    In view of this statement we are satisfied that proposed constitutional arrange-
ments have a reasonable prospect of working satisfactorily and Alliance is therefore
prepared to extend its support to establishment of these arrangements and to
co-operate and participate with the Government at all levels as before. We therefore

trust that for this purpose members of Alliance will be re-appointed to the various councils, boards and committees of which they were previously members. But in this connection you will appreciate our concern that all our members who have resigned should be afforded the same consideration in order to ensure co-operation at all levels.

We do, however, feel that there are other aspects of Federation agreement as it stands which merit further consideration and we understand that it will be Your Excellency's intention to discuss with Their Highnesses the Rulers on 15th July the request of Alliance for a Commission to report on these matters." *Ends.*

3. Following is text of my reply dated 7th July to Tunku Abdul Rahman.

Begins. "I have to thank you for your letter of 6th July on the subject of constitutional arrangements to provide for introduction of elections and am glad to receive your assurance that Alliance will give its support to establishment of these arrangements, together with expression of its wish to co-operate and participate with the Government as before.

In the circumstances I hope *"status quo"* before resignations will be restored as soon as possible so that Alliance may be able to give this support and co-operation. But as resignations have extended to councils, boards and committees in States, it will be necessary for me to consult Their Highnesses the Rulers in this regard and I intend to take first opportunity of doing so". *Ends.*

335   CO 1030/193   12 July 1954

[Regional policy and the future of the commissioner-general]: minute by Sir J Martin on discussions with W D Allen[1]

[The compromise reached over federal elections was followed by Alliance victories in the town council elections of Ipoh, Taiping and Telok Anson in Aug and in the first state elections of Johore and Trengganu in Oct. In Dec the Alliance won municipal elections in Kuala Lumpur, Malacca, Penang, Klang, and Port Swettenham, though not in Butterworth and Seremban, and in Feb 1955 it gained all elected seats on the Penang settlement council. For the CO, where Lennox-Boyd succeeded Lyttelton at the end of July, these months were a period of stock-taking (see 335–343): significant advance on the Malayanisation of the administration, closer association with Singapore and other fronts was arrested pending the outcome of the federal elections which, it was announced in Mar, would take place on 27 July 1955. Meanwhile the FO, service ministries and chiefs of staff reviewed Britain's position in the aftermath of the Geneva conference (see 324, note) and the Manila treaty, 8 Sept 1954, by which Australia, Britain, France, New Zealand, Pakistan, the Philippines, Thailand and the USA agreed to the formation of the South-East Asia Treaty Organisation.]

Consultation with the Foreign Office as authorised by the Secretary of State[2] has been delayed by the absence of Mr. W.D. Allen, the Assistant Under-Secretary in charge of the South East Asia Department at Geneva and then in Washington (while the Head of the Department has remained continuously in Geneva); but I was able to see Mr. Allen on the 10th July.

Mr. Allen said that, as a result of the negotiations relating to Indo-China, Mr. Eden

---

[1] W D Allen, diplomatic service, 1934–1969; attended Geneva conference on Indo-China, May–July 1954; deputy under-secretary of state, FO (FCO), 1967–1969.   [2] See 324, note 7.

had in the last few months taken a much closer personal interest in affairs in South East Asia than had been possible previously. Mr. Allen was fairly clear that Mr. Eden now felt that Mr. MacDonald had about reached the end of his usefulness and would be reluctant to agree to a further extension of his appointment beyond the end of the present year. The Foreign Office had not, however, worked out any very clear ideas about what should happen afterwards, i.e. whether a new Commissioner-General should be appointed with much the same functions as Mr. MacDonald or some change should be made in the organisation. Mr. Allen seemed to think that, if it was still necessary to retain some special organisation to deal with the various local international negotiations which tended to centre in Singapore as well as for defence co-ordination, someone much more lower powered than the present Commissioner-General might suffice and threw out the suggestion that possibly the Foreign Office requirement (though not that in relation to defence co-ordination) might be met by appointment of a fairly senior Foreign Service official to the staff of the Governor of Singapore. In any case, however, it will be difficult to reach a firm conclusion until we saw what emerged as a result of the Geneva Conference. If, for example, there was an elaborate SEATO structure corresponding to NATO, with Headquarters in the region, it might be necessary to have a fairly high powered United Kingdom representative; but on the other hand there might only emerge some form of internationally guaranteed arrangement requiring no elaborate administrative structure. In any event, Mr. Allen thought that Mr. Eden would prefer not to take any final decision about the future of Mr. MacDonald's appointment until we had made up our minds on the question of replacement.

Mr. Allen was of course familiar with the fact that the principal reason put forward by the Foreign Secretary in proposing extension of the present appointment last October was that we could not withdraw Mr. MacDonald without damage to our interests and to the general position in South East Asia, since the situation there remained uncertain and Mr. MacDonald's removal would be taken to mean that our interest in the area was lessening. He thought, however, that the present was a moment when, in view of our obviously close interest in the region and the negotiations for some form of international agreement, it was hardly likely that such an interpretation would be put on a change in this particular appointment.

Mr. Allen said that he was leaving for Geneva with Mr. Eden today, but that he would inform Mr. Barclay (Deputy Under Secretary of State)[3] of the position and suggest that there should be an examination (in which the Colonial Office might join) of our requirements in the way of an organisation of this kind in South East Asia, so as to submit proposals to Ministers which they could consider before coming to a conclusion regarding Mr. MacDonald's future. In this connection I said that we should probably find it useful to consult with Sir Donald MacGillivray when the latter is here (on present plans) at the end of this month. We agreed that, for the present, Mr. MacDonald would have to be told that, in view of pre-occupation with the Geneva Conference and uncertainty regarding the situation which would emerge from the current negotiations, it would not be possible to come to any definite conclusion for some weeks regarding the future of his appointment.

(I should add that I explained to Mr. Allen the present position regarding the work of the Joint Co-ordination Committee.)

---

[3] R E Barclay, later Sir Roderick, was deputy under-secretary of state, FO, 1953–1956.

The reply to Mr. MacDonald's enquiry can conveniently be included in answering his letter of the 5th July ((15) on SEA.81/02 about leave plans). When that has been done the present file should recirculate for consideration of possible alternative arrangements, assuming that Mr. MacDonald is not to be retained.[4]

---

[4] After further discussions CO and FO officials concluded that there was a case for retaining MacDonald until a lower-ranking replacement could be found, see 338.

336   FO 371/111852, no 5   8 Aug 1954
'Note on relations with the United States, China and the Colombo powers': note by Mr M J MacDonald for Sir I Kirkpatrick

Our relations in Asian affairs with the (i) United States, (ii) the People's Republic of China and (iii) the "Colombo Powers"[1] are three factors which can affect profoundly the issue whether there will be peace or war in Asia. The following are a few brief comments on these matters, made almost wholly from the point of view of an observer in South-East Asia.

(i) The United States
2. The conduct of American foreign policy towards Asia during recent months has left the United States with few friends, many enemies and almost universal critics amongst Asian Governments and peoples. It has done America's reputation shattering harm, appears sometimes to Asians to support the Communist contention that the United States are the real "war-mongers" in the world, and has left the United States virtually isolated here except for the support of some of the least influential Asian nations, like Siam and Chinese Nationalist Formosa. Yet fundamentally the Americans believe in and are striving for similar political ideals to those which most Asian Governments support. It is appalling that American statements and actions have caused such gigantic misunderstandings, and that the vast influence which America could exert for good has been turned to grave disadvantage to us all.

3. For the United States are not the only sufferers. In spite of the United Kingdom Government's remarkable success in pursuing a different policy at the Geneva Conference—which has distinctly increased our reputation and influence throughout Asia—we are regarded as being either too much under American influence or else too incapable of countering it to achieve adequate independence in international affairs. American policy is generally regarded as dominating all Western policy towards Asia, and the Asians are inclining to feel increasingly pessimistic about the chances of fruitful understanding and co-operation between them and "the West."

4. If we are to maintain a reasonable measure of sympathy and, ultimately, agreement by the majority of Asian countries with "Western" policy, the United Kingdom must:—

(a) continue to pursue, as far as the overriding necessity for co-operation with the United States permits, its own unfettered foreign policy towards Asian affairs, and

---

[1] A grouping of five Asian states (Burma, Ceylon, India, Indonesia, and Pakistan) which took its name from a meeting in Colombo, Apr–May 1954. The Colombo powers supported the agreements reached at the Geneva conference but, with the exception of Pakistan, disapproved of SEATO.

(b) seek by every possible means to influence American policy—and the statement and conduct of that policy (for often these are more at fault than the policy itself)—in the same direction.

5. Unless the misunderstanding and hostility which is growing between America and Asia is checked, enmity between the two may become for a period irreconcilable—with grave results.

(ii) Communist China

6. The contacts between the British and Chinese representatives at Geneva have clearly led to some (at least) slight improvement in political and diplomatic relations between their two countries. If we can take advantage of this situation to achieve gradually a further improvement—without its causing a serious deterioration in Anglo-American relations (which is admittedly difficult in present circumstances)— the result might be a real relaxing of international tension in Southern Asia. We must be careful of course, not to fall into any Chinese Communist "traps."

7. There is one aspect of this which has particular importance to us in South-East Asia. One of our major problems, and dangers is the existence of considerable populations of "overseas" Chinese in several countries in the region. The difficulty is that the great majority of them still owe their primary loyalty to China, are liable to yield to pressure from the existing Government in Peking (whatever its political complexion), and are therefore now a potential "fifth column" for further Communist advances in South-East Asia.

8. This tendency has been supported in the past by:—

(a) the policy of successive Chinese Governments that all "overseas" Chinese remain Chinese nationals debarred from becoming nationals of the countries of their adoption; and,

(b) the complementary policy of the local Governments in treating their Chinese residents as foreigners, and refusing them citizenship rights.

9. It appears that during their recent conversations with Mr. Chou En-lai, Mr. Nehru in Delhi and U Nu[2] in Rangoon both urged the Chinese Prime Minister to change the traditional Chinese policy, and that Mr. Chou said something to the effect that his Government might make a declaration that "overseas" Chinese should become nationals of their country of adoption or else cease to interfere in local politics. Such a declaration would have a great effect for good amongst the Chinese in South-East Asia, and in particular would help us in Malaya to realise our policy of turning the primary loyalty of the local Chinese from China to Malaya. Admittedly Mr. Chou may be at least partly insincere in his professions, and may have some ulterior Communist motive in suggesting a declaration of the kind; nevertheless whatever his purposes, we could exploit such a statement greatly to our advantage.

10. I urge therefore that we should:—

(a) encourage Mr. Nehru, U Nu (and Indonesian leaders also) to continue to put judicious pressure on Mr. Chou to confirm and publicise the suggested new policy;

---

[2] Chou En-lai was premier of the People's Republic of China, 1949–1976 and foreign minister, 1949–1958; Jawaharlal Nehru was prime minister of India and minister of external affairs, 1947–1964; U Nu was prime minister of Burma, 1947–1956 and 1957–1962.

(b) use our own increased influence with the Government in Peking—if Mr. Trevelyan[3] judges that prudent—towards the same purpose.

(iii) The "Colombo Powers"

11. The success of our policy in South-East Asia depends partly on general sympathy and, if possible, active support for it by the Governments and peoples in the region, and by those of India, Pakistan and Ceylon. If these are estranged from us and oppose our policy, it has comparatively little chance of success; but if they approve and support us, it has a good prospect. This is one direction in which the Americans have taken a wrong turn, for they seem to underestimate the importance of securing the understanding of public opinion in Southern Asia. Nothing in United Kingdom policy has been more admirable than our close contact throughout the Geneva and subsequent negotiations with the "Colombo Powers." It has made a most friendly impression in Asia, given many Asian leaders a clear understanding of our motives and aims, increased our influence throughout Asia, and prevented a much worse division of opinion than now exists between "the West" and Asia from arising.

12. The Governments of the "Colombo Powers," as a whole, are irresolute and weak in their recognition of the Communist threat to their countries and the world, and their belief in "neutrality" makes our task of averting that threat exceedingly difficult. Nevertheless, they are slowly but surely learning the facts of international life, and are moving gradually towards the adoption of more positive and helpful foreign policies. I have had unique opportunities, during periodic visits to some of their capitals over the last six years, to watch this evolution in their thinking. In Rangoon, for example, the development has been continuous and marked, if slow, and the change in thought exists not only amongst responsible Ministers, but also amongst many prominent local journalists and other fashioners of public opinion. I believe that in most of the "Colombo" countries these processes will continue, if we remain patient and understanding in our relations with them, and especially if the United Kingdom Government keeps in close, friendly, influential touch with their Government—and can prevent the Americans from taking drastic actions which will disastrously alienate them.

---

[3] Humphrey Trevelyan was HM chargé d'affaires in Peking, 1953–1955.

337 CO 1030/67, no 1   14 Sept 1954
'United Kingdom policy in Malaya': CO memorandum for UK high commissioners in Commonwealth countries

[This paper was one of a series of colonial appreciations prepared for the use of UK high commissioners posted to Commonwealth countries.]

A united Malayan nation, self-governing within the Commonwealth, is the aim of United Kingdom policy in Malaya. It is the aim not only of the present Government but also of the Labour Party. There is no reason to doubt that it is an aim which commends itself to the ordinary people of the United Kingdom, who have long been making their contributions towards it through material aid provided out of taxation and through the men who from innumerable families up and down the country have gone to serve the Malayan Governments, to help develop the Malayan economy, or to fight the Communist terrorists in the Malayan jungle. We are pursuing this aim because the people of Malaya want self-government, because without the kernel of nationhood self-government is an empty shell, and because in a multi-racial society nationhood is unattainable without unity. We believe that it will be in the best interests of Malaya, when self-government comes, to remain within the Common-wealth and continue to share in its political and economic strength, but it has always been made clear that that decision will be left to the free choice of a self-governing Malaya.

2. A statement of aims does not, however, of itself constitute a policy any more than the determination to climb a mountain maps a route to its summit. The climber cannot go straight up as if he were in a lift. He must follow the lie of the land. Occasionally, as he edges around the obstacles in his way, he may seem to be going in the wrong direction altogether even while each traverse or circuit is bringing him nearer the top. The route to the goal for Malaya is as difficult, and the obstacles as stiff, as any facing the traveller through Malaya's own jungles, across her rivers and over her mountains.

3. Malaya is at the tip of a peninsula between the great land masses of India and China, with Burma, Siam and Indo-China as buffers. Any Chinese convulsion sends a tremor down through the buffers or across the sea to be felt first among the Malayan communities of Chinese origin and to spread from these to the Malays themselves and to the minorities in Malaya. It is as if the mountaineer had to plan his route at a time when the geological masses were themselves liable to shift. But he cannot take the possibility of earthquakes into account. If he did he would achieve nothing. He is bound to go on as if the main landmarks would remain at least stable enough for recognition. He must deal with the immediate obstacles within his compass.

4. The largest of these obstacles are the Emergency, the racial mixture of the population, a political structure involving nine Malay States and two British Settlements (to say nothing of the separate Colony of Singapore) and an economic dependence on two primary commodities—tin and rubber.

5. *The Emergency* began in 1948 when the Malayan Communists abandoned the political struggle and turned to "direct action." Besides the initial advantage of surprise, they held certain strong cards. The first of these, which is still of value to them, was the fact that four-fifths of Malaya (a country about the size of England) is jungle, ideal for a guerrilla campaign. In addition, the Japanese war had had two significant effects. It had undermined people's faith in the power of the British to protect them, and it had led to a dispersal of many Chinese to remote and isolated homesteads where they could easily be forced to provide food and recruits for the terrorists, themselves nearly all Chinese. There was also, of course, the traditional Communist appeal, always attractive until compared with the Communist record in action, to liberation from "feudalism" and "imperialist exploitation." One card the Communists never held. They have throughout consisted almost entirely of Chinese; and without attracting substantial Malay support—of which there is no sign—they could not, even if Communism did not enter into the question, plausibly represent themselves as a Nationalist movement. They are in fact wholly indifferent to the legitimate aspirations of Malayan Nationalists, whether Malay or Chinese; their sole aim is to impose upon Malaya the alien and repugnant creed of Communism.

6. In dealing with the Emergency, United Kingdom policy has been essentially

simple and straightforward. It was clear from the start that civil and military effort would have to be combined against the terrorists. While the Security Forces maintained vigilant and relentless pressure in seeking out and destroying the terrorists in action, the great mass of law-abiding people had to be convinced that they could be protected, or protect themselves, from armed bands, and that a better life than that offered by Communist "liberation" was within their reach.

7.   The basis of advance, both military and civil, has been the re-settlement in the "New Villages" of the Chinese who had dispersed into the jungle fringes. By now more than half a million have been moved from their isolated holdings into these new communities, in which they can organise themselves for defence, where this is still necessary, and enjoy, often for the first time, the amenities of civilised life. Much progress has been made by denying food to the terrorists and preserving it for the civil population, by protecting the rubber plantations and mines so that few workers have been thrown out of employment, by expanding the educational and health services, and by encouraging the people to interest themselves in the conduct of their own affairs through the development of Local Government. When and how the Emergency will end no one can predict with certainty, if only because it is impossible to gauge the future influence and intentions of the Chinese People's Government. But to-day the terrorists are at least contained and frustrated and no more than a hard-core of about 4,000 remains. Restrictive controls and regulations are being progressively relaxed. Some, like the power of mass detention, have been abolished throughout the country; and in eight areas, covering nearly a quarter of the population, the principal restrictions have been lifted.

8.   Even without the Emergency the other obstacles confronting United Kingdom policy in Malaya would still have been formidable. *The problem of creating a united nation of a number of different races* is never easily solved. In Malaya, the two main races, the Malays and the Chinese, together amounting to nearly five-sixths of the population, and roughly equal in numbers, are deeply divided. There is practically no inter-marriage and each race clings tenaciously to its own language, outlook and customs. The Malays, as the indigenous race, enjoy a preponderance of political power and are reluctant to admit the Chinese to an equal share in it without practical evidence that the Chinese look to Malaya as their permanent home and the only fount and object of their loyalty. The Chinese, who largely sustain and control the economic life of the country, increasingly look to a greater part in its Government, without which they are reluctant to turn their backs on China and commit themselves unequivocally to a new allegiance. They are powerfully drawn by tradition and emotion towards the country of their origin, whether their eyes turn to Peking or to Formosa; and in the present state of all Eastern Asia they cannot but be acutely conscious of the imminence of metropolitan China. The Malays have virtually no middle class, and are mainly peasants with little share in the country's industrial or commercial life, although they largely support the public service and the police; they are still deeply imbued with a sense of loyalty to their hereditary Rulers. The Chinese have a large and powerful middle class and no aristocracy or hereditary rulers. The Malays are Moslems, whereas it is hardly possible to over-rate the importance to the Chinese of the pig in their economy and everyday life. The Malays for the most part live in small villages scattered up and down the coast line and along the river banks, while the Chinese tend to be concentrated in the towns and industrial areas. Substantial communities of Indian and Pakistani descent—totalling approximately

three-quarters of a million out of a total of six million—with smaller groups of Europeans, Eurasians, Ceylonese and others, add to the problem of creating a united Malaya.

9. The most that a Government can do directly to weld different communities into a single body of citizens is exceedingly limited—probably no more than to establish a framework within which the different races may come together if they themselves wish to do so. The aim is to create this framework at every level; that the village school, the teacher training college, the Army, the Police, the Civil Service, the Scout and Guide movement, the business world, the University, should be open to all races and should cater for the needs of each equally. But so far it cannot be pretended that any very rapid progress has been made in translating the aim into reality. The Chinese show no eagerness to enter the Army, the uniformed ranks of the Police and the higher grades of the Civil Service, now for the first time thrown open to them; and in the plans for a national rather than communal system of education they see a threat to the cherished traditions of Chinese culture. The Malays take little advantage of new opportunities to enter the world of business and commerce. And yet, in spite of the difficulties, progress is made: in the Women's Institute movement, for instance, or the field of adult education, where common interests draw Malay, Chinese and Indian naturally together. Most of all, the experience of working democratic institutions, including those of Local Government, must be trusted to bring the different communities together: as one learns to be a shoemaker by making shoes, so one learns to be a citizen by exercising a citizen's rights and performing his duties. In some of the New Villages Chinese, Indians and Malays are working well together on their local councils; and in Federal politics, though racial issues still lie barely below the surface, each of the two main political groups professes to represent members of all communities.

10. Federal politics are themselves complicated by *the constitutional structure of the country*. Legally the presence of the British in the Malay States (as distinct from the two British Settlements of Penang and Malacca) depends upon treaties between Her Majesty the Queen and the Malay Rulers, by which Her Majesty undertakes the responsibility for the defence and external affairs of their States. Although they have ceded certain executive and legislative powers to the Federation, the Rulers regard themselves as, and within certain limits are, independent sovereigns. We have no power to depose them even if we should wish to do so, and we cannot alter the Federation Agreement of 1948 (which established the Federation of Malaya in its present form and is in effect the constitution of the country) without their consent. But nine independent sovereigns (ten if we include Her Majesty in her capacity of Queen of the Settlements), who may well disagree among themselves, are too many for so small a country. If the new nation is to have any chance of standing on its own feet among its much larger neighbours its government must be an unitary government in fact, whatever its legal form.

11. The Rulers vary in their application to public affairs. All, however, have considerable influence, direct or indirect, as guardians of the Moslem faith and as champions of the "special position of the Malays," which the High Commissioner is bound by the present Federation Agreement to protect. It [is] always dangerous to underestimate the loyalty which hereditary monarchs who are also religious leaders can command among their own people. It was partly on this that the attempt in 1946 to form a more unified state, the Malayan Union, came to grief; and any attempt to

revise the Agreement of 1948 could only be initiated with the utmost caution.

12. These considerations necessarily influence the pace of political advance. The Rulers and their entourages are at the centre of the conservative opposition to constitutional reform, especially to reform based on equal rights and opportunities for members of all races who have made their permanent home in Malaya. The agreement earlier this year on constitutional development providing for elections to the State, Settlement and Federal Legislatures, and for a majority of elected members to the Federal Legislature was achieved only after prolonged negotiations and against the natural inclinations of the Rulers, and represents the furthest point to which they can at present be persuaded to advance. Most legislatures, however, once they acquire an elected majority, tend to make the running for more liberal institutions without any need of outside stimulus. The Government can do little more than give discreet encouragement to these natural processes and hope that in the course of time the Rulers will achieve some sort of *otium cum dignitate*[1]—with a position, perhaps, between that of an 18th century Bishop and an hereditary Lord Lieutenant.

13. Even so, true political unity would still be lacking so long as the Federation is seperated [sic] from the natural capital of the peninsula, Singapore. Strategically, the two territories must be defended as a single unit: economically they are largely interdependent. Nevertheless, there are formidable difficulties in the way of their unification. Singapore is a Chinese city; and it is natural that the Malays in the Federation should fear that the accession of nearly a million Chinese would give the Chinese the same predominance in politics as they already enjoy in economic affairs. On the other hand, the Chinese businessmen of Singapore are most unwilling to link their fortunes to those of a region where political power rests largely in the hands of another race with a specially protected position. For these reasons, and also simply because the two administrations have in fact been separate since the war, the policies pursued in the two territories in recent years have tended more and more to diverge.

14. It is an objective of the United Kingdom Government to see that this process is arrested and if possible reversed. A Committee of local politicians and leading officials from each territory, under the Chairmanship of the Commissioner-General for South-East Asia, is at present considering how policy and administration could better be co-ordinated between the two territories, and whether any form of constitutional association is possible.[2] The Committee has not yet reached the constitutional part of its agenda and, given the extreme difficulty of the problem, is unlikely to propound any early solution. It has, however, completed its examination of the problems of day-to-day co-operation, and is at present preparing its interim report. If practical co-ordination can be attained by administrative arrangement that will in itself have achieved much.

15. Finally, there is *the economic problem*. Immediately after the war attention was concentrated on restoring production of tin and rubber, both urgently needed and each commanding a high price. As long as the price kept up, both the Federation and Singapore could count on balancing their ordinary budgets with handsome surpluses; and, even with the Emergency to pay for, it was possible to estimate for a substantial and much-needed development programme. But when the tin and rubber

[1] ie dignified idleness.
[2] See part II of this volume, 300, and 324.

prices go down, as they have in the last two years, the whole economy sags. A real slump would put an end to any immediate hope of building up a solidly-based Malayan nation.

16. Now, it is clear that, whatever can be done to diversify Malay's [sic] economy, to build up secondary industries or diminish reliance on imported food—and progress is being made in all these fields, especially in improved rice-growing—tin and rubber will long remain the country's main sources of wealth. There is consequently a double problem—first, so far as possible to avoid the wide fluctuations in price and demand that have done these industries so much harm in the past; and second, to ensure that the industries themselves are efficiently run. The first calls for consultation and agreement between the main producing and consuming nations of the world in order to try to achieve a measure of stability. Such consultations are being diligently pursued by the Federation and United Kingdom Governments—one of their recent results has been the signature of the International Tin Agreement. As for the second, new prospecting areas for tin must be opened up; in the rubber plantations low-yielding trees must be replaced by improved varieties; and research into new uses for natural rubber must be prosecuted to enable it to compete with synthetic. In all these activities the initiative must come primarily from the industries themselves. The contribution from Government comes in other ways. The economic pattern of Malaya, relying on primary products for its income, is much the same as that of other under-developed countries. For its natural wealth to be fully developed investment must be encouraged; for investment to be forthcoming a reasonable degree of security must be ensured; for security there must be a satisfied population: to satisfy the people the country's natural wealth must be seen to be coming back to them in protection from their enemies, in wages, social services and general improvement in living standards. A Government can provide some, but in the nature of things not all of the spokes of the wheel, and do something but not everything to keep it turning.

17. Such in outline are the terms in which United Kingdom policy in Malaya is defined and pursued. At present we are at a watershed. Ahead of us lies the new unexplored region of government based on the electoral principle. How the Rulers, the different races, the different political parties, the business interests, the ideological war itself will emerge from a few years' experience of constitutional government, it would be rash indeed to predict. Nor can we gauge how strong outside influences will be nor precisely in what directions they can pull. But we can help to set Malaya on the path which we ourselves believe to be best; and in an uncertain world concentration on the immediate steps ahead, without attempting to penetrate the further mists, is as likely a method as any to bring us to the goal.

338   CO 1030/193, no 6   30 Sept 1954
[The role of the commissioner-general]: letter from Mr Lennox-Boyd to Mr Eden about MacDonald's future

I perfectly understand your inability to have a word with me about Malcolm MacDonald's future before I go to East Africa on the 1st October. I do want to discuss it with you sometime because it is, I think, the sort of question which we could settle much better that way than in correspondence; but obviously you have no time this week for relatively minor matters like this.

I am writing because I shall not be back until the 18th October and Malcolm, who is due to return to this country from Canada on the 13th, will probably be leaving for Singapore again on the 20th. It may thus turn out that we cannot have our talk before he goes back to Malaya and I therefore think that I ought now to let you know briefly what are my own views about his position, especially as I gather that they differ to some extent from yours.

I understand that your own view is that Malcolm's term should be extended yet again until the end of 1955, and that you had it in mind to tell Reading[1] to speak to him on those terms in Ottawa. I must, however, ask that Reading should not approach Malcolm until you and I have had our talk unless you can accept my own view that the time has come to make a change, that this should take place as soon as possible and that in all the circumstances, including decent warning to Malcolm, we should aim at getting a new man into the job by the middle of next year.

You will remember that at the end of 1952, when Malcolm got his last extension but one, Oliver Lyttelton was not particularly enthusiastic about it but was content to accept your view that for reasons of foreign policy he should continue for a time as Commissioner General. Generally speaking, it remains true today, as it was then, that Malcolm has comparatively little to contribute on the Colonial side; indeed, I have good reason to believe that his influence in the British territories of South-East Asia has for some time been declining. Last year, when Oliver Lyttelton supported your recommendation that Malcolm should be invited to stay on until the end of 1954, his main reason was the work of the "Joint Co-ordination Committee" which has been considering under Malcolm's Chairmanship means of achieving closer association between the Federation of Malaya and Singapore. The Committee has now completed the first and less contentious half of its task, that of examining means of co-ordination within the framework of the existing constitutions: it has not yet begun the second and much more difficult half, consideration of constitutional changes designed to that end. This is likely to prove very controversial and to take a long time: since both territories are to introduce new constitutions next year and will consequently be absorbed in their own domestic politics, there is every chance that the Committee may make little or no further progress for at least a year to come. In these circumstances I do not think that the work of the Committee is in itself such as to justify retaining Malcolm against what seems to me the powerful balance of advantage in replacing him as soon as possible.

I do not question the continuing need for a Commissioner General in South-East Asia, and I think that he should continue to be someone clearly established personally as well as by virtue of his office as standing not only apart from but also above our Ambassadors, Governors and High Commissioners in the area. But Malcolm has now been in Singapore for more than eight years and, as I have said, I think that his influence in the British South-East Asian territories is on the wane. Moreover, I wonder if he has not become so Asian-minded that he sometimes tends, in his anxiety to get the Asian point of view across to London, to overlook the importance of getting the views of Her Majesty's Government across to the leaders of

---

[1] Lord Reading was parliamentary under-secretary, 1951–1953, and minister of state at the FO, 1953–1957.

the local communities. Again, I think that we must bear in mind the likelihood that, if serious trouble broke out in South-East Asia—that is, full-scale warfare or something near it—we should almost certainly want to have there someone who could serve as a resident Minister of State and assume heavy executive responsibilities which do not fall to the lot of the Commissioner General. Malcolm seems to me quite unsuited to such duties. Finally, as a result of the Indo-China settlement, we are at present enjoying a relative lull and I think that we should use it to replace Malcolm as quickly as possible with someone who could get to work establishing his own personal position before the lull came to an end and new crises had to be faced. In addition, the timing of constitutional changes in both the Federation of Malaya and Singapore would fit in well with a change in the person of the Commissioner General about the middle of next year, since by then the effective government of Singapore will very largely have passed into the hands of elected unofficials, and they will also be in a majority in the Legislature of the Federation; it seems to me that there will be obvious advantage in having the new man on the job with the least possible delay after these changes have taken place.

   Although I think that the time has now come for Malcolm to leave Singapore, he has been a good servant of the State for many years and has still a lot of value to give in his right place. I therefore hope that when he does leave South-East Asia, whether in nine or fifteen months' time, we shall find him a suitable niche elsewhere. But we can discuss that together with the main question when we have a chance.[2]

---

[2] In Feb 1955 Eden visited Malaya on his return from the first council meeting of SEATO in Bangkok and later reported his 'doubts about the existing organisation for co-ordination, not only between the civil and military elements within Malaya, but also between the various Governments under the general supervision of the Commissioner-General for South-East Asia' (CAB 128/28, CC 21(55)1, 7 Mar 1955). In Apr Eden succeeded Churchill as prime minister and instructed Sir N Brook, secretary to the Cabinet, to examine the future functions of the office, see 348.

339   CO 1030/67, no 13   15 Nov 1954
[Trend of events in SE Asia]: minute by Mr Head[1] to Sir A Eden expressing his apprehension

I feel that I should write to you about my apprehension concerning the general trend of events in South East Asia.[2]

   I think the way in which the average literate Malayan or Chinese sees the situation is something as follows.

   Since 1947 Europeans have either voluntarily withdrawn or been forced out of the

---

[1] Antony Head, later Lord Head, was secretary of state for war, 1951–1956, minister of defence, Oct 1956 – Jan 1957, UK high commissioner to Nigeria, 1960–1963, and UK high commissioner to Malaysia, 1963–1966.
[2] At this point in the text, Eden scrawled on his copy of Head's minute, 'Rather late in the day'. He wrote similarly scathing marginalia as he read on, see notes 5 and 6 below. Eden was partly provoked by some unguarded remarks made by Head to the press during his SE Asian visit, and he minuted Sir Ivone Kirkpatrick: 'So far all he has done is to make speeches to weaken Laos and Cambodia. Now he goes on record to blame us for anything that goes wrong. I don't trust the man' (FO 371/111917, no 15, 17 Nov 1954). Eden's considered reply to Head was more diplomatically phrased, see 340.

whole of Asia excepting South Korea, Japan and Formosa in the American sphere and Hong Kong, Borneo and Malaya in the British sphere. During the same period India, Burma and Ceylon have become independent and adopted a neutral policy. Again, during this time Communism has spread over the whole of China and now most of Indo-China.

So far as future prospects are concerned he believes that Laos and Cambodia will shortly become engulfed by Viet Minh and he sees every sign of a weak and ill-governed Siam already being penetrated by Communist infiltration. Indonesia has a weak Government which can scarcely control the country and there too there are strong Communist cells which, although they could not hold down Indonesia, are working hard in a political and security climate favourable to subversion and infiltration.

With this general background the people of Malaya consider their own situation. They know that so long as the emergency lasts, there will be a considerable number of Imperial troops in Malaya and that their security is thereby guaranteed. However, they also know that British policy is to grant to Malaya self-government and independence. This they interpret as meaning that the British do not intend to stay in Malaya indefinitely and that the granting of independence will involve ipso facto the withdrawal of Imperial troops. If this happens they believe, rightly in my opinion, that an independent Malaya without British troops will be incapable of holding back Communist subversion and infiltration and that the eventual domination of Malaya by the Communists in the cold war will be inevitable.

I believe that the above is a fair summary of local opinion.

On the other hand, a good deal has been done to bring about an organisation whereby the resistance to Communism in South East Asia can be strengthened. The SEATO treaty has brought in Pakistan, Thailand and the Phillipines [sic] to the Five Power group.[3] Nevertheless their inclusion makes it difficult for a speedy resumption of defence planning on a high level because on security grounds their inclusion would presumably not be acceptable. At the same time, planning in the Five Power agency has been suspended and it does not seem that any planning progress can be made within the ANZAM[4] concept.

I had a long meeting when I was in Singapore with the BDCC although, unfortunately, Malcolm MacDonald was not there. Nevertheless, it was quite evident that BDCC planning has been restricted to an examination of the defence of Malaya in a hot war. What I believe is urgently needed now is a joint Australian, New Zealand, American and British planning organisation which can consider the whole situation and make proposals for stiffening up the defence of Malaya against subversion etc., in a cold war. I believe that this is far the most likely threat and that if we are to save Malaya we must also do everything possible to help Siam resist Communist infiltration.

So far as I can make out, Australia is tending to hold back until she is sure that America really means business in South East Asia and America is holding back until she is quite satisfied that we really mean to stay in Malaya indefinitely[5] and make strong efforts to resist the tide of Communism in South East Asia as a whole.

---

[3] See 335, note.
[4] An arrangement, not a formal agreement, dating from May 1948 for the co-ordination of the defence plans of Australia, New Zealand and Britain in the Malayan area.   [5] Eden: 'Nonsense'.

I believe that the gradual penetration of all South East Asia by C~~
eventual loss would be a reverse of the very first importance in the co~
believe it to be target No.1 in the Communist plans for the cold war.[6] Lastly, ~
that if the position deteriorates gradually during the next few years it might br~~
about a very strong American reaction later (rather as was the case in Indo-China)
which might lead to a serious danger of war.

If, therefore, the gradual deterioration is to be avoided, and if the eventual
domination of South East Asia by Communism is to be prevented without the risk of
war, I believe that we should now consider all possible methods for strengthening the
position there and preventing further subversion and infiltration. I believe that much
remains to be done in the planning field before definite proposals can be put up to
SEATO; and I also believe that time is of great importance. From what I have seen
and heard, it once again looks as though the initiative for starting realistic steps on
these lines lies with the British.

I would suggest that there are at least three things which might be done as soon as
possible.

1. We should consider the best method of setting up a high powered planning
team representing Australia, New Zealand, America and Britain to examine joint
measures which could be taken to halt Communist subversion and infiltration in
South East Asia.
2. In order to stiffen resistance in Malaya and indeed, inspire greater confidence
about our long term determination to protect Malaya, we should consider making
a statement that we are determined to honour our pledges concerning progress to
self-government and independence; but that we are equally determined to
guarantee that independence against the tide of Communism by providing the
necessary Imperial forces for that purpose. Such a declaration would remove a lot
of doubt and misunderstanding.
3. I would suggest that our post SEATO policy for the defence of South East Asia
(especially in the cold war) should be discussed by the Defence Committee at an
early date so that there is time for any subsequent investigation to be completed
before the Commonwealth Prime Ministers Conference in January.

---

[6] Eden: 'Great discovery!'

340   CO 1030/67, no 12   13 Dec 1954
[Trend of events in SE Asia]: letter (reply) from Sir A Eden to Mr Head

I should like to offer some comments on your analysis of the present situation in
South East Asia enclosed with your letter of November 15.[1]

I shall not comment upon your estimate of educated opinion in Malaya as this is a
matter for the Colonial Secretary. I see from recent reports that the political leaders
in Malaya have recognised in public statements that until the emergency is ended
Malaya's advance towards independence is bound to be delayed. I should hope that
long before independence is finally achieved we shall have made plans to provide for

---

[1] See 339.

the future defence of the country, whether by continuing to station Imperial troops there or by training and equipping indigenous forces sufficient for the task. On the other hand, although the Vietminh successes have no doubt raised the morale of the terrorists for the moment, I am doubtful subject to the views of the Colonial Secretary, whether public opinion in Malaya can be so pessimistic about the prospects in Indo-China, Siam and Indonesia as to justify a public declaration that we intend to maintain troops in Malaya even after independence. I should have thought that this might only play into the hands of the local extremists; it would certainly provoke an adverse reaction elsewhere in Asia. In my view it is preferable that we should continue to emphasise our determination to halt the spread of Communism, if not at its present limits, at least on the borders of Laos, Cambodia and Siam.

I have long believed, with you, that the greatest danger to our interests in South East Asia is that of Communist subversion and infiltration in the cold war. This, as you know, is also the view of the Chiefs of Staff. The root of the trouble lies in Indo-China. I regard the stiffening of the present administrations in the three Associate States[2] as the most urgent problem we have to face in South East Asia. As the Americans and the French, together with ourselves are the only powers immediately capable of influencing events in this area, I have been pressing these two Governments to agree to tripartite discussions as a preliminary to wider talks under the Manila Treaty.[3] Only by determined and effectively co-ordinated policies can we hope to arrest the alarming decline into chaos in Vietnam, to put more heart into the Laotians and to check the present drift towards neutralism and perhaps also Communism in Cambodia.

As regards the wider field of defence planning, I agree with you that, whilst the Manila Treaty marks a welcome step forward, it cannot be regarded as an effective planning instrument. Here again, the real effort can only be provided by those powers which have an effective defence contribution to make. With this in view, as you no doubt know, we recently agreed with the Commonwealth Relations Office and the Chiefs of Staff that the first step should be to get the Australians and New Zealanders firmly committed to the defence of Malaya and, on this basis, to approach the Americans. Discussions are in progress with the Australians and New Zealanders and I hope that the planning meetings which are now beginning in Singapore will prepare the way for decisions to be taken at the Prime Ministers' conference.

Meanwhile the Americans are pressing for an early meeting of the Manila Treaty Council in Bangkok.[4] We have agreed to the setting up of a Working Party in Washington to discuss the proposed agenda. The Americans think this should be confined to matters of organisation and procedure. I am pressing for a rather later meeting but a more solid agenda.

To sum up, the problem of South East Asia and the dangers which threaten us in that part of the world have been very much in my mind; and as you will have seen from recent telegrams I have been doing all I can within the framework laboriously erected at Geneva and Manila to induce the Americans and the French to join us in energetic action to defend our position.

I am sending a copy of this letter to Lennox-Boyd for any comments he may have.[5]

---

[2] ie Cambodia, Laos and South Vietnam.   [3] See 335, note.
[4] SEATO's council met for the first time at its headquarters in Bangkok in Feb 1955.
[5] See 343.

341   CO 1030/174, no 10   26 Jan 1955
[Security in Malaya]: despatch no 94/55 from Sir D MacGillivray to Mr Lennox-Boyd on the conduct of the emergency

[This despatch and two following ones (342, 345) were written in response to a CO circular letter of 24 June 1954 in which Lloyd asked colonial governors to consider writing periodic despatches 'in a colloquial style' for circulation among ministers outside the CO and, in certain cases, among ambassadors and high commissioners (see BDEEP series B, vol 1, R Rathbone, ed, *Ghana*, part II, 152, note). The printed version of this despatch is at CO 1030/403, no 12. The first paragraph, which refers to Lloyd's request, is omitted here.]

. . .

2. In this first of a new series of periodic appreciations, it is natural that I should choose as my subject the state of the six and a half year old Emergency, since the suppression of Communist terrorism still claims priority of attention over all our other endeavours. The pall of fear which lay upon the country two or three years ago has lifted; public confidence in the ability of Government to contain terrorism is greatly enhanced; the public now freely use the main roads and railways, and the restrictions imposed by the Emergency Regulations have been removed from "white" areas[1] containing over one third of the total population. Even so, the Emergency remains a great deal more than a nuisance, and it would be a grave mistake to think that its end is in sight. The complete destruction of Communist terrorism in Malaya must be a slow business, as I shall try to show, and no early release from it should be expected, unless there should be some radical change in the policy of the Malayan Communist Party or in the international outlook.

3. In an appendix[2] to this despatch figures are given, quarterly, of the number of incidents and of Security Force and terrorist casualties over the five year period 1950 to 1954. The changes in conditions of security can in one way be measured by these figures, although they are not an entirely reliable guide. Taken by themselves they would appear to indicate, for example, that there has been no appreciable improvement since the beginning of 1953, whereas, in fact, the improvement in conditions generally, although not spectacular, has been steady and continuous. It must be agreed, however, that the great change for the better took place during the last half of 1952, and that, since about the middle of 1953, there has been no further striking change in the position. The cause of the really great improvement of 1952 has been a matter of some controversy and detractors from General Templer's great achievements in Malaya have endeavoured to attribute it in large part to a change in Communist policy. It is true that by 1951 the Malayan Communist Party had realised that indiscriminate terrorism was alienating many who had been prepared to support them, and that they decided, therefore, to engage in a more selective campaign of attacking military and para-military objectives. Accordingly, in October of that year, they issued new directives and these began to have effect by the middle of 1952. The steep decline in the number of civilians killed and missing (from a monthly average of 56 in 1951 to 10 in 1953) can no doubt be attributed in part to these Communist directives, but, since the directives also required attacks on military and para-military objectives to be continued, it might have been expected that, while the

---

[1] See part II of this volume, 303.   [2] Not printed.

civilian casualty rate went down, the casualty rate among the Security Forces would go up. Yet the reverse was the case; the Security Force casualty rate also went down (from a monthly average of 52 in 1951 to 8 in 1953), whereas the rate at which the terrorists were accounted for was maintained at its previous level. There is little to support the contention that the decline in terrorist activity in 1952 was due largely to Communist directives. The improvement was due primarily to the greater effectiveness of the Security Forces in operations against the terrorists, backed by better measures of protection of the civilian population and a consequential restoration of confidence in the authority of Government. The training of the Special Constabulary, the re-organisation, training and equipment of the Home Guard, the fruition of measures initiated in earlier years, including the resettlement—begun in 1950—into compact villages of over half a million rural Chinese most of whom were formerly occupying squatter holdings along the jungle fringes, and the resiting in compact groups of the dwellings of many thousands of estate workers, were among the principal measures which afforded this protection. At the same time, these measures made it easier to prevent the civilian population from furnishing supplies to the terrorists.

4.   The decrease in terrorist activity which was thus forced upon the terrorists from 1952 onwards has made it much more difficult for the Security Forces to find them. Moreover, the greater part of the terrorist force now consists of men who have been in the jungle for several years, men seasoned in jungle life, experienced in jungle warfare, long subjected to Communist indoctrination and determined to see the thing through; most of the waverers and the weaklings have already been eliminated. This may well be the main reason for the decline in the surrender rate from an average of 31 monthly in 1953 to the present level of about 17. Most of the successful Security Force contacts with the terrorists have been the result of information, rather than of chance encounter, and the best information has, in the past, come from surrendered terrorists. The effect, therefore, of the lower surrender rate, combined with the decline in terrorist activity, has been greatly to reduce the number of contacts and this has been reflected in the rate at which terrorists have been eliminated since 1953. The killing or capture of every terrorist represents a much greater effort on the part of the Security Forces today than in 1951 or 1952 when terrorist activity made the opportunities for contact with the terrorist forces far more frequent.

5.   Today, M.C.P. militant effort is largely concentrated on keeping themselves a force in being, in the hope, no doubt, that there will, in due time, be a turn of events in South-East Asia favourable to them, and that they will once again be able to resume an aggressive role. There is certainly evidence that they are finding it more difficult to obtain food, clothing, medicines and other necessities. The severity of the shortages they are experiencing in some areas is indicated by recent atrocities committed by them upon civilians, such as the two Indians at Sungei Siput— ordinary foremen unconnected in any way with Government who were garotted and disembowelled in front of their wives and the estate labourers. Such acts of horror are contrary to the Politburo directive not to oppress the civilian population, and they are, undoubtedly, dictated by a local need to terrorise in order to secure supplies.

It is also clear that the Malayan Communist Party are taking care to conserve their stocks of arms and ammunition. Until recently there were no indications of a shortage of these and it seems that no serious attempt has ever been made to obtain supplies of arms from outside Malaya. There is still no evidence that supplies are reaching them by sea or across the land frontier in any appreciable quantities. The supplies acquired during and immediately after the Japanese Occupation have, hitherto, more than met their needs. These supplies, however, have been steadily whittled down by Security Force action during the last few years, and there is evidence that a part of their remaining stocks has deteriorated in their jungle armouries to the point of unserviceability. The seizure of arms and ammunitions has clearly been the main objective of many recent terrorist attacks.

Nevertheless, despite their apparent need to conserve arms and ammunition, and despite their increasing difficulties in supplying themselves with the necessities of life, there is no sign of any general cracking of the morale of the hard core of the Malayan Communist Party. They are still able in certain States, notably Johore, Perak and Negri Sembilan, to take sporadic aggressive action, and they do so whenever they see an exposed target—wherever there has been a slackening of vigilance by a Security Force unit, or a sign of defection among the Home Guard, or the dropping of routine precautions on the part of a planter. Whoever drops his guard may still get a bloody nose, even in the most unexpected places.

In short, the Malayan Communist Party have so far succeeded in maintaining an armed force in the field. Their present armed strength is thought to be not much less than 5,000, and, although recruitment has been no more than sufficient to replace losses, it seems that they are still able to obtain as many recruits from the civilian population as they wish. The majority of present day recruits are youngsters, some of only fourteen or fifteen years of age. The young Chinese have the predilection of all Asian youth for the ultra left and it is not difficult to interest them in Communism; at the same time the bandit is, traditionally, an ideological hero with them, and his exploits and his life in the jungle have the appeal of Robin Hood. In some areas, especially in Johore where recent road ambushes of Security Forces and attacks on Police and Home Guard posts have added to their stocks of weapons, there has been discerned a definite relationship between these successful attacks and recruitment, the seizure of arms by the terrorists being followed by recruitment to their ranks in the same areas. This seems to confirm the view that they still have little difficulty in obtaining recruits, but that recruiting is restricted by the number of weapons at their disposal. Any general negligence in precautions against terrorist attack might result in serious losses of arms and ammunition, and a consequent recrudescence of widespread terrorism.

6. By mid 1953, following the spectacular improvement in the state of the Emergency, the morale of planters and other civilians was high; some were optimistic that an early end to the Emergency was in sight, and many became complacent. At the same time there was concern over the economic and financial positions. The price of rubber had dropped from its peak of 230 cents a lb. in February, 1951, to 140 cents a year later later and 58 cents by December, 1953, and the price of tin, which had also reached its peak in February, 1951, at 740 dollars a picul, had fallen to an average of 480 dollars in 1952, and to under 300 dollars by August, 1953.

The surplus balances of the Federation, which had been built up during the boom years of 1950 and 1951 despite the high cost of the Emergency, were being rapidly depleted, and there was demand on all sides for Government economy. During 1952 every request made by General Templer for funds for Emergency purposes had been supported by the Legislative Council's Standing Finance Committee. By 1953 the attitude had changed and there was pressure for the swollen expenditure on the Emergency to be cut down. Indeed, the optimism of that time appeared to warrant such a course. Fortunately, little further expenditure was necessary to complete the resettlement of the rural Chinese into protected villages. Moreover, there appeared to be justification for substantial economies in the Police Force, the strength of which, regulars and specials together, was therefore reduced by 23,000 from a total of 71,500 in March, 1953, to a total of 48,500 at the end of 1954, the cost of the Force being cut from $159.5 million in 1953 to $132.8 million (estimated) in 1955. This inevitably necessitated the pruning of the number of police employed on rubber estates and mines and in the protection of New Villages and the placing of a greater reliance on the Home Guard. At the same time, the Home Guard strength was reduced from 239,000 to 170,000. Further reductions, to be effective in 1955, had been planned early in 1954, but it has now become apparent that the situation does not justify these, and General Bourne[3] is of opinion, which I endorse, that the strength of the Police Force (both regulars and specials) should be held at present numbers throughout 1955, and that the Home Guard should not be reduced below 160,000. Since the early days of the Emergency, the Police Force has been under the strain of either rapid expansion or rapid contraction, and the decision to keep its strength static for at least a year will relieve it of the diversion of effort which almost continuous re-organisation has hitherto entailed. General Bourne has also taken the view that the reduction in the strength of British Police Leiutenants [sic] (from 750 to 450) has been carried too far and that there is, partly in consequence of this, a lack of leadership of the police units employed on operations against terrorists and on food control duties. The strength of the Police Lieutenants is therefore being temporarily increased from 450 to 600, and, in addition, 117 more Police Inspectors (Asians) are being recruited.

The optimism and complacency of the latter part of 1953 have waned, and this is particularly noticeable among the European planters, many of whom are critical of the reduction in the number of Special Constables allocated for their protection on estates. Four planters were killed by terrorists in 1953 and six in 1954, and it is a sad fact that, in almost every instance, their deaths must be attributed to lapses on their own part in maintaining the security precautions required of them and not to the lack of a sufficient protective force. (The number of planters killed in 1951 was twenty-three). There is also a general feeling among planters that there has been some slackening of measures designed to prevent food being supplied to the terrorists and that this must be attributed to the severe reduction in the number of Special Constables employed. There may indeed have been some slackening, and steps are being taken, which in a few really bad areas will extend to the compulsory communal cooking and storage of rice on estates and New Villages, to tighten up food control measures.

7. Apart from a regular Police Force of 23,500, a Special Constabulary of 25,000 and a Home Guard of 170,000, there are 23 battalions of troops, along with ancillary services, engaged in the Emergency in the Federation. Eight of the battalions are of the Federation Army, paid from Federation revenues; there are seven British

---

[3] GOC, Malaya, and director of operations, 1954–1956.

battalions, six Gurkha, one Fijian and one Rhodesian. There are also many units of the Royal Air Force and some of the Royal Navy. The total personnel of these three Services in the Federation is 38,500, making with the Police a grand total Security Force of 87,000, excluding the part time Home Guard. The gross cost to Her Majesty's Treasury of units of the Army, Navy and Air Force employed on duties connected with the Emergency has been put at approximately £65 million per annum. In addition, a grant of £6 million in aid of the Federation's Emergency expenditure was made by Her Majesty's Government in 1954,[4] and, while it is estimated that, by the exercise of rigid economy, by curtailing the development of social services and by new taxation, the Federation can "get by" in 1955 without another grant-in-aid, the surplus balance will be so depleted by the end of 1955 that further grants-in-aid are likely to be required thereafter. The cost of the Emergency to the Federation's Treasury was £24 million in 1953, a figure which dropped to £20 million in 1954. This is apart from expenditure on the Federation Military Forces and the regular Police Force which would be necessary were there no Emergency, and which in 1954 amounted to £10 million. (This year, the Federal Government is expending 35 per cent of its total revenue under the Defence and Police heads). In short, the gross cost to Her Majesty's Government and the Federation Government together of the military, police and home guard forces engaged in Emergency duties and of measures designed solely to combat militant communism in Malaya, is not far short of £100 million a year.

8. It must often be a matter for wonder on the part of those who do not know conditions in Malaya why it takes so large a body of trained troops and police at such high cost to reduce to impotency so small a force of terrorists. The answer lies, as it always does in the case of guerilla warfare, partly in the physical features of the country and partly in the attitude of the inhabitants towards the insurgents.

9. The dense jungle which covers four-fifths of Malaya, with its forest fruits and edible roots, its fish bearing rivers, its swamps and its aborigine denizens, provides what must be the most ideal country in the world for any insurgent force. It cannot be changed; the jungle is not neutral to the forces of law and order; it is a permanent handicap to them; and it constitutes the main reason why the future Governments of Malaya, if they wish to maintain our standards of law and order, will ever have to devote more of their revenues to internal security forces than do countries whose physical features are less formidable. Our own Force 136[5] found, during the Japanese occupation, that small units of armed men could hide and feed themselves in the jungle for long periods. This has also been the experience of the last six and a half years during which the Malayan Communist Party has taken all the advantage given by the Malayan terrain. It was a part of the plan contained in the Politburo's directives of 1951 to withdraw the Party's senior commands into the deep jungle and there to establish operational bases and centres where the Party's political and military workers could be retrained without being molested. However, they have found this to be a much more difficult and slower process than they had thought. The aggressive action of the Security Forces penetrating the deep jungle, destroying the terrorist jungle camps and cultivations wherever found, disrupting supply and courier routes, bombing hideouts and camps, has kept the Malayan Communist

---

[4] See 306.   [5] See part I of this volume, 43, note.

Party confused and on the move. If they had not been harrassed in this way, had they been left free to build up their jungle bases, the Malayan Communist Party would undoubtedly be able to take more aggressive action than they can today. As it is, most of their militant effort is now devoted to maintaining themselves and avoiding contact with the Security Forces. It is General Bourne's tactical plan to take yet more offensive action in the jungle, to strike closer to the heart of the terrorist high command, and to deny them the use of those remaining jungle areas which hitherto it has been possible for them to dominate without much interference. (It is interesting to note that the proportion of high ranking terrorists killed to total eliminations is now increasing). This plan involves the freeing of more troops for operations in the jungle, and, in consequence, an increase of police and home guard responsibilities in other areas. It also places a premium on those troops, such as the Special Air Service Regiment and the Gurkhas, having the training and experience which fit them to operate for long periods in the jungle.

10. One of the most effective measures in this deep jungle campaign has been the establishment of jungle forts designed primarily to win over to our side the thousands of aborigines who, in the past, have often been the eyes and ears, and to some extent also the providers, of the terrorists. It was contended at one time that these aborigines should be removed from the jungle and resettled outside it. Experiments showed this policy to be impracticable. Moreover, the effect of it would not have been advantageous to our cause. The terrorists would still have been able to live in the jungle, and we would have deprived ourselves of a main source of information about their movements. The aborigines working on our side in the jungle can be as useful to us as they have been in the past to the terrorists. The jungle forts, of which there are now eleven, provide the aborigines not only with protection but with medical aid and elementary schools, and they serve also as trading posts at which they can sell their jungle produce at a fair price and buy their simple needs. A recent estimate puts the total number of aborigines in Malaya at between 50,000 and 60,000. Some 29,000 of these normally inhabit the deep jungle. Before the establishment of the jungle forts, and in the face of scarcely any opposition, the Malayan Communist Party was able to exert a considerable degree of influence over most of these jungle dwelling aborigines. At least 25,000 were out of touch with Government administration in any form, and the majority of these were under some degree of terrorist influence. Many of them were actively assisting the terrorists and have been known to attack Security Force patrols. As a result of the new policy of taking administration and protection to the main aborigine areas, about 22,000 have gradually been brought under Government influence. There remain three or four thousand in small scattered groups still under terrorist control, but it is intended to establish more jungle forts in 1955 and to try and win over these remaining groups.

11. As General Templer and General Bourne have often stated, if the whole civilian population would cooperate by denying supplies to the terrorists, the Emergency would be over within a year or less. It is not only the aborigines who help the terrorists. The greater part of the terrorists' food and all their medical supplies and clothing still come from the towns, the New Villages and the estate labour lines. Despite the resettlement of rural communities into compact protected areas, the rationing of rice and stringent control over the movement of food and other essential commodities, there is still a regular flow of supplies to the jungle and "protection"

money is still being paid. This is a problem provided by the Chinese rather than by the other elements in the civil population. It is true that some Malays in remote areas are induced by offers of high prices to supply small quantities of food; the Tamil labourer also supplies some, normally under threat and more particularly in the few areas where there are Tamils among the terrorists; but the bulk of the supplies for the Communist armed forces is furnished by the Chinese, who constitute 37% of the whole population. The reasons for this continued support of the Malayan Communist Party by a large section of the Chinese community in Malaya are various and will be the subject of a subsequent despatch.

12. The conclusions to be drawn from the present situation are:—

that any slackening of security force pressure will result in less public security and a consequent decline in public morale, and a nascent belief in the ultimate ability of the Malayan Communist Party to dominate certain areas of Malaya;

that in order to maintain this pressure the Security Forces must be kept at not less than their present strength;

that by the energetic pursuit of measures already effectively applied, such as the tightening of control over food and other supplies, the extension of the administration of the aborigines and the taking of the struggle deeper into the jungle, we can bring about some further measure of improvement;

but that, so long as the bulk of the Chinese population withhold their whole-hearted support from the Security Forces, we must expect this further improvement to be limited.

342 CO 1030/174, no 9 28 Jan 1955
[Malayan Chinese and the MCP]: despatch no 104/55 from Sir D MacGillivray to Mr Lennox-Boyd on Chinese support for MCP and MCP strategy

. . .

In my Confidential despatch No. 94/55 of the 26th January, 1955,[1] I reached the general conclusion that no early end to the Emergency in Malaya can be looked for so long as large sections of the Chinese community continue to give support to the Malayan Communist Party and thereby enable the communists to keep their armed forces in being. A discussion of the reasons for this continued support for the Malayan Communist Party was left over to this subsequent despatch.

2. The principal reason for this support is not so much that China is today a communist country, but that 95% of the armed forces of the Malayan Communist Party is Chinese. In comparison, the Chinese constitute only 4% of the Police Force and 5.1% of the Federation Military Forces, whereas the percentages of Malays in these forces of law and order are 86.9 and 89.2 respectively. Many of the Chinese in Malaya are China born and their connections with China are still fresh. Remittances of money are sent regularly to their relatives in China. The great majority

---

[1] See 341.

understand only a Chinese dialect and Peking Radio makes a greater appeal to them than does Radio Malaya—a chauvinist appeal which transcends communism. Though anxious to remain in Malaya, they have not yet acquired a Malayan outlook or any feelings of loyalty towards Malaya or her Governments. Moreover, the attitude of the Malays towards the Chinese has not always helped to generate such feelings, for many Malay leaders feel that the Malays cannot retain their major share in the control of Malayan affairs unless they continue to deny to the Chinese the full rights of citizenship. In short, the Chinese are not readily assimilable. Thus, race and an absence of loyalty to the Malayan Governments are stronger factors in this question of aid to the insurgents than is communism. In general, the trouble is not that the Malayan Chinese are communists, but that they remain Chinese.

3. There are also particular influences which cause many Chinese to continue to give material support to the Malayan Communist Party. These vary from class to class. By the peasant Chinese it is no longer given out of sympathy with a national movement as it was during the time of the Japanese occupation when the Malayan Communist Party was fighting a long-standing enemy of China's; nor is it given, except rarely, owing to sympathy with communist ideology. The motive more often lies in sheer fear of reprisal or else in nothing more than family affection. The ties of race are strong with the Chinese; those of family are stronger still, and the Chinese terrorist has many relatives in the villages. This is what makes the denial of supplies so very difficult. A peasant woman who has a hungry son in the jungle will not be deterred from feeding him by threat of prosecution, detention or deportation. Rather she must be persuaded of the futility of her son's cause so that she may in her turn persuade him of it and urge him to surrender. But before she can be so persuaded, she must herself have put trust in the Government's promises to surrendered terrorists that they will be fairly treated and must believe that the Government offers better prospects for herself and her son than do the communists; she must believe that the Government's plans for schools, health services, a sufficiency of agricultural land to cultivate, and decent conditions of life generally, under the administration of an efficient and incorrupt public service, are more likely to be practicable and fulfilled than are the promises of the Malayan Communist Party. No amount of propaganda can be a substitute for tangible progress with such plans. Before the scattered Chinese peasant population was resettled in the New Villages, most of them were outside Government influence, had little understanding of the Malayan Governments and had no opportunities to participate in the administration at any level; they regarded Government, in their traditional Chinese way, as something alien and Government officials as mainly tax gatherers who should be kept clear of whenever possible. They had never viewed Government as in [an] instrument to which they themselves could belong and in which they could take part. This attitude of mind does not change quickly, and has constituted a strong barrier to Chinese co-operation with Government in its struggle against the Malayan Communist Party. It is being steadily broken down by closer administration of the villages, by the provision of social services, by the establishment of Local Councils through which the villagers can administer their own affairs with Government guidance, by civics courses, and so on. It is a slow process but undoubtedly the attitude of many of the village communities is now changing to one of greater friendliness and trust in the Government's intentions, of diminishing sympathy with the Malayan Communist Party and of more willingness to resist the demands made by the Party's agents.

4. With other sections of the Chinese population there are different
withholding the full co-operation which is so essential if the Emerge
ended. With the shop-keepers, the owners of small tin mines and rubber estates, the
operators of public transport, the saw millers and the timber merchants, probably
the strongest motive is self-interest, a desire to protect their property from
communist attack by the easiest means, by the payment of "protection" money
(extortion money as we prefer to call it) and by avoiding public association with
Government measures.

5. Among the educated class, and this applies also, although with lesser force, to
all other sections of the Chinese community, the reluctance to co-operate openly
with Government in Emergency measures is due to apprehension as to what the
future holds in store for them in Malaya. This, coupled with the Chinese habit of
insuring against all eventualities and their inclination for compromise, has made
them determined to sit on the fence as long as the future remains so uncertain. The
jungle is not neutral, but the Chinese are. The rout of the British from Malaya in
1942 is still fresh in the memory of many and the recent rapid growth of the prestige
of Communist China, the success of communist arms and the spread of their
influence in the very countries to the north which only fourteen years ago had
preceded Malaya as victims of Japanese aggression, have led many to doubt whether
the West can check the spread of communist influence in South East Asia. They
remember the fate of the Chinese who were pro-British or anti-Japanese when the
Japanese invaded Malaya; they were singled out for torture and execution. Today the
Chinese in Malaya want to make certain they will not jeopardise their own future by
taking a stand against Communist China. Those who in 1953 began to come down off
the fence when the Emergency took a turn for the better have been watching with
deepening apprehension the march of events to the north of Malaya, and some have
thought it wiser to resume their old positions on the top of it. There were many
Chinese, especially among the Straits-born, who looked hopefully to the Manila
Conference of last September for assurances that practical steps would be taken to
stop further Chinese aggression, and who were discouraged by the apparently
ineffective outcome. Nothing short of the establishment of a S.E.A.T.O. with real
teeth in it will bring the great body of the middle-class Chinese in Malaya off the
fence and nothing could do more to secure their co-operation in Emergency
measures and thereby to bring the Emergency to an early end.

6. The growing influence of Communist China in world affairs has also brought
about a change of attitude towards her and towards communism on the part of the
Chinese in Malaya, and particularly among the well educated youth. The fall of Dien
Bien Phu, the great part played by China at the Geneva Conference on Indo-China,
and the subsequent visits to China of Mr. Attlee, Pandit Nehru, U Nu and Mr. Dag
Hammerskjold[2] have all helped to build up her prestige and put her in the news and
make her a country in which her nationals can take pride. At the same time, there is
a feeling that the Nationalist rump in Formosa is a spent force. It appears to many
Chinese that there is emerging a new China and that it is a country of reform and
reconstruction. They attach to it a new aura of glamour. It is this aura, far more than
any frustrated demand for higher education, which has recently attracted many
young men and women to China from Malaya. Over 1,400 Chinese of the student age

---

[2] Secretary-general of the UN, 1953–1961.

group left for China from the Federation and Singapore in 1953; and over 2,000 in 1954. Many of these were locally born. Some of them, after whatever instruction they may undergo in China, will no doubt find employment there. Indeed, reconstruction programmes in China will be able to absorb most of them. Others will wish to return to Malaya sooner or later, if only to see their relatives, and it is clear that before they are permitted to leave China they will have become completely indoctrinated in Communism. It is this growing prestige of China, this new appeal it is making to youthful enterprise, which is awakening a new interest and pride in the land of their fathers among teachers and students in the Chinese schools, and making it more difficult for the Malayan Governments to foster in them that Malayan outlook which is essential to Malayan unity. The present unrest in the Chinese schools[3] is due largely to this revival of interest in China, and, since China is a communist country, there is also an upsurge of interest in, and sympathy with, communism.

7.   There is also among many Chinese a growing realisation that self-government may be coming to Malaya much sooner than they had previously thought likely. Many of them are apprehensive lest a self-governing Malaya may be dominated by the Malays, who might give the Chinese short shrift. They know that so long as the British are responsible for the Government of Malaya, they will be treated fairly and their commercial interests will be protected. But many are fearful of an independent Malaya which might well be dominated by the Malays and some would even prefer to have a communist regime, on the assumption that under such a regime Chinese interests would be paramount or, at least, safe-guarded. This factor emphasises the need for the constant repetition of the assurances contained in H.M.G's directive of 1952[4] that H.M.G. will not lay aside their responsibilities in Malaya until they are satisfied not only that communist terrorism has been defeated, but that the partnership of all communities which alone can lead to true and stable self-government has been firmly established.

8.   It is always possible that, either out of despair or as a matter of policy, the Malayan Communist Party will itself attempt to end the present stalemate in Malaya by calling off the military struggle and concentrating all their effort on political activities, which is what the communist parties in most other countries of South East Asia are now doing. But such decision is less likely to be taken in Malaya than in Peking. So far, the leaders of international communism seem to have regarded the continuance of Emergency conditions in Malaya as advantageous to their cause, arguing, no doubt, that it is a drain on Malayan and British financial resources, and that, by retarding Malaya's progress towards self-government, it may generate attacks which they hope will enable the Malayan Communist Party to emerge as a leader in a struggle for national liberation, thus delivering Malaya into the hands of international communism. There are, however, indications that recent instructions, while not requiring that terrorism should be called off, demand that greater attention should be paid by the Malayan Communist Party to the establishment of an "anti-British national united front". This was one of the stated objectives in their 1951 directives. It requires the penetration of all forms of social, economic and political organisations.[5] So far, they have not had great success in this. The trade unions are on their guard against it, and only in isolated cases has successful

---

[3] See 345.   [4] See part II of this volume, 268.   [5] cf part II of this volume, 284, and 311.

penetration of unions been suspected. The Chinese element of the Home Guard has undoubtedly been affected in several areas, but there are no signs of successful attempts to suborn the remaining elements of the Security Forces or of the Civil Service. Greater success has been achieved by the Malayan Communist Party in some of the Chinese schools, especially in secondary schools, where some communist cells have been formed.

9. Whether the leaders of the Malayan Communist Party would follow an instruction from Peking to bring about a cease fire[6] is a matter of some doubt and presumably Peking would not give such an instruction unless they knew that it would be obeyed. These leaders must know that their record is such they would not be accepted back into civilian life in Malaya and that, if they were to call off the armed struggle, they would have to depart from Malaya. They would probably be very suspicious of their reception in China and it is doubtful if they would relish the idea of a future anywhere except in Malaya, where they were born and bred. Their ambition is to dominate Malaya, not to further the cause of communism elsewhere. They might however, if things became too hot for them in Malaya, or if directed to discontinue the armed struggle, be prepared to slip away into Indonesia or Thailand and continue to direct political penetration in Malaya from there. It is also questionable whether it would be in the ultimate interest of the British position in Malaya for militant communism to be called off completely and whether it would not be better for it to continue yet awhile at a level reduced to the point where it would be no more than a nuisance value. If communist terrorism should cease altogether in Malaya there would no doubt be demands, which it would be difficult if not impossible to resist, for the establishment of Chinese consuls and for the recognition of a lawful communist Party, through which agencies Communist penetration of the political life of the country would be stepped up.

10. Even as things are today the greatest danger to the British position in Malaya lies in the penetration of the political parties. They are obvious targets for Communist "national united front" activities. It is on this account that it is important to associate the leaders of these parties with the present struggle against communist terrorism, to commit them to the side of the free world, and keep constantly before their minds the gravity of the threat of communism to Malaya and to their own positions. Now that the majority of the population no longer go about their daily business in fear of communist terror, or shackled by the restraints of Emergency Regulations, there is a tendency for Asian civilians to regard the Emergency as a matter which no longer concerns them directly, and one which can be left to the British to bring to an end. There is much danger in such an attitude; the terrorist threat cannot be reduced to impotency without active Asian support, and it was therefore with a view to identifying Asian public opinion, and the political parties in particular, more closely with Emergency measures, that General Bourne and I recently decided to invite unofficials to serve on the Director of Operations' Committee and on the State, Settlement and District War Executive Committees. This step has been warmly welcomed in the press and by the public generally. It has caused a marked renewal of interest in Emergency operations on the part of the political leaders and has gained their support in public for these operations.

---

[6] See 350–353.

These leaders, Malay and Indian as well as Chinese, have also begun to show a greater appreciation of the danger of communist attempts to associate the Malayan Communist Party in the people's minds with the demand for independence for which all the lawful political parties stand. They did not fail to notice, for example, the prominent use made by one platoon of the Malayan Races Liberation Army of the word "Merdeka"[7] in pamphlets which they left behind after a recent raid on a police post, "Merdeka" being the slogan of the United Malays National Organisation. These political leaders now stress in public that they strive for independence by constitutional means and not through bloodshed and terror, and that the form of independent Government they seek is very different from that which the communists have in mind.

Although there is no clear conception in the minds of the public of how self-government will work in practice or of the practical advantages it will bring, there is a gathering support for the idea, particularly among the Malays. Few of them have any knowledge of the lower standards of living which exist in the neighbouring independent countries of Burma, Indonesia and Thailand, and, in that ignorance, the idea that independence is a panacea for all ills, is something infinitely desirable, and, moreover, attainable has caught on firmly. A political leader who is not a professed nationalist will get little following in Malaya today. It is not difficult for the communists to represent to a public which is politically inexperienced that the British, despite declarations to the contrary, are denying to Malaya the independence which this public is being led to regard as an Elysium, and that political leaders who associate themselves with the British administration are "stooges" and traitors to the cause of Malayan nationalism. So long as the Emergency is regarded as largely the concern of the British, political leaders who identify themselves too closely with Emergency measures may thereby find their positions undermined by extreme nationalists within their own party. They have not failed to note, for example, the decline of Dato Sir Onn's influence and public following since he became Member for Home Affairs, accepted a Knighthood, and identified himself thereby with the policy of the British Government. It is not therefore difficult to appreciate why it is that other leaders, such as Tunku Abdul Rahman and Cheng-lock Tan, whose political views in private conversation are moderation itself, while prepared to associate themselves publicly with the Director of Operations in the war against communist terrorism, in public take a strong nationalist stand, vehemently attacking "Colonialism" and "British imperialism" and demanding independence at the earliest possible date. If they did not do so, they would not long retain their positions as leaders of major political parties, as we would lose the influencial support which they are now giving to Emergency measures and which is valued by the Director of Operations. We must, it seems, take the rough with the smooth. The attraction of the cry for independence is probably less pronounced amongst the Chinese but their leaders feel that with the possibility of early self-Government and the withdrawal of British authority they must seek a political partnership with the Malays in order to secure for themselves a place in the future government of the country and go along with them in the demand for independence.

11.   To summarize:—by breaking down the traditional distrust of the Chinese for

---

[7] ie independence.

Government, by committing their leaders publicly to our side, by giving them greater stake in the country, thereby strengthening their loyalty towards it, and by convincing them that the British Government will not relinquish their ultimate authority in Malaya until a true and peaceful partnership of the Malayan races has been established, much can be done to secure their co-operation against communist terrorism. The majority of them will, nevertheless, continue to sit on the fence so long as militant communism outside Malaya continues to threaten; and the best chance to secure that co-operation of the Chinese which is essential for the destruction of militant communism in Malaya lies in the establishment of a S.E.A.T.O. of such a nature as will put heart into those who now fear that Communist China may eventually be able to dominate the country.

343   CO 1030/67, no 14   9 Feb 1955

[Trend of events in SE Asia]: letter from Mr Lennox-Boyd to Mr Head. *Enclosure:* CO memorandum 'United Kingdom aims in Malaya, and means by which they might be achieved, with special reference to defence'

I am writing to you about your minute of the 15th November, 1954,[1] to Anthony Eden, about the trend of events in South East Asia. I first learned of it from his letter to you D 1193/15 of the 13th December,[2] of which he was good enough to send me a copy. My Private Secretary subsequently got a copy of your minute from yours.

2. On many of the issues at stake it is clear that there is not a great deal of difference between the three of us, and I would agree with much of what both you and Anthony have said on the subject. I shall shortly be circulating a recent despatch from the High Commissioner for the Federation of Malaya which shows that he, too, goes most of the way with us.[3] Meanwhile, I enclose a copy of a paper setting out in very broad terms my own view of the present position and future prospects in Malaya, with special reference to defence. It was written before the High Commissioner's despatch reached me but nothing that he has to say conflicts with the general conclusions at which I had already arrived.

3. I think that you over-rate the clarity of thinking of "the average literate Malayan or Chinese"; and I would agree with Anthony that such public opinion as exists in Malaya is cautious rather than pessimistic. He is right in saying that the political leaders in Malaya have lately recognised in public statements that the Emergency necessarily acts as a brake upon the country's progress towards self-government, although they have not yet gone so far as to acknowledge that self-government is out of the question until the Emergency has come to an end: their present attitude appears to be that, if the Emergency were still dragging on when self-government had in other ways become an immediate possibility, they would want to make arrangements with Her Majesty's Government to continue the war against the Communist terrorists within the framework of a self-governing Malaya. This, of course, bristles with difficulties; but they are bridges which we shall not reach for quite a long time to come and I therefore think that we need not now worry about the best means of crossing them.

---

[1] See 339.   [2] See 340.   [3] See 342.

4. For the rest, I endorse all that Anthony has said about the general situation in South East Asia, and it seems to me from your minute that you are in broad agreement with us.

5. The only further point that I want to argue is the question of public statements about our intention to protect Malaya in the long term. In the despatch to which I have referred the High Commissioner for the Federation himself stresses "the need for the constant repetition of the assurances contained in Her Majesty's Government's directive of 1952 to Templer that Her Majesty's Government will not lay aside their responsibilities in Malaya until they are satisfied not only that Communist terrorism has been defeated, but that the partnership of all communities which alone can lead to true and stable self-government has been firmly established". Up to a point I agree, but I am certain that we must exercise great caution in deciding the character and timing of any such statements. For one thing, we have already made a good many of them, the latest being the reiteration by the High Commissioner himself in a New Year broadcast of the assurances in the 1952 directive which I have just quoted. Too frequent repetition of our determination to secure the defence of Malaya against external aggression would undoubtedly debase this particular currency and tend, if anything, to excite suspicion, especially if our protestations continued to lack sufficient visible, tangible support in the shape of forces on the ground, in the air and at sea. In particular, I agree with Anthony that any sort of bald declaration that we intended unilaterally to maintain troops in Malaya even after self-government had been attained would be unprofitable and damaging.[4]

The right line seems to me that set out in the enclosed paper. We must keep the Malayan political leaders convinced that we are entirely sincere in our intention to help them on towards self-government as fast as is consonant with the real long-term interests of the country; and we must also persuade them that we are right in our judgment of those interests. For my part I want to keep the pace reasonably slow, and I think that we can do so. To succeed in this we must pursue two lines of policy in parallel. First, the ordinary day-to-day handling of the political situation must include a steady, sympathetic course of political education, conducted chiefly by the High Commissioner and his advisers in the Federation but also by the mobilization of opinion in this country and by any other suitable means that come to hand from time to time. For instance, I hope to do something to that end personally in the course of a visit which I propose to pay to Malaya during the Easter recess.[5] In other words, we must in practice go ahead with constitutional advance as fast as the hard, material facts of life will allow; we must satisfy the Malayan political leaders of the reality of those facts; and we must get them to see that the primary condition of overcoming the obstacles to self-government is the whole-hearted co-operation of them and their followers in beating the Communist terrorists, in improving race relations, in building up a stable economy and a sound administrative machine, and in making satisfactory arrangements for defence against external aggression. On the political side we have made a good beginning with the new constitution which is to be introduced this summer, and I see no reason to be despondent about where and

---

[4] Although Eden made a reassuring statement of British intent during his visit to Malaya (see 338, note 2), businessmen continued to demand something more definitive guaranteeing their capital investments (CO 1030/67, minutes by MacKintosh, 27 Apr, and Hopkinson, 2 May 1955).

[5] In fact Lennox-Boyd did not visit Malaya until Aug 1955.

how we go from there. It is the second parallel of policy which urgently demands special attention.

What is now required above all else is unmistakable proof that we mean business in the fight against Chinese Communism. (I use both the last two words advisedly since what keeps most of the Chinese in Malaya sitting on the fence is much more the force of racial consciousness than any inclination to Communism as such.) The argument developed in the last paragraph of the enclosed paper is given additional point by a statement in the High Commissioner's despatch to which I have already referred. He says:—

> "Nothing short of the establishment of a S.E.A.T.O. with real teeth in it will bring the great body of the middle class Chinese in Malaya off the fence and nothing could do more to secure their co-operation in Emergency measures and thereby bring the Emergency to an early end."

In the long term, too, this would help to convince the peoples of Malaya how gravely we estimate the threat of aggression by Communist China against the non-Communist countries of South East Asia, and how powerful are our resolution and our capacity to prevent the threat from materialising or defeat the aggressors if an attack is launched. If we succeed, as I believe we can, in persuading the Malayan political leaders that they cannot do without our protection, both now and as far ahead as can at present be seen, that we are anxious to give it them and that we can make it effective, then, as I have said, we shall have a lively hope of stiffening resistence [sic] to Communist terrorism and so hastening the end of the Emergency, and thereafter of ironing out any possible conflict between Malayan political aspirations and the needs of Imperial defence. So far the prospects are not at all bad. Of late, not only have the political leaders in Malaya publicly recognised the menace of the Emergency and committed themselves more openly than ever before to the fight against the Communist terrorists; more than that, the leader of the United Malays National Organisation (and in this it may be taken that he spoke also for the Malayan Chinese Association) has recently said in public that even a self-governing Malaya would have to rely upon Her Majesty's Government for protection against external aggression. If we can rapidly build upon the ground, plain for all to see, a massive organisation for defence, there will be little need for further general statements about our intentions; unless we can do so, such statements will achieve nothing.

I am sending a copy of this letter to Anthony.

Enclosure to 343[6]

The United Kingdom Government are openly committed beyond any possibility of withdrawal to two propositions about the political future of Malaya. First, they have

---

[6] This top secret paper was sent to Singapore in July and A G Gilchrist (Singapore) reported to W D Allen (FO) that it 'provided the right reassurances about H.M.G.'s policy for the Commanders-in-Chief and enabled us to carry them with us'. Gilchrist went on to stress the need to make it clear to Britain's allies, the general public and, above all, to Malayan politicians that it was the government's long-term intention 'to link the granting of independence to the conclusion of a satisfactory Defence Agreement' (FO 371/116915, no 12, 11 Aug 1955).

undertaken to help Malaya along the road towards self-government as fast as is reasonably possible. Second, they have given assurances that, although they confidently hope that a self-governing Malaya would choose to remain within the Commonwealth, the choice would lie with her and she would be free to leave it if she wanted. Any attempt now to qualify these undertakings would be disastrous; indeed, our hopes of retaining Malaya as a stable and contented part of the Commonwealth both before and after self-government very largely depend upon our ability to convince the political leaders of the country, and its peoples as a whole, that we are entirely sincere in these protestations.

On the other hand, we must also do everything possible to make them realise that in our view the United Kingdom Government would betray their trust in the country, and leave it doomed to destruction from within or without, if they withdrew before certain conditions essential to successful self-government had been satisfied.

These are, first, that the Emergency must either be brought wholly to an end and its recrudescence rendered unlikely, or at least be reduced to the level of sporadic banditry such as is always liable to afflict a country with a political, economic and geographical character like that of Malaya. Since despite our best efforts we cannot ensure that even the more limited of these aims will quickly be achieved, progress towards self-government is bound to be slow, and it is conceivable that the grant of self-government would depend among other things upon agreement on both sides to special arrangements for United Kingdom help in dealing with what, if anything, still remained of the Emergency.

Second, the gap between the two main races in Malaya, the Malays and the Chinese, is still both wide and deep. A number of bridges have been thrown across it in recent years but it would have to be closed to a far greater extent than at present before we could be sure—and we must be sure—that there was little likelihood of self-government leading to serious communal strife. The outlook is not without promise and it should be possible to pass more confident judgment upon it in a few years' time when, as seems probable, the Alliance of the United Malays National Association [sic] and the Malayan Chinese Association has been tested as the party in power under the new constitution to be introduced this year.

Third, the economy and administrative fabric of the country must be sufficiently developed and stable to sustain the burden of self-government. Here the state of the Emergency is again crucial since those conditions can hardly be attained so long as the country's resources remain committed to it on the scale of today. Relieved of that, Malaya's prospects are in other ways tolerably encouraging.

Finally, the grant of self-government would require agreement upon measures which would at once afford the country security against external aggression and provide the free world with the firm base for defence against Communist attack which it is now proposed to build up round and upon Malaya itself.

So long as we can persuade the Malayan political leaders of the complete honesty of our intentions there seems no reason why we should not also persuade them that satisfaction of these conditions is essential to their future welfare, including their hopes of successful self-government, and that the greater their co-operation in all matters of this kind, the more rapid and safe will be their advance.

In this context it is scarcely possible to exaggerate the importance of defence. Within the framework of A.N.Z.A.M. and the Manila Treaty, the United Kingdom and the other Commonwealth and foreign powers interested in defending South East

Asia against Communist subversion or aggression must build up a really powerful defensive system with Malaya as its centre and focus. This would have two massive advantages. First, nothing could contribute more to confidence that the Federation Government can and will destroy the Communist terrorists; such confidence would more than anything else help to produce the popular support without which the Government cannot bring the Emergency to an end; and given that support, the Emergency could be brought to an end quite quickly. Second, the creation of a massive system of defence based upon Malaya would serve to bring home to its peoples that they are surrounded by grave external dangers, while at the same time demonstrating to them that their friends in the Commonwealth and other non-Communist States are determined and able to protect them. The more these things were realised the more sober and co-operative should be the attitude of the Malayan political leaders and their followers towards the conduct of the Emergency, their political progress and the part which, when self-government came, they would still have to play in the defence of themselves and the rest of the free world in South East Asia.

344   CO 1030/230, no 4   11 Feb 1955
[Malayanisation of government services]: despatch no 169/55 from Sir D MacGillivray to Mr Lennox-Boyd on the recommendations of a committee of inquiry

I have the honour to refer to the Proceedings of Legislative Council for its meeting of 6th May, 1953, at which the following motion, moved by Mr. M.P. Rajagopal,[1] was agreed to by the Council:—

> "That this Council resolves that Government should forthwith appoint a Committee to investigate and explore avenues whereby locally domiciled Malayans with necessary qualifications and experience could replace as far as possible the expatriate officers in all Administrative, Executive, Advisory and Technical Services so as to enable local Malayans to shoulder proper responsibility in the administration of this country."

In accepting this motion on behalf of Government the Chief Secretary stressed that the advancement of Malayans to positions of fullest responsibility was entirely in accordance with Government policy but that there could, at the present time, be no question of removing expatriate officers from the service prematurely in order to create vacancies for locally domiciled officers; further, that the motion required to be interpreted within the limits of Government's policy of accepting for local appointment only Federal Citizens and locally-born British subjects and of the Government's obligation under Clause 152 of the Federation Agreement to treat impartially all serving officers of whatsoever race.

2. For these reasons when the resolution was considered by Executive Council at its meetings on 23rd June, 1953, and 14th July, 1953, it was agreed that the terms of reference proposed for the Committee were lacking in definition and alternative

---

[1] MTUC nominee on the Federal Legislative Council, 1948–1955.

terms were discussed. After due consideration my predecessor accepted the advice of Executive Council that a Committee of Inquiry should be constituted with revised and more comprehensive terms of reference. The precise terms adopted may be found in the opening paragraph of the Report of the Committee of which three copies are enclosed.[2] The members of the Committee are listed on page 9 of the Report and it will be noted that Mr. Rajagopal, who had moved the motion in Legislative Council, was one of them.

3. The main recommendations of the Committee may be grouped as follows:—

(a) *Scholarships and Training:* Paragraphs 5, 6, 7, 8, 13, 14, 15 & 17 of the Report
(b) *Maintenance of standards:* Paragraphs 9 & 10
(c) *Speed of Malayanisation:* Paragraph 11
(d) *Expatriate recruitment:* Paragraphs 12 and 16.

In the following paragraphs I give a short statement of my conclusions under each of these heads.

4. *Scholarships and training.* I consider that the Committee's recommendation that the award of scholarships and training grants, apart from some exceptions in the case of Malays, should in future be limited to those professions where there are no openings in this country apart from Government service itself, is generally sound. The Standing Committee on Scholarship and Training Schemes, which is the central body responsible for training policy, has already allocated training funds for the year 1955 on the basis of the Committee's recommendations and in accordance with the detailed departmental recommendations given in Part II of the Report. An annual sum of about one and a half million dollars has been made available for training schemes and this sum, together with the assistance that may be expected from State Scholarship Boards, the Colombo Plan and Colonial Development and Welfare funds should suffice to ensure progress with the Malayanisation of the service at the rate contemplated in the Report. Figures in regard to this are given in Appendix II of the Report. It is clearly important, as suggested in paragraph 8 of the Report, that both Federal and State training funds should, so far as possible, be allocated with a view to implementation of the Committee's recommendations, if adopted, and I have recently set up a Committee with a view to ensuring co-ordination of policy in the award of Federal, State and Settlement scholarships.

5. *Maintenance of standards and speed of Malayanisation.* The unanimous recommendation of the Committee that there should be no lowering of standards required for the higher posts in the Government service is of the greatest importance and is most reassuring. The Committee has taken, too, a realistic view of the speed at which Malayanisation should proceed, although this view has not met with universal public approval. The possibility has been envisaged that a too rapid implementation of the Malayanisation policy by, for instance, a deliberate policy of non-renewal of contracts of expatriate officers might lead to a large and rapid intake of young qualified men, resulting in a too high proportion of junior and inexperienced officers in Division I of the Public Service. This might be expected to lead not only to a lowering of efficiency but also to the formation of a bottleneck in the normal promotion ladder at a later date. No immediate danger of this situation arising in any

---

[2] *Report of a Committee on the Malayanisation of the Government Service*, Aug 1954. Enclosures with this despatch are not printed.

service is foreseen however. In the professional departments it may for some time to come be found difficult to secure a sufficient number of qualified and suitable candidates to replace normal wastage. Nevertheless, the recommendation in paragraph 11 of the Report is clearly a most desirable safeguard.

6. *Expatriate recruitment*. It has for some time been the policy of the Government to limit expatriate recruitment to the minimum that is consonant with the maintenance of sound standards and efficiency in the public service. The guiding principle is that expatriate recruitment should only be undertaken where qualified and suitable locally demiciled candidates are not available. The extent to which such limitation is possible varies considerably in the different services; in professional and technical departments it is to be expected that there should not yet be a sufficient number of properly qualified candidates of Malayan birth, since there still is a general shortage of facilities for the study of the basic sciences in Malayan schools. The implications of this situation are discussed by the Committee and the progress which has been made in advancing Malayans in the technical branches of the service, in spite of this difficulty, is most reassuring. Wherever it can be foreseen that Malayan candidates will shortly be coming forward, as a result either of private or of Government sponsored studies, vacancies are being retained within departments and expatriate recruitment, if essential as a temporary measure, is approved on short-term contract terms only. In many departments, however, certain specialist posts must inevitably be filled by expatriates for some years to come and the time is not yet ripe to discontinue altogether the recruitment of expatriate officers on permanent terms. It is appreciated that in general the best and most promising material is obtained from the United Kingdom when it is possible to offer a choice of appointment on a permanent or contract basis.

7. It might have been thought that there would be no difficulty in filling locally vacancies in the non-professional and administrative services, but unfortunately this has not yet proved to be the case. The opening of the Malayan Civil Service to non-Malay officers has assisted by increasing the field from which administrative officers may be drawn, but it does not yet appear that expatriate recruitment can cease entirely. The position in this respect will shortly be reviewed in connection with proposals for recruitment in 1955. Expatriate recruitment to the gazetted ranks of the Police Force has now virtually ceased, except for specialist appointments, although some further recruitment of Police Lieutenants on contract from abroad is contemplated.

8. The shortage of locally domiciled candidates of high calibre and with a good general education has also been demonstrated by the difficulty of obtaining Division I recruits for the Customs Department where over thirty vacancies now exist. The standard required locally for entry to this service is an Honours Degree. Expatriate recruitment on a permanent basis is regarded as inevitable and the vacancies are being advertised in the United Kingdom, Australia and New Zealand.

9. As was to be expected, the press gave the Report wide publicity which was not always favourable. "The Malay Mail" of 15th October urged that Malayanisation of the Malayan Civil Service in particular and of all departments should be expedited. It was suggested that there should not be too much stress on qualifications; more opportunities should be given to experienced serving officers even if they did not have the academic qualifications normally required. "The Straits Times", in a leading article on October 20th, urged strong and positive action to implement the

recommendations of the Committee, and stressed the need to admit more non-Malays to the Malayan Civil Service. An unfavourable comparison was drawn between the progress made in Malayanisation in the Federation and the progress made in Singapore. By the vernacular press the Report was given a mixed reception. The Malay daily newspaper "Majlis" enquired why more qualified Asians were not coming forward for entry to Government service and suggested that discrimination in favour of the expatriate officer in matters of pay and promotion was the basic trouble. Other Malay papers were also critical; "Warta Negara", a Penang daily paper, thought that the lack of qualified Asians was the direct responsibility of the British Government for not having raised the standard of education, and this was also the line taken by a Singapore weekly paper "Warta Masharakat". The Chinese press, however, was favourably disposed and commented that, although the Committee's report was not perfect, it was sufficient to show the sincerity of the Government.

10.   In view of the general tenor of newspaper criticism, I would particularly remark that in all questions of recruitment to and promotions within the public service and of the selection of candidates for Government training schemes I shall shortly be in a position to benefit from the advice of the projected Public Service Commission. In the meantime, until that body is constituted, the interim Public Service Appointments and Promotions Board has been set up which, although not authorised to discharge all the functions of a Public Service Commission, does provide the suitable local machinery necessary when expatriate recruitment is giving place to local recruitment. The functions of the proposed Public Service Commission and the reasons for its establishment are described in Legislative Council paper 9/54, of which I enclose a copy for ease of reference. The Interim Public Service Appointments and Promotions Board[3] has now been discharging its duties for nearly a year and during that time it has scrutinised with particular care all cases in which expatriate recruitment on a permanent or on a contract basis is proposed. Where it is considered necessary to engage an expatriate officer for any appointment other than those excluded from the purview of the Board, the full circumstances of the case are submitted to the Board for its consideration and advice. So far the Board has, without exception, approved all such proposals put to it and it is my considered opinion that, despite certain comments in the less responsible newspapers, the informed public as a whole has confidence in the members of the Board and in their recommendations.

11.   I now propose to seek the advice of Executive Council on the Report and the Council's agreement in principle to the implementation of the Committee's recommendations. Before doing this, however, I have thought it desirable to furnish you with copies of [the] Report and I should be glad to know whether you wish to offer any comment on the issues raised. *I should be grateful for an early reply to this despatch.*[4]

---

[3] Chaired by C R Howitt who after 1958 deputised for Dato Hamzah bin Abdullah.

[4] MacGillivray's proposal to seek the Executive Council's agreement was later shelved pending the outcome of the federal elections. Malayanisation was reviewed after the federal elections and during the secretary of state's visit to Malaya in Aug 1955, see 354, 359, para 6 and 365–370.

345   CO 1030/51, no 69   2 Mar 1955

'Federation of Malaya: the Chinese Schools': despatch no 232 from Sir
D MacGillivray to Mr Lennox-Boyd

The Chinese schools have for some time been, and remain, a matter of great concern
to the Government of the Federation of Malaya, and it may be appropriate, therefore,
that they should be the subject of a despatch in the "periodic" series.[1]

2.   To understand the present attitude of these schools to the Government, and to
understand the policy of Government with regard to them, it is necessary to sketch
in the background. Some idea of the history of the development of the schools is
necessary because the manner of their development has a bearing on the present
situation.

3.   Until the end of the Manchu dynasty Chinese schools in Malaya were few and
small, organised for the most part by clans and studying, through the medium of the
clan dialect, classics dealing with philosophy, morals, filial piety and religious
ceremonies and commentaries on government administration. These classics were
learnt noisily by rote, the pupil's first book starting, perhaps, "Man by nature is
good."

4.   Events in China from 1912 onwards were eagerly followed by the Chinese in
Malaya. There was an increased interest in education and the national language
movement throughout the peninsula. One of the chief aims of education became the
instilling of patriotism—Chinese patriotism. This feature of the rapidly-increasing
number of schools was encouraged by the Kuomintang Government through the
Chinese Consulates and special educational emissaries. Their task was the easier as
text books and teachers nearly all came from China. Portraits of Sun Yat Sen and
reproductions of his last orders to his comrades mushroomed upon classroom walls.
The old style schools died hard, but by 1925 there were few left, though two or three
of the old dialect schools persisted even after the second world war.

5.   The Governments of Malaya paid scant attention to Chinese schools in the
early days. However, schools in which the medium of instruction was English were
open to the children of all communities, but these existed mainly in the larger towns.
The great majority of the Chinese who came to Malaya to trade and to find
employment in the rubber and tin industries were men, and there was practically no
inter-marriage with the indigenous peoples. Therefore, the problem of providing
education for Chinese children did not become one of great importance or
significance until an influx of Chinese women in the 1920s and 1930s caused a
marked change towards equality in the sex ratio. Even so, the Governments of
Malaya tended, and with reason, to regard the bulk of the Chinese population as
transient and consequently did not feel any compulsion to make special provision for
either English or Chinese vernacular education for the children of this community.
It would, indeed, have been difficult, politically, to justify large expenditure from
public revenue on the education of young persons who, it seemed at that time, were
not likely to regard Malaya as their permanent home. The Chinese who did not prefer
English schools, or who could not obtain places in those schools for their children,
were left, therefore, to provide education of their own contrivance.

---

[1] See 341, note. Like others in this series this despatch was printed for confidential distribution.

6. From 1920 onwards, however, some financial assistance was given to the Chinese vernacular schools. This was in return for a measure of control. It was realised that the schools were becoming instruments for propaganda for China's politics, and in 1920 legislation was introduced for the registration and control of schools and teachers. Control was in the hands of the Chinese Protectorate, and it was limited for the most part to the checking of undesirable expressions of Chinese nationalism in the schools. Chinese schools were regarded more as a political than as an educational problem.

7. This brief historical background to the development of China's vernacular schools would not be complete without reference to a Government policy statement towards education made in 1933. The world trade slump which started in 1929 seriously affected Malaya, and it was found necessary in 1933 to economise in expenditure on education. It was resolved to increase fees in English schools and to freeze grants-in-aid to Chinese schools at their current overall total. In announcing this the Government went on to say that Government was committed to providing Malay education and that education for the Malays must take priority over all other forms of education. The Chinese were told that if this policy did not suit them they could always send their children to China. All sections of the Chinese community bitterly resented this declaration of policy. The British Chinese and others who saw the value of English education, declared that the Government was, by making English education more difficult to obtain, betraying her responsibilities to British subjects in the Straits Settlements, and denying to the youth of Malaya an education which would in the future contribute largely to the building up of a multi-racial community with its interests and loyalties centred in Malaya. These early exponents of the "Malayan" idea deplored the fact that Government was forcing large numbers of Chinese who had settled in Malaya to regard themselves as a separate and unwanted unit. The effect of this decision of Government was that, as soon as trade improved, the Chinese community hastened to provide more Chinese schools for the rapidly increasing numbers of children being born in Malaya.

8. I now turn to more recent times. The expansion of Chinese vernacular education continued after the second world war. The war and the Communist victory in China virtually put an end to the hitherto normal movement of Chinese to and from China. The Chinese population became of necessity, therefore, more settled, and a very large natural increase in the birth rate demanded the provision of yet more schools. The Communist victory in China also provided an additional reason for increasing facilities for secondary education, since it was considered by many parents no longer desirable to send their children to China for higher education.

9. Government put in hand a considerable expansion of English education, and it is of interest to note that in 1954 out of a total enrolment of 158,000 in the English schools (Government, aided and private), 80,000 were Chinese. But Government was not in a position to meet all the educational needs of post-war Malaya and the new insistent demand for education on the part of the Malays absorbed a great part of the resources available. The Chinese, still left largely to their own resources, recognised the serious position which was facing their children, and money was forthcoming to finance a further rapid expansion of vernacular schools. There are now 1,160 Chinese schools in the Federation with a total enrolment of 245,000 pupils, a figure which represents over one quarter of the total number of children attending all types of schools. The great majority of them are in the primary schools, and in the lower

standards of these schools the wastage is considerable, many parents, for economic reasons, being unable to support their children at school after they have obtained an elementary grasp of the three Rs. There are 19,000 children in Chinese secondary schools. Here again the wastage is marked, less than 2,000 being found in the second three years of the six-year course. This should not be taken as indicating a lack of desire for higher studies in Chinese; indeed such desire is traditional among Chinese secondary school pupils, and there is at present no real outlet for this desire within Malaya. Although the actual number of pupils who could take full advantage of higher education in Chinese beyond the secondary school stage is small, they become a focus of discontent, and the absence of opportunities for further education within Malaya, coupled with the new appeal which China has for youth as a country of reform and reconstruction, has caused a steady flow of Chinese secondary school children to China during the past two years, often in the face of strong opposition from their parents.

10. A part of the recent expansion of vernacular education is attributable, also, to the Government's policy of resettlement in new villages of a rural population formerly so scattered as to make adequate protection from the Communist terrorists impossible and the provision of social services impracticable. Schools have been built in the resettled areas and staffed with the aid of Government grants, and have provided for many children of formerly isolated squatters their first opportunity of a school education.

11. The Chinese school has undoubtedly gone far to meet a need, but unfortunately it has failed to meet the greater need of the new Malaya. The promoters of Chinese schools cannot be blamed for this. They have played their part according to their understanding of the immediate situation, and their actions must be seen in their historical context. It is only in the last three or four years that the full significance of the Chinese school to Malaya has been appreciated. It has been realised that, if the Chinese community is to become a partner in the future Malayan nation, then the Chinese youth of the country must be given an education which will enable them to take their place in the social, political and economic life of the country. This the Chinese school does not do. It has also been realised that the Chinese school, particularly the secondary school, is still open to political influence and is the target of both the Malayan Communist Party and the Communist Party of China.

12. With few exceptions, Chinese schools have little in common with any other type of school in Malaya. Dr. William P. Fenn and Dr. Wu Tek-yao, who were invited by the Government to report on Chinese education in Malaya in 1951,[2] were unable to refute the criticism that the schools:—

> "are China-conscious to a degree that is not required by the present situation and that limits their consciousness of being a part of Malaya. Whatever the cause, the fact is that fostering of old loyalties instead of encouraging new tends to turn the child's gaze backward rather than forward. Commendable desire to preserve cultural values often blinds to the need of association with the community in which the child is to live and to the importance of participation in its development."

---

[2] See part II of this volume, 227, note 4.

The disciplinary system, methods of teaching Chinese subjects and to a large extent the curriculum were still, until very recently, those of the schools of Nationalist China. The teachers, being for the most part from China, have little understanding of Malaya and its needs. Furthermore, the pre-war tendency for China's politics to be reflected in the schools has continued to some extent since the war. In this connection, and also in connection with other weaknesses noticeable in Chinese schools, the system of school management has been, and still is, a contributory factor. The Committees of Managers are composed of the school supporters or contributors. Few managers have ever known anything about education, and clan, personal and political prejudices have led in the past to frequent changes in staff and a general feeling of insecurity among Chinese school teachers.

13. In 1951 and 1952, Government gave considerable thought to the problem presented by Chinese vernacular schools and decided that urgent steps must be taken to bring the schools under close control and to ensure that the curriculum of the schools should be more suited to Malaya's needs. At the same time it was proposed that Government should assume increasing responsibility for the provision of a common type of education for the children of all communities. This proposal, translated into law in 1952 by the Education Ordinance, envisaged attendance at Government schools by children of all races who would be instructed in the medium of either Malay or English according to the preponderance of Malay or non-Malay children in the area in which the schools were provided. The teaching of Chinese and other languages would be given if there were a sufficient demand from parents, and the extent to which those languages would be taught was to be left to the discretion of the Director of Education.

14. The national school proposal was made at the same time that measures were being taken both to bring Chinese schools under the closer control of the Education Department, and to revise the curriculum used in the schools. These measures were thereby associated in the minds of many Chinese with the national schools policy. There was an immediate outcry against the new Education Ordinance, and opposition was also raised to the steps being taken to improve Chinese schools, on the grounds that Government intended to get rid of Chinese schools and destroy Chinese culture. The mainspring of the opposition came from secondary school teachers and headmasters of primary schools who saw a threat to their livelihood. This fear was camouflaged by the appeal to Chinese racial sentiment which was stimulated by the China-minded Chinese, whether pro-Nationalist or pro-Communist Government. So great was the feeling aroused over this controversy that many, even of those Chinese who wished to see the introduction of national schools or at least the extension of the English school system, lent their support to the opposition, being led to believe that Government was determined to extinguish Chinese culture.

15. The economic situation of Malaya and the shortage of trained teachers prevented Government from making significant progress in implementing the national schools policy, and, although opposition remained strong to the national school principle, the passage of time allowed feelings to become calmer, and a more reasonable approach to be made to other matters affecting Chinese schools. Text book revision has proceeded satisfactorily, and English, and to a lesser extent, Malay, are being taught to an increasing extent. In order to remedy instability in the primary schools, Government has increased its financial aid to these schools, in

particular by a scheme of grant-in-aid based on direct salary contributions. Conditional upon the introduction of this scheme was acceptance of a scheme of service for the teachers which was designed to provide security of tenure and to bring them more under the control of the Education Department than of the School Management Committees. This scheme was opposed at the outset, being regarded with suspicion in the light of the proposals for national schools. The agitation against it fizzled out and almost every Chinese primary school qualified to do so has now entered the scheme. Government has also done much to assist the schools in the finding of suitable staff. In 1954 there were 1,200 teachers in training in Government organised and financed classes for Chinese language teachers in addition to those in training as teachers of English, art, physical education and domestic science in Chinese schools. Inspection of schools is better and visits by Inspectors who advise more than they seek faults are more welcome.

16.   The Chinese can no longer complain with justification that the Malayan Governments are not interested in the education of Chinese children, or that an altogether insignificant proportion of total Government expenditure on education is devoted to the Chinese community. Whereas in 1950 the total Government annual expenditure on the Chinese vernacular schools was $1·73 million, this had risen to over $19 million by 1953; moreover, since over 50 per cent. of the pupils in English schools are Chinese, the total expenditure by Government on the education of Chinese children in schools of all types had reached the figure of $37 million by 1953. This figure compared with $43 million per annum spent on the education of Malay children and $11 million on the education of Indian children; so that expenditure is now roughly in proportion to the respective population figures of the three principal races in the Federation; and Government is spending slightly more on each Chinese child attending school than on each Malay child.

17.   In 1954, Government, being unable to provide national schools, sought to make a beginning towards that end by offering to provide, at Government expense, teachers for "English medium national type classes" in the vernacular schools. It was hoped by this means both to meet in part the demand for English education, and at the same time to demonstrate the sincerity of Government's intentions not to eliminate Chinese culture, by arranging to teach Chinese (Kuo Yu) to an extent not less than is being taught at present in vernacular primary schools. At the same time, straitened financial circumstances obliged the Federal Government to announce that as from 1st January, 1955, it would not be possible to make any increases in the grants-in-aid in order to assist in the further expansion of Chinese schools by the addition of classes in which the medium of instruction would be Chinese. This restriction on the expansion of vernacular education applied equally to the Malay and Indian vernacular schools. This new programme re-opened the national school controversy, sentiment once more ruled the day, and the leaders of the opposition gained so complete a control of the situation that it has proved impossible to explain the significance of the programme to parents and others who would, it is firmly believed, welcome the proposal, if they understood it, to provide teachers for English medium classes.

18.   Opposition to Government's educational policy is without doubt now being exploited by the Communists and a serious situation is developing in that middle (secondary) school pupils, who by tradition participate in political activities, are being encouraged to organise themselves into a body in defence of a system of

education which will fit them for a place in Red China's society rather than that of Malaya. However, opposition to the Government's present programme is widespread and cannot entirely be attributed to undesirable influences.

19. Since the war, an increasing number of Chinese have realised that the education provided in Chinese schools is not suited to the needs of children who will be the Malayans of the future. The study of English has been recognised as desirable, and there has been a persistent demand, even before the national school was mooted, for the extension of English schools and the teaching of English in the vernacular schools. The more thoughtful of School Committee members have appreciated the fact that the burden of education is becoming heavier than can adequately be shouldered by private individuals. If the vernacular schools are to become useful and efficient instruments of education, they must be improved in very many respects, and these improvements can only be made with Government help. Nevertheless, School Committees are proud of their achievements in the last 30 years and resent any suggestion that their public services have only resulted in institutions which are harmful to society. The "Malayan" idea is new; so is Government's desire to provide education for the children of the Chinese community as a whole. They feel that, if the Chinese are to be partners in the Malayan nation, then the schools which they have provided largely from their own resources should be accepted in the educational system of the country. They also feel that it is fair that Chinese children should be taught the Chinese "national" language which is the passport to Chinese culture. The Chinese are usually open to compromise, and they hope to reach a compromise whereby a balance would be struck in the teaching of Chinese and English in the vernacular schools. The Education Ordinance, however, contemplated the eventual elimination of Chinese schools or their conversion to national schools in which the Chinese language would be relegated as a subject of a very minor nature in the curriculum. The statements issued by Government since 1952 to assure Chinese that there is no intention to eliminate Chinese schools or culture have fallen on deaf ears and, apparently, there will be no change in the attitude of the bulk of the Chinese community until the law is amended to guarantee the teaching of an adequate amount of Chinese as a subject in school curricula and perhaps also a sufficient number of hours per week in which the teaching will be in the Chinese medium. The opposition to any such amendment comes from the Malays, among whom there is an increasing demand that Malay should be the national language. The best time to obtain from the Malays an amendment of the Ordinance to an extent that will satisfy Chinese sentiment and allay present Chinese suspicions may come when, as is generally expected, the UMNO/MCA Alliance sweeps into office at the Federal elections at the end of July, and while the feeling of Sino-Malay partnership based on compromise should be at its strongest.[3]

---

[3] MacGillivray handed Eden, who visited Malaya at this time, copies of this despatch as well as documents 341 and 342. Impressed by the political importance of Chinese schools and concerned lest financial stringency hobbled the government's approach to the problem, on his return to Britain he offered to assist the CO in the matter, see 347.

346   CO 1030/163, no 1   2 Apr 1955

[Closer association of British territories]: despatch no 3 from Mr M J
MacDonald to Mr Lennox-Boyd

I have the honour to address you on the subjects of closer political association
between Singapore and the Federation of Malaya, closer political association between
the three Territories in British Borneo, ultimate closer association between the
Malayan and the Bornean groups of countries, and certain related topics.

A. Malaya and Singapore

2. As reported in my Savingram No. 12 of February 11, the Joint Co-ordination
Committee is about to commence its examination of its third Term of Reference.[1]
Useful preliminary progress in this work can be made during the next few months. As
you know, the two Attorneys-General are preparing a memorandum on the
alternative constitutional forms which closer association could take, for tentative
consideration by the Committee at a meeting in the next few weeks. We cannot
however attack the problem in a major way until the Elections in both Singapore and
the Federation are over. The Election results will probably cause some changes in the
membership of the Committee, which may to some extent affect the chances of it
succeeding in reaching agreement on a plan for a political partnership between the
two territories. But I hope that, whatever the Election results, the reformed
Committee will confirm the impression given at the Committee's last meeting, that
the leaders in all parties in both countries are ready to make the Committee the
instrument for planning closer political association.

3. I think that the prospects of this are quite good, and that if the Committee is
prudently and yet boldly guided, all the difficulties can be overcome and a
satisfactory accord reached. The Committee offers by far the best chance of finding a
solution to the problem agreeable to Her Majesty's Government and to the peoples of
the Federation and Singapore. We should therefore make the most of this
opportunity.

4. We should seek to achieve agreement on the Committee as early as possible. I
hope that its first meeting after the Federation Election can be held in September. It
will not be easy to arrange frequent meetings, for its members will be even busier
after the new Governments are formed than they are now, and hitherto we have
found it impracticable to hold meetings more often than once a month. Probably,
therefore, we cannot hope to progress more speedily than that. On that basis I hope
that the Committee would complete its task within the course of 1956. If this can be
done, we shall then have a draft agreement on the main principles, and perhaps also
many of the major details, of a Constitution for the combined Federation and
Singapore. This may involve substantial changes in the Federation of Malaya
Agreement, which would then have to be negotiated. After that an appropriate body
should be appointed to do the detailed drafting of the new Constitution for the
combined territories. We should aim at all this work being completed, and the new
proposals being adopted by both Legislatures within the next four years, before the
next Elections in Malaya.

---

[1] See 324, minute by Martin.

5. In my opinion we should aim at getting the Joint Co-ordination Committee to do more than work out the principles of closer association between the two territories as covered by item 3 of the present Terms of Reference. By extending the Terms of Reference at an appropriate time we should seek to get the Committee to make recommendations on the broad outlines of:—

(a) a Defence Agreement between the combined Federation/Singapore Government on the one hand and the United Kingdom Government on the other, (perhaps with the Australian and New Zealand Government as partners) and
(b) new constitutional machinery for political cooperation between a self-governing Malaya and the United Kingdom within the Commonwealth.

In paragraphs 6 to 11 below I comment on (a) and (b).

B. A defence agreement

6. One of our political objectives in the Malayan territories is self government within the Commonwealth. Our efforts will be in vain if the result of self-government, when it is established, is that the Malayans promptly lose their liberty through cold war or hot war conquest by a Communist or other foreign aggressor. We shall not fulfil our trust to them unless we ensure that the self-governing Malaya is effectively protected, so that it continues to be self-governing. That is a vital interest not only of the Malayans themselves, but also of the peoples of the United Kingdom and the rest of the Commonwealth, who wish strategically important Singapore, with its hinterland and surroundings, to remain part of the free world.

7. I think that the Joint Co-ordination Committee is an admirable body to discuss the broad terms of a Defence Agreement. We shall have to consult with the Malayan leaders on this all important question sometime, and the sooner the better. The Joint Co-ordination Committee is likely to be as good and reasonable a body of local leaders as will appear at any time in the next few years, and we should take advantage of our friendly discussions with them on other major political questions to settle this one. The two problems of how to create constitutional forms for a combined Federation/Singapore which shall eventually be self-governing, and how to protect that self-governing unit are related. During the Joint Co-ordination Committee discussions on closer association we shall certainly have to consider the appropriate constitutional machinery for co-ordination in defence. I propose so to guide the discussion that the fact of Malaya's inability to defend itself without considerable outside aid becomes obvious. From that discussion we can turn naturally to the proper ways and means of providing the necessary aid.

8. I shall not attempt to discuss here what should be the principal features of a Defence Agreement between the United Kingdom and Malaya. If it is agreed that we should attempt to get the Joint Co-ordination Committee to tackle the problem, then we should in due course set our Service and Civil advisers the task of preparing proposals.

C. Membership of the Commonwealth

9. Our assumption is that the combined Singapore/Malaya, when self-governing, will remain a member of the Commonwealth. We should get this confirmed by the Joint Co-ordination Committee.

10. I believe that we should also use the Committee to try to plan a new

relationship, unprecedented in the Commonwealth, between the United Kingdom and the self-governing Malaya. On all previous occasions when a nation in the Commonwealth has become self-governing, constitutional links between it and the United Kingdom have been virtually broken, except for the maintenance of the Crown and the appointment in most cases of a Governor-General. British participation in the conduct of internal and external policy has ceased, and the tie between the two Commonwealth members has become tenuous. That was a result of the zealous nationalism of the newly independent members of the Commonwealth, which infected "white" dominions like Canada, South Africa and Australia as much as the later "brown" dominions of India, Pakistan and Ceylon. Excessive Nationalism, however, is now out of date. Every free nation in this dangerous world is dependent on co-operation and support from other free nations. Certain problems, such as those of defence and foreign relations, transcend national boundaries.

11. I wonder whether we cannot now evolve somewhere in the Commonwealth a new constitutional concept to express this idea. The experiment of self-government in Malaya may be a good opportunity to attempt it. I suggest that we should discuss with the Malayan leaders the possibility of a formal Council being established representing a partnership between Malaya and the United Kingdom in common questions of defence and foreign relations. Possibly some other matters also might lie within its responsibilities. The Council would be consultative, and its membership would be half British and half Malayan. I shall not attempt in this despatch to pursue the proposal in any further detail; but again, if it is a good idea, I suggest that the Joint Co-ordination Committee would be an appropriate body to examine it. The conception could arise naturally in the course of the Committee's discussions.

D. The Borneo territories

12. As you know from my despatch No. 1 of February 4th, we are now attempting to bring representatives of the three Territories in British Borneo together on a Joint Council with certain executive powers. Such a body will perhaps not carry us very far in establishing combined government for the three countries, but it will be an important first step, and from it further developments might take place fairly rapidly. I need not write more on the subject now, beyond saying that I hope that we can achieve our immediate purpose about the end of this year.

E. The greater confederation

13. Our ultimate objective is a Confederation between the five present territories of the Federation of Malaya, Singapore, Sarawak, North Borneo and Brunei. We have already agreed that this should be achieved in two stages: first by the combination of (a) Singapore and the Federation and (b) the three Borneo Territories as separate entities; and second, by bring [sic] together these two groups under one appropriate constitutional government. Nothing should be done, therefore, under Sections A and D of this despatch which would prejudice our ultimate aim. Whatever is done regarding the proposals in Sections B and C should also be negotiated with a view to the agreements including the Borneo Territories either from the start or at a later date.

14. In Singapore and the Federation many politicians in every racial community already favour the idea of a Confederation between the five territories. I for one have been sedulously planting the idea in their minds, and in the minds of local

journalists, over the last eight years, and urging them to give public expression every now and then to this ultimate aim, so that the people are gradually educated towards it. Leaders in all parties have occasionally referred to it in speeches, and the press have given it quite favourable publicity. I expect that the matter will be raised by some members during the Joint Co-ordination Committee's discussions about closer association between the Federation and Singapore.

15. Because of the political "backwardness" of the Borneo Territories, we have not initiated similar private discussion on the subject there, and the Bornean leaders are perhaps less aware than those in Malaya of our grand design. Possibly we should begin to propagate the idea in Sarawak, North Borneo and Brunei. But, although it would be good to get this problem settled at not too distant a date, the time for that has not yet arrived. The more urgent problems referred to in Sections A, B, C and D above need settlement first; and beyond letting individual members of the Joint Co-ordination Committee air their views on the subject I suggest that it should not be pursued in the immediate future by that Committee. Later the membership of the Committee might be expanded to include representatives from Borneo, to examine the problem.

16. This despatch contains only my own provisional reflections on these subjects. I have not discussed them, except sometimes in the most general terms, with the High Commissioner of the Federation or the Governors of Singapore, Sarawak and North Borneo. I thought it better to put them to you, Sir, in a tentative form first, so that we here may receive your guidance on the general principles involved before we proceed further. I am sending copies of this despatch to the High Commissioner and Governors for their consideration.[2]

---

[2] CO officials expressed doubts about MacDonald's optimism and their minutes provided the basis of Lennox-Boyd's reply on 2 June, see 349. Meanwhile, the future of the commissioner-general was being reviewed by a committee chaired by Sir N Brook, see 348.

347 CO 1030/51, no 64   6 Apr 1955

[Education policy]: letter from Sir J Martin to W D Allen[1] on its political importance and the need for funding. *Enclosure:* extract from a letter from Sir J Martin to A E Drake, 5 Aug 1954

At lunch the other day we had a word about your very welcome letter of the 8th March telling me of the discussion which Sir Anthony Eden had had with MacGillivray in Kuala Lumpur about education in Malaya.[2] I told you how timely your letter was, since the subject is one which gives us great concern and it is our intention to consider it most carefully with MacGillivray during his proposed visit to this country in June.

We entirely agree about the great political importance of the whole question, and it is only too true that our policy has recently been badly set back by the straitened financial circumstances of the Federation. I do not think that I can better express our views on both points than by letting you have the enclosed extract from a letter

---

[1] See 335, note 1.   [2] See 345, note 3.

which I wrote to the Treasury in August of last year. You will see from it that the main points which weigh with us are:—

(a) the present educational programme is only a holding operation and not really a plan of development;

(b) yet for the following reasons educational development is of fundamental importance to the whole future of the Federation;

(c) for one thing, like many other dependent territories, the Federation combines a rapidly increasing population and a rapidly awakening political consciousness;

(d) second, only through education is there any real hope of bridging the gulf between the two main races of the country, which are almost equal in numbers but utterly different in most other ways;

(e) third, the most serious threat to the Federation is Communist subversion rather than violence, and there could be no better breeding-ground for Communism than a population (of whom more than half are under twenty-one) both uneducated and bitterly aggrieved on that account; and

(f) H.M.G. have repeatedly assured the Federation that they will give the country all necessary help not only in fighting the terrorists but also in its plans for social and economic development.

I am about to write to MacGillivray telling him that this is one of the main subjects which we shall want to discuss with him in June, suggesting that we ought then, in view of its vital importance, to consider what we should like to do if the financial obstacles could largely be overcome, and asking him to be prepared to go into the matter with us on those lines. It might at some stage during those talks be very helpful if I could ask you to join us and I hope that you would be willing to do so.

If we are to achieve anything on the scale which seems to be politically as well as educationally, necessary, it will undoubtedly involve substantial financial help from H.M.G., and we should, of course, be most grateful if we could enlist the aid of the Foreign Office in any attempt to secure such help. The simple fact is that the military forces now maintained in Malaya are costing H.M.G. something like £65 million a year, and furthermore, to carry out our present plans for building up our defences in Malaya against external aggression will inevitably require heavy additional expenditure both capital and recurrent. But these immense sums are likely to have been spent in vain unless the educational problem can be solved. The cost of a proper solution is so small compared with the expenditure on defence, but so necessary to ensure this success, that we are convinced that every effort must be made to find the money.[3]

Enclosure to 347

. . . I have described MacGillivray's plans as constituting a modest programme of educational expansion. But in fact they are in many respects rather in the nature of a braking operation than of an acceleration. This is particularly the case in regard to the severe reduction in the number of places available, in relation to the school-age population as a whole, both in the vernacular primary schools and in the English

---

[3] See 364.

secondary schools. It may indeed be argued that the proposed reduction is too drastic and that it will prove politically impossible to apply the brake so hard, though MacGillivray thinks that there is a chance of selling the scheme. But despite these reductions we think it justifiable to describe the plan as progressive, since it will bring the educational system nearer to the national school ideal embodied in the 1952 Education Ordinance. Financial considerations must defer the ideal solution of replacing vernacular and English schools with truly national schools. But the maintenance of the present percentage of school age population in the English primary schools and the introduction of "English" teachers in other schools will be a definite contribution towards the ultimate aim of national education.

I cannot overstress the fundamental importance of educational development to the future of the Federation of Malaya and to the interest of H.M.G. in the country. It is not only the importance common to most territories with a rapidly increasing population and awakening political consciousness; even in these respects the Federation is today a special case sinces its proportion of children of school age to the total population and its rate of population increase are amongst the highest in the world, while the country is about to take a great and inevitable stride forward politically which will carry it further in one step than almost any other Colonial territory has moved at a comparable stage. There are at least three other factors of even greater importance which we cannot afford to forget. First, in the Federation's unique racial position, with two main races almost equal in numbers and utterly different in practically all other respects, education has by far the most significant part to play of any of the measures by which we can hope to attain our declared and essential aim of building a united Malayan nation. Second, we have always—and rightly—maintained that in dealing with the Emergency the shooting war is only one tine of a two-pronged policy; the other is the need to win the hearts and minds of the people, and there again education is of first importance. Third, even were the Emergency to come to an end the struggle against communism would continue, probably a still harder struggle against an enemy insidiously bent upon perverting ordinary nationalism and subverting the minds of the people and particularly the young. I need hardly elaborate the dangers which would then arise among a people already predominantly youthful if they included large numbers of young men with a bitter grievance about their lack of education, especially young Chinese with the vast power of Communist China no great way off. Indeed, that this communist threat is already upon us may be seen from the recent disturbances among Chinese students in Singapore and the present remarkably heavy flow of young Chinese going from the Federation to metropolitan China for education and, of course, indoctrination. In our view all this means that education offers the most important key to the problem of Malaya as a whole; and if we delay in oiling the lock thoroughly over the next few years we may find that that key will no longer turn in it. It is no exaggeration to say that the result might well be disastrous not only for our own position of influence in South East Asia but also for the wider Imperial interests in defence and other matters to which the stability and loyalty of Malaya are indispensable.

H.M.G. have said that they will stand behind the Federation. The statement made in 1950, which has been reiterated since, was that H.M.G. are "willing to give Malaya all the assistance that may be shown to be necessary both for the effective prosecution of the anti-bandit campaign and to enable her to go ahead with her plans of social and economic development". It was then stated to be the desire of H.M.G.

that "the heavy burden that Malaya is continuing to bear in the common effort against Communist banditti should not be allowed to impede, for financial reasons, this very necessary development programme". Without those assurances the Federation Government could not confidently have pursued the essential educational development which has taken place during the last few years; and reliance upon that encouragement remains equally necessary for pursuit of the aims now proposed for the next five years to come. It is against that background that we have, after full consideration, endorsed MacGillivray's view that he must add to his draft estimates for 1955 provision for the first instalment of a five-year education plan on the lines which I have described. . . .

348 CO 1030/193, no 54   16 May 1955
[Future of the commissioner-general]: personal minute no M(E)13/55 by Sir A Eden to Mr Lennox-Boyd. *Annex:* minute by Sir N Brook to Sir A Eden, 13 May 1955

[Eden succeeded Churchill as prime minister on 6 Apr 1955 and appointed Macmillan foreign secretary, Lord Home Commonwealth secretary and Selwyn Lloyd minister of defence. Maintaining his specialist interest in foreign affairs, Eden instructed the secretary to the Cabinet to examine the future of the commissioner-general's office. Chaired by Sir N Brook, a committee of top civil servants discussed the matter on 15 Apr and 4 May. Although Sir T Lloyd pointed out that the colonial function of the commissioner-general could be fulfilled in other ways, the committee concluded that regional defence, foreign affairs and Commonwealth relations warranted retention of the post. Two further meetings on 13 June and 3 Aug dealt with staffing. In June it was announced that Sir R H Scott would be the new commissioner general and he took up the appointment in Sept (see CAB 130/109 and FO 371/116969).]

I asked Sir Norman Brook to review, with officials of the Departments directly concerned, the future functions of the Commissioner-General, South East Asia. His report is attached. It seems to me to be on right lines and I hope you will find yourself in agreement with it.

If so, our next task is to find the right man for the job. I think we should meet to discuss this very soon. Meanwhile I hope you will be thinking of possible candidates.

I am sending a similar minute to the Chancellor of the Exchequer, the Foreign Secretary and the Secretary of State for Commonwealth Relations.

Annex to 348

Prime Minister
You asked me to consider, with officials of the Departments directly concerned, the future functions of the Commissioner-General, South East Asia. I now submit our conclusions and recommendations.

2. The nature and functions of this post have undergone various changes. These are reflected in the current definition of the Commissioner-General's functions, as stated in the two lengthy directives which constitute his charter. We think it would be wise at this stage to sweep all this away and make a fresh start.

3. The main purposes for which a senior British representative is now needed in South East Asia are as follows:—

(i)   The United Kingdom has great interests and major responsibilities throughout South East Asia, but these are divided among a number of different authorities (Ambassadors, Governors, High Commissioners and Commanders-in-Chief) each of whom is primarily interested in his own part of the area. We need someone there who can advise on general policy for the area as a whole and has sufficient authority to promote co-operation, and to resolve differences, between United Kingdom representatives or authorities in different parts of the area.

(ii)   The United Kingdom must have a permanent representative on the Council of the recently established South East Asia Treaty Organisation (S.E.A.T.O.). He should be a person of standing who can speak with authority in respect of the whole area.

(iii)   The situation in Indo-China is likely to be critical for some time and we need a senior man on the spot to watch closely its possible repercussions on the rest of South East Asia.

(iii) [sic] The Australians have recently appointed a single representative[1] for the whole area, based on Singapore, and the New Zealanders are likely to do the same.[2] We do not wish to give the impression that our responsibilities and interests in this area are being surrendered to Australia or New Zealand.

4.   It is, however, very doubtful whether it would be expedient to attempt to define precisely, in a detailed directive of the kind given to his predecessor, the powers and duties of the post of Commissioner-General as we now envisage it. Anything like a charter defining his powers in relation to the other United Kingdom authorities with whom he would have to deal would almost certainly cause more difficulties than it resolved. There is also the difficulty that membership of the Manila Treaty, while it includes Australia, New Zealand and Pakistan, excludes some countries of South East Asia, such as Burma, in which the Commissioner-General should take a close interest.

5.   We believe that the authority of the new Commissioner-General should derive, not from any formal charter defining his powers and duties in detail, but from his personal standing and influence. We therefore recommend that he should be appointed by the Prime Minister, though he would continue to report through the Foreign Secretary and the Colonial Secretary respectively. It would then be clear that, as the Prime Minister's representative, he was the senior United Kingdom authority in South East Asia. His appointment should be based mainly on his representation of the United Kingdom at S.E.A.T.O., although it would be recognised that he had additional functions which were not directly connected with S.E.A.T.O. He could be given a broad directive in the form of a personal minute from the Prime Minister describing briefly his general tasks. This might follow the lines of the attached draft.

Her Majesty's approval would need to be sought for this change in the nature of the appointment.

6.   If you approve these recommendations on functions, we can consider what

---

[1] Sir Alan Watt was Australian commissioner in SE Asia, 1954–1956.

[2] Foss Shanahan was commissioner for New Zealand in SE Asia, 1955–1958.

staff the new Commissioner-General would require. We believe that his success will depend very largely on his personal influence and authority. The exercise of this will be hindered, rather than helped, by his having a large staff. We believe that it should be possible and advantageous to reduce the existing numbers.

[DRAFT DIRECTIVE]

1. You are appointed to be the Commissioner-General for the United Kingdom in South East Asia.

2. You will be the United Kingdom Council Representative for the South East Asia Collective Defence Treaty, designated in accordance with the decision taken at the first meeting of the Treaty Council held at Bangkok in February, 1955. You will be responsible in this capacity for promoting on behalf of Her Majesty's Government in the United Kingdom the general purposes and principles of the Treaty and for dealing with all matters falling within the purview of the Council Representatives.

3. You will advise Her Majesty's Government in the United Kingdom on the general conduct of British policy in South East Asia and will be responsible for ensuring, as necessary, co-ordinated action by the competent authorities in British dependent territories in South East Asia and the United Kingdom representatives in other countries in that area. You will not, however, exercise direct administrative functions in any of the British territories.

4. You will preside over the British Defence Co-ordination Committee (Far East) and as its Chairman will concern yourself with questions of defence policy affecting, not only South East Asia, but the whole of the B.D.C.C.(F.E.) and ANZAM areas.

5. You will maintain contact through the United Kingdom High Commissioners with the Governments of independent Commonwealth countries having interests in South East Asia.

6. You will report through the Foreign Secretary and the Colonial Secretary, respectively, on questions concerning each of them but you may on occasion refer directly to me on matters of general concern.

349   CO 1030/163, no 2   2 June 1955
[Closer association of British territories]: despatch (reply) no 150 from Mr Lennox-Boyd to Mr M J MacDonald

I have the honour to acknowledge the receipt of your secret despatch No. 3 of the 2nd April, 1955, about closer association between the British and British-protected territories in South East Asia.[1]

2. The despatch has been read with great interest. It puts forward a number of important ideas about the future scope of the Joint Co-ordination Committee which demand careful deliberation.

3. As you say, it is not possible to carry the work of the Committee much further until after the election in the Federation of Malaya in July and there has been time to assess the attitude of the newly elected Governments in the two territories towards the issues raised by the Committee's third term of reference. It will in my view be

[1] See 346.

desirable to avoid giving the impression that an attempt is being made to hurry the newly elected Governments into conclusions before they have had time to settle into their own harness and fully to consider the far-reaching questions involved. Meanwhile, it will, I think, be advisable to confine activity to the preparation by officials of any papers which may be necessary and to defer any endeavour to formulate a definite programme for the completion of their Committee's work. Moreover, I consider that there is some danger that any detailed discussion at this early stage about arrangements for self-government may reinforce the influence which already lead some time Malayan political leaders to expect and demand the final stages of constitutional development before the territories are in fact ready for it.

4. I should also like to give further thought to the issues raised in paragraph 5 of your despatch. Adequate arrangements for the defence of Malaya are a necessary condition to the grant of self-government but I should want to consider further whether the Committee would be the best body to consider the terms of an agreement on the subject or whether they might not when the time comes better be considered direct with the Government or Governments concerned.

5. I was most interested in your suggestion that there should be some new constitutional relationship between a self-governing Malaya and the United Kingdom within the Commonwealth. I should be grateful if you would let me have your ideas on the subject in more detail so that I may consider them further. Clearly our thinking on this subject should be carried a fair way towards the formulation of specific proposals before the suggestion is broached, even tentatively to Malayan political leaders.

6. I trust that it may be possible to discuss these various matters with you when you return to London. Meanwhile I take this opportunity to express my appreciation and gratitude for all that has been achieved under your guidance to lay the foundations for the structure which will, I trust, in time to come, and in whatever shape is found appropriate, hold together the British territories in South East Asia in ever closer association, for the benefit of their peoples and the prosperity and well-being of the region.

7. I am sending copies of this despatch to the High Commissioner and the Governors.

350 CO 1030/319, no 7   19 June 1955

[Communists' first peace offer]: inward telegram no 347 from D Watherston[1] to Mr Lennox-Boyd

[As the authorities established ascendancy over the MRLA, Malayan communists turned to political methods. Since the end of 1952 the British had been on their guard against MCP infiltration of political parties and trade unions (see part II of this volume 284, and 311), and in Jan 1955 MacGillivray accepted the remote possibility of the communists calling a ceasefire (see 342, para 9). In Apr Chou En-lai adopted a more conciliatory approach to colonialism at the Bandung Conference. Meanwhile, although Tunku Abdul Rahman accepted that independence would not be achieved until the emergency had ended, he believed that an amnesty might speed up the process, with the result that the

---

[1] Watherston was standing in for MacGillivray during the latter's absence in London.

Alliance included in its electoral manifesto the promise of a general pardon to all 'communist terrorists'. This initiative was complicated by a letter from MRLA headquarters suggesting peace talks. Received on 10 June by the UPAM in Kuala Lumpur, rather than by the authorities directly, a rough translation was taken to London by MacGillivray. The federal government, having satisfied itself that the document was authentic and anxious to agree a response before the letter leaked to the public, worked fast to persuade the Executive Council and Malayan leaders to reject the MCP's offer. Their grounds are contained in a paper which was transmitted in this telegram for London's prior approval.]

My immediately preceding telegram.

Following is text of paper.

Begins. An examination of the Malayan Communist Party's offer to negotiate—June 1955.

Introduction

1. A letter dated 1st May 1955[2] and posted in Haadyai Siam on 7th June was delivered to the United Planting Association of Malaya (U.P.A.M.) in Kuala Lumpur on 10th June. It was written in Chinese and purported to come from the "Supreme Command H.Q. of the Malayan Races Liberation Army". A translation of the letter has already been sent to Colonial Office under cover of savingram No. 707/55 dated 15th June, 1955. The signature on the document is unknown to the police.

2. A second letter understood to be in precisely similar terms, the examination of which has not yet been completed, was delivered to Col. H.S. Lee, who informed H.E. the O.A.G.

3. It is possible that copies may also have been sent to other people.[3]

Authenticity of the document

4. Although no conclusive evidence has been found indicating that the document does, in fact, originate from the highest Malayan Communist Party (M.C.P.) level, an examination of the text leaves little doubt that this is so. Its general tone and phraseology point to Communist Party origin and various allusions in it are in striking conformity with current international Communist propaganda—e.g., the reference to the Afro-Asian Conference,[4] the denunciation of the establishment of military bases in Malaya, the presentation of the orthodox Communist thesis on "sham independence", and use of the phrase "Asians killing Asians" and the reference to the Sino-Indonesian negotiations on Chinese dual nationality. A point in conformity with recent M.C.P. propaganda is the rejection of the Alliance Amnesty proposal.

5. For these reasons it appears improbable that the document could have originated from some non-Communist source (motivated perhaps by some other political or purely mischievous considerations).

6. The possibility has also been considered that the document might have originated from some dissident M.C.P. member or group (possibly wishing to end the emergency independently of the leadership). This, however, has been rejected. Not only is the discipline of the M.C.P. such that no such autonomous attempt could

---

[2] See 352, annex.

[3] Leong Yew Koh, Tan Siew Sin and *Utusan Melayu* (Singapore) were known by the authorities to have received copies.

[4] Held in Bandung (Java) in Apr 1955.

hope to command a following, but only the leaders would be capable of writing in this currently orthodox manner, and it is known that, although there has been a difference of view among the leaders regarding the relative advantages of violence and subversion, this difference is not of such an order as to be likely to result in an autonomous move of this nature.

7. The document is therefore accepted as being authentic. It represents a step in full conformity with recent developments in international Communist policy. The unusual clarity and cogency of its style point to a high origin in the M.C.P. hierarchy—indeed it is likely that the document is based on a draft emanating from Communist China, so closely does it follow the current Cominform line.

The M.C.P.'s motives in choosing this time and method of approach

8. In considering the M.C.P.'s motives in making this proposal, it must be remembered that their long-term policy will not have changed. It remains their aim to oust the Government and put a Communist Government in its place. The nature and timing of the M.C.P.'s proposal can probably be explained by three inter-connected motives. First, it must be apparent to the M.C.P. that their guerilla tactics have been mastered and that not only have they no hope of gaining military success, but by continuing terrorism they are severely handicapping their attempts to create a united front. It is well, therefore, that we bear in mind that the M.C.P. have approached us as an armed force which is conscious of failure. Secondly, since the proposal almost certainly derived from the policy decision taken at international Communist level, it could only have been made after Moscow and Peking evolved their current tactics of the peaceful settlement of disputes and the substitution of neutralizing and penetration methods. Thirdly, it may well have been argued by the Communists that any settlement of the emergency would be best achieved before the Malayan National Parties attained power, since otherwise the latter would be able to claim credit and thus win public prestige. The resulting confusion at a time of elections might be aimed to upset the present balance of the political parties and we accept as a commonplace of Communist policy towards Asian countries that the Nationalist parties, while being united against the Colonial powers, must at the same time be shown to be incapable of satisfying national aspirations in order that the public may in due course be induced to turn to the Communist Party. Thus it seems evident that the local needs of the M.C.P. today coincide with international Communist policy and that it has been calculated that this situation can best be explored before the election of the new Federal Government.

9. The method chosen was probably governed by two factors. First, the same consideration of preventing an access of prestige to the national parties may explain why one letter was addressed to the President of U.P.A.M., in that it could be assumed that he would pass it to the Government and so ensure that they would take the lead in negotiating any settlement. Secondly, the M.C.P. presumably wanted to ensure that pressure would be brought to bear on the present Government. They therefore sent copies to M.C.A. leaders and possibly to other political leaders not yet known to us, anticipating political pressure probably followed by a leakage to the press and finally followed by extensive public pressure on the authorities. They calculated that the Government would have great difficulty in handling the delicate situation that would immediately arise.

The M.C.P.'s probable terms for a settlement

10. The document itself gives some indication of the terms which the M.C.P. would put forward in any negotiations for a settlement. It states that "the war must be ended, the emergency regulations must be abolished and the democratic freedom and rights of the people must be safeguarded to enable a general election to be carried out in a peaceful and democratic atmosphere". Later on, the document describes the Alliance amnesty proposal as "not satisfactory" and "any attempt to force people to surrender" as "completely unreasonable". From these statements, as well as what is known of Communist technique generally, we may expect that the minimum M.C.P. demands would be:—

(a) cease fire during negotiations;
(b) recognition as a legal political party;
(c) immunity from punishment for its members and followers who have taken part in the armed struggle;
(d) abolition of the emergency regulations.

Consequences of negotiating

11. If we agree to negotiations the M.C.P. would, in the traditional Communist manner, come to them determined not to compromise. Therefore, unless the Government were prepared to meet M.C.P. demands the negotiations would fail.

12. The effect of meeting the M.C.P.'s demands would be to return to the conditions of 1948, before the emergency was declared. The situation in the Federation would then be:—

(a) The Government would have recognized a party which for seven years has been in armed rebellion against it, whose members have committed atrocities against the people, and whose policy has been treason.
(b) The Communist terrorist organization would make a token surrender with their arms as did the MPAJA in 1954 [1945], but like them would leave arms dumps hidden and keep their terrorist organization in being clandestinely.
(c) The M.C.P. would be able to work openly and, aided by the threat implied from their past record and the continuance of their secret terrorist organization, intimidation would distort political development. With the ending of the emergency there would be uneasy peace until the M.C.P. was strong enough to defeat the Government of the day and to take over the running of the country.
(d) The large section of the public which has consistently opposed Communism would suffer a grave loss of morale, with resultant weakening of the country's opposition to the M.C.P.
(e) Without the assistance of the emergency regulations it would be impossible to control the clandestine activities of the M.C.P.
(f) An M.C.P. demand would certainly develop for abolition of the Banishment Ordinance and the Registration of Societies Ordinance and for return of those who have been banished or deported to China.

13. The result would be that the M.C.P. would be in a far stronger position than any Communist party in Western Europe, where Communism cannot dominate to so great an extent by fear and where it is not backed by the racial ties that exist between Chinese in Malaya and their kinsmen in Communist China. The M.C.P. would, in a

short time, be in a stronger position than it was in 1948, because it would have gained by experience, and would have the open support and encouragement of Communist sympathizers throughout the country and would by its very re-emergence as a legal political party have frightened the waverers. There would be grave doubts in the minds of the people of the country and of South East Asia, and especially of Thailand, about the determination of the democracies to oppose the advance of Communism. They might see in negotiations a similarity with events in Indo-China.

14. If negotiations were started and the Government refused to compromise, the only result could be cessation of the negotiations. Unsuccessful and terminated negotiations would in themselves be a considerable victory for the M.C.P. The very fact that negotiations were starting would raise the hope of the country that the outcome would be peace and failure could not but result in a tremendous disappointment and consequent drop in morale with the Government receiving the odium of breaking off peace talks. That the Government had recognized the M.C.P.'s strength and position sufficiently to negotiate with it would enhance the M.C.P.'s prestige and power.

15. In short, to embark on negotiations would be to take the first step down a slippery slope with inevitably disastrous consequences for Malaya. No such line of action can be contemplated.

Courses open

16. There appear, therefore, to be two alternative courses:—

(a) Out of hand rejection of the Communist approach (course A).
(b) Rejection of the Communist approach, accompanied by an alternative offer (course B).

Course A

17. As regards out of hand rejection, the M.C.P. offer seems to make possible for the first time an early cessation of armed terrorism and might well react most unfavourably to outright rejection without any alternative. The Government would be accused of prolonging the emergency unnecessarily and some of those who have cooperated to oppose terrorism might well begin to hesitate in their purpose.

18. Lesser result of the rejection out of hand of such an offer would be to provide the M.C.P. with opportunities to pose as the only group promoting peace, thus rendering the Malayan people susceptible to their "United Front" propaganda.

19. The disappointment that would be felt throughout the country might result in such loss of popular support that the Government would have considerably greater difficulty in continuing to prosecute the emergency successfully.

Course B

20. Adoption of the second course, rejection of the offer accompanied by an alternative offer, would show that the Government is indeed anxious to stop the emergency as soon as possible, but only on conditions which would give the country a fair prospect of free political development. Since total surrender is out of question at present and individual surrenders are proceeding only slowly, an amnesty offer is the only practicable alternative. We are sure that it would not be accepted by the

M.C.P. as a body, but numbers of the less resolute members might well take advantage of it.

21. Moreover, the offer would make clear that it is even more within the power of the M.C.P. than of the Government to bring about an end to the emergency immediately, by accepting the Government's counter offer of an amnesty, which could produce an immediate cessation of hostilities without the inevitable delays which go with negotiations. The M.C.P. offer will have been as much of a surprise and matter of bewilderment to the majority of the Communist terrorists as it will be to the public. Although by direction they may step up attacks on Security Forces in order to threaten the Government and give the lie to the thought that they may be defeated, a large number of Communist terrorists will undoubtedly feel a loss of sense of purpose and will be particularly susceptible to an amnesty offer, combined with continued offensive Security Force psychological warfare operations.

Timing and method

22. In making a reply the wisest course appears to be to issue a statement having the full support of the Director of Operations Committee. This statement would reject the offer, refer to the present surrender policy[5] and say that active considera-tion is being given to the question of an amnesty. Before making any such statement there would be advantage in trying to force the M.C.P. leaders to come forward and associate themselves unequivocally with the offer of negotiations. We would do this with the object of ensuring that M.C.P. leaders could not disclaim responsibility for the offer after we had rejected it.

Conclusions

23. Our conclusions are as follows:

(a) The document appears to be an authentic offer by the M.C.P. to negotiate;
(b) the M.C.P. has chosen this time and method to make the offer because, negotiating with the present Nominated Government, they identify themselves with the masses, at the expense of the political parties which are about to contest the elections;
(c) acceptance of the offer to negotiate could only lead to acceptance of the M.C.P. terms or acceptance of the responsibility for failure of the negotiations. The former would inevitably lead to domination by the M.C.P. of the country, if not immediately, certainly in due course and the latter to loss of morale in the country and an increase of M.C.P. prestige;
(d) an outright rejection of the offer would lay the Government open to the charge of unnecessarily prolonging the emergency and would cause a loss of public support;
(e) the wisest course appears to be to issue a statement having the full support of the Director of Operations Committee, rejecting the offer, referring to the present surrender policy, and saying that active consideration is being given to the question of an amnesty. *Ends.*

---

[5] See 352, para 8. The government's psychological warfare campaign (eg drops of leaflets, broadcasts from 'voice aircraft' and schemes of rewards for informants) stressed the reasons for and methods of surrender.

351 CO 1030/319, no 20   23 June 1955
'Malayan emergency': minute no PM(55)36 by Mr Lennox-Boyd to Sir A Eden on the communists' first peace offer

Prime Minister

You should know that a number of individuals and organisations both inside and outside Malaya have recently had the same letter purporting to come from the Supreme Command Headquarters of the Communist terrorists, offering to negotiate a peace. I am satisfied that this letter is authentic.

The High Commissioner and I regard this as encouraging evidence that the Communist terrorists recognise that they are losing the shooting war, and that they are apprehensive about the effect upon them of the appearance in the Federation of a Legislature with a majority of elected representatives.

This letter offers the Federation Government a very useful opportunity to involve the Communist terrorists in serious loss of face, but to secure this the first public statement about it must come from the Government. Time is thus extremely short since the letter has been widely distributed and may at any moment be published through agencies outside the Government's control.

The Federation authorities have been working at top speed during the last few days to secure the agreement of Executive Council, Director of Operations Committee and the main political parties to the reply to be made to the letter. They have succeeded admirably and, with the support of all those groups are now about to publish a statement in terms of the most welcome firmness. The statement will demonstrate the hypocrisy of the Communist terrorists' offer and state that the Government has no intention of negotiating with them, adding that it keeps its existing surrender policy under constant review so that it can be modified at any time if it should appear that a greater or lesser measure of "amnesty" would hasten the end of terrorism. Owing to the overriding need for rapid action in the matter I have been unable to consult my colleagues about it and it will not be possible to arrange for simultaneous publication of the statement here; but I will publish it and the Communist terrorists' letter as soon as possible, and the delay should be brief.

Later today, however, I will send you copies of the letter and of the public statement in what will in all material respects be its final form.[1]

Meanwhile, the Federation authorities are urgently examining the question whether or not this statement should quickly be followed up with an offer to the Communist terrorists of some sort of "amnesty".

The High Commissioner and I have for some time been viewing with apprehension the dangerous possibility of public demand in Malaya for a negotiated peace. If any such negotiations were undertaken they could not but redound to the advantage of the Communist terrorists and it is therefore a source of great satisfaction to us that the leaders of public and political opinion in the Federation have agreed so readily and firmly to reject the present offer.[2] In our view this should, as I have said, gravely damage the Communist terrorists and lead to a marked stiffening in public morale.

---

[1] See 352.
[2] Eden replied the same day: 'I agree but what will they do after the election?'

352   CO 1030/319, no 31   23 June 1955

'Malayan government rejects negotiations with terrorists': CO press release for publication on 24 June. *Annex:* 'Translation of letter from communist terrorists'

The Government of the Federation of Malaya has issued the following statement on an offer by the Malayan Communist Party of Negotiations to end the Emergency:—

1.   The Government's attention has been drawn to a letter received by representatives of certain interests in the Federation purporting to come from Supreme Command Headquarters of the Communist terrorists.

2.   The full text of the letter is attached.

3.   As will be seen, the letter makes certain proposals for negotiating an end to Communist terrorism in the Federation. The Government has no doubt that these proposals come from the leaders of Communist terrorism. It has considered them and, on the unanimous advice of the Director of Operations Committee, issues the following statement:—

4.   The letter claims that the terrorists have not been defeated. The facts are that they have suffered severe defeat in Pahang, and their organisation has been split in two and no longer has control over its various branches. Defections from their ranks are occurring almost daily throughout the Federation. They realize full well that, weakened in numbers and spirit, they cannot gain their object by the continuation of terrorist methods and of their so-called armed struggle.

5.   Consequently, by sending this letter they hope to change their tactics by exploiting the natural desire of the people for peace and to persuade them to relax the fight against Communism. It is a typical Communist "peace offensive". The ultimate aim of Communism remains unchanged. It is to overthrow as early as possible whatever established Government may be in power and to substitute for it a Communist regime. We all know that this is not the way to freedom. The Communists view with distaste the forthcoming elections and the move to self-government by elected representation. It seems they want now, before the recognized national political parties have contested the elections, to suspend temporarily the Communist armed struggle and to revert to other forms of subversion, whilst keeping themselves free to renew their terrorism when it suits them. This letter is therefore a last-minute attempt to spread confusion and uncertainty amongst the political parties. They who have fought and committed countless atrocities against the people of Malaya without regard to race or creed, now pose as the purveyors of peace.

6.   We have seen these sudden shifts in Communist policy before and we shall not be misled by this one. We have not forgotten the chaos the Communists attempted to bring about between 1945 and 1948.

7.   Knowing the true purpose of the Communist offer and these motives which underlie it, the Government rejects it absolutely and has no intention of negotiating with the Communist terrorists.

8.   If the Communists genuinely wish to end the Emergency they can do this today. Liberal terms of surrender are already offered to them and are known to all, as is being demonstrated by many who are taking advantage of them. They are aware

that no one who has voluntarily surrendered since July 1949 has been tried on a capital charge but they have been fairly dealt with and well-treated. Furthermore, as stated on the 17th January, Government keeps the surrender policy under constant review so that it can be modified at any time if it should appear that a greater or lesser measure of amnesty would hasten the end of terrorism.

9. While reaffirming its desire for peace, the Government will not accept the Communist type of peace. The responsibility of the Government is to ensure that conditions exist in Malaya which will enable its people to move forward towards independence without the fear of Communist domination in any form.

Annex to 352

In accordance with the orders of the Supreme Command HQ regarding the problem of ending the war and achieving independence in Malaya by negotiation, I issue the following statement:—

(1) The one and only object of our struggle is a peaceful, democratic and independent Malaya. If only this is possible, we are willing, always, to strive by peaceful means, to achieve the aforesaid objective. It goes without saying that the achievement of independence in Malaya, through peaceful means, would be beneficial, not only to the Malayan people, but to the British Government and the British people as well.

However, it must be pointed out that up till now, the British Government, under various pretexts, is still continuing its colonial rule. It has maintained an indifferent attitude over the resolutions of the Afro-Asian Conference regarding the rights and self-determination of the people, and matters concerning the peoples of protected territories. At present, there is a common basic characteristic in the constitutional system prevailing in Singapore and the Federation of Malaya. The British Government has wide powers relating to defence, foreign affairs and finance. The British Governor or High Commissioner has the power to veto the laws passed by the Legislative Council. Foreign troops have the right to be stationed throughout the whole of Malaya. Moreover, they have the right to establish and to enlarge military bases in various parts of Malaya, which are only used for the benefit of foreign countries. If this state of affairs is not rectified, Malaya will never achieve independence, and democractic [sic] freedom, and the rights of the people will not be reliably safeguarded. Hence, there is a possibility that, in the interests of foreign countries Malaya may be dragged into a war of Asians killing Asians—the people will have to pay the grievous price of a war, which they have no right to question, and which does not further their personal interests. These facts cannot be concealed by the partial election, or the full election in the future, of members of the Legislative Council.

(2) In order to strive for peace and to achieve independence in Malaya, it is imperative that, firstly, the war must be ended, the Emergency Regulations must be abolished and the democratic freedom and rights of the people must be safeguarded, to enable a general national election to be carried out in a peaceful and democratic atmosphere.

All the various political parties, guilds and associations, and the people of various communities and walks of life of Malaya, who are sincerely and truthfully striving for independence, regardless of the various strata to which they belong, their stand in respect of independence or their demeanour in the past, can and should be united together to vigorously strive for the achievement of their common objective of ending the war and achieving independence in Malaya, by peaceful means.

Hence, we are of the opinion that the representatives of various political parties, guilds, associations and communities should endeavour to hold a round table conference at an early date, to thoroughly discuss the problems of ending the war and achieving peace and independence in Malaya with the object of reaching unanimous agreement, conforming with the actual state of affairs of Malaya. Such an agreement will definitely expedite the ending of the war, and the achievement of peace and independence of Malaya— it will be a major contribution towards a policy conforming with the personal benefits of the various strata of people throughout the country.

We would manifest a positive and co-operative disposition towards this conference. It is without doubt that, due to various races having their own special problems and various differences in political outlook, there certainly will be many discrepancies and disagreements in the opinions of persons attending this conference. But, as all will have the same objective, should all manifest an attitude of mutual understanding and respect for each other, and seek out the views common to all, and permit differences of outlook to be discussed in a democratic spirit, a unanimous agreement on major important problems will definitely be reached at the conference. In this respect, the success of the Afro-Asian Conference and the successful negotiation between the Governments of China and Indonesia on the question of dual nationality have set good examples for the peoples of Malaya.

(3) The amnesty proposal put up by the Alliance leaders of the UMNO, MCA and MIC is not satisfactory to us. In order to end this warfare early, and to show our sincerity in this matter, we are willing to compromise by holding negotiations on the basis of this proposal with the British Government, and come to a reasonable agreement. At the same time, we are willing to have discussions with the UMNO, MCA and MIC and any other political parties which support the ending of the present warfare by negotiation.

We must point out that any attempt to intrigue and force people to surrender is completely unreasonable and illusive. The present situation is this: It is almost 7 years now since the Emergency started, and in spite of the thousands of methods adopted by the British Government to liquidate us, it has failed to do so, and neither has it defeated us in war, because we are supported by the great masses of people, and hence we will never be defeated in this war. With regard to this point, Mr. Lyttelton, the former Secretary for Colonial Affairs had to use the term "possible" in his speech to the British Rubber Manufacturers' Association on 24th March last year. He said: "It is possible that we will never achieve complete victory". The complete victory which he referred to is similar to the victory in Europe and the victory over Japan. We confidently believe that the situation within and without Malaya is daily favouring the independence of Malaya, and that the time-factor is favourable towards the people of Malaya and is unfavourable to the colonial rulers who insist on continuing colonial rule.

(4) With regard to the holding of meetings in the jungle, especially in making arrangements for the first meeting, as this would cause difficulty and inconvenience to both parties, we are willing to send our representative to Kuala Lumpur to make arrangements for the meeting, provided that the British Government will guarantee us the safe conduct of our representative. If the British Government agrees to direct negotiation or allows the responsible political parties to have discussions with us, you can inform me at any time through the radio or through the Press. On receipt of your notice, I will start on my journey (to Kuala Lumpur) immediately.

On our side, the door to negotiation in the past, present and future is always open. We are now making one big step forward. For this reason, whether negotiations materialise or not solely depends on the attitude of the British Government.

Signed: Ng Heng[1]
Representative of the Supreme
Command Headquarters of the
Malayan Racial [sic] Liberation Army
Dated: 1.5.1955

---

[1] The official view was that this was a pseudonym.

353   CO 1030/319, no 35   27 June 1955
[Communists' first peace offer]: minute no PM(55)38 by Mr Lennox-Boyd to Sir A Eden

Prime Minister

In my minute of the 23rd June[1] about the Communist terrorists' offer of negotiations I said how glad I was that the leaders of public and political opinion in the Federation of Malaya had agreed to reject it. You replied that you agreed but asked what the politicians were likely to do after the election.

I see no reason at present to fear that they will attempt to withdraw from the position which they have now taken up in relation to negotiations, but I think that they may well revert to a proposal which the Alliance already have in their programme for some sort of so-called "amnesty". In fact, by "amnesty" they do not mean what the term connotes in normal usage: what they have in mind is rather an open guarantee, subject to a time-limit, that any surrendering terrorist will not be prosecuted, although other conditions will have to be attached to the surrender. The proposal for a general "amnesty" has its dangers for the following reasons. The existing surrender policy is in fact a running "amnesty" since, although no guarantee has ever been given to the terrorists that those who surrender will not be prosecuted, no prosecution on a capital charge has in fact been brought against a surrendered terrorist since 1949. Consequently, over the years confidence has been built up among the terrorists that they will not be so prosecuted, and that they will be decently treated if they surrender. If a general "amnesty" were declared and failed, we

---

[1] See 351.

should have to revert to the existing surrender policy but the confidence of the terrorists in it would inevitably have been at least badly shaken; and until it could be restored there would almost certainly be a sharp reduction in the present very satisfactory level of surrenders, especially among ranking terrorists. On the other hand, I believe that, if it becomes politically expedient to attempt some sort of "amnesty", there are ways of avoiding this risk. I have already indicated my views on it to the Federation authorities and they are now going into the question as a matter of urgency. I will let you know of any developments as they occur.

I am grateful for your interest in the question and it encourages me to repeat the suggestion which, I understand, has already been made to you, that you should see the High Commissioner, Sir Donald MacGillivray, while he is over here. He is out of London at present but will be back again from the 11th to the 13th July inclusive. I am sure that you would find it very well worth while to have even a short talk with him and I greatly hope that that will prove possible.

354 CO 1030/230, no 11 [July 1955]
'Malayanisation of the public service in the Federation of Malaya': CO brief for Mr Lennox-Boyd

Views of the Alliance
The Malayanisation of the Public Service in the Federation is one of the main planks in the programme of the U.M.N.O.–M.C.A.–M.I.C. Alliance which is likely to emerge from the elections on the 27th July as the dominant party. The other political parties are also committed to Malayanisation in greater or less degree. The Alliance has summarised its proposals as follows:—

> "To Malayanise the Public Service substantially within the first term of office; to accelerate the rate of Malayanisation by replacing expatriate officers (on abolition terms) by Malayan officers; and to allow no further recruitment of expatriate officers without prior reference to the Executive Council;
> to provide training facilities to fit present Malayan officers for higher posts;
> to give more scholarships to both serving Malayan officers and to students fresh from school;
> to protect the rights of pensioners".

> A fuller statement of the Alliance's proposals is at pp. 12–13 of the "Alliance Platform for the Federal Elections", a copy of which is at Annex "A".[1]

The Committee on the Malayanisation of the Government Service
2. The Federation Government have already given considerable thought to the question of Malayanisation. In July, 1953, a Committee on the Malayanisation of the Government Service was constituted to investigate the extent to which higher posts in the Public Service are at present filled by Malayans and the prospects of increasing the number of Malayans in such posts. The Committee reported in August, 1954: a copy of its Report is attached as Annex "B". The Committee examined the position in

---

[1] Annexes not printed.

detail in each Government Department and reached certain general conclusions (the latter are at pages 2–8 of the Report). It found that there are very few Malayans at present in the Public Service who have the necessary qualifications and experience now required for appointment to the higher posts (page 3, paragraph 2), and that, although the supply of qualified Malayans would increase over the years ahead, there would still be a serious shortage of good local candidates in most Departments. The Committee drew attention to the dangers which would result from the admission of Malayan candidates with inferior qualifications and advised against the artificial creation of vacancies in order to hasten Malayanisation (page 6, paragraph 11), declaring that Malayanisation should not, as a general policy, proceed faster than the normal occurrence of vacancies. The Committee's Report was the subject of a despatch (No. 169/55 of the 11th February, 1955) from the High Commissioner, a copy of which is at Annex "C".[2] Paragraph 6 of that despatch on the subject of expatriate recruitment, is of particular importance.

3. No action has been taken on the Committee's Report pending the Federal elections and the constitution of a new Executive and Legislative Council. The Federation Government decided that, during the months immediately before the elections, the political parties could not be expected to take a sober and balanced view of the subject, and, since there was no demand for discussion of the Report the question was put into cold storage until after the elections.

Views of the high commissioner

4. The question of the course which the Malayanisation campaign would be likely to take when the new Executive and Legislative Councils have resumed Office was discussed between Sir J. Martin and Sir D. MacGillivray during the latter's recent visit to London. Sir D. MacGillivray said that the Alliance leaders knew that the proposal in their election Manifesto to replace expatriate officers by Malayan officers in the near future on abolition terms was no more than an electioneering promise. The leaders themselves realised that there were not enough suitably qualified Malayans to take the place of expatriates and that the question of abolition terms had still to be worked out. The Alliance had also proposed that no further recruitment of expatriate officers should be allowed without prior reference to the Executive Council. Sir D. MacGillivray believed that this was a demand which could be met, provided that such reference was confined to classes of appointment and did not involve Executive Council being consulted on individual cases.

5. In this connexion the High Commissioner hoped that the proposed Public Service Commission would be able to give sound advice to the Executive Council on the question of recruiting expatriate officers. (Legislation to set up a Public Service Commission is at present in train, but consideration of the Bill has been suspended until after the new Legislative Council has taken office. A copy of the Legislative Council paper on the subject of the establishment of the Commission is attached to the High Commissioner's despatch at Annex "C"). Thus, if the Public Service Commission were to recommend that expatriate officers were required for certain types of posts, the High Commissioner thought it would be legitimate for this recommendation to go to the High Commissioner in Executive Council. The Executive Council might agree that this recommendation was justified at the time

---

[2] See 344.

but might foresee that suitably qualified Malayans were likely to become available within the next five years or so and therefore call for the appointment of expatriates on contract terms only and not on permanent and pensionable terms. Sir D. MacGillivray considered that the anxiety of the political parties in the Federation to ensure that as and when local men became qualified over the next twenty years or so there should be vacancies for them and that the way should not be blocked by numbers of expatriates on permanent and persionable terms was a reasonable one. Acceptance of this system would also have the salutary result of making Ministers face up to the current market rates necessary to secure men on contract and to the immediate burden of paying the resulting gratuities.

6. Sir D. MacGillivray thought that if such a system were accepted, he would not be able to get any more administrative officers on permanent and pensionable terms. This would mean that he would get no Chinese speaking officers. He would try to secure a few on permanent and pensionable terms on the understanding that they would all be trained in Chinese and deal with Chinese affairs, but if, as was likely, he failed to secure them, he would have to propose that some Malayans recruited as administrative officers must be prepared to become Chinese specialists. In general, the High Commissioner believes that one of the great difficulties in the future will be to resist a demand from politicians for lowering the standards for admission to the Public Service. Such a demand would not, he thought, be supported by senior Asian members of the Service. If and when he was faced with it, he proposed to take the line that one must rely on the expert advice tendered by the Public Service Commission as to the standards necessary.

Dissolution of the Malayan establishment

7. A further subject which should be mentioned in this context is the dissolution of the Malayan Establishment which took effect on the 1st July, 1954. The Malayan Establishment was set up in 1934 to control the distribution among States and Settlements in Malaya of the senior Government officers who had been recruited from abroad and were liable for service throughout Malaya. Although the Malayan Establishment was a useful instrument in the conditions of pre-war Malaya with its multiplicity of authorities, by 1952 when there were only two parties in the Malayan Establishment Agreement—the Federation of Malaya and the Colony of Singapore—it had become apparent that the Malayan Establishment system was in need of revision. A Committee was accordingly set up to consider the future of the Malayan Establishment Office: it reported in November, 1952, recommending that the Malayan Establishment Office be abolished and its present functions absorbed by the Service Branch and the Establishment Office of the two Governments; that each officer must be regarded as on the establishment of the Government under which he may be serving at the time, provided that the right to be considered for service and promotion in both territories is preserved for all officers of the Malayan Establishment; and that there should be free transferability between the two territories for all officers whenever it is considered desirable by both Governments. A copy of the Federal Legislative Council Paper summarising the question is at Annex "D".

8. The Malayan Civil Service Association addressed the Secretary of State in March, 1954, petitioning against the dissolution of the Malayan Establishment, and The European Civil Servants' Association of Malaya (T.E.C.S.A.M.) also declared that they were opposed to dissolution. The Secretary of State replied saying that, in his

view, immediate practical considerations required the dissolution of the Malayan Establishment but that he fully realised the importance of facilitating transfers between the Federation and Singapore, and of considering the claims of officers in both territories for promotion posts in either territory. A copy of the Malayan Civil Service Association's letter and of the Secretary of State's despatch are at Annex "E".

355 CO 1030/51, no 71   14 July 1955

'Memorandum explanatory of Sir D MacGillivray's proposals for national schools in Malaya': memorandum by CO Far Eastern Dept

[Following Eden's support for MacGillivray's proposals for national schools (see 345 and 347), the CO considered an application for Treasury funding and sent a copy of this memorandum to A E Drake, assistant-secretary at the Treasury (see also 364).]

The different races in Malaya think of themselves primarily as Malays, Chinese or Indians and only secondarily, if at all, as Malayans. No plans for defence against communist aggression from without and subversion from within can have a full chance of success so long as the people are thus left without a common outlook on fundamental questions. It is therefore urgently necessary to create a united Malayan nation, aware and proud of being Malayan. This is not to say that a new and united Malaya would, by its mere existence, necessarily prevent the country from going communist or from seeking to join the neutrals. But it would provide one of the essential conditions—probably the most important—under which efforts to hold Malaya for the West would have a good chance of success.

2. The process of nation-building, although recognised as essential by the authorities and some sections of local opinion, has so far made slow progress. The situation can be radically changed by one means only, reforms in the educational system which will make it an effective stimulant to national consciousness. The need is for schools, dedicated to promoting Malayan unity, in which children of all races may grow up together, learning each his mother-tongue as a subject of study but being taught through the medium of a common language. The common language must be the *lingua franca* of the country, English. Only thus can racial exclusiveness, at present fostered by the vernacular system of education which predominates in Malaya, be broken down.

3. The desirability of building new schools of this kind has been officially accepted since the enactment of the Education Ordinance of 1952, in which they are described as "English-medium National Schools". But, owing partly to Chinese opposition and partly to lack of money, only one such National School has so far been brought into existence.

4. In 1953 the number of children of primary school age was 1,141,000, 610,000 of whom were enrolled in vernacular schools and 90,000 in English schools (the rest receiving no education). A step towards creating a true educational melting-pot is now being taken by the conversion of the English primary schools into National-type schools. Moreover, the greater part of such secondary education as is available is already of this type, as are the Teacher Training Colleges and the University of Malaya. But this alone will not suffice, as is indicated by the enrolment figure for vernacular schools. It is estimated that the minimum addition with which it might

be hoped to turn the scale is 300 new English-medium National Schools, giving 168,000 new places in all.

5. It is accordingly proposed to build these schools over the next 13 years (work on 50 new schools being started in each of the years 1956 to 1962), together with 2 more Teacher Training Colleges to staff them, at an estimated total cost of some £27 million.[1] The schools will have 560 places each and will be carefully sited in selected rural areas, where they should become so many strong points in the struggle against communism. If they are successful, their effect on the community will be out of all proportion to their numbers.

6. The Federation Government have not the money to pay for this scheme. Moreover, although an elected Government in the Federation would be happy enough, if funds were available, to sanction expenditure of this order on education, it is unlikely that it would willingly devote the money to building schools of this particular kind. If, therefore the scheme is to go through Her Majesty's Government must bless it and "underwrite" it financially. It is hoped that after the elections the new Government may be persuaded to proceed with the scheme from local resources on the understanding that Her Majesty's Government, when considering year by year the general financial needs of the country, would take the cost of this scheme into account, as they already take account of certain other of the Federation's financial commitments.

---

[1] To their embarrassment officials of the Far Eastern Department later discovered that the figure £27 million was incorrect and that the scheme involved constructing 300 national schools at a cost of £44.6 million spread over a number of years.

356 CAB 129/76, CP(55)81   20 July 1955
'Federation of Malaya: constitutional development': Cabinet memorandum by Mr Lennox-Boyd

[Anticipating renewed pressure for constitutional change once the federal elections were over, Lennox-Boyd planned a visit to Malaya between 21 Aug and 2 Sept, during which he hoped to take the initiative along lines outlined here. Drafts of this paper contained a longer introduction on the following theme: 'It is, therefore, very necessary to dispel the idea that self-government and the retention of British protection are incompatible', and politicians in Malaya should be brought 'face to face with the hard facts of how they are to ensure their survival against hostile forces' (CO 1030/70, no 1).]

The first elections to the Federal Legislative Council in Malaya will take place on 27th July and will result in a Council with a small majority of elected members.

2. All the major political parties contesting the elections have already committed themselves to secure the establishment of some sort of Commission to examine the constitution with a view to recommending a rapid advancement towards self-government.

3. It is certain that after the elections pressure for such an advance will mount rapidly and, unless the initiative is first taken by us, it will lead to extravagant and competitive claims by political leaders for early self-government, taking no account of the fact that the Federation of Malaya will for some time to come be quite unable without outside help to defend itself against external aggression, to maintain internal security or even to balance its budget. It is therefore important to anticipate this

development and to bring the leaders of political opinion in the Federation to face the need to make satisfactory arrangements to ensure their survival against hostile forces before they proceed to the more congenial task of discussing the next stage of development towards internal self-government. If we do not make the next move, others will, with really embarrassing consequences.

4. The constitution of the Federation of Malaya is embodied in an Agreement between Her Majesty and the Rulers of the Malay States.[1] I suggest that the next step should therefore be to negotiate the substance of a new agreement incorporating satisfactory arrangements about certain fundamental points. The negotiations might take place between a team from the United Kingdom representing Her Majesty as one of the principals and a team representing the Rulers as the other principal. The leaders of political opinion in the Federation could participate as advisers to the Rulers. The objects of the talks would not be to negotiate any new constitution, but to incorporate in a new agreement satisfactory arrangements to cover the following points, before there is any further discussion of advance towards internal self-government.

(a) *Her Majesty's Government's responsibilities for the defence of the Federation.*—It is clear that the Federal Government will not be able to provide or pay for the forces necessary to protect it, unaided, from external aggression for many years to come, if ever. We should, therefore, seek from the Rulers a reiteration of their desire that we retain this responsibility; and to enable us to fulfil it when Malaya has become internally self-governing, the Rulers and their advisers should be asked to agree to provide the necessary facilities and to guarantee these by incorporation in the new agreement. This part of negotiations would in effect result in a form of agreement covering the establishment of United Kingdom military bases in the Federation.[2]

(b) *The maintenance of internal security in the Federation.*—The threat to the internal security of the Federation arises partly from the physical features of the country, partly from the plural nature of its society, but mainly from its close proximity to Communist China and its satellites, combined with the existence in the Federation of a large Chinese population. This imposes an unusually grave security threat which requires larger forces to meet than the Federation Government will be able to provide for some time to come. It will, therefore, be necessary for us to give some assistance, at least in the transitional period before full internal self-government: and it would be desirable to incorporate in the new agreement a clear and definite statement on the extent and manner of this assistance.

(c) *Reconsideration of the financial relationship between Her Majesty's Government and the Federation.*—It is clearly incompatible with even internal self-government that we should continue virtually to underwrite the financial position of the Federation generally and certain specific programmes, in particular those for education and the replanting of rubber. It is necessary to reach some settled

---

[1] Federation Agreement of 1948.

[2] This paragraph took into account the relevant section of the Report on Colonial Security by General Templer, commissioned by the Cabinet after his return from Malaya. Templer pointed out that the costs of local defence, on the one hand, and advances towards self-government, on the other, posed a complicated problem which should 'be tackled as a matter of urgency' (CO 1030/70, no 2).

formula on the extent of our financial assistance. The objective of such an agreement should be to ensure that any assistance which has to be given during the period of transition towards self-government can be tapered off during that period. Full self-government and financial dependence are not compatible and even if it might eventually be necessary in the special circumstances of Malaya to devise some means of assistance after full internal self-government has been granted, no such suggestion will be made to Malayan leaders at this stage. It is also necessary that there should be specific agreement in regard to any further financial assistance which may be necessary to finance development projects during the transition period. In the absence of such formulae and agreement it must be expected that there would be irresponsibility by the Federal Government in financial matters.

(d) *The relationship of Her Majesty's Government in the United Kingdom to the Federation*.—This would determine the status and functions of the High Commissioner and his authority and responsibility in relation to such matters as defence and external affairs.

Opportunity might also be taken to seek agreement on two other issues in the course of these talks.

(e) *A Malayan nationality*.—The present citizenship laws are unsatisfactory in that they deny citizens' rights to large sections of the Chinese community and they stand in the way of the possibility of a satisfactory agreement with China on the subject of dual nationality. They also tend to admit as subjects of the United Kingdom and Colonies persons whose loyalty to the Crown is doubtful. There might, therefore, be great advantage in the recognition of a special Malayan nationality. This is a matter of such importance that it could properly be the subject of negotiation between Her Majesty's Government and the Rulers at the highest level.

(f) *The composition and terms of reference of a constitutional commission*.—If agreement were reached on the points enumerated at (a) to (e) above, then there would seem to be no good reason why proposals for further constitutional change, with a view to a further measure of self-government within a limited field, should not be worked out by a body consisting mainly of Malayans, with the addition of some expert advice about constitutional forms. In other words, the way should be clear for the appointment of a Commission to review the remaining points of the constitution as incorporated in the present Agreement and to make recommendations which would then be likely to be acceptable to us without putting us in the embarrassing position of having to reject popular demands on the grounds of security and defence.

5. The further constitutional change envisaged in the preceding paragraph could properly embrace the question of the constitutional position of the Rulers in a democratic form of government based on universal suffrage—a question that could only satisfactorily be solved by local discussion and agreement.

6. It is very desirable that the idea of negotiating the framework for further constitutional change towards self-government should be put to the Rulers and accepted by them at an early date. To leave the matter until there is strong pressure for the early appointment of a Commission to consider these changes, or until Malay nationalism has gathered further momentum or until the Emergency has petered

out and is no longer a present threat to the security of Malaya, might prejudice the satisfactory outcome of negotiations in regard to British bases and the fundamental issues of responsibility for external and internal defence. I therefore propose to discuss this matter during my forthcoming visit to the Federation with the Conference of Rulers and the elected Ministers of the new Federal Government and to try to reach agreement with them in principle on the need for such high-level talks.

7. I invite the agreement of my colleagues to the following propositions:—

(a) that we should seek to secure a new agreement with the Rulers, with the safeguards for the future I have set out above, before discussing any further advance towards internal self-government; and
(b) that I should discuss this proposal with the Rulers and with leaders of political opinion in the Federation during my forthcoming visit to Malaya.

357 CO 1030/70, no 6   [July 1955]
'Future constitutional development in the Federation of Malaya': CO brief on CP(55)81[1] for use by Mr Lennox-Boyd in Cabinet

Timing of proposed negotiations
The negotiations will probably take some time. It is unlikely that it will be possible to complete them at one series of meetings. Both parties are likely to wish to have an interval for reflection and consultation between the first meetings which will serve to clear the ground and enable them to put forward their respective proposals and the second series of meetings at which an attempt would be made to reach agreed solutions. It would probably be convenient for the one series of meetings to be held in the Federation and the other series in the United Kingdom. It is for consideration whether it would be more convenient for the first series of meetings to be held in the United Kingdom where the Secretary of State could more easily preside over the vital opening discussions, or in Malaya. The idea that the first series of meetings should be held in Malaya would receive strong local support and would follow the precedent set in the discussions leading up to the latest Nigerian Constitution. It will be necessary to give the new Government which will emerge from the elections on the 27th July, some time to settle down and formulate their ideas before the talks start.

2. The timetable for the discussions might therefore be:—

(a) January or February 1956 – Preliminary discussions in Malaya or London
(b) April or May 1956   – Final discussions in London or Malaya.

Composition of negotiating teams
3. It is suggested that the United Kingdom team should be led, at least in the decisive stages, by the Secretary of State himself. He is unlikely to be able to spare the time to be present throughout the discussions, and it would be desirable for him to have a deputy of sufficient standing to act for him when he cannot be present.
4. The teams should be of equal numbers and kept as small as possible in the

---

[1] See 356.

interests of efficiency. Each team will, of course, be attended by advisers as necessary. A team of at least six will be needed to represent various interests in the Federation and it is suggested that this number be adopted. The composition of the teams might therefore be on the following lines:—

United Kingdom team
Secretary of State for the Colonies
Colonial Office official
Legal Adviser (Sir Kenneth Roberts-Wray)
A Treasury official
A Ministry of Defence representative
Two officials from the Federation of Malaya
  (Chief Secretary and Attorney General)

Note: It is for consideration whether the High Commissioner should stay aloof or whether he should replace the Chief Secretary in which case he could be held to hold a watching brief for the Straits Settlements.

Federation of Malaya team
Three Mentri Mentri Besar representing the Rulers.
Three politicians representing the major parties.

5. *Federation of Malaya's need for help from the United Kingdom*
A note is attached[2] giving an indication of the extent to which the Federation is financially dependent on aid from the United Kingdom. Her Majesty's Government have repeatedly given assurances that they will not abandon Malaya to the hostile forces which threaten it and that satisfactory arrangements will continue to be made to safeguard the country from external aggression and internal subversion. The fulfilment of these two objectives involves the third proposition that the different races in the Federation must cooperate together to build up a united Malayan nation. The present citizenship laws hamper the achievement of this last requirement, hence the proposed discussion of a Malayan nationality mentioned in the following paragraph.

6. *A Malayan nationality*
A note on the qualifications for Federal citizenship is attached. These qualifications which depend in the case of non-Malays on the place of birth of the parents, make it very difficult for many Chinese to acquire citizenship in a country where there has been and is no adequate register of marriages and births to make it relatively easy to produce the necessary proofs. This is in part responsible for the fact that the electorate in the forthcoming elections will be over 80% Malay although the two communities are nearly equal in number. It is one of the main objectives of Chinese political leaders to acquire "jus soli" or the right of Federal citizenship for all persons born in the Federation. The Malay political leaders are hesitant to grant this.

The above citizenship difficulties do not apply in the Straits Settlements. Everyone born in the Settlements is a citizen of the United Kingdom and Colonies and can easily qualify as a Federal citizen by local residence.

7. *Composition and terms of reference of a constitutional commission*
There has been some local disagreement about the composition of any such

---

[2] Annexes not printed.

commission. The Alliance have tended to favour a commission drawn from outside the Federation and recruited from the countries of the Commonwealth while Party Negara has tended to favour a local commission. It will be necessary in due course to reach local agreement on this point.

8. *Constitutional position of the rulers*

The position of the Rulers is bound to change as the constitutions of their States develop. In the past they have exercised their authority through an administration headed by a Mentri Besar appointed by the Ruler at his discretion with the aid of a nominated legislature. Developments are leading towards popularly elected State legislatures and it seems likely that in future the Mentri Besar will become a political figure relying on the support of the legislature and occupying the position of a Prime Minister in a democracy. The implications of this change on the position and powers of the Sultans must be worked out locally. It will also be necessary to consider the future powers and responsibilities of the Conference of Rulers and whether these might not be delegated to an Upper House.

9. *Present constitution*

A note is attached showing the composition of the Executive and Legislative Councils under the new Constitution.

Treasury amendments

10. Treasury consent to the circulation of this paper was necessary as it involves financial matters. They gave this subject to two amendments which are underlined. The purpose of these amendments is two-fold:—

(a) to reiterate the general Treasury principle that self-government and financial dependence are incompatible.

(b) to reserve the position of the Treasury over the grant of aid to the Federation after complete internal self-government is attained.

Sir Donald MacGillivray was consulted over the Treasury amendments and agreed to them.

358   CAB 128/29, CM 25(55)8   21 July 1955
'Malaya': Cabinet conclusions on CP(55)81[1]

The Cabinet considered a memorandum by the Secretary of State for the Colonies (C.P.(55)81) seeking approval for the basis on which the Colonial Secretary should begin to discuss with the Rulers of the Malay States a revision of the present arrangements governing the constitutional position of Malaya.

The Colonial Secretary said that there were a number of fundamental points on which he proposed to have preliminary discussions with the Rulers of the Malay States and leaders of political opinion in the Federation, in the course of his forthcoming tour. The points on which it was essential for the United Kingdom to keep the initiative in the development of plans for self-Government in Malaya were:—

---

[1] See 356.

(i)   the United Kingdom Government's responsibility for the defence of Malaya;
(ii) the maintenance of internal security in the Federation;
(iii) reconsideration of the financial arrangements with the Federation;
(iv) the relationship of the United Kingdom Government to the Federation;
(v)   the question of a Malayan nationality, and
(vi) the question of setting up a Constitutional Commission.

In discussion, the following points were raised:—

(a) Malaya was relatively prosperous at present and it should be made clear to its people that, if their aim was full self-Government, they must as a corollary make every effort to pay their own way. If, as seemed likely, we were to be obliged to provide them with considerable financial assistance for a long period, we should endeavour to ensure that the future security of our commercial interests in Malaya was safeguarded. Our financial stake in the Federation was one of the buttresses of the sterling area.
(b) It was suggested that we should not miss any opportunity of strengthening the link between Singapore and Malaya. The present position under which the two areas were constitutionally on a different footing was anomalous. On the other hand, unification with Singapore would weaken the Rulers.
(c) Australia and New Zealand had both now agreed to keep troops in the area in precaution and should be kept informed of the progress of the Colonial Secretary's negotiations. It was also desirable that the South-East Asia Collective Defence Treaty Powers[2] should be kept informed.
(d) The present relationship between the Governor of Singapore and his new Chief Minister (Mr. Marshall)[3] was unsatisfactory and had been brought to a head by two motions tabled in the Singapore Chamber for the following day. *The Colonial Secretary* said that he hoped that Mr. Marshall would remain in office until he arrived in Singapore.

The Cabinet:—

(1) Approved the proposals in C.P.(55)81, subject to the points made in discussion.
(2) Invited the Colonial Secretary, in consultation with the Commonwealth Secretary and the Minister of State for Foreign Affairs, to arrange for the Governments of Australia and New Zealand and the South-East Asia Collective Defence Treaty Powers to be kept informed, as necessary, about the progress of his discussions on constitutional development in Malaya.

---

[2] ie Australia, France, New Zealand, Pakistan, the Philippines, Thailand and the USA. See 335, note.
[3] David Marshall, leader of Singapore's Labour Front, became chief minister of Singapore after the elections of Apr 1955; he resigned in June 1956 when he failed to win a British commitment to full internal self-government by Apr 1957.

359 CO 1030/70, no 42   30 July 1955
[Secretary of state's visit to Malaya]: letter from Sir D MacGillivray to
Mr Lennox-Boyd

When, a fortnight ago, you discussed with me in London the proposal that you
should, when in the Federation next month, discuss with the Rulers' Conference and
political leaders the question of the manner in which consideration should now be
given to further constitutional development, you decided to put to the Cabinet a
paper[1] proposing:—

(a) that you should seek to secure a new agreement with the Rulers containing
certain safeguards for the future before discussing further advance towards
internal self-government, and
(b) that you should discuss this matter with the Rulers and with leaders of
political opinion in the Federation during your forthcoming visit.

2. The Malay Rulers never like to rush things and always like time to consider
new propositions and to discuss them among themselves and with their principal
Malay advisers before committing themselves to any view. They are never likely to
forget the strong reaction of their subjects to the so-called MacMichael treaties. It
was with this consideration in mind that I advised that, in advance of your meeting
with the Rulers, they should be given an indication of the suggestion you propose to
make to them that early negotiations should take place between representatives of
the two parties to the Federal Agreement with a view to determining certain
fundamental issues, such as external defence and future financial relations. It was on
this advice that you signed a letter to each of the Rulers notifying them of your desire
to meet with them in Rulers' Conference during your visit and attaching a note
indicating the substance of your proposals. It was left to me to draft and attach that
note.

3. I have not yet heard the outcome of the consideration of your proposals by the
Cabinet[2] and I have, therefore, not yet despatched your letter to the Rulers. I have,
however, notified them that you regret that time does not permit you to visit each of
the State capitals and that, therefore, you hope it will be convenient for them to meet
with you in Kuala Lumpur on the 23rd August.[3] I have also conveyed to them
invitations to dine that evening so that they may now make their plans to come to
Kuala Lumpur on that date. Meantime, the situation has been somewhat changed by
the overwhelming Alliance victory at the Federal Elections, where they have
captured 51 of the 52 seats for elected members and received 80% of the total votes.[4]
The Alliance election campaign was really fought on the single platform of early
independence and the Alliance can therefore justly claim that they now have a
mandate from the people to press for this. In yesterday's "Straits Times" Tunku
Abdul Rahman is quoted as saying that "The British Government cannot ignore the
fact that our tremendous success resulted from this issue of independence and
nothing else" and that "talks on a fully elected legislature and independence will be
opened when the Colonial Secretary, Mr. Alan Lennox-Boyd, arrives here next
month". He is reported to have gone on to say that "Constitutional reform will

---

[1] See 356.   [2] See 358.   [3] See 367.   [4] See 361.

absorb the thoughts of the new Government" and that the present constitution is not workable and that the Alliance will call for the appointment of a special commission. This report also indicates that Tunku Abdul Rahman is contemplating abandoning the idea of an independent commission from outside Malaya and is ready to accept what we know to be the Rulers' view that the commission should come from within Malaya but with an outside Chairman. The Tunku, however, modifies this view with a suggestion that the Chairman should come "from India or Ceylon or some other country" rather than from the United Kingdom.

4. All this emphasises the need for early agreement that certain fundamental issues should be negotiated first and that, while you are here, there should be discussions as to the manner in which these issues can be settled. Since, however, Tunku Abdul Rahman has now indicated that the Alliance proposes to raise the matter of constitutional reform with you, I think it might be better tactics to hold your proposals until the Alliance leaders have themselves opened the subject. If, however, I were now to send to the Rulers a note giving an indication of your proposals there is no doubt that this would get to the ears of the Alliance before they would have an opportunity of discussions with you (it has never been possible to depend on the secrecy of communications to the Rulers regarding political issues) and I think this might very well impair relations between them and ourselves at this delicate stage. Moreover, I understand from Raja Uda and the Keeper of the Rulers' Seal that the Rulers will undoubtedly wish to raise certain matters with you, amongst these being the proposal for a special commission to study the problem of further constitutional reform, and that they will, in any case, meet together before their meeting with you, to discuss these matters among themselves. In these circumstances It would, on balance, be a disadvantage to send to the Rulers, in advance of your meeting with them, a note outlining your proposals, and it would, I think, be better both at this meeting and at your discussion with the Alliance leaders to hold these proposals in reserve until you have heard what representations they themselves may have to make. There might, however, be some advantage if I were, meantime, to try and find out what would be the likely reaction to your proposals both on the part of the Rulers and on the part of the Alliance leaders should you decide to put them forward formally at your meetings with them. I could do this by tentative and non-committal suggestions in conversation with the Alliance leaders. I shall be glad to know if you would wish me to do this. Such informal conversations might prepare the ground for you and it might be as well to know how the land lies before you yourself become involved or seem to be committed in any way to specific proposals.

5. If you agree that it is best not to send any note at present to the Rulers, I shall be very grateful if you will sign the revised letters to the Rulers which I am sending to MacKintosh and which I will ask him to return to me. I am sorry to bother you with this at a time when you will be fully engaged with Singapore problems. If you would like to discuss the position with me, I could come down to Singapore and see you at any time you may appoint on Monday.

6. I should mention that, as a result of statements made by Alliance leaders, and the Alliance's sweeping victory at the polls, the expatriate element of the Civil Service are extremely anxious about their future and that the Staff Associations will wish to make representations to you about this when you are here. It is, I think, very necessary that they should be given firm reassurances and also that the present

position in regard to expatriate staff should be made clear to the political leaders on the lines of the statement contained in your personal telegram to Nicoll, No. 21 of 18th May, the relevant extract from which I enclose for ease of reference.[5] I am writing separately about this. This question of the position of expatriate officers is, incidentally, one which might be added to the fundamental issues for discussion and settlement between representatives of the two parties to the Federal Agreement before any consideration can be given to further advance towards self-Government.

P.S. Until recently the Alliance have indicated that they proposed, if they were returned to power at the elections, to try and make the new Constitution work. Indeed, in the exchange of letters[6] between myself and Tunku Abdul Rahman last year in regard to the "nominated reserve" Members of the Legislative Council, which letters were published, he stated that the Alliance was "satisfied that the proposed constitutional arrangements have a reasonable prospect of working satisfactorily and the Alliance is, therefore, prepared to extend its support to the establishment of these arrangements". But recent events in Singapore appear to have influenced the Alliance's attitude towards this, and you will note from my quotation from the "Straits Times" that the Tunku now appears to take the stand that the new Constitution is unworkable. It can work only if there is good-will and a genuine attempt to make it work until such time as it is replaced by something else. I fear that, if no prospect is held out of very early discussions of constitutional issues, the Alliance will take a leaf out of Marshall's book and try and force our hand by endeavouring to demonstrate that the present constitution does not work in practice.

I have not been able to see Tunku Abdul Rahman since the results of the Election were known. He is away in Johore taking a rest over the Malay public holiday (and making contact with Marshall) and I shall not now see him until Sunday morning.[7]

---

[5] Not printed.   [6] See 334.   [7] See 360.

360   CO 1030/225, no 3   3 Aug 1955
[The new Executive and Legislative Councils]: inward telegram no 451 from Sir D MacGillivray to Mr Lennox-Boyd on the federal elections and the appointment of Tunku Abdul Rahman's Cabinet

Tunku Abdul Rahman came to see me on Sunday morning for a discussion of the various matters which have to be settled following the Alliance's success at the polls. Since then I have had two other meetings with him on Monday and the following summarises the main points on which agreement has been reached. The intention was that an official announcement should be made of the appointments to Ministerial posts on the 5th August after I had had time to communicate to the Rulers, in accordance with the new Clause 72(2A) of the Federal Agreement on the proposed rearrangement of certain Portfolios and the names of the persons who are to be appointed as Ministers. But the appointments have now appeared in full in this morning's newspapers. I have not been able to ascertain who was responsible for the 'leak', but Tunku Abdul Rahman assures me that he was not (corrupt gp. ? the culprit).

2. I first disposed of the question of Tunku Abdul Rahman's own title and agreed to 'Chief Minister'. Although the position differs from that in Singapore, there seemed little point in withholding the title which he clearly expected to be given.

3. We next discussed the filling of the five reserved seats on Legislative Council on which I was bound by the undertaking[1] given last year to consult with the Leader of the Party winning the greatest number of elected seats. You will recollect that the purpose of these seats was to give a voice in the Council to any major element which did not secure adequate representation through either the electoral or nominating processes. These processes had produced a Council consisting of 50 Malays, 22 Chinese, five Indians, two Ceylonese, one Eurasian and 12 Europeans (including five Officials), a total of 92, leaving the five reserved seats and the representative of Malacca Settlement, who cannot be appointed yet since the Settlement Council has been dissolved pending Settlement elections. I told Tunku Abdul Rahman that it seemed to me that there was no major element other than racial elements which was not adequately represented, but that, in relation to population figures, I considered the Chinese and Indian communities to be insufficiently represented and that I would wish three of the reserved seats to go to Chinese and two to Indians (preferably local-born Indians); this would give the Chinese 25 seats (and possibly one more from Malacca) and the Indians 7. He at once accepted this view. I then expressed a wish that two of the seats should, if possible, be filled by women as there would otherwise be only one woman on the Council; although he himself was willing to appoint Mrs. Oon[2] and one Indian lady, the Alliance Executive would have nothing of this and, in the end, the Chief Minister has not been able to meet me on this point. He then put forward the following three names, which I was able to accept:—

(i)   H.S. Lee
(ii) S.M. Yong[3]—a Kuala Lumpur lawyer and prominent member of the M.C.A.
(iii) A. [sic] L. Devaser[4]—a prominent member and former president of the M.I.C.

There was some discussion spreading over the three meetings in between each of which the Chief Minister consulted with the Alliance Executive in regard to the remaining two seats. The M.I.C. pressed strongly for the second Indian seat, but the M.I.C. command support from only a section of the Indian community and are already more than adequately represented on the Council. Eventually agreement was reached between myself and Tunku Abdul Rahman to appoint M.N. Cumarasami—a local-born Indian lawyer with no political affiliations. The Chinese members of the Alliance are as yet unable to reach agreement amongst themselves as to the third Chinese and for the present this seat is being left vacant.

4. The next question to be settled was that of Ministerial appointments. The Chief Minister has been having considerable difficulty with the Chinese and Indians over this. The following are the finally agreed appointments:—

Chief Minister and Minister
for Home Affairs   Tunku Abdul Rahman
Minister for Transport   H.S. Lee

[1] See 334.   [2] Oon Beng Hong, member of the Federal Legislative Council, 1949–1955.
[3] Legal adviser to the Alliance National Council.
[4] Kunden Lal Devasar was president, Malayan Indian Congress, 1951–1955.

Minister for Natural Resources	Dr. Ismail bin Dato Abdul Rahman
Minister for Education	Dato Abdul Razak bin Hussein
Minister for Health and Social Welfare	Leong Yew Koh
Minister for Labour	V.T. Sambanthan
Minister for Local Government Housing and Town Planning	Inche Suleiman bin Dato Abdul Rahman
Minister for Agriculture	Inche Abdul Aziz bin I Hak [sic]
Minister for Works	Inche Sardon bin Haji Jubir
Minister for Posts and Telecommunications	Ong Yoke Lin.

Biographies will be sent by savingram. Only major change is creation of post of Minister for Agriculture by removal of certain Departments for over-burdened Natural Resources Portfolio. I am relieved that it has been possible to keep the number of Ministries down to ten. The Executive Council will now consist of these ten plus the three *ex-officio* Members and the Minister for Economic Affairs (Spencer) and the Secretary for Defence (Humphrey),[5] making a total of 15, the minimum number permitted by the Federation of Malaya Agreement.

5. The Chief Minister asked for five or six posts of Assistant Minister at our first discussion, but has since reduced this to two only on the understanding that further appointments may be made later when experience has been gained of where the need will be greatest. The two appointments I have agreed are:

(a) Senior Assistant Minister for Home Affairs	Che Bahaman bin Samsuddin[6]
(b) Assistant Minister for Education	Too Joo [Joon] Hing.[7]

6. The question of precedence was one which clearly exercised the Chief Minister to a considerable degree and I think it probable that he had discussed it with Marshall when he met him in Johore Bahru on 29th July. I pointed out that the position in the Federation with regard to the Malay States differs from the position in Singapore, but plainly it would have been a 'sticking' with him that he must have precedence over the Chief Secretary. I have accepted this and, as I think it would be undesirable for there to be any large block of expatriate officials coming immediately after the Chief Minister, I have used the authority given me by the proviso to Clause 27 of the

---

[5] A H P Humphrey, secretary for internal defence and security, 1953–1957.

[6] Joined MAS in 1925, promoted to MCS in 1937, senior assistant minister for home affairs Aug 1955 to 31 Aug 1957 when he became minister for natural resources.

[7] As assistant to Dato Abdul Razak he sat on the Razak education commission in 1955–1956, see 364, note 3. He would also play a part in setting up the Baling talks, see 385, note 6, and 391, note.

Federation Agreement to assign the following order of precedence among Members of the Executive Council –

(i)   Chief Minister
(ii)   Chief Secretary
(iii)   Minister for Transport
(iv)   Attorney-General
(v)   Financial Secretary
(vi)   Minister for Natural Resources
(vii)   Minister for Economic Affairs
(viii) Secretary for Defence

and then the remaining Ministers in the order shown in paragraph 4 of this telegram. I specifically asked the Chief Minister whether he wished to have a Deputy or Second Minister and he replied that he did not. Whole course of my discussions with the Chief Minister has been exceedingly amicable and, possibly [? apart] from the question of precedence, there was no sign of any wish to dictate terms.

7.   The first meeting of new Executive Council will take place on 9th August and the new Ministers will enter upon their duties on that day.

361   CO 1030/225, no 4   8 Aug 1955
[Federal elections]: despatch no 958/55 from Sir D MacGillivray to Mr Lennox-Boyd reporting the conduct and results of the elections to the Legislative Council

I have the honour to inform you that polling for the first elections to the Legislative Council of the Federation of Malaya took place on July 27th, 1955. The elections resulted in an overwhelming victory for the U.M.N.O.-M.C.A.-M.I.C. Alliance who secured 51 out of the 52 elected seats. The machinery of polling worked smoothly and the day passed without any major incident.

2. *The electorate*
Registration of electors commenced on October 18th, 1954, and ended on December 1st, 1954. There was a short period of supplementary registration in January, 1955, for the benefit of those who had applied for naturalization or registration as State Nationals prior to the commencement of the period of registration of electors but whose papers were not ready in time to make them eligible to register. A total of just over 1,280,000 persons were registered as electors. Registration was voluntary and was planned as a field operation, the registering officers visiting every town, village, and other residential unit in the country at least once during the registration period at a pre-arranged time. It is estimated that the number of persons qualified to register was probably in the region of 1,600,000 and, on the basis of this estimate, over 75% of those who possessed the qualifications on October 18th, 1954, completed an application form and had their names entered on the electoral registers. Over 84 percent of the resultant electorate are Malays, just over 11 percent are Chinese and the remaining 4½% consist mainly of Indians. Among Malay electors there are nearly as many women as men, but men outnumber women in the ratio of two to one among Chinese electors and in the ratio of more than four to one

among Indian electors. Approximately three out of four of the electorate had the opportunity of voting for the first time on July 27th; most of the electors in Johore, Trengganu and Penang, in Municipal and Town Council areas and in some local council areas had had the opportunity of voting at previous elections.

3. Polling districts and polling stations
Before the beginning of the period of registration of electors, the country had been divided into 1,504 polling districts with one or more polling stations provided for each district. There were 1,679 polling stations in use on July 27th and, at some of these stations, polling facilities were duplicated to enable the staff to cope with the large number of registered electors.

4. Administrative arrangements for polling
The Legislative Council Elections Ordinance provides for the appointment of a Supervisor of Elections for the Federation, a Deputy Supervisor of Elections for each State and Settlement and a Returning Officer and as many Assistant Returning Officers as may be necessary for each constituency. The Supervisor of Elections was appointed on 23rd June 1954, after the completion of his duties as Secretary of the Constituency Delineation Commission. During the ensuing three months small election departments were created at headquarters in Kuala Lumpur and in the several States and Settlements. As a matter of policy, the fulltime staff employed on elections work remained few in number and, both during the period of registration of electors and during the period of preparation for polling itself, a large number of Government officers in other departments shouldered additional commitments in connection with the elections. The Returning Officers were for the most part District Officers; the Settlement Secretaries of both Penang and Malacca were Returning Officers and a number of Municipal and Town Council Presidents in the larger towns were appointed Returning Officers for the appropriate constituencies.

5. Elections Advisory Committee
In December, 1954, a Committee consisting of eight Members of Legislative Council selected from the main political parties, two State Secretaries and one Settlement Secretary, and three other officials were appointed to advise the Chief Secretary, as the Member of the Federal Government responsible for the arrangements for the Federal Elections. This Committee held four meetings in the early months of 1955. During the course of these meetings important matters of policy relating to polling were discussed and the legislation relating to elections was reviewed and recommendations made for its amendment.

6. Training of staff
The Deputy Supervisors and the Returning Officers were trained at a series of briefing meetings held during the months preceding Polling Day and were issued with full written instructions. A film entitled "A Model Polling Station" was prepared by the Malayan Film Unit in consultation with the Supervisor of Elections and this film, together with written instructions and lectures, were used for the training of Presiding Officers and clerks employed in the polling stations. Approximately 7,000 persons, most of whom were Government officers, were trained for polling station duties in this way.

7. *Postal voting*

Members of the Police Force and of the Armed Forces who had registered as electors and persons officially employed on July 27th in polling stations outside their own constituencies were given facilities for voting by post. Preliminary estimates indicate that a very high proportion of the postal ballot papers were returned to the Returning Officers. Had postal voting not been introduced, many members of the Police Force and of the Services would not have been in a position to exercise their right to vote.

8. *Nomination day*

On Nomination Day, 15th June, nomination papers were accepted by Returning Officers from 129 candidates. In only one of the 52 constituencies was a candidate returned unopposed. The following table shows how the candidates were distributed among the political parties:—

	Malays	Chinese	Indians	Total
UMNO/MCA/MIC Alliance	35	15	2 (including 1 Ceylonese)	52
Party Negara	29	1	–	30
Pan-Malayan Islamic Party	11	–	–	11
National Association of Perak	8	1	–	9
Labour Party	–	2	2	4
Perak Malay League	3	–	–	3
Perak Progressive Party	1	–	1 (Ceylonese)	2
Independents	16	1	1	18
	103	20	6	129

9. *Polling day*

Over 1,000,000 electors cast their votes. Making allowance for the fact that one constituency (Wellesley North) was uncontested, more than four in five of the registered electorate voted. Polling was particularly brisk throughout the morning and, at many polling stations, some 60 percent of the electorate had voted by mid-day. Women were particularly numerous at the polling stations during the first few hours of voting. The considerable publicity on voting procedure which had been given both by the political parties and the official organisation helped the polling machinery to operate smoothly; explanations of voting procedure had, however, to be given by the Presiding Officers to a number of voters, particularly elderly Malay women. There were few cases of voters going to the wrong polling stations.

10. *Votes rejected*

Bearing in mind the illiteracy of many of the voters and the fact that comparatively few had any previous experience of voting, a surprisingly small number of ballot papers had to be rejected. The percentage of rejected ballot papers was about 2½ percent of the total number of votes cast.

11. *The election results*

The Alliance victory was expected but the overwhelming nature of that victory was a surprise to many observers. Alliance candidates obtained approximately 80 percent of the votes cast. The deposit of $500/– is forfeited by a candidate who fails to obtain more than one-eighth of the total valid votes counted; 43 out of the 77 candidates opposing the Alliance suffered this fate. No other Party obtained as much as one-tenth of the total number of votes cast for Alliance candidates and the only seat lost by the Alliance was obtained by a Pan-Malayan Islamic Party candidate by a very small majority. By parties, deposits were lost as follows:–

(a) Thirteen out of the thirty Party Negara candidates.
(b) Two out of the four Labour Party candidates.
(c) Five out of the nine National Association of Perak candidates.
(d) Two out of the three Perak Malay League candidates.
(e) Both the Perak Progressive Party candidates.
(f) Five out of the eleven Pan-Malayan Islamic Party candidates.
(g) Fourteen out of the eighteen Independent candidates.

12. *Police preparations*
The Police, in conjunction with the staff of the Returning Officer in each constituency, surveyed each polling station and its precincts before polling day. An average of three police officers were on duty at each polling station. Following recent amendments to the Election Offences Ordinance, no canvassing was allowed within fifty yards of the polling station limits. Despite the crowds and long queues of voters at many of the polling stations, crowd control was excellent and the police arrangements have earned the highest praise in all parts of the country.

13. *Air lift of ballot boxes*
The Royal Air Force gave valuable assistance by lifting some of the ballot boxes from isolated polling stations to the place of count. This operation, which was conducted mainly by helicopter, had the effect of expediting the counting of votes in some constituencies and of minimising the risk of interference by communist terrorists.

14. *Political party organisation*
The election results are a clear indication of the strength and efficiency of the Alliance machine and of the weakness in organisation of the other political parties. The adoption of the system of party symbols gave further advantage to the party with the most efficient organisation and resources. It is not at present possible to forecast what effect the overwhelming nature of the Alliance victory will have on the elections to seven State Councils which are due to take place between September and November. In Malacca, where nominations for election to the Settlement Council were received on August 4th, Alliance candidates were returned unopposed in all of the eight Settlement constituencies and it seems possible that the same thing may happen elsewhere, for example in Pahang and Kedah where all candidates opposing the Alliance at the Federal Elections lost their deposits.

15. The smoothness with which the elections machinery functioned was in a very large measure due to the careful and detailed preparations made by Mr. T. E. Smith[1] of the Malayan Civil Service who was able, as Supervisor of Federal Elections, to see

---

[1] T E Smith joined the MCS in 1940; he was secretary to the Constituency Delineation Commission, 1954, and superviser of elections, 1955; author of *Population growth in Malaya* (London, 1952).

the whole major operation through from the time when constituencies had first been delineated in the middle of last year. His foresight and the pains which he took to give precise instructions as to their duties to the very large number of officials employed on polling day were responsible for the high degree of success that was achieved.

16. A full report on the Elections is now in the course of preparation and should be complete by the middle of September.[2]

---

[2] Federation of Malaya (T E Smith), *Report on the first election of members to the Legislative Council of the Federation of Malaya* (Kuala Lumpur, 1955).

362   CO 1030/225, no 7   15 Aug 1955

'The elections in the Federation of Malaya': FO circular intelligence telegram no 147 to selected HM representatives overseas reporting and commenting on the results

The first General Election in the Federation of Malaya took place on July 27, 1955. The Election was held to fill the fifty-two elected seats (out of a total of ninety-eight of whom the other forty-six are for nominated members) in the new Federal Legislative Council. The new Council's term of office is for four years. Registered voters totalled 1,280,000 of whom well over a million were Malays and only some 180,000 Chinese. Although Malays make up rather less than half the total population of the Federation they comprise about five-sixths of the electorate. The reason why the Chinese and Indians are so poorly represented is that large numbers of them are not Federal citizens, and many who are citizens failed to register on the electoral rôle.

2. Of a total of 129 candidates fifty-two represented the Alliance which is a grouping of three important communal parties, the United Malays' National Organisation (U.M.N.O.) the Malayan Chinese Association (M.C.A.) and the Malayan Indian Congress (M.I.C.) The Alliance have summed up their policy in the slogan "Independence in Four Years." The most important item in their programme was their request for the setting up of a special Independent Commission composed of members appointed from outside Malaya to make recommendations for constitutional reform leading to self-government and to study the problem of Federal citizenship. The Alliance also proposed "to Malayanise the Public Service substantially within the first term of office by replacing expatriate officers by Malayan officers." On the subject of the Emergency, the Alliance declared that if successful in the Elections, they would propose a general amnesty for all Communist terrorists; if, however, this amnesty were rejected, they would mobilise all the country's resources and seek all foreign aid to intensify the campaign against the terrorists and bring it to a successful conclusion.

3. Of six other parties contesting the Election, the second largest was the Party Negara or "Nation['s] Party," a predominantly Malay organisation which put up thirty candidates. In its manifesto, the Party Negara put forward as its aims independence by 1960, Malayanisation of public administrative posts and a fully elected Legislative Council. The Labour Party is a small organisation which had only

four candidates in the Election. Its programme had much in common with that of the Alliance and the Party Negara, but differed from them in that it envisaged a union of Singapore and the Federation of Malaya and a common Malayan nationality. The Labour Party was the only party in the Federation to criticise the Federation Government's recent decision to reject the negotiation offer put forward by the Communist terrorists (my Intel No. 128).

4. The poll resulted in a sweeping victory for the Alliance which won fifty-one out of the fifty-two seats: the remaining seat was won by a candidate of the Pan-Malayan Islamic Party, a newcomer which stands for a strengthening of Islamic influence in the conduct of Malayan affairs. It had generally been expected that the Alliance would win a majority, but the complete collapse of the Party Negara came as a surprise. All its candidates were defeated including Dato Onn, the Secretary-General who had long been prominent in the political arena. The polling, which passed off without incident, was heavy by any standards, the average figure being 80 per cent. In general it was heavier in rural than in urban areas; for example, a poll of over 89 per cent. was recorded in one of the rural constituencies in the State of Negri Sembilan. Over one million people went to the poll; of whom approximately 800,000 voted for the Alliance; 75,000 voted for the Party Negara; 40,000 for the Pan-Malayan Islamic Party, and about 32,000 for the various independent candidates; the Labour Party polled under 5,000 votes. As leader of the Alliance, Tungku Abdul Rahman assumed the post of Chief Minister in the Federation Executive Council and also that of Minister for Home Affairs. The other portfolios (apart from those reserved for official non-elected members) have all been assigned to supporters of the Alliance.

5. It is a matter for satisfaction that such a large percentage of the electorate voted. Much of the credit for this is due to the Federation authorities who had undertaken an extensive publicity campaign to impress on voters that they had both the right and duty to vote. It is also encouraging from the point of view of racial relations in Malaya that an electorate which is predominantly Malay returned the fifteen Chinese candidates put up by the M.C.A. component of the Alliance. The Party Negara had originally hoped to win successes by putting up Malay candidates in those constituencies in which Chinese candidates of the Alliance were standing.

6. It is possible that their outright victory at the polls, coupled with the example of the recent behaviour of political leaders in Singapore, may tempt the Alliance leaders to jump their fences too fast, but it is fair to say that in the past they have shown themsleves responsible and co-operative. It is also possible that in the absence of a powerful opposition party, some degree of tension may develop between the various elements which make up the Alliance: for example, for some time there has been a certain amount of friction in the U.M.N.O. between the nationalist Right wing who see co-operation with the M.C.A. and the Chinese community as a disagreeable political necessity and those members of the party with more liberal views.

7. Although the Alliance hold all but one of the elected seats in the Legislative Council, it should not be assumed that other points of view will not get a hearing in the Council. For example, the nominated representatives of the States and Settlements, the representative[s] of Scheduled Interests and the High Commissioner's nominees may be expected to express their own points of view.[1] It is, however, to be

---

[1] The new Legislative Council conisted of 99 members as follows:—
   1 speaker

regretted that there is no organised and responsible opposition party to present a reasonable and constructive opposition case.

8. One of the first matters to which the new Government are devoting their attention is the question of an amnesty offer to the Communist terrorists (paragraphs 5 and 6 of my Intel No. 128 refer). Shortly before the Elections Tungku Abdul Rahman said at a meeting of the Director of Operations Committee that he hoped that the new Government would be able to declare an amnesty towards the end of August or beginning of September. It is also to be expected that when the Secretary of State for the Colonies visits the Federation at the end of August, Tungku Abdul Rahman will raise with him the question of a further revision of the constitution of the Federation.

9. Paragraphs 1 to 5 except the last sentence of paragraph 5 above may be used freely. Paragraphs 6 to 8 are for your confidential information only.

---

52 elected
 3 *ex-officio*
11 representatives of states and settlements
22 members for scheduled interests (*viz* 6 commerce, 6 planting, 4 mining, 2 agriculture,
     4 trade unions)
 3 members for racial minorities
 2 official members
 5 nominated reserve.

363 DEFE 7/494, DCC (FE)(55)32   [20 Oct 1955]
'Defence agreements': note by the British Defence Co-ordination Committee, Far East, of a meeting with Mr Lennox-Boyd on 17 Aug

[Before visiting Malaya, Lennox-Boyd was briefed in Singapore on defence matters by the committee which consisted of Sir R Scott (the new commissioner-general), General Loewen (c-in-c, Far East Land Forces, 1953–1956), Air Marshal Fressanges (c-in-c, Far East Air Forces and British military adviser to SEATO, 1954–1957) and Vice Admiral Scott-Moncrieff (c-in-c, Far East Station, 1955–1957.]

At our 154th Meeting on 17th August at which the Secretary of State was present, the following points in regard to the situation in Malaya as it is now developing were made:—

(a) An essential prerequisite of any measure of independence for Singapore and Malaya was a defence agreement which adequately protected the interests of the U.K., Commonwealth and South East Asia. It was and had always been the policy of H.M.G. ultimately to afford to any territory which had reached the stage of self government the opportunity to opt to remain either inside or outside the British Commonwealth. Nevertheless there could be no question of making such an offer in circumstances where the terms of a defence agreement could not be fully implemented.

(b) The political climate at the moment both in Singapore and the Federation was favourable for raising the question of a defence agreement, although it might not be as favourable in, say, a year['s] time. Although both Governments realised that their interests regarding defence coincided with ours, they might in future be embarrassed by any success the Communist inspired elements might achieve in prejudicing the public against any agreement which would be satisfactory to the United Kingdom.

(c) Negotiations on defence agreements with the Governments could not be divorced from other problems of self-government and would eventually involve constitutional matters.

(d) The Governments of Singapore and Malaya should be gradually brought face to face with their responsibilities regarding defence by bringing them in on discussions of local defence problems.

(e) It was therefore essential, in view of (b) to (d) above, to establish as soon as possible the broad principles of any defence agreement. To this end the Commanders-in-Chief had already initiated a paper stating their requirements; this would be processed through the BDCC and eventually presented to H.M.G. through the Chiefs of Staff. It was expected that talks on certain constitutional questions between H.M.G. and the Government of Singapore might open about April next year, and possibly some months earlier between H.M.G. and the Government of the Federation. The aim should be to make this paper available in London in adequate time for the first of these talks.

(f) Singapore and the Federation must be considered as a whole for defence purposes. Whether or not these two territories were amalgamated politically at some future time, there would, at the appropriate time though not necessarily at the outset, be advantage in tripartite talks between their respective Governments and H.M.G. in regard to defence matters.

2.   The paper foreshadowed in paragraph 1(e) above is attached at Annex I.[1] It is divided into two main headings

(a) Basic Minimum Safeguards.

(b) Additional requirements in Emergency and War.

Under these we have listed in some detail the many points which we would wish to see covered. We realise that the list is very comprehensive and that what is eventually decided will be the result of prolonged negotiations. In this respect the situation in Singapore and the Federation is complicated by the fact that military installations are widely scattered.

3.   We have made no attempt at this stage to give our views on issues of major policy such as who would be the eventual signatories and whether one or more different types of agreement would be required. We feel that the discussions and even decisions on the points we have listed should not await agreement on these matters of major policy, negotiations concerning which are likely to be equally prolonged.

---

[1] Not printed.

364 CO 1030/51, no 81   20 Aug 1955
[Education policy]: outward telegram no 91 from Sir H Poynton to Sir
D MacGillivray reporting discussions with the Treasury about the
funding of national schools

We have had further discussions with the Treasury about your scheme for new
National Schools.[1] We all recognise the importance of the scheme on political as well
as on educational grounds in the long-term interests both of the Federation and of
H.M.G. But, as you will be aware from the Chancellor's statement on the 25th July,
H.M.G. attach very great importance at this time to a reduction in Government
expenditure, especially in expenditure overseas, and the Chancellor has asked the
Secretary of State to pay special attention to this need.[2] It is against this background
that we have had to consider your request.
    2. We feel that the right principle is for the National Schools programme to be
treated as an integral part of the Federation's development programme, with the
implication that:—

(a) the capital cost of the Schools over the next five years should be included in
the development programme; and
(b) the annual recurrent charges should be accepted on the ordinary budget.

With Treasury agreement, we suggest that you should seek the agreement of your
Ministers to this course.
    3. If H.M.G.'s attitude has to be indicated, you can say that we think such a
programme would be right and, if the Federation's finances should take the course
that H.M.G.'s assistance to the budget generally has to be considered, H.M.G. would
obviously be more likely to help if the Federation Government is pursuing policies in
education and elsewhere of which they approve. But in saying this it should be made
clear that H.M.G. cannot guarantee or underwrite this or any other programme, and
the school programme would necessarily have to come up for review if the
Federation needed H.M.G.'s assistance.
    4. We know that the above does not go as far as you would wish, but we very
much hope that by taking the lines suggested you will be able to persuade Ministers
that the National Schools programme shall be put in hand at once. I repeat that we
fully share your view of the importance of this programme.
    5. It is possible that, at the time the development programme, as expanded by
this scheme, is being discussed with your Ministers, the question of Malaya's future
independence may also be under discussion or being aired. In that event, you should
contrive in the course of the discussions to remind them of our principle that there
can be no political independence until the Federation can stand on its own feet
financially and to warn them that they would do well to weigh carefully the financial
implications of an expanded development programme from that point of view.

---

[1] See 345, 347 and 355.
[2] On 25 July Butler presented a set of deflationary measures to the House of Commons. In conveying the
chancellor's determination to reduce overseas financial commitments, however, Sir Herbert Brittain of
the Treasury did hold out the possibility of support (in addition to expenditure on the emergency) if
Malayan finances took a turn for the worse. This, as J A C Cruikshank of the CO minuted, appeared to
represent 'an astonishing concession by the Treasury' (CO 1030/51, no 780.)

6. Please show this telegram to the Secretary of State when he arrives.[3]

---

[3] Lennox-Boyd discussed the matter with MacGillivray and they concluded that there was no point in the secretary of state saying more to Alliance leaders than 'to exhort them in very general terms to plan for a really forward policy of National School' (MacGillivray to Poynton, 11 Sept, CO 1030/51); see also 370, paras 33–34. A committee was appointed, under the chairmanship of Dato Abdul Razak to formulate education proposals. It held its first meeting in Sept 1955 and produced the so-called 'Razak report' in May 1956, see 415.

365 CO 1030/70, no 35   22 Aug 1955
[Talks in Kuala Lumpur between Mr Lennox-Boyd and Tunku Abdul Rahman]: letter from Tunku Abdul Rahman to Mr Lennox-Boyd containing points for immediate attention and early decision

[This letter is subsequently referred to as a memorandum. Though dated 22 Aug, a copy was handed to MacGillivray on the previous day.]

I have the honour to address you on various aspects of Government which call for immediate attention and early decision. I shall confine myself to only the most urgent of these matters.

2. *Constitution*. The Federation's electorate has returned the Alliance to office with a clear mandate to get Independence for our country by constitutional means and in the shortest time possible. It is proposed, therefore, that in order to achieve this end, the present Constitution of the Federation of Malaya should be revised. According to the Federation of Malaya Agreement 1948, Her Majesty's Government and Their Highnesses the Rulers have given an assurance that "progress should be made towards eventual self-government in Malaya." The first national election has already been held, and the Alliance was returned by an overwhelming majority, unprecedented in the history of free elections. We consider, therefore, that the time is now ripe to effect constitutional changes necessary for the fulfilment of the assurance referred to above, as otherwise the electorate will have cause to doubt the sincerity of Her Majesty's Government, Their Highnesses the Rulers and those whom they have returned to power. The first step will be to appoint a Special Independent Commission in order to review the present Constitution and to make recommendations for its revision. We request that Her Majesty's Government and Their Highnesses the Rulers will be graciously pleased to appoint such a Commission without delay. We propose that the Chairman of such a Commission should be someone from outside Malaya and that a proportion of the members of the Commission should also come from abroad, preferably from the Commonwealth countries, and that such appointment be made after consultation with the Federal Executive Council. In our opinion, only such a Commission would be able to exercise complete impartiality in the inquiry into the Constitution. We feel confident that the Commission composed of members, rich in experience of constitutional and political matters, would be able to bring a fresh approach to the problems of our country. They would be able to produce an unbiassed report on the constitutional reforms which will fit this country for full responsible self-government and independence in the shortest time possible.

3. *High Commissioner's veto powers*. While it may be necessary for the High Commissioner's powers of veto to be retained in this transitional stage of the country's development and progress towards self-government, we urge that, as this country now has a majority of elected members in the Government, the High Commissioner should only exercise these powers on the recommendation of the Chief Minister.

4. *Internal security*. At this stage of our progress towards self-government, we concede that it is proper to leave all matters affecting external defence to Her Majesty's Government. However, all matters affecting internal security including the Police and local Armed Forces should be the responsibility of the Minister for Home Affairs. We feel confident that we are able to accept, and capable of discharging, these responsibilities with satisfaction. This will also serve as tangible proof of the sincerity of Her Majesty's Government to grant us self-government and independence.

5. *Finance*. According to Part XI of the Federation of Malaya Agreement, finance is the responsibility of the Federal Government and, therefore, we consider it appropriate that a Malayan should be appointed Minister of Finance to take over the responsibilities connected with finance and that the Financial Secretary, who now performs these duties, should serve under the Minister.

6. *The public services*.

(a) *Recruitment*. The power of recruiting expatriate officers for the Public Services including Legal and Judicial (hereinafter called the Public Services) has in the past been exercised by the Colonial Office, and no reference was made to the Federal Executive Council. Such a practice is no longer acceptable in view of our Malayanisation policy. There should be no further recruitment of expatriate officers into the Public Services without prior approval of the Federal Executive Council.

(b) *Malayanisation*. With regard to the question of Malayanisation of the Public Services, we would like to give our assurance that it is not the intention of our Party to carry out such measures as would be detrimental and prejudicial to the interests of serving officers. We propose to deal with the problems arising from our Malayanisation policy in the following manner:—

(i)   Members of the Public Services who wish to continue in service and are acceptable to our Government will carry on under exactly the same terms as heretofore;

(ii) Those whose services are no longer required will have their services terminated in accordance with their terms of employment;

(iii) Those who do not wish to serve our Government will be allowed to leave the service, and if they are entitled to compensation; such compensation will be awarded accordingly.

In order to give effect to our policy of Malayanisation, a Public Services Commission should be set up without delay, and a Malayan should be appointed as its chairman.

7. *British advisers*. We feel strongly that among the first steps that must be taken to convince the people of this country that we are definitely progressing towards self-government and independence, is to abolish the post of British Advisers. Under the respective State Constitutions, the British Advisers are advisers to Their

Highnesses the Rulers while, in actual practice, they have no duties to perform other than serving as symbol of colonial authority. The post of British Adviser is a sinecure, and a heavy charge on public funds. It has been agreed that the post of Mentri Besar shall be a political appointment. With elected Councils of State and the post of Mentri Besar recognised as a political appointment, we consider it redundant to retain the post of British Advisers.

8. *Councils of state and settlement councils.* Since Her Majesty's Government and Their Highnesses the Rulers have accepted the principle that there should be an elected majority in the Federal Legislative Council, it is only logical and proper that this principle should also be applied to the Councils of State and the Settlement Councils. Only with such elected majority will the Councils of State be able to perform their proper function of advising Their Highnesses the Rulers in the administration of their respective States. We would like to point out that in the Malacca Settlement Council, there are only eight elected seats in a council of 24. This is totally inappropriate, and is a glaring anomaly to the Penang Settlement Council in which there is an elected majority. Malacca should also have an elected majority in its Settlement Council. We have been informed that the elected members of the Malacca Settlement Council have decided to withdraw from the Council by way of protest. We feel it is our duty to tell you that such withdrawal may have serious repercussions throughout the Federation. We hope, therefore, that you will give this matter your immediate attention and take steps to remedy the position in the Malacca Settlement Council as soon as possible.

9. *Amnesty.* The Alliance proposes to take every step possible to ensure peace, happiness and prosperity in the Federation. The Emergency has been going on for nearly eight years, and if we continue employing the present methods of fighting, it is difficult to see when the Emergency will end. We intend, with the approval of Her Majesty's Government, to offer amnesty to the terrorists on such terms as may be considered acceptable to both sides. With this in view, I have been working with the Director of Operations Committee to draft these terms, and they are now ready. The offer of amnesty will be made at the opportune time.

10. Sir, we hope you will give these matters your earnest consideration. We do not expect an immediate answer to our representations, but would request you to let us have your replies within a reasonable time, so as to enable us to report back to our people.

366 CO 1030/70, no 46   [Aug 1955]
[Talks in Kuala Lumpur between Mr Lennox-Boyd and Tunku Abdul Rahman]: note by Sir D MacGillivray of a meeting on 22 Aug

The Secretary of State met Tengku Abdul Rahman this morning and had an hour['s] talk with him, the High Commissioner being present.

After congratulating Tengku Abdul Rahman on his election success, the Secretary of State said that he had seen, and just had time to glance at, the copy of the memorandum[1] addressed to him by Abdul Rahman which Abdul Rahman had given

---

[1] See 365.

the previous day to the High Commissioner. Tengku Abdul Rahman then presented the original of this memorandum.

The Secretary of State said that he would give most careful consideration to the points raised in it and Abdul Rahman said that, of course, he did not expect an immediate reply to any of the matters raised. They were matters for discussion.

The Secretary of State then referred to Abdul Rahman's proposal for the appointment of a Constitutional Commission, indicating that the was not unsympathetic to this proposal. There were, however, certain issues, such as external defence, internal security, financial autonomy and the future of the civil service, which would have to be discussed and settled before such a Commission could be appointed. These were hardly matters which were appropriate for consideration by a Commission of the kind Abdul Rahman had in mind but were matters for direct negotiation between the two parties to the Federation Agreement. There was then some general discussion of these subjects. As regards external defence, Tengku Abdul Rahman said that he recognised that this must remain the responsibility of H.M.G.; however, he thought that the responsibility for internal security could be passed, not immediately but at some future time to be agreed upon, to the Minister for Home Affairs. As to the civil service, there was no intention on the part of the Alliance to victimise officers and indeed they hoped that many British officers would choose to continue to serve in Malaya. They would be treated fairly. However, it was important that Malayan officers should be given positions of responsibility especially in posts such as those of District Officers. Malayan officers were now lacking in confidence in themselves, and it was essential that they should be given this confidence. The only way to do this was to put them in responsible positions

The Secretary of State said that it would be useful if, in his discussion next day with the Rulers, he could indicate to them the way in which Abdul Rahman's mind was moving on these constitutional issues. He would like, therefore, to let the Rulers know what Abdul Rahman's proposals were. Abdul Rahman said that he would have no objection to the Secretary of State doing this.

In discussion over the need to build up the Federation Security Forces to the point when they would be strong enough to assume sole responsibility for internal security, mention was made by the High Commissioner of the importance of developing the Federation Military College at Port Dickson. At this point, Abdul Rahman mentioned that his son's application to enter the Federation Military College had been rejected and that he had not even been granted an interview. He had, therefore, had to send him to Dehra Dun[2] for training as an officer.

In regard to amnesty, the Secretary of State said that he understood that a great measure of agreement had been reached locally as to the terms which might be offered; and that there was no intention of opening negotiations with the M.C.P., nor to give them any kind of recognition as a lawful party. Tengku Abdul Rahman confirmed that this was so, but he indicated that he envisaged, at some future time, that those members of the M.C.P. who showed that they had given up the attempt to establish a Communist regime in Malaya and were prepared to set about their political ends by constitutional means, should be permitted to join a lawful political party. He went on to say that there were members of his own party who were extremists, and might even be prepared to join forces with the M.C.P. in order to

---

[2] A military academy in Uttar Pradesh, north India.

attain their own ends—which was independence. These members of his party had believed that independence should be sought by force of arms; however, he had persuaded them that this was the wrong course and, provided that nationalism was given expression, he thought that his party would always be ready to seek independence by constitutional means only. He said that the only answer to communism in Malaya was nationalism.

The Secretary of State said that he understood that it was desired to make the declaration of amnesty at an early date so as to forestall any second peace offer that might be on its way. Abdul Rahman said that he thought that a very early declaration should be made. The Secretary of State then said that of course it would be necessary to inform other interested parties, for example, the Thai and Australian Governments, in advance of the issue of the declaration, and that some time would be required for this after final agreement had been reached on the terms of the declaration. The High Commissioner said that he thought that it would not be practicable to make the declaration until the first week of September. Abdul Rahman indicated that such timing would be agreeable to him. The Secretary of State said that meantime it might be necessary for Abdul Rahman to say something to the press. Abdul Rahman admitted that this was so, and after some discussion it was agreed that an interim statement should be made by him to the press, somewhat on the following lines:—

> "I have discussed the question of an amnesty with the Secretary of State, the High Commissioner and the Director of Operations. A very considerable measure of agreement has been reached and an announcement will be made at a later date. Much thought had already been given to this matter in the Director of Operations Committee and, in the Government's view, there is no justification for any negotiations with the Communist party or intention to countenance in any way recognition of the Communist Party".

Abdul Rahman said that he had in fact arranged to give a press conference after he, along with other Ministers, had had the further meeting with the Secretary of State which he understood had been arranged for 6 p.m. on Tuesday. He would of course clear with the Secretary of State answers he proposed to give the questions he anticipated would be asked by the press. He would keep to generalities and would not detail the proposals set out in his memorandum. It was agreed that he would clear finally tomorrow evening the wording he would use in regard to the amnesty proposals.

There was some discussion in regard to the Malacca Settlement Council and the High Commissioner explained the present position and suggested that the arrangements just introduced should be given a trial. He had reduced the number of official nominated seats from 8 to 3, thus reducing the size of the Council to 19. Moreover, in making appointments to the Nominated Council he had made certain that the position of the Elected Members on the Settlement Council was fairly reflected. He had, in fact, appointed 4 out of the 8 Elected Members to the Nominated Council; furthermore, he had undertaken that, once the new Council was established, its constitution could be reviewed by a special committee, should there be a desire for this.

367 CO 1030/70, no 41   25 Aug 1955

[Talks in Kuala Lumpur]: record by the secretariat, Kuala Lumpur, of a meeting between Mr Lennox-Boyd and the rulers at 9.30 am on 23 Aug

[These notes, together with the record of the meeting with members of the Executive Council (see 368), were sent to the CO by M Power, MacGillivray's private secretary, on 3 Sept. Present at the first meeting on 23 Aug were: Lennox-Boyd, MacGillivray, MacKintosh, all the rulers (except the Sultans of Johore and Kedah who were represented by the Regent and Raja Muda respectively), and the nine *mentris besar*.]

The Yam Tuan of Negri Sembilan, presiding at the Conference, made an address of welcome to the Secretary of State, to which the Secretary of State replied.

2. The *Presiding Ruler* then said that there was one important subject which the Conference would like to discuss with the Secretary of State. It was a subject which much exercised the minds of the Rulers. It was the request that the Alliance was making for the appointment of a Special Committee to review the Constitution. The Conference of Rulers had last year appointed its own Committee to examine the question of further constitutional reform. This Committee had made recommendations on a number of minor matters and a number of minor amendments to the Federal Agreement had been made in consequence. The Committee had also recommended that there should be a thorough review of the Federal Agreement undertaken by some suitable body and the Conference of Rulers had accepted this recommendation in principle. The Conference now felt, however, that there should be some preliminary discussions either in Malaya or in England to "clear the air" before there was a detailed examination of the Federal Agreement.

3. The *Mentri Besar, Selangor*, on behalf of the Sultan of Selangor, said that it should be kept in mind that the Agreement was one between His Majesty and Their Highnesses. Their Highnesses felt that before further consideration was given to the proposal that there should be appointed a Commission to deal with problems of the internal constitutional machinery, discussions should take place on certain fundamental issues between representatives of Her Majesty and Their Highnesses. These discussions might take place here or in London, but it might be appropriate if they should at least begin in London. It was Their Highnesses' proposal that these representatives should include political leaders.

4. The *Secretary of State* replied that it was very right to recall to mind the fact that the Federal Agreement was an agreement between His Majesty and the Rulers. This was the very basis of the present responsibilities of the British in the Malay States. He agreed with Their Highnesses' view that before any Commission could be appointed to undertake a review of the Federal Agreement, there should be preliminary talks on important issues and decisions taken on these issues, these decisions then forming, so to speak, the framework within which the further review of the Agreement could proceed. He greatly welcomed the Rulers' proposal that the Malayan delegation to such preliminary talks should include some of the political leaders. Her Majesty's Government would welcome representatives of the Conference of Rulers to a conference in London, the purpose of which would be to reach an understanding on a number of subjects that the Secretary of State considered required early consideration and settlement.

5. The *Presiding Ruler* said that the Conference would like to hear from the Secretary of State what these subjects were.

6. The *Secretary of State* then briefly mentioned the subjects he had in mind. First, the question of the defence of Malaya against external aggression. Clearly it was still far beyond the ability of the Federation to meet this requirement from her own resources, and this was a responsibility therefore which must continue to be discharged by Her Majesty's Government. But Her Majesty's Government would require to have certain facilities, such as the use of land, to enable her to discharge them under circumstances of full self-government in internal affairs. It would be necessary to have detailed discussions as regards this, along with H.M.G.'s military advisers. The Secretary of State then invited comment on the proposal. He said he would be glad to know whether Their Highnesses wished H.M.G. to continue to bear responsibility for external defence. After a pause the *Presiding Ruler* indicated that the Rulers felt this was a big question and would wish to have time to discuss it among themselves before giving a firm answer. The *Secretary of State* said that of course he understood that, and that all he wished to know was whether Their Highnesses thought it might be a suitable subject for discussion at the proposed London conference. Their Highnesses replied that they thought it would be a suitable matter for discussion.

7. The *Sultan of Trengganu* then asked whether the question of training would come into this. The *Secretary of State* replied that certainly it would, although this would be more a matter affecting arrangements for internal security than for external defence; he had in fact been about to mention the problem of internal security.

8. The *Secretary of State* then said that he thought the second matter for discussion at the Conference would be internal security. It was likely to be a long time before the threat to internal security in Malaya would be lightened. How was the threat to be met? How adequate to meet the threat were the forces now available to the Federation? How fast could these forces be built up to the necessary strength? This was where the question of training, referred to by the Sultan of Trengganu, was very relevant. What would be the cost of forces of the strength necessary to secure an adequate standard of public security? To what extent could this cost be met from the Federation's own resources? How was the gap to be filled?

From the financing of internal security would arise other financial matters, particularly the question of financing the Federation's development plan providing for expanding social services. Self-government would be a mockery without financial autonomy. Therefore if there was to be a further step towards self-government there would have to be a new settlement of financial arrangements with H.M.G.

Fourthly, there was the question of the future essential relationship between H.M.G. and the Federation. In other words, what would be the future position of the High Commissioner? What would be his executive authority? It might be desirable to circumscribe this within a limited field in which he would have absolute discretion.

Then there was the question of the future of the public services. It was H.M.G.'s genuine intention that the men and women of Malaya should take an increasing part in the public services. The British Government was fully committed to the policy of Malayanisation. Side by side with this went the position of the British officers. How was their future to be safeguarded? These were things that would also have to be discussed.

With these things out of the way we could turn to examination of internal constitutional changes. He would be very glad to know if Their Highnesses had a general feeling that matters such as these ought to be discussed now. He asked no more than that. Particulars of an agenda for the proposed conference would require further examination and of course the agreement of the Conference of Rulers.

9. The *Raja of Perlis* said that he was doubtful whether it was desirable to hold the Conference as soon as early in the new year. It would be necessary for the Rulers Conference to hold previous discussions and there would be little time for these if the Conference were to take place in four or five months time. There followed some discussions as to this. It was pointed out by the *Secretary of State* that, even if the Conference were held in January or February, and agreement reached on all points, it would probably not be possible to appoint the proposed Constitutional Commission and to get it on the ground until nearly a year later. The Rulers expressed their view than [that] an early date for the Conference would be desirable. They also agreed that the subjects mentioned by the Secretary of State were subjects which should be discussed at such a conference. The precise date for the conference, the composition of the Malayan delegation, and the terms of reference were matters which would be discussed later with the High Commissioner. It was agreed that it would be desirable to have a meeting of the Conference of Rulers at the end of September for this purpose.

10. The *Secretary of State* then informed the Rulers' Conference that the Chief Minister had the previous day handed him a memorandum containing certain proposals, and had agreed that he could tell Their Highnesses of the Chief Minister's ideas. One of these proposals was that there should be appointed a Special Independent Commission to review the Federal Agreement. There were also other specific suggestions regarding the High Commissioner's powers, finance[,] internal security, and the public service. These were all matters which would come within the purview of discussion at the proposed London Conference. There were, however, two matters raised in the Chief Minister's memorandum which directly affected Their Highnesses, and were particularly their concern.

The first of these was the position of the British Advisers. The Chief Minister felt that their posts had become redundant. The Secretary of State said he would like to hear the views of the Rulers as to this. *Raja Uda* said that it was true the conditions which had prompted the appointment of British Advisers had changed. One of the main reasons for their appointment originally was to keep the balance between the races, to see that the Chinese and Indian minorities got a square deal. Now that there were Chinese and Indians on the Federal and State Legislative and Executive Councils, the need for the protection of Chinese and Indian interests was not so great. The *Secretary of State* replied that he entirely appreciated this point. The *Presiding Ruler* said that they would like to discuss this matter later among themselves and with the High Commissioner at their next meeting.

The *Secretary of State* said that the second matter which directly concerned them related to the Councils of State. The Chief Minister felt that there should be elected majorities on these Councils. The *Mentri Besar, Perak*, replied that this was a matter which had been discussed at length by a Committee representative of all the Select Committees appointed by each State and Settlement Council to consider the introduction of elections to State and Settlement Councils and that, with the exception of Penang, there had been unanimous agreement that at the first stage there should be a majority of unofficial members but a minority of elected members. The Secretary of State did not take this point any further.

368   CO 1030/70, no 41   25 Aug 1955
[Talks in Kuala Lumpur]: record by the secretariat, Kuala Lumpur, of a meeting between Mr Lennox-Boyd and members of the Executive Council at 6 pm on 23 Aug

[The first paragraph lists the names of those who attended as follows: Mr Lennox-Boyd, Sir D MacGillivray, Tunku Abdul Rahman, D C Watherston, Colonel H S Lee, M J P Hogan, Dr Ismail, Dato Abdul Razak, Mr Leong Yew Koh, Mr V T Sambanthan, Enche Suleiman, Enche Abdul Aziz, Enche Sardon, Mr Ong Yoke Lin, and A M MacKintosh.]

2.   The Secretary of State opened the meeting by referring to the press conference which the Chief Minister and some of the Ministers were intending to hold later in the evening and drew attention to the following matters:—

(a) He said that he fully realised that at this conference the Chief Minister and other Ministers would inevitably be pressed for statements about further constitutional developments and the correspondents would inevitably seek information as to what had transpired in the conversations that had taken place with the Secretary of State. In these circumstances, he hoped that it would be clearly understood and made apparent that anything which had transpired so far was purely tentative and exploratory and that no one had been committed in any way. He stressed that he also had colleagues and that before reaching any firm understanding on these matters, it would be necessary for him to consult with them. The Chief Minister expressed his agreement with this and said that in the memorandum which he had given to the Secretary of State he had specially pointed out that the Secretary of State would no doubt want time to think over the points which had been raised.

(b) The Secretary of State drew attention to the tendency very apparent in some of the draft answers which had been prepared for the press conference for the Chief Minister to refer to 'my Government'. He felt it was desirable to bear in mind that we are at a transitory stage in constitutional development and that the Government was in fact the High Commissioner and the whole of Executive Council as a body, which carried collective responsibility for the government of the country.

(c) The Secretary of State drew attention to the terms in which the Chief Minister was proposing to answer the question about amnesty and suggested that the reference to the Director of Operations should be couched in somewhat different language so as to indicate that the Chief Minister would wish to consult with the Director of Operations about questions affecting the amnesty even if he considered himself quite free in certain circumstances to act in this matter without prior authorisation from the Director of Operations. The Secretary of State drew attention to the difficulty of the Chief Minister taking any step in regard to amnesty in a purely personal capacity, since it would be virtually impossible now for the public or the Communists for that matter to distinguish between Tunku Abdul Rahman in a purely personal capacity and Tunku Abdul Rahman as Chief

Minister in the Government. Some discussion then developed on the proposed statement that there was no intention of negotiating with the Communist Party or recognising the Party. A number of the Ministers felt that they wished to modify the latter statement and Dr. Ismail pointed out that they would be placed in an embarrassing position in the future if, having said that they would not recognise the Communist Party, they were subsequently advised by H.M.G., after some possible future eventuality, such as the admission of the Chinese Communist Government to the United Nations, that it would be appropriate to recognise the Communist Party. They felt, therefore, that they should not purport to preclude themselves indefinitely from any such course. It was generally agreed that this difficulty could be avoided by making it clear that in repudiating any idea of negotiation or recognition, they were contemplating the Malayan Communist Party which was engaged in subversion in Malaya.

(d) The Secretary of State drew attention to the proposed statement about Australian troops and indicated that he thought the mention in its present form of opposition to a war base could give rise to misapprehension and unfavourable press publicity. It would be unfortunate if the impression went abroad that the Australian troops were not wanted. Soldiers sent overseas were usually reluctant enough to be parted from their homes and friends in any event, but if in addition they were given the impression that they were unwanted the whole effect on the troops and those who sent them would be unfortunate. The Chief Minister indicated that no country would wish to have its territory made a war base and the scene of fighting if that could properly be avoided but of course the Alliance was very glad to have the assistance of the Australians in dealing with the present Communist armed terrorism. The Secretary of State replied that whilst he appreciated the desire of the Ministers to avoid involvement in hostilities, he took it that all were agreed that if the arrival of the Australian troops was likely to contribute to deterring any external aggression against the territory of Malaya, it was a development to be welcomed. The proposed answer might, however, easily give the contrary impression particularly if the press isolated and headlined the phrase relating to a war base. It was generally agreed that this could be avoided by altering the phrase so as to make it read that if the intention was merely to establish a war base the Alliance would not have welcomed the development, but since the Australians were coming to help in the struggle against the Communist terrorists and as a deterrent to external aggression the Chief Minister and his colleagues were glad to see them here.

3. The Secretary of State then turned from matters arising out of the press conference to the general question raised by the desire of the Chief Minister and the Alliance for further constitutional advancement. He drew attention to the heavy tasks which await the Ministers in the normal administration of the government of the country—tasks which he felt would absorb a very great deal of their energies and from which it would obviously not be desirable to distract them unduly by constant pre-occupation with constitutional change. He recognised however that they would not wish to feel that they were standing still and that was a wish with which he had every sympathy. They regarded this as a transitional phase and therefore would like to know that their constitutional position was not static but progressing onward to self-government and independence, an independence which he hoped would lie

within the British Commonwealth. Practically every country associated with Great Britain which had eventually established itself as an independent state, since the American Colonies first broke away, had chosen voluntarily and spontaneously to become a part of the Commonwealth family and he hoped that Malaya would choose the same course. He wished to assure the Chief Minister and his colleagues with all the sincerity at his command that it was the firm and accepted policy of Great Britain, accepted by all parties, that the goal for Malaya was that of self-government and independence and it was the intention of himself and his Government to carry that policy into effect. His Government did not regard this course as being in any way a retreat but rather the fulfilment of their whole purpose in their relations with dependant territories.

4. He was accordingly very ready and glad to consider with the Chief Minister and his colleagues what further steps should be taken along the road which they were both determined to follow. He had noted the proposal for an Independent Commission to consider and make recommendations on further constitutional changes and that might be a convenient way of tackling the problem but it must of course be borne in mind that the Constitution of the Federation rested primarily and fundamentally on an Agreement between the Queen and the Rulers and there could be no changes in the terms of this document except by the consent of the parties to it.

5. It seemed to him—and he stressed that the ideas which he was now putting forward were purely tentative and that he was stating them merely for the purpose of indicating to the Chief Minister and his colleagues how his mind was working on the problem—that it would probably be necessary as a next step to consider certain fundamental issues for the purpose of determining the framework within which constitutional questions could be considered.

6. H.M.G. had undertaken to protect the Malay States against external aggression. For this purpose it is necessary to have certain facilities, land, etc. In addition, H.M.G. was providing much assistance in the maintenance of internal security.

7. The finance involved in such matters as these was a fundamental issue as was the question of any more general financial support that might be involved in maintaining a part not only in the struggle against subversive Communist influences but in ensuring the well-being and happiness of the people as a whole. These were matters that would require study, because it is not easy to reconcile demands for full internal self-government with measures of outside financial assistance. Financial assistance is normally accompanied by some control.

8. In addition the High Commissioner's position in the future and the position of the Public Services are matters on which it is probably desirable to reach some measure of understanding before proceeding to examine the best methods of introducing the next steps towards democratic self-government whether by way of a fully elected Council with an Upper House or otherwise.

9. The Secretary of State went on to say that the idea that had been taking shape in his mind was that a conference probably in London, and probably very early in the new year, to discuss these matters so as to clear them out of the way with a view then to enabling a Commission or Committee or conference, whatever was thought best, assembling for the purpose of making recommendations on further internal changes. He had, he said, already discussed this idea with Their Highnesses the Rulers this morning. While Their Highnesses were not of course in a position to

security commitment and of the Federation's programme for the development of its social services and economic resources; certain aspects of the High Commissioner's authority; and the position of the members of the public service. I therefore proposed that these important issues should be examined early next year at a conference in London between representatives of the parties to the Agreement, and that that conference should at the same time consider the proposal that a commission should be appointed to examine the internal constitutional structure of the Federation and give some thought to the composition, terms of reference and timing of any such commission.

4. I understood from Their Highnesses the Rulers that an approach on these lines might commend itself to them; and they expressed to me the hope that the Malayan delegation at such a conference would include a number of the Federal Ministers. As you know (and indeed we agreed at our last talk) any recommendations by a conference of this kind which involved amendment of the Federation Agreement would require the assent of the Conference of Rulers. As I see it, the purpose of the conference would be, by examining and defining certain fundamental issues, to establish the framework within which any constitutional commission could go to work.

5. It would of course help me a good deal if you and the other Alliance Ministers felt able to let me have your views however tentative, before I leave the Federation on the 2nd September.

6. In the seventh paragraph of your letter you express the view that it is no longer necessary to retain the post of British Adviser. As you know, the post of British Adviser derives from each of the Agreements entered into between Her Majesty and the Ruler of each State: and in accordance with those Agreements the cost of the British Adviser, with his establishment, is a charge on the revenues of the State. The matter is not, therefore, one of direct concern to the Federal Government. I have, however, mentioned it to the Conference of Rulers and have asked the High Commissioner to obtain their considered views upon it.

7. I shall reply to you separately about the particular matter of the Malacca Settlement Council which you have raised in the eighth paragraph of your letter.

8. We have already discussed the proposal, which you mention in the ninth paragraph of your letter, that there should be a declaration of amnesty to the communist terrorists and have reached a considerable measure of agreement. I hope that complete agreement can be obtained before the end of this month, so that the declaration may be made as early as possible in September.

370 CO 1030/70, no 37 2 Sept 1955
[Talks in Kuala Lumpur]: record by A S H Kemp and A M MacKintosh of a meeting between Mr Lennox-Boyd and members of the Executive Council on 1 Sept

[Kemp, acting secretary to the federal government, drafted this record and MacKintosh added amendments, especially in para 6. In addition to those who attended the meeting on 23 Aug (see 368, note), the following were present: C J Thomas (financial secretary), O A Spencer (minister for economic affairs), A H P Humphrey (secretary for defence) and Kemp.]

The *Secretary of State* opened the meeting by expressing his regret at having to leave the Federation on the following day and the hope that, before he next visited Malaya, he would have an opportunity to meet some of those present in London and to cement the friendships which had been formed during his present visit.

2. He referred to the Memorandum which had been handed to him by the Chief Minister at the beginning of his visit and to the letter which he had sent in reply after the preliminary talks with the Chief Minister and a discussion with the other elected Ministers.[1] This reply could not in the circumstances be conclusive on all points, since there were several matters which must be left for later discussion, but he wished to say that nothing had been passed over merely because it was difficult to answer.

3. The question of a *review of the constitution* had been the subject of preliminary discussions with Their Highnesses the Rulers[2] in which, meeting them in Conference as he was for the first time, he had taken great care not to give them the impression that there was any attempt to hurry them into hasty decisions and had therefore not pressed for an immediate reply. He understood, however, that Their Highnesses were intending to have a special meeting this month at which the subjects mentioned by him would be further discussed.

4. He had already explained to the elected Ministers the general lines of what appeared to him the best approach.[3] He was anxious that there should be no misunderstanding about the intentions of Her Majesty's Government, whose view was that the process of granting self-Government and independence to the territories in the Commonwealth was not one of disintegration but of development, along the lines which offered the best prospects for the spread of free democratic ideas and peace throughout the world.

5. He could give an assurance that there would be no attempt on the part of Her Majesty's Government to put obstacles in the way of political advance in the Federation. Since, therefore, there was agreement on the goal in view, he felt that there was no need for a rigid attitude at this stage on the steps to be taken to attain that goal. He himself had a dislike of laying down fixed timetables in matters of this kind because they often became an embarrassment later; given that there was an atmosphere of mutual trust and a community of aims, as he hoped there was, the necessity for an exact timetable tended to disappear.

6. On the subject of the proposed *Constitutional Commission*, he suggested that a conference should be held in London early in 1956 to face up to various important issues such as Internal Security, Finance, the Public Service and the relationship between H.M.G. & the Federation as represented by the High Commissioner's powers. Once agreement had been reached on these matters the way would be clear to consider the terms of reference, composition, etc., of a Commission to examine the internal constitutional problems of the Federation.

7. He had mentioned this approach both to Their Highnesses the Rulers and in his letter to the Chief Minister. It would now be very helpful to have the reaction of the Chief Minister and his colleagues to this suggestion for clearing up the important questions which he had mentioned and deciding on the framework of the constitutional review. He was himself prepared to recommend to his colleagues in the Cabinet that there should be a constitutional Commission later, and if the Alliance

---

[1] See 365 and 369.   [2] See 367.   [3] See 368.

agreed on preliminary talks it would be on the understanding that the principle of such a Commission was accepted. It would, however, be impossible for Her Majesty's Government to announce its acceptance until Their Highnesses the Rulers had agreed.

The *The Secretary of State* then sought the view of the Members of the Council on his suggestions.

8.   The *Chief Minister* said that he had answered the Secretary of State in part in his speech in the Legislative Council on the previous day. He and his colleagues were not averse to the idea of the London conference but they did wish to have an assurance that it would be followed by the appointment of a Commission, and if this were given they would agree to the proposal.

9.   The *Secretary of State* said that Her Majesty's Government could not state its acceptance of this principle of a Commission without first obtaining the consent of Their Highnesses the Rulers, but he would undertake to send a reply on this point as soon as he had received a definite indication of the attitude adopted by the Conference of Rulers towards the Commission.

10.   The *Minister for Agriculture* suggested that Their Highnesses, having received a Memorandum from the Alliance some months previously, had already had some time to consider their attitude and must by now have formulated some ideas.

11.   The *High Commissioner* pointed out that although the idea of a Commission had been known to them for some time the suggestion for preliminary talks was new.

12.   The *Secretary of State* said that in all probability Their Highnesses had begun to formulate their ideas and it was significant that they had themselves proposed that representatives of the Alliance should take part in the discussions.

13.   The *Chief Minister* said that, although there was no great urgency in the matter, he and his colleagues were most anxious to see the principle of an independent constitutional Commission established.

14.   The *Secretary of State* said that he would communicate the views of Her Majesty's Government on this point as soon as possible.

15.   The *Minister for Natural Resources* said that in the event of any conditions being attached to the acceptance by Their Highnesses the Rulers of the principle of a Commission, the Alliance must have the right to reconsider its attitude. The Secretary of State agreed.

16.   The *Secretary of State* then made mention of various points which he considered should be borne in mind in framing the agenda for the talks in London.

He would regard the question of the relationship between Her Majesty's Government and the Federation as being one subject for discussion, and the *High Commissioner's powers* were one aspect of this relationship.

17.   There followed some discussion on the exercise of these powers, and the view was expressed by the Chief Minister and other Ministers that, now that there were elected Ministers on the Council, the High Commissioner's power of veto, which they recognised as necessary, should be exercisable not in his discretion but on the advice of the Council.

18.   The *Secretary of State* said in answer to a question that the powers of the Governor which had been the subject of discussion recently in Singapore were the discretionary powers to be exercised in consultation with the Chief Minister. He had felt that the matters covered by these powers, which included the appointment of

Junior Ministers and the grant of leave to Ministers, were proper matters for the Chief Minister's advice and had accordingly agreed that where the phrase "in consultation with" was used it should in future mean "on the advice of". The Reserve Powers of the Governor had not been called in question either in Singapore or in the Gold Coast.

It was noted that these powers had never been used in Malaya since the coming into force of the Federation of Malaya Agreement, the last occasion having been in the days of the Malayan Union for the purpose of introducing Income Tax.

19.　The Secretary of State then turned to the question of *Internal Security* which he said would be a matter of very great concern as the terrorist tactics of the Malayan Communist Party were superseded by new tactics of subversion. It was, in fact, a problem of quite unpredictable magnitude, and the points to be borne in mind in dealing with it were, first, that Her Majesty's Government had had considerable experience in dealing with this kind of thing in other parts of the world and, second, that the expense involved in dealing with it satisfactorily might well be beyond the capacity of the Federation to meet.

20.　He said that there were several difficult questions connected with Internal Security, which he did not propose to discuss at this stage. Although he approached them with an entirely open mind, he might feel bound to adopt a very definite standpoint in the London talks. He would not wish there to be any misapprehension as to his feelings, which were that there were strong arguments against the transfer of responsibility for Internal Security until more was known of the nature and size of the menace to be met. It must be remembered in this connection that Malaya was a key-point in the free world's defence against the spread of Communism.

21.　He emphasised that his remarks did not imply any lack of confidence in the Alliance Members of the Council; what he had in mind was that it might be necessary for the Federation to rely on outside assistance to meet its commitments and that it would be natural that the provision of such assistance should carry with it a say in the conduct of affairs.

22.　The *Chief Minister* said that there was no question but that Her Majesty's Government should have a strong say in both the external and internal aspects of Defence Policy, but his feeling was that generally speaking the details of the internal arrangements should be determined locally by the elected Government with the minimum of interference from outside, that the conduct of operations should fall within the sphere of an elected Minister and that similarly the Secretary for Defence should exercise his functions under the directions of a Minister.

23.　The *Secretary of State* said that he entirely agreed with the policy of associating the people of the country with matters of this kind but that he considered it too early to talk of the transfer of the powers of direction until more was known of the shape of the dangers to be met. He wished for the present merely to make it plain, to avoid any misunderstanding later, that he saw considerable difficulties in the way of any arrangement which would impose on Her Majesty's Government an obligation to provide assistance in this sphere without at the same time conferring any right to direct the policy to be followed.

24.　The *Secretary of State* then said that he had mentioned the Alliance views on the *British Advisers* to Their Highnesses; their position rested primarily on the State Agreements between Her Majesty and Their Highnesses and it would be necessary to await the reaction of Their Highnesses before saying anything further.

25. Turning to the question of the *Public Service*, the *Secretary of State* said that many expatriate civil servants had become largely Malayan in outlook during the course of their service. He sympathised with the feelings of the Alliance on recruitment, but he had a protecting duty towards serving holders of Secretary of State's appointments. He had done his best during his visit to allay the understandable anxiety of members of the Public Service about their future. He had found little or no desire among them to leave the country; on the contrary they had many ties to bind them to it and felt that they might still have a useful contribution to make in the future.

26. The *Chief Minister* said that Malayanisation was not a new policy; the difficulty was not over its acceptance but over the method of implementation; in this respect the Report of the Malayanisation Committee was entirely unsatisfactory to the Alliance.

27. In the course of ensuing discussion the *Chief Secretary* said that considerable progress had been made in the last five years and he hoped soon to produce figures and information on training for the Council.

28. The *Minister for Natural Resources* expressed the view that the effort was concentrated too much on the Administrative Service and that not enough attention was being paid to the Technical Service. *The High Commissioner* agreed that more facilities for technical training were needed and that steps should be taken to provide them.

29. In connection with the Chief Minister's reference to the bitterness which had been occasioned in the Police Force in the past by the promotion of Police Lieutenants to higher ranks and the lack of Malayanisation, the *Secretary of Defence* said that some 24 per cent of Div. I Police Officers were now Malayan, that Police Lieutenants were not permanent officers and that promotion of expatriate officers serving on contract had been stopped; so indeed had the new recruitment of expatriate officers, so that Malayanisation was now a natural process.

30. The *Minister for Agriculture* said that the process was not fast enough, having regard to the 4-year period on which the Alliance programme was based. The *Secretary of State* stressed the importance of maintaining the efficiency of the Police Force.

The *Minister for Natural Resources* expressed the view that something less than 100 per cent efficiency should be accepted as part of the process of Malayanisation. He also referred to the difficulty that the appointment of suitable Malayans to the Public Service generally was retarded by the lack of vacancies due to holding of the higher posts by expatriate officers.

31. The *Chief Minister* said in conclusion that it was not the wish of the Alliance to do away with all the expatriate members of the Public Service in 4 years; it still wished to have their services, but in the capacity of officers of the Federation Government.

The *Secretary of State* added that this again was a matter for discussion in the proposed preliminary talks.

32. On the subject of *Amnesty*, the *Secretary of State* said that he had examined the wording of the Declaration adopted by the Council at its last meeting and had endorsed it on behalf of his colleagues. He would now watch the results of the Declaration with the closest attention and with hope for its success.

33. The *Secretary of State* then enquired about the progress in the creation of

National Type schools, which appeared to him a most desirable development.[4]

The *Minister for Education* said that the principle had been accepted but that the form proposed was not satisfactory either to the Malays or to the Chinese; a Committee would be appointed in the next few weeks to seek a satisfactory solution both on the best type of National Schools and on the amendment of the Education Ordinance.

34. The *High Commissioner* emphasised the urgency of creating acceptable National Schools where the children of all races could be educated together; it was generally agreed that this kind of school formed an important bastion in the defence against Communism.

35. Finally, in taking his leave, the *Secretary of State* expressed his warm thanks for the welcome which he had received in the Federation and said that he would look forward to seeing some members of the Council in London in the new year.

---

[4] See 364, note 3.

---

371   FO 371/116941, no 67/9   20 Oct 1955
[Amnesty talks with the communists]: inward telegram no 646 from Sir D MacGillivray to Mr Lennox-Boyd on the risks involved in a meeting between Tunku Abdul Rahman and Chin Peng

[On 8 Sept Tunku Abdul Rahman made good his electoral promise (see 350, note) and offered an amnesty to 'all who have taken up arms against the Government of the Federation of Malaya and those who have consorted with them', but he insisted he was not offering to negotiate with communists. The MCP responded immediately and proposed a meeting with the chief minister to achieve a ceasefire. In the weeks that followed and to the growing consternation of the British (see 373–382), the MCP set out its programme to end the war through negotiation while the Tunku appeared willing to end the emergency by whatever means. On 28–29 Dec a meeting took place at Baling (NE Kedah) between Chin Peng, Chen Tian (head of propaganda, MCP) and Abdul Rashid Mahiden, on the one side, and Tunku Abdul Rahman, Tan Cheng Lock and David Marshall, on the other.]

Your telegram Personal No. 138.

Amnesty.

I had a long talk with Tunku Abdul Rahman on the 18th October, and there was a further meeting in Singapore yesterday attended by Scott, Black,[1] Rahman, Marshall, Bourne, MacKintosh and myself. Rahman now takes the line that he must listen to what Chin Peng has to say, even if Chin Peng does not confine himself to points arising out of the terms of amnesty.[2] He says that Chin Peng is likely to ask for:—

(1) Recognition of the Malayan Communist Party.

(2) An assurance that those surrendering will not be deported.

(3) An assurance that those surrendering will be allowed to play a part in the political life of the country and will not be detained for more than a very short period.

---

[1] Sir Robert Black, governor of Singapore, 1955–1957, and of Hong Kong, 1957–1964.
[2] The four, brief terms of the amnesty declaration were confined to surrender procedures.

(4) The release of present detainees, and

(5) The repeal of the Emergency Regulations.

He says that (1) would have to be rejected straightaway but that he must be able to discuss points (2) to (5) and any other points raised by Chin Peng. He recognises that he would not have the authority to agree to anything at the meeting, and that after hearing what Chin Peng had to say and after discussion of these points with him he would have to refer them to me. I have emphasised that his meeting with Chin Peng was agreed to only on the understanding that it was for the purpose of clarification of the terms of the amnesty and that there would be no negotiations. To this he replies that the public now realise that the amnesty itself will not bring an end to the emergency and are looking to this meeting to do so; that there is growing public opinion in favour of negotiation and that he could not now go to the meeting if he were authorised merely to explain the terms of the amnesty.

2.   To what extent Rahman has been affected by the march of events and to what extent he has foreseen this development it is difficult to judge. There has certainly been a recent change in the public attitude. The amnesty is now 6 weeks old. It is evident that the terrorists, having had ample warning of its declaration, conducted intensive anti-amnesty propaganda in their ranks and among the masses organisation, tightened discipline and warned that defection would be severely punished. This, it must be admitted, has been effective since there have been few surrenders. The public reaction to the amnesty was at first favourable. It was accepted as a sincere and determined effort to end the emergency. As the weeks pass, however, without any sign of mass defection in the Communist ranks, there is less and less confidence that the amnesty by itself will bring an end to the emergency, and it is for this reason and because the people wish to be rid of an emergency now over 7 years old that there is growing feeling among them that there should be talks which might include a measure of negotiation despite the risks.

3.   I fear therefore that we are faced broadly with two alternatives:—

(a) To insist that the meeting should be for the sole purpose of explaining the terms of the amnesty and that any attempt by Chin Peng to discuss points not arising out of these terms should be resisted. If we do this there is a real risk that the Alliance will use their "secret weapon" of resignation from Councils at all levels; represent to the public that the British have refused to allow Rahman to meet Chin Peng even to hear what he has to say; and that it is therefore clear that the British do not (repeat not) want to end the emergency, but deliberately wish to keep it alive in order to deny independence to Malaya. There would then be a strong anti-British campaign by UMNO with consequential diminution of support given us in the prosecution of the emergency by the public and possible loss of morale in the police and Malay Regiment.

(b) To agree that the Chief Minister should hear what Chin Peng has to say and to discuss point with him but not (repeat not) to commit us in any way to agreement on any point. The Chief Ministers[3] would then report back and we would then have to consider with them how far we could go to meet their points. It might well be that we would then not be able to agree with Rahman and that he would resign, representing that he could have brought the emergency to an end on terms

---

[3] ie Tunku Abdul Rahman and David Marshall.

acceptable to the public but that the British had frustrated a reasonable solution.

4. At present I incline to the view that the greater risk lies in course (a) but I am having a full appreciation made of the full implications of each course! It may take 4 to 5 days to complete this.

5. Should course (b) be followed it seemed, from yesterday's meeting, that with Marshall's help Rahman could be persuaded to agree that:—

(i)　any undertakings given to Chin Peng would not be operative till the terrorists have all surrendered and handed in their arms and unless we were reasonably satisfied that no caches of arms had been left in the jungle as in 1946;
(ii)　the right to deport must be retained and
(iii)　although those parts of the Emergency Regulations required for the purposes of the shooting war would be revoked, those essential to combat subversion (especially the right of arrest and detention) would be retained either in the form of Emergency Regulations or, as in Singapore, in the form of special public security legislation. It seemed though that it might be more difficult to persuade him that:—

(a)　certain of the present detainees could not be released without real threat to public security and
(b)　It would be necessary either to deport the Politburo or to detain them at least for a considerable period. His ultimate attitude would no doubt depend on his estimate of the extent to which he could carry public opinion with him in insisting on the early release of all present detainees and of the Politburo, and the degree of control the Government could exercise over the security situation that would then arise.

6. The greater danger in course (b) lies in the possibility that Chin Peng would ask for an assurance that independence would be granted to Malaya by a stipulated date. The Chief Ministers would, of course, have to support this demand and I am afraid I would not now put it beyond Abdul Rahman to have this possibility in mind.

372　CAB 129/78, CP(55)162　　　　　　　　　　21 Oct 1955
'The constitutional position in Singapore and the Federation of Malaya': Cabinet memorandum by Mr Lennox-Boyd

I am shortly circulating to the Colonial Policy Committee a detailed analysis of the situation and major problems in Singapore and the Federation of Malaya.[1] In the meantime the Prime Minister has suggested that the Cabinet would be interested to read a shorter account of my recent negotiations in those territories. As my colleagues were in close touch with the discussions in Singapore at the time, I have

---

[1] The Cabinet Colonial Policy Committee was set up in Oct 1955 to consider 'problems arising from constitutional development in colonial territories and other problems of Colonial policy'. Chaired by the prime minister, its membership consisted of the foreign secretary, Commonwealth secretary, colonial secretary and minister of defence. Its papers for 1955–1957 are at CAB 134/1201, 1202, 1555 and 1556. CAB 134/1203 and 1551 contain minutes and memoranda of the Colonial Policy (Official) Committee.

recounted these in an appendix to this paper.[2] I should like in what follows to complete the picture with an account of my talks in the Federation of Malaya and of the developments which have since taken place.

2. On 21st July (C.M.(55) 25th Conclusions, Minute 8)[3] the Cabinet approved certain proposals which I had put forward for the line which I should take in discussing constitutional matters with the Rulers and political leaders in the Federation. I proposed that I should insist that, before there could be any fresh consideration of a further measure of internal self-government in the Federation, it would be necessary to have talks in London on a number of vital issues on which it was, in our view, essential to reach agreement as conditions precedent to examination of other constitutional questions. The most important of these were external defence, internal security, the financial relationship between Her Majesty's Government and the Federation Government and the general constitutional relationship between the two Governments. Subject to that, we could accept the proposal for a commission to review the constitution of the Federation within the limits set by prior agreement upon the vital issues. Both the Alliance and the Rulers had already adopted the idea of some such commission, although they held different views upon its composition.

3. The order of my negotiations in the Federation was as follows. I first had a long talk with the High Commissioner and the Chief Minister, Tunku Abdul Rahman, at which I outlined my ideas and ascertained that the Chief Minister's first reaction to them was broadly favourable.[4] I told him that I proposed next to discuss them with the Conference of Rulers, and he agreed that that was the right course. I then discussed them in some detail with the Conference of Rulers.[5] Their initial reaction was also broadly favourable but they said that they would like to have more time to consider the matter; and it was therefore arranged that they should meet the High Commissioner again for that purpose in September. The meeting took place on 29th September and the Rulers confirmed their agreement to my proposals. After meeting the Rulers I had two further meetings with the Alliance Ministers, first informally and second at a session of the full Federal Executive Council.[6] Their main interest has throughout concentrated on securing agreement to the appointment of a constitutional commission, which took pride of place in their election manifesto, and they at first showed some hesitation in accepting the need for preliminary talks in London. In the end, however, they did accept it, and I for my part agreed in principle to the appointment of the proposed commission on the understanding that the London talks took place first.

4. The High Commissioner has now written to the Chief Minister, setting out exactly what is proposed and seeking his formal agreement. As soon as he has had a satisfactory reply from the Chief Minister he proposes to issue a press statement, which will be published simultaneously here.

5. The proposed agenda for the London talks is as follows:—

---

[2] Not printed. During his visit to Singapore Lennox-Boyd agreed to hold constitutional talks with a Singapore delegation in London. These took place in Apr 1956: the British offered a fully-elected assembly but their refusal to grant complete internal self-government led to Marshall's resignation as chief minister in June.

[3] See 358.   [4] See 366.   [5] See 367.

[6] See 368 and 370.

(1) The future relations that should exist between Her Majesty's Government in the United Kingdom and Their Highnesses the Rulers and the Governments of the Federation of Malaya in regard to:—

  (a) External defence;
  (b) Internal security;
  (c) Finance.

(2) The future of the Public Service.
(3) The powers of the High Commissioner.
(4) The terms of reference, composition and timing of a Commission to review the constitution.

6. I will, of course, consult the Cabinet when I have worked out in detail the lines which I would propose to follow in dealing with the various items on the agenda for the London talks.

373 FO 371/116941, no 69   22 Oct 1955
[Amnesty and talks with the communists]: outward telegram (reply) no 140 from Mr Lennox-Boyd to Sir D MacGillivray

Your telegram No.646.[1]
  Amnesty.
  I am anxiously awaiting your further appreciation promised in paragraph 4 and trust it may take less than four or five days.
  2. In meantime I must tell you frankly of misgivings which your telegram has aroused. As you know, Rahman was publicly committed to meeting before I was consulted and I only agreed on clear understanding that sole purpose of meeting was to clarify the terms of the amnesty. I feel most emphatically we should stand by that. If Rahman listens to terrorists' views on other matters this will inevitably lead to discussion of them and in effect to negotiation.
  3. I know you will take above views into account in framing your fuller appreciation which I now await.

---

[1] See 371.

374 CO 1030/27, no 1   23 Oct 1955
[Amnesty and talks with the communists]: inward telegram no 140 from Sir R Scott to Sir A Eden assessing the risks

Your Telegram No. 199.
  Following personal for Prime Minister from Scott.
  Begins. Malaya and Singapore: Amnesty.
  In this and my next telegram[1] I summarise my first impressions.
  2. The AMNESTY issue turns on two factors: the strength or weakness of the Communists, and whether we can trust Rahman (Chief Minister in Malaya). To avoid

---

[1] See 375.

overloading what will anyway be a lengthy telegram, I propose to discuss the amnesty mainly in terms of Malaya, because Rahman is the doubtful quantity at the talks themselves. Once they are over, the outcome will have a profound effect on Singapore as well. Marshall (Chief Minister, Singapore) is going to them in a fatalistic and aprehensive [sic] mood.

3. There are indications that the end of the emergency may be in sight, because the Communists no longer want to keep it going. So much can, I think, be accepted: but why and how urgently do they want it ended?

4. *Communist motives.* They have no hope of military victory. They are belatedly recognising that for some time the Malayan Communist Party has been out of step with the new theme song "peaceful coexistence". Perhaps what weighs most with them is Rahman's success as leader of the fast growing Nationalist movement, a movement which moreover threatens (from the Communist viewpoint) to be led by Malays rather than Chinese.

5. These factors seem to me to explain why the Communists want to abandon force and concentrate on their other techniques, subversion and penetration of the Nationalist movement. But it does not necessarily follow that they are in a hurry. They can carry on, at any rate for a time, they have probably taken the measure of Rahman, and they must expect concessions.

6. It is unlikely that Rahman will break with the Communists at the talks, though of course they may still lead to nothing if the outcome is repudiated by H.M.G. Therefore, if the meeting does not end the emergency, the Communists no doubt plan to put the blame on H.M.G. and not on Rahman, a plan to which he would no doubt lend himself. Marshall would find it hard to avoid taking the same line. Neither can afford to be branded as "running dog of the Imperialists" or "Colonial stooge". From the Communist point of view, blaming H.M.G. would serve the double purpose of identifying Communism with the Nationalist cause and of isolating the British not only from many of the Chinese but from many of the Malays as well.

7. Rahman claims that the situation has changed since his talks with the S. of S. for the Colonies,[2] that the agreed terms of the amnesty have clearly not gone far enough, that public opinion in the Federation is tired of the emergency and that he has a mandate from the people to end it on the best terms he can get.

8. He is unfortunately in a tearing hurry. He wants to end the emergency (or at least to have settled the terms) before going to London to pursue his other election promise of independence. He does not believe that the Communists are under pressure to come to terms soon, and he does not trust H.M.G.'s motives in urging caution, advice which he interprets to show that we should prefer to continue the emergency in order to preserve Colonial rule and to procrastinate on negotiations for independence. He has an overwhelming Parliamentary majority, the local forces and police are largely Malay, and for his own ends he will keep legal powers to detain without trial. He is therefore serenely confident of his ability to absorb the Chinese terrorists into the community and to deal with any who give trouble (an assessment which incidentally betrays his lack of experience and which, in my view, is highly questionable). He is indifferent to the effects on Singapore.

9. *Clarification or negotiations?* I think we are making a mistake if we do not see (not, of course, for public admission) that the forthcoming talks with the Commun-

---

[2] ie in Aug–Sept 1955, see 365–370.

ists will be negotiations carrying far more risks than if they were merely to clarify the announced terms of an amnesty. It should be possible to persuade Rahman to make the opening gambit that he has come to clarify the terms of amnesty and that he wishes to be told the points which the Communists find obscure. But he will not refuse to listen, whatever proposals the Communists may make; and it is significant that he wants to make elaborate arrangements for the press to be near the meeting place. Local and world public may therefore get Rahman's version of it even before he has reported back to the High Commissioner.

10. It should also be possible to get him to refuse to make any personal commitments (at any rate at the first meeting) on the plea that he cannot commit H.M.G. and in any case must consult his colleagues: But I do not rule out that he may in the end go beyond the policy of H.M.G. in concessions on the vital issues of (a) period of detention for present and prospective detainees, (b) deportation and (c) political activities.

11. The Communists will no doubt want to start talking as soon as possible to Rahman and then spin them out to exploit his hurry to the full. If Rahman is so bent on coming to terms with the Communists that we cannot count on him sticking to his brief, the outcome (not necessarily of the first meeting but of the last) will strain H.M.G.'s relations with him, perhaps to breaking point. In Singapore public feeling would also run very high. It could be the end of Marshall and the beginning of another crisis graver than any hitherto.

12. In all this gloomy speculation I am looking some way ahead. My analysis may or may not be right: but I am strongly of the opinion that an analysis is needed to guide H.M.G. in the immediate issue—tactics in respect of the forthcoming talks with the Communists.

13. My forebodings have prompted me to consider whether it would be wise to prevent the meeting. This, indeed, could be done, and simply. If H.M.G. were to lay down conditions for the meeting which Rahman could not accept, he would call it off. For this purpose it would be sufficient to prescribe clarification on a strict interpretation of the terms of the amnesty and warn him in advance that H.M.G. would repudiate anything more. Another way would be to insist on the presence of a British observer. Neither the Communists nor Rahman would accept that, and the meeting would not take place.

14. But this would create a new situation whose consequences would have to be weighed with the greatest care. Rahman might not resign immediately, though he would certainly put his account of this development before local and world public opinion. Many Malays, as well as Chinese, would give ear to his allegations that H.M.G. were double-dealing and for their own ends frustrating the end of the emergency. Friction with the Government could easily develop to the point where Rahman would resign or the High Commissioner find himself forced in any case to suspend the constitution. These developments would incidentally suit the Communists excellently. I cannot assess how the situation might develop thereafter. There might be some elements of another Palestine in it, many of the Chinese hostile, many of the Malays non-co-operative, mounting anti-European feeling, the Communists strengthened and our ability to deal with them weakened. The situation could no doubt in time be brought under control—at a cost, to be measured also in terms of world opinion—but I am not sure that we should be any better off at the end than we are now.

15. Nevertheless, an estimate of the results (for Malaya, for Singapore and elsewhere) of suspending the Constitution may be a prudent exercise because it may be forced upon us by Rahman in any case. But, on balance, and despite my anxieties about the outcome, I do not consider that H.M.G. should stop the meeting. Looking back, it is hard to see how action by H.M.G. could at any stage have prevented it. Once the decision was taken to begin constitutional evolution before militant Communists had been extirpated (a decision which itself was in the circumstances both inevitable and right), it was certain that sooner or later Elected Ministers would try to end the emergency in their own way. And now H.M.G. are too deeply committed.

16. If this conclusion is accepted, our task is to consider very carefully our tactics with Rahman. Short of stopping the meeting, every possible safeguard must be introduced against the worst risks inherent in it. In my forecast of the outcome in para. 11 above, I have deliberately assumed the worst. But that is by no means inevitable, given tolerance and flexibility in our policy. Advice or events may bring home to Rahman the dangers of haste. Marshall has learnt a lot in six months. Rahman is also learning. Moreover, there will be more than one meeting: let us consider tactics for the first and decide tactics for the second in the light of the outcome of the first and of the way Rahman has behaved at it. It may be worth while to bring him to London to review the position after the first meeting, at which we must expect him to exceed instructions. Unless he has given away something vital, where we can muster public support behind us in repudiating it, it would not, in my view, be wise to permit a complete breach between H.M.G. and Rahman to occur in the context of the amnesty.

17. The right tactics to my mind are to give him written clarification of the terms of the amnesty offer, going somewhat beyond what was envisaged in the summer; warn him in writing that H.M.G. fully reserve the right to reject proposals going beyond these terms (but not going so far as to say that we shall reject them); warn him in writing against the dangers of allowing the terrorists to figure as heroes after an amnesty and against the dangers of subversion for both Malaya and Singapore; and orally explain (as a personal view of the High Commissioner) that he will no doubt have to listen to whatever the Communists have to say but that he should be careful to avoid committing himself even to a promise to consider a Communist proposal, though he is, of course, at liberty to reject outright.

18. A personal message from the Colonial Secretary to Rahman, timed to reach him shortly before the meeting, might be very valuable. It could wish him luck, remind him of the heavy responsibilities that lie on him and the world-wide interest that will be taken in the meeting, state that it is the sincere aim of H.M.G. to bring the emergency to an end as soon as possible so that the resources of the country can be devoted to raising living standards of the people and to economic development, and express the conviction that Rahman and Marshall will be able to make invaluable contributions to these ends without concessions which, by endangering Malayan security, will impede orderly progress towards independence.

19. In addition, we can I think, count on Marshall to do what he can for his own sake to prevent Rahman from being too rash. But Marshall does not trust him and it is difficult to say how much influence he has over him: and, in the last resort, Marshall would find it almost impossible to disassociate himself publicly from a line taken by Rahman. *Ends.*

375 CO 1030/27, no 2   23 Oct 1955

[Risks to British interests in Malaya and Singapore]: inward telegram
no 141 from Sir R Scott to Sir A Eden

My immediately preceding telegram.[1] Following personal for Prime Minister from
Scott.

Begins. Malaya and Singapore: General Impressions.

In the long run the welfare and safety of Malaya and Singapore point to their close
association. The present trend, because the Malays fear a Chinese-dominated
Singapore and the large Chinese population in Malaya, is the opposite.

2.   Both Rahman and Marshall are genuinely anti-Communist, but the former is
more afraid of the Chinese swamping the Malays than of Communists dominating
both. He gives the impression of aiming at old-fashioned Moslem dictatorship, with
some democratic trappings, ready if need be to deal ruthlessly with Chinese who give
trouble.

3.   Marshall, on the other hand, has to accept the fact of an overwhelming
Chinese majority in Singapore. His anxiety is Communist subversion, and his aim is
a non-Communist City State, where all communities can live and trade in harmony,
a modern venice [sic] on a British Socialist pattern.

4.   Both men desire good relations with the U.K. and the Commonwealth (I have
reservations about both in other respects, but I do not accept that either is
anti-British); and both wish to be on very friendly terms with their neighbours
especially those to the west, Indonesia, Burma, India. It is significant that these three
countries are not Members of S.E.A.T.O. and that all three are neutralist in outlook.
Rahman is frankly aiming at complete and early independence in two or three years.
Marshall professes to want Self-Government without complete independence. In this
he may well be sincere: he is obsessed by the fear of Singapore turning more and
more to China and he sees security in maintenance of a British connection. A Chief
Minister of Chinese stock might think differently.

5.   Because of his precarious majority Marshall is trying (with some success) to
strengthen his position by splitting the Opposition, and for this purpose and to
improve his electoral prospects he ardently desires early progress in respect of
numbers of seats, multilingualism, and widening the franchise. He realises that
these measures may boomerang against him in election time, but his attitude is that
Chinese residents of long standing, if given the vote, may support him—whereas, if
denied it, they will infallibly make a Left turn.

6.   As usual in situations like this the attention of the politicians and the public
centres on constitutional development. There is general ignorance of and indiffer-
ence to economic and defence problems, though in these respects both Malaya and
Singapore are far from self-sufficient. To take a single example, unless law and order
and stable efficient government are maintained in Singapore, trade will stay away.
Without trade it has no *raison d'être*.

7.   Marshall and Rahman display considerable naiveté in matters economic.
Marshall, for example, wants a Central Bank for Singapore so that Singapore can
keep U.S. dollar proceeds of her exports—though, in fact, Singapore's function is in

---

[1] See 374.

the main that of broker, middleman and transit depot. Exports are mostly re-exports. Rahman thinks that, with the end of the emergency, he will have vast sums at his disposal to promote social welfare and economic development—though, in fact, the emergency is being financed largely by the U.K. taxpayer and the end of the emergency will bring serious unemployment and budgetary difficulties for Malaya.

8.   They are equally ill-informed in the defence field, and it is going to be very difficult to get satisfactory Defence and Bases Agreements with either Malaya or Singapore or, having got them, to be sure that they will be respected. It is urgent that we should begin to discuss them soon, with both territories. We here cannot, however, get very far until a number of difficult defence and financial decisions are taken by H.M.G. An example is the scale and duration of financial contributions from the U.K. to the cost of local forces. This could be one of our strongest cards in negotiations.

9.   These problems are already under study in London. I mention them to emphasise their significance in the political as well as in the defence field. Without British bases and forces in South East Asia we shall not be able to discharge our defence commitments in this area, including those in respect of Hong Kong. Over the whole field of Western policy in Eastern Asia due weight will not be given to British views unless we can bear our share of military action. The withdrawal of British forces from the area would have a profound effect in Australia and New Zealand and greatly accelerate the present trend to dependence on the U.S.

10.   If it is important that we should maintain forces and bases in this area, we should try not to ask for so much that our demands will invite certain refusal by Malaya and Singapore. Bearing in mind that the main threat to the area in the forecast future is from subversion in all its aspects, it will be necessary to decide, within the framework of U.K. global defence and economic policy and after the most careful appraisal of political prospects in Malaya and Singapore, what minimum defence needs cannot be met except by facilities in these two territories. It may be worth while to consider dispersing (say, to the Borneo territories or even to Australia) such of the facilities as are needed for our defence purposes in the area but which need not necessarily be sited in Malaya and Singapore. Then, having reduced our requirements to what is really essential and must be met by Malaya and Singapore, it will be necessary to consider how to secure their agreement. For this purpose inducements, both political and financial, may be necessary.

11.   It will be necessary also to consider action in the event of definite failure to secure acceptable Defence and Bases Agreements. The stakes are so big that it may in the last analysis be necessary, whatever the consequences, to stand firm on vital defence requirements, at any rate on Singapore Island even if this provokes a crisis, widespread disorders and suspension of the Constitution, with some of the features of the Cyprus situation including Enosis (with China). Such a course of events would have widespread repercussions and is certainly not to be contemplated lightly. It is, therefore, of the highest importance that, from the outset of our negotiations on defence, we should know what is vital and what is not. Otherwise, there is a real danger that we may provoke an unnecessary crisis by pitching our demands too high and that when we begin to yield we shall find it hard to avoid putting in jeopardy something that really matters. I am not, of course, suggesting that we should start by presenting minimum demands: we need some freedom of manoeuvre.

12.   As I see it, the essential long term interests of H.M.G. in Malaya and

Singapore lie in the economic and defence fields, to be secured by establishing stable non-Communist Governments in Malaya and Singapore, with the trappings and most of the substance of independence, friendly to the U.K. within the Commonwealth, within the Sterling Area, and by adequate Defence and Bases Agreements with them. The time table of progress to this end seems to me to be of less importance. Our best chance of attaining the long term objective is, to my mind, by a flexible attitude to the problem of constitutional development. A programme that is too slow may carry as much risk as one that is too fast. *Ends.*

376   FO 371/116941, no 76   24 Oct 1955
[Political situation in Singapore and Malaya]: report by Lord Reading on his visit

During the week from October 15 to October 22 that I spent in Singapore it was inevitable that I should hear much discussion of the local situation. The Commissioner-General, the Governor and the Chief Minister of Singapore all talked to me frequently on the subject and in addition I attended a meeting presided over by Sir R. Scott at which Mr. Casey, Mr. Pearson, Mr. MacDonald[1] of New Zealand and I were able to have a very useful discussion with the three Commanders-in-chief. I was also present at a small luncheon at Government House at which Sir D. MacGillivray, General Bourne and Mr. Halloway, the Defence Secretary from Kuala Lumpur, talked over with the Governor and Chief Minister of Singapore the tactics to be followed later in the afternoon with Tungku Abdul Rahman. After his discussion with them the Tungku came to see me and gave me his views. It may, therefore, be of some value if I try to set down certain impressions, which though they are necessarily superficial, are at least up-to-date.

2. As I see the situation, the flash-point is the Federation. Although there is a certain atmosphere of strain and agitation in Singapore, Mr. Marshall could hold the position there without excessive difficulty, if it were not bedevilled by events in the adjoining territory. The early head-on collision between the Governor and the Chief Minister on the constitutional issue may prove to have been a blessing, in however effective disguise at the time. It has led them to take each other's measure at an early stage in their relationship and each has emerged from the tussle with an increased respect for the other. Even when the decision has been acute between them, their conversations have never descended to angry words on either side. The Governor is satisfied that the Chief Minister is learning rapidly and coming on well. The Chief Minister is credited with expressing the same opinion about the Governor in almost identical terms! Anyhow they meet frequently and amicably and the Chief Minister, from what he said to me, clearly finds it a comfort to be able to take his troubles to the Governor and to enlist his experience to counter his own freely admitted inexperience. Mr. Marshall is resolutely anti-Communist and has shown great

---

[1] Richard Casey (later Lord Casey), minister for external affairs, Australia, 1951–1960; governor-general, Australia, 1965–1969; Lester Pearson, secretary of state for external affairs, Canada, 1948–1957; prime minister, 1963–1968; Thomas MacDonald, minister of defence, New Zealand, 1949–1957; minister of external affairs, 1954–1957.

courage in introducing a Bill to authorize drastic security regulations which are mainly, if not wholly, directed against Communist activities.

3. If they could be insulated from the effects of events in the Federation, matters in Singapore might well move on a steady course and at a reasonable pace. But unfortunately Singapore is at the moment being stampeded by the Federation, where the Tungku is setting a course and a pace which may well result in the situation in both territories rapidly getting out of hand.

4. I can perhaps best present the picture as regards the Federation in the terms of my own talk with the Tungku. He made it quite plain at the outset that he had every intention of using every means in his power to bring the emergency to an end. He insisted that he had pledged himself in the election-campaign to do so and that, if he failed, he would at once become discredited. On the other hand, success would give the best and probably the only chance of creating a united country. I suggested that he had only just been elected with a substantial majority and that it seemed early days to talk of being overthrown. But he insisted that his position would be fatally undermined by delay. Time was vital. People were watching closely to see whether or not he was able to redeem his pledge. His final opinion was that a military solution was no longer possible. (General Loewen, the Commander-in-Chief, Far Eastern Land Forces, disagrees entirely, as does also General Bourne, who had tried his hardest earlier in the afternoon to convince the Tungku of his error, but had made no impression at all). The Communists, some 3,000 strong, were comfortably established in villages on the Siamese border, which they were free to cross and recross at will. Their presence increased the prosperity of the villages and was, therefore, welcome. These hide-outs were so remote and inaccessible that they could never be reached by troops. The only way to terminate the emergency was, therefore, negotiation. It was useless for him to meet Ching Pen [sic] unless he was in a position to make reasonable concessions. The terms of the amnesty were really no advance on the terms offered two years ago. He must have a discretion to make a more favourable offer, if the course of negotiations required it. If he were given a reasonably free hand, he could gain his objective and, once the emergency was at an end he would be free to turn his attention to the rooting out of subversive activities.

5. In answer to a question from me he said that he was not frightened of the Communist forces being set free to reinforce covert subversion. In his view, having accepted the terms, they would be anxious to re-establish themselves and show themselves good citizens, anyhow for some years to come. He brushed aside my comment that he might be bartering the chance of a permanent settlement for a very temporary and probably quite illusory advantage. He is obviously determined to bring about the talks at almost any cost and quite unprepared to recognize the dangers implicit in them

6. So headlong has been the rate of advance in the past weeks that no-one has yet had a chance to ascertain the Tungku's views on defence arrangements after independence, if indeed he has any. There are those who suspect him of a desire to emulate Sir J. Kotelawala's[2] earlier intention of making his country "the Switzerland of the East". He is evidently a very vain man and it may be that personal vanity is an element in the policy that he is persuing [sic]. But the main impulse seems to come from his desire to clear the ground of obstacles to the achievement of independence

---

[2] Sir John Kotelawala, prime minister, Ceylon, 1952–1956.

in the very near future. He may well relish the prospect of pointing to his own rapid success in putting an end to a situation which the British had proved unable to solve in spite of all their efforts and all their resources and using his success both as an agreeable tribute to his own self-importance and a valuable boost to his campaign for independence.

7.   But whatever his precise motives may be, the current of events is uncomfortably swift and strong and becoming still swifter and stronger and, unless some check can be speedily and effectively imposed, it seems to me not unduly pessimistic to say that it may sweep over the weir the present however recently established order not only in the Federation but in Singapore as well.

8.   The effects of such a "dégringolade"[3] upon the whole of the region and beyond it are neither difficult nor agreeable to foresee. The Tungku is set upon holding these talks, which in conversation with me he compared in importance to those held at Pan-mun-jon,[4] and if he is not given the latitude that he wants, it is fairly certain that he will refuse to pursue the project at all and will then publicly lay the blame for the continuance of the "emergency" upon the imperialistic obstinacy of Her Majesty's Government, alleging that they are unwilling to see achieved a peace which might result in the speedy relaxation of their grip on the country. He will now have been further encouraged by a statement, urging the value of the talks being held, issued by the Prime Minister of Thailand, who would have been much better advised in his own and his neighbours' interest to keep a discreet silence.

9.   I suspect also that he has been further stimulated in his obstinacy by Mr. Nanda,[5] the ministerial leader of the Indian delegation at the Colombo Plan Conference, who absented himself for a day in order to go up to Kuala Lumpur and lunch with the Tungku. Nanda, though capable enough, is a tense and angular personality, nurtured on the condensed milk of Gandhi-ism, who informed the Singapore Press that he was not anti-communist because "I have something that gives all that Communism can give and more". (He did not add whether he also had something that takes away all Communism can take away and more). I should judge him to be at the same time an able economist and a mystical socialist and no friend of Britain. I think it as reasonable to assume that he urged the Tungku on; he certainly reproduced and pressed upon Mr. Marshall on his return to Singapore the full Tungku gospel.

10.   These jet-propelled tactics are naturally causing both the Governor and Mr. Marshall, as well as the Commissioner-General, great anxiety. Patience and calmness are not amongst Mr. Marshall's obvious qualities but he wants to handle his problem in his own way and he sees acute danger of the situation slipping out of his control. He already has in Singapore a formidable hard core of Communists, who know him to be their bitter enemy. He now has to face the prospect of this hostile element being reinforced by a powerful contingent released by the ending of the emergency in the Federation for fresh and perhaps not less rewarding activities. Moreover, in the sacred name of coexistence they may be welcomed in Singapore probably as friends and quite possibly as heroes. For they are after all Chinese and so are more than 80%

---

[3] ie a sudden deterioration.
[4] Peace talks, held at Panmunjom between July 1951 and July 1953, resulted in an armistice (though not a peace treaty) in the Korean war.
[5] Gulzarilal Nanda was minister for planning and irrigation and power in the government of India.

of the population of Singapore—but not Mr. Marshall. And he cannot keep them out of the island, for whatever powers he might take could not be effectually exercised along the border, even if the resources at his disposal were far larger than they are, or are ever likely to be.

11. He, therefore, sees himself and his immediate supporters engulfed by a rising tide of mixed Chinese Communism and Chinese racialism, against which he feels that he has no defences. He kept on repeating to me, whenever we met: "I am a very worried man" and I am afraid that his anxiety is not without cause. It is not that he is lacking in courage or resolution; he just does not see the answer to what he regards as an inexorable development, unless steps can be taken without any delay to nip it in the bud in the Federation. Nor is he alone in his appreciation of the problem or his sense of its urgency.

12. The swift and incalculable changes in the situation are certainly baffling and the policy decisions to be taken by Her Majesty's Government are complicated by the Tungku's generally recognized unreliability. Mr. Marshall dislikes and deeply distrusts him and is violently resentful at having been led into a trap as regards his own attendance at the proposed meeting. He is still uncertain whether he will in the end participate, if it takes place, since he feels that, if he finds himself unable to go all the way with the Tungku, he will be branded as no more than a "stooge" of the British and will be seriously weakened in his relations with his own people.

13. Her Majesty's Government have presumably to decide whether they will:—

(a) refuse authority to go beyond the published terms of the amnesty and thereby risk the prospect of the talks never taking place or breaking down at a very early stage, with all the consequences of charges of imperialistic motives, of failure to move with the spirit of the times into a world of coexistence, even of unnecessarily sacrificing the lives of British soldiers in warfare which, but for their inflexibility, could be discontinued tomorrow.

or (b) allowing some further measure of latitude in spite of all the difficulties of specifying the nature and extent of the concessions which may be offered and all the dangers of the Tungku deliberately exceeding his authority and coming to terms which, however acceptable to large sections of local opinion, Her Majesty's Government could not possibly ratify.

The Colonial Secretary has himself paid so recently what was generally regarded by all with whom I spoke as a most valuable and timely visit to the area that I should not have considered recording these impressions if I had not been assured that the scene had significantly changed, and not for the better, in the short time that has passed since he was there.

377 FO 371/116941, no 69/A 24 Oct 1955

[Amnesty and talks with the communists]: inward telegram (reply) no 654 from Sir D MacGillivray to Mr Lennox-Boyd

Your telegram Personal No. 140.[1]

Amnesty.

On despatch of my telegram No. 646[2] I asked my Senior Advisers to assess the implication of the alternative courses. They (the Chief Secretary, Attorney General, Commissioner of Police and the Director of Intelligence), after taking account of the views expressed in your telegram Personal No. 140, reported unanimously last night after full discussions over last three days. I think you should see their report in full and, although it is long, I am sending it in five parts.[3]

2. General Bourne and I accept the conclusions in this report. We are convinced that Rahman will insist on listening to Chin Peng and on having discussion with him at least on some points, and that he would have very considerable public support in so insisting. We are also convinced that unless he is allowed to do this he will call the meeting off and lay on us the blame for missing an opportunity to end the Emergency. This would probably lead to an open breach between us and the Alliance. This is just what the Communists want most. We feel very strongly that the consequences of such a breach at the present time would greatly weaken our position in Malaya. Moreover, this breach would be likely to lead to dissension in the ranks of the Alliance itself and the emergence of Malay/Chinese antagonisms to an extent that would jeopardise the chances of establishing the United Malaya under a strong democratic Government which is the only answer in the long run to Communist penetration. We feel that far our best bet is a strong Alliance Government working in harmony with us and that the chance of this would be lost if the Alliance leaders should get it into their heads that we do not wish the Emergency to end and that we are using the Emergency as an excuse to delay self-Government. Our firm opinion is therefore that the meeting must be allowed to take place and that we should not now make a stand on an issue on which public opinion would not be on our side.

3. On the other hand, we also feel strongly that the M.C.P. must not be allowed to emerge from the jungle apparently undefeated. We would be likely to have a considerable body of public opinion in Malaya on our side if, later on, it should be necessary to take a stand in order to prevent this. I feel sure, however, that Rahman himself would not wish to go so far as to allow the M.C.P. this advantage since obviously it would threaten his own position and he is not so blind as not to see that. The Sunday Times yesterday in its leader summarised as follows a view which many people here will support:—

> "Chin Peng is anxious to call off the shooting war because he knows he can't win it; on our side we should be ready to come to terms with him because this would leave us the trouble and the pain of continuing a vastly expensive jungle war. But there must be no tendency on our part to conduct these negotiations in an atmosphere of 'equality'. On Chin Peng's side is a ragged

---

[1] See 373. [2] See 371.
[3] The report, which was ten pages and 29 paragraphs long, was sent as inward telegram no 655, 24 Oct (FO 371/116941, no 69/B).

379   CAB 128/29, CM 37(55)4   25 Oct 1955

'Malaya': Cabinet conclusions on Mr Lennox-Boyd's statement about Tunku Abdul Rahman's plan to meet Chin Peng

The Colonial Secretary said that the Chief Minister in Malaya, Mr. Tunku Abdul Rahman, had embarked upon a course of action which must give grounds for alarm. As the amnesty announcement of 8th September had failed to achieve any result, the Chief Minister felt it necessary that he should go into the forest himself to hold discussions with Communist leaders. Refusing to be dissuaded from this course, he had at first agreed to refrain at such a meeting from opening negotiations and from according recognition to the Communist Party, but to confine himself to further explanation of the terms of the amnesty. Later he had taken the view that the amnesty offer had not gone far enough and that he must be allowed, for the purpose of a meeting with the Communist leaders, a mandate to settle the situation as best he could. The High Commissioner, who had been instructed to remind Mr. Rahman of the undertaking he had given earlier, had replied that he felt that it would be impossible to dissuade the Chief Minister from entering into discussion with the Communist leaders, and that, if unacceptable conditions were imposed, the Chief Minister might well resign and so place himself in a position to cast the blame upon the Government at home for obstructing a course of action which could be represented as opening up a prospect of bringing the emergency to an end. The Commissioner-General, South-East Asia, had endorsed this view. The Government of Malaya was not, of course, the responsibility of the Chief Minister but of the High Commissioner in Executive Council, and the Chief Minister would have to report to the Council on his return. While it would be open to the Executive Council to reject any agreement or understanding with the Communists into which the Chief Minister had entered, it could be expected that any such act would precipitate a crisis of first importance. We should have no alternative but to stand firm in such an event and it would be right for us to do so.

The Prime Minister supported this view.

The Cabinet were informed that Mr Marshall,[1] the Chief Minister of Singapore, whose attitude towards Communism was more resolute and who would therefore have been a strengthening influence at the proposed meeting with Communist leaders, was now reconsidering his decision to be present.

The Cabinet:—

Took note of the Colonial Secretary's statement.

---

[1] See 358, note 3.

380 CAB 134/1201, CA 2(55)1 28 Oct 1955
'Malaya': Cabinet Colonial Policy Committee minutes on the forthcoming talks between Tunku Abdul Rahman and the communists

The Committee[1] were reminded that the Cabinet had been informed at their meeting on the 25th October[2] that it would not be practicable to dissuade the Chief Minister, Tanku [sic] Abdul Rahman, from holding discussions with Chin Peng and other Communist leaders. It had at first been explained that any such discussions should be confined to an explanation of the terms of the amnesty, but it was likely that Abdul Rahman could not be restrained from entering into some sort of negotiations with the Communists.

The Committee were informed that the High Commissioner had expressed the view (in telegram No. 659 from Malaya)[3] that the best way in which to stiffen Abdul Rahman's attitude in these discussions would be to make it clear that the end of the shooting war was now no longer regarded as a necessary condition precedent to the grant of self-government to the Federation. The general belief in Malaya, founded on certain authoritative statements, was that we insisted that the shooting war must end before self-government could be granted.

The Colonial Secretary said that he did not think the authoritative Government statements quoted in paragraph 1 of telegram No. 659 need be interpreted in such a way as to rule out the possibility of discussions about the next stage of the Federation's progress to self-government until the shooting war was over. He did not agree with the suggestion which the High Commissioner had made that the United Kingdom Government should announce publicly that they no longer regarded the shooting war as an obstacle on the road to self-government for Malaya. A public statement in such terms would be misunderstood. But, he suggested, it might be possible for the High Commissioner, in briefing Abdul Rahman for his meeting with the Communists, to say that he had been informed by the Colonial Secretary that, although the shooting war was not yet at an end, internal security conditions in Malaya had improved to such a degree that the United Kingdom Government no longer regarded them as an obstacle to further progress on the road to self-government.

The Prime Minister said that he was apprehensive lest a message to Abdul Rahman on the lines suggested by the Colonial Secretary should be regarded as a commitment on the part of the United Kingdom Government to make progress towards self-government for Malaya, whatever the outcome of the Chief Minister's talks with the Communists. Might it not be better to use the possibility of progress towards self-government as a threat, by warning Abdul Rahman that if his meeting with the Communists led to any sort of compromise prejudicial to our essential interests, there would be no hope of further progress towards self-government?

In discussion, it was suggested that a warning of this sort might take a less threatening form. The High Commissioner could point out to Abdul Rahman that if his meeting with the Communists resulted in a deterioration of the internal

---

[1] Present: Eden, Salisbury (lord president), Lennox-Boyd, Crookshank (lord privy seal), Selwyn Lloyd (minister of defence) and Reading (minister of state, FO).
[2] See 379. [3] See 378.

situation, this would be bound to have an adverse effect on progress towards self-government.

The Colonial Secretary said that he thought the argument would be of greater value if it was expressed in a positive or constructive way. This could be done, without entering into a final commitment to make progress, while the shooting war continued, towards self-government, if the instruction to our High Commissioner were on the following lines:—

> "In briefing Abdul Rahman, you (the High Commissioner) might say, for his own information, that if in the course of his explanations he does not compromise on any of the points to which we attach importance, we would, even though the shooting war has not yet ended, be prepared to consider whether internal security conditions have not improved to such a degree that we no longer regard them as an obstacle to further progress on the road to self-government."

The Committee were in general agreement that the instructions to the High Commissioner should be on these lines.

The Committee also agreed that it would be necessary to inform the Governments of Australia and New Zealand in confidence of the likelihood of a meeting between the Chief Minister of Malaya and the Communists, and to tell them what action was being taken to encourage the Chief Minister to avoid agreeing to any compromise prejudicial to our essential interests.

The Committee:—

(1) Invited the Colonial Secretary to send instructions to the High Commissioner, Federation of Malaya, on the lines agreed.[4]

(2) Invited the Lord Privy Seal, in consultation with the Colonial Secretary, to arrange for the necessary confidential information to be sent to the Governments of Australia and New Zealand.

---

[4] In his telegram to MacGillivray (no 145, 29 Oct 1955, FO 371/116941, no 76), Lennox-Boyd urged that every effort be made to persuade Tunku Abdul Rahman to do no more at the talks than clarify amnesty terms. In the event of the Tunku insisting on fuller discussions with Chin Peng, he should be informed, amongst other things, that the British government would reserve the right to reject proposals going beyond the amnesty and would in no circumstances agree to the recognition of the MCP or the release of 'hard core' communists. Lennox-Boyd also warned against 'the dangers of allowing the terrorists to figure as heroes after an amnesty'. The secretary of state agreed with the high commissioner that it would not be advisable for a senior British official to attend the talks but rejected MacGillivray's suggestion that he 'make a public statement in Parliament to the effect that HMG no longer regard the shooting war as an obstacle on the road to self-government'. He did so on the ground that it would be misunderstood and 'be represented as a retreat from the position previously held'. In spite of the Colonial Policy Committee's decision that Lennox-Boyd instruct MacGillivray to reassure the Tunku privately about the British commitment to Malayan self-government, the secretary of state had second thoughts about the wisdom of this and, as document 381 explains, chose to withhold this passage from his telegram.

381   FO 371/116941, no 77   31 Oct 1955

'Federation of Malaya': minute no PM(55)78 by Mr Lennox-Boyd to Sir
A Eden on the forthcoming talks between Tunku Abdul Rahman and
Chin Peng

Prime Minister

The Colonial Policy Committee at its meeting on the 28th October agreed on the instructions which should be sent to the High Commissioner of the Federation of Malaya on how to handle the Chief Minister's forthcoming talk with Chin Peng, the Communist leader.[1] In particular, the Committee agreed upon what the High Commissioner might say to the Chief Minister about the effect of the continuation of the shooting war on progress towards self-government.

2. As you know, on further reflection I felt considerable doubts whether the instructions given would have the right effect. The statement which the High Commissioner was authorised to make might be interpreted by the Chief Minister as meaning that progress towards self-government does not depend on an impartial assessment of the security situation while it seemed to me that the terms of the assurance might sound so uncertain and evasive to the Chief Minister as to cast doubts on our sincerity and motives in agreeing to the discussions next January. With your agreement, therefore, I omitted this passage from the telegram as sent and promised a further communication on the point. It was left that I should discuss the matter with the Head of my Far Eastern Department, who is due to return this evening from Malaya, and then raise it again in the Colonial Policy Committee at its meeting tomorrow.

3. You will, however, now have seen the High Commissioner's telegram No. 669 in which he says that he will be discussing the matter in his Executive Council on the 1st November and asks for guidance before then.

4. The High Commissioner and the Commissioner General are both convinced that it might be of decisive value to be able to assure the Chief Minister of the Federation that further progress towards self-government does not depend upon the ending of the shooting war. The Governor of Singapore in his personal telegram No. 139 reports that the Chief Minister in Singapore has independently suggested that assurance to this effect would be of immeasurable value. I myself feel that our agreement to the talks next January, which will include discussion of a commission to examine changes in the constitution leading to an advance towards self-government, implied that we did not consider that continuation of the shooting war which was then going on necessarily precluded such an advance. In these circumstances I think it important that we should say something on this point sufficiently positive not to imply that we are receding from this position or intending to use the continuation of the shooting war as a bargaining counter.

5. I should therefore like to be able to authorise the High Commissioner to speak on the following lines to the Chief Minister.

> "The attitude of H.M.G. towards progress towards self-government remains as it was when agreement was reached to discussions next January and to the

---

[1] See 380.

establishment of a commission to review the constitution. Although H.M.G. fervently hopes that the Emergency can be brought to an end within the amnesty terms, they do not consider that its continuation at the present level need in itself prove an obstacle to the establishment of such a commission and to the consideration of its recommendations, provided that no concessions are made to the Communists during the forthcoming talks which would affect the ability of the Federation Government to keep the internal security position under control."[2]

---

[2] A telegram on these lines was sent to MacGillivray on 1 Nov. The most significant amendment to the wording was the substitution of 'provided that nothing transpires during the forthcoming talks' for 'provided that no concessions are made to the Communists during the forthcoming talks' (FO 371/116941, no 76, outward telegram no 146.)

---

382 FO 371/116941, no 80   8 Nov 1955

[Meeting between Tunku Abdul Rahman and Chin Peng]: inward telegram no 691 from Sir D MacGillivray to Mr Lennox-Boyd

Your telegrams Personal No. 145 and No. 146.[1]

We had already done all we could to persuade Rahman to confine himself to clarification of the terms of the amnesty and it had become quite clear that he would not (repeat not) agree to do so. He had first made this clear at the meeting in Singapore on 19th October and as reported in my telegram No. 669 he subsequently committed himself publicly to listening to what Chin Peng has to say. I had also learned that insistence that he should confine himself to clarification would certainly lead to (corrupt gp. ? resignation) of the Alliance.

2. Conclusion of Council business on 1st November gave members of Executive Council an opportunity to express their views on the nature and scope of meeting with Chin Peng. I made the points (paragraphs 11 and 12 of my telegram No. 655)[2] that there is a considerable field for discussion within the limits of the amnesty terms but that discussion with Chin Peng of other matters, such as the repeal of the Emergency Regulations, would amount to our acknowledgment that Chin Peng had a right to a voice in policy making and would raise the meeting to the level of negotiations on equal terms. There appeared to be general assent or at least appreciation of this point of view on the part of most of the Alliance Ministers. I am sending by bag the relevant extract from the minutes. These have not (repeat not) yet been confirmed by Council.

3. The Chief Minister has reiterated his intention of doing no more than listening to what Chin Peng has to say and coming back to report to me. In Executive Council he expressed his appreciation of the importance of not (repeat not) allowing the Communists to appear in the guise of victors but thought that this could be achieved by insisting that all who surrender should be held for investigation. It may be significant and an indication of his line of thought that he added, after a slight pause, "even if this was only for 3 or 3 [sic] days".

4. Other Ministers said little on the subject of meeeting with Chin Peng itself,

---

[1] See 380, note 4 & 381, note 2.   [2] See 377, note 3.

probably for fear of expressing views which might not coincide with those of the Chief Minister. But Dr. Ismail emphasized the importance that was attached by the Alliance and the people generally to ending the Emergency at the earliest possible moment and brought out the point that sense of urgency was increased by the fact that Her Majesty's Government has made the ending of the Emergency a condition of the grant of self-government. Ong Loke Lin [sic][3] went so far as to say that the effect of this condition on many people's minds was to make them feel that Chin Peng held the key to the situation. Ismail said that he thought Her Majesty's Government should now (repeat now) take the initative by indicating that further progress towards self-government was not (repeat not) independent [sic] upon the prior termination of the Emergency although at outset of Council meeting some four hours earlier when we had been discussing draft press release relating to London Talks I had felt justified in giving Council the gist of your telegram Personal No. 146 (which had just reached me) neither Ismail nor any other Minister referred to it and they presumably felt that it did not (repeat not) go far enough to meet their point.

5.   Discussion in Executive Council seemed to give added weight to arguments in my telegram No. 659[4] in favour of a statement on lines of first sentence of that telegram. I would therefore again urge the importance of a public statement and I will telegraph further on this in a day or two. It might appropriately be made in my speech at the opening of the Budget Meeting of Legislative Council on 30th November and this would I think be about the right date for making it.

6.   With regard to the two written communications which you suggest should be made to the Chief Minister, I greatly fear that to put all these points to him in writing would create an atmosphere of distrust and would have the reverse of the effect desired. It would be likely to impel him to go up to and beyond the limits set simply in order to avoid being called a "British stooge". I am inclined to think that the best arrangement might be for me, with the Director of Operations present, to have a final discussion with him just before he goes to the meeting. Provided I feel I could then do so, (corrupt gp. ? without creating) the impression that we distrusted him, I would have a record made of this discussion and give him a copy of that record. He already fully understands and accepts (a) and (b) of paragraph 3 of your telegram Personal No. 145 and is on record in Executive Council as having agreed that the M.C.P. must not be recognised (but see paragraph 10). It is on the other points that difficulty is likely to arise, especially such matters as the detention of 'hard core' Communists (see paragraph 3 above) and the right of deportation.

7.   A paper is being prepared here containing an appreciation of the extent to which it would be safe to go in response to requests by Chin Peng for clarification of the words of the amnesty, "Restrictions will have to be placed on their liberty". This paper will also include an appreciation of the extent to which it would be safe to go in response to demands which would be likely to be made by the Chief Minister for the repeal of the Emergency Regulations and the release of all present detainees in the event of the surrender of the M.C.P. and the end of the Emergency. This paper will be sent to you as soon as it is ready, in a few days time. It will include statement of probable effect of a breach with Alliance and resignation of Ministers.

8.   I am grateful for your suggestion that you should send Rahman a personal message just before the meeting. I will telegraph separately on this.

---

[3] Ong Yoke Lin, minister of transport.   [4] See 378.

9.   I am also grateful for the suggestion in your fifth paragraph that you might, as a last resort, invite Rahman to come to London. The desirability of this step would, of course, depend on the situation at the time. My present guess is that Rahman will not wish to arrange a second meeting with Chin Peng before the London constitutional talks and that he will plan to use the fact that [?he] could reach a settlement with Chin Peng on terms which had a large measure of public support here, although unacceptable to Her Majesty's Government, in order to advance in London his demands for early self-government.

10.   "Singapore Standard" report this morning that Rahman told the Standard before he left yesterday for Indonesia⁵ that he was prepared: "To talk about the recognition of the M.C.P. if the subject is brought up for discussion", at his meeting with Chin Peng.⁶

---

⁵ The Tunku's first journey overseas as chief minister was to Indonesia at the invitation of President Sukarno.
⁶ In order to prepare for easier negotiations at the forthcoming Anglo-Malayan constitutional conference in London, the Cabinet Colonial Policy Committee agreed on 24 Nov to authorise the high commissioner to announce publicly that the continuation of war would not stand in the way of advance to self-government. MacGillivray made such a statement in the Federal Legislative Council on 30 Nov. See CAB 134/1201, CA 6(55)2.

383   DEFE 7/493, no 3   8 Nov 1955

'Negotiations on defence with Malaya and Singapore': minutes (NDMS/M(55)2) by the Ministry of Defence of an inter-departmental meeting¹
[Extract]

The Chairman said that the Colonial Policy Committee were about to consider a paper by the Minister of Defence on the general line to be taken on defence matters in the forthcoming negotiations with the Federation of Malaya and Singapore. Against the general background that we could not hinder the steady progress of the territories through self-government to independence, defence arrangements fell to be considered under two heads:—

(i)   The short term, in which nominal responsibility for internal security would presumably pass to the local governments but Her Majesty's Government would retain responsibility for foreign relations and external defence. During this stage the local governments would have to build up indigenous forces for internal security purposes. The Chiefs of Staff had recommended a force of 12 Battalions organised as a Division in the Federation, a Brigade Group for Singapore, and small naval and air components. These recommendations would be put to the Malayan and Singapore authorities before the January talks began.

(ii)   In the second stage the local governments would assume responsibility for foreign relations and defence, thus becoming independent Sovereign States. It was

---

¹ The meeting was chaired by Sir R Powell (deputy secretary, Ministry of Defence, 1950–1956; permanent secretary, 1956–1960) and attended by officials from the Ministry of Defence, the Treasury, the Admiralty, the War Office, the Air Ministry, the FO, CO (MacKintosh) and CRO.

hoped that they would remain within the Commonwealth and that they would join SEATO. The continued presence of U.K. and Commonwealth forces would, in our view, be necessary but their presence would have to be justified on these wider grounds.

2. It was clear that at a comparatively early stage in the discussions the question of a bilateral defence agreement would come up. The object of the present meeting was to discuss the general content of such an agreement and to draw up a provisional programme of work. The B.D.C.C. study, which had been circulated to the meeting, formed a useful starting point.

3. *Mr. MacKintosh* said that the scope of the talks in January had been modifed. It was now envisaged that there would be a conference lasting two or three weeks, the main objects of which would be to set up a constitutional Commission and to discuss arrangements for defence and the general scope of a defence agreement. It was not intended that the conference would get down to detail. If all went well the conference would be followed by the detailed negotiation of a defence agreement, both in London and locally, which would proceed in parallel with the setting up of the Constitutional Commission. The Commission would take a year to eighteen months to report, so that there should be adequate time for drafting the defence agreement. It would, nevertheless, be of the greatest value to have the general outlines of an agreement ready well in advance.

4. So far as the form and content of the agreement was concerned, *Mr. MacKintosh* urged that the specific provisions should be kept to the practicable minimum. There was a far greater chance of getting the co-operation without which any agreement would be bound to fail if we did not pitch our initial demands too high or in terms which would lead the Malayan and Singapore authorities into believing that we were attempting to take back through the agreement any apparent concessions which had been made in the political field.

5. The representatives from the Federation of Malaya would arrive in this country during the third week in January. We should aim to have any necessary briefs on defence in the hands of the Commissioner General and the High Commissioner, by the middle of December.

6. So far as the duration of the agreement itself was concerned, the Colonial Office view was that it should be open-ended with provision for review and, if necessary, re-negotiation by mutual agreement but not for termination when the governments moved from self-government to independence.

7. *The Chairman* said that in view of the time-table the present Committee should aim to meet again in about three weeks' time with a view to putting any necessary briefs into final shape. The Colonial Office would meantime be keeping the High Commissioners [sic] informed of work in progress. In particular, the Minutes of the present Meeting would be circulated both to them and to B.D.C.C.

8. The following general points were made in discussion:—

(i)   The C.R.O. would wish to keep the Australians and New Zealand governments closely informed of progress. The agreement would have to be drafted with their requirements in mind and the long term position of the Commonwealth Strategic Reserve would need very careful handling. There was a particular danger that the Australian Government would be influenced against our proposals for financing the deployment of the Strategic Reserve, which they were now considering, if they were given reason to believe that the long term deployment of the Strategic Reserve was already in doubt.

(ii) The question of financial assistance would have to be considered in two stages; as applying to self-government and as applying to independence. Continuing financial assistance to an independent country raised difficult questions of principle. In general, the Treasury would wish to examine the question of financial assistance in the broad context of the financial standing of Malaya and Singapore as a whole and not merely in relation to their defence obligations, still less to the facilities which they continued to make available to us.

(iii) We should in considering the form of the Agreement make as much use as possible of existing agreements between independent Sovereign States, i.e. the U.S./Philippine agreement, the agreement to the stationing of U.S. forces in the U K , and the NATO Status of Forces agreement. . . .

384 CO 1030/75, no 4 [Nov 1955]
'The London talks: Alliance demands and the extent to which they might be met': memorandum by D C Watherston

Present political background and likely developments
It must be recognised that the Chief Minister and his colleagues will be going to the London Conference[1] with one object in mind, namely, to obtain a promise of the grant of independence, almost certainly with a date attached to it, and agreement on certain concrete steps to be taken in the immediate future in the direction of attaining that independence.

2. The Ministerial numbers of the delegation will go with the eyes of the whole country fixed on them and they will know that, unless they come back substantially with what they will be asking for, there will be widespread disappointment and dissatisfaction and they would, in fact, be committing political suicide.

3. The political opponents of the Alliance have steadily been organising themselves during the months since the new Government took office. They can be relied upon to cash in on the growing feeling of uneasiness in the country that, so far, the new Government has come out with no concrete schemes of social improvement or indeed, shown signs of implementing any of the schemes in its election manifesto. Its energies have been almost entirely devoted to (a) ending the Emergency by means of an amnesty and talks with Chin Peng, and (b) preparations for the constitutional talks in London. Success in the first of these is still distinctly problematical and, if the Chief Minister is not successful in achieving the target the Alliance has set itself in London, it could lead to the party losing the overwhelming support which it possesses at present. The Malays—and it must not be forgotten that they make up 85% of the electorate—would look for more extreme nationalist leadership.

4. The attitude of the Chinese is not so easy to forecast. The M.C.A. leaders, the majority of whom are pro-K.M.T., have always recognised that the Chinese in the Federation can never be sure of a fair deal when the country achieves self-

---

[1] Held at Lancaster House between 18 Jan and 6 Feb 1956.

government unless they can secure acceptance of the principle of the *jus soli* and so obtain a voting strength proportionate to the Chinese population. Remembering the present voting strength of the Malays, the M.C.A. leaders know that they have no hope of getting this policy accepted unless they give full support (with large financial backing) to the Malays in the Alliance, and they will continue to give that support and press for citizenship to be included in the terms of reference of the Constitutional Commission for which the Alliance has asked. But the M.C.A. has few roots and the bulk of the Chinese in the Federation—including particularly the labourers in new villages and the Chinese who have been educated in the Chinese vernacular Primary and Middle Schools—are much more China-than-Malaya-minded and, without necessarily being Communists, they have a great pride in the achievements of the Chinese Peoples' Government in the international field. With the prospect of the end of the Emergency, and the return of erstwhile Communist terrorists and detainees to the normal life of the country, there is a real danger of a steady spread of left-wing theories among Chinese and their admiration for China is likely to make them ready to accept them. The left-wing leaders—equally with the M.C.A. leaders—would realise that they could not attain their ends without Malay support and they would make common cause with the extreme Malay nationalists, being careful not to give prominence to their communist ideology but disguising it as nationalist.

5.   The Alliance leaders see these dangers and they know that they can maintain their present following only if the outcome of the London Conference can be represented as a real victory for them. The consequences of the talks failing to reach a satisfactory agreement would be extremely serious. The Alliance Ministers would almost certainly resign and so would all Alliance members of the Federal/State/Settlement/Municipal/Town/Local Councils. There would be a demand for new elections and the probability is that the Alliance would be as successful as last time but that their programme would be more far-reaching and would be violently anti-British. The moderate Ministers would be dropped. There might well be mass demonstrations which would be a serious threat to the internal security of the country in the control of which reliance might not be able to be put upon the Police or the Local Forces. A separate and fuller appreciation on the probable situation that would arise has been prepared.

Alliance demands
6.   It will be as well to consider that the Alliance Ministers are likely to demand and then how far we would wish to go to meet them, and how much further we could go if this became necessary to prevent the talks breaking down. Finally, it would be necessary to decide which of their demands we would not be prepared to concede even if the refusal led to a break-down, in the full knowledge of the likely consequences of such a break-down.

A constitutional commission
7.   In the first place, the Alliance has asked for an independent Commission to review the constitution. The appointment of a Commission, without any commitment as to its nature, has already been agreed in principle by H.M.G. and the composition, terms of reference and timing are to be discussed at the London talks. Assuming agreement is reached, some time will elapse before such a Commission could start work. The names of suitable persons for appointment as Chairman and as

members of the Commission would have to be agreed by the three interested parties, *viz*., H.M.G., the Rulers and the Alliance Ministers; these persons would have to be approached and would have to disentangle themselves from their present commitments; and they would then have to assemble in Malaya. It would probably be impossible for them to start work before June, 1956, at the earliest, and doubtful if they could begin before July or August. The task to which they will be addressing themselves will be a formidable one and, if the members of the Commission have no previous acquaintance with Malaya, they will take a little time to acquire essential background knowledge. Representations will be made to the Commission by every shade of interest—political, racial and economic. So far as the Alliance is concerned, we know that they are contemplating a legislature consisting of a Second Chamber and a fully-elected Lower Chamber. This is likely to involve consideration of the respective spheres and powers of the Federal and of the State and Settlement Governments. It will also involve consideration of the delicate question of the powers and functions of the Conference of Rulers. Further, the Alliance contemplates the Commission going into the exceedingly complex and controversial question of citizenship and nationality. Without going into further details in this paper, it is sufficiently clear that the Commission could not hope to produce its report in any shorter period than many months and possibly even as much as a year.

8. Looking beyond the stage of the submission of the Commission's report, whatever steps are taken to speed up the processes of consultation, considerable time will inevitably be taken up in consideration of the Commission's recommendations by H.M.G., the Rulers and the Federation Government. When agreement has been reached, the formal processes of framing amendments to the Federation Agreement and of passing legislation through Legislative Council have to be undertaken and there might well be other matters such as the re-delineation of electoral constituencies, or the registration of additional categories of electors if there was to be any change in eligibility for Federal citizenship, which would have to be dealt with before the revised constitution could actually be brought into force. It is unlikely, however, that the Malays would accept as a valid reason for any appreciable delay the time needed for the introduction of new citizenship provisions; but there would be bound to be strong pressure from the Chinese for this as otherwise the new elections would, like the last, be on the basis of an electoral roll which is 85% Malay.

9. The conclusion to be drawn from this is that it would be impossible for any constitutional changes of this kind to become effective before the latter part of 1957; even January, 1958, might prove to be too early a date to achieve. It is intended to examine the terms of reference of the Commission and its composition in a separate paper.

385   CO 1030/27, no 10   1 Dec 1955
[Meeting between Tanku Abdul Rahman and Chin Peng]: letter from Sir D MacGillivray to Sir J Martin on arrangements

I enclose a document[1] recording the decisions taken at a meeting held here on the

---

[1] Not printed.

26th November to discuss arrangements for the meeting between the Chief Ministers and Chin Peng. This meeting was attended by the ten persons mentioned in the distribution list at the end of the document.

You will note that it is proposed to agree that the Security forces within the cease-fire area will remain in base and to insist that there should be no movement either by them or by the Communist terrorists during the talks. It is also proposed to agree that there should be no air reconnaissance over the cease-fire area during the cease-fire period. (This cease-fire period has not yet been defined, but is likely to be from about ten days before the meeting until ten days after it.) There may be danger in such an arrangement, for, if there is to be no air reconnaissance, the C.T.s could, without our knowing it, move their forces under cover of the jungle to within striking distance of the place where the talks are to take place and, if the outcome of the talks should be unsatisfactory to them, make an attack on the place and kill or carry off the Chief Ministers and others attending the talks. There has been treachery in the past on the part of the M.C.P. leaders (see pages 39 and 68 of Harry Miller's book "Menace in Malaya"),[2] and I would not put it past them to break the condition that there should be no movement of their forces in the jungle during the cease-fire period. It will be necessary, therefore, for us to take the precaution of moving additional troops into the area before the period of cease-fire begins, and particularly to build up our forces in and near the meeting place.

The passage[3] which the Secretary of State authorised me to include in my address to the Legislative Council yesterday to the effect that Her Majesty's Government see no reason to regard the continuance of the Emergency at its present level as an obstacle in the Federation's advance towards self-Government has been very well received, and I am sure will be very valuable in stiffening public opinion against negotiations. Yesterday evening, Abdul Rahman made a broadcast in which he quoted this important passage correctly (and, incidentally, misquoted me elsewhere) and ended his broadcast with the following sentences:—

> "His Excellency also mentioned that these last few years had seen great strides in constitutional developments. These advances, he said, had been made possible by the measure of trust which had been established within the Federation Government, between the political parties, and H.M.G. "It is this spirit of trust", (I quote), "and this spirit of goodwill that has made possible these advances." I am sure the people are happy to hear the assurance coming, as it did, from Her Majesty's representative in his address to the Council. I am sure that the people of Malaya will join with me in an expression of thanks to Her Majesty's Government."

The Chief Minister and the Executive Council agreed that I should include in my speech the statement that the Chief Minister "was prepared to meet Chin Peng, and only Chin Peng, in order to clarify the already declared amnesty terms", and that "the Chief Minister is not prepared to negotiate in any way at all, although he is ready to listen to what Chin Peng has to say." Moreover, in reply to an oral question in the

---

[2] Harry Miller was chief correspondent of the *Straits Times* based in Kuala Lumpur; *Menace in Malaya* (London, Harrap) was published in 1954.
[3] See 382, note 6.

Legislative Council yesterday, he declared that his meeting with Chin Peng "will be neither negotiations nor peace talks."

In paragraph 3 of the Secretary of State's telegram Personal 145 of the 29th October,[4] the suggestion was made that I should make it clear to Abdul Rahman in writing that my consent to his being allowed to listen to Chin Peng was given on certain definite understandings. In paragraph 6 of my reply, No. 691 of the 8th of November,[5] I said that I thought that to put these points to him in writing would create an atmosphere of mistrust and would have the reverse of the effect desired. I suggested that, instead, I should have a final discussion with him before he goes to the meeting, and, provided I felt I could do so without creating an impression of mistrust, have a record made of this discussion and send him a copy of that record. In view of what is now recorded in paragraph 2 of Part II on page 4 of the attached document, and of what is recorded in the Executive Council minutes and in the Hansard of the present Legislative Council meeting, I do not think it is necessary, and indeed not desirable, for me to send Abdul Rahman a note of record of our final discussion before the meeting takes place. Since early November there has been a distinctly favourable change in Abdul Rahman's attitude towards the Chin Peng meeting, and I do not think we need now have the same degree of concern as to its outcome that we had a month ago. What I would propose to do is to see him before he leaves for the meeting, hand him the letter from the Secretary of State and to wish him good luck.

Before, however, the next meeting takes place between Chen Tian and Wylie and Too Joon Hing (on 13th or 16th December),[6] I would endeavour to get Abdul Rahman to agree that instructions should be given to Wylie and Too to the effect that they must make it clear to Chen Tian that, if Chen Peng does not turn up for a meeting on the 28th of December under the arrangements now given, then

(a) the Amnesty will be terminated, and
(b) there will be no further question of a meeting and talks.

I am sending a copy of this letter and of the enclosure to the Commissioner-General and the Governor of Singapore.

---

[4] See 380, note 4.   [5] See 382.
[6] I C Wylie (deputy commissioner of police) and Too Joon Hing (assistant minister for education) had their first meeting with Chen Tian (head of propaganda, MCP) on 17 Oct at Klian Intan (a village in Upper Perak and a few miles from the Thai border) where they discussed arrangements for talks between Tunku Abdul Rahman and Chin Peng.

386 CO 1030/27, no 13   [Dec 1955]
'Talks between the chief ministers of the Federation of Malaya and Singapore and Chin Peng': draft CO memorandum

[This would appear to be a draft memorandum intended for ministerial circulation. It was not, however, presented to the full Cabinet (CAB 129 does not contain a version), nor was it discussed by the Cabinet Colonial Policy Committee, which met on 25 Nov for the last time in 1955 and did not reconvene until 4 Jan 1956 (see CAB 134/1201).]

I have now heard from the High Commissioner for the Federation of Malaya that these talks may take place on the 28th of this month. Marshall has always been opposed to the talks; and in my view he can be relied upon to give nothing away at them so long as Abdul Rahman is also prepared to stand firm. Abdul Rahman's attitude has recently stiffened a great deal and it is even possible that he may yet agree to call off both the talks and the amnesty. Nevertheless, it is important that we should let the High Commissioner and the Governor of Singapore know well in advance what concessions to Chin Peng we would be willing to countenance, and on what issues we must insist on standing firm even at the risk of a break with the Alliance Government in the Federation.

2.   The High Commissioner has sent me a most useful appreciation of the problems involved in ending the Emergency on terms outside the declaration of amnesty. I do not think that I need trouble my colleagues with the whole document (which is long) but I attach copies of two appendices to it, one (Appendix A to this memorandum)[1] dealing with the consequences of a break with the Alliance, and the other (Appendix B)[2] setting out in tabular form the main issues involved, the main factors affecting them and the High Commissioner's conclusions upon them.

3.   The recent attitude of Abdul Rahman suggests that he may be prepared to take his stand well in advance of what we would regard as our last ditch positions; but the High Commissioner's appreciation of the consequences of a break with the Alliance seems to me so grave—and I would not dispute it in essentials—that I accept the view underlying the Appendix B, that we should have as few "sticking-points" as possible.

4.   In general, as I see it, we have two aims—first, to prevent the Malayan Communist Party from saving anything material from the wreck of the shooting war, and second, so far as possible to limit their capacity for subversion when the shooting war is over. The first of these aims requires that the Communist terrorists must be prevented from coming out of the jungle on terms which could suggest that victory lay with them rather than with the Federation; and it also requires that the arrangements for their surrender should include providing the Government with the information necessary to enable them to collect the great bulk of the terrorists' arms and ammnunition. (I think that at any rate the hard-core should be detained at least until the Government were satisfied about this.)

5.   The second of these general aims requires that when the shooting war ends the power to arrest, detain and control should be retained either in Emergency Regulations or in ordinary law. (My own view is that the Emergency Regulations should so far as possible be abolished, those which it is necessary to retain being translated into permanent or semi-permanent legislation.) That is one of the two sticking-points recommended by the High Commissioner. The other is refusal to recognise the M.C.P. unless power is retained to detain or to deport the hard core. An important implication of this is that in the view of the High Commissioner and his advisers we should in the last resort by prepared to recognise the M.C.P. so long as powers to arrest, detain and control are retained. On the other hand, the High Commissioner has told me that General Bourne does not agree and thinks that we should on no account agree to recognise the M.C.P. I agree with General Bourne.

6.   There are estimated to be some 3,000 Communist terrorists in the jungle. Of these:—

---

[1] See 387.   [2] Not printed.

(a) 2,500 are regarded as being of little security significance;

(b) 500 are believed to be hard-core Communists; and

(c) 50–100 are really dangerous Communists.

I suggest that our attitude to these three categories should be as follows:—

(i)   those in (a) could be released fairly soon, after investigation by the Special Branch;

(ii)   those in (b) would require fuller investigation and, if they could not be deported, would have to be detained, or kept under close police supervision, until they were no longer a security risk; and

(iii)   those in (c) could not, for as far ahead as we can see, be set free in Malaya at all: every effort should be made to deport them, failing which they would have to be indefinitely detained.

That is what, in my view, we should aim at but, subject to insistence upon the two sticking-points to which I have referred in paragraph 5 above (the point in paragraph 4 is of rather a different order and seems to me to be implied by paragraph 5), I do not think that we need insist rigidly upon them if to do so would involve us in a break with the Alliance.

7. It will be seen from Appendix B that (i) to (iii) in paragraph 6 above could be modified in a variety of ways but I do not think that we can at this stage usefully pursue the matter in further detail. The two Chief Ministers have firmly undertaken that, if the talks take place, they will avoid commitment on any of these matters and will return to discuss with the High Commissioner, the Director of Operations and the Governor any proposal by Chin Peng which they have not already rejected out of hand. We shall then have an opportunity to consider any of these points again in the light of the advice of the High Commissioner and the Governor upon them.

8. I therefore seek my colleagues' agreement to instruct the High Commissioner and the Governor on the general lines of this memorandum.

387 CO 1030/27, no 21   [Dec 1955]
'Consequences of a break': memorandum prepared by Sir D Mac-Gillivray's senior officials concerned with defence and intelligence

[This paper was received in the CO and forwarded to the Chiefs of Staff Committee on 21 Dec. It addresses the probable consequences of a break between the British and Alliance governments were the latter to make concessions to the communists with respect to either (i) the retention of present powers to arrest, detain and control or (ii) the recognition of the MCP without detention or deportation of hard-core communists.]

The consequences of a break with the Alliance Government, on any of the fundamental issues, are outlined below.

(a) *Public Opinion*

(i)   UMNO would back the Chief Minister and he would try to use this support and the weight of public opinion to force us to give way.

(ii)   The M.I.C. would support him. Some of the MCA leaders would not agree with him but would fall in with the wishes of the majority and present a united front.

(iii) The Chinese in the villages because of their desire to end the Emergency would follow the Chief Minister in order to obtain peace.

(iv) Although the Rulers or some of them might not wish to support the Chief Minister it would be most unlikely that they would publicly express this view.

(v) There would then be a tremendous but not quite unanimous weight of public opinion against us inside the country. Certain elements would support us but the only vocal section would be the British. It would be claimed that it was unreasonable not to allow the Chief Minister to end the shooting war on reasonable terms.

(vi) Free world opinion, except in certain countries of South East Asia would probably not be so strongly against us. The dangers of negotiation arising out of discussions would be recognised.

(b) *Preliminary steps to a break*
It is probable that:—

(i)   The Chief Minister would arrange for the press to know why the meeting with Chin Peng had failed. He would let it be known that he had been willing to end the shooting war on the terms offered but the High Commissioner had compelled him to reject the offer.

(ii)   He would continue to act constitutionally maintaining the normal Government of the country.

(iii) He would privately guide public opinion to demonstrate on his behalf.

(iv) He would wait for this public opinion to mount before he took further action.

(v)   Then with this vociferous support, he and his ministers might resign from Executive Council but remain in Legislative Council arguing that they had been forced to take this step as their advice to H.E. and the wishes of the people had been disregarded.

(vi) If these steps failed to obtain a reversal of decision from the High Commissioner he would use his "secret weapon"—the signed resignation slips of all Alliance members of Council at all levels throughout the country.

(c) *Consequences of a break*

(i)   The Alliance ministers of Government might resign. Their resignations would be followed by the resignations of all Alliance members of the Federal/State/Settlement/Municipal and Town Councils. Responsible elected Government would end.

(ii)   They would set up a demand for new Elections. At present there is no prospect of any other party coming into power in these circumstances.

(iii) There would be vociferous and active resentment against:—

(i)   The British Government
(ii)   British Officials;

(iv)   There might well be mass demonstrations, which would be a serious threat to the internal security of the country, in the control of which reliance might not be able to be put upon local Military or Police forces.

(v)   The situation might well be aggravated by the essential use of British and

Gurkha troops in a civil security role.

(vi)   Malay support for the prosecution of the Emergency would cease, and this might well extend to the possibility of the MCP getting recruits in rural Malay areas.

(vii)   There could be a very increased rate of defection amongst Home Guards with their arms.

(viii)   Information from the public as regards movement of terrorists, etc., would diminish and civil disobedience might well extend to a refusal to comply with food control regulations.

(ix)   Military initiative against the terrorists would be gravely affected.

388   CO 1030/410, no 1   22 Dec 1955

[Withdrawal of British advisers from the Malay states]: letter from Sir D MacGillivray to A M MacKintosh on the rulers' reluctant agreement. *Enclosure*: circular letter from Sir D MacGillivray to the rulers, 28 Nov 1955

I wrote to the Rulers on 28th November on the subject of the British Advisers as in the attached copy of my letter. I asked them to meet me by themselves at King's House yesterday to let me know their views. They came without their advisers, and informed me briefly that they had discussed the matter together and had come to the conclusion that it would be unwise to resist the political pressure for the removal of these posts. They had obviously come to this decision with great reluctance.[1] It seems clear therefore that the Rulers' representatives will receive instructions to join with the Alliance Ministers in the request which will undoubtedly be put forward at the London Conference for the withdrawal of the British Advisers. I enclose a note[2] on the subject which Watherston prepared before he left here.

In discussion with the Rulers yesterday, I put forward the suggestion that, if it should be agreed in principle at the London talks that these posts should be abolished, it would be unwise to proceed to do so with unseemly haste. I pointed out that the State Agreements and Constitutions and the Federal Agreement would all have to be amended first; that at least the majority of the present British Advisers would have to be allowed to retire on pension on abolition terms; that it would be only right to give them due notice; and that there would be practical problems of the disposal of their Residencies and the allocation of their remaining duties to be settled. I also said that it might not be necessary, or indeed desirable, for all of them to go at the same time; that there might be a practical need to retain them in those States, for example Johore and Perak, where the Emergency remained a serious problem for a longer period than in those other States, such as Kelantan, Trengganu

---

[1] Sultan Ibrahim of Johore was particularly intractable. He insisted, in a letter to MacGillivray on 1 Dec, that 'I must have a British Adviser otherwise works cannot be carried out smoothly'; he complained to Lennox-Boyd about 'the way the Government is now being run in this country'; and he questioned the competence of Malay politicians (CO 1030/375, no 13). The dispute over the withdrawal of advisers rumbled on for another year, see 435.

[2] Not printed.

and Pahang, where there no longer exists a serious Emergency situation. I suggested further that the State Agreements might be amended at the same time, but in such a way that effect to the change could be given at any time within say twelve months of the amendment of the Agreements. I also proposed that if this was done the timing in each case could be agreed upon between me and the Ruler concerned, but that in any case the withdrawal of the British Adviser would not take effect until at least six months after such agreement had been reached. The Rulers indicated that something on these lines would generally be agreeable to them. I think, therefore, we must contemplate the withdrawal of the British Advisers beginning some time towards the end of next year and concluding perhaps by mid-1957.

Enclosure to 388

I have the honour to address Your Highness on the subject of British Advisers.

2.   Your Highness will recollect that when the Secretary of State, the Rt. Hon'ble Mr. Alan Lennox-Boyd, met with the Conference of Rulers in Kuala Lumpur on the 23rd August[3] he informed the Conference that the Chief Minister, Tunku Abdul Rahman, had the previous day handed him a memorandum containing certain proposals,[4] and that one of these related to the position of the British Advisers. The Chief Minister had expressed the view that these posts had become redundant and the Secretary of State said that he would be glad to have the views of the Conference as to this. The Presiding Ruler replied that the Conference would wish to discuss the matter among themselves and that the views of the Conference would be conveyed later to me for transmission to the Secretary of State.

3.   This is a matter which will, no doubt, be discussed in the course of the meetings which are being held in Kuala Lumpur, preliminary to the London talks, between the representatives of Your Highnesses and the Alliance Ministers who will form the Malayan delegation at those talks. I hope, also, that Your Highnesses will agree to discuss the matter at the Conference of Rulers to be held on the 21st December and will be able to acquaint me with your views when we meet on the 22nd December. The matter will undoubtedly be raised during the course of discussions in London, and I shall be glad to have my friends' views in advance.

4.   The abolition of the post of British Adviser, or even its replacement by a post not having the same status and functions, would, of course, entail amendments to the State Agreements (Clauses 4–6), the State Constitutions, and the Federal Agreement (Clauses 90 and 98).

5.   I am sending a copy of this letter to the Keeper of the Rulers' Seal.

---

[3] See 367.   [4] See 365.

389   CO 1030/75, no 2   [22 Dec 1955]
'Federation of Malaya constitutional conference': memorandum by the
CO Far Eastern Department on aims, agenda and tactics. *Minute* by M
L Cahill[1]

The purpose of the conference
We are going to the assumption that what the Alliance hope to secure as a result of
the Conference (although not as an immediate result) is that Federation Ministers
should be granted complete responsibility for the internal government of Malaya. We
are at the same time assuming that the Alliance leaders do not at this stage expect to
be given control over defence and external affairs and that H.M.C. would not in any
case be prepared to concede such such control. H.M.G. are, of course, committed to
granting self-government to Malaya, and it is suggested that they should take part in
the Conference on the understanding that they would be prepared to agree to the
Alliance demands for internal self-government, and would negotiate with the
Alliance on this basis: defence and external affairs would, however, remain "reserved"
subjects. There is one major issue, however, which lies half way between the
"reserved" subject of defence and those more purely domestic matters which could
be transferred to local Ministers without undue difficulty – the issue of internal
security. Is control of the Federation's own military forces, the Police (regular and
special), and the Home Guard, together with responsibility for the custody of those
detained under the Emergency Regulations, to pass to an elected Minister or to
remain with a British official? This is likely to prove one of the most troublesome
items on the agenda.

After the conference
    2. The Alliance are not expecting us to concede all their demands at the
Conference table, although they undoubtedly hope that certain concessions will be
made straight away (see paragraph 4 below). They envisage that an independent
Constitutional Commission should be set up as a result of the conference to examine
their proposals for constitutional reforms; this Commission will probably take as
long as twelve months or so to produce its report, which will then have to be
considered by H.M.G. and the Federation Government. In the field of defence we
expect the Conference to produce, at the most, no more than a broad measure of
unanimity: the details of a Defence Agreement would have to be worked out during
the months after the Conference has taken place. When these major issues of the
revision of the constitution and a Defence Agreement have finally been settled, we
could amend the Federation Agreement accordingly, incorporating in it the heads of
the Defence Agreement between H.M.G. and the Federation Government and the
new constitutional provisions recommended by the Constitutional Commission.

The main headings of the agenda
    3. The items on the agenda fall into five main categories. First there are matters
relating to *defence and internal security*. A committee on this subject has been
meeting at the Ministry of Defence for some weeks now, and we shall be in a position

---

[1] Assistant principal in the CO.

to confront the Delegates with concrete proposals. The subject of *financial responsibility and economic development* has not received so much attention, but the Federation authorities have drawn up a certain amount of preparatory material and we shall very soon be discussing the matter fully with the Treasury. *The future of the Public Service* will be included in the agenda: it is not expected that the Alliance will make any far-reaching demands in regard to the Malayanisation of the Government Service, but the subject will have to be discussed if only to clarify and secure the position of expatriate officers. A further item will be the question of the composition, timetable and terms of reference of the independent *Constitutional Commission* which the Alliance have requested should be set up. We have not yet given any detailed thought to the question of the composition of the Commission, but we envisage that it will be quite small (with, say, half-a-dozen members): the Chairman should come from the United Kingdom, and an Australian and an Indian might well be included among the members. This item raises the more general subject of the *relationships between H.M.G., the Federation Government and the Malay Rulers*: one aspect of the latter subject which will call for special attention is the subject of the powers of the High Commissioner.

The immediate demands of the Alliance
4.   In addition there are a number of matters in regard to which the Alliance have declared that they consider that concessions should be made without delay and without reference to the Constitutional Commission. Detailed briefs will have to be prepared on these five subjects, which are as follows:—

(i)   Control of internal security. (See paragraph 1 above).
(ii)   Restrictions on the powers of the High Commissioner. (The Alliance ask that what they described as the High Commissioner['s] "veto" power should be exercised only after consultation with the Chief Minister).
(iii)   The abolition of the posts of British Adviser. (This question was on the agenda of the meeting of the Conference of Rulers to be held on the 21st December).[2]
(iv)   The appointment of a local Minister to be Minister of Finance. (This is a demand which it is considered could be met without difficulty.)
(v)   The question of immediate financial assistance from H.M.G. (This question is part of the more long-term question of the economic development of the Federation—see paragraph 3 above—but the Alliance Ministers hope that they will be able to return to Malaya with pledges of an immediate increase in the level of financial assistance granted by H.M.G. to the Federation.)

Minute on 389

Mr. MacKintosh
The following is a summary of the points made when you and Mr. Newsam[3] discussed the note opposite with Sir J. Martin this morning.
2.   The Alliance were in no hurry to take over control of the Federation's *external affairs*: it was to some extent galling to them that Malaya should be excluded from membership of international bodies, but they realised that they were not in a

---

[2] See 388.   [3] R W Newsam, principal in the CO, 1948; transferred to the CRO, 1957.

position to staff diplomatic missions etc. As regards *defence*, it was quite reasonable that local ministers should have control of the Malay Regiment and other local forces while H.M.G. retained control of the strategic reserve. It was desirable that the arrangements in force in the Gold Coast, under which the Governor consulted local ministers on "reserved subjects", but was not obliged to act on their advice, should be introduced in the Federation.

3. Sir J. Martin said that although the Conference would clearly not settle everything, he hoped that it would produce some concrete results. Mr. MacKintosh agreed and remarked that the subjects of the Constitutional Commission, the Defence Agreement and the future of the Public Service were the only main matters which would require further consideration.

4. On the subject of finance, it was pointed out that the Treasury would be unlikely to look favourably on suggestions for increased financial assistance, at a time when Malayan finances were buoyant. It was suggested that our aim should be to induce the Treasury to agree to grant financial assistance to the Federation, not on a year-to-year basis but for a period of several years.

5. On the question of the *Constitutional Commission* it was pointed out that the Alliance and the Rulers had rather different views on the character of the Commission. It was suggested that the Chairman of the Commission and one of its members might come from the U.K. and that other members might be drawn from Australia, India and Canada. The Department would start considering possible names for the post of Chairman.

6. As regards the *High Commissioner's powers*, Sir J. Martin agreed that the present position, whereby the Executive and Legislative Councils were simply advisory, was anomalous.

7. It was agreed that the question of *internal security* would be the crucial one. We might well aim at the Gold Coast arrangement, whereby a local Minister is responsible for the administration of the police, but operational control of them remains vested in the High Commissioner.[4] In the last resort we ought to be prepared to allow operational control over the security forces to pass to the Federation Ministers: General Bourne and Mr Carbonell[5] were themselves agreed that this was a risk which might have to be taken. The question of seeing that there was a continuing flow of information through intelligence channels might present some difficulties, but it was suggested that the arrangements in force in India might provide a useful precedent. The repercussions on Singapore of transferring responsibility for security forces in the Federation would have to be borne in mind. We should also keep Sir T. Lloyd's point about the arrangements in Barbados in mind when we prepared our brief on the subject.[6]

8. On the subject of the *British Advisers* there was much to be said for Mr Watherston's suggestion that a senior British official should remain in the State in an appropriate post after the position of British Adviser had been abolished.

9. It was agreed that a paper should be prepared for the Cabinet[7] setting out the general purpose of the Conference and drawing special attention to the subjects of

[4] See BDEEP series B, Vol 1, R Rathbone, ed, *Ghana*, Part II, 120–123, 128, 130–133.
[5] W L R Carbonell, commissioner of Malayan police, 1953–1959.
[6] On which see BDEEP series A, vol 3, D Goldsworthy, ed, *The Conservative government and the end of empire 1951–1957*, part II, 247.   [7] See 394.

finance and internal security which would probably be the most troublesome. In the paper the Secretary of State would ask for freedom of manoeuvre – if necessary, he could consult the Cabinet again in the course of the Conference. It could also be pointed out in the paper that the recommendations of Conference would not be binding, although H.M.G. would have to consider themselves bound to a very large extent by them.

M.L.C
23.12.55

390 CO 1030/75, no 7   29 Dec 1955

[Constitutional conference]: letter from Sir D MacGillivray to A M MacKintosh on Alliance demands

This replies in part to your Secret and Personal telegram No. 804[1] of the 22nd December asking me for short notes giving my latest views on the lines which should be taken on the various issues likely to be raised by the Malayan delegation.

2. An analysis of the speech made by Abdul Rahman to Legislative Council on 3rd December, a copy of which I sent to Martin with my letter KHY 92/55/A of the 7th December, would seem to indicate that the Alliance appreciate that the next major constitutional change can only come about as a result of consideration of the recommendations of the Constitutional Commission and that it is very unlikely that the Commission will be able to report in time for such change to have effect much before the end of 1957. They feel that their own position would be insecure if they should indicate that they are content to wait that long before there is any further advance whatever towards self-Government, and they would therefore like to have something on account, so to speak, to put forward as an immediate achievement of the London conference. I think they would agree that whatever "immediate" concessions they should obtain at the conference should not have effect for some months, perhaps not until 1st August, by which time there would have been two opportunities (the May and the July meetings of the Legislative Council) to pass such legislation as these concessions might necessitate.

3. Abdul Rahman's speech of the 3rd December (and that which he made on Christmas Day at the U.M.N.O. Annual General Assembly went no further) would appear to show that the Alliance is now prepared to allow the High Commissioner's "veto powers" to stand for the present and to have them considered by the Constitutional Commission. It probably suits them quite well that the Executive Council should remain advisory to the High Commissioner for the time being; they know that their advice must normally be accepted and the position leaves them with something in hand to tilt against pending the outcome of the Constitutional Commission. What then it seems they wish to obtain immediately are:—

(1) *A date for independence.* Until recently their intention was, I think, to ask that this should be July 1959, i.e. four years after the Federal Elections. This was in keeping with their Elections Manifesto. They wish to remain within the Commonwealth, but with nine Rulers and two Settlements just who would be the head of

---

[1] Corrected upon receipt in the CO to read 'telegram No. 181'.

the independent State and just exactly where allegiance would lie, is not I think yet clear to them. Abdul Rahman has never attempted to define "independence" and yet he has publicly committed himself to obtaining a date. Some formula with a date attached to it will undoubtedly have to be found if he is to satisfy U.M.N.O. and retain his position. The matter has been made the more embarrassing for the Alliance leaders by:—

(a) the motion passed by the [Party] Negara Annual General Assembly early this month that independence should be achieved by the 1st January, 1957, and
(b) the motion passed by the U.M.N.O. General Assembly last week that independence by 31st August, 1957, should be sought. Abdul Rahman told me that this was an embarrassing motion which he had not felt able to oppose and that the only amendment he had thought it wise to obtain was one which added the words "If possible".

(2) *Control over finance.* They will, I think, be satisfied with a Minister for Finance responsible for the subjects which the Financial Secretary is responsible for now, leaving a Minister for Economic Affairs for the present. The effective date might be 1st August 1956 (see my letter KHY 92/55/A of 28th December).

(3) *Control over internal security.* I hope they will agree to limit their demand to responsibility for the administration of the Police, Prisons, Detention Camps and the Civil Defence organisation, leaving the Federation Military Forces and the Volunteer Units for the time being with the Secretary for Defence. I think Her Majesty's Government would be wise to agree to this, subject to the safeguards set out in my letter KHY 95/55 of 28th December.

(4) *Malayanisation of the public service.* They will ask for the abolition of the posts of British Adviser and this I think should be agreed, effective from about the end of next year. The Rulers have already accepted this as inevitable. (See my letter KHY 18/54 of 22nd December.)

I think we should try and take the question of the safeguarding of the position of the expatriate officer as far as possible. Indeed, I think we should endeavour to secure in London more than agreement on principles (your telegram 801 of 22nd December refers). We should endeavour to get a compensation scheme in three phases agreed to in all important particulars and drawn up in some detail, leaving blank only the dates for implementation of phases 2 and 3 and the actual rates of compensation (which will no doubt require actuarial assessment).

We are likely to run up against two demands from the Malayan delegates, and these I think must be resisted strongly. The first will be a demand that a number of superscale posts (particularly in the Police Force) be reserved for Malayans and that promotion of expatriates to these posts be frozen. This would be tantamount to a break with the traditional Service principles of promotion and would be contrary to Clause 152 of the Federation Agreement. I would not object to the creation, as in the Gold Coast, of a number of supernumerary superscale posts to which Malayans could be appointed in order to gain experience of superscale duties and to become fit for promotion to yet higher posts, but this I understand is unlikely to appeal to the Alliance Ministers. The second proposal which I think must be resisted is one which would, in effect, convert the compensation scheme from a voluntary one to a compulsory one. There is undoubtedly a small number of expatriate officers who are out of harmony with constitutional developments and resent taking instructions from Asians. They ought to go; and I hope they will go voluntarily as soon as a scheme for premature retirement is announced. But Abdul Rahman would like the scheme to include powers to make them go with due notice and with compensation. If the scheme should include such power, the effect on the Public Service would be very bad and a great majority of expatriate officers would elect to go as soon as the scheme was effective. We must, therefore, resist any attempt to make this scheme a discriminatory one. On the other hand, if an officer should show that he is not prepared to accept and work with the new set-up and yet should refuse to go voluntarily with compensatory addition to pension at stage 2 of the scheme, I would not hesitate to use the existing power under the Pensions legislation which authorises me to retire him in the public interest. This power would of course be reserved to me and would not be exercised under political pressure, and there would remain the right of appeal to the Secretary of State.

I think we must insist that before any concessions in regard to the abolition of British Advisers or control over finance and internal security become effective, there should have been passed satisfactory legislation providing for:—

(a) a Public Services Commission, and
(b) at least stage 1 of a premature retirement scheme providing for the right to retire on proportionate pension without compensation.

I would prefer that such legislation should be in the form of additional clauses to the Federation Agreement rather than by ad hoc legislation, thus ensuring that there would be no amendment of the legislation without the prior approval of the Queen and the Rulers.

The recent appointment by the Secretary of State of a Deputy Director of Agriculture from outside Malaya has perturbed the elected Ministers and I feel sure that the Secretary of State will be faced with a request by the delegates at the Conference that no further appointments should be made by the Secretary of State from outside the Federation without the approval of the Executive Council. Since the Singapore Government has refused to honour the agreement reached between the Governments of the Federation and Singapore at the time of the break-up of the joint Malayan Establishment, I think it likely that the delegation will also seek an assurance that there will be no transfers of expatriate officers from the Singapore Establishment to the Federation without Executive Council approval in each case. They fear that Malayanisation may the more quickly be achieved in Singapore by means of one-way transfers to the detriment of Malayanisation in the Federation. Unless Singapore is prepared to honour the agreement of last year, I fear that the Federation also will be forced by political pressure to refuse to give effect to it.

(5) *The appointment of a constitutional commission.* I feel sure we should agree to the appointment of a Commission just as soon as practicable, subject to the approval of the Rulers' Conference. I think we should also agree that the terms of reference should be so framed as to indicate that full internal self-Government is the immediate target. As regards the composition of the Commission, I understand from the Sultan of Kedah that the Alliance has now agreed[2] that the

---

[2] MacGillivray added in manuscript in the margin: 'I cannot confirm this from any other source'.

Commission should be appointed from within Malaya with only a Chairman from outside. If the Malayan delegation is unanimous as to this, I do not think their views should be resisted, provided the Chairman is personally acceptable to H.M. Government.

4. As far as I know the Alliance have no other demands to make. If that is so and provided they are content to let the Executive Council remain advisory to the High Commissioner, I now incline to think we should let the High Commissioner's position remain as it is until after the Constitutional Commission has reported. As you are aware, the position is not entirely satisfactory in that there are no reserved subjects, but, rather than disturb it, I think we might take a chance, so long as the present Alliance Ministers remain in office, and trust that good relations will see us through future difficulties.

5. I have dealt in this letter with matters the Alliance are likely to raise, in so far as it is possible to forecast them. I have not dealt with two matters which H.M.G. is anxious to have new understandings on (a) financial support and (b) military bases. I will be writing separately about these in a few days.

6. It has not been possible for the Alliance Ministers, preoccupied as they have been with their first budget, with the Chin Peng meeting and a host of other things, to give the time they would have liked to give in the last few weeks to preparations for the London Conference. They have not been able to formulate their demands in any detail or to work out their implications; nor have they been able to have any detailed discussion with the Rulers' representatives and they are relying on their nine days with them on board ship to achieve an identity of view on several subjects. It will therefore be very difficult to say before they arrive in London what are the points on which they do not see eye to eye or on which one party or the other may have reservations.[3]

---

[3] See 392.

391   CO 1030/30, ff 3–16   [29 Dec 1955]
'Report by the chief minister of the Federation of Malaya on the Baling talks': draft summary by Tunku Abdul Rahman of the verbatim record

[Tunku Abdul Rahman, David Marshall and Sir Cheng Lock Tan met Chin Peng, Chen Tian and Abdul Rashid Mahiden at Baling, northern Kedah, on 28 and 29 Dec. Too Joon Hing, Malayan private secretaries to the government team, interpreters and stenographers were also present. The verbatim record, taken from tape-recordings, was considered on 10 Apr by the Federal Executive Council which recommended the preparation of this summary (see CO 1030/29 and CO 1030/31).]

The background

At the beginning of June 1955, a letter was received from the representative of the "Supreme Command Headquarters of the Malayan Racial [sic] Liberation Army", stating that the Malayan Communist Party was prepared to negotiate the ending of the Emergency and the restoration of peace in Malaya. On June 24th, 1955, the Federation Government, while reaffirming its desire for peace, rejected this offer to negotiate and stated that if the Communists genuinely wished to end the Emergency, then they should do it immediately by accepting the liberal terms of surrender which were well known to all. Both the letter and the government statement were issued to the press.

2. On September 8th, 1955, shortly after the Alliance Government came into power after the first Federal Elections, an amnesty offer was announced by the Chief Minister. The terms of this offer are attached at Appendix.[1] Subsequently contact was made with a representative of Chin Peng, the Secretary-General of the Malayan Communist Party, so that a meeting could be held to discuss these terms. The Chief Minister made it clear that he did not propose to negotiate with Chin Peng and that he intended only to explain the amnesty terms and to consider any proposals regarding them which the M.C.P. might put forward.

The meeting

3. On this basis a meeting was arranged and took place at Baling on the 28th and 29th of December, 1955.

4. On the Government side the principals were Tunku Abdul Rahman, the Chief Minister of the Federation of Malaya, Mr. David Marshall, the Chief Minister of Singapore, and Dato Sir Cheng-Lock Tan. On the Communist side the principals were Chin Peng, Chen Tian and Abdul Rashid Mahiden.

5. The talks were held in four sessions:—

    28th December, 1st session, 2.30 p.m.—3.30 p.m.
                   2nd session, 3.40 p.m.—5.45 p.m.
                   3rd session, 6.30 p.m.—8.05 p.m.
    29th December, 4th session, 10.50 a.m.—12.48 p.m.

First session

The present position and the amnesty offer

6. Tunku Abdul Rahman opened the meeting by thanking the Communists for the confidence they had shown in coming out to the meeting. He reminded them that he was not standing in judgement over them but was there to explain the amnesty terms. He then detailed the political changes which had been taking place in the country and explained that his election victory was based on one big promise "that colonialism must end and that this country must be given freedom". He then mentioned the High Commissioner's announcement at the last Legislative Council meeting that self-government would be given to Malaya despite the Emergency. Since then the UMNO Assembly had passed a very important resolution to the effect that independence for Malaya must be given by the 31st August, 1957, and "I have no doubt in my mind whatsoever that we shall, if possible, achieve this aim and that there will be no conditions attached to that independence". He explained that the words 'if possible' had been included to allow a smooth hand-over, and that while the Alliance were strong enough to be able to demand immediate independence they had not done so because there were many important matters arising out of it that would be bound to take a little time. He himself was leaving on the 1st January to take part in round-table talks with the British Government. "I have no doubt that the talks will produce results and will be successful".

7. The Tunku went on, "Before my party came into power . . . I said that I wanted

---

[1] Not printed; see 371, note.

to bring peace to this country and I really meant it. But in my opinion there is no way of bringing about peace other than to offer suitable terms for the surrender of the Communist Party against whom the Government is fighting today. They have been, in the view of the Federation Government, fighting the lawful authority—that is, the Government of the Federation of Malaya. That is the position". For that reason he explained that the Emergency Regulations had been necessary, but that he and his colleagues—and the rest of the people of Malaya—wanted "to see the end of the trouble so that we can declare independence and make the country peaceful, happy and prosperous. Malaya includes Singapore for this purpose. That is why, as you know, Mr. Marshall is here to take part in the talk [sic], and Dato Sir Cheng-Lock Tan, my partner and colleague and founder of the Alliance, is here for the same reason." In view of the disturbances in the country and the atrocities being committed and the laws enforced to deal with them, he could not do more than to say that "if they accept the amnesty everyone will be pardoned—that is the main theme of the amnesty". He then went on to explain the amnesty terms in full, and added that the Government had carried out its part of the terms with regard to local cease-fire, but unfortunately the Communists on their part had continued offensive action, a recent example being the Kea Farm outrage. As a result, cease-fire arrangements had been suspended by the Government, although the Security Forces would be on the alert to help those who wished to accept the amnesty offer. He understood that they had rejected these amnesty terms and would like to know the reason, but first he asked Mr. Marshall and Dato Sir Cheng-Lock Tan if they had anything to add.

8. Mr. Marshall said that as far as he was concerned "It has been a campaign of hate that has corroded our civic life, a campaign of violence, brutality and atrocities that has achieved nothing except misery of the people. We understand that there are some genuine nationalists in the movement. I distinguish between nationalists and those who seek to make us a Colony of a foreign ideology". He appealed to the nationalists to realise that the constitutional, peaceful methods the rest of the country had been pursuing were the methods along which their welfare lay, and that violence could only breed violence and misery. To them he would say, "You are welcome back to the healthy stream of constitutional progress with your fellow citizens. We will forgive your past delusions and errors if you yourselves are now conscious that along that path only misery for the people lies, and are prepared to come in and live in peace with the rest of the population". He added, while the Federation had suffered most, Singapore had suffered as well and that if the campaign of hate and violence could be ended so that all good men could join together in the formation of a democratic nation, then all else was detail which could easily be worked out.

9. Tunku Abdul Rahman then stressed that "I did not come here as the spokesman for the British Government, neither am I the stooge or running dog of colonialism. I am the servant of the people and I represent the people who have elected me to power, and I do genuinely seek peace for this country". He then made it clear that the Communists were free to say what they liked, and that no one would object.

10. Chin Peng then spoke for the first time:—

"First and foremost, I wish to say that it is precisely because we realise that you are not the spokeman of the British Government and are not the running dog of the

British Government, the stooge of the British Government, that we have come out to meet you at the risk of our lives. I am not exaggerating when I say that we came out at the risk of our lives, because the present situation shows that the British armed forces are still in a superior position even though the cease-fire agreement will stand for ten days after the meeting. The British armed forces possess more modern equipment and therefore are still in the superior position.

I am not coming here to argue questions of ideology, but if questions of peace are to be discussed we are fully prepared to do so. Peace is the common demand of all people. We also hope that peace will be realised early so that the misery of the people can be reduced. War is war. War will certainly bring misery to the people and will also bring hatred". He thought it unnecessary to discuss at the meeting the question of responsibility for the present war in Malaya, and said that "the reason why we reject the Amnesty offer is very simple, because the conditions offered in this Amnesty Declaration differ little from the existing surrender terms, but we are prepared to discuss this question. In the Amnesty terms the principle is to disregard past behavior [sic] and this shows a conciliatory spirit with which we agree". But he added that the terms were quite different from those generally understood. The Tunku had mentioned that if they stopped the armed struggle, then they could enjoy equal status so that they could fight for independence by constitutional means. But the Amnesty terms did not contain such a point.

11. Tunku Abdul Rahman replied that he wanted the Communists to come out so that they could all fight together for independence for Malaya by constitutional means, and he intended that sentiment to be conveyed under paragraph 5 of the amnesty offer, which read:—

> "Those who show that they genuinely intended to be loyal to the Government of Malaya and give up their Communist activities will be helped to regain their normal position in society."

Then everybody would be the same, but "first you have got to convince us that you will be loyal to Malaya". In his view being anti-British did not indicate loyalty to Malaya. "You have to prove that this is the country to which you really owe your allegiance". The position was in his view that "today the people in Malaya, one and all regard the Communist activities as something entirely foreign to the Malayan way of life. They regard the Communist Party as belonging to a power outside this country, and consider its members give allegiance to that foreign country and not to Malaya". That was why it was necessary for the Communists to prove their loyalty so that they could take their place in society like anybody else.

12. Referring then to Chin Peng's claim that the amnesty terms were no different from the surrender terms, Tunku Abdul Rahman said "There is this difference—the pardon which we promise those who surrender. Before the amnesty they were liable to be prosecuted. That is not so under the amnesty as this gives absolute pardon for any crime which may have been committed before the date of the amnesty, or which may have been committed in ignorance of the amnesty. There is also this difference—the surrender terms were made by the Government of Malaya, the amnesty is made by the representatives of the people".

Second session
13. Dato Sir Cheng-Lock Tan pointed out that the M.C.P. consisted mostly of

Chinese and it was the Chinese community who had suffered most from terrorism in the last eight years and who particularly wanted peace and an end to the Emergency. They hoped that this meeting would achieve that. "There is no hope of the M.C.P. winning. Why waste money unnecessarily on the Emergency? There is no point in that. The vast majority of the people of this country are not in favour of the Communists because they are not working for a prosperous Malaya, and communism sets class against class and causes disorder. The other reason is that communism is distasteful because it causes violence". Peace could be attained if the Communists would come out of the jungle and become peaceful citizens, loyal to Malaya, and he added, "Communism is like a disease, sucking out the blood of Malaya, and will cause the ruin of the country".

14. Tunku Abdul Rahman then referred to the manifesto issued by the M.C.P. and said that if the manifesto really represented the M.C.P.'s aims then it contained many points which were in fact part of Government policy and the Dato agreed that on that basis there should be no quarrel between the M.C.P. and the people. The Tunku then asked Chin Peng what he had to say about the amnesty offer.

Loyalty to Malaya

15. Chin Peng then asked to have two points cleared, the first being, "May I know the actual meaning of 'Loyalty to Malaya'?". Tunku Abdul Rahman replied that one of the things the Malayan people expected was that the Communists would give up their communist activities, activities such as were being carried on today. He also referred to subversive activities, including those in Singapore, and compared the communist advocacy of class warfare unfavourably with the present democratic system under which the wealthy were taxed so that their money could be distributed for the welfare of the country. He also alluded to the position of the Rulers as Heads of their States and of their religion in those States and pointed out that they were constitutional rulers and important to the Malays as guardians of customs and adat [Malay custom]. Loyalty to Malaya would include acceptance of the position of the Rulers and agreement to uphold their dignity. "Loyalty to the democratic system established constitutionally is better than any system advocated by the Communists".

16. Dato Sir Cheng-Lock Tan added that if a man wanted to live in Malaya, he should assume the responsibilities and duties of a good citizen.

17. Mr. Marshall then defined loyalty as "Respect for the peoples' welfare, respect for the individual personality, harmony and harmonious relations between the races and an effort to achieve the common good by constitutional means, loyalty to the government of the day, and loyalty to the constitutional processes in bringing about such changes which we sincerely believe are for the welfare of the people. Not hatred or violence: they are not part of a democracy. Absolute dedication to the welfare of the country, not seeking to make it a province of another foreign ideology, but absolute dedication to this country itself and to the people". He then suggested that the discussion should return to the amnesty terms, as Chin Peng himself had said that he did not want to discuss ideology. He believed with Tunku Abdul Rahman that the amnesty terms were honourable. They gave an opportunity to the nationalists to come back to the main stream of healthy public life and to assist in promoting a great nation. Malaya[,] in his view, had a tremendous international status, if racial harmony and democratic processes could be preserved. Within that context and in the light of term 5 (of the amnesty offer) just what was it that the amnesty sought?

"Firstly, put down their bullets and fire-arms, and come back and seek harmonious relations, away from hatred".

Recognition of the M.C.P.

18. Chin Peng said that he still wished to clear certain points. "May I know whether the giving up of communist activities means the dissolution of the M.C.P.?" The Tunku replied 'Yes', and added "Giving up communist activities means they have to dissolve the Communist Party". Chin Peng then asked whether on the Government side there were any other suggestions. The Tunku replied that he had no other suggestion except to say that they should come out and take their place in society. Mr. Marshall said "I agree with that". He then added that he recognised that sincerity and dedication of some of the Communists, but abhorred that this should be utilised for the evil ends of hatred, violence, disorder, chaos, bitterness and misery. The two territories were on the point of achieving independence and the help of all true Malayans was required to achieve a "glorious future". Malaya was in a "magnificent position to join East and West". The Communists could do their share as human beings in this process but to date their activities had instead been a set-back to economic development. The Communist way was definitely wrong, as it was out of step and merely delaying the progress of the people. It was associated in Singapore with brutality, violence and hatred, and the Communist Party could not be recognised. If, however, in the years to come they sought to re-form the Party, that would be for the government of the day to consider, "but let me say now for the people of Singapore and in respect of the Government of Singapore, we will not recognise the Communist Party at present, because it has been too long associated with the activities that all humanity abhors".

19. It was then made clear that in both territories the communists were now fighting the elected governments. In view of the fact that they were still fighting, the Tunku asked "How can you ask us to recognise the Communist Party?"

> *Chin Peng*: "Actually speaking, in the past the Government with whom we fought, against whom we fought, was not an elected government".
> *Mr. Marshall*: "This year, it is."
> *Tunku*: "That is why we have offered them amnesty."

He reminded Chin Peng that a year ago he and the Dato had been prepared to enter the jungle in order to bring about peace. The fighting of the Emergency obviously required a lot of money, and that involved not only Malaya but the Commonwealth, from which money and other resources had to come.

> *Chin Peng*: "I fully realise this point."
> *Dato*: "Why not stop fighting?"
> *Chin Peng*: "The point is this, as a member of the M.C.P. we still believe in our ideology. We will never allow ourselves to be forced by others to give up this ideology, but wish to put our ideology to the people to decide, if that is possible. Now the Government request us to give up this ideology. As a citizen, of course, we have obligations, but at the same time we must have freedom of thought, the right of freedom of thought, but the Government's point is that they don't want this."

Tunku Abdul Rahman then pointed out that the Alliance Manifesto up-held all the five freedoms, and added that the Communists "say they want the people to decide whether or not to accept their ideology or accept ours. Now, speaking for myself, I have no doubt whatsoever that if they were allowed to take part in free elections, the people would choose our system".

Chin Peng: "Yes, I know that too, I agree".

21. The Tunku continued that the Communist and Malayan ideologies were not the same. The people preferred their own way of life, and the Communists must accept the way of life accepted by the majority. Chin Peng admitted that during the last year political progress had been made in Malaya and it was because of this that he believed the time had come when the Communists should co-operate to end the Emergency. Chin Peng continued: "We came here with sincerity in the hope that we can solve our problems, this problem. I have made it quite clear just now that we cannot accept the Amnesty conditions as they are now, because these conditions require us to dissolve the Communist Party. On this issue I want to request the Ministers of both countries to tell us whether or not there is any further grounds for discussion".

Tunku: "No, if you are returning to the question of whether we are prepared to recognise the Communist party—no".

22. The Ministers then offered a half hour adjournment if the Communists wished for more time to think things over, but Chin Peng continued "The question which I brought out just now is the primary question, the most important question".

Mr. Marshall: "Is it suggested that if the Communist Party is not recognised, they intend to continue to subject the peoples of both territories to this hatred and violence which can bring no good to anybody?"
Chin Peng: "It is a difficult question. We do not mean to say that if the Communist Party is not recognised the Emergency will be carried on, — that we are to blame".
Mr. Marshall: "What does he mean? What else does it mean?"
Chin Peng: "The statement presents some difficulty. Did you mean just now that if the Communist Party is not recognised and the Emergency is to be carried on with the resultant sufferings to the people, that we are to blame?"
Mr. Marshall: "It is a simple question. Just because the Party will not be recognised, you are proposing to subject the two Governments of the territories and the people of the two territories to continued miseries through violence and hatred, violence and hatred which you yourselves admit can produce no worth-while results. Is Communism so tied up with violence and hatred that it must be continued even when it becomes injurious to Communism? We cannot believe it. You have seen 8 years of struggle—what has happened to you—misery for yourselves as well as for the people, misery for your own colleagues and your friends. I have seen them. They believed and they suffered—for what? What have they achieved?"
Chin Peng: "Now I reiterate once more that if the Emergency is to be continued the blame should not be thrown only on one party or on one side. Of course we realise that war brings misery and sufferings. The question is: With what means can we end the Emergency or war?"
Tunku: "Give up. Prove yourself loyal to this country . . . absorb yourself into

society like everyone else. That is the only way".

Chin Peng: "But does that mean that we should swear to the Government that we are going to give up our ideology?"

Tunku: "No, not ideology – it is their activities which I mentioned. One's ideology is what one thinks, what one believes in. Activities are different. Especially activities to enforce the acceptance of one's ideology."

Chin Peng: "Does that mean then that if we are prepared not to achieve our aims by violent means or by force, then we will be recognised?"

Tunku: "No. When you come out and you surrender, your ideology and your beliefs are you own business."

Chin Peng: "This is a simple question, let us be frank. We can adopt a certain measure, a certain method. For example, we will preserve our Communist Party, but will join forces with the Alliance—I mean join the Alliance. Then will not the Alliance blame us for over-throwing the Government through subversive activities? I mean if we do it that way, we are not frank, we are not sincere. Another way is that since we are Communists we might as well declare to the people that we are Communists. We do not wish to join other political parties and then to do our scheming or intrigues. That is why we want this question of recognition of the M.C.P. to be solved."

Tunku Abdul Rahman reiterated that the country could not accept recognition of the Communist Party because communist activities had been associated with murder, with atrocities, with acts of violence of every kind. "That is why, therefore, we cannot recognise it."

Chin Peng: "The question of recognising or otherwise of the Communist Party perhaps is not to be decided by the Alliance alone—we wish to clarify this matter. We want to know, we wish you to clarify whether or not the Alliance is the final authority for saying whether the Communist Party will be recognised or not."

Tunku: "At the moment, the Alliance is the Government of the country—this was not so before. I said this just now. I did indirectly refer to the people this question of recognition and the way I did it was to ask the people to say whether they accepted the Amnesty terms which I issued or whether they did not accept them. If they did accept them they were to hold demonstrations everywhere. If they did not then no demonstrations were to be held. The results were that they held demonstrations which, perhaps, in the history of Malaya have been unparalleled."

The Tunku then referred in more detail to these demonstrations, and to the work of the Alliance in bringing together all races. Now he wanted to bring peace to all the people of Malaya. There was room in the country for everyone.

23.   Mr. Marshall asked for an answer to an important question. It had been made clear to Chin Peng that the Governments of the Federation and Singapore would not be prepared to recognise the Communist Party. "Now, is there any purpose in continuing these discussions? It is a fair question, please reply with frankness."

Chin Peng: "May I make one more point clear—the matters discussed in this house: are such matters to be approved by the British Government?"

Tunku: "If I decide, and Mr. Marshall agrees with me, that will be all."

Mr. Marshall: "The British Government, of course, may disagree with the course of action, but as far as we are concerned, we take our own decision."

Third session

24. At the beginning of the third session, Chin Peng referred back to Mr. Marshall's enquiry whether, since it had been made clear that the two Governments were not prepared to recognise the M.C.P., there was any purpose in continuing these discussions. He asked whether this was intended as an ultimatum. Mr. Marshall replied that it was not and that what he meant was that, if the Communists considered recognition to be a sine qua non, then did they think it would serve any useful purpose continuing the talks? Chin Peng accepted this explanation and said that they would return to the question of recognition later.

Independence

25. Chin Peng then asked "May I know if the British Government has given full guarantee for independence to Malaya?" The Tunku replied 'Yes' and added that the assurance had been given to the Legislative Council and that a Constitutional Commission would be set up to examine all issues connected with the transfer of power. Chin Peng then asked whether the transfer of power included the transfer of internal security to the elected government. The Tunku replied that it did and that this was one of the things which he was going to England to obtain even before independence. Chin Peng then asked whether, if the Communists continued the armed struggle, it would set back progress towards independence. The Tunku replied that there would be no set back to independence itself but that the continuation of the Emergency would cause a lot of misery to the people. He repeated that the Communists would be fighting the elected government.

Recognition of the M.C.P.

26. Chin Peng then returned to the question of recognition of the M.C.P. and asked for a fuller explanation. The Tunku then stated that Malaya was quite unlike other countries where the Communist party was recognised because in Malaya the Communist party was composed of very few nationals of the country and was moreover actually fighting the elected government. "To ask us to recognise you as a Party, so that you can disperse throughout the country to organise your communist activities, naturally you must understand that the people of this country would not accept that." Chin Peng then took up the point whether the difference was ". . . because most of the members of the Communist Party in Malaya are Chinese." Mr. Marshall replied at once that as far as Singapore was concerned that had nothing to do with it. The point was that the Communists were exercising violence against the people of Singapore and against the elected government of Singapore, and that their activities were therefore traitorous, and he strongly resented the suggestion that because the Communists had a large Chinese element that that was why their ideology or their activities were considered traitorous. The Tunku added that in the Federation the situation was slightly different because there the Malays felt that the Communists owed allegiance to China "because, as you yourselves said, there are more than 90% Chinese in your Party." Because there were so few Federal citizens, Malays or Indians in the Party, he did not consider that they could call themselves "the national party of this country". Chin Peng then asked whether, if the M.C.P. were confined to Federal citizens, it could be recognised, but the Tunku made it clear that they had to prove their loyalty to the country first.

Detention and investigation

27.   Chin Peng then asked what their position would be if they came out. The Tunku explained that they would first be held for investigation. This was not like the situation at the end of a war because in this case the Communists were not going to leave the country afterwards, some of them intended to live here. An investigation was therefore necessary to ascertain whether they were going to stop their un-Malayan activities. Chin Peng stated that they did not wish to come out like prisoners and be detained in prison. The Tunku explained that there was no question of prison, but that special camps would be established and that the sole purpose of the investigation to find out whether they were going to be loyal to the country or whether they were going to carry on their subversive or other activities to enforce their alien ideology. In the past when that ideology had not been accepted the Communists had tried to enforce it by violence, killing innocent people, and indulging in acts of brutality and hatred. If they were allowed to come out freely as members of the public, ". . . you might feel there were people against whom you wanted to take revenge . . . you might go into his house and slaughter him in cold blood." With all these possibilities he would be denounced as an irresponsible leader if he allowed that sort of thing to happen in order to bring about peace.

28.   In reply to a query by Chin Peng as to the length of detention, the Tunku said that it would only be for as long as was necessary to carry out the investigations. It would not be like detention under the Emergency Regulations, and it was possible that the investigation could be carried out very speedily. Committees of Enquiry would be set up straightaway, and . . . "we want to extract a promise from you that you will not carry on your activities; which we say are not loyal to Malaya and are prejudicial to the interests of Malaya and Malayans. We will want you to sign a declaration to that effect." Mr. Marshall added that those who were released would be assisted to settle in society and that any who wished to return to China could do so. Every facility would be given to them and they would be treated in a manner compatible with the dignity of human beings. The Tunku mentioned that under the terms of the amnesty those who surrendered would be helped to rehabilitate themselves in society. Even though many who had helped the Government might object to such help being given to the Communists, he himself considered that it would not be fair to expect them after living in the jungle for so long to be able to obtain employment immediately on coming out. He mentioned the Kemendore Agricultural Settlement, in which rehabilitation was given to those surrendered Communists who required it, and stressed that there was no intention to putting the Communists into camps and then forgetting them. Chin Peng thought the question of assistance was of secondary importance and that the more important question was that of restriction of freedom. The Tunku replied that there would be very little restriction except for the first few months when they would have to report where they were. This Chin Peng refused to accept. The Tunku explained that they could not be allowed "to go free just like that", and that the Government must protect itself and make sure that nothing untoward happened. Even what the Government was proposing might lead to incidents which, in that case, could not be helped, because at least precautions would have been taken. He summed it up by saying "There would be restriction on movement for a certain period of time, but not after you have shown yourselves to be like the others. Then restriction on movement will be removed. You will be free to go wherever you like, but we have got to take

precautions just to be sure."

29.   Chin Peng said that for the dignity of man, if this principle was insisted upon then they would have to carry on with the struggle. "Although we are comparatively weak in strength, we are quite confident we can carry on the struggle, even for a long period."

Mr. Marshall: "Forgive me asking, but what are you struggling for?"
Chin Peng: "It is very simple, just for the dignity of man."

Mr. Marshall said that using deeds of violence to enforce their views on a population that does not want them was hardly compatible with the dignity of man. Their struggle only resulted in misery, both for them in the jungle and for the rest of the population. He could see no "dignity of man" in that. The dignity of man required sacrifice for the welfare of Malaya as a whole. Chin Peng admitted that their outlook on this question was quite different, and that they were not prepared to argue on it.

30.   It was at this stage that the talks really broke down. Chin Peng came back time and again to the points on which the Communists insisted: recognition of the M.C.P., no detention, no investigation and no restriction on movement. It was, however, made clear by the Chief Ministers that after the investigation had been carried out and restriction of movement removed, then those Communists who remained in Malaya would be allowed to take part in politics and to join recognised political parties, but would not be allowed to form a Communist Party under another name.

31.   At the end of the session Mr. Marshall pleaded with them to try and consider the question soberly and to remember that there must be some sacrifice on their part. The Chief Ministers informed the Communist representatives that they would be prepared to meet them again on the following morning if they so wished.

Fourth session

Summary of the position

32.   The position was summarised by the Tunku at the beginning of this session in his opening remarks:

> "Yesterday, the discussion revolved around three points. First, recognition of the Communist Party. We have told you in no uncertain terms that we would not agree to recognition of the Communist Party. Next is detention. On this point you said you would not want to be detained or investigated. But I think I have explained to you (although I do not know whether you understood it or not), that the period of detention would be only for as long as is necessary to hold the investigation, no longer than that. I think I have explained to you the difference between the detention which you understand and the detention which we propose in the case of surrendered Communists. Correctly speaking, it is not detention at all; we intend to hold you for investigation. You, I understand, do not agree with that. You propose that as soon as agreement is reached whereby there shall be peace, you should then be allowed to come out and go wherever you like, freely. To that we cannot agree for the reasons which I explained yesterday. Then again, you suggested that there should be no investigation held to ascertain whether you are loyal or

not. We feel that investigation or an inquiry, if you like the term better than 'investigation', must be held. Investigation does rather suggest investigation into all your past acts. What we aim to do exactly is to ascertain whether you want to be loyal citizens of the country or not. For that reason I would rather call it an 'inquiry'. Then there was the third point, which was suggested by you and amplified by the Chief Minister, Singapore. For those of you who wish to go to China, or for that matter to any other country, we would be pleased to help you to go. For those people I don't think an investigation would be necessary at all. All we need to know from them is where they want to go. Then arrangements will be made for their passage and pocket money will be given to them—enough to see that they are well looked after in that country. I reiterate again that only those persons who want to stay in Malaya and make their homes in this country will be investigated. I hope we can come to some agreement on these points, and I think it would be better to come straight to the point without beating about the bush. I appreciate that you have got to obtain the best possible terms before you can agree to surrender, and I understand that attitude. So I would like to hear what you have to say."

33. *Chin Peng*: "If the conditions as laid down cannot be changed, then I am not empowered to accept them."
Tunku: "How can they be? As I say, they cannot be so changed that we give up investigation—that would be absolutely wrong."
Chin Peng: "There is no need for me to repeat what I said just now. What I have said just now is very, very clear."
Mr. Marshall: "I think we have cleared one point—that those who are free can take part in political activities. But we must have investigation and perhaps they would like to discuss the question of duration of this investigation, accepting the principle that that is something which the people will require, then I think this line of thought might be fruitfully discussed."
Chin Peng: "This is a question of principle. I am not empowered to discuss this principle. My answer in this matter is very plain."

Laying down of arms
34. Chin Peng then continued: "The present Government, although it is a popularly elected government still is not an independent government."
Mr. Marshall: "Tell him we recognise that fully".
Chin Peng: "Under such circumstances, therefore, when we bring out our suggestions we have got to have regard to this situation. If those popularly elected Governments of the Federation and Singapore have self-determination in matters concerning internal security and national defence, then all problems could be solved easily. As soon as these two Governments have self-determination in internal security and national defence matters, then we can stop the war immediately."
Tunku: "Is that a promise? When I come back from England that is the thing I am bringing back with me."
Chin Peng: "That being the case, we can straightaway stop our hostilities and also disband our armed units."

Mr. Marshall: "You say that as soon as the two Governments have control of internal security and national defence you will end hostilities and lay down your arms and disband your armed forces. Mr. Chan [sic] Tian, is this right please?"

Tunku: "There is one word "self-determination.""

Chan Tian: "Not self-determination—full power to control internal security."

Tunku: "One of the purposes for which I am going to England is to get control of internal security. When I do get that, are you saying that you are prepared to accept our terms and lay down your arms, if the terms come from me?"

Mr. Marshall: "What do you mean by 'national defence'? Do you mean control over all internal forces?"

Chan Tian: "National defence includes control over all armed forces within the country."

Mr. Marshall: "You say 'national Defence' means control over the armies within the country?"

Chan Tian: "At least local forces."

Mr. Marshall: "Local forces? Fair enough. Would you in those circumstances then accept these terms?"

Chan Tian: "To give an example—control over the Malay Regiment, the Federation Regiment."

35. The point was then raised that, whereas the Chief Minister of the Federation was going to London immediately, the Chief Minister of Singapore would not be leaving until April, and whether the offer had to wait on Mr. Marshall's return, but Chin Peng clarified this by saying "If Tunku obtains control in such matters concerning internal security in February—and national defence—then we will stop our hostilities at once and we will not wait for the results of Mr. Marshall's mission."

36   Chin Peng then clarified his offer by making it clear that the laying down of weapons did not mean handing them over to the Government. "May I repeat, the downing of weapons is not equivalent to the handing over of weapons to Government. If only the M.C.P. is recognised; if only we are not subject to restriction of our liberty, it is possible for us to surrender our weapons." He thought that the mere laying down of arms, as interpreted by him, was what was required under the amnesty terms, but the Tunku made it clear that these terms required that the arms should be handed over to the Government, as otherwise it would mean that they could be taken up again at any time.

37. Mr. Marshall then returned to Chin Peng's offer and read out a note which he had prepared, and which he asked the Communist representatives to initial. This read as follows:—

> "As soon as the Federation obtains control of internal security and local armed forces, we will end hostilities, lay down our arms and disband our forces."

Chin Peng said that he was prepared to accept this but with an addition, "It does not amount to accepting the present amnesty terms." Chin Peng said that he was not prepared to consider the question of the present amnesty terms or any extension of them.

Surrender

38. Chin Peng then returned to the question of investigation, which appeared to

him to imply surrender. The Chief Ministers made it clear, however, that since there were 7,000,000 people in Malaya and only about 3000 Communists, the welfare of the 7,000,000 must come first. As Mr. Marshall said, "The welfare of the 7,000,000 must come first. Now that we have elected governments and we are on the verge of independence it cannot be said that your struggle is for independence. I appeal to you to think of the welfare of the people as a whole, even if it means a certain humiliation for the 3000. If you seek the welfare of the people you should not put your pride before their welfare." Chin Peng, however, said that he had made it clear that as far as investigation was concerned he had no authority to accept it. He admitted, however, that their numbers were small. The Tunku said that if many of the leaders and a large number of their followers went back to China and those who wanted to remain were very few, then he might forego investigation and the only condition would be that they would have to report where they were. Even this reporting, to Chin Peng, had a touch of surrender which was unacceptable.

39. The Tunku replied that some surrender was inevitable. "As I said yesterday our ideologies are completely at variance . . . Therefore if you do not come out to surrender, we would rather not accept you in our society. If you want to have peace in this country, one side must give in—either we give in to you or you give in to us." He was not prepared to allow a situation where Malaya might be divided as had happened in the case of Korea and Vietnam. Malaya was too small and he had, therefore, to be frank with them and say that it was they who must surrender.

40. The Chief Ministers, before leaving, then appealed to the Communist representatives to think of the general welfare of the people and informed them that if, in the future, the Communists were prepared to show any change of attitude, they would not consider their pride in coming to meet them again.

392   CO 1030/132, no 3   5 Jan 1956
[Constitutional commission]: letter from Sir D MacGillivray to A M MacKintosh on the views of Tunku Abdul Rahman

[The Malayan delegation to the constitutional talks consisted of four representatives of the Alliance (Tunku Abdul Rahman, Dato Abdul Razak, Dr Ismail and Colonel H S Lee) and four representatives of the rulers (Dato Panglima Bukit Gantang, Abdul Aziz bin Haji Abdul Majid, Dato Wan Idris and Dato Nik Kamil). Accompanied by two secretaries (T H Tan for the Alliance and Abdul Kadir Samsuddin for the rulers' representatives), they embarked from Singapore on New Year's Day, and during the voyage to Karachi on board MV *Asia*, they worked out a common approach to key constitutional issues. From Karachi they flew to London where they were met by Sir J Martin, who, replying to a casual question from Abdul Razak—'Are you going to make things difficult for us?'—reportedly said, 'No, we are going to give it to you on a golden platter' (William Shaw, *Tun Razak: his life and times*, Kuala Lumpur, 1976, p 106).]

I spoke to Tunku Abdul Rahman the day before he left here about the composition and terms of reference of the Constitutional Commission. He told me that he really hadn't had time to think about this, nor to discuss it with the Rulers' representatives, but that he would do so while on board ship. When I pressed him for his views he said that the Alliance still had it in mind that the Commission should be composed of persons with knowledge of constitutional development in other Commonwealth countries. He thought that they might be drawn not only from Great Britain but from Canada, Australia, India and possibly Ceylon. The Alliance had no particular names in mind. I told him that I thought the Rulers were still of the view that the Commission should be composed of Malayans with a Chairman from the U.K., and that this view was based on the grounds:—

(a) that such a Commission would be much more likely to make recommendations which would find the greatest measure of acceptance, both by the Rulers and the Alliance, and

(b) that an outside Commission might not appreciate the special position of the Malays to an extent that a Malayan Commission would.

Abdul Rahman replied that he thought it might be possible to accommodate the Rulers' view on this matter by having a mixed Commission, half the members being Malayan and the other half being drawn from Commonwealth countries. I am myself rather doubtful whether a mixed Commission of this kind would be satisfactory, unless perhaps the Malayans should merely have the status of assessors. In any case it would be extremely difficult to select four or five Malayans who would be acceptable to all parties concerned, and presumably it would be impracticable to have a much larger number. The problems which the Commission will have to tackle are going to be so very intricate that I now incline to think they would be beyond the capacity of a purely Malayan Commission, and that despite the risks that the recommendations might prove to be quite unacceptable to any of the parties concerned, it would be best to place this extremely difficult task in the hands of a small body of experts drawn from the U.K. and Commonwealth countries. The calibre of the Commission will have to be very high, since the problems will be unusual and of great complexity.

Since the Malayan delegation view on this matter may not have crystallised even after a few days together on board ship, it is, I think, desirable that before the talks start we should form our own opinion as to what sort of Commission is likely to be best from H.M.G.'s point of view, and then endeavour to obtain acceptance of that opinion. I see no great objections and some advantage in a Commission drawn from Commonwealth countries, as suggested by Tunku Abdul Rahman, provided great care is taken over the selection of the individual members. Since the Alliance themselves seem to have no names in mind, they might readily, in the interests of speed, accept any names which the Secretary of State was able to put forward, provided these were names of sufficiently eminent people. I suggest, therefore, that we should have some names ready to propose.

The same applies to the terms of reference. Abdul Rahman had no ideas as to this, other than that they should be wide enough to enable the Commission to make recommendations for a constitution suitable under conditions of full self-Government and providing for the retention of the Rulers as constitutional heads. He was, however, rather doubtful as to whether they should be wide enough to embrace the question of citizenship, and suggested that this was a problem which might be tackled by some other body. H. S. Lee, on the other hand, quite evidently has it in mind that citizenship should be one of the principal matters for consideration by the Commission, and, largely on this account, he desires that the Commission should be drawn from outside Malaya and should not be one composed of Malayans. He has told Gray that he thinks the terms of reference should be so wide as to include matters such as future land policy.

393 CO 1030/72, no 11   5 Jan 1956

[Financial consequences for Malaya of constitutional change]: letter
from Sir D MacGillivray to A M MacKintosh. *Appendix* 'A': 'Assurances
by Her Majesty's Government about financial aid to the Federation of
Malaya 1950–1954'

As Thomas[1] informed you, in his demi-official letter dated 8th November, it was the
intention to supply a series of financial memoranda to the Federation delegates to
the London talks. The proposal has had to be abandoned mainly because the
Ministerial Committee entrusted with the preparation of the Development Plan
memorandum has not completed its task. In the circumstances I thought it advisable
to let each delegate have a copy of a memorandum on financial and monetary policy
which Thomas and Spencer have prepared for their general guidance. The delegates
have asked numerous questions on financial matters, both orally at meetings and by
written questionnaires, and each delegate has been supplied with written replies. I
enclose two copies[2] of the written answers and the memorandum, together with
supporting documents, for your information.

2. One of the main purposes which I intended the series of financial memoranda
to serve was to demonstrate the effect of the Federation's financial independence of
Her Majesty's Government and to bring it home that it will be impossible, without
some external financial assistance, for the Federation to do more than a fraction of
what the Ministers would like to do during the next few years in the fields of social
services and economic development. Her Majesty's Government has, on several
occasions, declared in general terms its intention to give financial support to the
Federation so that its social and economic development should not be retarded by
the heavy financial burden imposed by the Emergency. These declarations have been
given wide publicity in the Federation and I attach, as Appendix "A", a summary of
them. These statements were made at a time of complete dependence upon H.M.G.
as the administering power and while control over expenditure was exercised by the
High Commissioner through a Financial Secretary who was an expatriate officer.
These conditions are changing rapidly and clearly the old formula must be
withdrawn, since first, if perpetuated, it would be likely to give rise to irresponsibility
by the elected Government in financial matters, and secondly because it is hardly in
keeping with the dignity and self-respect of a self-Governing territory. It should
therefore, I consider, be one of the objectives of the London talks to secure by
agreement the withdrawal of the old guarantees on the grounds that they are no
longer appropriate to the changed status of the Federation.

3. It is likely, however, that the Federation delegates will in the course of the
London talks ask the U.K. Government for continued financial assistance. Indeed, H.
S. Lee, one of the delegates, has told Thomas that they would ask not only for
permission to raise loans in London to help finance their Development Plan, but for a
free grant of $100 millions as well. These requests, if made, will doubtless be
supported by the general argument that the Federation has suffered, and is suffering,
in the common cause by fighting militant communism and will be morally entitled

---

[1] C J Thomas was financial secretary, 1955, and financial adviser, 1956, Federation of Malaya.
[2] Not printed.

to further assistance even after the Emergency has come to an end and self-government and independence achieved.

4. Whatever may be the merits of that general argument, I cannot believe that the financial relations between Her Majesty's Government and the Government of the Federation can be satisfactorily governed in the future merely by reference to former assurances. With the achievement of self-government, and the consequent loosening of the Secretary of State's influence upon the Government's financial policies, the maintenance of those assurances in their present form would, I feel sure, be an incentive to extravagance, if not irresponsibility, in financial matters because the Federation Government would be able to plead, as justification for over-spending, that it placed absolute faith in those explicit assurances of financial aid in case of need. I do not think that the cautionary sentence in the October 1952 assurance that "In considering any help that may be required later, Her Majesty's Government would, of course, have to take into account the extent to which the Federation had shown "self help" by e.g. increasing taxation and raising local loans" would be very helpful, for it is already apparent that the Alliance Government is unwilling to increase taxation and also to resist proposals for increased expenditure. It rejected all proposals for increased taxation which would have reduced somewhat the estimated budget deficit of $50 millions for 1956, and was unmoved by the Singapore Government's strong plea for increases in Pan-Malayan taxes, such as income tax. It was only with difficulty that the Government was persuaded to resist extravagant claims for increased wages and salaries from its daily-rated employees and the General Clerical Service and to refuse to take the disputes to arbitration. Moreover, the Alliance Government has reversed the policy of its predecessor and re-introduced a guaranteed price for padi. This could be a costly business. So far, I do not think much harm has been done, and it must be admitted that there were strong political and other arguments for refusing to increase taxation when the 1956 esimates were presented to the Legislature and for granting some increase in wages and General Clerical Service salaries, as well as for re-introducing a guaranteed price for padi. What I fear is that under conditions of self-government the Government will be quite unable to resist the popular clamour for the fulfilment of the election promises of the Alliance and that the Alliance will expect Her Majesty's Government to combine to underwrite the cost on the basis of past assurances.

5. This position may well arise quite soon if an elected Minister of Finance replaces the Financial Secretary at an early date. I dealt with this question in my demi-official letter to you KHY 92/55/A dated the 28th December 1955, in which I expressed the opinion that Her Majesty's Government might find it advisable to accede to this demand. In the circumstances it seems to me to be most advisable, during the coming talks in London, to define which some precision the nature and amount of the financial assistance which Her Majesty's Government will be prepared to give in the future, and the conditions which will have to be fulfilled before aid will be given.

6. I think it could be fairly contended that Her Majesty's Government has carried out the first four general undertakings mentioned in the Appendix to this letter, and that the only further assistance which the Federation might fairly claim under them is permission and assistance to raise sufficient loans in the London Market to provide the balance of funds (say £20 millions) required between now and the end of 1960 to carry out a reasonable revised Development Plan.

7. There remain the undertakings on the specific subjects of Education and Rubber. As to Education, the Alliance Government is already committed to some variation of the Education policy advocated in the White Paper, which was the policy Her Majesty's Government undertook to support, and may well substitute for it a policy unlikely to command unreserved approval. Moreover, it has already gone beyond the limits agreed in that White Paper by undertaking to admit to the English primary schools the 8,000 applicants of the age of seven years for whom the expansion programme approved in the White Paper made no provision. This step alone will cost an extra $456,000 in 1956 rising automatically to nearly $5 million by 1961. The two undertakings about rubber are subject to fairly effective safeguards and could not be expected to become effective except in the most adverse circumstances. I suggest that we should endeavour to withdraw, by agreement, these past undertakings and to replace them by an undertaking to make a free grant of a fixed amount for a specific purpose, and I make a proposal to that end in the succeeding paragraphs.

8. As you know, the Alliance delegation to the London talks will press very hardly [sic] for internal security to be put in charge of an elected minister who would be responsible for both the Police, the Prisons and the Federation Military Forces. While I think we can allow the Police and Prisons, which constitute self-contained organisations, to be placed under an elected minister, it would be best if the Federation Military Forces should not come under his direction at present, since they do not constitute a self-contained organisation and are closely integrated with the Imperial Forces and dependent on them for much of the higher organisation and services without which they cannot operate at all as an independent fighting force. However, we shall undoubtedly be pressed strongly to allow these Military Forces to be the responsibility of an elected Minister at once, and even if we are able to resist that pressure for the present it will undoubtedly be necessary to hand over this responsibility at a fairly early date. It is most desirable, therefore, for political reasons, that the Federation Military Forces should be made into a self-contained organisation as soon as practicable. To do this it will be necessary to form, equip and train the necessary units of service troops without delay. The capital cost of equipment and accommodation will be fairly heavy and I suggest therefore that Her Majesty's Government should, when arguing against the Alliance request for immediate responsibility for their Military Forces, offer to meet the capital cost of equipping and accommodating the special units which, I am advised, would amount to some $12 millions, and also the additional recurrent cost involved for a period of two years. (See the enclosure to my savingram No. 1587/55 of 28th December.) When making this offer an undertaking should be given that the work of equipping and training will be pushed forward with all speed and that, as soon as it is complete, the Federation Military Forces will be placed in charge of an elected minister. I advise that absolute priority should be given to making what already exists self-contained and that expansion of the Forces by the addition of battalions of either the Malay or the Federation Regiments should be permitted only to such extent as would not retard the pace at which this first priority can be achieved. The undertaking of H.M.G. to pay the full cost ($62.5 million) of initial equipment and camp accommodation for the previously planned expansion of the Military Forces should however remain unchanged. It would be made clear that the offer was in substitution for the undertakings about Education and Rubber.

9. To turn to the more general financial questions which are likely to be raised during the London talks. The Alliance delegates are clearly much interested in the subjects of exchange control (with special reference to the Federation's large dollar surplus), sterling balances, currency control and the founding of a Central Bank. We have been at some pains to explain to them the practical advantages of remaining within the sterling area and of retaining the present system of currency control. They are all, I am assured, united in the determination not to take joint action with Singapore, which they regard in many ways as a parasite of the Federation, in these matters. The advice given them in the answers to questionnaires and memoranda take account of this determination which, I foresee, may effectively prevent the formation of a Malayan Central Bank, although the Alliance would very much like to have a Federation Central Bank even though its functions were severely restricted.

Appendix 'A' to 393

A. *General assurances*
1. December 1950. Reply by the Secretary of State to a Question by Mr. Champion (agreed by Treasury).

> ". . . Her [sic]³ Majesty's Government, as they have always been, are willing to give Malaya all the assistance that may be shown to be necessary both for the effective prosecution of the anti-bandit campaign and to enable her to go ahead with her plans for social and economic development. It is Her Majesty's Government's desire that the heavy burden that Malaya is continuing to bear in the common effort against communist banditry should not be allowed to impede, for financial reasons, this very necessary development programme".

2. January 1952. Secretary of State's Despatch noting with general approval the Ordinance covering the Loan Programme (agreed by Treasury).

> ". . . I wish to take this opportunity to re-state the undertaking previously given by Her [sic] Majesty's Government, i.e. that Her Majesty's Government will stand behind the Federation to the extent shown to be necessary in carrying out its approved Colombo Plan Programme."

3. September 1952. Facts of which the Secretary of State authorised the High Commissioner to remind the Finance Committee in connection with the 1953 Budget (this arose out of a request by General Templer for an £8 million grant, which was *not* put to the Chancellor of the Exchequer).

> ". . . in the past Her Majesty's Government had specifically recognised that the Development Plan must go forward and that the financial assistance, which had been readily forthcoming, had made the fullest allowance for development needs and had been calculated on a basis which left the Federation with reasonable working reserves. In other words, previous assistance had not been calculated on a narrow grant-in-aid basis, and it could be assumed—and my authority can be quoted for this—that in future

---

³ Queen Elizabeth II succeeded King George VI on 6 Feb 1952.

Her Majesty's Government will consider the Federation's claim for financial assistance on a basis no less generous".

4.   October 1952. Statement which the Secretary of State authorised the High Commissioner to make to Legislative Council during Budget Session (agreed by Treasury).

". . . It is Her Majesty's Government's view that the Federation Government can plan for the defence and development of the country in the confidence that Her Majesty's Government will not permit the burden of Emergency expenditure to retard these plans. The past assurances are quite explicit and the rather gloomy immediate budget prospects may be considered in the light of these assurances. In considering any help that may be required later, Her Majesty's Government would, of course, have to take into account the extent to which the Federation had shown "self-help" by e.g. increasing taxation and raising local loans".

The Secretary of State expressed the hope that the above statement would "convince doubters that Her Majesty's Government are committed to whatever assistance may be necessary and will never let the Federation down".

B. *On specific subjects*
5.   October 1954. Education. Statement authorised by the Secretary of State to be made by the Member for Education in Legislative Council during the Debate on the White Paper (agreed by Treasury).

". . . The High Commissioner represented fully to Her Majesty's Government (i.e. during his talks in London in the summer of 1954) the present situation in which the Federation is placed in this matter of education. It is clearly recognised that there must be expansion of our educational services and that additional expenditure on education is quite unavoidable. Her Majesty's Government has always recognised and continues to recognise that a well planned programme of social and economic development is essential, not merely as a solution of the Emergency but as an essential part of the progress and development of this country, and I am sure Honourable Members will share with me the gratitude I feel to that Government for having reiterated its previous undertakings to stand by the Federation in the evolution of those social services. The Federation must, however, play its own full part in meeting its future requirement and work towards the achievement of improved educational services according to a clear and approved plan. Her Majesty's Government recognises the need of the Federation Government to proceed with a programme of education which is likely to increase expenditure to be met from Government revenues by as much as $10 million each year for the next five years, bringing the total expenditure on education from Government revenues to $150 million by 1959 and, subject to the Federation making its own maximum contribution from local resources, will take this programme into account should it be necessary for the Federation Government to seek financial assistance from Her Majesty's Government in the future".

6.   October 1954. Rubber. Statement authorised by the Secretary of State to be

made by Federation Government to the R.P.C. arising out of the Mudie Report[4] (agreed by Treasury).

".... Government accepts in principle that with production costs at their present level, and when prices are below 70 cents a pound, adequate replanting would be beyond the unaided resources of the industry without effective financial assistance from the Government either by reductions in export duty or by other comparable means".

7. April 1955. Rubber. Statement authorised by the Secretary of State.

".... H.M. Government recognise the vital importance of the rubber industry to Malaya's economy and subject to the Federation making its own maximum contribution from local resources towards meeting any loss to the Government which the scheme may involve will take the implications of the scheme into account should it be necessary in the future for the Federation Government to seek financial assistance from H.M. Government".

---

[4] *Report of the Mission of Enquiry into the Rubber Industry of Malaya* (chairman, Sir Francis Mudie), Kuala Lumpur, 1954.

394   CAB 134/1202, CA(56)3   7 Jan 1956

'Conference on constitutional advance in the Federation of Malaya': memorandum by Mr Lennox-Boyd for Cabinet Colonial Policy Committee

|MacKintosh had a major hand in drafting this memorandum on which Lennox-Boyd commented on 6 Jan: 'I think this is an outstandingly good paper, & I am in full agreement with it'. Copies were circulated to Cabinet ministers and a summary was telegraphed to MacGillivray. On 12 Jan it was discussed by the Cabinet Colonial Policy Committee chaired by Eden (prime minister) and attended by Selwyn Lloyd (foreign secretary), Home (S of S for Commonwealth relations), Walter Monckton (minister of defence) and Lennox-Boyd. In a note accompanying the paper, Lennox-Boyd pointed out that 'the subject is of great moment and intricacy' and sought agreement 'that I should try to guide the Conference along the lines which I have proposed . . . . and that I should be free to diverge from them, if necessary, on all but major issues' about which he would reserve his position for further ministerial consultations. As regards internal security, the Colonial Policy Committee agreed that, if pressed, the government should be prepared to transfer administrative control of the local military forces as well as the police, provided that Malayans accepted that the high commissioner would retain ultimate responsibility for internal security as envisaged in clause 19 of the Federal Agreement of 1948. On the matter of defence, the committee concluded that the point had been reached when the government should try to secure the right to retain a Commonwealth strategic reserve in Malaya after independence. The committee noted that the financial proposals were acceptable to the chancellor of the exchequer. Finally, the committee decided that Australia and New Zealand should be informed of the general lines to be taken at the conference. Subject to these amendments, the paper was approved by the committee and a revised version (namely CP(56)12) which is still retained) was considered by the full Cabinet on 17 Jan, see 400. See also CAB 134/1201, CA 2(56)2, CAB 21/2883 and CO 1030/70.]

Background
This Conference is due to open on Wednesday, 18th January, and is expected to last for some two to three weeks. Three groups will participate—first, a delegation from

the Federation composed of four leading members of the Alliance, headed by the Chief Minister, and four representatives of Their Highnesses the Rulers, second, the High Commissioner and a number of his senior advisers and, third, myself and my advisers, who will as necessary include representatives of other interested Departments.

2. I originally agreed with the Alliance and the Rulers that the main subjects on the agenda should be:—

1. The terms of reference, composition and timing of a commission to review the constitution.
2. Defence.
3. Internal security.
4. Finance.
5. The future of the public service.

It later became clear that we should have to deal with a number of other subjects of lesser importance, with which I need not now trouble my colleagues. As a result of preoccupation with other more immediate problems it has not been possible for the Alliance Ministers to give as much time as they would have liked to preparations for the Conference; nor have they been able to have detailed discussions with the Rulers' representatives. I therefore do not yet know definitely how far the two sides of the delegation will come to the Conference with an identity of view, or what is to be asked of us. It appears, however, from the latest report to reach me that the Chief Minister proposes to seek the immediate grant of:—

(i)   Control of internal security.
(ii)   Control of finance.
(iii) Malayanisation of the public service.

He is said to regard these as amounting to self-government. I understand that by "control of finance" he means only the appointment of an elected Minister of Finance in place of the present *ex-officio* Financial Secretary. I see no difficulty about this. I shall deal later with the questions of internal security and Malayanisation.

(iv) The appointment of a constitutional commission instructed to prepare for the introduction of what he calls "full independence" by the 31st August, 1957, if possible.

By this he is reported to mean full control of external affairs and defence, "though treaty arrangements on these could be made with Britain."

3. Certain matters will have to be determined during the course of the Conference but its aim will not be to reach detailed agreements on all the main items; it will rather be to agree in broad terms what should be done, the details being left to be worked out later where necessary. Nor will the conclusions and recommendations of the Conference immediately bind Her Majesty's Government, the Federation Government or the Rulers: before they become binding they will be referred back to all three parties for study and approval. This is due to insistence by the Rulers that their representatives at the Conference should in no sense be plenipotentiaries and that the Rulers would hold themselves free to consider the recommendations of the Conference without prior commitment to accept them. In view of this, although the delegation will to a large extent regard Her Majesty's

Government as committed to anything that may be provisionally agreed at the Conference, I propose to make it clear that we must retain the same freedom as the other parties to study the recommendations before finally approving them.

General approach

4. We must be prepared to go a very long way with the delegation on the fundamental question of political advance, and to do so with the readiness from which we may reasonably hope to derive all the advantages that can flow from establishing an atmosphere of goodwill and understanding early in the Conference. If we do not approach this major issue boldly we will in the end be driven back upon our final positions in an atmosphere which will do no good to our future relations with the territory. It is scarcely possible to exaggerate the strength of feeling in the Federation about self-government; and the Alliance could hardly be in a stronger position to pursue it. It was the main plank in their election campaign, and as a result they were swept into power with victory in 51 of the 52 constituencies for the Legislative Council. There is, of course, still a wide gulf between the Malay and Chinese races, and no one could to-day say with any confidence how or when it will be bridged. This may well give rise to grave problems when the territory becomes self-governing, but meanwhile we must accept the fact that the two races are completely united in the demand for self-government and that we no longer have anything to gain by arguing that relations between them must be more firmly and harmoniously established before self-government can be granted. Another, more immediate, problem is the settlement of the considerable differences of outlook between the Rulers and the politicians. I propose not to let myself be made a party to any disputes which may emerge between them during the Conference, and to insist that relations between the Rulers and the political leaders in the Federation are essentially matters which they must settle among themselves.

5. But the decisive consideration is that the Alliance can claim that in seeking self-government they demonstrably enjoy the enthusiastic support of practically the whole country. (Apart from the Sultan of Johore, few, if any, of those who may believe otherwise would dare to day so.) It would also be difficult to offer any conclusive refutation of the argument which the Alliance would almost certainly use, should it seem necessary, that, probably with some continuing help from us in a number of ways, the Federation is as well equipped for self-government as the wholly independent Asian countries by which it is surrounded. Few of them are face to face with anything like the same problem of Communist violence and subversion, but I see no effective counter to the answering argument that a determined Malayan Government with full responsibility for their own internal affairs could deal more successfully with the Communists than a "Colonial" régime running a country anxious to be rid of it. In this connection it is significant to recall that our recent statement that we no longer regarded the continuation of the shooting war at its present sort of level as an obstacle on the road to self-government had an excellent effect upon the Alliance Ministers and public opinion generally and was a real blow to the Communist terrorists.[1] The indications are that, if we accept the Alliance view on this, we shall be able to secure satisfactory agreements on defence and the other issues of particular concern to us. If, on the other hand, we do not go far enough

---

[1] See 382, note 6 and 385, para 3.

with them on the question of self-government, we shall in all probability not only fail to secure such agreements but also find ourselves faced with a refusal to co-operate in the administration of the Government and a serious deterioration in internal security. We know that the Chief Minister has in his possession signed letters of resignation from all members of his party who are also members of all councils from the Legislative Council downwards. Without them, none of the councils could in practice survive. These letters have only to be dated and submitted to produce a situation in which the High Commissioner would be forced to assume direct administration of the affairs of the territory. Moreover, the sympathies of nearly all local members of the public service and police, the great majority of whom are Malays, would lie with the Chief Minister and his colleagues. Faced with a hostile public, at least unco-operative and perhaps quickly turning to active opposition, we should find ourselves benefitting [sic] only the Communists; and sooner rather than later we should have to concede in the most unhappy circumstances what we could earlier have granted with an air of generosity, the support of world opinion and the promise of loyal co-operation. The tide is still flowing in our direction, and we can still ride it; but the ebb is close at hand and if we do not make this our moment of decision we shall have lost the power to decide. Not far off the French have shown us what can happen if such a tide is missed.

Constitutional commission

6. In the last analysis, if the delegation are adamant in demanding that the constitutional commission should prepare a scheme for full self-government, we shall at least have to consider whether we can agree. On the other hand, I hope to obtain agreement to the more modest proposal that the terms of reference of the commission should be so drawn as to set it the task of preparing a scheme only for internal self-government, excluding defence and foreign affairs. Nothing less than this will serve. The subjects with which the commission will have to deal will include the structure of the legislature; the question whether or not there should be an Upper House; citizenship; the relation between the Federal Government and the State Governments; and the position of the Rulers. The commission will thus be faced with a heavy task and I would hope to set it to work as soon as possible since it would be of some tactical value to agree with the delegation that the commission should aim at completing its work, if possible, in time for its recommendations to be agreed and put into effect by 31st August, 1957, as proposed by the Chief Minister. Until recently it seemed likely that the demand would be for a commission mainly, if not wholly, composed of persons from outside the Federation, and that we should be asked to find most of them from other Commonwealth countries and not from the United Kingdom alone. In that case I would seek agreement upon a fairly small body with a chairman and at least one other member from the United Kingdom. According to my most recent information, however, the delegation are likely to propose a commission composed entirely of Malayans except for a chairman from outside the country. I see no need to make an issue of this question, but I shall insist that, in view of the responsibilities of Her Majesty's Government, the chairman must be someone acceptable to us, and I shall seek to have it agreed that I should myself look for a suitable person.

7. It is plain from past experience and from the very nature of things alike that, even if I succeed in obtaining agreement to an interim period during which

self-government is limited to internal affairs, that cannot last very long. It would, however, be invaluable in preparing for an orderly handover, and particularly in allowing local Ministers an opportunity gradually to learn how the machinery of internal security ought to work and what is its proper and essential relation to external defence. I shall deal with this aspect of the matter more fully later. But if we recognise the inevitability of the advance to full self-government before very long, it would be foolish not to extract from that such advantage as we can. I therefore further propose to agree that the constitution should again be reviewed at the end of two years from the introduction of internal self-government in order that, in the light of its operation during that time, the grant of full self-government should be contemplated.

Defence

8.   On this programme responsibility for external defence would remain with the High Commissioner right through to the beginning of full self-government. Among other advantages this would allow time for the careful preparation of a defence agreement designed to have effect from the date of full self-government. It is already in practice essential that the High Commissioner should consult his Executive Council on any defence questions which directly involve the Federation Government, and this arrangement would necessarily continue. I also propose, however, that, as in the Gold Coast, the High Commissioner should have a small advisory committee of Ministers whom he could at his discretion keep more closely in touch with problems of defence, although he would not be bound to accept their advice. This should provide for a valuable process of education. It had earlier been thought that a defence agreement would be a major matter for the Conference to consider, certainly in broad terms and possibly even in some detail; and discussions on the subject have been going on between the interested Departments in London, and also in Malaya. If, however, my present plan succeeds, discussion of defence need presumably go no further than an attempt to reach agreement in principle that there should in due course be a formal agreement providing for our right to maintain the Commonwealth Strategic Reserve in the Federation, for the facilities which that will require and for arrangements ensuring that our forces will be able to function effectively in the event of war. We should also make it clear that these arrangements must allow for the participation, both in force and in planning, of Australia and New Zealand. I hope that the Federation Government will ultimately join the South-East Asia Treaty Organisation. It is too early to move in that direction at present, but the period of internal self-government will, I trust, help to produce that result.

Internal security

9.   Internal security poses a problem of crucial importance and great difficulty. Hitherto we have always taken the line that until the stage of full self-government was reached the Governor of any dependent territory must retain ultimate responsibility for internal security, and in particular for control of the police. In the Gold Coast even to-day, for instance, the Governor still controls internal security, advised by a committee of the Cabinet but not bound to accept (or necessarily even to seek) their advice. Until quite recently the Chief Minister of the Federation intended to ask for immediate control over the military forces as well as over the police, but my latest information is that a study of the problem of making the military forces self-

contained and independent of Imperial units may have convinced him that this is impraticable, and I am also told that his colleagues hope to persuade him to be content with the transfer of responsibility for the police.

10. The High Commissioner, the Director of Operations, the Commissioner of Police and the Chief Secretary (who is the Minister at present responsible for internal security) all take the view that this request should be granted. Their view is based mainly upon two arguments—first, that the Alliance are so set upon obtaining this concession that refusal on our part might result in the breakdown of the whole Conference; and, second, that internal security will in any case be better safeguarded if controlled by co-operative local Ministers than if we retain nominal control in the face of constant opposition from Ministers and, as a result, probably also of growing unreliability among the great mass of the locally-recruited members of the internal security forces themselves. Nor can we ignore the fact that the delegation are likely to be fortified in their attitude by Chin Peng's statement in the recent discussion of the amnesty offer that the Communist terrorists would be prepared to lay down their arms and leave the jungle when control of internal security had passed to an elected Government in the Federation.[2]

11. While I agree that it would be impolitic to resist in principle the idea of the early transfer of responsibility for internal security, I hope that practical arguments can be developed in the forthcoming talks with a view to avoiding any change during the period before the introduction of internal self-government. The main point would be the difficulty of making any such change without affecting the intelligence and operational machine during the immediate future, when the shooting war must be prosecuted with the utmost vigour.

12. If, however, despite this, it appears necessary to make some gesture in response to the Chief Minister's demand for the immediate transfer of the control of internal security, I would propose to go no further than to agree that the Minister for Home Affairs (a portfolio at present held by the Chief Minister) should take over responsibility for prisons, detention camps and the civil defence organisation, and for the administration—but not the operational control—of the police. "Operational control" would be regarded as covering the operations of the Special Branch and the Director of Intelligence's organisation. Responsibility for the Federation military forces and the volunteer units would remain with the Secretary for Defence. Whether or not any such concession has to be made, I think it important to obtain a clear understanding that at all stages, including that of full self-government, the police should retain the independence and freedom from political influence in the ordinary conduct of their civil duties which they at present enjoy and which in the United Kingdom is regarded as a cardinal principle. This would mean, for example, that the Commissioner of Police would retain sole responsibility for police investigations and prosecutions, where necessary dealing direct with the Law Officers on such matters. I further hope that it will be possible to agree upon the early establishment of a police service commission which would at first advise the High Commissioner on such matters as appointments, promotions to gazetted rank and discipline, and would, when internal self-government, and later full self-government, came, continue in existence as a [sic] independent body.

13. The core of the whole problem is, however, what we agree to do about

---

[2] See 391, para 34.

internal security when internal self-government is introduced. My own view is that we should at once agree that, subject to an important understanding relating to the essential interests of the Federation itself and to our responsibilities for its protection, the introduction of internal self-government should carry with it the transfer of control of internal security. The understanding would be that, because of the enduring mutual interest of the Federation Government and Her Majesty's Government in the United Kingdom in the defence of the territory, and because of the impossibility of dissociating that defence from internal security, both Governments should recognise their common interest and concern in the machinery for security intelligence and counter-subversion. This machinery is at present on the whole soundly constructed and operationally efficient: it is essential to keep it so since otherwise the dangers of internal subversion will gravely and rapidly increase and adequate arrangements for the defence of the territory cannot be sustained. Her Majesty's Government's continuing responsibility for defence therefore requires that the product of the work of the intelligence security machine and of the police Special Branch must continue to be equally available to the High Commissioner as well as to local Ministers; and Ministers for their part must recognise Her Majesty's Government's special interest in the maintenance of the efficiency of that machine after it is handed over to their responsibility. Moreover, so long as the shooting war continues, because of our enormous contribution to sustaining it, both in troops and in other ways, the High Commissioner must retain responsibility for the conduct of operations. During the period of internal self-government, in addition to maintaining the intelligence security machine at full efficiency, our objects should be to make local Ministers thoroughly conversant with its nature, functions and operation and to go ahead as fast as possible with the training of Malayans in its work, in order that when the time for full self-government arrives the machine can continue to do its job without loss of efficiency. For this it will be particularly important to ensure that every encouragement is given to British officers to remain at their posts, certainly during internal self-government and, it is to be hoped, even thereafter. Without this the whole plan is likely to be jeopardised.

14. There remains the question of Singapore, where the problem of internal security is still more serious and difficult. It is bound to arise in my discussions with the delegation from the Colony which is due to come to London in April; and it would have been satisfactory if I felt that I could approach it on the same lines as I have proposed for the Federation. Unfortunately, however, as I see things at present, any demand that the control of internal security should at an early date be handed over to local Ministers in Singapore will have to be resisted. I believe that a reasonable arrangement could be arrived at with Marshall and his colleagues, but we have to recognise that he is a phenomenon of limited and probably brief duration, and that there is in sight no other potential Government which we could safely entrust with this responsibility. Even more than in the Federation our whole defensive position in Singapore depends upon it. While facing this, I do not think that we can let it affect our attitude towards the Federation. If we turned the Federation down because of Singapore we should run into grave trouble with the former without saving ourselves similar trouble with the latter; whereas, if we can secure a contented Government in the Federation we shall be in a stronger position should it be necessary to take a different and tougher line in Singapore.

Finance

15. It is not possible to consider the question of finance in any great detail since the Government of the Fedration have not yet completed a review of their financial resources and of the demands to be made upon them during the next five years. There have been suggestions, however, that the delegation may have ambitious projects in mind for the future and that the demands which it may present for assistance may be substantial. For the present, however, it should be assumed, in the absence of any clear evidence to the contrary, that the delegation will accept the principle that full self-government carries with it the obligation of financial self-sufficiency and that the Federation should then cease to look to the United Kingdom for general financial assistance, except in so far as that assistance may be made available by loans for development through the London Market. Even when the Emergency comes to an end Her Majesty's Government will continue to have heavy financial commitments in the Federation as a result of their continuing responsibility for its external defence. Apart from this, Her Majesty's Government have at present certain further financial commitments, actual or potential, in respect of the Federation. These are:—

(i) A promise to consider financial assistance if the Emergency and the programmes for rubber replanting and expanded educational services involve the Federation in agreed expenditure which cannot be met after the maximum possible use has been made of local resources.

(ii) A new grant of £4 million from Colonial Development and Welfare funds for use in the period ending the 31st March, 1960.

(iii) A grant of up to £7.2 million for use up to 1962 towards the capital cost of the expansion of the local armed forces.

(iv) A promise to consider loan assistance should the Federation be unable to make local arrangements to finance its contribution to the Buffer Stock under the International Tin Agreement.

16. No change need be caused to these arrangements by a degree of constitutional advance which falls short of full self-government, but it is necessary to consider how they might be modified when the Federation becomes fully self-governing. The commitments which Her Majesty's Government have assumed under paragraph 15 (i) would lapse; the Federation did not require a grant towards the cost of the Emergency in 1955, none will be needed this year and there is no present reason to expect that any will be needed in 1957. There remain the types of assistance listed under paragraph 15 (ii), (iii) and (iv). I believe that the United Kingdom interest in preserving a friendly Malaya will be best served if we avoid any suspicion of exacting a price for the grant of full self-government by withdrawing the specific monies already promised. I therefore propose—

(a) that arrangements should be made to enable the Federation, should it attain to full self-government before the 31st March, 1960, to continue to receive assistance up to the limit in paragraph 15 (ii);

(b) that the Federation should continue up to 1962 to be able to count upon financial assistance from Her Majesty's Government as already promised for the capital cost of the expansion of her armed forces, and that, if necessary, this assistance should be increased beyond the figure of £7.2 million quoted in paragraph 15 (iii), to cover the capital cost, as may be agreed, in connection with any further expansion of those forces; and,

(c) that the arrangements in paragraph 15 (iv) should remain in force.

The future of the public service

17. "Malayanisation," or the staffing of the Public Service by local officers, has been the accepted policy of the Federation Government for a number of years. The delegation is certain to press for complete Malayanisation as quickly as possible, and political pressure will undoubtedly tend in the direction of removing overseas officers more rapidly than the country's true interests will allow. While agreeing that all reasonable steps should be taken to accelerate Malayanisation, I propose to remind the delegation of the grave damage which their administration will suffer if overseas officers leave before there are adequately qualified local officers to replace them. The aim should be, not to replace overseas officers by local officers tor the sake of doing so, but to build up a loyal and efficient service in which, while Malayanisation proceeds, both local and overseas officers can feel assured that their conditions of service will continue to be governed by traditional service principles and that there will be no discrimination on racial or political grounds. A public statement to this effect by Federation Ministers on the lines of statements made by the Prime Minister of the Gold Coast and by Nigerian political leaders would go far to remove uncertainties and to reassure staff. I shall endeavour to obtain the agreement of the delegation that such a statement should be made.

18. A loyal and efficient service can be secured only by the establishment of an independent Pubic [sic] Service Commission entirely free from political influence. There is as yet no Public Service Commission in the Federation and I propose to urge the delegation to see that one is set up forthwith and to ensure that it is a truly independent body commanding the respect of both the Government and the Public Service.

19. I must also make it my task to safeguard the interests of those overseas officers for whom I am responsible and to secure agreement to a fair scheme of compensation for those whose terms and conditions of service and career prospects are affected by constitutional changes or by Malayanisation. Details of such a scheme will have to be worked out in consultation with the Government and the Staff Associations concerned but I propose to press for a scheme in two stages on lines similar to those followed in the Gold Coast. So long as I am able to exercise, through the High Commissioner, ultimate control in essentials over the terms and conditions of service of those officers for whom I am responsible, the scheme would permit all such officers to retire on earned pension plus a compensatory addition. When by reason of constitutional or other changes, terms and conditions of services are no longer under my control, the scheme would provide for officers to be offered lump-sum compensation. Those officers who stayed on would retain indefinitely the right to leave at any time with due compensation. They would have to become members of the local Service and forgo my protection, but they would remain members of Her Majesty's Oversea Civil Service (where applicable) and continue to be eligible for transfer and promotion to other territories.

20. I assume that the Conference will result in constitutional changes requiring the immediate introduction of the first of these two schemes, but I also propose that it should be clearly and publicly established that a full lump-sum compensation scheme will be worked out at once and introduced at the right moment.

395   CO 1030/70, no 76   9 Jan 1956
[Constitutional conference]: inward telegram no 15 from Sir D
MacGillivray to Mr Lennox-Boyd

Your telegram Personal No. 4.

Following for Martin.

I agree entirely with your paragraph 4[1] and would only add the point that if the Alliance should be dissatisfied with the outcome of the London Conference they will not return to Malaya with the determination to rally the country in an all out effort against Communist terrorism and are more likely to seek a settlement with the Communists on terms which might in the end constitute a new and greater threat to internal security.

2. Events during the last week before the delegation sailed have encouraged the Alliance leaders to press their demands further than they had previously intended. First came the U.M.N.O. general meeting on 25th December at which they were pressed by their more extreme element and were unable to resist the resolution seeking "independence" by August 1957. Then came the Chin Peng talks and the suggestions that if the Elected Ministers in the Federation could obtain control over internal security (including the local military forces) then a solution could be found to the Emergency.[2] There then followed the emotional influence of Merdeka shouting crowds on the delegation's departures from the airport at Kuala Lumpur and on the quayside at Singapore. On the day before their departure the Alliance Council agreed to ask for "independence by 31st August 1957 if possible" and for immediate control over the Federation local military forces as well as over the Police and prisons. Press reports from Bombay seem to indicate that the Rulers representative[s] will support these demands. The information contained in your paragraph 9 is therefore no longer up to date.[3] During the 24 hours before leaving Kuala Lumpur, Abdul Rahman twice stated publicly that Her Majesty's Government had already agreed in principle that the Elected Ministers should be responsible for internal security and that the Alliance was going to London merely to work out the details. He must be aware that this advance was not being achieved on account of Chin Peng's conditional offer but had been obtained by the Alliance before the Chin Peng meeting took place. He would not wish it to appear that he was beholden to the Communists for this achievement or to allow them to get a measure of credit for it.

3. It would now seem that if responsibility for Police, prisons, Home Guard and local military forces and finance were to be transferred from the Secretary for Defence, and the Financial Secretary to Elected Ministers as soon as practicable after the London Conference the Alliance leaders would publicly claim that this was self-government in internal affairs and that "full independence" would follow upon the recommendations of the Constitutional Commission. It was not clear, however, by the time they left here whether or not they have in mind any curtailment of the High Commissioner's authority at this stage. They have never been able to explain

---

[1] MacGillivray refers throughout to Martin's telegram of 7 Jan containing the summary version of the secretary of state's memorandum, see 394. Para 4 of Martin's telegram relates to paras 4 and 5 of 394 (ie 'General approach').

[2] See 391, para 34.   [3] See 394, para 9, last sentence.

what they mean by restrictions upon the High Commissioner's "veto powers". Just before he left H.S. Lee was speaking of the Ministers being "controlled by the overriding authority of His Excellency [sic] in Council". It seems to me that we must try and get this straight at the London Conference at the outset, or else we shall not know where we stand in discussing the vital and difficult question of internal security. If they are content to accept that at this next stage the High Commissioner should retain a special responsibility for internal security as envisaged by Clause 19 (1) (b) of the Federation Agreement[4] and may in the last resort act against the advice of the Executive Council in the exercise of this special responsibility, and if it is also recognised that, so long as British and Commonwealth forces are required for internal security purposes, the Director of Operations must be responsible to the High Commissioner and not to an Elected Minister then I see no great difficulty in agreeing in principle that the Member of the Executive Council responsible for the local military forces, Police, etc. should be an Elected Minister. I should add that the view of officers responsible for internal security expressed in paragraph 10[5] of your telegram applies with equal force to the request for control over the local military forces. The Alliance are now so committed publicly to obtaining responsibility for internal security and the local military forces that they will have to return with something which on the face of it gives them this responsibility. It will therefore be necessary to go further than proposed in your paragraph 11.[6]

4. Should it be agreed that the local military forces be the responsibility of a Minister then we might consider the desirability of establishing a Federation Army Council over which the Minister would preside. This Council would administer the Federation land forces. At present the G.O.C. Malaya Command is by law in command of these forces. So long as this is so it would not be practicable for a Federation Army Council to be established with full powers, subject to the local Legislature, of control over those forces since the G.O.C. who also commands Imperial troops, would thereby become virtually subordinate to the local Legislature and a local Minister. It would be necessary first to amend the law so as to provide for an officer of the Federation Army to be placed in administrative command of that army which would however remain under the operational command of the Director of Operations for purposes of the anti-Communist campaign. I am sending by bag a paper on this subject.

5. I agree with your paragraph 5[7] but would include "the special position of the Settlements" and "the safeguarding of the rights of minorities" amongst subjects with which Commission will have to deal. There has been a lot of loose political party talk here about a single Malayan nationality and a single sovereignty, but the problem as to just where the allegiance of an independent Federation and its armed forces would lie is conveniently ignored. A Federation of the nine Malay states alone would be an easier proposition. During the last week I have consulted the Nominated Councils in both Settlements and have found concern among the Members, other

---

[4] ie 'In the exercise of his executive authority, the High Commissioner shall have the following special responsibilities, that is to say: . . . the prevention of any grave menace to the peace and tranquillity of the Federation or any Malay State or Settlement comprised therein.'

[5] See 394, para 10, except for the last sentence which was not transmitted to MacGillivray.

[6] See *ibid*, para 12, on the proposed responsibilities of the minister for home affairs.

[7] See *ibid*, para 6, on the terms of reference for a constitutional commission.

than the Malay Elected Members, lest some constitutional arrangements should be made which would sever their direct allegiance to the British Crown. None of the delegation comes from the Settlements and on this issue would be likely to speak from the standpoint of the British Protected Persons and aliens in the Malay States, rather than from that of the British Subjects in the Settlements. The Penang Nominated Council made it clear that, should it become necessary for Penang to be separated from the Federation they would on no (repeat no) account wish to be joined with Singapore.

6. Your paragraph 13.[8] Press reports of discussions on board the "ASIA" indicate that they will also ask for a Minister for Commerce and Industry, Spencer becoming an adviser to the Minister. If this is proposed I recommend it should be agreed to although I do not know if Spencer would stay and he might have to be offered abolition terms.

7. Should a Minister for Finance be agreed to then I think we should seek at this stage to withdraw the obligation under paragraph 14 (1)[9] of your telegram substituting an undertaking to provide the money required to make the Federation Army self-contained at the earliest possible moment (see my letter to MacKintosh KHY 92/55/A of 5th January).[10]

8. Your paragraph 16.[11] I favour a premature retirement scheme in three stages, the first being retirement on earned pension without compensation. I note you make no mention in this paper on the proposal to withdraw the British advisers. You know my views as to this.

9. I am sorry I cannot be more helpful but ideas must remain fluid until we can see more clearly what the Alliance itself has in mind.

---

[8] See *ibid*, para 2(iii), on the demand for the appointment of an elected minister of finance.
[9] See *ibid*, para 15(i), on proposed financial assistance.
[10] See 393.   [11] See 394, para 17, 'The future of the public service'.

396 CO 1030/72, no 17   Jan 1956
'Federation of Malaya talks: finance': CO Far Eastern Department note

This note is intended to summarise (for the purpose of informal discussion in the Colonial Office) the main views expressed in the memorandum prepared by officials in Malaya to brief the Delegation on financial matters. It includes a few tentative comments on the memorandum and takes account of a brief talk with Mr. Spencer immediately after his arrival. It does not comment on the High Commissioner's letter KHY 92/55/A of the 5th January,[1] which will be dealt with separately after discussion with Sir Donald MacGillivray. Mr. Selwyn[2] is preparing another note on the general economic background of the territory, which was not available when this note was prepared.

2. There is no reason to think that the Delegation will take the initiative in putting up a detailed case for financial aid from Her Majesty's Government or that their chief interest is in the financial aspects of the progress towards full self

---

[1] See 393.
[2] P Selwyn was appointed economist, 1950, and senior economist, 1959, in the CO.

government. Nevertheless the Delegation may well stress the need for complete financial autonomy as a pre-requisite of full self government: (among the appendices to the memorandum there is a short note on the financial measures taken when Ceylon achieved full self government) and there may also be proposals for additional United Kingdom assistance towards e.g. their development programme, so it seems that we should be ready with at least some preliminary comments based on the information we have so far been given. It is in any case highly probable (and Spencer confirms this) that the Delegation will raise the following:—

(a) question of appointing a Finance Minister and possibly also a Minister of Commerce and Industry.

(b) relations with the sterling area and the treatment of oversea capital.

(a) will be dealt with in connection with Sir D. MacGillivray's letter referred to in a paragraph 1 above, (b) is covered in the following paragraphs.

3. In part A of the memorandum dealing with relations with the sterling area etc. it is clearly shown that Malaya pulls a great weight for her size in the sterling area team, as is demonstrated by the fact that in the period 1950–1954 Malaya earned surpluses of about £400m. and £240m. with the dollar and O.E.E.C.[3] areas on visible account, far larger than any other member and comparing with United Kingdom deficits of £1,525m. and £860m. Malaya also had in the same period a favourable visible balance with the rest of the sterling area, but an unfavourable balance with other countries. Even after including an unfavourable balance on invisibles, Malaya had achieved an overall favourable balance in her oversea trade to the extent that Malayan sterling balances had increased by about £110m. from 1950 to 1955. On the other side proper weight is given to the value of direct United Kingdom aid and all the main advantages of remaining a member of the sterling area (security, stability and wide convertibility of the currency, access to the London market, easy realisation of investments etc.) are fully stressed. The conclusion, with which I think we would not wish to quarrel, is that while it might be technically possible for the Federation of Malaya to have a separate currency, the likely disadvantages outweigh possible advantages and that the Federation would be very well advised to stay within the sterling area.

4. It seems not improbable that the Delegation, influenced partly by the example of the fully self governing members of the Commonwealth, may accept the view that the Federation should stay within the sterling area. This is a point of great importance in itself and also because it may influence Singapore's attitude in the matter. (We gather from Mr. Spencer that Singapore may not have such strong official advice as that given in the Federation to remain within the area). Given this general attitude and the need to encourage it, it may be necessary to make some concession on the Exchange control front, though there are obvious difficulties about this. As is pointed out in the memorandum the Federation already has virtually complete freedom to import from the Dollar area through a combination of the normal colonial dollar programme procedure and a special arrangement whereby Malaya can import dollar goods through the Hong Kong free market. This latter arrangement however involves a 5 or 6% commission.

---

[3] Organization for European Economic Cooperation (succeeded by the Organization for Economic Cooperation and Development or OEDC in 1961).

5. The memorandum suggests that the Federation should indicate its desire to remain in the sterling area provided that on the achievement of full self government it is accorded all the privileges of full membership of the area and provided that meanwhile some specific recognition is given to its special services to the area. This might take the form of: (a) separate representation in some form at future meetings of Commonwealth Finance Ministers; (b) greater freedom to import dollar goods and to trade with neighbouring non sterling countries so long as the territory continues to contribute on a major scale to the sterling area's dollar earnings. There is a third suggested condition—support by Her Majesty's Government in obtaining loans on the London market; this is mentioned separately below. (a) and (b) are clearly points which present difficulties and which will require further detailed consideration in consultation with the Treasury when the Delegation's precise views are known, but it is suggested that meanwhile the preliminary views of Economic General Department should be sought. It seems likely that some formula may have to be devised to give the Federation a greater measure of freedom to import dollar goods (otherwise than through Hong Kong), pending the attainment of full self government.

6. Part B of the memorandum simply sets out the present arrangements for currency control and is intended to be read with Part C which deals with the possibility of establishing a Central Bank. This whole matter is to be the subject of a special enquiry by a member of the Bank of England and Sir Sidney [sic] Caine[4] and it is unlikely that the Delegation will raise the subject pending the result of the enquiry. It is however worth noting that the memorandum advises against the early creation of a Central Bank but suggests that the possibility might be explored of instituting as a first step some kind of State Bank, operating in conjunction with a Currency Board, which could later if necessary be expanded into a full Central Bank. The memorandum suggests that any report on the possibility of introducing a Central Bank should comment on the practicability and desirability of evolution in this way, and also on the question of compensation to Governments for assets of the currency funds transferred to the Bank. Emphasis is rightly given to the need to preserve external and internal confidence in the currency and finances of the territory in any arrangements to set up a Central Bank. We can be sure that the Financial Secretary will make his points to the mission of enquiry when they are in Malaya and there appears to be no need to comment at this stage.

7. Part D of the memorandum discusses budgetary policy and financial relations with the States and Settlements. The merits of orthodox financing and a balanced budget are rehearsed and it is stressed that borrowing should normally be confined to productive purposes. Scope is seen for some increased taxation and the hope is expressed that within four years the cost to the Federation of defence and internal security could be brought down from its present figure of about £27m. to about £15m. per annum. Given this sort of reduction the Federation should be able to balance its budget in future while still providing some modest expansion of the social services and a fairly substantial amount of capital for productive purposes. The memorandum emphasises the need for the States to realise that in the course of progress towards full self government they and the Federation Government must

---

[4] Sydney Caine, who had been a member of the Financial Mission to Ceylon, 1951, and chaired the British Caribbean Federation Fiscal Commission, 1955, examined the matter with G M Watson of the Bank of England.

stand or fall together in the matter of finance and that they must be prepared to accept economies when necessary in the interests of the territory as a whole. The financial provisions of the Federation of Malaya Agreement as amended from the 1st January, 1956 are thought to be better than those previously in force but clearly to leave room for improvement. A comprehensive financial agreement between the States and the Federation Government is thought to be a most desirable part of any new Constitution. The question of Federal/State financial relations is a very complicated one which I think we should not wish to take up with the Delegation at this stage.

8. Of the appendices to the memorandum the only ones which appear to need mention at this stage are those on the development programme and the raising of loans. Malayan Ministers have not yet had time to revise the 1955–60 Development Programme and we do not know what shape they will finally wish to give it. We are not therefore in a position to engage in the normal development plan exercise or to commit ourselves in any way about development finance. It is worth noting however that Departmental proposals for Capital Expenditure, including security, during the period amount to some $1,371.1m., of which some $496.6m. represents continuing approved expenditure, leaving some $910.1m., attributable to new schemes. Total development expenditure of $776.6m. was thought to be practicable over a similar period by the I.B.R.D. mission. The Federation Budget contains no separate development or capital estimates and it is not possible on present information to say what rate of capital expenditure was achieved in 1955. However, mainly on the grounds of physical capacity, the Financial Secretary doubts whether it would be possible to achieve a capital programme of much more than $600m. over the period. This figure is somewhat less than the funds which might be available ($700m.), given London market loan finance of about $100 [m.] and I.B.R.D. loan finance of about $60m. Subject to a detailed check it seems that all special funds of any significant size are taken into account in calculating the contribution from local revenue sources except the Currency Fund. It seems that the latter could, if necessary, contribute (from the Federation's share of $\frac{3}{5}$ths), say, $50m. The assets of the Fund stand at about $800m. and up to 15% of this may be invested in local securities. The Savings Bank seems already to have invested almost up to the permitted limit. The possibility of London market borrowing up to $100m. over the period up to 1960 cannot be accepted without reserve but it would seem reasonable to aim at this target. It is not possible to comment on the proposal to obtain $60m. from the I.B.R.D. in the absence of information about the project or projects in mind, but given a suitable project and ability to meet the local costs there seems no reason why the I.B.R.D. should not seek investment in the Federation if political and economic conditions remain stable. The possible sources of development finance are listed by the Financial Secretary as:—

		$m.
(a)	Brunei Loan	40
(b)	Employees Provident Fund	300
(c)	Budget appropriations	60
(d)	Reserve Fund	140
(e)	London borrowing	100
(f)	I.B.R.D. Loan	60
		700

to which may be added
Colonial Development and Welfare unspent
  balance approximately: 35
and possibly Currency Fund contribution, say   75
  say   810 or £96.5m.

The budget appropriations' total of $60m. over the 5 years seems prima facie on the low side, especially in view of the hoped for reduction in the cost of internal security. Admittedly with the increased recurrent costs which will have to be borne, particularly in the latter part of the period, as a result of the development programme it is desirable to avoid any overestimation of this figure, but further examination might nevertheless show that it could be increased.

397 CO 1030/132, no 20   13 Jan 1956
[Constitutional problems of independence]: note by Sir K Roberts-Wray. *Annex*: note by Roberts-Wray, 'The constitutional position of an independent Malaya

It looks as if complete independence for the Federation of Malaya may become an actual proposition in the foreseeable future, and the time has come, in my opinion, to consider the novel and very difficult constitutional problem to which this will give rise. I attach a note which merely states the question without any attempt to answer it. I have been thinking about it in a vague way for four or five years, but have not yet discovered a satisfactory answer, unless Malaya were to become a Republic. I am sending copies of this note to Mr. Hogan, the three Assistant Legal Advisers and Mr. Rushford[1] (who is going to assist on the Malayan discussions beginning next week). Any contributions will be gratefully received.

Annex to 397

There is no precedent for giving complete self-government (what used to be called "Dominion status") to a country which is almost entirely under Her Majesty's protection, though the problem will be somewhat similar when Nigeria reaches the final stage. There were, of course, Protected States in India and Pakistan at the time of the Indian Independence Act, but they could be regarded as appendages to British India which was part of Her Majesty's dominions. It seems inconceivable, however, that the Malay States could be regarded as appendages to the Settlements. Independent Protected States would be a contradiction in terms, because Protectorates (in international law they are the same as Protected States) are essentially dependent countries for which some other State is internationally responsible. In a place like the Gold Coast, it is, I think, possible for Her Majesty's protection to be continued after independence, her powers and jurisdiction being exercised through the Government of that part of the country which is part of Her Majesty's dominions, but one could not suggest establishing a Government for Penang and Malacca to

---

[1] A R Rushford was senior legal assistant, 1954–1960, and assistant legal adviser, 1960–1966, in the CO.

exercise the Queen's right as Protectress in the States. Even assuming that the Settlements remain part of Her Majesty's dominions, it is difficult to see what the position of the Queen will be unless the Federation becomes a Republic like India and Pakistan, when the Queen will merely be recognised as Head of the Commonwealth. It seems a trifle odd to have States with hereditary Rulers within a Republic, but I believe that is still the position in India.

2. The above merely states the problem. I do not know the answer, but we ought to start trying to work out at least one answer and, if possible, two or three for consideration.

398   DEFE 7/493, no 5   16 Jan 1956

[Defence aspects of constitutional talks]: minutes (NDMS/M(56)1) by the Ministry of Defence of an inter-departmental meeting on 9 Jan

The Chairman[1] said that the object of the meeting was to discuss the Defence aspects of the forthcoming talks with Malaya against the background of the paper (C.A.(56)3)[2] which the Secretary of State for the Colonies had submitted to the Colonial Policy Committee.

The Colonial Office briefly outlined the procedure and programme for the conference with the representatives of Malaya. To a large extent the actual pattern of the talks would depend upon the circumstances and the attitude adopted by the Malayan representatives but, broadly speaking, they hoped to persuade them to accept that their constitutional development should take place in three main phases. During the first phase the Constitutional Commission would be set up to examine the complicated question of the structure of the legislature, the relation between the Federal Government and the State Governments, citizenship, and the position of the Rulers, and it was hoped that the Malayans would recognise the necessity for the U.K. to continue as at present to be operationally responsible for internal security as well as for external defence. The second phase would be the implementation of the recommendations of the Constitutional Commission in about August 1957 when the Federation would become responsible for internal self-government and would take over full control of internal security, external defence and foreign affairs still remaining the responsibility of the U.K. The third phase of the grant of full self-government would probably come about two years later in 1959, this being the minimum period which we considered desirable for the education of the local Ministers into the full responsibilities of office. It might well be, of course, that this period would be much shorter. At the appropriate time negotiations would be opened on a detailed Defence Agreement covering the stationing of U.K. and Commonwealth Forces in Malaya and establishing rights to the use of bases and other necessary facilities.

The Chairman said that the substance of our defence requirements should be made known to the Malayans during the course of the conference lest there should be any misunderstanding at a later date. It would be necessary to reach agreement in

---

[1] Sir Richard Powell, see 383, note 1. Also present were: A M MacKintosh (CO), R C C Hunt (CRO), A D Peck (Treasury), A M Allen (Treasury) and W D Allen (FO).
[2] See 394.

principle that a defence agreement should be negotiated providing for the maintenance of such forces as we thought necessary for the external defence of the territories and for the discharge of our international obligations under ANZAM and SEATO, it being made clear that these forces would consist of U.K. forces and the Commonwealth strategic reserve. We should need to continue using facilities in Malaya on something like the present scale but the disposition of forces would have to be determined in the light of strategic requirements. A broad formula covering the requirements on which agreement in principle would need to be reached would have to be worked out and included in the brief to Ministers.

The Commonwealth Relations Office said that Australia and New Zealand had previously been given to understand that the negotiation of a satisfactory Defence agreement would be an essential preliminary to any constitutional advance. The programme now outlined, if accepted by Malaya, represented a change of emphasis which would need to be carefully explained to Australia and New Zealand. They would also need to be informed of the terms of any broad formula put forward at the conference and it was proposed to keep them in close touch with the course of the discussions.

The Colonial Office said that the timing and extent of the handover of responsibility for internal security presented the greatest difficulty. During the first phase it might be necessary to make a gesture of some kind by handing over responsibility for prisons etc. and the administration, but not the operational control, of the police. We should probably have no option but to accept that control of internal security would pass to Malaya with the introduction of internal self-government. If, however, the shooting war had not ended and U.K. troops were still involved, we should have to insist that responsibility for the conduct of operations should remain with the High Commissioner. It was hoped that this problem would not arise until after August 1957 and that by then some acceptable arrangements could be worked out to fit the circumstances. The Colonial Office realized that the question of handing over internal security while possibly retaining operational control of the use of U.K. troops and the negotiating of a defence agreement covering our responsibilities for external defence could not be used in themselves as arguments for delaying constitutional advancement.

The Treasury said that there were no major financial implications in the proposed defence agreement in its present draft form. Under the constitutional programme outlined, the Treasury accepted that in the main we should honour existing financial commitments to Malaya but with the grant of full self-government, they assumed that Malaya would become financially independent.

The Foreign Office said that it seemed undesirable to broach directly in the talks the question of membership of SEATO. The Federation of Malaya was already being associated with the discussions of the various committees of SEATO and was being encouraged to send observers. *The Meeting* agreed that it would be better to allow this association to develop in the expectation that Malaya would come to realize the aims of SEATO and the benefits of membership.

The Meeting then discussed the draft preamble to a defence agreement circulated by the Ministry of Defence (N.D.M.S./P(56)1). A few drafting amendments were suggested and the meeting invited the Commonwealth Relations Office to submit amendments covering a more direct reference to the presence of Commonwealth Forces in Malaya.

The Meeting also discussed the question of departmental representation at the forthcoming talks. *The Colonial Office* said that it might be necessary to set up a separate working party on Defence, possibly under the chairmanship of the Minister of State, on which they would wish to have a representative of the Ministry of Defence and, possibly, of the Chiefs of Staff. It was agreed that either Sir Richard Powell, or Mr. Cary,[3] as appropriate, would represent the Ministry of Defence.

---

[3] M Cary was assistant secretary, Air Ministry, 1951–1956.

399   CO 1030/70, no 84   16 Jan 1956
[Target date for full self-government): minute by A M MacKintosh to Sir J Martin on the British response to the Alliance demand

As a result of our meeting with the Secretary of State on Saturday morning there is one major change of policy in relation to the Malayan Conference which it is most desirable for the Secretary of State to agree with his colleagues in Cabinet tomorrow. You will remember that Sir D. MacGillivray told us that, as a result of a long talk which he had had with the Tunku on Friday evening, it was clear that the Alliance would insist that the terms of reference of the constitutional commission should instruct it to prepare a scheme for full self-government; that the Rulers' representatives would almost certainly support them in this; and that we should not succeed in restricting the commission to the extent hitherto proposed. On the other hand, Sir D. MacGillivray was also clear that if we agreed to this we should not in fact radically change the timing of developments, since the task of the commission would be so great, and the work to be done upon its recommendations before they could be put into effect (including the holding of fresh elections) so complex and extensive that the timing which we have previously contemplated for the introduction of full self-government, that is, 1959, would not be substantially advanced. Moreover, the Tunku has indicated that, if he obtains agreement to a plan on these lines, he will seek to avoid any major changes in the Federation Agreement in advance of the introduction of full self-government. Thus, our acceptance of the Alliance proposals for the commission will not only avoid the risk of frustrating an amicable settlement of the major issues before the Conference but will also leave the High Commissioner in a stronger position between now and 1959 than we are likely otherwise to secure. Since the Alliance leaders have publicly committed themselves to the 31st August, 1957, if possible, as the target date for full self-government, while at the same time privately acknowledging that in practice this target is not feasible, we should be prepared to agree that full self-government should come about as soon as possible. This would leave it open to us to make the best tactical arrangement that we could in relation to the date of the 31st August, 1957.

2.   The Secretary of State will also want to tell his colleagues that it now seems likely that the delegation will ask for a small commission consisting entirely of people from outside Malaya. He might indicate that he would therefore propose to aim at a commission consisting of a United Kingdom Chairman, one other U.K. member, and some three other members from Australia, Canada and India respectively.

3.   Sir D. MacGillivray has seen this minute and agrees with it. We both feel, in

view of Saturday's meeting, that it may make all the difference in the world to the success or otherwise of the Conference if the Secretary of State can enter it with freedom to go as far as I have indicated above.

400   CAB 128/30/1, CM 4(56)3   17 Jan 1956

'Malaya': Cabinet conclusions on policy to be pursued at the constitutional conference

The Cabinet considered a note by the Colonial Secretary (C.P.(56)12) covering a memorandum[1] outlining the policy to be pursued at the forthcoming Conference on constitutional advance in Malaya.

The Colonial Secretary said that the main lines of the policy which he proposed to follow had already been approved by the Colonial Policy Committee. There were three particular points to which he wished to draw the Cabinet's attention. As regards *internal security*, he expected the Malayan leaders to press that the local Government should have administrative control over the local military forces, as well as the police, operational control remaining with the Director of Operations. The High Commissioner and his advisers had recommended that this request should be granted, subject to an undertaking that residual control over internal security and control over security intelligence would continue to rest with the High Commissioner until the end of the present emergency. In addition, until full self-government was attained, the High Commissioner would have authority under his existing powers to reject the advice of local Ministers on questions of internal security.

As regards *defence*, it had been felt that we should be in a stronger position at this stage, than when full self-government was about to come into effect, to obtain guarantees covering our right to continue to maintain forces in the Federation both for its defence and for meeting our obligations under ANZAM and SEATO. He would attempt, therefore, in the forthcoming negotiations to reach agreement on a broad formula which would embrace these guarantees.

On the question of a *constitutional commission*, it was now known that the Malayan leaders would ask that the commission should be empowered to prepare plans for full self-government as well as for the intervening stage of internal self-government. The stage of full self-government would not be reached before 1959. This timetable would not, however, be advanced by empowering the constitutional commission to prepare a scheme for full self-government, for the preparation of the scheme and of plans for putting it into operation would be a lengthy task. He understood that the Malayan leaders, if their proposals in regard to the constitutional commission were accepted, would not seek for any major changes in the Federation Agreement during the intervening period. The High Commissioner would therefore retain his residual powers under the Agreement until full self-government had been introduced.

The Malayan leaders proposed that the constitutional commission should be composed of members from outside Malaya: they contemplated a commission of four members drawn from the United Kingdom, Canada, Australia and India.

---

[1] This is retained, see 394, note.

The Cabinet's discussion turned mainly on the question whether this opportunity should be taken to attempt to obtain appropriate guarantees to safeguard the future of our economic interests in Malaya when the stage of full self-government had been reached. On this, it was pointed out that the Malayan leaders could not be expected to enter into an agreement limiting their freedom of action in such matters as taxation after full self-government had been attained, and that safeguards of the kind we sought would be of little value if a Government wishing to pursue a discriminatory policy towards United Kingdom or foreign interests were eventually to come into power in Malaya. On the other hand it was argued that the protection provided by formal undertakings would be of value even if a time came when Malaya was governed by less conservative elements. Moreover, Malaya would continue to depend on the United Kingdom and other Commonwealth countries for her defence for an indefinite period, and it was reasonable that this dependence should be associated with an assurance that our economic interests in Malaya would continue to be respected. It was agreed that further consideration should be given to the possibility of securing some assurances on this point in the course of the forthcoming negotiations.

The Cabinet:—

(1) Approved, subject to the point recorded in Conclusion (2) below, the proposals for constitutional advance in Malaya contained in C.P. (56) 12.

(2) Agreed that an attempt should be made in the forthcoming negotiations to secure assurances to safeguard the future of United Kingdom economic interests in Malaya.

(3) Invited the Chancellor of the Exchequer, the Colonial Secretary and the President of the Board of Trade to consider, in consultation, the form and scope of the economic safeguards which might be sought.[2]

---

[2] See 403.

401   CO 1030/129, no 27   [Jan 1956]

'Federation of Malaya conference: constitutional commission': CO memorandum (FMC3) on terms of reference and composition

Her Majesty's Government have already agreed that following the Conference a commission should be appointed to review the constitution. One of the items on the agenda will therefore be the terms of reference, the composition and the timing of this commission.

2. We do not know exactly what the delegation wish this constitutional commission to do. It has been reported that Tunku Abdul Rahman has it in mind that the commission should be instructed to prepare for the introduction of what he calls "full independence" by the 31st August, 1957, if possible. It is not clear what he means by full independence but he is reported to mean that it should include full control of external affairs and defence, "though treaty arrangements on these could be made with Britain".

3. *Terms of reference*
Although it is possible that the delegation may insist that the constitutional

commission should prepare a scheme for full self-government, we should hope to obtain their agreement to the more modest proposal that the terms of reference of the commission should be so drawn up as to set it the task of preparing a scheme only for internal self-government, excluding defence and foreign affairs.

4. There may be some difference of opinion among the delegation about the subjects with which the commission should deal. In particular there may be a difference of opinion between the Chinese and Malay elements of the Alliance on the question whether the commission should consider the problem of citizenship. It is suggested that the terms of reference should be wide enough to enable the Commission to deal with citizenship as well as other such subjects as the structure of the legislature; the question of whether or not there should be an Upper House; the relation between the Federal Government and the State Governments; and the position of the Rulers. On the last the delegation is likely to be unanimous in desiring that the position of the Rulers as constitutional heads of their States should be respected. The High Commissioner has suggested that two other subjects to be covered should be the special position of the Settlements and safeguards for the rights of minorities.

5. The delegation has not produced any draft terms of reference for the commission. It is suggested that a draft on the following lines might be put forward for discussion:—

> "To examine the Federation Agreement and to make recommendations to Her Majesty's Government in the United Kingdom and Their Highnesses the Rulers which would result in the introduction of self-government within the Federation, external defence and external affairs alone remaining the responsibility of Her Majesty's Government through the High Commissioner. In making its recommendations the Commission should regard itself as bound by the agreements reached as a result of the Conference in January, 1956, between the Secretary of State for the Colonies and a delegation from the Federation of Malaya, as approved by Her Majesty's Government and Their Highnesses the Rulers."

It will almost certainly prove necessary to elaborate this draft by specifying some at least of the main subjects to be covered, but our own candidates for insertion cannot be determined until after discussion with the High Commissioner.

6. If the delegation are adamant in demanding that the constitutional commission should prepare a scheme for full self-government it will be necessary to consider further whether or not to agree to this demand.

Composition

7. There has been a division of opinion between the Rulers and the Alliance on this matter. The Rulers have favoured a commission drawn from within the Federation of Malaya, whereas the Alliance have pressed for an independent commission whose members should be chosen from other Commonwealth countries.

8. The problems which the commission will have to tackle are going to be so intricate that they may be beyond the capacity of a purely Malayan commission. There would therefore seem to be some practical advantage in placing this extremely difficult task in the hands of a body of experts drawn from the United Kingdom and Commonwealth countries. The calibre of the commission will have to be very high

since the problem will be unusual and of great complexity.

9. It is suggested that the balance of advantage lies in a small commission whose members should be drawn from Commonwealth countries and that we should favour this but that we should not press for it should the delegation show a strong and united preference for a commission from within the Federation. In this latter event we should strive to have one or two really sound constitutional advisers – perhaps one lawyer and one experienced administrator, possibly with political experience— attached to the commission. If the first alternative is preferred nominations for membership should be sought from the Commonwealth Governments concerned. The Australian and Canadian Governments have already been asked by the Alliance whether they would be prepared to assist in making the services of someone of sufficiently high calibre available and their reaction has been favourable. Apart from Commonwealth members there should also be at least one United Kingdom member as well as a United Kingdom chairman.

10. Whatever the composition of the commission the chairman should be a person from the United Kingdom. In view of the responsibilities of Her Majesty's Government it is essential that the chairman should be someone acceptable to them and it is suggested that the Secretary of State should insist that he himself should pursue the search for a suitable person. A discussion on possible names will be initiated on a separate file dealing with the composition of the commission (FED. 36/1/015).

Size of commission

11. If it is decided on the insistence of the delegation that a commission should be composed of members selected from within the Federation it will probably have to be fairly large in order that all the various interests may be represented on it.

12. If, however, it is agreed that the commission should be composed of members from other Commonwealth countries under a United Kingdom chairman then it would be desirable in the interests of efficiency to keep the commission small.

Timing of the commission

13. The object would be to get the commission to start work as soon as possible. It will take some time to select and appoint a commission and it will have a heavy task to do. It would be of tactical value if it were possible to agree that the commission should aim at completing its work, if possible, in time for its recommendations to be agreed and put into effect by the date proposed by the Chief Minister, the 31st August, 1957.

Recommendations

14. It is recommended that our objects should be to obtain agreement to the following:—

(a) the terms of reference should be the preparation of a scheme for internal self-government excluding defence and external affairs;
(b) the commission should be a small one under a United Kingdom chairman with at least one other United Kingdom member and other members drawn from the Commonwealth;
(c) that the selection of the commission should be undertaken by the Secretary of

State: selected and agreed Commonwealth Governments concerned should be asked to suggest names for membership;[1]

(d) if the delegation insist upon a Malayan Commission it would have to be much larger and should be fortified with advisers from outside; and

(e) the commission should start work as soon as possible and aim at completing its task in time for its recommendations to be put into effect by the 31st August, 1957.

---

[1] Lord Simonds, a former lord chancellor and currently a lord of appeal, was the CO's initial preference as chairman but Lord Reid was appointed. The other members were jurists from Britain (Sir Ivor Jennings), Australia (Sir William McKell), India (Mr B Malik) and Pakistan (Mr Justice Abdul Hamid). Canada was not able to provide a suitable nomination in time (see CO 1030/129 and 130, and DO 35/6274 and 6275).

402 DEFE 7/493, no 6   26 Jan 1956

[Anglo-Malayan defence agreement]: minutes (NDMS/M(56)2) by the Ministry of Defence of an inter-departmental meeting attended by Sir D MacGillivray   [Extract]

1. *The Meeting* had before it a note by the High Commissioner for the Federation of Malaya (N.D.M.S./P(56)2) which suggested that consideration should be given to the possibility of concentrating our military bases in Malaya in a few areas situated in the two settlements of Penang and Malacca.

2. *The High Commissioner* said that in putting forward this proposal for consideration whilst he was in London, he had not had the opportunity of discussions with the B.D.C.C. (F.E.). Until quite recently military planning for the continued presence of British Forces in Malaya had been based on the assumption that control would remain with us for perhaps another ten years. It was now clear from the course of the discussions with the Malayan representatives that the constitutional advancement of Malaya towards self-government would take place in a much shorter time. In his view, the prospects of maintaining amicable relations with the Federation in any treaty with them under which we could station forces and maintain bases in Malaya, would be immensely improved if our forces were concentrated in particular areas as, for example, the American Forces were concentrated in the Philippines. The danger of having foreign troops scattered in small pockets all over Malaya, frequently in sensitive spots, was that this would lead to friction and misunderstanding and would be regarded as a continuing affront to the nationalist sentiment which would be exploited by the political opposition and by subversive elements. The Service Departments were at the moment considering plans for large-scale permanent works projects for the accommodation of their units and the High Commissioner suggested that these should be reviewed before they had proceeded too far with the object of forestalling the objections which the Malayans might make on political grounds. Although the Malayans had not yet given any positive indication of their attitude, he considered that their thinking would undoubtedly tend towards the viewpoint set out in his note and might well lead to some hard bargaining when negotiations were begun on the Defence Agreement covering the stationing and use of facilities in Malaya.

3. *The Chairman*[1] said that our experience in defence treaty relationships with other countries and particularly with Ceylon and Libya lent support to the view put forward by the High Commissioner. Before the U.K. entered into negotiations on the Defence Agreement, we should have to examine how far it would be practicable to concentrate our units in the manner suggested. There would undoubtedly be difficulties if the proposal led to very large-scale expenditure by the U.K. on new facilities, but it was right that at a time when there were plans for a number of new developments, we should consider carefully whether these would fit in with a long term policy of some concentration of our bases in Malaya in order to establish a favourable atmosphere for the treaty.

4. *The Commonwealth Relations Office* said they supported the views expressed by the High Commissioner and considered that the question of location of the bases was bound to be raised by the Malayans as soon as negotiations began. . . .

---

[1] Sir R Powell.

---

403 CO 1030/72, no 29   [Feb 1956]
'Safeguarding UK economic interests in Malaya': draft Cabinet memorandum by Mr Lennox-Boyd advising against a formal agreement

The Cabinet, in its consideration of the policy to be pursued at the Malayan Constitutional Conference, agreed that an attempt should be made in the present negotiations to seek assurances to safeguard the future of United Kingdom economic interests in Malaya, and invited the Chancellor of the Exchequer, the President of the Board of Trade and myself to consider the form and scope of the economic safeguards which might be sought.[1] The following appraisal of this question is the result of those consultations, with which the Secretary of State for Commonwealth Relations has been associated.

2. The present Government of the Federation of Malaya has already given some attention to the role of overseas capital and private enterprise in the present and future development of the country, and public assurances of fair and considerate treatment were given in the High Commissioner's address to the Legislative Council on November 30th, 1955, an extract from which is attached as an Appendix.[2]

3. My colleagues and I have considered whether any further advantage would accrue from an attempt to embody those assurances in some more formal agreement. The advantages of a more formal agreement may be summarised as follows:—

(i) It might encourage the Federation Government to resist pressure from individual interests in Malaya desirous of squeezing out United Kingdom competitors;

(ii) it would set out Malayan rights as well as obligations, and so give the Malayan authorities concrete realisation of the advantages of their economic relations with the United Kingdom;

---

[1] See 400.   [2] Not printed.

(iii) it might serve to support the morale of United Kingdom interests in Malaya; and

(iv) it would serve as a basis upon which to make representations to the Federation Government, particularly if the present Ministers had less moderately-minded successors.

4. On the other hand, such an agreement could only have a limited value, for the following reasons:—

(i) It could do little more than codify the treatment which the Federation Government of the time was willing to extend to United Kingdom interests, and if negotiated now might need re-negotiation at the time of a transfer of power;

(ii) it might be regarded as a limitation upon sovereignty to be dispensed with as soon as possible, and its provisions as a maximum entitlement;

(iii) the well-being of commercial interests in Malaya will depend less upon a legal document than upon the friendliness of economic relations with the United Kingdom and upon the cultivation of goodwill between the interests themselves and those with whom they deal; and

(iv) specifically, if we seek formal assurances at this time, we might forfeit goodwill by appearing to doubt the integrity of the present Government and the value of their recent declaration.

5. This question is not a new one. No agreement was negotiated—although one was at one time intended—with India and Pakistan at the time of the transfer of power in 1947; but the difficulties which our nationals with business interests in India or Pakistan have encountered are not of the sort that could have been avoided by an agreement. An agreement might provide for consultation with us before action was taken which might be prejudicial to United Kingdom business and commercial interests, and for adequate compensation in the event of expropriation or acquisition. (The Government of Burma agreed to provisions in these terms). But in practice the Governments of India and Pakistan have "consulted" us about many of the matters which have caused difficulty. Our businessmen would no doubt have liked to have been assured that their interests would not be nationalised, that the high (but non-discriminatory) Indian taxation would not harm them and that the legislation on Managing Agencies in India would not affect their operations. But we could not have asked for such assurances. The fact is that the sort of assurances we could expect to secure in any formal agreement are not as valuable to us as the recognition of mutual interest and the establishment of understanding and cordial relations between the commercial interests and the local governments.

6. Having weighed all these considerations, my colleagues and I are of the opinion that no attempt should be made at the present juncture to seek any formal agreement with the Federation Government on this question. We do, however, feel that the opportunity of the present discussions should be taken to invite the Federation Delegation to reiterate their Government's past assurances, and for a statement in this sense to form part of the report of the Conference. I am proceeding accordingly. I shall represent to the Delegation that the repetition of these assurances, which relate to all oversea interests, would be to their own advantage in ensuring a prosperous economy for Malaya.

7. I shall report to the Cabinet the result of my approach. Whatever statement

emerges should provide us with a basis for the subsequent financial and commercial discussions with the Federation Government which will be necessary, nearer the time of the transfer of power, to reach understanding upon such matters as the Federation's position in the sterling area, past and future borrowings on the U.K. capital market and the maintenance of certain preferences which Malaya at present extends to the United Kingdom.[3]

---

[3] This approach was agreed by Macmillan (Treasury), Thorneycroft (Board of Trade) and Home (CRO) on the understanding that Lennox-Boyd would persuade Tunku Abdul Rahman to agree to the insertion of a statement in the conference report. As it happened, the circulation of this memorandum was deferred indefinitely: Lennox-Boyd spoke to this effect in Cabinet on 8 Feb, see 404, and an economic statement was inserted in the conference report and later approved by Cabinet, see 405, Annex C, and 406.

404   CAB 128/30/1, CM 9(56)7   8 Feb 1956
'Malaya': Cabinet conclusions on agreement reached at the constitutional conference

The Colonial Secretary reported to the Cabinet that the agreement reached in the Conference on Constitutional Advance in Malaya was due to be signed that afternoon. The agreement contained satisfactory assurances on external defence, internal security, finance and the position of expatriate officials. It would also incorporate assurances regarding the future of United Kingdom economic interests in Malaya. The Departments concerned had agreed that it would not have been practicable to safeguard these interests by binding undertakings,[1] and the business community in Malaya had not urged that undertakings of this nature should be secured.

It had been agreed that Lord Reid, who had consented to act in that capacity, should be the Chairman of the Constitutional Commission. This would include representatives from Australia, Canada, India and Pakistan together with a second representative from the United Kingdom. The terms of reference of the Constitutional Commission would not be published until they had been approved by the Cabinet and by the Council of Rulers. It was foreshadowed that, when Malaya achieved full self-government, the exercise of sovereign functions would rotate among the Rulers in turn. The fact that Her Majesty was Sovereign of the Straits Settlements of Malacca and Penang had presented some difficulty in this connection, but the terms of reference of the Constitutional Commission would contain a formula making it clear that The Queen's position would be in no way prejudiced by the arrangements foreshadowed. He had agreed, in deference to the wishes of the Malayan leaders, that the report of the Conference should express a hope that the Constitutional Commission would complete their task in time for full self-government to be brought into effect by August 1957.[2]

---

[1] See 403, note 3.

[2] In an exchange with the Tunku on 27 Jan, Lennox-Boyd had insisted on flexibility as regards the timetable, saying that 'he was prepared to discuss this question of a target date on the clear understanding that it might in the event prove impossible to meet it and that no pledge was given and no accusation of bad faith on the part of Her Majesty's Government should be levelled if it should prove impossible to complete the task by the published date' (minute by R C Ormerod, 30 Jan 1956, DO 35/6274).

The Cabinet:—

(1) Took note of the Colonial Secretary's statement.

(2) Invited the Colonial Secretary to circulate a written report on the results of the Conference.

405   CAB 129/79, CP(56)47   21 Feb 1956

'Federation of Malaya': Cabinet memorandum by Mr Lennox-Boyd on the constitutional conference. *Annex* C: 'Notes on the main conclusions and recommendations of the conference'

I attach at Annex A a copy of the agreed Report of the Conference on Constitutional Advance in Malaya, and at Annex B[1] an extract from the Report of the General Purposes Committee of the Conference, as approved by the Conference in Plenary Session, containing material relating to the proposed Constitutional Commission which was not included in the Report of the Conference as a whole. The Report of the Conference contained a number of typographical and other minor errors which have been corrected for publication of the Report as a White Paper in, I hope, the next two to three weeks.[2] I do not expect my colleagues to read these two documents in full, and I therefore also attach at Annex C notes upon those recommendations of the Conference to which I think it necessary expressly to draw their attention.

2.   The Conference was undoubtedly of success. Its Report deals with all the issues which we set out to settle; and the conclusions and recommendations upon them are comprehensive and free from ambiguity. Agreement was reached on all points within the limits authorised by the Cabinet on 17th January (C.M. (56) 4th Conclusions, Minute 3).[3] These agreements are far-reaching, but we had all recognised beforehand that it was right to go a long way in order to obtain an amicable settlement, and they include satisfactory safeguards for all our vital interests. The business of the Conference was throughout conducted in an atmosphere of goodwill and I have no doubt that the Malayan Delegation has returned to the Federation with feelings of genuine cordiality towards Her Majesty's Government and the British people. In a farewell letter to me Tunku Abdul Rahman, the Chief Minister, wrote:—

> "We feel, as we return, that there has been laid down a most excellent basis for the continued improvement of relations between the United Kingdom and a self-governing Malaya within the Commonwealth and for increased friendship and understanding between our two peoples. I can assure you of my personal co-operation and support on all matters agreed upon".

It is, above all, upon this goodwill and co-operation that we must in future depend for the security of British and Commonwealth interests in the Federation of Malaya.

3.   I have already sent the High Commissioner a despatch asking him to convey the Report of the Conference to Their Highnesses the Rulers and to ask them to

---

[1] Annexes A and B not printed.

[2] See *Report of the Federation of Malaya Constitutional Conference held in London in January and February, 1956* (Cmd 9714).

[3] See 400.

express their views upon it. The Conference of Rulers is to meet for this purpose on Tuesday, 28th February. Since the Report was unanimously agreed by the entire Delegation, including the representatives of the Rulers, I expect Their Highnesses to endorse it. I have told the High Commissioner that I hope before 28th February to inform him by telegram of the views of Her Majesty's Government upon the Report; and I have said that, should Her Majesty's Government approve its recommendations, I would propose, if those recommendations are also approved by the Conference of Rulers, to submit them to The Queen for Her Majesty's approval.

4. I therefore ask my colleagues to approve the Report of the Conference, including the proposals for the Constitutional Commission contained in the Report of the General Purposes Committee of the Conference. As I have said above, those conclusions and recommendations to which I think it necessary expressly to draw my colleagues' attention are set out in Annex C.

Annex C to 405

I. *General*
As a result of the Conference, constitutional development in the Federation of Malaya over the next few years will pass through two phases. The first phase, which the Report of the Conference refers to as "the interim period", is that before the Federation attains full self-government within the Commonwealth. The second phase is that following the attainment of full self-government within the Commonwealth. It will be convenient to deal with the conclusions and recommendations of the Conference under these two heads.

II. *The interim period*

(1) *The high commissioner's powers* (Annex A, Appendix C, paragraph 32)

(a) *The reserved legislative power.* This remains unchanged.

(b) *The reserved executive power.* The High Commissioner will in future act on the advice of the Executive Council unless he considers it expedient in the interest of public order, public faith or good government to reject their advice. Before acting contrary to their advice he must obtain the prior approval of the Secretary of State, and give the Chief Minister an opportunity to make representations to the Secretary of State, *unless* he considers that the interests of public order, public faith or good government are too urgent, in which case he may act against the advice of the Executive Council without any prior approval. These arrangements do not apply to matters relating to external defence and external affairs, in which the High Commissioner will retain complete discretion.

(2) *Defence and internal security* (Annex A, paragraphs 7–24)

(a) *Defence.* Responsibility for external defence will remain entirely with the High Commissioner, but in order to prepare for the assumption by the Federation Government of responsibility for external defence, there will during the interim period be an External Defence Committee, including Malayan Ministers, with the High Commissioner as Chairman, to discuss matters relating to the external defence of the Federation. It will have no executive powers and will be purely advisory to the High Commissioner.

(b) *Internal security.* A Malayan Minister for Internal Defence and Security will assume responsibility for the administration of the police force and the Federation armed forces. So long as the Emergency continues, operational command of the police force and the Federation armed forces will remain with the Director of Operations. The present Director of Operations Committee will, however, be replaced by an Emergency Operations Council, with the Minister for Internal Defence and Security as Chairman and the Director of Operations among its members. A Police Service Commission will be set up to deal with appointments, promotions and discipline in the higher ranks of the police force. It will be completely free from political influence. For the administration of the Federation armed forces there will be set up, under the Chairmanship of the Minister for Internal Defence and Security, a Federation Armed Forces Council modelled upon the Army and Air Councils in the United Kingdom.

(3) *Financial and economic matters* (Annex A, paragraphs 28–37)

(a) *Minister of finance.* The Financial Secretary, at present a member of Her Majesty's Oversea Civil Service, will be replaced by a Malayan Minister of Finance.
(b) *Exchange control.* The Federation Government will continue to regulate its dollar expenditure in general conformity with the policy followed by the Sterling Area and in consultation with Her Majesty's Government.
(c) *Financial assistance.* This will continue on the same lines as at present.

(4) *The public service* (Annex A, paragraphs 38–61)

(a) *Public Service Commission.* A Public Service Commission with executive authority will be set up from 1st July, 1957, to deal with appointments, promotions and discipline in the Public Service. It will be independent and free from political influence. Before that date the present Public Service Appointments and Promotions Board will remain advisory to the High Commissioner.
(b) *Compensation scheme.* A scheme will be introduced in two phases. Until 1st July, 1957, members of Her Majesty's Oversea Civil Service will be permitted to retire on earned pension even if they have not served for the ten years normally required for pension purposes. After that date they will be free to retire when they will and entitled to lump-sum compensation in addition to their earned pension. It will also then be open to the Federation Government to dispense with an oversea officer's services on payment of the due compensation and pension. The scheme contains various other elements, but those are its main lines.

(5) *Constitutional changes* (Annex A, paragraphs 62–73)

(a) *The high commissioner's powers.* See (1) above.
(b) *The Executive Council.* The Financial Secretary will be replaced by a Malayan Minister of Finance (see (3)(a) above). The Secretary for Defence will disappear and matters of external defence will be handled by the High Commissioner himself, matters of internal security being handled by the new Minister for Internal Defence and Security. The Minister for Economic Affairs (at present a member of Her Majesty's Oversea Civil Service) will be replaced by a Minister for Commerce and Industry, who may be either an unofficial or an official. The Chief Secretary

and Attorney-General will continue to remain members of Her Majesty's Oversea Civil Service and to have seats in the Council.

(c) *The Legislative Council.* There will be no significant change except in consequence of the changes noted in (b) above.

(d) *The British advisers.* The British Advisers to the Rulers will be withdrawn within about a year's time. Their functions have already been overtaken by constitutional change and they no longer have an essential part to play in the administration of the Federation. There was therefore no good ground for opposition to the collective view of Their Highnesses the Rulers and Alliance Ministers that the British Advisers should be withdrawn.

III. *Constitutional commission* (Annex B, paragraphs 18–22)

(1) *Composition*
The proposed composition of the Commission is set out in Annex B. The Lord Chancellor very kindly agreed that Lord Reid should be invited to be Chairman and he has accepted. The United Kingdom member seems likely to be Sir Ivor Jennings, Master of Trinity Hall, Cambridge. The Governments of the other Commonwealth countries concerned are being approached through our High Commissioners with requests to suggest suitable members.

(2) *Terms of reference*
The terms of reference are set out in Annex B.

There was some difficulty with the Malayan Delegation about the position of Her Majesty the Queen in relation to the British Settlements of Penang and Malacca, but the Conference ultimately recorded a clear understanding that nothing in the terms of reference should be taken to prejudge the recommendations of the Commission on this matter. It was also clearly understood by the Conference that (iv) of the terms of reference will not preclude the Commission from recommending that British subjects and subjects of the Rulers should retain their status as such even if they acquire the proposed common nationality for the whole of the Federation.

(3) *Timing*
It was agreed that the Commission should be set up as soon as possible and that every effort should be made to avoid delay in the introduction of full self-government. The Alliance had committed themselves so deeply over the date of August, 1957, in this connection that it simply had to be accepted as the aim. The Malayan Delegation explicitly recognised, however, that this aim was almost certainly unattainable, and that it was very unlikely that full self-government could be introduced before the spring of 1958 at the earliest. Tunku Abdul Rahman firmly stated that he and his colleagues would—and could successfully—defend any delay beyond August, 1957. The composition of the Commission should help in avoiding any criticism on grounds of delay.

IV. *Full self-government*

(1) *Defence and internal security*

(a) *Defence.* A Working Party under the Chairmanship of the Commissioner-

General for the United Kingdom in South East Asia will be set up as soon as possible to prepare a treaty of defence and mutual assistance between Her Majesty's Government and the Federation Government. It was agreed that the Australian and New Zealand Governments should be invited to nominate observers at its meetings. Its terms of reference are:—

"To consider and make recommendations on the detailed provisions of a Treaty of Defence and Mutual Assistance between Her Majesty's Government in the United Kingdom and the Government of an independent Federation of Malaya, bearing in mind the following general principle:—

The Federation Government
(a) will afford to Her Majesty's Government in the United Kingdom the right to maintain in the Federation the forces necessary for the fulfilment of Commonwealth and international obligations:
(b) will continue to afford to Her Majesty's Government facilities needed in the Federation for the maintenance and support of these forces, which would include the Commonwealth Strategic Reserve:

Her Majesty's Government in the United Kingdom

(c) will undertake to assist the Federation Government in the external defence of its territory:
(d) will consult the Federation Government in regard to the exercise of their rights under the Treaty".

The intention is that the Treaty should be signed when full self-government is introduced. The agreement reached in the Conference meets in full the requirements which we had set ourselves beforehand.

(b) *Internal security.* It was agreed that, even after the attainment of full self-government, it would be essential that the present effective security intelligence machine should retain its efficiency, and also that, in view of its importance in the field of external defence as well as of internal security, its working would remain a matter of joint concern to Her Majesty's Government and to the Federation Government. (The Conference decided not to include in its published Report its agreed conclusions and recommendations on security intelligence. They are contained in the Report of the Defence and Internal Security Committee of the Conference).

(2) *Financial and economic matters*

(a) *Financial assistance.* It was recognised that the attainment of full self-government implied the principle of financial self-sufficiency, but it was agreed that certain particular measures of financial assistance by Her Majesty's Government would continue to be available to the Federation Government even after full self-government had been attained, and that, if the Emergency had not by then been brought to an end, Her Majesty's Government would still be prepared to consider with the Federation Government whether the financial needs of the Federation would justify special assistance from Her Majesty's Government towards meeting the cost of the Emergency over and above the substantial assistance which will continue to be given through the forces and services provided by the United Kingdom to sustain the fight against the communist terrorists.

(b) *Overseas investment.* The Conference recorded the repeated assurance by the Malayan Delegation that it would remain the policy of the Federation Government to encourage overseas investment, industry and enterprise to look to Malaya with every assurance of fair and considerate treatment and without fear of discrimination. This included continuation of the present policy whereby the overseas investor could, after payment of local taxes and obligations, remit to his country, within the framework of ordinary and reasonable exchange control requirements, funds for the payment of dividends and for the repatriation of his capital.

(3) *The public service*

The arrangements for a Public Service Commission and a lumpsum compensation scheme set out in II(4) above will remain in operation.

(4) *The constitution*

The constitutional pattern proposed for a fully self-governing Federation of Malaya will emerge from the work of the Constitutional Commission described in III above.

406 CAB 128/30/1, CM 16(56)11 22 Feb 1956
'Malaya': Cabinet conclusions on CP(56)47[1]

The Cabinet had before them a memorandum by the Colonial Secretary (C.P.(56)47) covering the report of the Conference on Constitutional Advance in Malaya.

The Colonial Secretary said that in Annex C of his memorandum he had listed the main points to which he wished to draw the attention of the Cabinet. All the issues before the Conference had been settled amicably and the agreed recommendations were within the scope of the authority which he had been given by the Cabinet on 17th January.[2] The Conference of Rulers in Malaya were meeting on 28th February to consider the report, and he would like to be able to inform the High Commissioner in Malaya before that date of the Government's views on the report.

In discussion the following points were made:—

(a) All the recommendations relating to defence and internal security had been considered and approved by the Chiefs of Staff and the Minister of Defence.

(b) *The Chancellor of the Exchequer* said that the financial arrangements appeared to be satisfactory. Although he had not yet had an opportunity to study them in detail, he was prepared to accept the financial and economic recommendations listed in Annex C of C.P.(56)47 on the understanding that they reflected fully the position agreed by the Conference.

(c) The outcome of the Conference would be generally welcomed by other members of the Commonwealth. In the Federation of Malaya a fund of goodwill had been built up and it would be unwise to attempt to postpone the meeting of the Rulers.

---

[1] See 405.

[2] See 400.

The Cabinet:—
(1) Approved the report of the Conference on Constitutional Advance in Malaya, including the proposals for the Constitutional Commission as approved by the Conference.
(2) Authorised the Colonial Secretary to inform the High Commissioner in Malaya of the Government's attitude to the report.

407 DEFE 7/494   21 Mar 1956
[Defence treaty working party]: inward telegram no 2 from Sir R Scott to Sir H Parker[1] on arrangements for talks in Kuala Lumpur

[The London conference having set an agenda to be completed by 31 August 1957 'if possible', work got underway on the financial provisions, constitutional commission, Malayanisation of the administration, and an Anglo-Malayan defence agreement.]

For Parker from Scott.
Your Tel. No. 3465: Malayan Defence Treaty Working Party.
This arrived after Cary[2] had left for London. It may help if I set out my comments at some length.
2. My original plan had been to start in the third week of March (repeat March) and in February I made provisional arrangements accordingly with the Tungku. At that time my idea was that the leader of the U.K. Delegation might come out in mid-March, spend a week doing preparatory work, then have the first meeting of the Working Party about March 20th or 21st, and perhaps two more meetings before the end of March with the U.K. side tabling some papers not earlier than the third meeting. Then an adjournment for a fortnight or so to let the Malays study the papers and thereafter meetings of the main party about once a week. I thought that sub-committees would have to be set up after the main working party had agreed in principle on the main points of the Draft Treaty. I saw the whole process as continuous and lasting for about three months i.e. mid-March to mid-June.
3. Colonial Office Tel. No. 27 of February 3rd spoke of the negotiations starting "as soon as possible" and then Tel. No. 36 spoke of winding up by the end of the year. I was (and still am) hopeful that we can do it in about three months. Even so I realised that such a long period would be personally inconvenient to the leader of the U.K. Delegation and those he brought from London. Nevertheless I did not believe it would be wise to compress it further because I attached great importance to beginning in a leisurely way. There are two reasons for this:—

(a) To establish an atmosphere of confidence and trust with the Malayan Delegation, and
(b) As they are completely inexperienced in these matters and as the Tungku told me that he was relying entirely on the U.K. Delegation to educate the Malayan team on these problems I thought we should not hurry at the beginning, but

---

[1] Parker, permanent secretary at the Ministry of Defence, 1948–1956, was to lead the UK delegation on the Malayan defence treaty working party.
[2] See 398, note 3.

devote the first two meetings to general explanations and to educating the Malay team without giving them any impression that we were rushing them.[3]

4. If we do not create an atmosphere of trust and confidence and if the Malays think we are rushing matters there is a risk that they will wish to bring in outside consultants perhaps even from other countries, i.e. the U.K., India, Ceylon or even elsewhere. This is why I put so much stress on a leisurely pace to begin with and on the educational process.

5. The delay in starting and the coincidence of the fasting month do not affect my views on these factors.

6. The risks attendant of further postponement are hard to assess. It might give rise to misunderstanding and suspicion in the minds of the Malays or they might think that we were waiting for the outcome of the talks in Singapore in order to link Singapore problems with their own. In addition there is always the risk of some quite unconnected issue vitiating the present extremely happy atmosphere, and so affecting the success of the defence working party. Examples of such issues are possible difficulties over the constitutional commission, status of Penang and Malacca, finance, policy in regard to the Communist terrorists, or arising out of the London talks on Singapore (a crisis in Singapore in May and June would be certain to affect the Federation of Malaya though it is not at present possible to say precisely how).

7. It is however quite possible that these apprehensions of mine are exaggerated and in any case a highly relevant point is the length of time you personally can stay. If your first visit is for only a month or so then it becomes important that your stay should cover at least a fortnight and preferably three weeks after Ramadan. Therefore if by postponing the start until April 30th we can keep you here at least until the end of May this to my mind is a very important consideration in favour of postponement.

8. Incidentally, I trust that the staff who are coming with you will not have to go back with you but will be able to stay at least three months if need be. They will be needed in the sub-committees.

9   I have set out above the pros and cons as I see them. Whilst my preference is still for an early start I leave it to you to decide after consultation with Cary.

10. If you decide to postpone your arrival till later in April so that we can have the first meeting of the working party say on April 30th, then I would suggest a programme on these lines:—

---

[3] cf Scott's record of an interview with Tunku Abdul Rahman on 28 Feb 1956 (DEFE 7/494): 'The Tungku said he saw no particular difficulty about this exercise. It was true that some of his own supporters strongly disliked the idea of any British bases in Malaya partly because they might be considered to be inconsistent with complete independence and partly because they might attract enemy attention in war. Malaya had had enough of war and did not want to be a target for the new weapons. But he had taken a strong line with his own supporters and said that it was part of the bargain reached in London that H.M.G. should look after the external defence of Malaya. He had complete trust in H.M.G.'s sincerity in this matter and that H.M.G. would not make impossible demands on Malaya for bases and facilities. If the Agreement was to be reached in a friendly spirit and if its terms were to be respected in the future, then it must be an Agreement which must be seen by both sides to be advantageous to them. If H.M.G. imposed a hard agreement there was always the risk that in the future the Malayan Government or people might reject it. He hoped that when we asked for facilities we would be able to point to international precedents. He cited in particular the Ceylon Agreements.'

First meeting of the working party April 30, second meeting on May 5 or 7, third meeting May 15 or 16. At this third meeting (i.e. after Ramadan) I would hope that it would be possible to table the outlines of the draft treaty. Then we can work much more intensively and have at least another three meetings (perhaps four) of the working party before the end of May. With luck the substance of the treaty and much of its wording will have been agreed in principle by then, and it may also be possible to set up sub-committees in the third week of May, i.e. even before the last couple of meetings of the main working party. Sub-committees can continue through June and you might come back in the fourth week of June for a fortnight to resolve as many of the outstanding points on the annexes as possible and to complete the whole exercise by say the end of the first week of July. If the exercise is by then not completed it should be possible at least to narrow down and define the points of issue which may then have to be considered in London. Indeed the working party or some of us might if necessary adjourn to London in July for this purpose when we could also have expert legal advice on the final detailed drafting of the treaty.

408   DEFE 7/494, no 102   28 Mar 1956
'Negotiation of a defence agreement with Malaya': minute by Sir H Parker to Sir W Monckton. *Appendices*: A–C

I shall be leaving on April 3rd for Singapore as leader of the U.K. delegation to negotiate a defence agreement with the Malayans. The object is to draw up a complete agreement which might be initialled by both sides and left for signature and ratification in about August 1957 when the Constitutional Commission has reported, its recommendations have been accepted, and Malaya becomes an independent member of the Commonwealth.

2. The negotiations will probably start on April 16th. Before then, I shall need guidance from Ministers on the limits within which I can negotiate, and the general principles which the Agreement should embody.

3. Both the Australians and New Zealand Governments are sending observers to attend the negotiations. It may be that the Federation will want to have separate agreements with the two Commonwealth countries or that they will accept that Australia and New Zealand should subscribe to the U.K./Malaya Agreement by an exchange of letters. Whatever happens, our aim is to preserve the position of Australia and New Zealand in regard to their participation in the Commonwealth Strategic Reserve stationed in Malaya and to see that they enjoy equal facilities, rights and powers with the U.K.

4. The draft text of a covering treaty which has been prepared by officials is at Appendix A. This has been seen and agreed in principle by the Commissioner General for South-East Asia, the High Commissioner of the Federation of Malaya and the two representatives of the Governments of Australia and New Zealand in Malaya (Sir Alan Watt and Mr. Shanahan). The Australian and New Zealand Governments have raised no points of any substance on the draft but they are continuing their detailed examination and will no doubt make any further comments through their observers.

5. It must be realised of course that for the purposes of political presentation in

Malaya, it will almost certainly be necessary to accept forms of wording differing from those drafted here in London.

6. The Commissioner General and the High Commissioner of the Federation consider that we should give greater emphasis to and set out in some detail the assistance to the Federation armed forces which the U.K. undertakes to provide in Article 2. They suggest that details of such assistance might be included in an additional annex to the Agreement. This would in their view give a better balance to the Agreement for purposes of political presentation and would facilitate negotiations. The wording of such an annex would need careful consideration in order to keep our commitments within reasonable and clearly understood bounds. A possible draft of the annex is being examined by the Treasury and the Service Departments. If, during the course of the negotiations, it becomes clear that its inclusion in the Agreement will have a favourable influence, I would propose to adopt this proposal, subject to agreement with London on the wording.

7. You will wish to note that in Article 7 dealing with consultation, our right to freedom of action in an emergency is safeguarded, the Federation are not given any power of veto and the area of consultation is limited. The Malayans attached great importance to the question of consultation during the London Conference, and it may be necessary to undertake to consult them over a much wider field that that defined in the present draft.

8. Article 8 may be necessary if the Malayans think that it is politically important that they should set a term to the Treaty. From our point of view a timeless Agreement would be preferable and appropriate between members of the Commonwealth and experience has shown that the enjoyment of goodwil is not to be determined by the terms set down on paper. If the Malayans press strongly, I suggest that I should negotiate a period as long as possible and certainly not less than 10 years. This is the shortest time in which the Federation could possibly have modest self-contained forces capable of assuming some limited responsibility for external defence.

9. It is proposed that there shall be two annexes to the covering treaty – Annex 1 describing the bases and facilities and the rights and powers we are allowed to exercise in meeting our commitments for external defence of Malaya and the preservation of peace and security in South-East Asia; and Annex 2 dealing with the status of our forces. In addition, as described in paragraph 4 above, there may be a further Annex 3 dealing with the forms of assistance which we shall extend to the Federation. The principal requirements under Annexes 1 and 2 set out in Appendix B. The Annexes also contain, on the precedent of other Treaties and Agreements, a good deal of subsidiary detail. The points listed in Appendix B are, however, essential to the working of the Agreement and I shall endeavour to preserve the substance of them intact. I hope I may be allowed to use my discretion on the details. The possible headings which might be included in the additional Annex 3 are shown in Appendix C.

10. I have no doubt that points will arise during the course of the negotiations on which reference back to London will be necessary. I hope it will be possible to keep this to a minimum and I am afraid that it is impossible to forecast at this juncture what may prove to be the real stumbling blocks.

11. If you yourself agree with the course of action suggested above you may wish to obtain the views of the Chancellor, the Foreign Secretary, Secretary of State for

the Colonies, the Secretary of State for Commonwealth Relations and your Service colleagues on these proposals. The most convenient way would probably be to write them a letter on lines following from this minute. I attach a draft.[1]

Appendix A to 408: Draft defence agreement with Malaya

Whereas the Federation of Malaya has reached the stage of full self-government and independence within the Commonwealth.

And Whereas the Government of the Federation of Malaya and Her Majesty's Government in the United Kingdom recognise their common interest in the defence of the territories of both and in the preservation of peace and security in South East Asia;

Now Therefore Her Majesty's Government in the United Kingdom and the Government of the Federation of Malaya have agreed as follows:—

Article 1. H.M.G. in the United Kingdom will assist the Government of the Federation of Malaya in the external defence of their territory.

Article 2. H.M.G. in the United Kingdom will furnish the Government of the Federation of Malaya with such assistance as may from time to time be mutually agreed for the training and development of the Federation's armed forces.

Article 3. The Government of the Federation of Malaya will afford to H.M.G. in the United Kingdom the right to maintain in the Federation such naval, land and air forces, including a Commonwealth Strategic Reserve, as H.M.G. in the United Kingdom consider to be necessary for this purpose and for the fulfilment of their international obligations and the safeguarding of Commonwealth strategic interests in the areas.

Article 4. The Government of the Federation of Malaya agree that H.M.G. in the United Kingdom may for the purposes of this Agreement retain and use the bases and facilities described in Annex 1 to this Agreement and establish such additional bases and facilities as may from time to time be mutually agreed.

Article 5. The conditions under which such forces may be stationed in the territory of the Federation of Malaya shall be as defined in Annex 2 to this Agreement.

Article 6. In the event of an armed attack or the threat of an armed attack against the territories or forces of either country or in the event of any other threat to the preservation of peace or security in South-East Asia, the Governments will come to each other's assistance and will consult together on the measures to be taken jointly or severally to ensure the fullest co-operation between the Governments for the purpose of meeting the situation effectively.

Article 7. When major changes in the size, character or deployment of the forces maintained in the Federation of Malaya under Article 3 of this Agreement are in prospect, H.M.G. in the United Kingdom will consult the Government of the Federation of Malaya and afford them an effective opportunity for comment before putting such changes into force. Similarly, the Government of the Federation of Malaya will discuss with H.M.G. in the United Kingdom any major administrative or legislative proposals which may affect the operation of this Agreement.

---

[1] Not printed.

(*Article 8.* This Agreement will remain in force for . . . years[2] and thereafter be terminable at one year's notice.)

Appendix B to 408: Principal requirements to be covered in the annexes

Annex 1—Bases and facilities
Security of tenure of the land either by retention of title or by means of a long-term lease.

Rights of disposal of land or property in the Federation or elsewhere.

The use of additional areas for periodical training and exercises.

Freedom of movement between the bases and in and over the territory and territorial waters of the Federation. (This to include unrestricted over-flying rights for military aircraft.)

Right to construct, develop and maintain facilities needed for the operation of the bases.

Right to make local purchases and employ local labour.

Right to install and maintain communication systems, navigational aids and postal services.

Annex 2—Status of forces
Rights of exclusive and concurrent jurisdiction, powers of arrest and custody on the lines of the current agreement with N.A.T.O.

The right to maintain Service police and to use civilian police within the bases.

Exemption for U.K.-based civilians from compulsory service.

The right to import and export freely without duty materials, equipment and supplies for the Forces and their accompanying civilian dependants and Service organisations.

(In the main these requirements follow closely the pattern of the N.A.T.O. Status of Forces Agreement.)

Appendix C to 408

Annex 3—Assistance to the Federation armed forces
General headings of the forms of assistance which the U.K. might wish to provide under Article 2.

(i)   Provision of personnel to assist in the administration and training of the armed forces of the Federation.

(ii)   Granting facilities, including instructional courses abroad for training members of the Federation forces.

(iii)   Providing expert advice and assistance in operational and technical matters.

(iv)   Agreement that the facilities within the bases may be employed for the maintenance and logistic support of the Federation forces.

(v)   Facilitate as far as possible the supply of arms and equipment.

(vi)   The maintenance of H.M.G.'s undertaking to finance certain capital costs of expansion of the Federation armed forces in an agreed programme.

(vii)   The fostering of the closest co-operation between the armed forces of the two countries, including joint training of unit formations.

---

[2] The duration of the agreement was left blank in this draft.

409   CO 1030/258, no 1   18 Apr 1956
[Political tension over nationality and citizenship]: inward telegram
no 249 from Sir D Watherston to Sir D MacGillivray

For MacGillivray.[1]

During the last two weeks there has been a rapid upsurging of feeling among the
Chinese over the question of nationality and citizenship. Opening phase of this
development was mentioned in paragraph 7 of my political report for March.

2.   The announced intention of the Chinese to put a memorandum to the
Constitutional Commission led to strongly worded resolutions being passed by some
branches of U.M.N.O. to the effect that *"jus soli"* was totally unacceptable to the
Malays. This stung the Chinese into asserting their position more vigourously [sic]
than before and they began to arrange public meetings throughout the country in
support of their claim. The Alliance then sought to play down mounting tension by:–

(a) the issue of instructions to U.M.N.O. branches in the name of the Chief
Minister tightening up discipline generally and in particular directing the
branches that they were not to pass resolutions on constitutional issues without
headquarters approval;
(b) an announcement that one memorandum would be put to the Constitutional
Commission on behalf of the whole Alliance.

3.   For the most part U.M.N.O. has responded well to the Chief Minister's
instructions and Malay opinion has been mollified by his statement that:—

(a) [? *jus soli*] is not included in the Alliance election manifesto;
(b) that it is a matter, in any event, for the Constitutional Commission, the
recommendations of which should not be anticipated. The Chief Minister is
emphasising in public the second of these two points.

4.   The M.C.A. finds itself in acutely difficult position. On the one hand it realises
that it owes its position in the Alliance to Malay votes and that the adoption of *"jus
soli"* now as a plank—the most important plank—in its political platform could only
lead to an open breach in the Alliance. On the other hand, it sees that the strength of
the demand for *"jus soli"* from the influential Chinese business class (which
constitutes the main support of the M.C.A.) is such that this class will abandon the
support of the M.C.A. unless it takes a stand on this question. If this support was lost
the M.C.A. might well disintegrate as it has never had any real roots among the rank
and file of the Chinese population.

5.   It is not surprising, therefore, that the M.C.A. attitude has so far failed to be
clear cut. On the 16th April after a meeting the previous day at Tan Siew Sin's house
in Malacca attended by most M.C.A. leaders (but significantly excluding H.S. Lee)[2]
the Press reported that the M.C.A. would prepare a separate memorandum for the
Constitutional Commission which would include a request for *"jus soli"*. As a
compromise it was stated that this memorandum would be passed to the Constitu-

---

[1] The high commissioner was in London at this time.
[2] The day after this meeting (ie 16 Apr) Lee was in Kuala Lumpur attending the meeting of the Malayan
defence treaty working party, see 410.

tional Commission through the Alliance National Council. Tan Siew Sin later denied that there was any rift in the Alliance and said that the M.C.A. still proposed to draft only the Chinese view for incorporation in the Alliance memorandum to the Constitutional Commission.

6. The newspapers, particularly English and Chinese, have had a considerable hand in whipping up public feeling in this issue so quickly but the opposition political parties are, of course, trying to turn the situation to their own advantage, thus Party Negara and Party Ra'ayat are openly opposing "*jus soli*" while the Labour Party of Malaya has announced that it will hold a public rally in its favour.

7. I discussed the position with the Chief Minister yesterday. He made it clear that it would be politically impossible for U.M.N.O. to adopt "*jus soli*" without qualification as its policy. He emphasised the great sacrifices which the Malays had already made by accepting the changes in the citizenship provisions which became law in 1952. Nevertheless, he said that he himself would be prepared to agree to the adoption of "*jus soli*" for all persons born in the Federation on or after independence day. By itself this of course would not of course satisfy the Chinese, but if something rather more than they already have could be done for those born before Independence Day there might be a basis for a compromise for the Constitutional Commission to consider.

8. Since the earlier paragraphs of this telegram were drafted this morning's papers have announced under banner headline plans for the formation of a Federation of Chinese organisations which would be a direct rival of the M.C.A. and would "fight for the legitimate rights of the Chinese". This bears out the forecast in paragraph 4 above. Those who have planned this move are:—

(a) Lau Pak Khuan, Chairman of the Perak Chinese Assembly Hall;
(b) Leong Chee Cheong, President of the Selangor Chinese Guilds.
(c) Lim Lean Geok, President of the United Chinese School Teachers' Association;
(d) Cho Yew Fai, Acting Chairman of the Selangor Chinese Assembly Hall.

It is reported that they propose to hold a mass meeting of non-Malays in Kuala Lumpur on 27th April with the object of electing a delegation to fly to London and press H.M.G. for the adoption of "*jus soli*". The Secretary for Chinese Affairs will endeavour to bring home to one or more of the sponsors of the meeting that no possible good can come of such a move as nationality and citizenship are matters on which the Constitutional Commission will be making recommendations and H.M.G. would not be prepared to come to any conclusions until the whole question has been fully examined by the Commission.

9. The Chief Minister is disturbed at the position which is developing and fears that despite his instructions to U.M.N.O. there is a risk of the Malays staging demonstrations if the non-Malays and particular[ly] the Chinese continue with their present designs and publicity continues to be given them. (This is especially the case during the fast month when tempers are notoriously brittle).

10. Person named at (a) paragraph 8 above is known to have been opposed to early independence and it is possible that this new group would rather see independence delayed that [sic] that it should come without "*jus soli*". Position of H.S. Lee in all this is obscure and I am seeing him later today.

410   DEFE 7/495, MDTWP(56)1   23 Apr 1956

'Malayan defence treaty working party': minutes by E N Larmour of the
first meeting held in Kuala Lumpur on 16 Apr

[Present: Sir R Scott (Chairman); Tunku Abdul Rahman, Haji Mustapha Albakri bin Haji
Hassan, Colonel H S Lee, Abdul Aziz bin Haji Abdul Majid, Dato Abdul Razak bin Dato
Hussein (Federation delegation); Sir H Parker, Major General T B L Churchill, Air
Vice-Marshall F J St G Braithwaite, C H W Murphy (UK delegation); F Shanahan (NZ
observer); Air Vice-Marshall A M Murdoch (Australian observer). Also present: L T G Sully
and E O Laird. Secretariat: Abdul Kadir, Group Captain C B E Burt-Andrews and E N
Larmour)]

After brief introductory remarks by the leaders of both delegations, the *New Zealand
Observer* said that his Government had strongly welcomed the agreement reached in
London about the transfer of power. The security of Malaya was indissolubly linked
with that of New Zealand, and the New Zealand Government were glad to have their
army and air force units helping the Federation Government in their operations
against the terrorists. The *Australian Observer* said that his Government too, with
their equally strong interest in Malaya, were grateful to both Governments for their
invitation to send an observer to attend meetings of the Working Party. The
Chairman then made a statement on matters of procedure and read out the Terms of
Reference of the Working Party as agreed at the London Constitutional Conference
in February.[1]

   2. *Tunku Abdul Rahman* said that it was the intention of the Malayan Delegation,
following closely the Terms of Reference, to work as a team with the U.K. Delegation
in order to produce a draft agreement which would be acceptable to both
Governments. He would be grateful however for a definition of the phrase
"international obligations" appearing in sub-paragraph (a) of the Terms of Reference.
Colonel Lee amplified this question by enquiring whether this phrase was limited to
existing obligations or whether *future* obligations would also be included. *Dato
Abdul Rasak* [sic] asked, with reference to the words "forces necessary" appearing in
the same sub-paragraph, who, (i.e. whether the U.K. or Federation Government or
both in consultation) would decide on what was "necessary" in this context.

   3. *Sir Harold Parker* said that these were important issues on which it might be
most helpful if he circulated a short note.

   4. *Sir Harold Parker* then went on to describe agreements broadly similar to that
about to be negotiated, which had been drawn up between the U.K. and certain other
countries such as Libya, Iraq and Ceylon. He also referred to the NATO Status of
Forces agreement. These were typical examples of the sort of thing he had in mind.
Their main value, for the purpose of the Working Party, was that they indicated the
kind of document that might eventually emerge. The concept behind the London
agreement on defence during the interim period had been that of a partnership, with
the Federation assuming responsibility for internal defence and the U.K. retaining
that for external defence. These functions did of course overlap, because of the
complicated nature of modern strategy and the structure of modern armies and air
forces. He undertook to circulate a note setting out in detail all the needs of a
modern army and air force in the way of bases, installations, living accommodation,

---

[1] See 405, Annex C, para IV (1)(a).

training areas, storage and maintenance depots, supplies and other administrative services.

5. Another problem that inevitably arose in negotiating a defence agreement was the question of jurisdiction over visiting forces. This always created difficulties, which with goodwill between the parties could be overcome. These difficulties, so far as they could be foreseen, should if possible be settled in advance. The NATO agreement was a good model.

6. Another problem was that of the employment of civil labour. This had advantages for the country in which the forces were stationed in that it reduced the number of people in uniform and gave employment locally; but it was a point which needed to be covered in any agreement.

7. One of the most difficult questions (which had been mentioned by *Enche' Abdul Aziz*) was the terms on which visiting forces could enjoy the use of land. Visiting forces must have the necessary facilities in which to work and train and if they were to be contented must have reasonable living conditions. There was always Treasury reluctance to spend large sums of money on buildings etc. unless there was some security of tenure. In Malaya, the U.K. Government had acquired land by several methods. Some was freehold, some was leasehold (especially in the States) and the leases varied in length. He thought some consolidation and clarification was required. The U.K. Delegation were fully alive to the importance of solving this problem in a way which would not infringe, or even appear to infringe, Malayan sovereignty. It was a question of balancing military needs with political possibilities.

8. The U.K. Delegation had no preconceived idea about the shape of any agreement that might emerge, but in general they deprecated a too loose and general form of words since this would almost inevitably lead to later argument, and thus impair relations between the contracting parties

9. *Tunku Abdul Rahman* then enquired how the U.K. proposed to follow up the points mentioned by Sir Harold Parker. *Tuan Haji Mustapha Albakri* thought it essential that Malaya should have from the U.K. a list of her minimum requirements to enable her to fulfil her obligations, both immediate and long-term. *Sir Harold Parker* promised to bear this point in mind. *Dato Abdul Razak* then enquired about the defence relationship that existed between the U.K. and other Commonwealth countries such as Australia and New Zealand. The *Chairman* explained that there was no formal obligation in the defence field with those countries; it was for instance entirely up to their Governments to decide whether or not they would join with the U.K. if she should become involved in a war. *Sir Harold Parker* pointed out that there was however in NATO an instance of a formal defence treaty link between the U.K. and another Commonwealth country, Canada, but this was largely co-incidental. In reply to a further question from *Dato Abdul Razak*, the *Chairman* explained that, even under the SEATO agreement, there was no formal obligation on the parties to do more than to take common action, *subject to their respective constitutional processes*, to resist aggression. He went on to explain that very few treaties compelled action to be taken by the contracting governments, and that almost invariably any obligations assumed were made subject to constitutional process.

10. *Sir Harold Parker* said that the U.K. could produce a list of the kind of subjects that needed to be covered in discussion. He thought that a form of treaty that might eventually emerge might be a short general agreement, to which could be appended annexures dealing with specific problems.

11. There was a brief further discussion on the extent and nature of the obligations that the U.K. had already assumed in respect of Malaya. The *Chairman* pointed out, that though the nature of an obligation might be easy enough to define, it was extremely difficult to forecast the nature of the threat, the relative strengths of the enemy and our own forces and therefore the extent of the effort that would be necessary to resist them.

12. *Colonel Lee* pointed out that it should be possible to estimate what forces would be required in the three phases which be foresaw:—

   (1) the duration of the Emergency;
   (2) the post-Emergency peace; and
   (3) war.

13. *Tunku Abdul Rahman* then raised the question of the duration of any agreement reached. The financial arrangements between Malaya and the U.K. were subject to yearly review and he wondered whether this might not also be applied to any defence agrement. There had been a good deal of criticism inside the Federation and outside, e.g. from India, to the effect that, though Malaya might nominally achieve independence, she would be still under military occupation. From the Malayan point of view it was important that he should have an honourable treaty which he could present to the Malayan people as such and which successor governments would also honour. *Sir Harold Parker* agreed that it was important that the result of the Working Party's deliberations should appear as a joint solution to a common problem. He felt however, that the arrangements at present applicable in the field of finance would not be suitable as regards defence.

14. The *Chairman* then suggested there were three aspects of the problem that should be dealt with:—

   (1) an objective study of the external defence requirements of Malaya;
   (2) the extent to which the U.K. could help to meet those requirements; and
   (3) the facilities needed by the U.K. for this and other U.K. defence purposes.

15. *Colonel Lee* then raised the question of the terms under which land was held by the Services in Malaya. *Mr. Murphy* explained that three-quarters of the total area was land that had been bought outright. Some, especially in the States, was held on leases of varying lengths. *Enche' Abdul Aziz* enquired whether any increase in Service requirements of land would follow from the obligations already assumed by the U.K. *Sir Harold Parker* explained that once the Emergency was over those troops now on active service conditions in the jungle, who might remain in Malaya, would require extra land for barracks and other installations.

16. *Tuan Haji Mustapha Albakri* then raised the question of the employment of non-Federation citizens in Service undertakings. *Mr. Murphy* and *Sir Harold Parker* thought that there was a misunderstanding about this. The point had been covered in the U.K. treaty with Libya and was one for consideration in this instance also.

17. After some further discussion on the question of land and of jurisdiction over visiting forces, *Tunku Abdul Rahman* suggested that it would be useful if the U.K. could produce a draft outline of a treaty together with an indication of the questions, such as land tenure, jurisdiction, facilities required, the employment of civil labour etc., which would need to be dealt with in annexes. *Sir Harold Parker* agreed that the U.K. Delegation would produce a draft on the lines proposed.

18.   The Working Party then approved the text of a draft communique for issue to the press and agreed to meet again on Friday, April 27, at 10 a.m.

411   CO 1030/258, no 4   23 Apr 1956
[Political tension over nationality and citizenship]: inward telegram no 254 from Sir D Watherston to Mr Lennox-Boyd

My telegram No. 249.[1]

Political Situation.

Tension has eased during the last three days and proposal to form a new Chinese organisation as rival to the M.C.A. appears likely to be dropped. Lim Lean Geok (see paragraph 8 of my telegram under reference) withdrew his support for his proposal within 24 hours; he is a left wing Chinese schoolteacher who was from the outset a strange bedfellow for the other three, who are businessmen with a K.M.T. background. Cho Yew Fai (paragraph 8 (d) of my previous telegram) has now issued a statement saying that his organisation would not support the formation of a rival body to the M.C.A., although it still favours a mass rally of Chinese associations on 27th April to discuss citizenship. Lau Pak Khuan, who is the leader of the anti-M.C.A. movement, is reported in the "Straits Times" to have said that for the time being at any rate he will not make an issue of M.C.A. leadership; but the "Singapore Standard" which has been taking a strong anti-M.C.A. line throughout has published a contrary report. I expect to learn more about his attitude from the Secretary for Chinese Affairs when he returns from Perak today.

2.   I have had a frank discussion with H. S. Lee on the situation. He confirms that Lau Pak Khuan and his associates, having been evicted from the M.C.A. last year, now see the "jus soli" issue as their opportunity to get their own back and to seize the leadership of the Chinese community from the present leaders of the M.C.A. who are ineffective and in whom they have no confidence. H. S. Lee himself was, of course, thrown out of office by the M.C.A. and the Chief Minister is certain that he has been giving support in the background to the latest move in the hope of regaining a position of influence for himself among the Chinese. It now seems possible that the price demanded by Lau Pak Khuan and the others for the withdrawal of opposition to the M.C.A. may be the strengthening of H. S. Lee's position in that Association.

3.   Meanwhile, at an M.C.A. meeting in Malacca on 19th April, attended by Chinese Guilds, clubs, associations and schools, Tan Siew Sin is said to have claimed that the Alliance had tacitly accepted the principle of "jus soli" and he assured his listeners that the M.C.A. would not swerve from their support for "jus soli". He argued however that in the interests of the Chinese themselves the matter must be taken carefully and in consultation with the other partners in the Alliance and he paid tribute to the restraint shown by U.M.N.O. leaders. Some of those attending the meeting do not however seem to have been convinced of the benefits to be derived from the (corrupt group ?M.C.A.'s) association with the Alliance, and one speaker suggested delaying independence until the citizenship question is settled, while another questioned whether if existing arrangements continued the Chinese could hope to retain their present rights.

---

[1] See 409.

4. In accordance with the Chief Minister's instructions to U.M.N.O. there has been little public reaction on the part of Malays during the past week to latest developments. It become clear towards the end of the week, however, that the Chief Minister was coming under strong pressure from U.M.N.O. to make a statement himself in order that the Malay case should not go by default. He first told me on 20th April that he considered it necessary that he should make a broadcast which would have the dual purpose of stating the Malay case to the non-Malays and of taking the heat out of the controversy. I pointed out that the broadcast would be listened to by Malays as well as non-Malays and I expressed disquiet that the effect on the former might be precisely the opposite to that which he intended. He accordingly very substantially altered his original draft, although even in its final form as broadcast last night there remained some passages which could lead to an aggravation rather than to a diminution of racial tension. Copy of broadcast follows by bag. Will telegraph press and public reactions as soon as they are available.

5. I was able to persuade Chief Minister to omit from his broadcast a strong attack on the press for the part which it had played during the past two weeks. Ya'acob, Director of Information Services, visited Singapore on the 20th April and had talks with editorial staff of "Straits Times" and "Standard" and "Nanyang Siang Pao." In consequence English newspapers have in the last few days given the matter less prominence and "Straits Times" leader of 21st April was a timely call for moderation. The Chief Minister had been talking of prohibiting entry of "Singapore Standard" into the Federation.

6. Although they have made clear their support for "jus soli", Indian leaders have sought throughout to stand aside from the argument between the Malays and the Chinese and have emphasised the necessity for restraint.

7. It is still early to sum up the results of the week's events, but the following points seem clear:—

(a) There is a very real and mounting disquiet among the Chinese on the "jus soli" issue; Chinese business leaders are dissatisfied with M.C.A. leadership and are anxious to see it take a stronger line; neither they nor other Chinese leaders wish however to split the Chinese community at this time and appear prepared to give the M.C.A. another chance, hoping that the stand they have made will strengthen the wavering hearts of the M.C.A. leaders and that it will also strengthen their hand against the Malays. M.C.A. leaders cannot, for their part, fail to have been impressed by the control U.M.N.O. has exercised over the Malays in contrast to their own uncertain hold over the Chinese.

(b) Malay leaders have however been made to realise the strength of their community's opposition to "jus soli" and the danger to their own position if they appear to favour it.

8. The week's troubles have therefore helped to bring home the realities of the situation to both sides and have shown up very clearly how difficult is the problem of citizenship. At the lower levels, Chinese and Malays probably regard each other now with greater suspicion than hitherto. Even if tension has eased for the moment, the potentialities for future tension have been increased.

412 CO 1030/258, no 7   1 May 1956
[Political tension over nationality and citizenship]: inward telegram
no 273 from Sir D Watherston to Mr Lennox-Boyd

My telegram No. 254[1]

Political Situation.

The tension has continued to ease and the acute stage of trouble appears likely to be over for the present at least, although there are still rumblings of protests from both sides.

2. The mass meeting in Kuala Lumpur of 1,000 delegates of 600 Chinese Associations on 27th April passed off quietly and the leaders for the most part succeeded in keeping the tone of the meeting moderate. No serious attempt was made to form a Federation of Chinese Organisations in opposition to the M.C.A. and the meeting contented itself with electing a Working Party to draw up a memorandum for the Constitutional Commission, the leading members of whom are the four mentioned in paragraph 8 of my telegram No. 249. The memorandum will press for the liberalisation of the Citizenship Laws and will not only include the claim for "*jus soli*" but also ask that aliens who have lived in Malaya for five years should be eligible to apply for citizenship. The case for multi-lingualism will also be included. At the meeting on the 27th April Lau Pak Khuan was clearly angered by the Chief Minister's reference to him in a message to "Malaya Merdeka", the official organ of the U.M.N.O., which he interpreted as accusing him of being a traitor to the cause of Malaya's independence, and the meeting as a whole seems to have seen this as an attack on those Chinese who were pressing for "*jus soli*".

3. The S.C.A. met Lau Pak Khuan as foreshadowed in paragraph 1 of my telegram No. 254, and found his attitude to be much the same as that described in paragraph 7 (a) of that telegram.

4. In general, the reaction[s] to the Chief Minister's broadcast have been better than I expected. All papers have recognised it as a timely call for moderation, but the Chinese press has seen in it signs that Malay feeling against the Chinese claim for citizenship concessions is strengthening, and the general manner of approach of the Chinese papers now is to analyse both the Malaya [Malay] and Chinese arguments in a spirit of apparent reasonableness, and thus to show how strong is the Chinese case. The most critical analysis of the Chief Minister's broadcast is contained in a lengthy editorial in the China Press which is usually regarded as H.S. Lee's mouthpiece. Lee himself has still not shown his hand, and no further evidence has been forthcoming of the possible development mentioned in the last sentence of paragraph 2 of my telegram No. 254.

5. The collapse of the proposal to form a rival body to the M.C.A. has enabled that organisation to recover in a large measure its position in the Alliance, although there is now greater Malay suspicion of its motives than hitherto, and the Malay press, including "Malaya Merdeka", has had some harsh things to say about the M.C.A. in the last week. The M.C.A. has, however, again told U.M.N.O. that it will co-operate in the preparation of a joint Alliance memorandum for the Constitutional Commission, and work on the preparation of this memorandum has begun. For the most part it

---

[1] See 411.

seems likely to be a statement of the agreed views of the Alliance leaders with addenda containing:—

(i) Malay argument for special provisions for their race being written into the Constitution; and

(ii) the Chinese case for *"jus soli"*.

U.M.N.O. leaders apparently realise that the Chinese may expect the M.C.A. to go further than this and privately I am told are prepared as a face saving measure, and to avert a split in the Alliance, to allow the M.C.A. to present a separate memorandum to the Constitutional Commission.

6. Apart from this uneasy restoration of the position of M.C.A., I have for the present nothing to add to the conclusions reached in paragraph 7 of my telegram No. 254. A more detailed assessment of the effect of the month's events will be attempted in the Political Report.

413 DEFE 7/501, no 4   7 May 1956

[The role of British troops in Malaya]: letter from Sir D MacGillivray to Sir J Martin on their role in the periods before and after independence

In his letter Def. 75/92/012 of the 16th April, Johnston replied to a letter from Humphrey about the limitation on the use of Australian and New Zealand troops stationed in Malaya.

Under the arrangements at present in force, a Government officer who has authority to call out troops (e.g. a District Officer in his capacity as a Magistrate, a senior Police Officer, or a Resident Commissioner in a settlement) has to address his request to a designated local Commander who is normally the senior military officer in the State or Settlement. That Commander has instructions from Headquarters, Malaya Command, that troops are to be made available in the following order of priority:—

(i) Federation Army;

(ii) British troops;

(iii) Gurkhas.

It is hoped that it will never be necessary to go below the first of these for the purpose of dealing with civil disturbances apart from the Emergency. I would therefore agree that, although there could be an awkward situation as envisaged by Humphrey, it would be reasonable to let sleeping dogs lie in the hope that circumstances will not develop during the interim period before full self-government in which Australian or New Zealand troops might be required under the existing laws to intervene to restore law and order and to be prepared, should such circumstances arise, to absolve them from their legal liabilities in this respect by administrative action.

I cannot imagine, however, that the Federation Ministers would wish British troops or any other troops of the Commonwealth Strategic Reserve to be available after independence for any internal purpose other than the Emergency. Nor, as Johnston pointed out, would H.M.G. wish it. I have discussed this with Sir Harold

Parker and it is proposed, if you see no objection, that the attention of the Alliance Ministers on the Defence Agreement Working Party be drawn to the legal obligation at present resting on United Kingdom and Commonwealth troops to intervene in internal security matters in the Federation; that the Ministers be asked for their views on the implementation of the law in this respect after independence; and that they be informed that H.M.G. in the United Kingdom considers that United Kingdom and Commonwealth troops should be to absolved of their responsibilities in this respect after independence and that the local legislation should be amended accordingly. It is possible that the Ministers will raise the question of the arrangements during the interim period either in the Working Party itself or on another occasion, such as during a meeting of the Emergency Operations Council. But if they do I can see no harm in their being informed of the arrangements described earlier in this letter.

So far I have dealt with the question of the use of United Kingdom and Commonwealth troops in the event of a civil disturbance apart from the Emergency. There remains to be considered the much more important question of the use of such troops after independence in operations against the communist terrorists should it still be necessary at that time to continue military operations on a scale not within the competence of the Federation's own armed forces.

We cannot contemplate postponing the date of independence on account of the Emergency. I do not believe that this would be any longer possible from the political point of view; moreover it will give great propaganda advantage to the communists and possibly give rise to a revival of misguided nationalist support of the terrorist organisation. Nor can we contemplate leaving the Alliance Government in the lurch by confining British and Commonwealth troops to their primary role, as defined in the Commonwealth Strategic Reserve Directive, and leaving Emergency operations to the police and Federation forces. Nobody can say what the position will be regarding the Emergency when independence comes. It is possible that the recent political changes may in time lead to a change in the present Emergency situation in our favour and that we shall be able to run down the Emergency to the point when it will be of nuisance value only to the communists; in that event the Federation forces would be adequate to deal with it. But it is more probable that the Emergency, although run down to a lower level than it is today, will still be beyond the ability of Federation forces alone to contain it and some outside assistance will still be needed, though perhaps on a smaller scale than at present.

If you accept this probability, it is necessary to consider what arrangements should be made to provide for the continued participation after independence of both United Kingdom and Commonwealth troops in operations against the communist terrorists. Clearly it would be impracticable to consider placing United Kingdom and Commonwealth troops under the immediate direction of the Federation Government; apart from anything else they might be ordered to do things repugnant to our ideas of public faith and morality. It would thus appear that we should seek to agree with the Alliance Ministers that there should be some kind of Joint Council responsible for the conduct of Emergency operations on which representatives of H.M.G. would have an equal voice with representatives of the Federation Government. It might be that such a Council could also deal with questions of external defence, but for the present I am thinking primarily of the need to work out suitable arrangements for maintaining adequate pressure on the communist terrorists after independence. I should be grateful if this matter could be given some thought. It is a matter which should be raised and settled in the Defence Agreement Working Party and an appropriate clause embodied in the Defence Treaty or is it preferably left for discussion at the time when the recommendations of the Constitutional Commission are under examination by the two Governments and the Conference of Rulers? I incline to the view that it is best dealt with now as part of the future defence arrangements.

If the Emergency conditions on independence are as I envisage and, for the sake of argument, it is concluded that we cannot contemplate the withdrawal of all United Kingdom and Commonwealth troops from Emergency operations and must there-fore propose that independence be delayed on this account, we would inevitably be faced with the same sort of unpleasant situation as arose a few months ago and the Tunku would be forced by nationalist opinion to consider the reopening of negotiations with Chin Peng and a settlement of the Emergency by making dangerous concessions to the communists against which he has so far stood firm. For these reasons some kind of Joint Council seems to be the only answer and I have little doubt that the idea will commend itself to the Alliance Ministers.

I am sending copies of this letter to the Commissioner-General, the Officer Administering the Government, Singapore and Sir Harold Parker.

414 DEFE 7/496   24 May 1956
[Defence treaty working party]: letter from Sir H Parker to Sir R Powell

As I am sending you another letter I thought I might supplement what I have said in my telegrams. During the last few days things have become very sticky here (in more ways than one, because both the temperature and the humidity have been extremely high even for K.L.).

2. Up till a few days ago both Rob Scott and I were reasonably hopeful. We realised that there were difficulties but we thought with a little give and take on each side that the gap could be bridged. After my private talk with the Tunku last Monday I became very pessimistic. He was extremely charming and we had a very friendly discussion. It became clear, however, to me at an early stage that he did not wish to use the talk as an off-the-record opportunity of exploring possibilities of reaching agreement.

3. I cannot say whether right from the outset the Malayans have had no intention of settling unless they got everything they wanted. My impression is that in the course of the negotiations their attitudes stiffened somewhat.

4. If this is the case it is rather important to see if one can discover the reasons for their possibly [sic] change in attitude.

5. There are, I think, three possible explanations. They are becoming increasingly concerned about domestic political implications. There is a distinctly disturbing article in this morning's Singapore Standard. It is headed "Cabinet rift on Bases" and the following is the relevant extract:—

> "The Agriculture Minister, Inche Abdul Aziz bin Ishak, today became the first member of the Federation's Alliance Cabinet to oppose the establishment of foreign military bases in Malaya.

'We have to be on guard against those powers who will drag us into war to serve their own ends. To establish military bases is to attract war and not to avoid it,' he declared.

In an article in this quarter's issue of "The War Resister," The Agriculture Minister said: 'This is why I have opposed and will continue to oppose the establishment of bases in Malaya'."

6. Aziz is, I am told, the man with whom Gerald Templer had a row over the articles which he wrote after attending the Coronation in his capacity as a journalist.[1]

7. The second difficulty arises from the lack of experience of the Federation Ministers in regard to international discussions. The Tunku feels that Ministers talk to Ministers because, unlike the established Dominions, he has had no experience of a High Commissioner in the normally accepted sense. This is a point which rather worries me. Malaya is near Dominion status, but will not reach it probably for another fifteen months. There is noone in Kuala Lumpur who can discuss with the Tunku from the U.K. point of view problems of mutual concern. The present High Commissioner's functions are quite different to those of a normal Dominion High Commissioner and I can well understand the difficult position in which he might feel he would find himself if he were asked to advance U.K. views. This really raises the question whether one should not anticipate the post-independence position by getting some U.K. representative here fairly soon. There may well be continuing discussions on location of bases where one may want on the U.K. side someone who is concerned with the political, as distinct from the purely military, aspects of the problem.

8. The third difficulty arises from the Tunku's desire to visit London. He has firmly made up his mind on this and I think it would be unwise to try and dissuade him. If he is coming to London I think his visit should not be too long deferred. I would advise September because I feel that the longer the Defence Agreement remains in a half completed form the greater the risk that it may come unstuck. There have been one or two leaks already. In general they have been rather less than I had anticipated. I should, however, be surprised if there were no further leaks in the course of the next two or three months.

---

[1] See part II of this volume, 237, note 2.

415 CO 1030/51, no 96   8 June 1956

'Monthly political report for May, 1956': savingram no 776/56 from Sir D MacGillivray to Mr Lennox-Boyd on the education policy of the Alliance   [Extract]

. . . Education

2. After citizenship, Education policy is probably not only the most contentious subject in Malayan politics but also the one most likely to give rise to friction between the Malay and Chinese partners in the Alliance Government. The Chinese in particular, have always been very sensitive on this subject and any attempts in the

past to infuse into Chinese education a more Malayan outlook have met with stern opposition. It was for this reason that the Chinese opposed the earlier "National Schools" policy, and that one of the first acts of the Alliance Government was to appoint, under the chairmanship of the Minister for Education, Dato Abdul Razak, a Committee of members of Legislative Council to devise a new Education policy.

3. Moreover, since the Alliance Government came into power, pressure has been growing among the Malays for greater use of the Malay language. Contact with Indonesia has fostered this pressure and the way in which in that country, Malay (in its Indonesian form) has been increasingly used has attracted both an attention and admiration from the Malays, which has been strengthened by Chinese demands for multi-lingualism.

4. It is not surprising, therefore, that the publication of the Education Committee's Report was politically the most important event of the month. Being fully aware that public opinion on this subject was suspicious, Abdul Razak took a great deal of trouble in the presentation of his Committee's Report. It was released a little over a week before the Legislative Council meeting at which he was to move a resolution proposing its adoption in principle, and before its publication he met the leading Chinese educationalists to persuade them in advance of its merits.

5. The Report itself is not easy to summarise and, indeed, it has been noteworthy that the newspapers, in dealing with it, have tended to pick out particular recommendations for comment rather than attempt to evaluate it as a whole. It seeks to foster the use of the Malay language by making it a compulsory language in all schools, both primary and secondary, and using it when possible as the medium of instruction in some secondary schools; at present, except in the Chinese Middle Schools, all secondary education is given through the medium of English. It also proposes the radical re-organisation of the Department of Education and teaching profession by placing primary education under the control of local authorities at Municipal and Rural District level, and by establishing an Inspectorate to maintain standards of teaching. The general effect of these recommendations will be to raise the position of the vernacular school teacher (which includes the vociferous Chinese school teacher) and to ensure a greater Government contribution towards the cost of Chinese education. Indeed, the cost of adopting the recommendations contained in the Report is possibly the most vital consideration; it is also the one which has received least attention.

6. First comments on the Report were favourable, particularly from the Chinese, from whom opposition was most feared. The truth is that in the past, Chinese school teachers have often been in the van of the opposition to attempts to give Chinese education a more Malayan outlook, because their own training is largely based on a Chinese curriculum; on this occasion, the prospect of personal advantage for them as a class, which the Report opens up, made them inclined to welcome its proposals. Some Chinese did make it clear that they would not be rushed into accepting the Report in its entirety in the few days available before it was debated in Legislative Council, but generally it seemed as if the first hurdle had been safely cleared.

7. It was not therefore from the Chinese but from the Malays that opposition arose and the Legislative Council meeting, at which the resolution to adopt the Report in principle was approved, was noteworthy for the strong criticisms of the Report for failing to promote the use of the Malay language quickly enough, which were voiced in rapid vernacular Malay—itself incomprehensible to most Chinese and

Indian members—by some of the extreme nationalist elected Malay members, mostly from the East Coast. The causes of this Malay opposition are many and include personal jealousy, but the most significant are probably:—

(a) a Malay reaction against the "jus soli" crisis provoked by the Chinese the previous month (Abdul Rahman's instructions prevented them from reacting directly on "jus soli" itself),[1] and

(b) some of the more extreme advocates of Malay nationalism in UMNO saw the Report as a stick with which to attack their moderate leaders.

In addition, the fact that the Report had been so well received by the Chinese was in itself enough to arouse the suspicions of the Malays.

8. This Malay revolt appears to have worried the Ministers, and in Legislative Council, Suleiman, the Minister for Natural Resources, his brother Ismail, who has now taken over the portfolio of Commerce & Industry, and Sardon Jubir, the Minister for Works and UMNO Youth Leader (he is about 40 years of age himself!) were put up in quick succession to silence the critics. Of the three, Ismail made the most vigorous speech, in which he pointed out that Malay, with its limited vocabulary was a poor prospect for a country hoping to grow quickly to full political and economic independence, and then charged his Malay opponents with themselves taking the Imperialist line that they are usually so ready to condemn, in trying to suppress the languages of all the people in this country except their own. Since the Legislative Council debate, Razak has been touring the country explaining the benefits of the Education Report and seeking to combat Malay opposition; the signs are that he is achieving a considerable measure of success, but, as is to be expected, other Malay political leaders are now trying to turn the opposition to the Report to their own political advantage and in a forthright condemnation, Boestaman, the Party Ra'ayat leader, said that if it were adopted, the Alliance could not hope to fulfil its election pledge (repeated by Razak only three weeks before) of making Malay the national language within the next ten years.

9. Meanwhile, the Chinese were finding that the longer they looked at the Report, the less attractive it became; further, the Malay opposition has tended to arouse the Chinese to a defence of their own position. They realise, however, that the crucial stage will not be reached until the new Education Ordinance, which is intended to give effect to the Report's recommendations, is published; it seems possible that at that time the Chinese will seek to introduce amendments designed to protect their own position and the indications are that the last has not yet been heard of the opposition to the Alliance's new Education policy.[2] Although the reactions have been a great deal milder, fundamentally the friction between the two communities has been apparent this month over the Education Report in the same way as it was on "jus soli" last month. . . .

---

[1] See 409, 411–412.

[2] The Razak report, see 364, note 3, was the basis for the Education Ordinance of Mar 1957, replacing that of 1952. Despite its commitment to the creation of an integrated national scheme of education, it retained the separate language-medium school system. Nonetheless, defenders of Chinese-medium schools attacked the legislation, and, under pressure from the MCA, the Malayan government agreed to review the Razak plan after the 1959 election.

416 CO 1030/230, no 22   1 June 1956

[Malayanisation]: letter from Sir D Watherston to J B Johnston on the discussions of the Malayanisation Committee

[The London conference set out general principles and procedures for the Malayanisation of the public service and agreed: (i) to establish, with effect from 1 July 1957, a Public Service Commission with executive powers and a compensation scheme; (ii) to assure officers of their continued employment until the compensation scheme was in place; (iii) to provide expatriate officers with the opportunity to apply for jobs in the public service after 1 July 1957; and (iv) to guarantee officers their full term of promised employment and their right to retire under the compensation scheme.]

In your letter of the 24th May you say you would like to be kept informed of developments on the Malayanisation Committee and so I am sending you a further paper[1] which was prepared following on the discussion which took place on the earlier paper enclosed with my letter of the 7th May.

The Committee discussed this paper a few days ago and agreed generally with the conclusions[2] contained in it. We are now setting to work on yet another paper in which we shall endeavour to make a case for the acceptance of the following principles:—

(a) That Government will not exercise its powers to dispense with the services of any expatriate officer, except for normal disciplinary reasons, before the 1st July, 1960, i.e., three years after the compensation scheme comes into force, and that a clear statement to this effect should be incorporated in the final scheme presented to the Staff side. This would be all that would be necessary in regard to departments in the first of the three categories[3] in the enclosed paper in view of the fact that broadly speaking, it can be expected that they can be completely Malayanised by 1960. There is, however, one important reservation which requires special consideration, *viz.* senior officers in the Police; we have not sufficient experienced Malayans in the Force at the moment to be able to take over all the senior posts within four years from now and the Chief Minister himself recognises this fact even though politically he may find difficulty in resisting pressure for Malayanisation of the top posts at an early date.

(b) The offer of further employment for say, 5 years to expatriate officers in the second of the three categories in the enclosed paper. This could either be by remaining on the permanent establishment or by being re-employed on contract. In the latter case, the officer would have to take his chance of re-employment; contracts would be offered on a selective basis and not automatically.

(c) The offer of further employment for a period of say, 8 years to officers in the third category. The same alternatives would apply as in the case of (b) above. We

---

[1] Not printed.

[2] In conclusion, the committee was asked to consider further recommendations regarding the 'expatriate retention period'. It was thought that those services that were being Malayanised at rates that were 'better than average' might be completely Malayanised by 1960; that those proceeding at an 'average' speed might become so at various dates between 1960 and 1965; and that those in the 'below average' category would not achieve total Malayanisation earlier than 1965.

[3] ie 'above average', 'average' and 'below average'.

are considering the possibility of long-term contracts up to a maximum of 10 years.

So far as one can judge, a large number of expatriate officers are thinking in terms of applying to go under the compensation scheme next year and of immediately offering themselves for re-employment on contract. Their reasons are sufficiently clear, namely that they wish to be assured that their compensation is secure and that they will be getting it at the present rates of exchange. It is here that the new scheme for a special list as part of Her Majesty's Oversea Civil Service[4] as recently announced for Nigeria is of greatest interest to us, more particularly for younger officers. We shall be addressing the Secretary of State officially about this very soon. It must be expected that the younger officers as a group will be looking for alternative careers and that the great majority of them are likely to ask to go as soon as possible after the 1st July next year. We have some very good officers in this category and the only way of keeping them in the service will be for them to be brought on to the new special list. They could then continue to serve in Malaya during the next few years when the need for them will be acute. They would have an assured future without the Federation of Malaya being committed to providing employment for them indefinitely; there are, in fact, advantages all round and the only difficulty, I imagine, is the contingent liability on H.M.G. should it be impossible to absorb them elsewhere at a later date.

The tentative programme which we have in mind at present is that we should endeavour to complete the work of the Compensation Working Party within the next four to six weeks and that by about the same time we should have an interim report ready from the Malayanisation Committee. Thereafter, we would hope to be in a position, not later than September or October, to publish the compensation scheme and to be able to inform all expatriate officers of what their prospects of further employment are likely to be. They would then be asked to state their intentions before the end of the year and we would have a much clearer picture than we have at present of the staffing position from the 1st July, 1957 onwards. The Malayanisation

---

[4] Provision for a 'special list' to which British officers might transfer was made in the scheme for an Oversea Civil Service established in May 1956. The special list was designed with Nigerian considerations particularly in mind. By offering conditions of service which would keep them as employees of HMG, the special list was devised in an attempt to persuade British officers in Nigeria to remain in post in the approach to regional self-government and then national independence. Officers transferring to the special list would remain in the service of HMG and then be seconded to an employing government. Their salaries and conditions of service would be negotiated between the employing government and HMG. Pensions and any compensation payments for which they might qualify on retirement would be paid to them by HMG and recovered from the employing government. Except in cases of ill-health, misconduct or inefficiency, the employing government was expected to give one year's notice before terminating the secondment of an officer and to consult HMG before introducing any reorganisation which might involve terminating the secondment of a considerable number of officers. The intention was to find continuous employment for all officers on the special list up to at least the age of 50. If, however, any officer became unemployed through no fault of his own, he would be kept on full pay (at HMG's expense) for as long as necessary up to a maximum of 5 years (or until he reached the age of 50, if that was earlier) while efforts were made to place him. If, in the last resort, suitable employment for an officer could not be found, he would receive his pension, plus any additional compensation for which he would have been eligible if he had remained in his former service, and not transferred to the specialist list. The details of the scheme were the subject of prolonged and at times acrimonious debate between the CO and the Treasury in Whitehall. For background, see BDEEP series A, vol 3, D Goldsworthy, ed, *The Conservative government and the end of empire 1951–57*, part II, 219–242.

Committee would then be re-convened and, if it appeared that a very large proportion of expatriate officers was asking to go, the Committee would have to consider what measures would be necessary to keep the Government machine working during the next critical years, including, perhaps, the offer of special inducements to selected expatriate officers to stay.

417   DEFE 7/496, no 25/11   12 June 1956
'Malayan defence agreement talks': minute by Sir H Parker written after his return to London

At the Constitutional Conference held in London in January and February 1956 it was agreed that a Working Party should be set up to study and work out the details of an Agreement between the United Kingdom Government and the Government of the Federation of Malaya in regard to defence arrangements and mutual assistance in defence matters.

2.   The terms of reference of the Working Party were set out in Appendix 'D' to the Report of the Conference.

3.   The Working Party met in Kuala Lumpur. It had its first meeting on April 16th[1] and its last one on June 5th. There were in all five meetings of the main Working Party. In addition there were a large number of meetings of sub-committees to discuss the detailed provisions to be incorporated in Annexes to the main Agreement.

4.   Australian and New Zealand Observers participated fully in the work, both of the main Working Party and of its sub-committees.

5.   Attached to this minute is a copy of the draft Report[2] of the Working Party to which is annexed the draft Agreement and the Appendices thereto.

6.   At the last meeting of the Working Party most of the outstanding differences of detail were resolved. The issues left over, so far as the Agreement itself is concerned, were:—

(i)   the wording of Article 6,[3] and
(ii)   the duration of the Agreement.

7.   On (i) the Malayans wish to limit their commitments. They would agree that the two countries should come to each other's assistance in the event of actual attack. In other circumstances they propose that there should be consultation with a view to deciding what action should be taken. We rely on Article 6 to empower us to take action in an Emergency without prior consultation with Federation Ministers. This applies not only to the defence of Malaya, but to the implementation of our international and Commonwealth obligations.

8.   It is difficult to say with certainty what underlies the Malayan approach but three factors probably come into the picture:—

(1)   newness as a nation;
(2)   a possible neutralistic trend; and
(3)   domestic presentation. .

---

[1] See 410.   [2] Not printed.   [3] See 408, Appendix A.

9. So far as the Tenghu [sic] is concerned the last factor is, I believe, the predominant one. At lunch after our last meeting he said to me: "You must ask Mr. Lennox-Boyd to help me in presenting the Agreement in my own country. I must not give my opponents grounds for attacking me. I know we cannot stand without your help in defence and, if the United Kingdom fell, Malaya would fall too."

10. I think this is the honest view of the Tenghu, although it is not that of everyone in Malaya, including one at least of the Tenghu's colleagues.

11. As regards duration, the Malayans would like no limit but with a provision allowing review from time to time at the request of either party. In suggesting this they are influenced by a desire to maintain the maximum degree of freedom and by considerations of public presentation.

12. I argued strongly the need for permanence and stability in any Agreement to which the Tenghu's reaction was: "We are friends. You must trust us."[4]

13. Although I pressed for either a limitless agreement, without tags, or, if a period were included, for a really long-term one, my personal view, shared I think by the Commissioner-General, is that we should be well advised, if the Malayans would accept, to agree to Libya terms. These, broadly, are that the agreement remains in force for 20 years but is subject to review after 10 years.

14. On the Annexes there remain three outstanding issues:—

(a) Land tenure.
(b) Contributions to Local Authorities in lieu of rates.
(c) Jurisdiction in running down cases.

15. Land tenure has proved a particularly intractable issue. Local practice varies according to the State or Settlement concerned. Our own past arrangements have been based on colonial status. The approach of the representatives of the Rulers in whom land vests has differed from that of Federation Ministers. Twice agreement was reached with the Keeper of the Ruler's [sic] Seal and the Mentri Besar of Selangor only for it to be rejected by Federation Ministers. Further discussions are taking place in Kuala Lumpur. These may be successful. The primary difficulty is one of presentation. What suits the Federation raises difficulties for the United Kingdom and vice versa.

16. The basis on which we make a contribution to the expenditure of Local Authorities can, I believe, be settled, though the detailed application of any agreed principle will involve a good deal of work.

17. Jurisdiction in running down cases may be a difficult detailed issue to resolve. In our view, if a member of the forces is involved in a traffic accident in the course of official duty, the primary right to jurisdiction rests with the Service authorities, i.e. if the circumstances warrant it he would be court-martialled. The Malayans claim that the primary right should rest with the civilian authorities and that proceedings should be taken, if at all, in the local courts. We support our view by N.A.T.O.

---

[4] In a minute to his minister of 29 June, however, Parker wrote: 'Whilst I agree that the Tunku's heart is in the right place I would stress the risk that developments either within Malaya or elsewhere in Asia may force him to the conclusion that a more cautionary approach to certain problems may be wise from his own domestic political point of view. In particular I would not go so far as to say that I regard Malaya's accession to S.E.A.T.O. as something which will follow more or less automatically within a reasonable period of Independence' (DEFE 7/496, no 6).

practice. The Malayans plead in aid existing practice in the Federation, which they say works satisfactorily and should not be changed on Independence.

18. To sum up. On the agreement itself Federation Ministers do not wish it to be claimed by their critics that they have given away their newly-found birthright. In addition they would like as much fluidity as possible. The issue is to some extent one of presentation though the present differences of view are rather more fundamental.

19. Are we to seek to obtain an agreement which is in terms bending [? binding] and durable, or should we accept an agreement which, in form, is looser, and rely for its maintenance on the continuance of good relations between the two countries? There are differences of opinion on this. I, personally, would take some risks.

20. On the question of the long-term location of Imperial troops the Federation representatives were most co-operative. They disliked the use of paddy[5] land for two R.A.F. stations. Otherwise they raised no major difficulties anywhere. The large Army areas north of Malacca and at Sungei Patani in South Kedak [sic] were agreed. The Malayan representatives would have accepted the site at Sungei Besi, south of Kuala Lumpur. The High Commissioner doubts whether politically it will be wise to continue to develop this area on which a good deal of money has already been spent.

21. In these circumstances I asked the Federation representatives to give the matter further thought before finally agreeing. The area at Sungei Besi is virtually at the stage when constructional work could start for accommodation for two Gurkha battalions. There are many practical advantages in proceeding with this scheme, but we do not want to spend more money and then find that the location is unacceptable on political grounds.

22. In my view it is essential that immediate progress should be made with some provision for rehousing the Army when the Emergency ends or substantially abates. Unless this is done the troops on withdrawal from the jungle will be condemned to emergency and extemporised arrangements. In such circumstances morale and discipline will deteriorate, trouble with the local population may develop and the whole agreement may be prejudiced.

---

[5] ie rice.

418 CO 1030/230, no 26   18 June 1956
[Malayanisation]: letter from Sir D Watherston to A R Thomas[1]

Thank you for your letter FED.103/266/02 of 29th May which crossed my letter of 1st June[2] to Johnston.

We will certainly do our best to persuade Ministers to give a "no compulsory retirement" undertaking to cover as long a period as possible. But it became evident some weeks ago that they were averse to treating all categories of staff in the same way. They recognise that they will need e.g. Mechanical Engineers for a long time to come. But they are firm in their view that certain Departments can be completely Malayanised within a few years. The scheme propounded in my letter to Johnston for a threefold classification[3] is about as far as they are likely to go.

The Ministers' difficulty is not that they question our arguments about their

---

[1] Assistant under-secretary of state, CO, 1952–1964.   [2] See 416.   [3] See *ibid*, note 3.

continuing need for staff but that they see serious political difficulties in accepting any general commitment to retain expatriate staff in large numbers after say 1962 (some of them would substitute 1960 for 1962). In political terms they can "get away with" a three or five year Malayanisation programme and the incidental consequence of retaining expatriate staff for the period of the programme. But no more than that. Their thinking tends to be conditioned by this fact plus a suspicion that most of their expatriate staff will go anyway, whatever time limit is set, and why should they make themselves unpopular over a longer time limit which is likely to be more effective than a short one? It is in part a question of confidence and the sooner the present period of uncertainty comes to an end the better.

On their side the expatriate officers are subject to some misgivings about their prospects of promotion if they stay on. It is one of the peculiar difficulties of a scheme for compulsory retirement before the normal age that it sets the expatriate officer at a disadvantage as compared with Malayan colleagues of equal or less seniority and merit. The expatriate will not remain in the service until the normal age for retirement and can on that account be passed over in favour of the Malayan who will stay longer in the service than he. I am putting this argument as the Ministers see it; they want to "bring on" their best Malayans as fast as possible in order to have men with suitable experience for the top jobs in a matter of a few years time at the most. Hence arises a pressure for giving Malayans undue preference now in promotion to junior and middle superscale grades. We realise well enough that if promotions are not made strictly in accordance with C.R.32[4] (and a clear undertaking to that effect given now) no amount of other promises will suffice to retain the expatriates in the 35–45 age group whose interests would be prejudiced by any departure from the accepted principles for promotion.

I put this point in writing to the Chief Minister last week, drawing his attention at the same time to the importance for the future of the service as a whole, after the expatriates have gone, of maintaining the principles laid down in C.R.32. The issue of promotions policy after 1st July, 1957, is therefore likely to be brought to a head shortly and the proposal is that an undertaking should be given that any expatriate officer with not less than two years' service ahead of him shall be eligible for promotion on the basis of official qualifications, experience and merit on parity with his Malayan colleagues.

This explanation may help to show that the question of a promise not to exercise powers of compulsory retirement is only part of a rather complicated situation. As I explained in the last paragraph of my letter to Johnston, we hope to persuade Ministers to have a second look at the situation early in 1957 when the consequences of any shortcomings in their original policy will be evident to them *and* to the critics whom they have to face. Two bites at the cherry are less satisfactory than one, but it may be the only way. No one can say yet how many expatriate officers will ask to go.

If we do find ourselves badly short of staff I have little doubt that the Federation would be willing to take Singapore officers on contract terms. But our Ministers are extremely sensitive to any proposal which would increase the number of expatriate officers entitled to retire with compensation. They would probably refuse to accept officers on transfer from Singapore for that reason and I do not imagine that any

---

[4] Colonial regulations.

Singapore officers would be willing to come if they were not entitled to go with compensation.

The next move is to submit to the Malayanisation Committee a draft interim report, covering among other things the proposals for expatriate staff set out in my letter to Johnston. The report has been drafted and we should know the Committee's reactions to it within a fortnight. I will keep you informed of the outcome.

419 CO 1030/230, no 27   28 June 1956
[Malayanisation]: letter (reply) from J B Johnston to Sir D Watherston

Many thanks for your letter of the 1st June[1] about developments on the Malayanisation Committee. Ambler Thomas also asks me to thank you for your letter to him of the 18th.[2]

We do recognise the reality of Ministers' difficulties in the political field. It is however very gratifying to see how firmly you are keeping the real problems before them. We are sure you are right in your "two bites at the cherry" policy. I think it is true to say that in other territories time rather than argument is what has made Ministers realistic on these subjects. Certainly in the Gold Coast, and to a lesser degree in Nigeria, the clamour for Africanisation has been in inverse proportion to the imminence of a European exodus. Unfortunately in Nigeria the degree of clamour and the behaviour of some of the Ministers have led to a situation in which none of their present assurances carry any weight. Things have worked out more satisfactorily in the Gold Coast where there has been just that much more time for Ministers to come down to earth.

I fear I must sound a warning note about the Special List of HMOCS. I know you recognise what heavy liabilities the Special List arrangement imposes on H.M.G. and I think it is only fair to warn you that a strong case will have to be put forward to convince the United Kingdom Government that a Special List arrangement should be applied in the Federation. The circumstances there are very different from those in Nigeria where the arrangements are essential in order to avoid a complete breakdown in the administration as a result of premature large-scale departures of overseas officers at a time when the supply of Africans coming forward to take their places is quite inadequate. Although the most forthcoming assurances have been given by all the Nigerian Governments that all overseas officers will be welcome to stay on indefinitely, there is ample evidence that without a Special List agreement there may well be such a withdrawal of expatriate officers that the processes of Government will collapse.

Conditions in the Federation are, happily, far from parallel. A reasonably satisfactory separate agreement was reached on Public Service matters at the London Conference and the supply of Malayans available to staff the public services is relatively much greater than in Nigeria. Indeed if this were not so, the Federal Government could hardly have insisted on the principle of compulsory retirement. Where a territory is in a sufficiently strong position to contemplate some measure of compulsory retirement it is not easy to make out a case for the United Kingdom Government to accept the heavy potential liabilities involved in a Special List

---

[1] See 416.   [2] See 418.

agreement. It would I think be necessary to show that the territory has exhausted every attempt to induce overseas officers to stay and that there was a real risk of a breakdown in the administration. This is of course only a preliminary view and we can discuss all this later on when the High Commissioner comes over in October. But we thought we ought to warn you that it will not necessarily be plain sailing.

420   CO 1030/230, no 28   6 July 1956
[Malayanisation]: letter (reply) from Sir D Watherston to J B Johnston

Thank you for your letter of the 28th June[1] in FED.103/266/02.

You may like to have the enclosed copy of the draft Interim Report of the Malayanisation Committee[2] which we hope to discuss at the next meeting on the 16th July. You will see that two paragraphs are missing—one about H.M.O.C.S. and the other about the continued application of traditional service principles in regard to promotions, etc., after the 1st July, 1957. In regard to the latter, I have been informed by the Chief Minister that, following my letter to him (to which I referred in paragraph 5 of my letter to Thomas of the 18th June),[3] he discussed the matter with his Ministers and they have agreed that expatriate officers remaining on the permanent establishment after the 1st July next year should be given an assurance of non-discriminatory treatment but that officers who take their compensation and then are re-engaged on contract should not be given any such assurance. This seems only reasonable and it is now becoming clear that Ministers dislike the latter arrangement. They would be open to political criticism that expatriate officers had been paid substantial sums in compensation for loss of career and yet were still in the employment of the Government. The draft paragraph on traditional service principles for discussion at the meeting is also enclosed.

On the other point—the "special list" of H.M.O.C.S.—we have been brought up a bit short by the latter part of your letter of the 28th June. Despite the fact that we shall, in a few years' time, have a substantial supply of Malayans coming forward to replace overseas officers, it will be quite possible for there to be a major breakdown of the machinery of Government if a large proportion of the 1,650 entitled officers under the compensation scheme decide to go. The reason why the Malayan delegation insisted in London on the principle of compulsory retirement was that there is an expectation of substantial numbers of Malayans becoming available particularly from 1960 onwards. Indeed, as you will see from the draft Interim Report enclosed, some Departments may be completely Malayanised by 1960, while others can be expected to become Malayanised during the succeeding five years. If there was no element of compulsion, Malayanisation could be materially delayed by the continued presence of overseas officers in substantial numbers. It is the next few years that are really critical.

It would surely be even more disastrous for H.M.G. if there were to be a breakdown here than it would be in Nigeria having regard to the strategic importance of South East Asia, the threat of Communism and the amount of British capital invested here. What we are now proposing to do is to invite the views of Executive Council on the

---

[1] See 419.   [2] Enclosures not printed.   [3] See 418.

scheme so that, if they are in favour of its being applied to the Federation we can make an official application which will be backed by strong arguments. The paper goes to Executive Council next week.

421   CAB 130/118, GEN 538/10   23 July 1956
'Report on political, economic and information measures in Eastern Asia': memorandum by the Official Committee on Eastern Asia for Cabinet Policy Review Committee

[The Cabinet Policy Review Committee was established by Eden in June 1956 with the purpose of reviewing the whole field of government expenditure in search of economies. It consisted of Eden (chair), Salisbury (lord president), Macmillan (Exchequer), Selwyn Lloyd (FO) and Monckton (Defence). In view of what was seen as a change in the methods, if not the objectives, of the Soviet Union, Eden informed the committee that the main threat to the UK position and influence in the world was now political and economic rather than military and that policies should be adopted to meet the changed situation. Eden added: 'The period of foreign aid is ending and we must now cut our coat according to our cloth. There is not much cloth. We have to find means of increasing by £400 millions a year the credit side of our balance of payments.' A paper by officials of the FO, Ministry of Defence and Treasury on 'The future of the United Kingdom in world affairs' (CAB 134/1315, PR(56)3, 1 June 1956) formed the basis of the subsequent reports commissioned by the Policy Review Committee but the full programme of subjects for review was never completed because of the onset of the Suez crisis (see BDEEP series A, vol 3, D Goldsworthy, ed, *The Conservative government and the end of empire 1951–1957*, part I, 21 and 25). The inquiry into Eastern Asia, which is the subject of the memo reproduced here, was an exception. The official committee, which was chaired by Lord Reading and composed of officials from the Treasury, FO, CRO, CO and Ministry of Defence, agreed the final draft of this report on 13 July (another copy on CAB 134/1315, PR(56)26). It was discussed by the Policy Review Committee on 25 July (see Goldsworthy, *op cit*, 27) and, as a step towards making savings and shifting expenditure from military to civilian objectives, it led to the establishment of a working party of officials on expenditure in Eastern Asia which reported in Feb 1957 (see 440).]

Part I: Introduction
The Committee was set up by the Policy Review Committee with the following terms of reference:—

"To examine political, economic and information measures for the mainte-nance and promotion of United Kingdom interests in Eastern Asia, bearing in mind that it is the objective of Her Majesty's Government to reduce military commitments in that area; and to report to the Policy Review Committee through the Foreign Secretary."

2.   Since no estimates of possible savings in military expenditure were or at this stage could be available to the Committee, we decided that our first task should be to examine our current expenditure in the area, which we defined as the whole of South and South-East Asia and the Far East from Afghanistan to Japan inclusive. This showed how small a proportion of our total expenditure in the area we devote at present to developing our dependent territories and to assisting the Commonwealth and foreign countries with technical and other aid.

3.   There is no doubt that during the past five or six years we have lost many opportunities for maintaining and extending our influence in the area. Not only have

we been obliged to reject a substantial number of requests made to us for assistance of all kinds but we have been unable ourselves to take the initiative in offering help. It is not surprising therefore that some of the countries of the area are beginning to look for help to the Soviet Union and China.

4. There are still opportunities open to us. If we fail to seize them now while at the same time we reduce our military strength, our influence throughout the area will begin to decline rapidly. But there is this in our favour, that even modest increases in the sums spent at present on non-military methods of maintaining our influence have a disproportionately great effect on our efforts to achieve that object.

5. Other Commonwealth countries Canada, Australia and New Zealand are also closely concerned in the problems of Eastern Asia, particularly in the sphere of defence and development. We should aim at concerting any new plans for development closely with the above Governments, whose financial assistance would also be valuable.

Part II. Current United Kingdom expenditure in the area

6. In 1956/57 non-military expenditure will be about £9.5 millions, of which in round figures £4.5 millions will fall to the Colonial territories, £1.6 millions to Commonwealth countries and £1.8 millions to other countries, the balance going to International Organisations in the area and other miscellaneous items.

7. This non-military expenditure will be broadly divided as follows:—

	£
Colonial Service Vote	625,000
Colonial Development Corporation	2,400,000
Colonial Development and Welfare	1,407,000
Colombo Plan	931,000
Representation Costs	1,846,000
Information Services	382,000
British Council	331,000
British Broadcasting Corporation	120,000
International Bodies	557,000
Miscellaneous	867,000
	£9,466,000

8. In addition to the annual expenditure tabulated certain Government loans or credits for special purposes have been and are in future likely to be extended to countries in the area. Other similar commitments may also have to be contemplated. The problems involved, however, are of a substantially different kind from those concerned directly with the presentation of the British standpoint or the development of British territories.

9. Total military expenditure in the area is difficult to assess. But on a balance of payments basis alone it will amount to £51 millions in 1956/57.

10. It is evident that at present the emphasis in our expenditure is very heavily on the military side, though the non-military expenditure is subject to marked variations from year to year and the figure of £9.5 millions cannot be taken as necessarily representative of our past and future commitments in the area. The basic question for consideration is whether this deployment of our resources is best suited to promote and protect our interests in view of the changed nature of the threat to them and the present state of our economy.

Part III: Future needs

11.   The Colonial Office, Commonwealth Relations Office and Foreign Office have for the purposes of this Committee drawn up their own tentative programmes for projects which in their view are the most urgently needed in the territories with which they deal. The extent to which these projects can be carried out must depend upon the money available. But certain general conclusions may be drawn from the Departments' statements about the form which any increased non-military expenditure might most usefully take in the event of a reduction of our military commitments.

(i)   Much needs doing in order to improve the security and welfare of our dependent territories, especially in regard to the problems of Chinese schools in Singapore, Malaya and Borneo, housing in Hong Kong and the development of the Borneo territories.

(ii)   The Colombo Plan must remain the chief instrument of United Kingdom economic aid to the independent Commonwealth and foreign countries. The funds we can supply are so small in relation to the development needs of the area that they must continue to be devoted primarily to the Technical Co-operation Scheme. But there is a strong case for increasing our contribution to that scheme (at present £1 million a year) and especially the amount of aid given to foreign member countries (at present only one-fifth of the total). With more money to spend we could also aim to accept a limited number of requests for small-scale capital aid. This would be of particular political advantage in those countries which are not yet sufficiently developed to benefit adequately from the Technical Co-operation Scheme. In order to prevent misunderstanding and to scotch any idea that capital aid on a large scale was being made available we should need to make at an appropriate moment a carefully worded statement of the exact amount of money involved and of the ways in which we proposed to spend it.

(iii) Both within S.E.A.T.O. and outside it we need to intensify the efforts already being made, especially through training courses in Malaya and the United Kingdom, to strengthen the administration and internal security of the independent countries of South-East Asia.

(iv) There are also measures of assistance to the armed forces of Asian countries which, although their military value may be small, nevertheless offer opportunities for the exertion of political influence which we cannot afford to ignore. These measures would include assistance in the expansion, development, equipment and training of the armed forces of certain countries in the area.

(v)   Any reduction in our military strength will make it all the more necessary to intensify our information and cultural activities. There is still, for example, an unsatisfied demand for the teaching of English. Increased activity in this field by the British Council and by our information services and the British Council in related fields could be a highly important means of maintaining our influence, especially in non-S.E.A.T.O. countries such as Burma, Ceylon, India, the Indo-China States, Indonesia and Japan.

Part IV: Illustrative programmes for additional expenditure

12.   We have set out below three programmes based on additional annual expenditure of £1 million, £2 millions and £3 millions respectively.

Items	Estimated cost (£'000) Programmes		
	I	II	III
Colonial Office			
1. Chinese education and contributions to general development in N. Borneo and Sarawak	250	500	800
2. Hong Kong—housing, social services, development and University	150	400	600
3. Expanding United Kingdom Information Services in Malaya and Singapore and British Council activities there and in N. Borneo and Sarawak.	100	100	100
Foreign Office			
4. Colombo Plan	150	250	500
5. Security measures	25	75	125
6. Information	10	110	110
7. Cultural activities	65	65	65
Commonwealth Relations Office			
8. Colombo Plan	125	250	350
9. Service items, e.g., training, military equipment	35	65	135
10. Information and British Council	55	125	155
11. Staff (non-information)	35	60	60
TOTAL (£'000)	1,000	2,000	3,000

13. These programmes are designed simply to illustrate what might be done with certain sums. Even the largest of them would be no more than a beginning towards meeting some of the more urgent problems confronting us in our own dependent territories and towards taking advantage of some of the opportunities still open to us in Commonwealth and foreign countries. They have inevitably been prepared in London without consultations with our various overseas representatives and with the Colonial Governments concerned.

14. Increased expenditure in South-East Asia even at the rate of £3 millions a year would not make certain of matching everywhere the Russian and Chinese effort. But that cannot be our aim. We should rather concentrate on certain key fields, developing tried policies rather than initiating new ones.

15. In many fields shortage of man-power and facilities is a limiting factor as well as shortage of money. In drawing up these illustrative programmes account has been taken of these shortages. They are therefore of necessity modest in relation to the needs of the area. In some fields the expansion of our activities might have to be gradual over the years. The essential thing is that the effort, once begun, should be sustained and where possible intensified as opportunities present themselves.

Part V: Recommendations

16. We recommend that the Policy Review Committee should:—

(i) indicate, if necessary on a provisional basis, the annual increase to be aimed at in non-military expenditure in the area, in the light both of whatever reductions in military expenditure may be decided upon and of other financial commitments in the rest of the world;

(ii) approve the general lines of such additional expenditure, as set out in this report;

(iii) authorise the Departments concerned, in consultation with United Kingdom representatives and Colonial Governments in the area, to formulate detailed schemes within the general framework of the illustrative programmes set out in Part IV of this report.

422   DEFE 7/501, no 15   28 July 1956
[Emergency operations]: letter from Sir D MacGillivray to E Melville[1] on the continuing role of British troops after independence

With my letter of the 17th July I sent to Martin a copy of my paper to the B.D.C.C. in regard to the direction and command of Emergency operations against the communist territorists after independence. This is a vitally important question, to which we have been giving further thought here, especially in the light of the Chief Minister's public statements reported in my telegrams Personal 21 and 505 of the 20th and 23rd July. (Incidentally, thank you for the very prompt reply to my first telegram authorising me to make a statement if necessary. In view of the Chief Minister's subsequent statement, the second paragraph of which was given sufficient local emphasis, I have not found it necessary myself to say anything.) I now enclose a memorandum[2] prepared by General Bower,[3] together with comments made thereon by Air Vice Marshal Kyle and myself. These further papers were considered yesterday at a meeting of the B.D.C.C. which I attended with General Bower. We were not able to reach agreement with General Loewen who insisted that the only possible arrangement militarily was the present one whereby the G.O.C., U.K. and Commonwealth forces is also Director of Operations. We agreed to disagree and a paper setting out our conflicting views is now being prepared for despatch to the Chiefs of Staff.

2. For the reasons explained in my previous letter it is, I think, important that the problem of command of the various forces which will be required for anti-terrorist operations after independence should be settled very early. Whatever solution is found to this problem it will inevitably take General Bower many months to make the necessary progressive administrative adjustments so that the new organisation can have effect from the date of independence. None of us here now think that this date can be any other than the 31st August, 1957.

3. The Chief Minister is genuinely optimistic that the Emergency will have been reduced to such a low level by August 1957 that the Federation Forces will be able to tackle it on their own. None of the Service Commanders and very few of the Chief Minister's colleagues share his optimism, and I cannot myself see any chance that, within little more than a year, the Federation Forces will be at such a strength and so trained and equipped that they will be able unaided to tackle the job. The M.C.P. are

---

[1] Assistant under-secretary of state, CO, 1952–1961.
[2] Enclosures not printed.
[3] GOC and director of operations, Malaya, 1956–1957.

at present lying low and conserving their forces in the hope that British troops will be withdrawn from active operations against them when independence comes and that then they will either be able to force the Federation to negotiate the kind of peace that would enable them to undertake political subversion quite freely, or that they will be able to resume their armed offensive with much greater success than in the past. It is important, I think, to make the Chief Minister see during the next six months how dependent the Federation Forces still are on the British Forces for administration, for air reconnaissance, for supply, for transport, for workshops and in many other ways, and what would be the implications of a complete withdrawal of British Forces from Emergency operations so long as the Federation's own Forces are so dependent and so long as the M.C.P. armed threat remains at anything like its present potential. I believe, however, that there is a real danger that the Chief Minister's nationalist emotions may overpower his judgement and that, as a part of pride, he would, when the moment of independence came, be prepared to take a great risk and declare that the Federation could deal with the Emergency unaided. It is possible indeed that the Federation Government might be able to do so, but only I think by using methods which we would not wish to be associated with, even by the secondment of British officers to the Federation Forces, and which in the end would inevitably lead to violent racial conflict. I believe that there may be a much better chance of the Chief Minister being realistic in this matter and agreeing that there should be continued assistance from British Forces after independence if this assistance could be localised. He has already hinted to me in conversation that he contemplates the need for British Forces "in certain areas". If we can say that we contemplate that by August next year the M.C.P. armed threat will be so diminished in the greater part of the country that it could safely be met by the Federation Forces alone, but that there will remain parts which, for yet a while, will still require the assistance of British Forces, then this prospect would be far more acceptable to the Chief Minister and his colleagues than the prospect of a prolongation of the present arrangements whereby British and Commonwealth Forces are employed all over the country. If he should accept this and if therefore the United Kingdom and Commonwealth Forces were to remain in the fight against the communist terrorists in a defined area or defined areas of the Federation, and if then it was found that the situation was getting out of hand in some other part of the Federation, it would be an easy matter quietly to extend the defined areas and to move United Kingdom and Commonwealth Forces to the aid of the Federation's Forces in the threatened part without any loss of face to the independent Federation Government. If, however, the new independent Government should be too proud or too confident to put forward a request for assistance from the U.K. and Commonwealth Forces at the moment of independence and if then they found, as I am sure they would, that the situation was getting out of hand, it would be extremely difficult for them to admit their mistake and ask for assistance. Rather than go cap in hand to H.M.G. for assistance at that stage, they might prefer to take the grave risk involved in concluding the Emergency by negotiation with the M.C.P.

4. I have therefore been discussing with Bower a plan whereby after independence United Kingdom and Commonwealth Land Forces would be used only in Perak, Penang and Kedah on Emergency operation duties, the whole of the rest of the country being left to the Federation Land Forces with assistance from the R.A.F. This would, I believe, have great political advantage, though I recognise that from the

administrative point of view it would present formidable difficulties to the military authorities and these might well prove to be the limiting factor. It would mean the brigading together on operational use of the Federation's military forces in one division in the south and the brigading together of all United Kingdom and Commonwealth land forces in one division in the north. At present the U.K. and Commonwealth forces and the Federation forces are mixed up together in Emergency operations, units of each being contained in both divisions; but sooner or later they will have to be separated out. It would mean that the Federation military forces would have to be made administratively self-contained within a year and this might well prove impossible. And it would mean that Asian personnel would have to live in barracks designed and built for Europeans (kitchens and latrines mainly affected) and vice versa. The plan would however have the advantage that Federation Forces only would be used in Johore where conditions are such that operations must be carried out more closely to the rubber estates and inhabited areas than they are in the north and where contact by the Forces with the civilian population is consequently more frequent and there are greater opportunities for friction between them. In the north, operations are to a much greater extent confined to the deep jungle which covers the central mountain spine and are of a nature particularly suitable to the Gurkhas who, it must be remembered, form the greater part of the British land forces in Malaya. The plan would have the grave disadvantage that the greater part of the country (all but Johore) would be deprived of troops available for use in aid of the civil power to suppress riots or civil disturbances, since it is already agreed that, after independence, U.K. and Commonwealth [? forces] could not be called upon to undertake internal security duties other than in engaging in the armed combat against the communist terrorists. I fear that this particular plan must therefore be abandoned as impracticable. However, we shall examine the practicability of a modified plan whereby U.K. and Commonwealth forces would remain brigaded together with the Federation forces for Emergency operations as at present, but with the operations of units of the former being limited to certain defined areas within the divisional areas of responsibility—say the worst part of Johore in the south and the whole of the State of Perak in the north.

5. If such a plan is to be practicable, then it would be necessary for General Bower to start making arrangements very soon. He is at present endeavouring to clean up Selangor and Negri Sembilan and there is some prospect that within three or four months there will be a great "White/Grey" belt across the country comprising most of Kelantan and all Trengganu, Pahang, Selangor, Negri Sembilan and Malacca, thus isolating Johore from the other terrorist stronghold in Perak, eastern Kedah and the frontier area. As soon as this belt has been established, Bower would be able to concentrate the great part of his military effort on Johore for, say, six to nine months, in the hope that by June next year the Emergency in the greater part of that State would be reduced to such a condition that there would be a good chance of the Federation Forces being able to finish it off on their own or at least to keep it under control. If Bower is to do this, and if he is to have a chance of giving orderly effect to the administrative arrangements for the reorganisation which the plan involves, the earliest possible decisions must be made.

In my view, we shall not get the Chief Minister to see this problem in proper perspective and get agreement of such a plan and on the Command organisation which is discussed in the attached papers until there has been discussion in a series of meetings round a table, the first meeting being devoted, as in the case of the London Conference earlier this year and the Defence Agreement Working Party, to educating the Malayans in the facts of the situation. I hope, therefore, that a Working Party, with composition similar to that set up for the negotiation of the Defence Agreement, can be established very soon and that Rob Scott will consent again to take the chair. I would hope that this could be agreed during August and that the Working Party can get down to work as soon as Rob Scott returns from his leave.

I am sending a copy of this letter to MacKintosh.

423 CO 1030/136, no 2   2 Aug 1956
[Constitutional commission]: letter from Mr Lennox-Boyd to Lord Reid on its work and speed

Many thanks for your letters.

I am very glad you find the other members of the Commission helpful and I do most sincerely hope you are making good progress with the work.

I need hardly say how concerned I have been at what you have said about Hall.[1] We here have the highest confidence in his ability and I feel sure he would have been able to play his proper part in the drafting of the report. I am sorry indeed that personal relations seem to have gone astray. I will no doubt hear more details from MacGillivray and Hall when they arrive here this week and it would perhaps be unwise of me to comment at this stage. One thing I feel I must say as between old friends, and that is that I do very much hope that it was realised that we had made a senior officer available in the person of Hall. As Head of a Department in the Colonial Office he must be regarded as roughly equivalent in rank to a Colonial Secretary in one of our territories overseas and I cannot but wonder whether some of the matters about which you have complained may have arisen from a misunderstanding of his proper status. Be that as it may, the matter is ended now and I can only hope that you will enjoy happier relations with his successor. It would have been enormously difficult for us to produce a second officer from here but I gather that it may be possible to provide one from the Federation and so avoid any loss of time or efficiency.

I very much hope this will be so, because I am more and more conscious of the urgent need for your report to be completed as soon as possible, and very troubled by a recent suggestion that you may not be able to complete it by Christmas. It now seems likely that the Tunku will be in London in the last week or two of December and it is most important from H.M.G.'s point of view that I should, if possible, be able to discuss the Commission's recommendations with him. You do, I know, recognise that after the Commission have reported the Federation Government, the Rulers and H.M.G. have all to study the report, make up their minds about it, and iron out any differences there may be between H.M.G. on the one hand and the Federation Government or the Rulers on the other. This may well take some time and if

---

[1] H P Hall, who was assistant secretary and head of the CO's Pacific Department before being seconded as secretary to the Reid commission, was replaced by E O Laird of the MCS. K J Henderson served as his assistant secretary. Reports of disharmony within the commission continued to reach London, see 443.

constitutional instruments are to be ready by the 31st August we shall have to work very quickly.

I say all this to you not of course officially as to the Chairman of the Commission, but privately as between old colleagues who have known each other for so many years, knowing how much you have H.M.G. interests in Malaya at heart. I am sure you will agree that those interests could be gravely imperilled if we reach the 31st August next year without an agreed constitution, if the Malayans then insisted—and there are precedents on which they can base themselves—that they should be given their independence and left to work out their constitution afterwards. You know as well as I do how real the possibility of this is, and it is for these reasons that I do beg you personally to do everything you can to complete the report before Christmas.

I quite understand why it is desirable to write the report outside Malaya and equally that, from the Malayan point of view, you might be thought to be under other pressures if it were written in the U.K. I note that you are suggesting that it should be done in Rome and I am sure that if this is the final decision our Ambassador will do all he can to help with arrangements. I wonder, however, whether at least some sections of the general public here might not be puzzled—and indeed I might have to answer Questions as to why this essentially Commonwealth party should have to write their report in a foreign capital. It occurred to me, therefore, to ask whether you had considered doing it in Malta. You might have better weather than in Rome, you could be very comfortably housed, Jennings would be within easy flying distance of the U.K.[2] (there are, I think, daily services), and of course no problems of foreign exchange would arise. I think in fact that it would prove less expensive and I am sure you will agree that we ought to take that into account.

In view of what I have said above about pressure of time upon us in all these matters and your decision to come to Europe to write the report, I hope it will not prove necessary to return to Malaya once more for its completion. I know you are anxious to avoid flying, and that would, I presume, mean that any return would so far as you are concerned involve the sea voyage once more and would accordingly impose greater delays. So far as I can see there would be no reason for your return to Malaya save to secure additional information or to canvass opinion in some new way and I would very much hope that the thoroughness with which I am sure you are going about your business during the present visit will make this unnecessary.

This is, of course, entirely a private letter and I have not said anything to the Governor of Malta about the suggestion I have made above. Perhaps you would let me know how it commends itself to you. In the meantime I send you all good wishes in your labours.

---

[2] Sir Ivor Jennings, who at the same time was Master of Trinity Hall, Cambridge, and chairman of the Royal Commission on Common Land Law, needed to be within easy access of London. Despite Lennox-Boyd's preference for Malta, the commissioners collated their findings and wrote up their report in Rome in late 1956 and early 1957.

424   CO 1030/136, no 3   14 Aug 1956
[Constitutional commission]: letter (reply) from Lord Reid to Mr
Lennox-Boyd

I received your letter[1] on 9th instant. You really need not emphasize to me the need
and difficulty of getting everything ready for August 1957. Ever since I started, that
date has been a nightmare to me. I know there were the qualifying words "if possible"
but, as might have been expected, that qualification has now quietly disappeared
from sight. In fact, since we started, we have been working at top speed—often
working or travelling on Saturdays and Sundays—and, if only because of the climate,
we cannot keep this pace up for very long.

2.   I was told, when asked to serve, that we were to begin work at the beginning of
May but as you know, through no fault of ours, we could not start until near the end
of June thus losing nearly two months.

3.   When my Commonwealth colleagues were asked to serve they were all told
that they would be away for a minimum of six months, probably for nine months and
perhaps for twelve. As the same estimate was given in three different parts of the
world I suppose it must have come from you and it meant that probably we could not
finish until the end of February and perhaps later. In spite of that estimate given to
them officially only a few weeks before, my colleagues willingly co-operated with me
in trying to speed things up.

4.   Christmas came in this way. At the beginning I asked MacGillivray what was
the latest convenient date—not the latest possible date—for our report to be
completed. He said Christmas and I said we would try to achieve that date. At that
early stage I could not, of course, say more than that and I now see that I was too
optimistic.

5.   It now appears to us to be impossible to complete our task by Christmas.
Several factors have contributed to this besides our late start. In the first place,
nothing was prepared for us either in London or here. Hall told me he had asked for
some preparatory work to be done here but that, in fact, nothing had been done
when he arrived. When I first saw MacGillivray he said not only that he had no
memorandum for us but that we could not even have his Officers to give evidence to
us. He only offered the absurd suggestion that we should formulate requests for
information on specific points and that, then, factual memoranda would be prepared
and submitted to us. I said how could we know what questions to ask until we had
made some study and I strongly objected to this idea of written notes passing to and
fro.

6.   In fact, we soon established business-like informal relations with the various
Government Officers whom we wished to consult and I would like to pay tribute to
the way in which they have all gone out of their way to help us. I make no complaint
at all that we were left to ferret things out for ourselves; things that you ferret out
stick better than things that are spoon-fed to you. But this method takes a great deal
of time and if, in the Spring, speed was regarded as important I find it very difficult to
understand why nothing was done by your people either in London or here to give us
more of a flying start, especially when they knew that our work had to start late. If

---

[1] See 423.

there was any idea that well-meant efforts to supply us with information would be ill-received, I was always there for consultation.

7. There are two other smaller matters which have contributed to lengthen our task. When I first saw MacGillivray he asked that we should deal not only with the Federal constitution but with the eleven State and Settlement constitutions which would also have to come into operation under the new set up. I said at once that we would be willing to do this but, of course, it has somewhat extended the scope of the enquiries which we have had to make. And finally, we are constantly finding that the actual methods of administration and taking decisions are very different from what one would expect on reading the existing law, etc. If I may offer an opinion, I think that most of these departures from the scheme laid down have been wisely made but we find that practice is so fluid that it is difficult to find out just what the present position is. We think it essential to find out just what is happening now before we consider our recommendations for the future because, with a view to a smooth transition, I at least feel that we ought not to recommend changes of existing practice except where we have good reason to do so.

8. We have now reached a stage at which we are being embarrassed by the fact that we have not yet received the views of any of the three parties chiefly concerned—H.M.G., the Alliance and the Rulers. I begged MacGillivray, a month ago, to give us your memorandum before we visited the Settlements but nothing has yet come. We have now finished our visit to Penang and go to Malacca this week, and it may be that we shall have to pay a second visit to Penang which would have been unnecessary if we had had your memorandum in time. I think we have established cordial relations with the Alliance leaders and, on sounding them, the best I can get is a hope that their memorandum will be ready by the end of this month.[2] A few weeks delay will have been well spent if, in the end, the Alliance can agree on all main points but, of course, they may not agree. The best I can get about the Rulers' memorandum is what seems to be a firm promise that it will be ready in mid September.

9. I told you before that we proposed to leave Malaya on October 1st. That has now proved to be impossible and we have booked accommodation in an Italian ship leaving Singapore for Naples on November 1st. After much discussion, we decided that we would lose less time than in any other way if we began our discussions here and let Jennings, and probably Hamid, fly from here to the United Kingdom about October 27th. This will enable Jennings to fulfil your commitments to the Ministry of Agriculture.[3] If it had not been for these commitments we could have gone to India and saved some considerable time. We decided to go to Rome solely because that seemed to save the most time if we were to enable Jennings to fulfil your commitments to Agriculture. I thought I had made that plain to you before. We all considered Malta but thought Rome better with this in view. Our Commonwealth members are not at all keen on Malta but if you could formulate your arguments for Malta we will certainly reconsider our decision. I might say, however, that most of us are not impressed by the money argument. Jennings tells me that flights to Malta take seven hours against four hours to Rome and are less frequent. Going to Malta will certainly mean a little extra delay and it will also mean a more strenuous time for Jennings but he does not wish that that point should be raised. I, however, wish to

² See 426.   See 423, note 2.

mention it because I feel that Jennings is going to have a very strenuous time indeed.

10. We have been so rushed that we have not been able to reach a decision about returning to Malaya. As you know, a second journey to Malaya was put to all of us as at least a possibility when we were asked to serve. Of course, when we come to discuss this question, any extra delay involved in returning here will weigh heavily with us.

11. I am sorry that you now find you want to discuss our recommendations with the Tungku in late December. This is the first I have heard of that and I can only suggest that, if it is vital for you to have our recommendations, you should ask the Tungku to put off his visit for six weeks or so. In view of all I have said I can really hold out no hope of getting our recommendations by mid December and I think it is a bit hard that now, for the first time, we are asked to make our recommendations within less than six months of our starting work.

12. The first paragraph of your letter shows that you are under grave mis-apprehensions as to the reasons which compelled us to get rid of Hall. In fairness to my colleagues and myself I cannot let it rest there. As soon as I have time I shall write to you on this subject and I shall mark my letter "Private" so as to avoid it being read by any junior Officer in your Ministry.

I am sorry this letter is so long but I could not make it shorter.

425 PREM 11/2298 22 Aug 1956

'Federation of Malaya': minute no PREM(56)69 by Mr Lennox-Boyd to Sir A Eden on the future of Penang and Malacca

[Unlike the nine Malay states of the Federation, Penang and Malacca were British territory and 'part of the Queen's dominions'. Reluctantly persuaded by MacGillivray to accept that the links between the Crown and the settlements would be severed by the constitution for independent Malaya, Lennox-Boyd decided to inform the prime minister and advise Buckingham Palace (see CO 1030/135).]

Prime Minister

There is a constitutional point in relation to the Federation of Malaya of which I think I ought now to inform you and those of my colleagues who are most closely concerned.

2. As you know, the Federation consists of nine Malay States under the Queen's protection, each with its own Sovereign Ruler, and the two British Settlements of Penang and Malacca. An independent Commission under Lord Reid is at present in the Federation, and is to recommend a constitution to come into effect when Malaya attains full self-government within the Commonwealth.

3. When the Commission was agreed upon with the Tunku, we reserved the right to submit to them the views of H.M.G. on certain matters. Among these was the future of the two Settlements. The position of the nine Malay States, which are not part of the Queen's dominions, is easy. Constitutionally they attain full self-government simply by the termination of Her Majesty's protection. Our problem is what should happen constitutionally to the two British Settlements, which are at present part of the Queen's dominions.

4. We have for some time been considering whether a way could be devised by

which, despite the fact that the Federation as a whole will become a self-governing and independent member of the Commonwealth, the two Settlements could continue to be part of the Queen's dominions and if this was constitutionally possible, whether we should put specific suggestions to this end to the Constitutional Commission.

5. After a great deal of thought and very full discussion with the High Commissioner, I have reluctantly come to the conclusion that such an arrangement is beyond the bounds of practical politics. If we insisted that the Settlements remain part of the Queen's dominions, and found some way of providing for this constitutionally, the inhabitants of the Settlements would inevitably feel they had a right to look to the Queen (or to her representative in the Settlements) for help and the remedy of grievances: no such help could be forthcoming, because we could not interfere in the affairs of an independent Commonwealth country, so that the most likely result would be to destroy present loyalty and affection for the British tradition, and possibly to bring the position of the Queen into disrepute. On the political side, it is clear that there would be great resentment and widespread criticism in the Federation if we attempted to keep the Settlements as part of the Queen's dominions: our proposals would be regarded as an attempt to keep a foot in the door of Malayan sovereignty, and would be stigmatised as showing our unwillingness to grant to the Federation as a whole the full self-government we have promised. Even in the Settlements themselves there would, I regret to say, be no majority support for any such move:[1] Malacca in particular is a stronghold of Malay nationalism. Apart from this, we might provoke, by such suggestions, much more radical and unwelcome proposals from the Malays themselves for the future of the Settlements.

6. There are constitutional difficulties, too, on which I will not elaborate save to say that it would be impossible for the Head of State of the Federation (who it has been agreed should be one of the Sultans) to act as Viceroy or Governor-General in respect of the two Settlements when he himself would not owe allegiance to Her Majesty.

7. All these considerations lead to the inescapable conclusion that, when the time comes for Malaya to become independent, the two Settlements will have to cease to be part of the Queen's dominions and become part of the new Federation of Malaya within the Commonwealth. I do not therefore propose to put any specific proposals to the Constitutional Commission on behalf of H.M.G. but to recommend to them that they should be guided chiefly by the wishes of the inhabitants of the Settlements and to inform them that it would be very acceptable to H.M.G. if, having done this, the Commission thought it possible to recommend some arrangement whereby the traditional link between the Crown and the Settlements would not be completely severed. (I have not however separately urged on the Commission that present inhabitants of the Settlements should be able without penalty to retain their present British citizenship).[2]

8. I have set all this out so that you may know at this early stage what the likely outcome will be. We shall not of course be able to reach any conclusions about the

---

[1] In the drafting of this minute to the prime minister, this point was included at Lennox-Boyd's express request; see CO 1030/135, minute by Lennox-Boyd, 17 Aug 1956.
[2] This point was included at Lennox-Boyd's express request, *ibid.*

final arrangements until the Constitutional Commission have reported. It seems at present unlikely that this will be before the beginning of 1957.[3]

9.   I am sending copies of this minute to the Foreign Secretary, the Commonwealth Secretary, the Home Secretary and the Minister of Defence.

---

[3] On this point Lennox-Boyd commented: 'The reference to early 1957 for Ld Reid's report is certain to elicit from the PM a Query as to how in general Reid & Co are now behaving. Do not hold this up on that account, but I would be grateful for a short note to PM on this. Can it now be slightly more reassuring? I wd also like to see Hall on Monday.' *Ibid*. See also 423, note 1.

426   CO 889/6, ff 219–239   25 Sept 1956

'Political testament of the Alliance': memorandum by Tunku Abdul Rahman for the Reid Commission. *Appendix*: 'Fundamental rights'

[This memo formed the basis of discussion between the commission and an Alliance delegation on 27 Sept (see 427).]

We, the Alliance, comprise the three main political parties in the Federation of Malaya: the United Malays National Organisation, the Malayan Chinese Association and the Malayan Indian Congress, which have allied themselves into a single movement for the sacred purpose of achieving independence for this country. With "Merdeka within 4 years" as our main platform, we were returned to power by the electorate at all levels from local to Federal Councils with unprecedented success. We, therefore, represent the great majority of the population of the Federation of Malaya.

The political testament, which we set out below, reflects the firm desire of the majority of the peoples of this country for a form of government which will ensure freedom, equality and unity of the new nation. We, therefore, desire that the future constitution of this country must provide for the establishment of a sovereign and fully independent State in which the people shall enjoy freedom and equality. This constitution shall also provide for a stable democratic government and ensure, peace and harmony amongst all its peoples.

Composition of new state
This sovereign and fully independent State should be a federation of the territories of the States of Johore, Negri Sembilan, Selangor, Perak, Kedah, Perlis, Kelantan, Pahang and Trengganu, and the Settlements of Penang and Malacca. Accordingly, it is necessary for Her Majesty the Queen to cede her rights over Penang and Malacca, and for Their Highnesses the Rulers to waive some of their rights over their respective territories in order to establish the Federation.

Each component part of the Federation should be called a State, and the constitution should provide for the admission of other territory or territories under terms and conditions to be agreed upon by the Federal Legislature.

Name of new state
The UMNO desires that the new State should be called MALAYSIA; the MCA would prefer the name MALAYA to be retained.

Head of state

In keeping with the dignity and prestige of a sovereign and fully independent State, Malaysia should have a Head of State entitled the Yang di-Pertuan Besar, chosen by Their Highnesses the Rulers from amongst themselves and shall hold office for a term of not less than three years. The Yang di-Pertuan Besar should be the constitutional head of Malaysia.

There shall at the same time be appointed by the Conference of Rulers a Successor of the Yang di-Pertuan Besar to be styled as the Yang di-Pertuan Muda who shall succeed as Head of State on the demise of the Yang di-Pertuan Besar.

Provision should also be made for the appointment of a successor within 24 hours in the event of the demise of both the Yang di-Pertuan Besar and the Yang di-Pertuan Muda. Should a successor not be appointed within 24 hours, provision should be made for the appointment by the Cabinet of a Council of Regency from among the Rulers.

Their Highnesses the Rulers

In accordance with the terms of reference of the Reid Commission, Their Highnesses the Rulers should continue to be constitutional Rulers of their respective States.

The Yang di-Pertuan Besar should also be the constitutional head of each of the States of Penang and Malacca. He should, however, appoint a representative, (to be called Persuroh Jaya) on the advice of the Prime Minister after consultation with the respective Executive Councils, to act on his behalf in each of these two States. Such representatives should hold office at the pleasure of the Yang di-Pertuan Besar.

Conference of Rulers

There should be a Conference of Rulers presided over by the Yang di-Pertuan Besar.

The legislature

The Legislature of Malaysia should be bi-cameral consisting of an Upper House, to be known as the Dewan Negara, and a Lower House to be known as the Dewan Raayat.

The Dewan Negara

The Dewan Negara would have 45 members. Each of the 11 States should have two elected representatives, and 22 prominent persons should be appointed by the Yang di-Pertuan Besar on the recommendation of the Government with a view, as far as possible, to ensuring that they reflect the national pattern of life in the country, including racial minorities. A President who would preside over meetings of the Dewan Negara, would be appointed by the Yang di-Pertuan Besar.

The term of office of the Dewan Negara should be five years. Members of the Dewan Negara must be nationals of Malaysia, and at least 35 years of age.

The Dewan Raayat

The Dewan Raayat should be fully-elected, with a Speaker to be known as the Yang di-Pertuan Dewan, who should be elected from amongst the members themselves. We, however, recommend that for the first life of the Dewan Raayat, the speaker should be appointed by the Yang di-Pertuan Besar.

Ordinarily the maximum life of the Dewan Raayat would be five years but the Yang di-Pertuan Besar may exercise his prerogative to prorogue, dissolve and in the event of national crisis to extend the life of the Dewan Raayat.

Members of the Dewan Raayat must be nationals of Malaysia, and at least 21 years of age.

Elections

The constitution of Malaysia should provide for parliamentary democracy, and it is therefore imperative that the Dewan Raayat should be fully elected. The election of members of the Dewan Raayat should be under the system of direct elections from single-member constituencies held once at least in every five years. Every national of Malaysia who has attained the age of 21 years should have the right to vote in such election.

The 22 representatives of the State in the Dewan Negara should be elected by the members of the Council of State from amongst themselves.

Powers of both houses

The Dewan Negara and the Dewan Raayat should have equal powers in initiating Bills, except Money Bills which should only be initiated by the Dewan Raayat.

Bills initiated and passed by the Dewan Negara should be passed by the Dewan Raayat before they become law.

Bills initiated and passed by the Dewan Raayat should be sent to the Dewan Negara, and, if not passed, such Bills should be sent back to the Dewan Raayat for reconsideration.

If, after reconsideration by the Dewan Raayat, such bills are not passed by the Dewan Negara within a period of 12 months from the date on which they were passed by the Dewan Raayat, they should automatically become law; in the case of Money Bills, they should automatically become law after 21 days.

The executive

The executive authority of Malaysia should be exercised in the name of the Yang di-Pertuan Besar by the elected government, headed by a Prime Minister to be known as the Perdana Mentri. There should be a Council of Ministers to be known as the Jumaah Mentri, presided over by the Perdana Mentri. Members of the Jumaah Mentri should be appointed by the Yang di-Pertuan Besar on the advice of the Perdana Mentri.

Judiciary

The Judiciary should be completely independent both of the Executive and the Legislature.

The fountain of all justice should be the Yang di-Pertuan Besar. In the dispensation of justice, there should be, besides the subordinate courts, a High Court with appeals therefrom to the Supreme Court. All judges of the High Court and the Supreme Court should be appointed by the Yang di-Pertuan Besar to hold office till they are 65 years of age. They may, however, be removed from office by an order of the Yang di-Pertuan Besar after an address by the Dewan Raayat, supported by the majority of the total number of members of the Dewan Raayat and by votes of not less than two-thirds of the members present and voting, has been presented to the Yang di-Pertuan Besar for the removal of the Judge on the ground of proved misbehaviour or infirmity of mind or body: provided that no proceedings for the presentation of the address shall be initiated by the Dewan Raayat unless notice of the motion to present the address is supported by not less than one-third of the total number of members of the Dewan Raayat.

The Supreme Court should also be vested with powers to decide whether or not the actions of both the Federal Executives and Legislatures are in accordance with the constitution. There should be from the Supreme Court a right of ultimate appeal to the Yang di-Pertuan Besar who, for the purpose of deciding on these appeals, should be advised by a body of law councillors especially appointed by him.

Division of legislative and executive powers between the federal government and state governments

(a) *General*

(1) The principle underlying this division of powers is that there should be a strong central government with States enjoying responsible government and having autonomous powers in certain specified matters.

(2) Under the existing constitution, the legislative powers of the Federal Government are enumerated in column (1) of the Second Schedule to the Federation of Malaya Agreement. The residuary powers vest in the States/Settlements. It is recommended that under the new constitution, the legislative powers of the States should be stipulated and that the residuary powers should be vested in the Federal Government. It is considered necessary, for the smooth and efficient running of the administrative machinery of the country as a whole, especially in times of national crisis, that the central government should have the residuary legislative powers.

(3) The legislative powers of the Federal government should continue to be as in column (1) of the Second Schedule to the Federation of Malaya Agreement. The States should have legislative powers in remaining matters to be specified.

(4) The States should have executive authority over matters on which the Federal government has legislative power as in column (2) to the Second Schedule, except in matters relating to education. Under the 1956 Education Report, the Federal Government is responsible for secondary and higher education and the local education authorities are responsible for primary education as well as trade schools. In education, therefore, State Governments have only supervisory power over primary and secondary education, working in conjunction with the Federal Government on the one hand and local education authorities on the other.

(5) We consider that the Legislative and Executive powers of the Federal and State Governments should be clearly defined. We do not consider that the provision of any consultative machinery such as the Conference of Federation Executives as existing at present would work in practice when both the Federal and State Legislatures are fully elected. It must be borne in mind that under a system of Party Government there is always a possibility that the Party in control of the Central Government may be different from that in any particular State, in which event provision of formal consultative machinery in the exercise of Executive powers would not be conducive to efficient Government. However, this should not preclude the possibility of Federal and State Governments making arrangement for purely informal consultations on matters of policy or otherwise as and when the need arises.

(b) *Finance*
The States should be financially autonomous whereas the power to raise revenue and the system of allocation of funds between the State and Federal Governments should be as in the Third Schedule and Part III of the Federation of Malaya Agreement.

(c) *Land*
(1) In matters of land administration, the Federal Government should have the power to acquire land anywhere in the country for any purpose of national importance after consultation with the State Government concerned. Such land should vest in the Federal Government, and a machinery be set up to put into effect full ownership including the right to sell or lease land so vested for Federal purpose.
(2) Any land at present reserved for a Federal purpose should vest in the Federal Government and Federal government should be allowed to have titles over such land. Any land acquired by the Federal government in future should similarly vest in the Federal government.

State Governments
The State Legislature should consist of a fully elected Council of State, with a Speaker.
Executive authority should be vested in an Executive Council, which should be responsible to the Council of State and presided over by a Mentri Besar (Chief Minister) who should be appointed by the Ruler of the State on the advice of the leader of the majority party in the Council of State. Members of the Executive Council should also be appointed by the Ruler on the advice of the leader of the majority party in the Council of State.

Fundamental rights
The constitution should secure and guarantee the fundamental rights normally enjoyed by free peoples, based on: —

1. Freedom of Speech and Expression,
2. Freedom of Assembly,
3. Freedom of worship,
4. Freedom from Want,
5. Freedom from Fear.

Principles of national policies
It is the objective of the Alliance Movement to ensure that the new nation should be prosperous and contented. Therefore, it is desirable to write into the constitution that, to achieve this aim, the government should endeavour to:

(a) Promote a sound social order and the welfare of the people;
(b) Remove illiteracy and provide free and compulsory primary education within the minimum period;
(c) Secure just and humane conditions of work;
(d) Secure ownership and control of natural resources, and ensure that their distribution shall subserve to the common weal;
(e) Provide equal opportunities to nationals to acquire land without prejudice to the system of Malay Reservations;

(f) Ensure that the economic system shall not result in concentration of wealth and the means of production to the common detriment;

(g) Ensure that all persons shall have the right to an adequate means of livelihood.

Common nationality

The constitution should provide for nationality laws that would build a peaceful and stable independent federation, with a contented and unified people whose loyalty is unquestioned and undivided, so that, in due course, the country can take its proper place in the comity of nations. To achieve this end, it is essential to have a nationality law which provides for a common nationality, to the exclusion of all others.

(a) *Citizens of Federation of Malaya*

We would, therefore, wish that all those who are Federal citizens by operation of law, registration or naturalisation on the date of the declaration of independence should be accepted as the first nationals of Malaysia.

In coming to this decision, we have taken due note of the fact that under the existing laws those born in Malacca and Penang are British subjects *and* automatically Federal citizens. Therefore, we consider that those born in these two territories before the date of declaration of independence should be nationals of Malaysia on and after the declaration of independence, but should be entitled to elect to retain their British nationality within a period of one year from the date of independence by making a declaration renouncing their Malaysian nationality. We would particularly stress the importance of applying the principle of common nationality in the case of those British subjects who automatically become the first nationals of independent Malaysia. This means that subjects to their right of election such British subjects, on becoming nationals of Malaysia, must lose the status of British subjects.

(b) *Those born in Malaysia after independence*

To ensure a common nationality, we would want the constitution to provide that those born in Malaysia on and after the declaration of independence should be nationals of Malaysia.

In the case of nationals born in Malaysia of alien parents on or after the date of the declaration of independence the UMNO considers that they should be free to choose their nationality after attaining the age of 21 years: and that there should therefore be a provision that such persons should cease to be nationals after attaining the age of 21 years unless they made a declaration of retention of nationality within a period of one year after attaining that age but this provision should not apply to persons who would, on such cesser have no national status.

The MCA and MIC do not agree with this proviso.

(c) *Those born outside Malaysia*

Any person born anywhere outside Malaysia after the declaration of independence and whose father at the time of the child's birth is a national should be eligible to become a national. There should be a system of registration after independence at consulates, legations and embassies of Malaysia abroad.

(d) *Wife of a national*
A women who is a legal wife of a national should be entitled, on making application therefor, to be registered as a national.

(e) *Minor children of nationals*
We also recommend that a person below the age of 21 born of a father who at the date of his birth was not a Federal Citizen under the Federation of Malaya Agreement 1948 but who subsequently acquired such citizenship or nationality shall after the date of independence become a national upon registration if he is ordinarily resident in the country.

(f) *Acquisition of nationality by naturalisation*
In the future independent Malaysia, those aliens who wish to become nationals must comply with the following qualifications:

(1) Be 21 years of age or above;
(2) Be of good character;
(3) Take the oath of allegiance and abjure allegiance to any other power or nation;
(4) Declare intention to reside here permanently;
(5) Have resided here for 10 out of the 12 years immediately preceding date of their application;
(6) Have a reasonable knowledge of Malay.

(g) *Transitional provisions*
However, we recognise the fact that a large alien population exists in the Federation of Malaya, and that the continued existence of such an element will not be in the interests of national unity. We consider it is vital to such unity that the nationals of the independent Federation should comprise all those who genuinely desire to make the Federation their home and the object of their undivided loyalty. We, therefore, consider it imperative as a step towards solving our alien population problem and in the interests of national unity, that in the case of these existing aliens there should be some relaxation of the qualifications to encourage those who genuinely desire to be nationals of this country to make this their home and the object of their undivided loyalty. For these existing aliens, therefore, we propose the following provisions:

(i) *Those born here before independence*
Those born in this country before independence should be entitled on registration to become nationals, provided they:

(1) Were born here and are 18 years of age or more;
(2) Are of good character;
(3) Take the oath of allegiance and abjure allegiance to any other country or nation;
(4) Declare intention to reside here permanently;
(5) Have resided here for 5 out of the 7 years immediately preceding date of their application;
(6) Have a simple knowledge of Malay.

For the above category of aliens the language qualification should be waived for a period of one year following the date of independence. The MIC, however, would prefer the period to be two years.

(ii) *Those not born here but are resident here up to date of independence*
Those aliens who were not born in this country but have been resident here before and up to the date of independence should also be eligible to become nationals, provided they:

(1) Are 18 years of age or more;
(2) Are of good character;
(3) Take the oath of allegiance and abjure allegiance to any other country or nation;
(4) Declare intention to reside here permanently;
(5) Have resided here for 8 out of the 12 years immediately preceding the date of application;
(6) Have a simple knowledge of Malay.

For the above category of aliens, the language qualification should be waived for a period of one year from date of independence for those above the age of 45 years. The MIC, however, would prefer the period to be two years, for all aliens in this category.

Renunciation of nationality
We recommend that provision should be made for nationals who are of full age and capacity to renounce their nationality by making a declaration to that effect.

Deprivation of nationality
We recommend that provision should be made for deprivation of nationality in any case where a national

(a) voluntarily acquires the nationality or citizenship of another foreign State or country; or
(b) being a woman who has acquired nationality by reason of her being a legal wife of a national, marries a man who is not a national and acquires his national status;

or, having obtained nationality by naturalisation

(c) has shown himself by act or speech to be disloyal or disaffected towards the State; or
(d) has done any voluntary act which is incompatible with his loyalty to the State; or
(e) has obtained naturalisation by fraud, false representation or concealment of a material fact.

We also recommend that no national should be deprived of his nationality for any of the reasons set out above, if as a result of such deprivation he would have no national status.

In accordance with the principles of national [? natural] justice, provision should also be made to give any national against whom an order for deprivation is proposed to be made the right to require that his case be referred first to a Committee of Inquiry.

Special position of Malays
While we accept that in independent Malaysia, all nationals should be accorded equal rights, privileges and opportunities and there must not be discrimination on grounds of race or creed, we recognize the fact that the Malays are the original sons of the soil and that they have a special position arising from this fact, and also by virtue of the treaties made between the British Government and the various sovereign Malay States. The Constitution should, therefore, provide that the Yang di-Pertuan Besar should have the special responsibility of safeguarding the special position of the Malays. In pursuance of this, the Constitution should give him powers to reserve for Malays a reasonable proportion of lands, posts in the public service, permits to engage in business or trade, where such permits are restricted and controlled by law, Government scholarships and such similar privileges accorded by the Government; but in pursuance of his further responsibility of safeguarding the legitimate interests of the other communities, the Constitution should also provide that any exercise of such powers should not in any way infringe the legitimate interests of the other communities or adversely affect or diminish the rights and opportunities at present enjoyed by them.

Definition of Malay
For the purpose of providing for the special position of Malays, it is necessary to have a definition of Malay. The privileges derived from the special position outlined above are intended only for existing nationals of Malay descent and their descendants. We therefore suggest the following as a definition:—

"A person shall be deemed to be a Malay, if
(1) He practises the religion of Islam;
(2) He habitually practises Malay Customs;
(3) He habitually speaks the Malay language; and
(4) He is a person, or the descendant of a person, who at the commencement of this Constitution
    (a) was domiciled in the Federation of Malaya, *or*
    (b) had been born in the territories comprised in the Federation of Malaya, *or*
    (c) had been born of parents one of whom had been born in the territories comprised in the Federation of Malaya."

General provisions
Language: We are *all* agreed that MALAY should be the national and official language of MALAYSIA.

We are further agreed that this recommendation should not prejudice the Alliance policy of preserving and sustaining other languages in the education system of the country.

The UMNO considers that the present system of the use of ENGLISH in the conduct of Government business should continue for a maximum period of 10 years or for such shorter period as the Legislature may decide.

The MCA and MIC, however, consider that it is not unreasonable to allow at the very least, the use of English, Kuo-Yu [Mandarin] and Tamil in Councils with the permission of the Chairman or Speakers for a minimum period of ten years and thereafter until such time as the Legislature should decide that the use of languages other than Malay is no longer necessary.

They also consider that the present system of the use of English and other languages in the conduct of Government business should be continued until the Legislature should consider it to be no longer expedient or necesssary.

Religion: The religion of Malaysia shall be Islam. The observance of this principle shall not impose any disability on non-Muslim nationals professing and practising their own religions, and shall not imply that the State is not a secular State.

Good character

For the purpose of an application for naturalisation a person shall be deemed to be of good character if he has not within the three years immediately preceding the date of his application been sentenced to death or to imprisonment, by whatever name called for a term exceeding 12 months for a criminal offence and has not received a free pardon.

Evidence of birth

In connection with the nationality provisions, we are fully conscious of the difficulties which have been met with in the past in providing acceptable evidence of birth, in cases where proper birth certificates cannot be produced.

We recommend that in the regulations and rules to be made for carrying into effect the new provisions for nationality, suitable provision should also be made for statutory declarations by the applicants to be acceptable as evidence of birth whenever proper birth certificates cannot be produced.

Amendments to the constitution

Amendments to the Constitution shall only be made if

(1) At least two-thirds of the total members of both Houses (Present and not present at the appropriate meeting) approve of the amendments

   and

(2) At least two-thirds of the State Legislatures also approve by simple majority vote such of the amendments as may affect the rights of the States.

Appendix to 425

The following fundamental rights shall be written into the Constitution:—

(a) Equality before the law;

(b) Protection of life and personal property;

(c) Freedom from arrest and detention except according to law;

(d) Protection against retrospective offences and punishment;

(e) Freedom of speech, expression[,] assembly and association;

(f) Freedom of worship, faith and belief;

(g) Freedom of acquire, hold and dispose of property;

(h) Protection against confiscation of property except according to the law and with due compensation;

(i) Protection against slavery and forced labour;

(j) Freedom to engage in trade and in the professions;

(k) Protection of children in employment of a hazardous nature;

(l) Freedom to profess, practise and propagate any religion, and to establish and maintain religious institutions;

(m) Protection of the languages and culture of all races, and of their schools and cultural institutions;

(n) Protection of the legitimate interests and rights of minorities.

427   CO 889/6, ff 281–290   27 Sept 1956
[Constitutional commission and the Alliance submission]: transcript of hearing   [Extract]

[Since fundamental rights, common nationality and the special position of the Malays were the most controversial issues considered by the commission, the verbatim transcript of their discussion is printed in this collection. For the members of the Alliance delegation, see 429, note.]

. . .

Fundamental rights

Chairman: There are two kinds of Fundamental Rights – those that are enforceable by the Court, as set out in page 10,[1] and those which are extremely varied and cannot be enforceable by the Court, but merely guides [sic] the future political parties as to what they should do. Now, you put in here quite a lot of the second class of Fundamental Rights which you really cannot guarantee. I am wondering whether you want them to be put in in such great detail or not at all? What do they do? They simply tie your hands and your successors? So far as they have any political effect; they have no legal right and, speaking entirely for myself, it seems to me to deflect the argument whether that is a good Bill or a bad Bill, it is a question of words whether it fits in with Article C of the Fundamental Rights in the Constitution which has become a matter of words, because every political party that ever was would say that they are trying to promote a sound social order and the welfare of the people. Whether it is democratic, totalitarian, right wing or left wing, they all say they are doing right. I wonder whether that gets you anywhere?

Tunku Abdul Rahman: All these can be taken out. The main thing is the Fundamental Rights. It was a suggestion from the M.I.C., and that was why it was put in.

Mr. Ramanathan: Whatever is not constitutionally enforceable, they could probably be taken out. Whatever rights should be protected by the Court would appear in the Constitution.

Chairman: Anything for the Court should be made sufficiently definite for the Court to enforce. As regards Freedom from Fear, I very much fear that no Court or Government could to that.

Dato Abdul Razak: That is true. We have given an Appendix.

---

[1] See 426, p 311.

Sir Ivor Jennings: All those listed on page 10, or do you really mean the list that is worked out in the Appendix?

Tunku Abdul Rahman: It was really put in on the suggestion of the Indian community as represented by the M.I.C. As far as U.M.N.O. and M.C.A. are concerned, it is immaterial whether it is in or not—if we have to mention other rights, then there are millions of rights.

Mr. Ramanathan: 1, 2 and 3 could probably stand—they are enforceable by the Court—and add to it the Appendix.

Chairman: I think it could be put into a form.

Tunku Abdul Rahman: We suggest five Fundamental Rights which are recognised by all countries in the world—(1) Freedom of Speech and Expression; (2) Freedom of Assembly; (3) Freedom of Worship; (4) Freedom from Want; and (5) Freedom from Fear. I think under all these heads you can put in anything you like.

Common nationality

Chairman: Let us go to Common Nationality. It looks as if there might be a little misunderstanding at the top of page 12.[2] Let me put this and see whether it is what you really mean. I think it is.

Tunku Abdul Rahman: Before you go to page 12—I have not discussed this with my colleagues yet—I think it is redundant to add under Common Nationality the words: "so that, in due course, the country can take its proper place in the comity of nations."

Chairman: That is really a preamble. Now, it is agreed that Malaysia, or Malaya, whichever it is to be, will be within the Commonwealth, and therefore from ordinary principles, all Federation citizens will be Commonwealth citizens automatically. They will have the two capacities of Federal citizens and Commonwealth citizens. In British legislation, Commonwealth citizen and British citizen are used to mean the same thing. It may be that most people have never been British subjects, and they would prefer to be called "Commonwealth citizens". That may well be so, it will be left to their option. I imagine you do not want to alter that rule under which wherever you go in the Commonwealth, you are not an alien, you are a Commonwealth citizen? That does not necessarily mean that you can get in, because in certain Commonwealth countries they keep out Commonwealth citizens—they have the power to do that. In Canada and Great Britain they never keep you out, and I presume that you wish to have a common standing within the Commonwealth; and I find it a little difficult to know just what you want to happen with regard to those who are at present. . .

Tunku Abdul Rahman: With regard to those born in Malacca and Penang, we say here "that those born in these two territories after the declaration of independence should be nationals of Malaysia". It means that they are subjects of Malaysia, but they can be citizens of the Commonwealth.

Dato Abdul Razak: There are two status. They are, at the moment, British subjects, but with the independence of Malaysia, they must declare themselves to be nationals of the new country. And then after they are new nationals, they can become Commonwealth citizens, whereas if they want to remain as British subjects, then they are not nationals of the new country.

---

[2] See *ibid*, p 312, para beginning 'In coming to this decision. . . .'

Chairman: That does not follow at all. There are many people with dual nationality and it does not cause much trouble. Of course, anybody who is a Federal citizen is, in the eyes of international law, a Malayan or a Malaysian. There is no question as to his nationality in international law. It is possible to have two nationalities both within the Commonwealth, or maybe one within and one outside. There are lots of people like that. It does not seem to cause much trouble.

Tunku Abdul Rahman: For a new nation, it will be rather troublesome later. It is all right for an established or old nation; it can make all sorts of laws. But, at this moment, our main interest is to try and bring these people towards one common nationality and that is the reason why we have provided in our terms of reference that there shall be a common loyalty, so that the loyalty of the people shall not be divided. They shall be for Malaya alone. We made no provision that those in Malacca shall be British subjects and at the same time citizens or subjects of Malaya. We will find that their interest, loyalty and everything else will be rather divided and that, we fear, will create different feelings among the people in this country. A person in Malacca will say that he is a British subject, so he can claim all the rights of a British subject, and at the same time can enjoy all the rights that a Federal citizen can have. There is bound to be a little feeling of jealousy from the side of the federal citizen who is only entitled to what is given to Federal citizens.

Chairman: I think you have made your views quite clear. Now we go on to the next point about those who are born here as aliens being free to choose on attaining the age of 21. In the ordinary way, I think the provision is that when you ask for a vote or a passport, you have to swear that you won't acknowledge or rely on any foreign citizenship which you may happen to have. Certain countries would not allow you to renounce and they will claim you after you get back after generations. You cannot effectively renounce. All you can say is that you won't do anything to rely on this—you won't take advantage of any right which may be given by these foreign countries. Can you really do more effectively than that, because that would apply and that would seem to meet the point you have in mind, I think—I am not sure.

Dato Abdul Razak: Once they have declared, that will satisfy us.

Chairman: I think, at the present moment, anybody who gets on the Voters Roll would have to sign a declaration of that kind.

Tunku Abdul Rahman: And when they apply for Passport, all they have to say is that they are citizens.

Chairman: Yes, I think that makes that clear. Now we go on to the slightly complicated—but I can well understand the reason for it—provisions on pages 13, 14 and 15[3] which you set out the "relaxations". First of all, the ordinary provisions at the bottom of page 13 which would apply to anyone who wishes to be naturalised but has not already had the requiste [sic] residence; and you go on to deal with those who already had the requiste residence—first, those who were born here, and secondly, those who were born elsewhere; and there is a slight, if not very large, difference between these two, and I appreciate how these proposals have come about and they are very clear. The first division of opinion, I think, is on page 15—about the period of relaxation of the language qualification. I presume the "one year" does not mean within a year that a man has to be registered, but that he has to apply within a year.

---

[3] See *ibid*, pp 313–314.

Mr. Ng Aik Teong: From the date of application.

Chairman: Now, two years is suggested. If it is the date of application, I wonder why it is thought that a year is too short a period in which to make application to be registered? Is there some practical reasons [sic] for it?

Mr. Ramanathan: It is only about the language test.

Chairman: Yes. If you apply within a year to be registered as a national, you do not have to take a language test if you were born in this country.

Mr. Ramanathan: We say two years.

Chairman: That is the proposal. I wonder why one year is too short to make application? Is there some practical reasons [sic] for it?

Mr. Ramanathan: Because most of them are in the estates, they might find it difficult to go through the process. It was thought that a longer period would be most satisfactory; it would be difficult to organise them.

Sir Ivor Jennings: In order to fill up forms?

Mr. Ramanathan: They have to fill up the forms and have them attested; they cannot do it in the estates.

Chairman: The practical difficulty, the other way, is that we do not want to postpone the next election too far. It has got to be postponed until you get your new Register and the rest of it. If it is two years, it will be rather difficult.

Mr. Ramanathan: The two years only for exemption from language test; of course there are other qualifications which they will have to satisfy. But if they apply in two years, there would not be a test. Another difficulty is that there will be thousands of applicants and all of them have to go through the test.

Chairman: That is all right, that will take a long time.

Mr. Ramanathan: They will have to come from the estates twice—once for the application, and another time for the test.

Mr. Ng Aik Teong: Actually, my lord, the practical difficulty, especially with regard to the Indians, as I understand it from certain District Officers, is that most of them are estate tappers. Firstly, they are illiterates, and secondly, they may work in an estate and after a year or so, they may join another estate. To apply, they must get two referees and they have to be Federal citizens. Very often, these estates tappers are only known to the Manager of the estate who is a European, who is himself not a Federal citizen, and therefore he cannot be a referee. The other person who can do so is the Conductor in the estate. He, being an Indian, is also himself not a Federal citizen and so cannot be a referee. So there is great difficulty in obtaining referees for these Indian tappers.

Chairman: That may take time.

Mr. Ng Aik Teong: That is the practical difficulty.

Chairman: You mean that in your application you have to supply somebody who can say, for instance, that you have resided here for 5 out of the last 7 years?

Mr. Ng Aik Teong: Yes, and also that he is of good character.

Tunku Abdul Rahman: The point is to overcome that difficulty. If 2 years is not enough, then 20 years even may not be enough.

Justice B. Malik: 2 is better than 1.

Tunku Abdul Rahman: If the suggestion is 2, then the proposal from the M.I.C. should be 4!

Mr. Ramanathan: With regard to the hurdle of the language test they can escape, but the other difficulties will be there.

Justice B. Malik: Is there any serious objection to two years?

Tunku Abdul Rahman: We feel, politically, it is untenable because the objection is very strong. If a real effort is made to be citizens of this country, it can be made very quickly indeed. We have gone through all that. When the proposal was made that the electors should be registered within such and such a time, efforts were made from our side, the U.M.N.O. and the M.C.A., to go all out and try to get people registered in a short time. If a real effort or attempt is not made by responsible Indian leaders, it will go on for five years. We are in the same party. In the case of M.C.A., the U.M.N.O. helped. If you really want to be registered it can be done within a year. I think it is not necessary to go to two years as most of the Indian labourers in this country want to go back; if they can, they would like to go back.

Mr. Ramanathan: The labourers are illiterate and they do not know the language.

Chairman: Is it possible to have an application which would comply with this and then to be followed up later, if there is any difficulty, by the man who vouches for the residence and the rest of it. Is it feasible to have a sworn application within a year stating all these things, and for the other evidence to be provided later? Is it feasible?

Tunku Abdul Rahman: That can be done. The main thing is to get them registered.

Chairman: They must send in their application within a year—I wonder whether that would cut across anything—but if for any reason he cannot get those people to vouch for the application, he can send that along later. Would that do? The man must send in within a year.

Tunku Abdul Rahman: That would do. The intention is to get as many people as possible living in this country to be nationals. A year is long enough.

Justice B. Malik: To make up their minds?

Tunku Abdul Rahman: Yes.

Chairman: The practical difficulty is to get two Federal citizens who could vouch regarding residence. But if they can be got later, that would seem to meet the objection.

Tunku Abdul Rahman: Yes, I think so.

Chairman: I do not think that is really going to be very difficult. I fully realise the objection to too long a period, but I do not think there is any other matter of difficulty on that.

Committee of inquiry

Chairman: Page 16,[4] Committee of Inquiry. You used the word "disloyal or disaffected" in the middle of the page, and you set up a Committee of Inquiry to enquire into a very vague charge. Is it necessary to put it quite as vague as that, or would it be better to go to the Court? I can see the possibility of abuse. It is not likely to happen but there is a possibility.

Tunku Abdul Rahman: Yes, for want of better arrangement.

Chairman: Now we come to the special position of the Malays. The point which I would like to have. . .

Dato Abdul Razak: On the question of the special position of the Malays, there is added a provision for review, and we suggested 15 years after the declaration of independence.

---

[4] See *ibid*, pp 314.

Chairman: This "special reponsibility": I take it you do not mean that the Yang di-Pertuan Besar would have that responsibility personally, but that he would act as a constitutional monarch and the responsibility would really be on the Prime Minister. Well, now, does this mean that the Prime Minister would override the States in this matter? The Prime Minister might say: "Well, I think it is time that some alteration was made" and the State may say: "No, it is not." Now, is this to be a Federal responsibility? Take, for example, Kelantan. We are told that the whole State of Kelantan, with very small exception, is not only a Malay Reservation but it is reserved for Kelantan Malays, and we are told that the reason is that they are so overcrowded that they owe their duty first to their own people to give them any land that is available. I am not saying whether that is a good or a bad thing, but that is the position. Now, is the new Prime Minister under this proposal to be able to say to the people in Kelantan: "This is a Federal responsibility"; and I think you are proposing that this should be altered? Is that the proposal?

Dato Abdul Razak: He will have Federal responsibility in Federal matters.

Justice A. Hamid: Who will protect them in regard to State matters?

Dato Abdul Razak: It will be the State.

Justice A. Hamid: It should be made clear—the Ruler in State matters and the Yang di-Pertuan Besar in Federal matters.

Chairman: That will be clear with regard to Malay reservation of land. Would you leave it as partly a State matter?

Dato Abdul Razak: It has to be State because land is a State matter.

Chairman: It may not be easy because the Prime Minister would say: "Now, I think there is too much Malay reservation in one State and not enough in another, and they must be brought into line." That would be difficult.

Dato Abdul Razak: It would be difficult.

Chairman: But you would be prepared to leave that subject to the provision that an extension of the privilege is not to be increased substantially because you say at the end, the privilege "should not in any way infringe the legitimate interests of the other communities". That would mean that you must not have more of these privileges than you have at present, I suppose.

Dato Abdul Razak: We do not want to reduce the legitimate interests of the others. What we have in mind is not to give Malay special rights by taking away the legitimate rights of other people.

Chairman: I think what you mean here—the Malays have certain rights at this moment, and of course every additional privilege is, to some extent, prejudicing the others because it is limiting the amount of land or the number of jobs they could get and so on; and I think what you have in mind was that there should be no substantial increase in the present rights and privileges but that they should gradually be diminished and that it should be the responsibility of the Prime Minister, in Federal matters, to regulate the way in which it should be diminished?

Dato Abdul Razak: In certain cases it should be increased—in business or trade the Malays have very few permits, and they should be given more, but by giving more we should not take away from what the non-Malays now have. That is the idea.

Tunku Abdul Rahman: The intention is to look from the Federal angle those main rights which the Federation has so far reserved for the Malays and we just maintain that without encroaching upon the States—the rights of the States—but in regard to various other things, I suppose in certain cases where it has really brought a great deal of hardship, it is provided—I see in the memorandum presented by the Rulers to the Commission—I think that it is mentioned in the Rulers' memorandum, page 39 (4). They have a provision for their own States and as land policy is a State matter, we do not want to encroach upon their authority; but I suppose it will be the duty of this Government to see that no undue hardship should be suffered by any particular people who are citizens of this country. Therefore when we talk of Malay rights here, it is no more than to say what is being done in the Federation alone. We do not actually refer to the States.

Chairman: I follow that. You are leaving the Malay reservation of land as a State subject really.

Tunku Abdul Rahman: Yes.

Chairman: And those other matters—education, the Public Service, trade and so on, and then you say that the Prime Minister—in effect, of course the new parliament—will be the master of that. Are you putting in any period for compulsory review or are you just leaving it at large?

Tunku Abdul Rahman: The suggestion is that there should be a review every 15 years.

Chairman: That would not mean, I suppose, that it was wrong to do anything before that?

Tunku Abdul Rahman: No. The present system of doing it is this: for instance, there is a condition that there should be three Malays appointed to every one non-Malay, but that particular rule has been relaxed from time to time. Even in the case of bursaries in the University, this year, they are all awarded to non-Malays. We stated that there should be three Malays to one non-Malay, but all the twelve appointed were non-Malays. It is the same with appointments to the Customs Service because we could not get enough Malay recruits. We therefore asked the Rulers to relax to allow non-Malays to be taken into the Service when we find that there are not enough Malays to fill the posts and in all cases it has been granted. That is a matter for departmental working out, but the main thing is that we say here under general terms of the special position of the Malays that it should be reviewed every 15 years, but that does not prevent the government of the day from relaxing the rule from time to time.

Chairman: I suppose 15 years' review would include both the States and the Federation—both Malay reservation of land and the matters for which the Federation is responsible.

Tunku Abdul Rahman: Yes. . . .

428   CO 1030/133, no 11   28 Sept 1956
[Constitutional commission]: letter from Sir D Watherston to Sir J Martin on his discussion with Lord Reid about procedure

I sent you on 21st September an interim reply to your letter FED 36/591/01 of the 10th December [sic: September] about the timing and handling of the report of the Constitutional Commission. I was able to see Lord Reid yesterday afternoon and to discuss procedure with him.

I emphasised the importance that you attached to the Commission sending the report in the first instance to the Secretary of State, but I found Lord Reid was quite uncompromising on this point. I found that he had discussed it with the members of the Commission and that the Asian members in particular—Malik especially—had expressed the view that they would not have accepted appointment to the Commission if they had thought that it was on any other terms than a joint request by Her Majesty The Queen and Their Highnesses the Rulers. Admittedly the invitation to serve on the Commission had come from the Secretary of State, but in making the offer he was specifically acting on behalf of The Queen and the Rulers.

I was unable to move Lord Reid at all on this point and he went on to say that he wished to make arrangements for printing either in Rome or in Geneva. He thought it was important that the copies on sale should not have been printed by H.M. Stationery Office. He also thought that it was more convenient for everybody including the Commission itself to have the report printed—provided adequate security arrangements could be made—than merely to have it cyclostyled. I pointed out that sooner or late H.M.G. would almost certainly wish to publish the report as a White Paper and equally we in Malaya would wish to publish it as a Legislative Council paper, so that both H.M.S.O. and the Printing Department here would have to print the report at some stage. I think he saw the force of this although he did not before the end of the interview say anything to detract from his earlier stand that printing should be arranged by the Commission itself.

It must be taken, therefore, that the Commission's present considered intention is to deliver its report simultaneously to the Secretary of State (for Her Majesty The Queen) and to the Keeper of the Rulers' Seal (for Their Highnesses the Rulers). This is most unfortunate, and Lord Reid himself recognises that it will be next to impossible to prevent leakage for more than a very short period after the report has reached the Rulers. He expressed the view during our discussion that for the Secretary of State to have the report first and presumably to prepare his own proposals for submission to the Rulers before the Rulers themselves had had time to study the report would be liable to lead to the gravest suspicion—he mentioned the word "MacMichaelism".[1] If, therefore, you wish to take the matter any further it can I think only be done by direct approach to Lord Reid by the Secretary of State himself, but I am afraid that it would meet with a rebuff.

During the course of our discussion Lord Reid did disclose, more than he has done before, the Commission's line of thought on one or two important matters. They had yesterday received the Alliance's memorandum, a copy of which is being sent to you separately, and a delegation from the Alliance itself.[2] On the State Constitutions they feel that it will be necessary to set out a blueprint of the recommended line of development which could be introduced at different times in different States. On the Settlements they are disposed to favour a head of the Settlement nominated by the Head of State on the advice of the Settlement Government without the Queen having any share in that nomination. They are not in favour of an elected President of each Settlement (or whatever other title might be appropriate).

On nationality and citizenship, in view of the opposition both from the Rulers and from the Alliance to retention by the present inhabitants of the Settlements of their citizenship of the U.K. and Colonies in addition to the new Federal citizenship or

[1] This is a reference to Sir Harold MacMichael's mission to the Malay rulers in Oct–Dec 1945.
[2] See 426, 427, 429.

nationality, the Commission is not disposed to recommend it. Their view is that the new Federal citizenship or nationality will carry with it (in common with other Commonwealth countries) the status of Commonwealth citizenship, i.e. that of a British subject, the expressions having identical meanings. The Commission do not therefore see any particular point, other than possibly a sentimental one, in permitting persons to retain their citizenship of the U.K. and Colonies.

I am sending a copy of this letter to MacGillivray.

429   CO 889/6, ff 241–247   9 Oct 1956
'Federation of Malaya constitutional commission: hearing of the Alliance Party': summary record (no CC 2167) of the hearing in Kuala Lumpur on 27 Sept

[The Alliance delegation consisted of Tunku Abdul Rahman, Dato Abdul Razak, V T Sambanthan, Mohamed Khir Johari, Yong Pung How, Ng Ek Teong, K Ramanathan and Senu Abdul Rahman. All five commissioners were present. Discussion followed points raised in the Alliance memorandum (see 426).]

On behalf of the Commission, Lord Reid welcomed the Alliance delegation and said that they were extremely glad to have from a body commanding so much public support such a full and helpful memorandum. The Alliance had offered to elucidate any points in the memorandum on which the Commission might like further explanation, and the Commission were glad to avail themselves of that offer.

Before turning to the memorandum, the Chairman referred to the question of publication. He said that when the Commission came to write their report they would, he thought, wish to refer to the Alliance proposals and either to give their reasons for accepting them, or, if they thought that in some way they would prefer to recommend a modification on any point, their reasons for suggesting such a modification. The Chief Minister said that it had already been agreed to publish the memorandum on September 28.

Head of state
The Chairman referred to the Alliance proposal that when the new Yang di-Pertuan Besar was appointed there should also be appointed at the same time a successor. Others seemed to think that it would be better to have a deputy so that when the term of office of the first Head of State came to an end there would be a fresh appointment and not merely a succession. Dato Abdul Razak said that it did not matter whether the person concerned was described as a deputy or as a successor. What was required was someone who could replace the Yang di-Pertuan Besar at short notice.

Mr. Hamid asked what were the implications of the sentence at the top of page 2 "It is necessary for Her Majesty the Queen to cede her rights over Penang and Malacca and for Their Highnesses the Rulers to waive some of their rights".[1] After discussion, the Alliance representatives made it clear that in their view this question was bound up with the necessity for the Federation to assume sovereignty. The

---

[1] See 426, p 307.

Chairman thought that this matter involved the question of residuary powers. It was not usual to have sovereigns as units of a Federation, but it was no doubt possible for the Rulers to be sovereigns within their own sphere and for the Federation to be sovereign within its sphere.

Name of the new state

The Chairman said that it was difficult for the Commission to make recommendations regarding the name of the new State as they were bound by their terms of reference which referred to the "Federation of Malaya". He thought that before the new Constitution was finally agreed the question of a name could be decided locally.

Heads of the settlements

The Chairman said that he wished to clarify the proposals in regard to the appointment of Heads of the Settlements. He assumed that the Constitutional Head of a Settlement would act directly on the advice of the Chief Minister of the Settlement in such matters on which the Settlement had powers under the Constitution, and that it would not be a question of referring to Kuala Lumpur. Dato Abdul Razak said the Alliance were thinking on the lines of the Queen and the Governor-General of the Dominions. At present there was a Resident Commissioner in each Settlement and he was the representative of the High Commissioner. He thought that constitutionally the Executive Council would advise the Ruler and that the Ruler would delegate his powers to the representative. After further discussion, however, the Alliance representatives agreed that, although the Yang di-Pertuan Besar would be the Head of the Settlements, he would appoint his representatives there who would exercise the same power as the Sultans in the States and who would give assent to Settlement legislation. They thought that the representatives should be appointed for periods of five years at a time.

Conference of rulers

The Alliance representatives made it clear that in their view the Conference of Rulers should be able to discuss matters concerning the Muslim religion and Malay custom, and to appoint the Yang di-Pertuan Besar but that the Conference should not have any political or executive functions. The Chief Minister wondered whether the question of the removal of the Yang di-Pertuan Besar should be a matter for the Legislature or whether it should be left entirely to the Conference of Rulers. The Chairman replied that this was a matter which the Commission would go into in some detail.

The legislature

The Chairman remarked that the report of the Commission would be written using English terms. The question of suitable Malay names for the Legislative Houses would not arise until the report came to be translated into Malay. Mr. Hamid said that it would be convenient for the Government at that stage to set up a nomenclature committee. The Chief Minister agreed.

Upper house

Referring to the proposals for the Upper House, the Chairman said that it had been represented to the Commission from some quarters that any nominated members should be in the minority, whereas the Alliance were now proposing that the number of elected members should be equal to the number of nominated members. As the nominated members would be slected [sic] by the Government he wondered why the Alliance attached importance to this.

Dato Abdul Razak replied that the intention was to prevent the States having too much say. The term of office in the Upper House would be for five years and the nominees might have to be changed when a new Government came into office. The expression "those who reflect the national pattern of life in the country, including racial minorities" was intended to include racial minorities, representatives of important commercial interests and elder statesmen or prominent people appointed in their own right.

Mr. Ng Ek Teong said that any schedule of interests to be represented by nominated members should be avoided to leave the widest scope for appointments. No one who was not a citizen of the Federation should be appointed, particularly as the Upper House would be able to initiate legislation. This principle should be followed even in the initial stages.

The discussion then turned to the question of whether the Upper House should represent the sovereignty of the States. On the one hand, as the President of the Chamber would be nominated by the Government it would appear that the elected State representatives would be in a minority. On the other hand, if one or two of the nominated members were to support the States' representatives in the Council then Federal legislation, excepting money bills, could be delayed for twelve months. Dato Abdul Razak said that both of these points had been taken into account in making the proposals.

Sir William McKell observed that since the proposal was that the representatives of the States should be members of the Councils of State this was not the same as direct representation of the people in the States. Mr. Ng Ek Teong thought it unlikely that legislation would be delayed because in most cases the members of the Councils of State sent to the Upper House would be members of the party with a majority in the Lower House. Sir William McKell asked to whom those members would owe loyalty—to the States or to the Federation? The Chief Minister replied that at the moment the Alliance controlled all Councils of State and loyalty was to the party. The situation might change in the future but the Alliance proposal was made to ensure that there would be a strong central Government.

After further discussion the Alliance representatives agreed that on page 5, line 5,[2] of their memorandum the words "from amongst themselves" could be deleted. The effect of this amendment would be to permit Councils of State to elect members to the Upper House who were not necessarily members of the Councils of State, thus widening the choice. The Chief Minister said, however, that they did not wish to prohibit simultaneous membership of both houses because of the shortage, especially in the smaller States, of suitable candidates. If at a later stage it was desired to change this practice it could be done by legislation.

The Alliance representatives agreed that special interests should be permitted to continue the practice of submitting names for approval by the Head of State.

The Chief Minister said that both houses should have the same term of office and should go out of office together.

---

[2] See *ibid*, p 309.

Regarding the appointment of a President of the Upper House and the appointment of a Speaker of the Lower House, Dato Abdul Razak said that the President of the Upper House should, in the initial stages at least, be appointed by the Head of State. In the Lower House, because of the difficulty of obtaining someone with the necessary experience, it would be desirable to allow for the appointment of a Speaker for at least one term of office.

The lower house

Dato Abdul Razak said that the Alliance proposal was that the membership of the Lower House should be fully elected. There should be no nominated members. Minorities and special interests would be represented in the Upper House. Mr. Malik pointed out that this differed from the situation in India. Dato Abdul Razak said that those interests were protected because the Upper House was to be allowed to initiate legislation.

It was agreed that the provision whereby in the event of national crisis the Yang di-Pertuan Besar could extend the life of Parliament required very careful consideration to prevent a party which had lost the confidence of the people extending its life in Parliament.

The executive

In reply to a question by Mr. Malik, the Chief Minister said that the Cabinet would comprise members of either or both of the houses and that they would have a right of audience in both houses. Ministers would, of course, be appointed from among the members of the houses. The "Council of Ministers" should be amended to read "The Cabinet".

The judiciary

Dato Abdul Razak amplified the last paragraph on page 6[3] of the Alliance memorandum and said that the phrase "on all matters" should be inserted after "right of ultimate appeal".

In explanation of the Alliance proposal that the right of ultimate appeal should be to a "body of law councillors", Mr. Ng Ek Teong said that it was hoped that some arrangement could be made whereby the advice of the Privy Council could be obtained. He agreed that the Privy Councillors could not be appointed by the Yang di-Pertuan Besar, but thought that the latter might be advised by the Privy Council. It was the intention that the Supreme Court should have power to decide the constitutional validity of all laws and regulations, whether Federal or State.

The Chairman said that if arrangements were being made for the establishment of a Judicial Service Commission, as well as other Service Commissions, it was of some importance that the Commission, in making their recommendations, should know what legislation the Government contemplated. Dato Abdul Razak said that the Government's proposals for legislation would be made known to the Commission. At the London Conference it was agreed that there should be provision for the appointment of a Public Service Commission, a Judicial Service Commission and a Police Service Commission.

---

[3] See *ibid*, p 310.

Division of powers

The Chairman said that the Alliance proposals in sub-paragraph (3) and (4) on page 7[4] advocated the continuance of the system whereby on certain subjects, upon which it had power to legislate, the Federal Government could delegate executive power to the States. This system might not be effective if the political party in a State was in opposition to the party in power in the Federal Government. Dato Abdul Razak said that powers should be clearly divided but that on this whole question the Alliance was subject to advice by the Commission.

The Alliance did not wish to be compelled to make use of consultative machinery except in the case of finance as stipulated in the terms of reference.

Finance

The Chief Minister agreed that the States should be made as financially autonomous as was reasonably practicable and that it might be necessary to go further than the Alliance proposal on page 9[5] of the memorandum.

Land

Dato Abdul Razak agreed that when land was required for federal purposes the Federal Government wished to pay the necessary fees and to receive a title. When the land in question was no longer needed for federal purposes there was no objection to its reverting to the State provided that appropriate payment was made by the State. Payment would be by negotiation.

The Chief Minister said that these were future intentions; it was not proposed to pay for land already in use for federal purposes as this would be too expensive. Dato Abdul Razak said that only where a title was given would payment be made.

State governments

The Chief Minister said that although the aim was to have fully elected Councils of State, there should be elasticity to permit the States to make the change gradually and in accordance with conditions. In the interim, however, financial autonomy should be given to the States. The safeguard would be to have an elected majority in the Councils of State. The Mentri Besar at this stage would not necessarily be an elected member. Even when the Councils were fully elected, provision should be made for an outsider to be appointed Mentri Besar with the concurrence of the Councils of State concerned. He would be obliged to resign if the Councils of State passed a vote of no confidence in him.

The Chairman asked whether the Mentri Besar would hold office at the pleasure of the Ruler or of the Council of State. Dato Abdul Razak said that he must hold office at the pleasure of the Ruler. Elucidating their proposals for this, the Alliance representatives agreed that before the next State Elections provision would have to be made for an elected majority in the Councils of State and for the Mentri Besar to be approved by those majorities. The Rulers would then have to make the necessary alterations to their State Constitutions to provide for fully elected Councils at an early date. The Rulers should also withdraw gradually from the Executive Council.

The Chief Minister thought that special interests should be represented in the Councils of State.

---

[4] See *ibid*, p 310.   [5] See *ibid*, p 311.

Fundamental rights

The Chairman pointed out that two kinds of Fundamental Rights were mentioned—those enforceable by a court and those which could never be enforced by a court. To include Fundamental Rights of the latter category might cause certain political difficulties. The Alliance representatives proposed that those Fundamental Rights which could not be enforced by the courts should be omitted.

Common nationality

The Chairman explained that if Malaya were to be a member of the Commonwealth, all Federation citizens would at the same time be Commonwealth citizens under United Kingdom legislation. The term "Commonwealth citizen" meant the same as "British subject". The advantage of being a Commonwealth citizen was that the person concerned was not an alien in any part of the Commonwealth.

The Chief Minister said that those born in the Settlements after independence would be citizens of the Federation but could also be Commonwealth citizens. Dato Abdul Razak thought that after independence British subjects must declare themselves to be Malayan nationals and lose their status as British subjects.

The Chairman pointed out that dual nationality had many precedents in International Law.

The Chief Minister said that the object was to unite the people of Malaya with one common nationality. It was undesirable that the people of the Settlements could be in a position to claim special rights above those accorded to Federal citizens.

The Chairman pointed out that with regard to aliens becoming citizens of the Federation there were difficulties in asking them to renounce their foreign citizenship. They could be asked to declare that they would not exercise any rights conferred upon them by their foreign citizenship. Dato Abdul Razak agreed that such a declaration would be satisfactory.

In reply to a question, the Alliance representatives said that in stipulating the period during which the language tests would be relaxed the intention of their proposal was that the application for citizenship should be made within the period. The M.I.C. representatives said that they wished the stipulated period to be two years instead of one because of the practical difficulties involved for estate labourers who had great difficulty in finding referees.

The Chief Minister said that it was necessary to create citizens as quickly as possible and that this would depend upon the efforts of the leaders, otherwise registration would drag on for years. He thought that there would even be no objection to incomplete applications being accepted for the purpose of immunity from language test, provided they were submitted within the stipulated period.

Deprivation of nationality

The Chairman suggested that to deprive someone of citizenship who had shown himself to be "disloyal or disaffected" was vague unless it were intended that the matter should be decided by a court, and the Chief Minister agreed.

Special position of the Malays

Dato Abdul Razak said the Alliance wished to add a proviso to their memorandum that the position should be reviewed 15 years after independence. He agreed that the Yang di-Pertuan Besar would have a constitutional, not personal, responsibility in this matter and that the same would be true of the Rulers in their States with regard to matters affecting the States, such as Malay reservations. Continuing, he said that it was not the intention generally that there should be any substantial increase in the present rights and privileges of Malays, but that, in certain cases, they should be increased; e.g., in business and trade where the Malays now had very few permits. It was however important that the legitimate rights of other communities would not be affected.

The Chief Minister said that although it was intended to review the position after 15 years, this would not mean that nothing could be done before then. Even now where insufficient Malays possessing the necessary qualifications were available, the quota system of entry into the Government service was relaxed. At the end of the 15 years it was intended that both Malay reservations and the matters for which the Federation were responsible would be reviewed.

Multi-lingualism
The Chief Minister said that it was the intention that every speech should be translated sentence by sentence into the National language. Mr. Yong Pung How added that it was not the intention to translate into other languages. The Chief Minister considered that the Chinese or Indian who felt that he must use his own mother tongue to express himself in the Council would not necessarily be unable to understand the proceedings in Malay.

A discussion ensued as to the practicability of using Kwok Ue [Mandarin] as a language which would be commonly understood by Chinese of all tribes. It seemed that most of the Chinese population had a fair knowledge of Kwok Ue. Mr. Malik said that in India if the Speaker was satisfied that a man could not adequately express himself in English or Hindi, he might be given permission to speak in his own mother tongue. Mr. Ng Ek Teong said that this would be an acceptable procedure.

Religion
The Chairman said that under this heading there was a discrepancy between the proposal on page 19[6] which stated that there should be no disability on non-Muslims professing and practising their own religions and the appendix which advocated freedom to profess, practise and propagate any religion. The Alliance representatives agreed that the proposal in the appendix should be followed.

Amendment of the constitution
The Chairman observed that the proposals made amendment of the Constitution difficult. The Alliance representatives agreed but thought this necessary.

Subjects of the ruler
The Chief Minister said that there was no objection to the Rulers describing Federal citizens resident in their States as their subjects. Dato Abdul Razak thought that a subject could obtain certain residential rights. Mr. Malik suggested that it would be difficult to reconcile those with the desire for common nationality. Mr. Hamid pointed out that on page 11 the Alliance said that "It is essential to have a Nationality Law which provides for a common nationality, *to the exclusion of all others*".

---

[6] See *ibid*, p 316.

The Alliance government
The Chief Minister said that during the transitional period after independence it would be necessary that his Government should continue as a caretaker Government. It would be convenient for this arrangement to last until the next elections in 1959. This arrangement need not necessarily be repeated in the States, however.

State constitutions
The Chief Minister asked whether the Commission would make recommendations with regard to the State Constitutions. The Chairman said that the Commission would be making recommendations, but whether these would be accepted or whether they should come into effect at once or after an interval was another matter. The Chief Minister thought that delay would be necessary in introducing fully elected Councils of State but not in other matters.

Conclusion
Mr. Ng Ek Teong said that the Alliance wished the new Constitution to be as flexible as possible to encourage the growth of conventions.
    The hearing ended at 12.45 p.m.

430 CO 1030/132, no 50   9 Oct 1956
[Constitutional commission]: letter from Mr Lennox-Boyd to Lord Reid on the State constitutions

> [The CO wished the commission to make recommendations for the state constitutions and to safeguard the position of the 'Queen's Chinese' (or British citizens) in the Settlements. To attempt the first, however, would risk confrontation with the Malay rulers who resisted Reid's interference in state matters, while the second would alienate UMNO which objected to dual nationality. In pursuing these objectives Lennox-Boyd tried not to antagonise either party.]

I have now had a chance to get MacGillivray's views on the extent to which the Commission should deal with the State constitutions, about which you wrote to me on the 11th September. I have also now seen the memorandum by the Rulers to which you referred and which I had not received when I wrote to you on the 27th September.
    On further consideration I do not think that there is any difference between the U.K. Government and the Rulers on this matter and I can accept the statement in paragraph 3 of the Rulers' memorandum.[1] I feel sure that, in making recommendations for the Federal constitution, the Commission will find it necessary and desirable to recommend in general terms the form of the various State constitutions without going into great detail. On some matters however you may be obliged to be specific. For example, when you make recommendations about the manner in which members of the Second Chamber in the Federal Legislature are to be selected or nominated, you will probably find it necessary to make specific recommendations

---

[1] Para 3 of 'Proposals of their highnesses the rulers made to the constitutional commission' contains a general statement favouring constitutional advance, whereas para 6 deals specifically with state constitutions (see CO 889/8/3, nos 22A, 25A and 50).

about the body or authority in the State which is to perform this function and the manner in which it should perform it. There may well be other matters affecting the State constitutions on which the Commission will wish to make comparatively detailed recommendations.

I take this opportunity to confirm your assumption that the Commission should deal in detail with the Settlement constitutions and make recommendations for new constitutions to replace the present ones.

As you know, the present relationship between the two Settlements and the Crown naturally leads the U.K. Government to pay particular regard to future arrangements for the Settlements and to have a special concern for the status and welfare of their inhabitants in the new independent Federation. Numerous representations I have been receiving from the "Queen's Chinese" all emphasise the special responsibility they regard H.M.G. as holding in respect of the Settlements. It would therefore be of great assistance to me if you felt it possible later in the year to let the Tunku and myself have some advance indication of what the Commission are likely to recommend about the Settlements. We should be especially interested to know your thoughts about the future citizenship of those inhabitants of the Settlements who are at present citizens of the U.K. and colonies and who either enjoy citizenship of the Federation or have the opportunity for doing so if they so wish; and also about arrangements for the appointment and status of the Head of the Government in the Settlements. As I mentioned in a previous letter, it would be particularly valuable if I were in a position to discuss your likely recommendations on these points with the Chief Minister when he comes to London at the end of December. I realise how hard-pressed you are with the vast burden of work and the many problems which face the Commission but I do very much hope you will be able to help in this way. An opportunity of preliminary discussion with the Tunku on these points may well be of crucial importance in preparing the way for the smooth and uncontentious acceptance of the Report of the Commission when the time comes for it to be published.

431   DEFE 7/501, no 33/1   2 Nov 1956

'Malayan defence agreement': CO record of a meeting chaired by Mr Lennox-Boyd and attended by Commonwealth representatives

[Extract]

[Present: Lennox-Boyd, R G Casey (minister for external affairs, Australia), Sir Clifton Webb (high commissioner for New Zealand), L R McIntyre (Australian High Commission), H G Lang (NZ High Commission), R C Chilver (Ministry of Defence), E Melville (CO), G W StJ Chadwick (CRO), R C Ormerod (CRO) and J D Hennings (CO, secretary). The meeting was cut short by events, as Lennox-Boyd put it probably in a reference to the Suez crisis, 'beyond my control'.]

1. *The Secretary of State* said that the major item of substance in the Defence Agreement which was still unagreed was Article VI.[1] The United Kingdom recognised that both Australia and New Zealand were vitally interested in obtaining a satisfactory formula for this clause which would ensure that the Agreement was an

---

[1] See 408, appendix A, and 417, paras 6–10.

effective instrument and would permit us effectively to discharge our Commonwealth and international obligations. The original United Kingdom proposal had provided for automatic action without reference to the Malayans in the event both of an armed attack or other threat to the preservation of peace, but the Malayans had rejected this on the ground that it would infringe their sovereignty. Had this proposal been accepted, it would in fact have done this and it would have accorded us rights which we had unequivocally denied the Americans when they set up bases in this country, for those bases cannot be activated without our consultation and agreement. The Malayans had originally suggested that all action should be dependent upon consultation with them, but in discussions in the Working Party they had been brought to realise that immediate action would be needed to meet an attack if Malaya were to be defended effectively; they had therefore indicated that they could accept a compromise under which the United Kingdom could act forthwith to counter an attack, but would consult them before acting in the event of a threat. This formula would mean that the United Kingdom could take immediate action in the event of an attack on any British territory. An attack on any other country or the threat of such an attack would be regarded as a threat to the preservation of peace in the area, and if the United Kingdom wished to take action in support of SEATO to meet it she would first have to consult the Malayans. This compromise however would pledge the Federation to the fullest cooperation with the United Kingdom, and any difficulties which might now been [sic] seen would disappear if the Federation herself joined SEATO. The Chief Minister had said that he had no doubt that the Federation would join SEATO after independence if it could clearly be seen that she had reached this decision of her own freewill, but the prospects of this would clearly be enhanced if it could be shown that the defence agreement in no way infringed Malayan sovereignty. The United Kingdom was anxious to conclude the agreement as quickely [sic] as possible in order to avoid the possibility that the Malayans might seek to make their acceptance of the compromise dependent upon concessions to them by the United Kingdom in other fields. There was also a risk that if we held out for our original version, the Malayans might seek to reopen negotiations on Articles I and III to our disadvantage. The United Kingdom had therefore come to the conclusion that, when discussions on Article VI were reopened in the Working Party, we should propose the acceptance of the compromise version.

2. *Mr. Casey* said that he understood that these United Kingdom views had been communicated to the Australian Government. He agreed that the compromise offered the best we could reasonably hope for, and he undertook to recommend it to his Government. He asked that he might be given a note setting out in summary form the rights which the compromise version would accord the United Kingdom in different situations, and it was agreed that this should be provided.[2]

3. *Sir Clifton Webb* confirmed that the New Zealand Government had agreed that the compromise should be accepted.

4. *Mr. Chilver* said that it was important that we should not lose sight of our main objective which was to secure in the Federation a firm, cooperative and realistic ally and to ensure that the defence agreement endured as a practical and effective instrument for as long as possible. The best hope for this lay in making an agreement

---

[2] See 432.

which was acceptable to Malaya and which clearly did not infringe her sovereignty.
. . .

432 DEFE 7/501, No 33/2   2 Nov 1956

[Malayan defence agreement]: note by Mr Lennox-Boyd for Mr Casey
on UK rights under the proposed agreement

The United Kingdom's rights under the Malayan Defence Agreement if she accepted
Sir Robert Scott's compromise on Article VI are as follows:—

(i)   the U.K. is permitted by Article III[1] to maintain forces (including a
Commonwealth Strategic Reserve) in the Federation for the purpose of affording
the Federation such assistance as she may require for her external defence (Article
I) and for the fulfilment of Commonwealth and international obligations (i.e.
ANZAM and SEATO).
(ii) Any action which the U.K. may wish to take (e.g. reinforcing those forces or
committing them to military operations) in furtherance of the purposes of Article
III would have to be taken in conformity with the provisions of Article VI;
(iii) This means:—

(a) if an armed attack is made against the territories or forces either of the
Federation of Malaya or the United Kingdom, the U.K. may take action
automatically without consulting the Federation first. The application of this
Article is therefore not confined to an armed attack on the Federation alone, but
could be invoked if an attack were made on any U.K. territory;
(b) if there is a threat of such an armed attack against the territories or forces
of either Federation of Malaya or the United Kingdom (as defined in (a) above),
the United Kingdom can take action to counter that threat after consulting the
Federation Government;
(c) similarly, the United Kingdom can take action to counter a threat to the
preservation of peace (e.g. it can act in support of ANZAM or SEATO) after
consulting the Federation.

The reasons which have led the U.K. to conclude that an agreement embodying
these terms would give all that can reasonably be hoped for are:—

(a) the Malayans are surpremely [sic] concerned to ensure that their sovereignty
is in no way infringed by any of the provisions of the Defence Agreement;
(b) the version of Article VI which the U.K. originally proposed would have
infringed that sovereignty since it would have enabled the U.K. to take whatever
action she thought necessary without consulting the Malayans, and would have
given her freedom of action which she has sought from no other independent
nation and which she has herself granted none. It would have been an analogy to
what the U.K. has asked of the Malayans if the U.S.A. had asked the U.K. to agree
that their strategic bombers stations [sic] in this country could take off on
bombing missions from British bases whenever the Americans judged it necessary

---

[1] For the original draft see 408, appendix A.

without first consulting H.M.G.; if such a request had been made the British Parliament and people could not be expected for one moment to have accepted it.

(c) The U.K. position in Malaya after independence will depend upon the goodwill of the Federation Government, and any action which the U.K. might take against the wishes of that Government whether or not it was countenanced explicitly or implicitly by the Agreement would certainly contravene the conception of full political independence which is being granted the Federation;

(d) an unfriendly government would have no difficulty in repudiating any agreement in such terms, but a friendly government could be expected to acquiesce or co-operate in any action taken by the U.K. in an emergency even though there might be little or no time for effective consultation; indeed, it would probably welcome such measures of reinforcement as H.M.G. might wish to take in the light of the military situation in the area. In this context, it is worth remembering that the Chief Minister has explicitly pointed out that the compromise text would pledge the Federation to the fullest co-operation with the United Kingdom in meeting any situation effectively;

(e) there is a real danger, which the High Commissioner for the Federation has confirmed, that, if the U.K. go back to the Malayans on the U.K. version of Article VI, Malayan suspicions of H.M.G.'s sincerity in granting them independence will be aroused. This may lead to an unwelcome demand to reopen negotiations on Articles I and III on the ground that in their present form they grant the U.K. too much freedom, moreover, although the Federation has indicated that they could accept the compromise version, they have not formally done so, and unless the U.K. offers to close with them on this, they may stand pat on their own original proposal which required consultation before any action whatever was taken and refuse to be budged from it.

This question should be seen against H.M.G.'s long-term objectives in Malaya, which are to secure a friendly, co-operative and reliable ally. It is to be hoped that when she is independent the Federation will join SEATO. The difficulties which may now be seen in Article VI would then vanish; it is known however, that Tunku Abdul Rahman is determined that the Federation should not take a decision on this question until she is independent so that it can be seen that she is acting of her own free will and is under no duress from us.

In the United Kingdom's view the best chance of gaining these ends, and of ensuring that the defence agreement will endure for as long a time as possible lies in granting the Federation her political freedom and in concluding a defence agreement which will be accepted popularly as in no way infringing her sovereignty.

The Working Party on the Agreement is resuming its meetings in Kuala Lumpur tomorrow, but if it is not possible to authorise discussions to be reopened then on Article VI, it is hoped to arrange a further meeting later this month, so that the Defence Agreement can be finally settled and got out of the way before the Tunku comes to London for financial discussions and before negotiations are begun on the report of the Constitutional Commission.[2]

---

[2] Partly because of the Suez crisis, the Tunku's attitude hardened against the 'compromise version' with the result that further amendments became necessary. Even so he put off agreement until the London talks in Dec 1956—Jan 1957 (see 441; also CO 1030/829–836 and DO 35/6264).

433   CO 1030/716, no 3   3 Nov 1956

[The Suez crisis]: outward telegram no 704 from Mr Lennox-Boyd to
Sir D MacGillivray containing a personal message for Tunku Abdul
Rahman

[Lennox-Boyd's message was a response to a telegram from MacGillivray reporting an
'atmosphere of bewilderment' and foretelling Malayan criticism of the Anglo-French
action against Egypt.]

Following Personal from S. of S. to MacGillivray.

I should be very grateful if you will pass the following personal message from me
to Tunku Abdul Rahman.

Begins.

My dear Tunku.

I realise that recent events in the Middle East will have caused you anxiety and that
you may well have found it a little difficult to understand the reasons which have
forced our Government to take the action we have done. I can assure you that our
only aim has been to stop a small war from developing into a far larger one with
disastrous consequences perhaps to the whole world. I will write on this at greater
length in my letter next week.

The Prime Minister has just spoken in the House of Commons and you may like to
have at once the exact words that he used. I am telegraphing the text separately.

I have no doubt that events will fully justify the action we have taken which we
know was bound to be temporarily unpopular in many quarters and even perhaps
puzzling to our friends.

Yours ever sincerely,
Alan Lennox Boyd

Ends.

434   CO 1030/716, no 4   8 Nov 1956

'Middle East crisis': inward telegram (reply) no 78 from Sir D
MacGillivray to Mr Lennox-Boyd

Middle East Crisis.

I am most grateful for guidance telegrams which have been sent, particularly for
the personal message to the Chief Minister contained your telegram No. 704.[1] It
arrived at a most opportune time and has, I feel sure, had an excellent effect. Chief
Minister had agreed a meeting of U.M.N.O. women, 3rd November, and had taken the
line that Malays and Muslims generally should take the situation calmly and pray
that the crisis should come to an end as quickly as possible without much loss of life
or property. He said that the Malays could not take sides in the affair because they are

---

[1] See 433.

still not free and independent. If they sided with the British, the Muslims in other countries would accuse them of not being in sympathy with them. But, if they sided with the Egyptians, they would be accused by the British of not being faithful to their Rulers who are going to give them independence soon, so they had to be neutral.

2. This statement, which was given a good deal of publicity, had a good effect and at a meeting which I held on 4th November of all Mentri Besar (who are in Kuala Lumpur for Budget meeting of Legislative Council), they said that their information was that the news from the Middle East was being taken reasonably calmly throughout the country. The Malay vernacular press has naturally been critical of Anglo-French action, but has on the whole been surprisingly moderate.

3. Yesterday's news of cease fire will undoubtedly have a salutary effect and it is most satisfactory that it has come before Friday, when there are risks of feeling being aroused by addresses made to gatherings of Malays and other Muslims at weekly prayers at the mosques.

435 CO 1030/375, no 28   27 Nov 1956
[Sultan of Johore and his British adviser]: letter from Sir D MacGillivray to Mr Lennox-Boyd on the Sultan's wish to retain his adviser

[The withdrawal of British advisers from the Malay states was a delicate matter. Alliance politicians were eager to see them go but the rulers (and especially Johore) were reluctant to agree to their departure. Lennox-Boyd had made it clear at the constitutional conference in Jan–Feb 1956 that the British government would not put pressure on the sultans, but, during Sultan Ibrahim's visit to London in Nov, the secretary of state did his best to point out to his highness the problems he would encounter should he persist in his demand for a British adviser after independence. MacGillivray wrote this letter in answer to Lennox-Boyd's request for advice in his talks with Ibrahim. By the time it reached the CO, however, it had been overtaken by events; diplomacy had prevailed and on 5 Dec Ibrahim informed Lennox-Boyd that he agreed to the withdrawal of the Johore adviser on 1 Feb 1957 (see also 388).]

I cannot easily answer in a few words the questions you have put to me in your telegram Personal 248 of the 15th November about the Sultan of Johore and his British Adviser. I am therefore replying by letter rather than by telegram.

2. I understand that since you saw the Sultan he has written to his Mentri Besar and asked him for a list of the British Adviser's duties. These do not amount to much on paper and when he gets a reply from the Mentri Besar the Sultan may find some "face saver" by taking the line that it appears that the duties have become so reduced that clearly he can dispense with the services of the British Adviser.

3. If, however, the Sultan should say when you meet him again that, if the Council of State refuses to pay for the British Adviser, he will pay his salary privately, I suggest that the line you might take is that Her Majesty's Government would be unable to accept the position of having a British Adviser who is paid out of private funds, for the reason that at present a British Adviser is constitutionally and by treaty not merely a public officer, but a representative of Her Majesty in a State, conveying to the Ruler on occasion the official advice of Her Majesty's Government. If he were to be paid out of the private funds of a Ruler, his whole status would be changed. It would be unreasonable to expect that an adviser so paid could be appointed or removed without the consent of the Ruler or could be required to observe the

directions of Her Majesty's Government. He would, in short, in fact, even if not in theory, no longer be a representative of Her Majesty. It would be impossible for Her Majesty's Government to consent to Her Majesty being nominally represented by a person over whom they could have no effective control; when at the same time they would be held responsible, as they inevitably would be, for his conduct and advice. It would be still more difficult for Her Majesty's Government to consent to bear such a responsibility when the elected representatives of the people had indicated that they no longer wished for Her Majesty's Government to keep such a representative in the State. It might be pointed out also that under the Johore State Agreement it is expressly provided that the cost of the British Adviser and his establishment should be "a charge on the revenues of the State of Johore". It would be inconsistent with the Agreement as it stands if the cost of the British Adviser was met not by the revenues of the State of Johore, but out of private funds. You will appreciate that such a change in the mode of remuneration is not a trivial matter, but involves the alteration of the entire status of the post.

4. It would, of course, have to be admitted that there would be no similar objection to the Sultan employing any person that he liked as his private adviser and paying for him out of his own private funds. But such a private individual could not be acknowledged by Her Majesty's Government as the representative of Her Majesty and should not bear the title of "British Adviser". It might further be pointed out to His Highness that the powers conferred upon the British Adviser by the Johore Constitution are conferred upon "the officer appionted by virtue of clause 4 of the Johore Agreement, 1948". A private adviser would not come within this description and consequently he would not be in a position to take part in the State Executive Council or Council of State or to exercise any other functions conferred by law on a British Adviser. Before he could be given any legal position at all it would be necessary to amend the Constitution. This could not be done in the face of opposition from the Council of State, since an amendment to the existing provisions of the Constitution can be effected only with the "aid and concurrence of the Council of State to be signified by resolution" (Article LVI(2) of the Johore Constitution).

5. The point made by His Highness that British Advisers have rendered and still render valuable services to Their Highnesses the Rulers can be gratefully acknowledged; but it might be suggested to him that a private adviser, not possessing any constitutional status or legal powers, would never be able to render the Ruler the services rendered to him in the past by the British Advisers. Moreover, the appointment of a private adviser of this kind would certainly be attacked as unconstitutional and it would be difficult to answer such an attack. By the Johore Constitution, an Executive Council is established to aid and advise His Highness in the exercise of his functions (Art. VIII). His Highness is bound to consult it as a general rule (Art. XVI). He may disregard its advice but he is required in every such case to give his reasons in writing (Art. XVIII). For His Highness habitually to seek the advice of one who is not among his constitutional advisers and to follow such advice in preference to that given by the constitutional advisers would obviously be contrary to the spirit, if not to the letter, of the Constitution, and could have no other effect than to cause a general political agitation which would, in present circumstances, be bound to shake the popularity, and therefore the influence and prestige, of His Throne.

6. You might finally point out to His Highness that even if it were possible (which

it is not) for the British Government to agree to be represented by a person bearing the title of British Adviser to the State of Johore, although he was privately employed by the Ruler, such an arrangement could not last beyond August 1957. On that date the British Government has agreed that it would grant independence to the territories comprised in the Federation of Malaya. This agreement was a tripartite one between Her Majesty's Government, the Alliance Ministers, and the representatives of Their Highnesses the Rulers, who spoke with the authority of all the Rulers including His Highness. It would be impossible for Her Majesty's Government, without being accused of a breach of faith, to continue to be represented in one of the States by an Adviser, presumably speaking on Her Majesty's behalf, and advising in that capacity a Ruler on the exercise of his powers, after the date fixed for independence. It follows that if a British Adviser were to be continued in the State of Johore it could only be for a few months. In those circumstances it would clearly be in the interests of His Highness to accept the inevitable, and to avoid antagonising political opinion in his State and involving himself in an undignified dispute with his own subjects on an issue on which success could, at the most, be but temporary.

7. As stated above the British Government could not, of course, prevent His Highness employing a private individual to advise him. But it would have to be made plain that he was not in any sense a "British Adviser", or a person having any authority whatever to speak on behalf of the British Government; nor could the British Government agree to provide or select such a person. Somerville[1] would almost certainly not stay under these circumstances, nor could any other serving officer of the M.C.S. accept the appointment. The M.C.S. is a Federal service under the control of the Federation Government, and it may therefore be assumed that no member of that service would be permitted by the Federation Government to act in the way suggested. It could not be argued that either the British or the Federation Government are under any obligation under the Johore State Agreement to provide an Adviser. The only obligation is on His Highness to receive one if provided. There would therefore be no means available to the British Government to overcome the resistance of the Federal Executive Council to making an M.C.S. officer available for private employment by the Ruler. It is of course just possible that some officer who resigned from the M.C.S. under the compensation scheme might be willing to enter into a private contract with His Highness. It is, however, virtually certain that no officer would wish to incur the unpopularity and frustration which would be involved by accepting this particular appointment, especially since he would have no legal powers or status whatever.

8. What I have written above is based upon the assumption that His Highness will take the line that, if the Council of State does not vote the necessary funds, he will pay them privately. A much more embarrassing position would arise if the Sultan took the line that under the Johore State Agreement the salary of the Adviser is a charge on the State Revenues; that therefore there is a treaty obligation on the State to provide the money and that if the State does not so provide it he will exercise his reserved powers under Art. XXXII of the Constitution. I do not think that there would be any legal answer to this course and it would in fact be difficult to deny his right to take it, in view of the fact that it was agreed at the London Conference that the British Advisers should be withdrawn only with "the concurrence of Their

---

[1] D A Somerville, British adviser, Johore, 1954–1957.

Highnesses the Rulers". This was agreed not only by Her Majesty's Government but also by the Alliance Ministers. I need not stress the practical difficulties and embarrassment to the British Government that would result from such an exercise of reserved powers.

9. In all the circumstances I suggest the safest line to take is, while mentioning the legal difficulties, and above all the difficulty of filling the post, to stress the practical disadvantages involved in His Highness entering into a head-on-collision with the only vocal political feeling in the State, with the consequent serious loss of popularity and influence, and a considerable weakening of the prestige which His Highness now enjoys amongst his people; and to press the point that a British Adviser who was the target of Alliance hostility would have little practical power and would be very much more of a handicap than an asset to His Highness, and that probably everything he was known to have advised would be opposed on that ground alone; finally, that, in any event, the departure of the British Adviser could be postponed only for about six months, since it is inevitable that Her Majesty must withdraw such an Adviser on August 31st, 1957, at the latest.

436 CAB 129/84, CP(56)279 10 Dec 1956
'Federation of Malaya': Cabinet memorandum by Mr Lennox-Boyd on Malaya's future right of appeal to the Judicial Committee of the Privy Council

The Federation of Malaya Constitutional Commission, under the Chairmanship of Lord Reid has discussed the future position and functions of the Judicial Committee of the Privy Council in relation to appeals from the Federation of Malaya after the grant of independence.

2. The basis of the appellate jurisdiction of the Privy Council from those Commonwealth countries which have retained the right of appeal, and from the Colonies, is the subject's right of appeal to the steps of the Throne. The jurisdiction and practice of the Privy Council depends upon the Judicial Committee Act, 1833, which provides that appeals brought before Her Majesty are to be referred to the Judicial Committee. The Judicial Committee is required to report to The Queen and the appeal is determined by The Queen in Council by an Order in Council. Constitutionally, therefore, the right of appeal, and its determination, depends upon the nexus between the subject and The Queen.

3. In Malaya, however, the constitutional position is somewhat different. Clause 83 of the Federation of Malaya Agreement, 1948, contained a request by the Malayan Rulers to Her Majesty to receive appeals to Her Majesty in Council from the Supreme Court of Malaya, and expressly conferred upon Her Majesty the necessary power and jurisdiction. The Agreement recorded the acceptance by Her Majesty of this power and jurisdiction, and was given the force of law by s.5 of the Federation of Malaya Order in Council, 1948. Further provision was made by local Malayan legislation (Ordinance No. 50/1949). This special arrangement preserved the essence of the constitutional position, viz. the appeal from the Malayan Supreme Court lies direct to The Queen and the function of the Judicial Committee as Her statutory body of advisers is unimpaired.

4.   Malayan Ministers wish to retain the right of appeal to the Judicial Committee but not within the present constitutional framework. They say that after Malaya has become an independent member of the Commonwealth Her Majesty will cease to be the Fountain of Justice in the Federation and will have no jurisdiction there. It would therefore no longer be appropriate for advice on Malayan affairs to be tendered by the Judicial Committee to Her Majesty, for no Order in Council made by Her Majesty could have effect in Malaya. Malayan Ministers have suggested that, in view of this alteration in the constitutional position, the Judicial Committee should be empowered to advise the new Head of State in Malaya in the same way as they now advise The Queen, and that their advice should be incorporated in an Order made by him and deciding the appeal.

5.   The Malayan proposal is entirely novel and raises important constitutional implications. Even assuming that it was decided to accede to it, an arrangement which involved the Judicial Committee advising not The Queen in Council but the Head of another State within the Commonwealth could not be brought within the existing provisions of the Judicial Committee Act, 1833. Special legislation would be needed but the grant of independence to Malaya will, in any case, involve legislation.

6.   The Lord Chancellor, whom I have consulted, agrees with me that it is of the greatest importance to the future development of the Commonwealth that the jurisdiction of the Judicial Committee should be preserved, and that there should continue to be a right of appeal not only from the new Malayan Federation but also from other Colonial Territories now approaching independence. What we decide to do for Malaya will inevitably have its influence upon the relationship of the Judicial Committee with these Colonial Territories and also with the older Commonwealth countries. The whole future of the Judicial Committee is, in our opinion, at stake and, if we can find a formula which will at once satisfy the aspirations of the Malayans and the susceptibilities of the older Commonwealth countries, we may be able to arrest the tendency in the Commonwealth to abolish the right of appeal for nationalist reasons. There is reason to believe that, in India and Pakistan, at any rate in legal circles, the decision to abolish the right of appeal is already being regretted.

7.   I suggest that these questions be referred as a matter of urgency for detailed consideration by a Committee of Ministers consisting of the Lord President, the Lord Chancellor, the Commonwealth Secretary, the Paymaster-General, the Attorney-General and myself.[1]

---

[1] On 13 Dec 1956 the Cabinet agreed to the appointment of such a committee (CAB 128/30/2, CM 100(56)2).

437   DEFE 7/501, COS(56)437   14 Dec 1956

'Use of Commonwealth forces on emergency operations in the Federation of Malaya after independence': joint note by the CO and the Ministry of Defence for the Chiefs of Staff Committee

[On 18 Dec the Chiefs of Staff agreed these recommendation subject to some amendments, the most significant of which are noted below.]

At the Malayan Constitutional Conference held in London in January, the United

Kingdom Government undertook, if requested by the Federation, to make its forces available in the Federation to continue the campaign against the Communist terrorists after independence. In the opinion of the Service commanders and of the High Commissioner that assistance will be essential if the tempo of emergency operations is to be maintained. Only 8 out of the 22 army units engaged in emergency operations are Malayan and these depend upon British administrative support. In addition, the FEAF which plays a vital role in these operations have no Malayan element. It is clear therefore that if the emergency were left to be conducted by the Federation Armed Forces alone, it would quickly deteriorate and force the Federation Government either to negotiate with the Communists or to try to crush them by repressive measures which might well lead to racial conflict. Even if in such a dilemma they agreed to seek Commonwealth* assistance the deterioration in the military situation would present a formidable handicap which would cancel out all the advances made in recent years towards the defeat of the terrorists. Our own and Commonwealth interests therefore clearly indicate that Commonwealth forces should continue without interruption to be used on emergency operations.

2. There was at one time a danger that the Federation in its anxiety to demonstrate that it was not militarily dependent upon the United Kingdom to a degree which would make its political independence nominal only, might decide to dispense with all outside assistance in fighting the emergency and go it alone. Our intelligence reports indicate that the terrorists have deliberately been lying low to encourage this intention. Recently, however, the Chief Minister has come to realise that the Federation will need the assistance of Commonwealth forces in fighting the emergency after independence, and within the last few days he has publicly stated that he will ask for this assistance. He may well not wish to make this request formally until after independence has been obtained, but it seems clear that he has been persuaded of the need before then to resolve the many problems of reorganisation necessary to give effect to the consequence of independence whereby the Federation will become exclusively responsible for the direction of emergency operations.

3. This calls in the first place for a new command structure. At present, the executive direction of emergency operations, under the Emergency Operations Council of the Federation Government, is the responsibility of the Director of Operations, who is also GOC Malaya Command. This officer is responsible ultimately to Her Majesty's Government in both these capacities so long as H.M.G. is responsible for the defence and security of the Federation. The Chief Minister, in accepting that he will have to call upon H.M.G. for assistance, does not doubt that it will be forthcoming under arrangements which scrupulously respect the Federation's newly-won independence and will clearly reflect, as the inevitable consequence of that independence, that the prosecution of the emergency is thenceforward the responsibility of the Federation Government and not of H.M.G. Any system which retained the GOC Malaya Command as the Director of Operations (even if it were possible for him to sustain a divided loyalty) would not satisfy this criterion, and if we are not willing to meet the Malayans on this, there is a grave risk that, whatever the

---

* The phrase[s] "Commonwealth" and "Commonwealth forces" are here used as meaning the United Kingdom, Australia and New Zealand and if need be other *oversea* Commonwealth countries in distinction to the Federation of Malaya and her forces. Malaya will, of course, be a Commonwealth country itself.

danger to themselves, they will decide to do without any assistance whatever. The utmost damage would be done to our relationships with them if it could be said that we were unwilling to honour the undertakings we had given except on conditions which infringed their independence.

4. The BDCC(FE) considered this problem earlier this year in a paper which has been circulated as an annex to COS(56)363. At that time, all the evidence suggested that the Federation Government would contend that the appointment of the GOC Federation Army as director of operations was the only practicable solution consonant with the principles set out in paragraph 3 above. The military objections to this proposal were set out in paragraphs 7 and 8 of the BDCC(FE) paper and are quite conclusive. As a preferable alternative the BDCC(FE) suggested also that the direction of operations should be vested in an executive operational sub-committee of the Emergency Operations Council. The Chiefs of Staff, however, have expressed the view that this proposal is unacceptable and would prove unworkable.

5. When attention was first directed to this problem, it was suggested that the political requirement that the direction of operations should be seen to be the exclusive responsibility of the Federation Government and the military requirement that there should be centralised direction under one officer could be met by appointing as Director of Operations an officer who would not combine this post with the command of either the Federation or Commonwealth Forces, and who would be the exclusive servant of the Federation Government and paid for by them; he could be a British officer released to their service and appointed with the agreement of all the governments whose forces would be placed under him *for operations*. The Chiefs of Staff, in discussions with the High Commissioner at their 102nd meeting, commended this proposal as likely to prove acceptable to H.M.G. This proposal had found no place in the BDCC(FE) paper, however, since at that time it was thought that the Federation Government would see political and financial objections to the appointment of another British officer in addition to the GOC Federation Army. On his return to Malaya, however, the High Commissioner had an opportunity to discuss this question informally with the Chief Minister in the presence of the Commander-in-Chief FARELF and the Commissioner General for the United Kingdom in S.E. Asia. It emerged from those discussions that the Chief Minister was likely to agree to the appointment after independence, as the exclusive servant of the Federation Government of a seconded British officer with the rank of Lieutenant General to be the director of operations. During a recent visit to this country General Festing, the C.-in-C. FARELF said that he supported this proposal and that a paper endorsing it would shortly issue from the B.D.C.C.(F.E.) That paper has not yet been received here, but since it will be necessary to discuss this matter with the Chief Minister and his colleagues when they visit this country later this month, the formal views of the Chiefs of Staff are sought upon it now.

6. It will be necessary also to define certain other matters concerning the employment of Commonwealth forces on emergency operations after independence.

7. The Federation Government are unlikely to be willing that the United Kingdom and Commonwealth forces should continue as now to be employed in operations all over the country and upon essentially police duties such as the supervision of food denial schemes which bring them into contact with the civilian population, nor would we wish this. They would probably accept that those forces should be used on essentially military operations in specifically "black" areas.

8. It is necessary also to ensure that our forces are not used under Federation direction upon operations of a type of which we might disapprove or which would expose them to unnecessary military risks. The appointment of a British officer as an independent director of operations would go some way to diminish this risk, since he can be expected to enjoy the confidence of Federation ministers whose servant he will be, and so able to exert influence on them to ensure that the operational uses proposed for Commonwealth forces paid regard to the views of their national authorities touching that employment. It is, however, suggested that in order that this, and other requirements may be clearly known, the Commonwealth Force commanders should be issued with directives specifying clearly the uses and manner in which their forces may be employed, on the lines set out in paragraph 21 of C.O.S.(56)363, and that they should also be members of the Federation Emergency Operations Council and should possess the right of appeal to their national authorities whenever they consider that the orders given them contravene the principles of their directives.[1] The Federation Government are understood to be generally willing to accept these proposals.

9. If Commonwealth forces are to be employed on emergency operations after independence, they will need facilities additional to those laid down under the Defence Agreement. It will also be necessary to provide that they shall be fully protected in respect of their acts in support of the Federation Government both by securing, as we intend under the Defence Agreement, that the primary right of jurisdiction in respect of offences committed while on duty should rest with the Commonwealth service authorities and also that they should continue to enjoy the powers and immunities at present conferred on them under the emergency regulations of the Federation Government, which should only amend them after consultation with the Commonwealth authorities concerned.

10. It is proposed that Ghurkas [sic] should be used on emergency operations in the same way as Commonwealth troops. We propose that the Foreign Office should consider whether this matter should be raised with the Government of Nepal, and, if so, how best this could be done. At a later stage the Commonwealth Relations Office will wish to consider whether the Indian Government should be told in general terms of our proposals.[2]

11. The Chiefs of Staff are therefore asked to agree:—

(a) That the Federation Government should be asked to agree that after independence a British Officer of the rank of Lieutenant General should be seconded to their service as Director of Operations.

(b) That this officer should not have command of troops, but that the commanders of the forces engaged on emergency operations (GOC Commonwealth Land Forces, AOC Commonwealth Air Forces, GOC Federation Army and Commissioner of Police) should place forces under him[3] for operational purposes.

(c) That a directive on the lines indicated in paragraph 8 above, the terms of which should be communicated to the Federation Government, should be issued

---

[1] The penultimate sentence in para 8 was amended by the COS Committee in order to confine directives to broad principles and to clarify the force commanders' right of appeal.

[2] The COS Committee deleted para 10.

[3] The COS Committee replaced 'him' by 'his direction'.

to the Commonwealth Force Commanders specifying the conditions[4] under which their forces may be used on emergency operations.

(d) That the commanders of the Commonwealth forces should be members of the Emergency Operations Council and should have a right to appeal to their national authorities if any operational use proposed for their forces contravenes in their opinion the terms of that directive.[5]

(e) That negotiations should be initiated in Malaya with the Federation author-ities with a view to agreeing the areas in which Commonwealth forces should operate on emergency operations after independence and the additional facilities they will require.

(f) That before any discussion[s] are initiated with Federation Ministers, the Australian and New Zealand Governments should be invited to consider these proposals and to say whether they agree that they provide satisfactory arrange-ments on the basis of which they can agree that their forces should continue to be employed on emergency operations.[6]

(g) That when Federation Ministers agreed in principle the arrangements for the use of Commonwealth troops the Foreign Office should consider whether this matter should be raised with the Government of Nepal and, if so, how best this can be done.[7]

---

[4] The COS Committee replaced 'Conditions' by 'Principles'.
[5] The COS Committee replaced 11(d) with the following: 'That the G.O.C. Commonwealth Land Forces, the A.O.C. Commonwealth Air Forces and when necessary the Flag Officer, Malaya, should be members of the Emergency Operations Council and that they should have the right of appeal to their national authorities before committing their forces if any operational use proposed for their forces contravenes in their opinion the terms of their directives.'
[6] The COS Committee inserted the following new sub-paragraph: 'That legal provision should be made to ensure that Commonwealth forces employed on emergency operations after independence are fully protected in respect of their acts in support of the Federation Government.'
[7] The COS Committee deleted para 11(g).

438   CO 1030/522, no 1   21 Dec 1956

[Report of the Reid Commission]: letter from Sir D MacGillivray to J B Johnston on controversial issues particularly the future of the Settlements   [Extract]

The latest forecast received from Rome[1] suggests that the report of the Constitution-al Commission may be complete by the end of January. If so, it is clearly essential that a decision be taken as soon as possible on how the Commission's report is to be handled on its arrival in Malaya; it is a subject to which we have been giving considerable thought.

2. The Commission's report is likely to arouse controversy on three main issues and the manner of its handling must be related to the likely effect on these issues; they are:—

(a) Citizenship and the privileged position of the Malays;

---

[1] Having collected evidence in Malaya, the commission completed its report in Rome.

(b) the relationship between the Federal and the State Governments;

(c) the status of the Settlements and the nationality of their inhabitants.

3. The Citizenship issue, if badly handled, could of course give rise to communal trouble. If, however, as seems likely, the Commission accepts in a large measure, if not in their entirety, the Alliance's compromise proposals, present indications seem to be that trouble can be avoided provided that (and it is a very important proviso) the acceptance at least in principle of the Commission's recommendations on this point can be announced at the time when the report is published.

4. I see little prospect of early agreement being reached between the Rulers and the Alliance on the future relationship of the Federal and State Governments, but I hope that both sides will be prepared to negotiate, and I would not expect this part of the Commission's report to give rise immediately to bitter controversy—anyway not of the most dangerous kind—since it will not be a racial issue. Public opinion is in my view unlikely to be aroused on this subject to any marked degree unless the Alliance later feels it necessary to arouse it as a means of inducing the Rulers to retreat from a stand which the Alliance may regard as reactionary and intransigeant. In whatever way we handle the publication of the Commission's report there is still therefore likely to be a measure of disagreement on this issue and probably the best that we can hope for is that the manner of negotiation will have been settled before the report is published; this would have obvious advantages.

5. The future of the Settlements is the most difficult of all the issues and it is the one in which H.M.G. is likely to be most directly concerned. With regard to other issues H.M.G. should be prepared to offer its good offices towards arriving at a settlement satisfactory to the contending parties but should endeavour to avoid any course directly taking sides or likely to involve them in any controversy. As regards the Settlements, three separate questions are involved.

(a) whether the direct link between the Settlements and the British Crown is to be maintained;

(b) who shall be the Head of the Settlement Government in an independent Malaya;

(c) what will be the citizenship status of the inhabitants of the Settlements.

In my view it is essential that H.M.G. should have decided on the line which it will take on these three issues before the report is published and, as far as possible, in advance of receipt of the report. I think this is practicable since I believe that the policy which H.M.G. should adopt is already fairly clear.

6. The Secretary of State has, I understand, already accepted the position that the direct link between the Queen and the Settlements should be broken;[2] my Memorandum of 19th July 1956 "Comments on Proposals by Her Majesty's Government contained in the draft Memorandum to the Constitutional Commission" is relevant. This in itself is likely to arouse some bitter protest from minorities—and it is essential that we should immediately be able to show that we are mindful of the interests of the Settlements under the new deal.

7. This could be demonstrated by our attitude in the matter of the manner of appointment of the Heads of the Settlements. I attach the extracts from the Memoranda by the Rulers and the Alliance to the Constitutional Commission[3] which

---

[2] See 425.   [3] The rulers' memorandum is not printed; for the Alliance memorandum, see 426.

contain their proposals on this point. Acceptance of the Rulers' proposals would, I am convinced, cause considerable trouble in the Settlements. Whilst the Alliance may claim to represent the majority of the people of the Settlements and may argue that its proposals are acceptable to them, I would myself expect some very vocal opposition to be aroused if they were accepted as they stand. The crux of the problem is that both the Rulers and the Alliance intend that the Rulers shall continue to derive their sovereignty from their own States but propose that the Heads of the Settlements shall be appointed by the Federal authority. Unless these appointments are made in a manner which has the support of the great majority of the people in the Settlements there is likely to be trouble in both Penang and Malacca. Many of the most loyal citizens in the Settlements have always placed their trust in British protection. They will be disappointed that the link with the British Crown is to be broken and the majority of them are only likely to be induced to accept the break if it is clear to them that the Settlements will retain their separate entity and adequate autonomy in an independent Federation of Malaya.

8. This issue is likely in any case to be a very controversial one and, unless carefully handled, it may arouse strong feelings. Much will depend on what the Commission recommends. If they should support the proposals of the Alliance or of the Rulers we shall be placed in a much more difficult position than if they were to support our own view that the appointment of the Heads of the Settlements is a matter for the Settlements themselves. However, it seems to me that the basis from which H.M.G. must start in handling this issue, as with the others, is one that accepts as fundamental the need to preserve, as much as possible, the present friendship between Great Britain and the Malayan peoples as a whole and to avoid entering into any dispute which would gravely endanger our future relations with the new independent country. If it is at all possible we should avoid controversy with the Alliance, particularly, and also with the Rulers, although a controversy with the Rulers would not be so dangerous. I think that, even as regards the Settlements, H.M.G. should therefore support as much as it can the recommendations of the Commission. It would clearly be very difficult for H.M.G. to reject the proposals of the Commission if, in doing so, it came into conflict with both the Alliance and the Rulers. It would be argued that H.M.G. had agreed to have these questions determined by an impartial Commission and that to reject that Commission's recommendations was an act of ill faith, and argued the existence of some sinister purpose. Moreover, I do not think that an attempt by H.M.G. to go against the views of the Constitutional Commission and in conflict with the Alliance and Rulers would have any great chance of ultimate success. It would be strongly opposed by the greater part of vocal political opinion. It would be difficult for H.M.G. to rouse much support either in Malaya or abroad because every argument based on justice to the people of the Settlement would be met by the counter-argument that the Commission, composed of independent and eminent judges, saw nothing unjust in their proposals. We could only base our arguments on the sentiment of a majority of the people in the Settlements. We might then be faced with the challenge that we should take a referendum. This we would wish to avoid, not merely because the taking of a referendum would greatly delay decisions and postpone the day of independence, but also because it would arouse emotions to an extent that might endanger the peace. On the other hand a referendum on this particular issue would not be likely to engender anti-British sentiments, at least not nearly to the extent that would be

aroused by a referendum on the subject of the retention of the Settlements as British possessions. Moreover, I believe that, on this particular issue of the manner of appointment of the Heads of the Settlements, the true sentiments of the majority of the people of the Settlements would be with us and that a secret ballot might show a result in our favour despite the strength of the Alliance machine. However, I think there would be a good chance of getting the Rulers and the Alliance to agree that the appointments should be made in accordance with the wishes of the Settlements. This is a safeguard which, I would suggest, should be regarded as fundamental and upon which H.M.G. should, if necessary, ultimately insist. If the point should be strongly pressed I think we might agree that the "Heads" should be formally appointed by the Yang di Pertuan Agong on the nomination of the Settlements but not in his discretion. I doubt the wisdom of committing ourselves publicly, at least at the outset, to a line which conflicted with the recommendations of the Commission and the views of the Alliance and Rulers and, therefore, if the report of the Commission should be against us on this issue and if we are not able, behind the scenes, to persuade the Rulers and the Alliance to our point of view, then it might be best when it comes to publication of the report, to reserve our position and merely to state in the accompanying statement something to the effect that consultation with the representatives of the Settlements would be necessary before final decisions were taken.

9. If, on the other hand, as one hopes will be the case, the Constitutional Commission makes recommendations with regard to the Government of the Settlements in line with our own views, I agree that H.M.G. should support them even although they may meet with opposition from the Rulers and the Alliance. In such a case we could retort on the Alliance and Rulers the argument set out above that all the parties had already agreed to an independent Commission to make recommendations. With the support of the Commission, H.M.G. can urge arguments of policy and justice with much greater force and would enlist a considerable body of public opinion. With regard to the Rulers' proposal, the Alliance might well be persuaded to disapprove of that, on the ground that its principal effect would be to increase the authority of the Rulers, which is already exercising a hampering effect on the Federal Government and, in consequence, on the plans and policy of the Alliance.

10. The question of the citizenship status of the inhabitants of the Settlements is less clear cut. Again both the Rulers and the Alliance have taken the view that dual nationality is impossible and that if an inhabitant of the Settlements wishes to remain a citizen of the United Kingdom and Colonies he cannot also enjoy citizenship of the Federation. There might be room for negotiation here in the light of the Commission's report, but the approach which H.M.G. should make to the problem is, I suggest, no less clear. It should be that it would be unjust to take from those inhabitants of the Settlements, who now possess it, the right by which they can vote as citizens of Malaya and are counted also as citizens of the United Kingdom and Colonies. Since Malaya will remain in the British Commonwealth and her citizens will enjoy Commonwealth citizenship, the retention of their present status as citizens of the United Kingdom for which some of the inhabitants of the Settlements are asking is surely unobjectionable. It would not of course be proposed that anyone born in the Settlements after independence should enjoy this privilege. I would hope, however, that it could be agreed that all those who are citizens of the United

Kingdom and Colonies before Independence would automatically become citizens of the Federation, if they so wished,—and would not be required to give up their U.K. citizenship, but should continue to possess it as a dual nationality, subject to the Master nationality principle when resident in the Federation. . . .[4]

---

[4] In the rest of the letter MacGillivray discusses probable local reactions to the report's main recommendations and the manner in which its publication might be handled to minimise controversy. Completion of the report was delayed, however, by the insistence of one of the commissioners, Abdul Hamid of Pakistan, to submit a minority report with respect to the Malays' special position. This, the British feared, threatened to inflame racial feeling and could be 'politically disastrous', see 439.

439 CO 1030/519, no 26E   2 Feb 1957
'Note of discussions in Rome on 29th January, 1957': note by Sir D Watherston of his discussions with the constitutional commissioners; views of Mr Abdul Hamid on the special position of the Malays

I arrived in Rome by air from London about 1.15 p.m. on the 29th January and was met by Mr. Henderson, Assistant Secretary to the Constitutional Commission. As the plane was early and as Lord Reid was not expected to be available until between three and four o'clock, my wife and I went on a sight-seeing tour with Mr. Henderson and returned to the Eden Hotel at about 4.15. During this time Mr. Henderson warned me that a serious situation had developed during the last few days owing to the attitude of Mr. Abdul Hamid who had prepared a memorandum dealing with a number of points concerned primarily with the position of the Malays, on which he differed from the other members of the Commission. He wished this memorandum to be put in as a separate note to be attached to the Commission's report.

2. I saw Lord Reid about 4.30 for an hour. He was clearly tired and worried; he asked me to read the four or five pages of Mr. Abdul Hamid's 30-page memorandum which dealt with the special position of the Malays. In this part of the memorandum Mr. Abdul Hamid had looked ahead to the situation twenty-one years hence when the Malays were likely to lose their numerical majority on the roll of Federal citizens and he advocated that special powers should be conferred by the constitution on the Head of State (in relation to Federal matters) and on the individual Rulers (in relation to State matters) to allow them to act against the advice of their Ministers and against a majority vote of Parliament (the Federal body) or of their State Council, as the case might be, in respect of matters concerned with the special position of the Malays.

3. Lord Reid said that Mr. Abdul Hamid had only very recently come forward with these views and with the other points dealt with in his memorandum which were concerned with State autonomy, particularly on such subjects as land and finance. He considered that Mr. Abdul Hamid had behaved somewhat strangely during recent weeks and he had actually maintained in so many words that he had the right to put forward fresh views as late as the day before the Commission signed its report if "he had a dream the night before". Lord Reid felt that the deterioration in Mr. Abdul Hamid's contribution to the Commission's work was partly due to the fact that he had no friends in Rome and that he felt very isolated. There had too been some

difficulty between him and Mr. Malik[1] presumably over the Kashmir dispute and they had not been on speaking terms for two or three days.

4.   Lord Reid was very concerned that a separate note by Mr. Abdul Hamid would have serious effects in Malaya and cause racial trouble. He thought, for example, that Dato Onn might very well make capital out of such a situation. He had been wondering whether, in view of the Commission's intention to sign its report on Sunday, 10th February, it might be possible for Mr. Abdul Hamid's note to be published separately at a later date as it could hardly be ready in time to go out with the report itself. He had enquired of the Colonial Office whether they felt that Mr. Abdul Hamid's note could be suppressed altogether but he realised that the effect would probably be that Mr. Abdul Hamid would resign from the Commission and he would then, of course, be at liberty to give his note to the Press and to make any other remarks to the Press that he felt inclined. All this could be exceedingly damaging.

5.   I enquired whether Lord Reid had represented to Mr. Abdul Hamid firstly that it made the position exceedingly awkward for the Commission, particularly in view of the time factor, for fresh views to be put forward at this very late stage, and secondly, that the effect of a separate note—in fact, a minority report—being written on such controversial matters might very well lead to serious racial friction in Malaya. Lord Reid replied that in fact both the arguments had already been put to Mr. Abdul Hamid at a meeting of the Commission and that they would be put to him again on the following day when the Commission would be going through Mr. Abdul Hamid's memorandum paragraph by paragraph. I gathered, however, that Lord Reid had not had any private discussions with Mr. Abdul Hamid on any of these matters but that all the discussion had taken place at full meetings of the Commission. Later in the evening, when my wife and I dined with Lord and Lady Reid, I asked him whether it might not be possible, in private conversation with Mr. Abdul Hamid, to represent more forcibly to him the dangers of a minority report on these subjects; Lord Reid replied that he did not think that it would be likely to have any effect.

6.   After dinner at a restaurant a short distance from the Eden Hotel, we walked back to the hotel and in the lounge downstairs met Mr. Abdul Hamid and Mr. Malik in a group of some six to eight people including Mr. Laird but not including either Sir William McKell or Sir Ivor Jennings. Mr. Abdul Hamid greeted me in a most friendly way and immediately asked Lord Reid if there would be any objection to his having five minutes private conversation with me. Lord Reid agreed and Mr. Abdul Hamid and I went over to a quiet corner of the lounge. He did not enquire whether I had had any discussion with Lord Reid and I did not, of course, disclose that I had seen or heard of his memorandum. He immediately launched on me a summary of it based on the theme that it was essential, in his opinion, that the Commission should accept in toto the representations made in the memorandum submitted to the Commission by the Alliance and that he did not consider that in some important respects the Commission's report was doing this. He mentioned his four main points, *viz*:—

1.   Citizenship
2.   Special position of the Malays

---

[1] The commissioner from India.

3. National language
4. Islam as the State religion.

He proceeded to discuss the last of these first but as I knew from his memorandum and from discussion with Lord Reid that his points on the special position of the Malays were by far the most important, I succeeded in switching him to that subject as quickly as possible. (Time was short as it was necessary for us to leave for the airport at 10.45 and it was then about 10 o'clock or after).

7. I said first that the prestige of the Commission stood very high and that there was little doubt that its report, if unanimous, would in all major matters be accepted, with nothing more than minor modifications here and there, by all the parties concerned—the Rulers, H.M.G. in the United Kingdom and the Federal Government. But a separate note on such controversial matters as those which he had mentioned to me could cause very serious racial trouble and I cited the recent riots in Penang as an example. I said that I fully realised that he, as the only Muslim member of the Commission, felt that special responsibility fell upon him for seeing that the Malays should be protected; I myself, from my long service in Malaya, had a great liking for and sympathy with the Malays. I was, however, exceedingly doubtful whether it was wise to include in the constitution provisions such as he had in mind and I proceeded to point out the difficult situation in which a Ruler would be placed if he exercised reserved powers to disallow legislation passed by a Federal or State Government. It could very well produce a state of affairs where the Government of a Federation or of a State could not be carried on and it might lead to a move for the removal of the Rulers altogether. I felt sure that it was not a suggestion which would find favour with the present Chief Minister. This last point seemed to surprise Mr. Abdul Hamid but he proceeded to explain that the sort of situation he had in mind was a non-Malay majority in the State Councils in say, Perak or Johore, with perhaps a non-Malay Mentri Besar and a decision by the State Government to revoke the Malay Reservations Enactment. I said that I thought that even in such a case it would be very unwise for power to be given to the Ruler to disallow legislation; it would be better to leave the decision with the legislature but perhaps to require something more than a bare majority. Mr. Abdul Hamid said that he thought that this suggestion was a valuable one and that he would consider it.

8. It emerged during the discussion that there was intense feeling between Mr. Abdul Hamid and Mr. Malik and that the former considered that the latter was in a sense a direct representative on the Commission of the non-Malay communities in the Federation. He quoted one or two instances of remarks made by Mr. Malik at meetings of the Commission—made no doubt entirely innocently—which he regarded as a deliberate affront. One of these was apparently a suggestion that a clause from the Indian Constitution should be incorporated in the Federation Constitution. Mr. Abdul Hamid said that he had never made any such suggestion that any clause from the Pakistan Constitution should be adopted.

9. We must have talked for at least twenty minutes. I then excused myself and we parted on friendly terms. I went upstairs and in the short time available, recounted as much of the discussion as I could to Lord Reid before leaving.[2]

---

[2] On 1 Feb Reid wrote to Lennox-Boyd: 'After a battle Hamid has agreed to curtail his note. I think he will leave out the worst bits, and the result though bad may not be disastrous. But I can't be sure of anything yet' (CO 1030/518, no 04).

440   CAB 130/122, GEN 570/1   4 Feb 1957

'Expenditure in Eastern Asia': Cabinet note by Sir N Brook. *Annex:*
report by a working party of officials

I was asked by Ministers, during the summer, to arrange for a working party of officials to study the pattern of United Kingdom expenditure in Eastern Asia[1] in the light of the assessment that the immediate threat in the area is political rather than military. The attached report examines the possibilities of transferring some resources from preparation for war to the economic and information measures needed to maintain and promote our influence in this area in peace. It is circulated for consideration in connection with the general review of defence policy.

Annex to 440

We were asked to prepare as a basis for discussion by Ministers suggestions for adjusting the pattern of United Kingdom expenditure in Eastern Asia in order to achieve, within a net reduction in total expenditure in the area, some transfer of resources from preparation for war to measures for maintaining our influence in peace in view of the assessment that the immediate threat in the area is political rather than military.

2. During the current financial year the approximate cost of maintaining the present forces in Eastern Asia is £96 millions. Non-military expenditure will be about £9.5 millions.

3. The Defence Committee have already approved certain reductions in the forces stationed in Malaya and Hong Kong, which will produce savings of about £4 millions in 1957–58 and about £7 millions a year thereafter. The withdrawal of United Kingdom forces from Korea, if successfully negotiated, will save another £2¼ millions a year. It may be hoped that further savings will result from the review of defence policy now in progress.

4. We have considered how part of these savings on defence expenditure could be applied to measures designed to increase the political influence of the United Kingdom in the area. The report of the committee, under the Chairmanship of Lord Reading (P.R. (56) 26),[2] indicated that the level of non-military expenditure in Eastern Asia was subject to marked variations from year to year, and that in addition to the total of £9.5 millions for 1957–58 there were certain Government loans or credits for special purposes which had been extended to countries in the area.

5. Since that report was prepared certain new commitments have arisen. The Government of the Federation of Malaya have made large demands for a contribution towards the costs of the emergency in Malaya. In recent negotiations, the United Kingdom has accepted a potential commitment which might be as much as £33 millions over the next five years or so—mainly a sum not exceeding £20 millions in 1957–61 towards the cost of the emergency and about £13 millions towards the costs of equipping and expanding the Federation's armed forces. Malaya is also receiving the balance of the Federation's Colonial Development and Welfare allocation which is

---

[1] See 421, note.   [2] See 421.

unspent at the date of independence. There will also be expenditure in Malaya in setting up the new office of the United Kingdom High Commissioner in Malaya on the achievement of independence by the Federation in August this year.

6. There may also be commitments under the Special United Nations Fund for Economic Development (SUNFED). The United Kingdom Government have accepted in principle the setting up of this Fund when military expenditure is reduced as a result of an all-round reduction in armaments. Some of the grants from SUNFED would go to Eastern Asia, but it is impossible at this stage to make any realistic assessment of the amount and timing of this commitment.

7. In view of the need for a general reduction in overseas expenditure, it is evident that there will be only limited scope for increasing non-military expenditure in Eastern Asia. Nevertheless, if our military strength in the area is to be reduced, increased reliance will have to be placed on non-military measures to maintain our influence in peace. In June last year, the Commissioner-General for South-East Asia emphasised the need for increased political and economic effort in the area and he has recently re-affirmed this view in a report on his annual conference of British representatives in Eastern Asia, held in Singapore in December.

8. In paragraph 12 of their report (P.R. (56) 26), Lord Reading's Committee suggested how an additional annual expenditure of £3 millions might be divided between the various non-military measures. The Departments concerned have reviewed the proposals incorporated in that report and have made certain adjustments to meet recent changes in circumstances. The following table summarises these revised proposals for additional expenditure:—

Items	Estimated cost (£'000)
Colonial Office	
1. Chinese education in North Borneo and Sarawak and contributions to general development in these territories	800
2. Hong Kong—housing, social services, development and University	600
3. Expanding United Kingdom Information Services in Singapore and British Council activities there and in North Borneo and Sarawak	100
Foreign Office	
4. Colombo Plan	500
5. Security measures	125
6. Information	110
7. Expansion of British Council activities in Burma, Indonesia, Japan and possibly the Philippines	65
Commonwealth Relations Office	
8. Colombo Plan	400
9. Service items, e.g., training	135
10. Information and British Council	165
	3,000

9. These proposals have been prepared without consultation with our overseas representatives or the Colonial Governments concerned. The list includes provision for additional expenditure on certain items, such as the military training of overseas

officers in the United Kingdom, the details of which are at present being considered separately.

10. We should point out that programmes of increased expenditure under the Colombo Plan would need to be built up gradually. It is not possible without notice and without constructing the necessary administrative machine to spend the large additional sums of money mentioned in paragraph 8. The figures in fact represent targets which we should expect to be able to reach within a period of two years or so needed to expand the administrative machine.

11. The additional expenditure on security measures proposed in paragraph 8 includes some provision for the training of intelligence officers from countries in Eastern Asia. The training of officers in intelligence, police and related work is a valuable form of assistance since it is to the advantage of the United Kingdom that the countries concerned should build up an efficient system for maintaining internal security. Discussions are at present taking place with the Government of the Federation of Malaya about the use of the Police College in Malaya for the training of police officers from neighbouring territories. Though the training would normally be provided on a repayment basis, some United Kingdom expenditure may be required, particularly if the Malayan Government are unwilling to co-operate and new facilities have to be established elsewhere.

12. The above proposals make no provision for additional expenditure on facilities for the teaching of English overseas. At the recent conference held by the Commissioner-General for South-East Asia in Singapore, there was unanimous agreement on the importance of expanding these facilities. A separate report on this general problem is being submitted to the Ministerial Committee on Overseas Information Services.

13. In other fields covered by our study we realise that there are also difficulties in considering the problems of Eastern Asia in isolation. For example, the claims for additional expenditure on development in Eastern Asian colonies ought to be weighed against the needs for development in other colonies, which on economic grounds may have better claims for assistance. Many of the projects outlined in paragraph 8 of this report will therefore need to be considered in a world-wide context before final decisions are taken. In particular the details of any proposals for additional expenditure on information projects in Eastern Asia will necessarily have to await the outcome of the general review of overseas information services which is being undertaken by the Ministerial Committee under the chairmanship of the Chancellor of the Duchy of Lancaster.

14. Subject to these qualifications, the suggestions in this report indicate the non-military measures on which additional expenditure could most usefully be incurred in Eastern Asia and illustrate how an increase in civil expenditure of £3 millions a year might be divided between these measures.

441 CO 1030/494, no 21   4 Feb 1957
'Discussions with Federation of Malaya, December–January 1956–57':
circular intelligence telegram no 26 from FO to HM representatives on
talks in London about the defence agreement and financial assistance

A delegation from the Federation of Malaya, led by the Chief Minister, Tunku Abdul
Rahman, visited England from the middle of December until mid-January. It held
discussions with Her Majesty's Government on the terms of a Defence and Mutual
Assistance Agreement between Her Majesty's Government and the Federation and
also on the financial assistance to be given by Her Majesty's Government to the
Federation in the first years of its independence.

Defence agreement
    2. These discussions had their origin in the Report of the Malayan Constitutional
Conference held in London in January–February 1956, at which it was agreed that,
when the Federation attained full self-government and independence within the
Commonwealth in the course of this year, Her Majesty's Government should be
permitted to maintain forces in the Federation for the fulfilment of their Commonwealth and international obligations and that they should also assist the Government
of the Federation in the external defence of its territory. A joint United Kingdom–
Malayan working party, the meetings of which were attended by observers from
Australia and New Zealand, was set up in Malaya under the chairmanship of the
Commissioner-General for the United Kingdom in South-East Asia to work out the
details of this Agreement. The working party quickly reached broad agreement, and
in the recent negotiations in London satisfactory agreement was reached on those
few points which remained outstanding from the deliberations of the working party.
    3. The Agreement provides that Her Majesty's Government shall assist the
Government of the Federation of Malaya in the external defence of its territory, and
shall have the right to maintain in the Federation such naval, land and air forces,
including a Commonwealth strategic reserve as are mutually agreed to be necessary
for that purpose and for the fulfilment of Commonwealth and international
obligations. There are four annexes to the Agreement dealing with: (a) the assistance
to be provided by the United Kingdom to the training and development of the armed
forces of the Federation; (b) bases, training and facilities to be provided for the
United Kingdom forces; (c) the status of those forces; (d) the arrangements under
which the United Kingdom Services may hold land in the Federation for the purposes
of the Agreement.
    4. The Agreement sets out the circumstances and manner in which United
Kingdom forces in the Federation can be committed to military operations, viz.:—

(a) Her Majesty's Government can take automatic military action to counter any
direct attack on the Federation of Malaya, Singapore, Sarawak, [North] Borneo,
Brunei or Hong Kong, or upon the United Kingdom or other Commonwealth
forces in those territories (including Federation forces);
(b) in the event of the threat of such an attack, Her Majesty's Government can
take action after consultation with the Federation Government; who are pledged
to offer the fullest co-operation;

(c) in the event of a threat to the preservation of peace in the Far East (e.g., a threat of attack or an overt attack on another country in the area) Her Majesty's Government can take action as in (b) above;

(d) in the event of a threat to the preservation of peace or the outbreak of hostilities elsewhere than in the Far East, Her Majesty's Government can withdraw her forces from the Federation at her discretion, but shall not be able to commit them to military operations from Malaya without first obtaining the consent of the Federation Government.

5. These arrangements in our opinion meet all the requirements that can reasonably be expected of an independent country. They accord us the automatic right to take action if we are directly attacked in the Far East or if the Federation is attacked. The consultation required under (b) and (c) above must, in the circumstances of independence, be construed to mean consent, but in her own interests the Federation is unlikely to withhold that consent if she were herself threatened. The Government of the Federation recognise, moreover, that a threat to our position in the Far East is a threat to the Federation since, if successful, it would impair our ability to provide effectively for her defence. In theory the requirement to consult the Malayans before taking action under (b) or (c) above is a limitation upon us, but even if the Agreement gave us a completely free hand, we could in practice take no effective action without Malayan goodwill and co-operation. It is clear from statements made by the Chief Minister that he intends that the undertaking of co-operation should be interpreted honourably by the Federation Government, and it is therefore most satisfactory that this undertaking extends to attacks or threats of attack upon other countries in the Far East. It is under this clause that we might wish to take action in support of ANZAM, and more particularly SEATO. The Federation is not yet a member of SEATO, and the Chief Minister has said that she will not take any decision on membership until she has gained her independence, since he is particularly anxious that her decision, when taken, should not appear to have been reached under any duress from us. We respect this attitude. We do of course hope that the Federation will in due time join SEATO, and the Chief Minister has said privately that it is his intention that she should. Throughout the negotiations the main preoccupation of the Malayans has been to ensure that nothing in the Agreement should appear to derogate from their newly won sovereignty. The Chief Minister has declared publicly that he is satisfied that the terms of the Agreement as now drafted fully respect Malayan sovereignty, and indeed, by agreeing that we may have the right to take action in support of SEATO from Malayan bases, while the Federation is not yet a member of that Organisation, he has shown a statesmanlike understanding of our position and of his country's own interests.

6. The Agreement contains no provision for duration or review, and the Chief Minister has stated that, since the Federation will never be able alone to provide for her own defence, he recognises that to all intents and purposes it will be perpetual. In order, however, to meet any criticism that the Federation had accepted a military dependence upon the United Kingdom which would make her political independence no more than nominal, it has been agreed that letters should be exchanged and published setting out the understanding, which is no more than the recognition of the obvious, that it will be open to either party at any time to propose a review of all

or any part of the Agreement. There was indeed a danger that if definite provision for duration or review had been made the Agreement might be brought into the local political arena at regular intervals and the present arrangements may well offer surer prospects of its enduring without being seriously challenged.

7.   One of the most difficult points in the negotiation concerned the question of the primary right of jurisdiction over United Kingdom servicemen accused of committing offences while on duty. We took our stand on the practice based on the NATO Status of Forces Agreement, but the Malayans pointed out that their civil courts at present possessed this right of jurisdiction and they argued that it would seem an inexplicable derogation from their sovereignty if they agreed that upon independence these courts should cease to have this power. In the end a compromise was reached under which the Malayans conceded that the Agreement should provide that the primary right of jurisdiction over these offences should rest with the United Kingdom Service authorities provided that it was at the same time agreed in a published exchange of letters that by administrative arrangement the present practices should be allowed to continue.

8.   In general we have good reason to be satisfied with the terms of the Agreement as providing the most hopeful ground upon which we can base ourselves for the discharge of our responsibilities and interest in defending South-East Asia against Communism. It says much for the good sense of the Chief Minister and his colleagues that they recognise that in this the Federation's interest marches with our own. We do not overlook, of course, that there is some opposition, from nationalist and neutralist elements in Malaya, to the policies of the present Government; the extent to which this criticism may be kept in check will depend upon the success which attends the efforts of the present Government in promoting economic and social development and in the continuing evidence of a fruitful and beneficial co-operation between the Federation and the United Kingdom.

9.   Two minor technical points still remain outstanding which should be resolved within the next few weeks. Thereafter, we expect to exchange letters with the Government of the Federation confirming that the Agreement as then negotiated shall be brought into effect on the day that the Federation becomes fully self-governing. The Agreement is a bilateral one, but it has been drawn in such a way that the other Commonwealth forces in Malaya enjoy the same position as United Kingdom forces. The Governments of Australia and New Zealand have been kept fully informed throughout the negotiations, and it is likely that their formal association with it can be secured by exchanges of letters between them and the Government of the Federation, and that it will not therefore be necessary for them to conclude separate agreements.

10.   The Agreement is concerned exclusively with external defence, and no provision is made in it for United Kingdom forces to be made available to assist the Federation in operations against the Communist terrorists. Her Majesty's Government have stated that they are willing that those forces should continue to assist in these operations, and the Federation Government has agreed that it will be necessary for them to ask for that assistance. Separate negotiations are now in progress with the Federation to agree the manner in which those (and Australian and New Zealand) forces shall be made available, and upon the command organisation under which they shall operate. A completely satisfactory arrangement is likely to be reached very soon.

Financial negotiations

11. As with the Defence Agreement these discussions arose from certain undertakings made at the Malayan Constitutional Conference. At that Conference Her Majesty's Government, in addition to agreeing to make available to the Federation after independence the unspent balances then remaining of a grant of £7.29 million promised her for the expansion of her armed forces and also the balances of her Colonial Development and Welfare Allocations, which on the 1st January, 1956, stood at £6.5 million and £4.4 million respectively, undertook to consider whether any further assistance might be given towards the expansion of the Federation's Armed Forces and towards the cost of the campaign against the Communist terrorists in Malaya, if that had not been brought to an end by the time of independence and if the Federation's financial needs justified such special assistance. It was agreed that detailed discussions could only be held when the Federation had completed the preparation on which they were then engaged of a programme of development for the period immediately after independence.

12. At the recent talks the Federation delegation submitted such a comprehensive development plan and sought assistance from Her Majesty's Government in implementing it under the following heads:—

(a) assistance in cash and kind towards the expansion of their armed forces;
(b) assistance in cash towards the cost of the emergency; and
(c) an exchequer loan at reduced rates of interest for development.

13. In the discussions it was recognised that political independence connoted financial self-sufficiency, and that it would be incompatible with this doctrine for the United Kingdom to grant exchequer assistance towards the development programme of an independent country. Her Majesty's Government agreed, on the other hand, that it would not be inconsistent with this doctrine to give assistance towards the cost of the Emergency or to the development of the Armed Forces which the Federation wished to create to fight it, since the Emergency was not the exclusive concern of the Federation alone, but was a part of the struggle against Communism in which the whole of the free world was engaged. In recognition of this, Her Majesty's Government is at present bearing the full cost of her forces engaged on emergency operations in the Federation, and will continue to do so. The emergency assistance discussed at these talks related to that expenditure on the Emergency which bore on the Federation. The Federation's estimate of the total assistance needed was based, however, on a number of assumptions about the future trend of her revenue and expenditure all of which could be challenged. Her Majesty's Government felt that a reasonable, but in no way harsh, estimate of those trends indicated that over the six-year period to which her development plan may be expected to extend, the Federation would nevertheless still discover a need for financial assistance, and they therefore agreed to make further assistance available over and above the two items mentioned in paragraph 11 above. This new assistance is as follows:—

(a) an additional grant of £1.3 million in cash towards the expansion of the Federation's armed forces;
(b) a grant of £5.5 million in kind of equipment, &c., for the Federation's Armed Forces plus the free transfer to the Federation of certain surplus installations of

the British forces in Malaya; details of these are not available as yet and no value can therefore be given to them;

(c) a cash grant of £3 million a year towards the cost of the Emergency in the three years to 1959, and a promise to contribute up to a maximum of a further £11 million in 1960 and 1961, the exact amount to be determined in 1960 when it will also be decided whether this further assistance shall be in the form of a grant or an interest-free loan or part loan, part grant.

14. The total value of the assistance which Her Majesty's Government has agreed to give the Federation from Exchequer sources in the period 1956–61 will at the lowest estimate exceed £27 million, and could exceed £38 million. In addition Her Majesty's Government has agreed that during this period the Federation may look to raise loans on the London market, while in accordance with principles already enunciated governing the activities of the Colonial Development Corporation in emergent territories, the Federation may expect certain assistance from this source.

15. This assistance falls some considerable way short of that for which the Federation asked.[1] Nevertheless, on any reasonable estimate, such as can now be made, it is likely to meet all the Federation's needs and to enable the Federation to embark confidently on its development programme. The Chief Minister has recognised that having regard to Her Majesty's Government's other commitments (including those she already has for her forces in Malaya) it represents a generous gesture, and it is our confident hope that it will be recognised in Malaya as evidence of the genuine goodwill and interest which we have and will continue to have in the prosperity and well-being of this new independent member of the Commonwealth.

16. All the above, with the exception of paragraphs 4–7 inclusive, the second sentence of paragraph 8, and the last sentence of paragraph 11, may be used at your discretion.

---

[1] E Melville (CO) reported to MacGillivray by telegram on 16 Jan 1957 as follows: 'To sum up, reason why Malayan requests were not met in full was not, as Tunku ingenuously said in Dublin, because "Britain is broke", but because Federation could not prove need for more. Assistance we have now promised is gesture of faith and good will, which has been agreed after far less rigorous scrutiny of Federation's proposals and needs than we normally apply, and will, in our view, enable Federation confidently to press ahead with development plan they have drawn up' (CO 1030/683, no 3).

442 CO 1030/522, no 6   13 Feb 1957
[Report of the Reid Commission]: outward telegram no 31 from Mr Lennox-Boyd to Sir D MacGillivray

Following for MacGillivray from Johnston.

Begins. Report of Constitutional Commission.[1]

Following are my first personal impressions.

Recommendations on Settlements seem acceptable.[2] Although appointment of Governor is to be made by Yang di-Pertuan Besar, he is to consult settlement and not (repeat not) Federal Government in making appointment. Governor is to be above

---

[1] *Report of the Federation of Malaya Constitutional Commission 1957* (Col no 330).
[2] See 425 and 438.

politics and once appointed is secured from any control or direction by Yang di-Pertuan Besar or Federal Government. Report and Constitution emphasise at many points complete equality of status of Settlements and States and of Governors and Rulers (Cp. Art 64 of Constitution which lays down precedence according to date of accession or appointment). Report also emphasises that Governor represents people of the Settlement. This seems to give us all we were anxious about. Only point we might contest is proposal for removal of Governor by two-thirds majority which seems unwise politically and unnecessary technically since appointment is only for 4 years.

2.   Citizenship recommendations as they affect settlements are also satisfactory, permitting retention of U.K. and Colonies citizenship without loss of Federal citizenship, and Commission have usefully dealt with this by reference to Malaya as a whole and have not tied it directly to position of people in the Settlements. This helps presentationally. Hamid's minority report (unfortunately entitled 'Note of Dissent') objects to persons now eligible for Federal citizenship because they are citizens of U.K. and Colonies (but who have not been registered as citizens) retaining for that reason *right* to be registered as citizens after independence; but this is not a major point, and he does not seem to object to general dual citizenship proposals.

3.   Report generally seems to offer some helpful compromises on difficult questions, but betrays regrettable lack of unanimity, many paragraphs beginning 'In the opinion of the majority' and many others saying that Hamid or McKell or Reid did not agree on some particular point. We can only wait and see how far this will be seized on by those who themselves want to disagree. Hamid's note of dissent has been much emasculated by comparison with version we saw earlier, and though its appearance is regrettable it does not look prima facie as if it will do all that much harm. Some of his practical comments on the drafting seem to have good sense in them, and the offensive passages about the doom of the Malays after twenty years have been completely excised.

4.   On general recommendations your opinion will be more valuable than ours, but it looks from here as though there may be difficulty over provisions which seek to compel States to enact their constitutions including certain essential provisions by 1st January, 1959 (paragraphs 184–188) with sanction that Federal Government can take over the State Government[s] if they fail. Reid has himself entered a note of dissent on this last.

5.   Fuller comments later. Main first impression is that problems of getting agreement are more likely to be between elements in Malaya than between those elements and H.M.G.[3] Citizenship provisions look potentially acceptable but complicated relations between Federal Government and States may take some ironing out. Grateful for your own first impressions however brief when you have seen the documents. I will try and get Lawson's[4] assessment of Rulers' likely reaction and telegraph it before he arrives. Please say soonest if there is any particular point you want put over to him if opportunity arises. *Ends*.

---

[3] The working party on the report, consisting of representatives of the Alliance and rulers and senior British officials, met for the first time on 22 Feb 1957, see 446, note.
[4] Neil Lawson QC acted as the rulers' legal representative at the Reid hearings.

443   CO 1030/518   18 Feb 1957

[Constitutional commission]: minute by J B Johnston on the behaviour of Lord and Lady Reid while in Malaya and Rome

The Secretary of State wishes to send a letter to Lord Reid to await his return from holiday in Sicily, thanking him for his work on the Constitutional Commission, and I attach a draft for consideration.[1]

2. I must say I found this a very difficult letter to draft, the more particularly because I had a long talk with Mr. Henderson, the Assistant Secretary of the Commission this morning. He has come to England for a medical checkup before returning to Malaya and I think there is no question that the strain of working for the Commission is responsible for the breakdown in his health which has made this necessary. I think I ought to record some of the impressions he gave me. He thought the Commission had finished up completely at loggerheads with each other, largely because of the extraordinary behaviour of the Reids who had set an example of self-concern and had been utterly and consistently inconsiderate not only of the staff of the Commission but of the other members. Mr. Henderson was quite certain that Mr. Justice Hamid's insistence at the last minute on producing a minority report was little more than an attempt to asert himself after his opinions and views had been consistently brushed aside by Lord Reid during the Commission's time in Malaya.

3. The rudeness with which the Reids visited almost everyone with whom they came in contact is scarcely credible. I cannot forebear [sic] from setting down a recent example. At Christmastime the Manager of the hotel at which the Reids were staying in Rome sent up to them with his compliments an enormous bunch of flowers from Sicily as a Christmas gift. Lady Reid's response was to write him a two-page letter telling him off for having failed to address them correctly!

4. I think I might also set down an example of the vice-regal and patronising attitude which caused so much resentment during the extremely leisurely progress of the Commission round Malaya, when it appears very little work was done. Leaving a lunch party given for them by the Mentri Besar of Johore, host and guests, who included the British Resident, went outside to the waiting car. Lord Reid stepped forward to open the door of the car for his wife to get in, but was called back by Lady Reid who said "Stop, Scott. They *must* learn". A silence followed since neither the Mentri Besar nor the British Resident, to whom Lady Reid had been rude at lunchtime, felt inclined to be told to open the door for her. I understand the silence was broken by an oath from the driver who leapt from his seat and opened the door himself!

5. I do not suggest that we should take cognizance of these stories and I would not wish to embarrass Mr. Henderson who passed them on to me. I only record them because I do not know what fulminations we may get from Lord Reid about lack of co-operation when he returns to this country, and I am anxious that if there are any complaints there should be no illusions about the context in which they arose. The Commission's report reflects the disharmony which prevailed throughout, and which I think we cannot but ascribe to the absence of real leadership. I think we must be profoundly grateful that the report is as good as it is.

---

[1] Not printed.

444 CO 1030/437   19 Feb 1957

[Commonwealth membership]: minute by I B Watt[1] to J B Johnston
on Malaya's application

We had a word yesterday about Membership of the Commonwealth, for Malaya. You told me that no steps have as yet been taken by the U.K. Government to arrange this, and I said I would let you have a note.

As you know, Ministers have said publicly that, whereas the grant of independence to a dependent territory is a matter for the U.K. Government alone, Membership of the Commonwealth is "a matter for the existing Members". Several times in recent years Labour Members of Parliament have tried to pin down Ministers with the question whether or not any existing Member has a right of veto, but Ministers have always succeeded in not being drawn.

Largely because of the susceptibilities of the Union of South Africa, the U.K. Government began to prepare for getting Ghana accepted as a Member as long as two years ago. It was recognised here that it would be necessary to play South Africa along patiently and tactfully, and the aim was to get the South African Government into a position where it would be as easy as possible for them "to agree not to dissent" when eventually the proposal that Ghana be accepted as a Commonwealth Member was formally put to them. There have thus been between the C.R.O. and the U.K. High Commissioner in South Africa exchanges of elaborate communications, during the past two years. At the same time U.K. High Commissioners in other Commonwealth capitals were instructed to keep the Governments to which they were accredited informed of all the important political and constitutional developments in Gold Coast, and, generally, to let them know that in due course the U.K. Government would be putting formal proposals for Ghana's Membership to them.

By the summer of 1956, the U.K. Government felt confident enough of its policy for Gold Coast for the Prime Minister, Sir Anthony Eden, to write to the other Commonwealth Prime Ministers, who were in London for the Conference, saying that it looked as though Gold Coast would get independence in the spring of 1957, and asking for their agreement in principle to accepting Ghana as a Member when independence came about. Each Prime Minister gave a written assurance of acceptance (Mr. Strijdom's was churlish, but he did agree).[2]

All that has been required in the past month i.e. once the legislative measures for Ghana's independence have been made effective in the U.K., has been for the C.R.O. to send Prime Minister to Prime Minister telegrams recalling the agreements in principle, given last summer, and asking them to confirm that they now agree in substance.[3] Replies giving this agreement in substance came back from all the Prime Ministers concerned straightaway. I expect that an announcement of Ghana's becoming a Member of the Commonwealth will be made on or about Independence Day.[4]

---

[1] See 307, note 1.
[2] See BDEEP series B, vol 1, R Rathbone, ed, *Ghana*, part II, 229; also *ibid* series A, vol 3, D Goldsworthy, ed, *The Conservative government and the end of empire 1951–1957*, part I, 146, 147, 149–154. Johannes G Strijdom was prime minister of South Africa, 1954–1958.
[3] See Rathbone, *op cit*, part II, 284.
[4] The Gold Coast became independent as Ghana on 6 Mar 1957.

I do not myself think that Malaya is as awkward a customer as Gold Coast has been, for various reasons; but I do feel that since there are only six months to go, assuming all goes well, before Malayan independence, it would be wise to start now to explain our policy for the achievement of that independence carefully to the Commonwealth Governments, and seek their approval in principle to Membership of the Commonwealth for Malaya at the same time as independence is achieved. The thing to do would be to work out with the C.R.O. suitable draft communications to the High Commissioners.[5]

---

[5] After the Anglo-Malayan London talks in May, the matter of Malaya's membership was put on the agenda of the July meeting of Commonwealth prime ministers, see 445, 447, 457 and 458.

445   DO 35/6281, no 3A   14 Mar 1957
[South Africa and Malaya's membership of the Commonwealth]: letter from Sir P Liesching[1] to H J B Lintott[2]

Now that Ghana has been accepted by the Union Government, not without hesitation and difficulty, as a fellow member of the Commonwealth, I have been considering the prospects opened up for us here by the near approach to independence of the next candidate for membership, namely the Federation of Malaya.

2. It might be thought that the principle of accepting these colonies as Commonwealth members has now been swallowed by the Union and that since that awkward corner has been turned there will be no great difficulty in the future. This comforting conclusion might in the case of Malaya find support from the reflection that she is remote and non-African and that her independence will have none of the direct impact on South Africa that the emergence of Ghana will inevitably have, and is indeed already having. But the conclusion is, of course, far wide of the mark. Commonwealth membership for non-White countries, implying an eventual preponderance of non-White Prime Ministers at Commonwealth Prime Ministers meetings, is a matter of intense interest to Union Ministers—and could well in the long run be decisive for their attitude to the Commonwealth connexion. Moreover the Union Government's view of Ghana's admission would not so much be that a principle had been established as that two principles had been breached. The correspondence that passed between Mr. Strijdom and Mr. Eden last year sufficiently indicates that in their view colonies should not be given Commonwealth membership unless they are in all respects ready for independence, as the Gold Coast was not (in their view), and that the Gold Coast should not have been promised "independence within the Commonwealth" without consultation with the other Commonwealth members.[3] The reasoning behind this latter argument was only recently vouchsafed to me by Mr. Strijdom—as you will remember from my letter of the 4th February—as being that colonies are automatically part of the Commonwealth only so long as they are administered by a member of the Commonwealth, and that once they cease to be so administered they cannot remain within the Commonwealth in any capacity without approval by the existing membership.

---

[1] UK high commissioner in South Africa.   [2] Deputy under-secretary of state, CRO.
[3] For references to this correspondence, see 444, note 2.

3. No doubt the Union Government's views on these matters are unacceptable to us and there is, I assume, no possibility of Malaya's progress to independence and Commonwealth membership being impeded on their account. But it is equally true that, unless we regard the Union's relationship with the Commonwealth as of no account, some attention must be paid to her Government's views.

4. As to the more formal point of "independence within the Commonwealth" this phase has already been publicly used to describe the immediate goal for Malaya—and was indeed so used before Mr. Strijdom took exception to it. But if we are to continue to use it something ought clearly to be said to Mr. Strijdom even if it must be to explain that we for our part do not accept his view of the formal position and that it does not appear to be shared by the other members.

5. On the more substantial point, of the readiness of Malaya for independence, I think it would be wise urgently to prepare, for communication to Mr. Strijdom, a realistic memorandum on the internal situation in Malaya comparable to that on the Gold Coast which I was able to use in 1955 (see the last paragraph of the record enclosed with my letter to Laithwaite of the 15th December, 1955). The latest document of this kind we have on Malaya is that enclosed with Ormerod's letter of the 29th February, 1956, but this would no doubt need to be edited and brought up to date. The Union Government have, of course, received the full accounts that have been sent to us from London about last year's Constitutional Conference and its results, including the report of the Constitutional Commission, but it is uncertain how much of this has reached Ministers themselves or what its impact has been. For this reason the memorandum ought I think to give a very brief account of where matters now stand.

6. If I were able to take such a document to Mr. Strijdom and to convey to him some message on the question of "self-government within the Commonwealth" it would, I am sure, serve to avert the immediate danger I see of resentment on the part of Union Ministers at being given no direct opportunity of commenting on matters about which in the case of the Gold Coast they had indicated to us their decided concern.

7. In the longer term the Union's continued membership of the Commonwealth is still an open question. The recent comments of Dr. Odendaal, the new National Party leader in the Transvaal (on which I shall be reporting separately) sufficiently indicates [sic] that the objective of the extreme Nationalists in that important province is still to take the Republic out of the Commonwealth—though that is by no means the end of the matter. On our side it may be that we are moving towards a situation in which we might ourselves be content to see her outside. But all this is for the longer term. Meanwhile I think it of great importance that on these matters of membership that could have a close bearing on the Union's ultimate decision we should be particularly careful to take them manifestly into our confidence, and—in the peculiar circumstances of this country—not to assume that silence on their part must mean consent.

446   CO 1030/524, no 31   1 Apr 1957

[Working party on the Reid Report]: letter from Sir D Watherston to
J B Johnston on the political background to current discussions

[Extract]

[The working party was chaired by MacGillivray and consisted of four representatives of
the rulers, four from the Alliance, the chief secretary (Watherston) and the attorney
general (T V A Brodie). It met for the first time on 22 Feb and finalised its recommendations for the revision of the report by 1 May. The papers of the working party are at CO
941/85. Meanwhile, in the wider political arena, the issues of citizenship and the Malays'
special position, proved particularly contentious. In Mar, as Malay opinion hardened
against Reid's recommendations, the Tunku had to battle with critics within UMNO to
win his party's authority to negotiate a new constitution based upon the Reid report.]

Although you are being sent a lot of material about our discussions in the Working
Party on the Constitution, I thought you might perhaps like to have a personal note
about some of the background which has not found its way into the telegrams. I will
make it as short as possible, as you must have been having an exceedingly trying time
over the Singapore discussions.[1] In fact, you cannot be looking forward with any
particular relish to the prospect of yet another conference with the Federation in just
over a month's time!

2.   The UMNO meeting at the end of last week was critical. The real danger was
that one didn't know for certain in advance what line the Tunku might take. There
had been signs that, if faced with a serious threat of revolt, he would have been ready
to fall in with the idea that Merdeka should come first and consideration of the Reid
Commission Report later. He has remarked more than once that Pakistan managed
to get on quite well without a constitution for eight years. However, I think he
realised that H.M.G. held the whip hand on this and would not be prepared to agree
to Merdeka on the 31st August unless certain essential matters were settled
first—the key issue being citizenship.

3.   In one respect, however, he was in a strong position at the UMNO meeting.
Dato Onn and his new associates have been concentrating their fire on the
inadequacy of the draft Constitution in so far as it fails to give an assurance of
permanency for special privileges for the Malays. They had not said so much about
citizenship. As you know, the Working Party has already agreed to substantial
alterations of the Articles dealing with the special position of the Malays and the
Tunku was therefore able to tell UMNO (he had carefully not let out the news earlier)
that the Malays' position would be adequately secured by amendments which had
been agreed in the Working Party. He and other Ministers had a fairly rough passage,
I gather, particularly over the Negri Sembilan proposal that decisions on the Reid
Report should be postponed, but they came out on top at the end with a clear
mandate for acceptance of the Commission's Report as a whole.

4.   We must, I think, look forward to the opposition parties switching their
attacks to the citizenship provisions. This is going to be much more embarrassing for
the Tunku and his Ministers because, of course, he has no room for manoeuvre. He
cannot retreat from the agreement reached last year and incorporated in the Alliance

---

[1] In Mar 1957 Lim Yew Hock led a second all-party delegation to London to renew discussions about
self-government for Singapore.

memorandum to the Reid Commission. No doubt Dato Onn will do his utmost to stir up feeling among the Malays and there is the distinct danger that H.M.G. may in due course find itself cast for the role of "whipping boy" on account of the necessity for safeguarding the position of the inhabitants of the two Settlements.

5. We have been having extremely sticky meetings on finance and land with differences of opinion, stoutly maintained on both sides, between the Federal (Alliance) representatives on the Working Party and the representatives of the Rulers. The Tunku has announced that these questions may have to be left over for decision after Merdeka. We shall do our best to avoid this, but, in the last resort, it may be necessary to fall in with this idea.

6. It looks as if the chief difficulty ahead is going to be over dual citizenship. The Tunku was very emphatic in rejecting it at the UMNO meeting, but in private conversation he seems to be ready to consider a compromise in the form of permitting the retention of citizenship of another country within the Commonwealth concurrently with citizenship of the Federation provided that reciprocal provisions in regard to the Federation are made by that other country. This, however, is a matter which must be left for discussion in London and a complete re-writing of the article in question will be necessary.

7. There is one other consideration which I cannot help feeling is bound, in due course, to affect developments here in one way or another. The draft Constitution requires elections to take place in 1959. So far as one can foresee at present, that will be a time which will not suit the Alliance at all. The glamour of Merdeka will have gone and there will not have been time for many of the projects in the Development Plan to produce results. It will be easy for the opposition parties to point out that all that the Alliance has done since it was elected in 1955 has been to increase taxation. The best possible time for the Alliance to go to the country would be before the end of this year. They can then cash in on having achieved Merdeka and be in the saddle for another four years. There is no sign at present that they are planning anything of the kind and, of course, it runs completely contrary to the principle that new elections should not be held until the new categories of citizens have had time to get put on the electoral roll. However, I think it is a factor which we must keep in mind during the next few months as one which may provide an explanation for any sudden change in Alliance tactics. . . .[2]

---

[2] In the last paragraph of this letter Watherston turns to a different matter—*viz* the agreement whereby the Federation was to have a representative on Singapore's Internal Security Council—and voiced 'considerable personal misgivings' over the arrangement.

447   DO 35/6281, no 5A   2 Apr 1957
[South Africa and Malaya's membership of the Commonwealth]: letter (reply) from H J B Lintott to Sir P Liesching. *Enclosure:* CRO memorandum on the internal situation in Malaya

Thank you for your letter SAR.303/73/1 of 14th March about membership of the Commonwealth for the Federation of Malaya.[1]

---

[1] See 445.

We are very grateful for your timely comments on the Union Government's attitude on this issue and for your further definition of Mr. Strijdom's views on independence within, and membership of, the Commonwealth generally.

In answer to the request in paragraph 5 of your letter, we have had prepared, and I now enclose a memorandum on the internal situation in Malaya which brings up to date the earlier paper of February 1956, to which you refer. There has not been time to consult the High Commissioner in Kuala Lumpur on its contents, but the note has been cleared with the Colonial Office and gives, I think, a fair and unbiased picture of the current Malayan situation. I hope that you will find it suitable as a basis for discussion with Mr. Strijdom.

As to the questions raised in paragraphs 2 to 4 of your letter, it is no use our denying that Mr. Strijdom has some logic on his side when he argues that Her Majesty's Government should not promise "Independence within the Common- wealth" without prior consultation with other Commonwealth members, because the mere fact that a country has been vouchsafed in advance the goal of full self-government within the Commonwealth, virtually commits other members to granting it membership in its turn. But political realities are more important than logic. To commit Her Majesty's Government to the principle of prior consultation as a preliminary step to granting a colonial territory its independence within the Commonwealth, would, in practice, be tantamount to giving any member country the right of veto on United Kingdom colonial policy. Mr. Strijdom will hardly need reminding that it has for long been the policy of successive United Kingdom governments that the colonial territories, as they reach the goal of self-government and independence, should remain within the Commonwealth. If, therefore, we were to admit that unanimous agreement among the existing member countries was required for a newly independent ex-colony to remain in the Commonwealth, we should be allowing other members to obstruct the implementation of decisions about independence which are for the United Kingdom Government alone.

The above also answers the additional contention that colonies, once they cease to be administered by a member country of the Commonwealth, can no longer remain within the Commonwealth. In practice, the membership issues has in all past cases been settled before the date of independence, so that a hiatus of the kind foreseen by Mr. Strijdom has in fact never arisen. Nor, of course, would it be our intention to allow things so to develop that a dangerous gap existed between the date of a colony's attainment of independence and its acceptance as a member of the Commonwealth. Clearly the membership issue must on every count be settled before independence is brought about.

You will be the best judge of how to handle this matter with Mr. Strijdom so as to secure his agreement about Malaya while avoiding an intolerable theological argument. But subject to your views, we suggest that in presenting the enclosed memorandum to Mr. Strijdom, you might wish to speak to him on the following lines.

As the Prime Minister will realize, the decision to grant independence to the Federation of Malaya was reached as long ago as February, 1956, when the Constitutional Conference, meeting in London, agreed that full self-government and independence within the Commonwealth for the Federation should be proclaimed by August, 1957. Furthermore, the terms of reference of the Commonwealth Constitu- tional Commission, which were at the same time approved by the Conference, stated that the Commission should make recommendations for a form of constitution "for a fully self-governing and independent Federation of Malaya within the Common-wealth". The Union Government, together with all other member countries, were kept fully informed at the time of these developments. (See for instance our telegram W. No. 27 of 8th February, 1956). Her Majesty's Government have no reason to believe that they gave rise to any doubt on the part of other member countries as to the aim which Her Majesty's Government were pursuing in regard to the Federation.

You might then go on to say that the United Kingdom Government do not fully appreciate the reasons underlying Mr. Strijdom's suggestion that once a colonial dependency ceases to be administered by a member government of the Common-wealth, it should not be regarded as remaining within the Commonwealth. The policy of Her Majesty's Government, as repeatedly stated by successive governments, is not only to bring the colonial territories stage by stage to the goal of independence, but to ensure that when they reach that goal they shall remain within the Commonwealth. The United Kingdom Government, as the administering power, is in the best position to judge when a colony is ripe for independence. It is of course the hope of Her Majesty's Government that each new candidate for independence within the Commonwealth will also be recognised by other Commonwealth govern-ments as a member of the Commonwealth. It would be impracticable for the membership issue to be left for discussion until after a colony had obtained its independence. So far this situation has been avoided. If Mr Strijdom's theory were to be accepted very considerable practical difficulties would follow. A juridical and constitutional vacuum would be created. The precise status of the emerging territory would be open to question and the link with the Crown or Sovereign would be, if only temporarily, interrupted.

In expressing the hope that the Union Government will agree, as in the case of Ghana, to recognize the Federation of Malaya as a member country of the Commonwealth as from the date of its independence on 31st August, you might, if you see fit, go on to emphasize the cogent political arguments which are advanced in the latter part of the enclosed memorandum in favour of this course. The case for accepting Malaya as a member of the Commonwealth in order to help her to resist Communism and to become a viable independent state capable of withstanding external and internal trouble (in contrast with, for instance, Indonesia) is of course of more general application. You may find it useful in speaking to Mr Strijdom to play up this argument.

I hope that you will shortly be receiving a message for Mr. Strijdom about possible dates for the next Prime Ministers' meeting, and that soon after we shall be able to let him have, through you, our suggestions for the items which might be included in the draft agenda of the meeting. It would certainly be our intention that the admission of Malaya to membership of the Commonwealth should be discussed at the next meeting, though whether we would put the item formally upon the agenda I do not yet know. I imagine that you might think it best to wait until we are in a position to put specific suggestions about the topics that might be discussed at the meeting before you deploy the arguments about Malaya.

In view of its general interest, I am sending copies of this correspondence to all our other posts for information.

Enclosure to 447

The Federation of Malaya is the largest of the six territories in Asia for the government of which the United Kingdom is still ultimately responsible. The British connection originated in trading ventures of the 18th and 19th centuries, and in 1829 [1826] the three areas Penang, Singapore and Malacca, were combined to form the Straits Settlements. In the later years of the nineteenth century treaties were concluded between Her Majesty The Queen and the Rulers of a number of the Malay States which then became a Federation with a British Resident General and a centralized system of government; and by the Bangkok Treaty of 1909 Siam transferred to Britain all rights of suzerainty, protection, etc., which she had over some of the Northern States. Up to 1941, when Malaya was overrun and occupied by the Japanese, the area consisted of three administrative units—the Colony of the Straits Settlements, the Federated Malay States and the Unfederated Malay States.

2. After the war a highly centralized Malayan Union was introduced. It became apparent that there was widespread dissatisfaction among the Malay section of the population over the constitutional position which they considered to take too little account of the rights of the Malay States. After a Conference in 1948 there finally emerged the Federation of Malaya Agreement of that year under which each of the nine States and the two Settlements of Malacca and Penang were to retain their own individuality but all were to be united under a strong central government. In 1951, the "member" system was introduced as the first step towards ministerial responsibility, and in 1955 a new Constitution was brought in which transferred to the elected representatives of the people most of the responsiblity for the government of the Federation. An election was held in July of that year at which the Alliance Party (formed by the union of the United Malay National Organisation (U.M.N.O.), the Malayan Chinese Association (M.C.A.) and the Malayan Indian Congress (M.I.C.)) was returned with an overwhelming majority. Discussions followed between the United Kingdom Government, the new Alliance Ministers and Their Highnesses the Rulers, at which it was agreed that a conference should be held in London early in 1956 to discuss the problems involved in advancing further towards self-government.

3. The Constitutional Conference, which ended in February, 1956, was attended by representatives of the United Kingdom Government, Their Highnesses the Malay Rulers and the Alliance Government. It produced an agreed Report on the steps necessary "to secure the early establishment of a fully self-governing and independent Federation of Malaya within the Commonwealth on the basis of Parliamentary institutions." It made recommendations which covered defence and internal security, financial and economic matters, the public services and future constitutional changes. The recommendations were divided to cover the interim period and the period after the attainment of independence.

4. The results of the Conference were widely welcomed in the Federation of Malaya, and its recommendations have received general support. The attention of political leaders has consequently been largely concentrated on putting into effect the recommendations for changes during the interim period.

5. The arrangements agreed at the Conference have made it possible for the Chief Minister and his elected colleagues in the Government to assume responsibility during the interim period for internal security within the Federation, and for the foundation to be laid for the administration of the Federation armed forces after the

Federation acquires full self-government, and they have introduced Ministers to the problems of external affairs and defence which will then confront them.

6. Concerning the period after the Federation becomes fully self-governing, the Conference agreed that the United Kingdom Government and the Government of the Federation should enter into an agreement upon external defence and mutual assistance in defence matters. Discussions have since taken place on the terms of this suggested agreement, and also on the financial assistance to be given by the United Kingdom Government to the Federation during the first years of its independence. As a result, a mutually acceptable agreement has been reached which provides that the United Kingdom Government shall assist the Government of the Federation in the external defence of its territory, and shall have the right to maintain in the Federation such naval, land and air forces, including a Commonwealth strategic reserve, as are mutually agreed to be necessary for that purpose, and for the fulfilment of Commonwealth and international obligations.

7. Satisfactory financial arrangements were also agreed upon, which, though falling some way short of what the Federation had asked, are nevertheless likely to meet all its essential needs and to enable the Federation confidently to embark on its development programme. The Chief Minister has recognized that having regard to the United Kingdom's other commitments (including those she already has for her forces in Malaya) these arrangements represent a generous gesture.

8. Looking further ahead, the 1956 Constitutional Conference agreed that an independent Constitutional Commission with members drawn from other Commonwealth countries, should be appointed in order to make recommendations to implement the accepted aim of a Constitution providing for full self-government. This Commission, which was appointed in the name of Her Majesty The Queen and of Their Highnesses the Rulers, under the chairmanship of the Rt. Hon. Lord Reid, has recently published its Report. The recommendations have been generally well received in Malaya and are now being studied by the United Kingdom Government, Their Highnesses the Rulers and the Federation Government, with a view to the formulation of agreed conclusions.

9. The Report envisages that Malaya shall become an independent Federal Secular State within the Commonwealth with a strong central government retaining the police in its own hands, but leaving land as a State subject and residual power also resting with the State Governments. There will be a Paramount Ruler, elected from among the Malay Rulers for a five-year period, who will have the functions of a constitutional monarch. Each State will continue to have its Ruler, Executive Council and Legislative Assembly. The Colonies of Malacca and Penang will be absorbed in the independent Federation of Malaya, and their direct link with the Crown will be severed. The Governor, who will be the Head of Government in each of these two Settlements, will be appointed in accordance with the wishes of the Settlements and will enjoy status with the Malay Rulers. The Settlements themselves will come into the Federation as States of equal status with the other Malay States.

10. The Alliance Party, despite some signs of internal strain and recent political setbacks (in local government elections last December they suffered a number of defeats) still controls all but one of the elected seats in the Federal Legislative Council, is dominant in the State Councils and even in the local government elections won 21 of the 31 seats at issue. It is the only party to bring together in one organisation political groups representing the major communities. The Communists

and their friends were trying in 1956 to form a united front; but they have still not achieved this aim. It is from this dominant position that the Alliance are leading the country to independence. [In Malaya, as elsewhere in Asia and Africa, the tide of nationalism flows strongly and is unlikely to slacken, but the Alliance, with their overwhelming majority, need not feel themselves under any strain to keep pace with an opposition constantly trying to outbid them in popular favour, and their approach to the question of self-government has been temperate and reasonable.][2] They have displayed good sense and realism and a welcome interest in getting on with the many essential tasks of government that press upon them in such fields as education and economic development. [Their leader, Tunku Abdul Rahman, has indeed publicly stated that there are only two alternatives for Malaya; to take the easy way of ending the conflict by throwing in their lot with the Communists, or to resist subversion with the aid of the United Kingdom and the West; that his decision is firmly for the latter alternative and it is for this reason that he is prepared to keep United Kingdom and other Commonwealth forces in Malaya after independence.] The Alliance also have the advantage of including among their leaders a number of experienced and level-headed men. Constitutional development in the Federation has followed an unusual course in that a ministerial system (the "member system" as it was called) was introduced long before any elections were held; and since it became clear well in advance of the first elections that the Alliance would almost certainly win them easily, it was possible for the High Commissioner to give some of their leading members experience of ministerial office even under the old Constitution. [Fortunately the Alliance for their part had at the top a small group of men capable of holding office effectively. Further, because most of the mature and educated Malays were in the public service, it was necessary under the old Constitution to allow some of the most senior and able of them to take part in politics.] Several of the most senior public servants also became important members of the Alliance and the party have consequently been able to bring to the councils of their Government useful experience of administration from within the public service as well as in command of it.

11.   Another factor conducive to stability is that Tunku Abdul Rahman, who is, of course, the undisputed leader of the U.M.N.O. as well as the Alliance, personally commands the warm support of the vast majority of the Malays throughout the Federation. He combines the prestige of Royalty (he is the half-brother of the Sultan of Kedah) with a genuine and unmistakable feeling for the main body of Malay peasants. Born in 1903, he was educated at Penang and at Cambridge, and later qualified as a barrister. From 1930 to 1951 he was a Civil Servant, but then resigned in order to become President of the U.M.N.O. [He has a certain intuitive sense of politics and is essentially sincere.] He has, [moreover,] made many sacrifices for the cause of Malayan nationalism and is generally regarded as the champion of the Malay race.

12.   Despite these factors there has nevertheless been a potential source of instability within the Alliance itself. The U.M.N.O. and the M.C.A. exist separately to further the divided interests of the two races, and each wtihin itself reflects the

---

[2] This memo was used to brief the governments of other Commonwealth countries on Malaya. It was circulated by telegram to UK high commissioners. The sections in square brackets were omitted from the telegrams sent to New Delhi, Karachi, Colombo and Accra.

suspicion of the other which still deeply pervades the Malay and Chinese peoples throughout the Federation. The Chinese resent the preponderant political power of the Malays and the Malays distrust the economic predominance of the Chinese. Hence the Chinese demand for equality in citizenship with the Malays and (among other reasons) Malay resistance to any increase in the political power of the Chinese. The proposals of the Constitutional Commission have, however, been specifically designed to satisfy the conflicting interests and allay the fears of the Malay and Chinese communities; these proposals strike a reasonable balance between the different interests within the Federation, and the fact that they have had such a generally good reception in Malaya is a good augury for future relations between the major communities and for the stability of the country.

13. The emergency situation is another ever present problem. The Communist terrorists appear to have realized that they cannot get their way by force, and have therefore been concentrating on preserving their strength and have limited action to the minimum necessary to make their presence felt and feared. (They have refused offers by the Chief Minister of a passage to China should they surrender). There is, however, little hope of completely eliminating them, and it seems clear that the terrorists will continue to pose a latent threat to, and constitute a considerable burden on, the new independent Malaya's resources. Fortunately one compensation for the emergency is that since 1948 it has kept most of the fanatical indoctrinated Communist cadres in the jungle, thus severely limiting the Malayan Communist Party's capacity for general subversion. As a result, the [legitimate] political parties and the trade unions are relatively free from Communist infiltration; indeed the leaders of the Alliance are stoutly and openly anti-Communist [and although the problem of Communism in the Chinese schools is serious, it is nothing like so grave as it recently proved in Singapore. The initial danger in Malaya was that Communism would ride on the nationalist band-wagon and, by constantly encouraging public opinion to believe that nothing but British intransigeance stands in the way of immediate self-government, goad the non-Communist political parties to behave as if that were true. By their championship of the nationalist cause for political advancement, and at the same time their unequivocal rejection of Communism, the Alliance have successfully spiked the Communist guns and have rallied the forces of "legitimate" nationalism on the side of the free world. As a result one of the major factors in the Malayan situation is that the Communists have been unable, as elsewhere, to exploit the nationalist theme.]

14. It none the less remains true that Malaya is in the forefront of the struggle for Communist domination of South East Asia. It is therefore all the more important that the Federation should continue to have the benefit of the moral backing of the Commonwealth connexion no less than the material support of Commonwealth forces to assist them in the struggle. [The issue is really whether it is to the advantage of the Commonwealth as a whole that the new independent Malaya should remain within the Commonwealth and so have this all important guidance and backing, or be left out on a limb to continue the struggle as an individual foreign country on their own. In the latter case, as Malayan Ministers themselves recognize, the chance of their being able successfully to resist the encroaching Red tide would be seriously reduced.]

448   CAB 134/1555, CPC(57)11   8 May 1957

'Report of the constitutional commission for Malaya': memorandum by Mr Lennox-Boyd for the Cabinet Colonial Policy Committee

[The working party having completed its revisions of the Reid Report, a Malayan delegation was due in London for final talks on 13 May. Lennox-Boyd accordingly briefed the Colonial Policy Committee on outstanding issues, notably: the selection of the governors of Penang and Malacca, dual citizenship, and appeals to the Judicial Committee of the Privy Council.]

Background

It was agreed at the Malayan Constitutional Conference in January/February 1956 that Malaya should become independent within the Commonwealth in August this year, and that a Constitutional Commission should be set up to recommend a form of constitution for the independent Federation of Malaya. The Report of the Conference (Cmd. 9714) was approved by the Cabinet on the 22nd February, 1956[1] and by The Queen on the 3rd March.

2. The Constitutional Commission (of which Lord Reid was Chairman) have now reported. Their Report has been reprinted as a non-Parliamentary White Paper (Colonial No. 330) and copies were circulated to members of the Colonial Policy Committee on 12th March (CPC (57) 8). Chapter XII of the Report contains a summary of the Commission's recommendations.

3. It is now necessary for the three parties concerned—H.M.G., the Malay Rulers and the Government of the Federation of Malaya—to reach agreement on the form of the new Constitution on the basis of the recommendations of the Commission.

The task of the constitutional commission

4. The Commission's terms of reference, agreed at the 1956 Conference, laid out the general political framework within which they were to advise. They were to provide for a federal form of government for the whole country as a self-governing unit within the Commonwealth, based on parliamentary democracy, and with a bicameral legislature. There was to be a strong central government though the States and Settlements should enjoy a measure of autonomy; the position of the Rulers, the special position of the Malays and the legitimate interests of other communities were to be safeguarded; there was to be a common nationality for the whole of the Federation; and the Head of State ("Yang di-Pertuan Besar", i.e. Paramount Ruler) was to be chosen from among the Rulers.

5. With the framework of government thus decided in advance, the main problems the Commission had to solve were:—

(i)   The relationship between the States and the Federal Government;
(ii) The relationship between Malays and Chinese (comprehending the thorny issue of citizenship);
(iii) The future of the Settlements. It will be recalled that the two Settlements of Penang and Malacca are part of the Queen's dominions, whereas the nine Malay States are each sovereign and merely under the Queen's protection.

---

[1] See 405 and 406.

The position of H.M.G. in the United Kingdom

6.   It is my view, and that both of the High Commissioner and the Commissioner General for the United Kingdom in South East Asia, that H.M.G. in the United Kingdom have two quite distinct degrees of interest in the recommendations of the Commission.

(i)   As regards the constitutional arrangements as a whole, they have a general interest in seeing that they are sound in principle, acceptable in Malaya, and such as to promote political stability and racial harmony. Apart from this benevolent concern, the general recommendations are a matter primarily for agreement between the parties concerned in Malaya, and H.M.G.'s attitude must be to promote agreement without becoming involved in the domestic argument.

(ii)   H.M.G. in the United Kingdom have a particular and specific responsibility for the future of the two Settlements of Penang and Malacca, since at present they form part of the Queen's dominions and their inhabitants are British subjects by birth, and also as regards the future status of other inhabitants of Malaya who are at present British subjects. H.M.G. are therefore a principal in any discussions and decisions about the future of the Settlements and about the future status of these persons. It has for some time been patent that the Commission was bound to recommend that Penang and Malacca should cease to be part of the Queen's dominions and become an integral part of the new Malaya. It is not possible to conceive of an independent Malaya in which two small areas remain under the sovereignty of the Queen. Indeed, any such arrangement, apart from its impracticability, might gravely damage the prestige of the Crown since it would encourage the inhabitants to believe they could look to the Crown for the redress of grievances, despite the fact that the Crown would have no authority in an independent Malaya. The Queen was therefore advised informally last year that it was likely that the Settlements of Penang and Malacca would cease to be part of Her Majesty's Colonial possessions and would become integral parts of the independent Federation of Malaya, which itself would acknowledge the position of the Queen as Head of the Commonwealth, of which it would remain a member.[2] Our prime concern has accordingly been that the Commission's recommendations should not relegate the two Settlements to a position of inferiority *vis-à-vis* the Malay States, and should deal fairly with their inhabitants and the other British subjects in matters of citizenship and otherwise.

The commission's recommendations

7.   I do not propose in this paper to examine in detail those recommendations of the Commission falling within the category I have described in paragraph 6(i) above. They have tackled the problems mentioned in paragraph 6 with skill and their recommendations seem to be generally acceptable in Malaya. The division of responsibilities between the Federal and the State Governments seems to be prudent and the handling of the Malay/Chinese problem which they have recommended does something for each of these two communities. Malay fears of Chinese domination would, to some extent, be met by the provision that certain special and important privileges accorded at present to the Malays should continue for fifteen years and should then be reviewed by the Malayan Parliament. On the other hand the fears of

---

[2] See 425.

the Chinese that they would be regarded as second-class citizens and that they might be victimised by a Malay Government would be safe-guarded first by the citizenship proposals, which would give the right of *jus soli* to all born after the date of independence and liberal facilities for enfranchisement for the present generations, and secondly by writing certain fundamental rights into the constitution (including clauses prohibiting discrimination on grounds of race). It is only right to add that the Working Party which, as mentioned below, has been considering the Commission's Report, has recommended a considerable number of modifications to the detailed proposals of the Report, including some of those specially referred to here, and other modifications may yet have to be agreed on. But there is no question of departing from the major principles of the Report.

8.   While therefore it might be possible to criticise details of the drafting of the Report and its appended constitution, there seems, subject to what is said below in paragraphs 12–18, no matter of principle in its general recommendations which need restrain H.M.G. from endorsing any agreement which may be reached locally upon them.

9.   As regards the Settlements the recommendations of the Commission (recommendations 97–100 of Chapter XII) also seem to meet our requirements. The Settlements are to come into the new Federation as States of equal status and powers to the Malay States. The Head of each of the Settlements is to be a Governor who, although he is appointed by the Head of State, is to represent and be responsible to the people of the Settlement, and there will be provision to give the Governors of the States due treatment in matters of precedence, etc. In my view these recommendations provide for the honourable entry of the two Settlements into an independent Federation in a way that should be acceptable to their inhabitants and to H.M.G. The recommendations on citizenship are in a somewhat different position. Many of the inhabitants of the Federation who cherish their present status as citizens of the United Kingdom and Colonies have been apprehensive that they would be forced to give up this citizenship in order to become citizens of the new Federation. I urged upon the Commission, in a memorandum on behalf of H.M.G., and the Commission recommended (recommendation 11 of Chapter XII), that dual citizenship should be provided for, so that the inhabitants of the Settlements need not surrender their status as citizens of the United Kingdom and Colonies in order to qualify as citizens of the Federation. As explained below, however, this proposal has not met with the favour of the present government of the Federation, and agreement on the point has still to be reached.

10.   Thus in my view, and subject to the points to which I draw attention in paragraphs 12–18 below, the recommendations of the Commission generally and in the matter of the Settlements should be fully acceptable to H.M.G.

Forthcoming discussions

11.   A Working Party consisting of representatives of the Rulers and of the Government, under the Chairmanship of the High Commissioner, has been considering the Commission's Report and endeavouring to reach agreement on its recommendations within Malaya. I shall be discussing these recommendations and those of this Working Party with a delegation from Malaya during the week beginning the 13th May. The Working Party's recommendations in substance amount to a general acceptance of the Commission's Report, although, as I have

indicated, a number of comparatively detailed changes have been agreed upon and others have been suggested and are still to be agreed. In general none of these raises major issues of policy of immediate concern to H.M.G., though the decision that Islam should be the state religion, with certain safeguards for other religions, has attracted publicity. For the reasons I have explained, I do not think it necessary that H.M.G. should seek to dispute arrangements for the future which have been agreed locally unless they concern the particular points in which H.M.G. have a direct interest. It is our interest that the new Constitution should be on the lines desired in Malaya and we have at this stage little power to impose our own ideas. There are, however, three matters which have emerged from the local discussions which are of sufficient importance and direct interest to H.M.G. to justify our taking a line of our own. These relate to the method of selection of the first Governors of the Settlements of Penang and Malacca, provision for appeals from Malayan Courts to the Judicial Committee of the Privy Council and provision in the law of the Federation of Malaya to allow dual citizenship within the Commonwealth.

Selection of the first governors of the Settlements of Penang and Malacca

12. The Commission recommended that each of the Governors of the two Settlements (which will become States) should represent and be responsible to the people of his State and independent of control of the Federation Government. For that reason, each should be appointed by the Head of State (Yang di-Pertuan Besar) after consultation with the Government of the State concerned. It will not, however, be possible for the Head of State to consult the Governments concerned over the appointment of the first Governors, who must assume office on the day the new constitution comes into force both in order to appoint the Chief Ministers of the States and also so that their administration can be carried on in the name of the Governors without interruption. The Commission therefore recommended that before the day on which the new Constitution comes into force there should be such informal consultation as will enable the Yang de-Pertuan Besar to appoint on that day someone acceptable to the peoples of Malacca and Penang. It has already become clear that as a result of this recommendation there is much lobbying going on to secure these two posts and the Chief Minister of the Federation is anxious to make sure that they are not sold to the highest bidder who would almost certainly not be a suitable first Governor. The Chief Minister and the High Commissioner have therefore proposed that, in order to ensure the appointment of suitable men, the first Governors of Malacca and Penang should be appointed by the Queen with the concurrence of the Conference of Rulers and that provision for this be made in the constitution. The motives for this proposed variation of the Commission's recommendations are clearly sound, the dangers feared by the Chief Minister are real, and I therefore propose to agree to the arrangement proposed. It will only affect the first appointments, future appointments being made in the manner recommended by the Commission. These first appointments would be for a period of two years before the end of which there will have been held elections to the legislative assemblies of the two States and new fully elected Governments will have taken office.

Appeals to the Judicial Committee of the Privy Council

13. The Constitutional Commission recommended that it would be desirable in principle that appeals to the Judicial Committee of the Privy Council should

continue to lie, although they considered that some change would need to be made to the existing procedure governing appeals in view of the fact that under the new Constitution Her Majesty will no longer be the Fountain of Justice for the Federation. I agree that it would be valuable to retain the link of appeals to the Privy Council and it has been ascertained from the other members of the Commonwealth from whom such appeals still lie that they share this view and would not object to modifications being made to the law governing such appeals in order to meet the circumstances of the Federation. A small committee under the Lord Chancellor has been considering the machinery necessary for this purpose and I have little doubt that it will be possible to reach agreement upon the proposals of that Committee with the delegation from Malaya who welcome in principle the continuation of these appeals.

Dual citizenship within the Commonwealth

14. The Constitutional Commission unanimously recommended that the law of the Federation should allow of dual citizenship within the Commonwealth and that citizens of the United Kingdom and Colonies, as well as of other Commonwealth countries, should be able to retain their existing citizenship on acquiring citizenship of the Federation.

15. This recommendation was most satisfactory, since it would preserve the existing rights of the inhabitants of the two Settlements which are the particular responsibility of H.M.G. The inhabitants of these Settlements at present are citizens of the United Kingdom and Colonies by right of birth and also possess the local citizenship of the Federation of Malaya. Many of these people have lived for generations in the Settlements and value their long enjoyed citizenship rights and they have strongly represented that they do not wish to be faced with the choice of surrendering their United Kingdom citizenship or of abandoning their political rights in the Federation and in the Settlements themselves. There are also many other inhabitants of the Federation who are at present citizens of the United Kingdom and Colonies and who share the interests and views of the inhabitants of the Settlements.

16. Unfortunately considerable opposition has arisen in the Federation to the idea of dual citizenship, mainly among the Malays, on the grounds that future citizens of Malaya should not have a divided loyalty. Much of this opposition derives from misunderstanding of the effect of dual citizenship. The delegation from the Federation is known to be coming here with certain reservations in the matter.

17. I hope to secure agreement to provisions which will in practice enable the inhabitants of the Settlements to continue to enjoy the same citizenship rights as they now enjoy. I think there is a possibility of securing agreement to a proposal which would permit the retention of citizenship of another country within the Commonwealth concurrently with the possession of citizenship of the Federation, provided that reciprocal provisions in regard to the Federation are made by that other country. Such an arrangement, which would in principle be the same as that recently agreed in the case of Singapore, would in practice preserve the existing rights of the inhabitants of the Settlements to hold both citizenship of the Federation and of the United Kingdom and Colonies. Persons born in the Settlements after independence would not, of course, continue to acquire thereby citizenship of the United Kingdom and Colonies.

18.   An arrangement on the lines just suggested is the best we can hope to secure and would adquately meet our desire to safeguard the rights in this respect of the inhabitants of the Settlements for whom H.M.G. has a particular responsibility. I will therefore do my best to secure agreement to it.

Future programme
19.   Once agreement has been reached with the Malayan delegation on the provisions to be included in the constitution of the Federation of Malaya, it will be necessary to have the relevant instruments prepared so that they may come into force on the 31st August. This will require legislation in the United Kingdom during the current session of Parliament and a place has been reserved in the Legislative Programme for a Bill. The short time available will not allow of the full constitution being drafted in time to be included in, or scheduled to, this Bill and it is therefore proposed that it should be an enabling Bill empowering The Queen to make provision by Order-in-Council for the new Constitution. Among the matters which will need to be provided for by or under this Bill are the transfer of sovereignty over the two Settlements from The Queen to the new Federation, the cession of Parliament's authority to legislate for Malaya and an amendment to the British Nationality Act, 1948, to recognise Federal citizens as British subjects and citizens of the Commonwealth. Various other consequential matters will also have to be provided for. Legislation will also be necessary in the Federation itself to endorse the new Constitution. Before the Order-in-Council is made and before the legislation is enacted in the Federation, it will, of course, be necessary for Her Majesty and the Rulers formally to conclude a new Agreement terminating the existing Agreement between His Majesty and the Rulers as a body and between His Majesty and each Ruler in respect of his own State and providing for the establishment of the new constitution.
20.   I invite my colleagues to approve the proposals outlined in paragraphs 6–18 regarding the forthcoming talks with the delegation from Malaya, and to take note of the timetable of events I have set out.

449   CAB 134/1555, CPC 7(57)1   13 May 1957
'Report of the constitutional commission for Malaya': Cabinet Colonial Policy Committee minutes

[Chaired by Lord Kilmuir (lord chancellor), the meeting was attended by Lord Home (CRO), Lennox-Boyd and Ormsby-Gore (minister of state, FO).]

The Committee had before them a memorandum by the Secretary of State for the Colonies (C.P.C.(57) 11)[1] about the recommendations of the Constitutional Commission, which the Malayan Constitutional Conference of 1956 had agreed should be set up to recommend a form of constitution for the independent Federation of Malaya.
The Colonial Secretary said that he was due to start talks that day[2] with a delegation from Malaya regarding the recommendations of the Constitutional

---

[1] See 448.   [2] See 450.

Commission and the comments which had been made upon it by a Working Party of representatives of the Rulers and of the Federation Government. The latter had proposed a considerable number of amendments to the Commission's recommendations, but in general these did not raise major issues of policy of immediate concern to Her Majesty's Government. Our concern in the matter was primarily the general one of seeing that the new constitutional arrangements were sound and were acceptable to the Malayans. In addition, however, we had a particular responsibility for the future of the two Settlements of Penang and Malacca, which at present formed part of The Queen's dominions and who [sic] inhabitants were British subjects by birth. We were not yet formally committed to the incorporation of these two Settlements within an independent Federation of Malaya, but there could be no doubt that such a transfer of sovereignty was inevitable: to try to maintain an authority over these two small territories within an independent Malaya would tend to prejudice the prestige of the Crown, and Her Majesty had therefore been advised informally last year that Penang and Malacca were likely to cease to be part of Her Majesty's Colonial possessions and to become instead integral parts of the new independent Federation. We had concentrated, therefore, on ensuring that the two Settlements were not placed in a position of inferiority in relation to the other Malay States, and this object had been achieved.

The Committee turned to consider three particular points which had arisen from local discussions on the constitutional arrangements:—

(a) The Constitutional Commission had recommended that the Governors of the new States of Penang and Malacca should in future be appointed by the Head of State (Yang di-Pertuan Agong) after consultation with the Government of the State concerned. Such a procedure would however be impracticable for the appointment of the first Governors, and the Commission had, therefore, proposed informal consultation to enable the Yang di-Pertuan Agong to make an acceptable appointment on the day on which the new constitution came into force. It had, however, become clear that such an arrangement might well have undesirable consequences. It was therefore proposed that the initial choice of the Governors of Penang and Malacca should be made by The Queen and the Conference of Rulers jointly, after consultation with the Chief Minister of the Federation. Such an arrangement could be accepted, provided that it did not in effect give to the Chief Minister the ruling voice in the matter.

(b) *The Lord Chancellor* said that the difficulties of reconciling continuance of appeals to the Judicial Committee of the Privy Council with the fact that, under the new constitution, Her Majesty would no longer be the Fountain of Justice for Malaya had been surmounted, and he and the Attorney-General had agreed upon a draft article for the new constitution: under the arrangement now proposed the Royal Prerogative would be exercised in the act of assent to the use of the Judicial Committee for this purpose.

(c) The Constitutional Commission had recommended that the law of the Federation should permit dual citizenship within the Commonwealth, so that citizens of the United Kingdom and Colonies would be able to retain their existing citizenship on acquiring citizenship of the Federation. Considerable opposition to such an arrangement, had, however, since arisen, largely from the Malayas [sic], on the score that loyalty would be divided. It was probable that such opposition was mainly due to a mis-understanding of the implications of dual citizenship, and the

Colonial Secretary was hopeful of securing an agreement on the lines of that reached at the recent Singapore Conference, whereby citizenship of a country within the Commonwealth could be retained concurrently with that of citizenship of the Federation, provided that reciprocal provisions in regard to the Federation were adopted by the Commonwealth country concerned. Part of the present difficulty might, however, be found to lie in the fear that subversive elements in the Federation who now enjoyed British citizenship might be able to avoid control by the Federation authorities by making use of British passports to visit Communist countries, and it might be necessary to consider special arrangement in regard to passports. *The Commonwealth Secretary* drew attention to the difficulties which had arisen in the past over consultation with South Africa over individual passport cases: any special arrangements made should preferably be on general lines.

The Committee approved the proposals made in C.P.C.(57) 11 for the conduct of the forthcoming talks with the Federation of Malaya and agreed to the preparation of an enabling Bill (for which a place had been reserved in the legislative programme) for the introduction of a new constitution. It would be difficult in the time available to draft the full constitution for inclusion in, or as a schedule to, the Bill: it was, however, for consideration whether this might not in fact prove to be desirable. It was noted that before the Order in Council was made providing for the new constitution, and before legislation endorsing the new constitution was enacted in the Federation, it would be necessary for Her Majesty and the Rulers to conclude a new agreement terminating the existing agreements and providing for the establishment of the new constitution.

The Committee:—

(1) Approved the proposals set out in C.P.C.(57) 11.

(2) Subject to the satisfactory conclusion of the forthcoming negotiations, authorised the preparation of a Bill on the lines mentioned in paragraph 19 of C.P.C.(57) 11.

450 CO 1030/496, no 1 13 May 1957

'Federation of Malaya constitutional talks': CO summary record FMI(57)1 of the first plenary session held in Church House on 13 May

[The talks were chaired by Lennox-Boyd and attended by MacGillivray. The Malayan delegation consisted of: Tunku Abdul Rahman, Dato Abdul Razak, Ong Yoke Lin, V T Sambanthan (Alliance); Mustapha Albakri, Tunku Ismail bin Yahya, Shamsudin bin Nain, Dato Panglima Bukit Gantang (rulers' representatives); T V A Brodie (attorney general); Neil Lawson (rulers' legal adviser); and E O Laird. The UK delegation consisted of: Lord Perth, Mr Profumo, Sir J Martin, Sir K Roberts-Wray, E Melville, J B Johnston, H Steel (CO); P H R Marshall (FO); G W St J Chadwick (CRO); G V Hart and J M Ross (Home Office); and N K Hutton and H P Rowe (parliamentary counsel). R W Newsam and I C Jackson served as secretaries.]

1. *Opening speeches*
The *Secretary of State* welcomed the Singapore [sic][1] delegation and expressed his pleasure at meeting them again. He drew attention to the success which had attended his earlier talks with a delegation from the Federation of Malaya and said

---

[1] A slip induced perhaps by the recent meetings in London with a Singapore delegation, see 446, note 1.

that he had little doubt that this success would be repeated on the present occasion.

The *Chief Minister* thanked the Secretary of State for his welcome and Her Majesty's Government for their hospitality to the delegation. He said that the Federation of Malaya looked forward to taking their place in the British Commonwealth of Nations as a full independent member. He explained that a working party in Malaya consisting of representatives of Their Highnesses the Rulers and of the Alliance Government, under the chairmanship of the High Commissioner, had considered the Reid Report and made recommendations which had been agreed in principle by the Conference of Rulers and the Alliance National Council. He believed that outstanding points had been reduced to a minimum. They concerned dual citizenship, whether Malay reservations should be extended to the Settlements, the mode of appointment of the first Governors of Malacca and Penang, and the question of appeals to the Privy Council. Since the working party had completed its work there had been doubts about the proposed method of appointment of the Yang di-Pertuan Agong. The representatives of Their Highnesses the Rulers and of the Federation Government would wish to consider this matter further among themselves and then put it to the Conference of Rulers. It would therefore not be possible to settle this point during the present talks.

2. *Work of the Conference*

The *Secretary of State* said that Her Majesty's Government were in general agreement with the recommendations of the Reid Commission and the subsequent recommendations of the working party in the Federation of Malaya, although he agreed there were certain points of principle which remained to be discussed. In particular, Her Majesty's Government attached importance to the citizenship provisions.

The *Secretary of State* suggested that there were two categories of matters to be considered, those which involved points of principle and those on which clarification and elucidation was required. He suggested that the work be organised as follows:—

(a) full plenary meetings should discuss all points of principle;

(b) a working party should be set up to elucidate and clarify detailed points and if necessary refer to the plenary meetings any points of principle which might emerge;

(c) the working party might be under the chairmanship of Sir John Martin. It might consist of the High Commissioner, two members from each side of the Malayan delegation, two members from the Colonial Office and legal advisers and Parliamentary Counsel. This membership need not be regarded as fixed and if the delegation wished to increase their membership they would be open to do so;

(d) as the Conference was informal there should be no Press communiqué issued at the end of each day's meeting but there should be an agreed communiqué issued at the end of the talks.

The meeting agreed to the above proposals.

The *Secretary of State* then explained the functions of Parliamentary Counsel. Their task was to give legal expression to the decisions reached in such a form as to eliminate ambiguities and inconsistencies. They were not concerned with policy. It was essential to him when introducing legislation in the United Kingdom Parliament to be able to assure the House that a workable document had been produced in this way. Because Parliamentary Counsel were incorporating drafts produced by many minds in both the Reid Commission and in the Federation working party in a single coherent document it was likely that their draft would differ greatly from the drafts with which all concerned were at present familiar. Parliamentary Counsel had already produced a first working draft covering many proposed Articles of the new Constitution which would be shown to the delegation during the discussions and the delegation would be free to ask any questions they wished about them.

The *Secretary of State* then turned to the question of ensuring that the final drafts produced by Parliamentary Counsel accurately expressed the agreed intentions regarding the Constitution. He suggested:—

(a) that Mr. Brodie and Mr. Lawson should remain available for consultation with Parliamentary Counsel for a fortnight after the conclusion of these talks while Parliamentary Counsel were completing their draft of the Constitution;

(b) that subsequently one of Parliamentary Counsel, accompanied by an official from the Colonial Office, should bring out the complete draft Constitution to the Federation of Malaya and be present to explain it and amend it as might be necessary when it was being considered there.

The meeting agreed to this procedure.

3. Appeals to the Privy Council

The *Secretary of State* said that he had seen with pleasure the recognition in the Federation of Malaya of the value of continuing appeals to the Judicial Committee of the Privy Council. He was glad to say that a formula had been devised which it was believed would enable these appeals to continue after independence. He promised to circulate this formula for discussion at a later meeting.

4. Citizenship

The *Secretary of State* said that citizenship was a difficult subject open to considerable misunderstanding. He explained that there were legal advisers present from the Home Office and other departments to explain any points of difficulty. The under-lying principle to which Her Majesty's Government attached importance was that the citizens of each Commonwealth country should enjoy wider rights as being members of the whole family of the Commonwealth; they did not wish to encourage divided loyalties. He invited the Chief Minister to explain the wishes of the delegation and the difficulties which they saw in the way of accepting the recommendations of the Reid Commission.

The *Chief Minister* said that there was general disquiet in Malaya over this question. They believed that the new nation would require a strong foundation and that this would be undermined unless its citizenship were clearly defined. They feared that if some of its citizens could have a second citizenship they would have a second loyalty and the whole concept would be endangered. What they wanted was to make it clear that all citizens of Malaya owed loyalty to Malaya alone.

In discussion the following points were made.

Article 24

The *Chief Minister* said that it was not clear what was involved in Commonwealth citizenship. There was a fear that any Commonwealth citizen from another

Commonwealth country might be in a position to claim rights in Malaya, including the right of entry, which might result in Malaya being swamped by them.

In reply the following points were made:—

(a) The acknowledgment of the status of Commonwealth citizenship would not in any way impair the Federation's control over the entry of Commonwealth citizens or indeed of the rights which they were prepared to accord to them in the Federation.

(b) A provision on the lines of this Article was more or less common form in the Commonwealth and was desirable as emphasizing the concept of a common family.

(c) This Article might be valuable to the Federation of Malaya in connection with Most Favoured Nation treaties. It would allow them to grant privileges to citizens of a Commonwealth country without having to extend the same privileges to citizens of a foreign country and would thus enable them if the Federation so desired, to extend special rights on a reciprocal basis to citizens of any other Commonwealth country.

The meeting agreed to remit this Article to the Legal advisers to consider whether it could be phrased more acceptably.

Article 22
Dato Abdul Razak explained that it was felt in Malaya that dual citizens would have the best of both worlds if they could enjoy citizenship rights in Malaya and also in their country of origin. It was also feared that the enjoyment of these dual rights might lead to dual loyalties.

In discussion the following points were made:—

(a) There was a difference between taking the voluntary step of acquiring another citizenship and exercising rights under a second citizenship already possessed by operation of law. It was inconsistent with Commonwealth practice to require that a person acquiring another Commonwealth citizenship should lose citizenship of the Federation

(b) There should be a distinction between the exercising of another citizenship rights in a foreign country and in a Commonwealth country.

(c) It might be possible to seek agreement on the lines that the acquisition of another citizenship should involve loss of Federal citizenship but that Federal citizenship should not be lost simply because a Federal citizen exercised in another Commonwealth country the rights he enjoyed as a Commonwealth citizen. This would enable Federal citizens to continue to enjoy their rights as Commonwealth citizens in, for example, the United Kingdom.

It was agreed to remit this to the legal advisers to consider a draft.

Oath of Allegiance
The *Chief Minister* said that the delegation were not satisfied with the oath proposed by the Reid Commission and would prefer a form of oath based on that in the form of VIII in the First Schedule to the 1948 Agreement. This point was connected with the discussion of Article 22.

The meeting agreed to remit this to the legal advisers to consider a draft.

Passports
Mr. Ong Yoke Lin asked whether it would be possible for a Federal citizen in Malaya who also had United Kingdom citizenship to acquire a United Kingdom passport. The *Secretary of State* said that a document on the question of dual passports within the Commonwealth was being prepared and would be circulated. He suggested that this matter be considered later.

5. *Future business*
The following future business was agreed.

(a) The working party would meet at 10.30 a.m. on Tuesday, 14th May to commence its work.
(b) The plenary meeting would he at 4 p.m. on Tuesday, 14th May.[2]

---

[2] The working party, chaired by Sir J Martin, met five times. In addition there were three further plenary sessions, on 14, 17 and 21 May (for a summary of the talks see CO 1030/494, no 25, FO intelligence telegram no 109, 20 June 1957). While the Tunku realised that dual citizenship would cause him problems on his return to Malaya, he spoke and wrote warmly of Lennox Boyd's 'broadmindedness, fairness and tolerance'. He assured the secretary of state that he would have 'no cause for regret, for, independent Malaya within the Commonwealth, will be the best friend of Britain' (CO 1030/493, no 45, Tunku Abdul Rahman to Lennox-Boyd, 28 May 1957).

451   CO 1030/439, no 82   21 May 1957
'Constitution of Malaya': letter from Mr G Longden[1] to Mr Lennox-Boyd about a meeting on 20 May between the Conservative Party's Far Eastern Sub-Committee and a Malayan deputation

The Far-Eastern Sub-Committee yesterday received a deputation from the Pan-Malayan Federation of Chinese Associations and the Malayan Party. I had heard from them only a few days ago, and we received them at the earliest opportunity.

The former body claims to represent 1000 Chinese organizations and two milliom [sic] of the $2\frac{1}{4}$ million Chinese in the Federation; and the latter claims to have scored signal successes against the Alliance during the local Elections last year especially in the two Settlements. Both deny that the M.C.A. and the M.I.C. are at all representative of the non-Malay population in Malaya.

As Peter Smithers[2] was at the meeting, and as these people yesterday submitted to you a Joint Memorandum setting out their case, I can be brief. But I did promise, in case you had no time to receive them yourself, to write to you before final decisions are agreed between you and the Tengku; because we felt that some part of their claims at any rate are just; and that they speak for people who have been outstandingly loyal to Britain for generations.

I. The most important one relates to *citizenship* which carries the *right to vote*.

(1) They allege that the Alliance has gone back on its Election promises when it

---

[1] Gilbert Longden, Conservative MP for SW Hertfordshire, 1950–1974.
[2] Peter Smithers, parliamentary private secretary to Lennox-Boyd, 1956–1959.

held out that anyone born in Malaya, or who had lived there for 5 years, would have the right to vote. (And, moreover, that there would be another General Election based on such franchise before Merdeka Day.)

(2) They allege that, owing to the definition of "Malay", Indonesians who come into the Federation will become voters before non-Malays who have lived there for generations.

(3) They consider that the proposed right to apply for registration within one year of M. Day[3] is not enough because of the time taken to approve these applications.

They therefore claim:—

(1) That everyone so applying should be able to vote *unless* his application is rejected within the year; and that there should be no language test for such persons.

(2) That the "jus soli" should apply to all existing citizens and not merely to those born after M. Day as the Reid Report recommends.

(3) (Perhaps above all) that the Reid Commission's recommendation that all those who are now citizens of the U.K. and Colonies should NOT have to renounce this right on becoming citizens of the Federation, should be accepted without question.

II. The delegation urge that the term "privileges" should NOT be used to describe the "*safeguards*" some of which they agree are necessary to the Malays. It certainly seems an unfortunate term.

They consider that the ratio of 4 Malays to 1 non-Malay is too unbalanced, especially in the case of the judiciary which must surely be manned by those most suitably qualified, irrespective of race.

III. *Sovereignty in the Settlements*
The delegation would like Her Majesty to remain Sovereign of the two Settlements, and to appoint their Governors as she does with the Dominions.

They claim that the *peoples* of the Settlements should have a say in the matter. (It occurred to me that the House of Commons has not been consulted nor has this question been raised in the Party Committee?)

IV. The questions of the *election of the Senate*, the *official languages* (on the Swiss model) and the *State Religion* do not seem of comparable importance with the other three matters raised.

I hope you will be able to consider these claims and, if you think fit, to insist on their acceptance by the Tengku. He is getting so much that I suspect he is not in a mood to be tiresome. My own respectful submission would be that it is most important to bring the Chinese and Indians in *from the start* as co-operators and not risk their becoming a powerful and organized racial opposition.

---

[3] ie *Merdeka* (independence) day.

452   CO 1030/439, no 83   31 May 1957
[Independence constitution]: letter (reply) from Mr Lennox-Boyd to
Mr G Longden

Many thanks for your letter of the 21st May about the deputation from the Pan
Malayan Federation of Chinese Associations and the Malayan Party.[1] As you know I
did in fact see both these delegations, so I do not think you will expect me to reply in
detail to your letter, particularly as David Perth[2] was able to give the Committee
some confidential information on this subject last Thursday.

There is perhaps just one thing I ought to say on a confidential basis. I personally
feel much sympathy with the sort of line these delegations have been taking. But I
have to recognise, and I think it would be helpful if Members of the Sub-Committee
recognised, that the people you saw represent only one point of view in the
Federation. (I do not think, incidentally, that they represent anything like 2 million
Chinese—they were careful in their memorandum to me to say they represented "the
interests of" 2 million Chinese). There is a quite considerable body of Malay opinion
who would claim with equal force that the Alliance Government was not representing them, and was letting them down in accepting recommendations of the Reid
Commission which they think are far too liberal in favour of the Chinese. Dato Onn
has been trying to work up feeling from the extreme Malay angle, and has been
backed up by a lot of the Malay nationalists, in trying to dig away Malay support from
under the Tunku. Indeed if they had had as much money as the Chinese command,
and could have afforded to send a delegation to London, you might well have been
listening to violent attacks on the Reid report for going too far in favour of the
Chinese. One has to remember that the Communist terrorists are practically all
Chinese and that the Malays do not find it easy to accept constitutional arrangements
which of their nature may embrace the bad Chinese as well as the good.

I say all this simply to indicate that it is not just a question of insisting that the
Tunku meets the demands of the Chinese in certain respects. His own Malay support
is pretty divided and much of it is just as extreme in the other direction. I have as
usual the thankless job of trying to produce a solution which is as fair as possible to
both sides and which he can defend before his Malay extremists, just as I must be able
to defend it in respect of the "Queen's Chinese" element as being reasonable and fair
all round. The result of all this obviously will satisfy neither of the extreme
wings—the Malays won't get all they want in the way of an upper hand over the
Chinese, and the Chinese won't get all they want in the way of complete and absolute
jus soli.

I am sorry to inflict such a long letter on you, but I am anxious that, at least on our
side of the House, these problems may be seen in the right perspective. What is at
stake is the continuance of British influence and the British connection in the
Federation. I believe that the agreement we have reached with the Tunku is the best
we could secure from this point of view.

---

[1] See 451.   [2] Lord Perth, minister of state, CO.

453   CO 1030/518, no 1   31 May 1957
[Independence constitution]: letter from Mr Lennox-Boyd to Lord
Reid on amendments to the commission's proposals

You have been very much in our minds in these last few weeks as we have been working through the constitution for Malaya. I was going to try and give you some account of the way in which the working party of Rulers' representatives and members of Government, which has been sitting in Kuala Lumpur, had suggested amendments and alterations to the original constitutional proposals, but I gather that Michael Laird was able to give you a pretty comprehensive picture of where we had all finished up.

Although there are of course a lot of amendments of minor importance, and some fairly major changes, I think it is true to say that the constitution you and your colleagues produced emerged triumphant from the concentrated attention of so many sectional interests and will be in its essentials the foundation of Malaya's independent life. The Rulers, as you know, changed their tune about Islam and they and the Government presented a united front in favour of making Islam a state religion even though Malaya is to be a secular state. We got agreement to the retention of appeals to the Privy Council and despite Malay attacks we have in fact preserved the essentials of dual citizenship for the people of the Settlements, even though the Malayans have not accepted the principle of dual citizenship as enunciated in your report. What they have agreed to is that those with two citizenships can keep them, and that they can exercise their other Commonwealth citizenship to the same extent as can Commonwealth citizens as a whole. Since in the United Kingdom Commonwealth citizens have all the rights and privileges of United Kingdom and Colonies citizens, this means that in fact the Settlements people will have the full exercise of both citizenships without let or hindrance. Things will be more restrictive for Indians and Pakistanis and Ceylonese, but they are in any case not allowed under, for example, Indian law to hold two citizenships.

Laird will have told you that as regards the state constitutions the working party adopted your own view rather than the majority report. We also got a good agreement on the appointment of the first Governors for Penang and Malacca. The Tunku was very much worried about what might happen if it were left to the Yang di-Pertuan Agong and we have agreed that the first appointments should be made jointly by the Queen and the Rulers before Merdeka Day.

All this and the many other points of detail on which changes have been made will be emerging in a White Paper before so very long, but I just wanted to write and let you know once more how grateful we are for the remarkably solid foundation that you and your colleagues have built for the independence of Malaya.[1]

---

[1] Despite this emollient tribute, bickering continued between Reid and CO draughtsmen over the wording and detail of the final constitution (eg CO 1030/486, nos 16 and 20). During the Lords debate on the Malayan Independence Bill on 29 July, Lord Reid criticised some of the drafting. Johnston told MacGillivray that the 'Minister of State [Perth] and ourselves were shocked at this egotistical and irresponsible statement by Lord Reid' (see DO 35/6280 and *H of L Debs*, vol 205, cols 245–251).

454   FO 371/129342, no 8   [May 1957]

'The outlook in Malaya up to 1960': note by the commissioner-
general's office

[This paper was one of a trilogy (the others being on the outlook in Singapore to 1960 and
the probable MCP attitude to terrorism after independence) considered by the British
Defence Coordinating Committee (Far East) on 7 June. It had been foreshadowed by
'Future of the Alliance government', Mar 1957 (see CO 1030/440, no 1). Although the
BDCC(FE) admitted that longer-term prospects were unpromising, it declined to endorse
this conclusion lest Whitehall used it as a pretext to cut essential expenditure in Malaya
(see FO 371/129342, no 8, D A Greenhill to J B Johnston, 11 June 1957). On 7 June P H R
Marshall (FO) minuted: 'Perhaps the somewhat pessimistic analyses which the papers
make—quite rightly no doubt on the basis of the evidence available—need not discourage
us unduly. Similar forecasts might have been made about the course of events in India
after Partition, forecasts which would have been correct in pointing to the dangers of the
situation and the potentialities of anti-British and left-wing tendencies, yet incorrect in
their underestimation of the powers of attraction of the western world. Perhaps it is
simply a question of the economic strength of the West in general and the U.K. in
particular. If we are strong, Malaya and Singapore will continue to be drawn towards us:
but weakness of the western economies will accelerate any drift to China and the Left.' In
Dec 1957 G W Tory, the first British high commissioner to independent Malaya, prepared
a brief, 'Malaya since independence', for the commissioner-general's conference at Eden
Hall, 16–19 1958. In it Tory drew attention to the following: tensions within UMNO
particularly over the defence agreement; the MCA's inability to command Chinese
support; the emergence of a socialist opposition in the form of the Party Ra'ayat (People's
Party) and the Labour Party; the declining threat of communist terrorism; continuity in
the economic life of the country and of UK interests; the unexpectedly rapid departure of
expatriate officers from government service; the Alliance government's reluctance to take
up attitudes on foreign policy questions and, despite its wish to cooperate closely with the
UK, the fading prospect of Malaya joining SEATO (see CO 1030/559, no 18).]

The future of the Federation of Malaya is of importance to the United Kingdom for
four main reasons:—

(a) as a source of essential raw materials and a very substantial dollar earner;
(b) as a country in which many £millions of British capital are invested;
(c) as a base for defence purposes; and
(d) as a symbol of British influence in the area.

2.   Any possible alternative to the present Alliance Government at present in sight
would certainly be less well disposed to the United Kingdom. The object of this paper
is therefore to try to assess the stability of the Alliance Government and its chances of
retaining power in the years following independence. The paper does not attempt to
look beyond the end of 1960 and is based on the assumption that during that period
there will be no dramatic switch in the external policy of Communist China, or any
significant change in the economic situation in Malaya—particularly in the price of
rubber.

3.   The Alliance began as a marraige of convenience through which the United
Malaya [sic] National Organisation (UMNO) secured the benefits of Chinese money
and business organisation and the Malayan Chinese Association (MCA), conscious
that they would get nowhere without Malay votes, hoped to extend their political
influence. The Malayan Indian Congress (MIC), very much a junior partner, was
accepted later by Tunku Abdul Rahman, mainly because of the UK Government's
statement that only after the three main communities had settled their differences

could any hopes of independence be entertained. The national elections of 1955 confirmed the predominant strength of Malay political power (the Malays still number more than 80% of the electorate) and UMNO's dominating position in the Alliance is well understood and accepted by all political leaders.

4.   The Alliance, in fact, in spite of an outward appearance of homogeneous unity, is a highly artificial grouping which blurs, but does not conceal, the predominating position of UMNO. It has been held together largely by the Tunku's personality and influence and his wise conciliation of the moderate elements in the political leadership of the Chinese and Indian communities. But above all the cementing force has been the Alliance's successful campaign for Merdeka. After the first enthusiasm of Merdeka has worn off, however, there is obviously a danger that the natural diversity of interest between the Malays, Chinese and Indians may again assert itself and that the Alliance may come under strong and conflicting pressures from interested groups in all communities. As more Chinese and Indians obtain the vote and extend their political as well as their commercial and business influence, UMNO may well feel that it can retain the support of the Malays only by forcing on the Alliance a more vigorous pro-Malay policy. The MCA leaders, and in proportion the MIC, might find themselves in these circumstances losing the support of the Chinese and Indian vote to the opposition parties, with the consequent danger of a split. Paradoxically, the strength of UMNO has to some extent reacted adversely on that of the MCA and the MIC. The latter have no deep roots in their own communities, and if communal tension should develop in the Federation they could scarcely survive as effective components of the Alliance.

5.   It follows, therefore, that the future of the Alliance and the position of its present moderate leaders, and in particular the Tunku, depend largely on the extent to which UMNO can control and moderate the demands of its followers. The Malays fear that their power is on the wane in their own country, and they can therefore be expected to press a strong communal viewpoint over the next few years. It was in fact the Malays who were the leaders of the demand for early independence, largely because they felt the need to gain control of their own country before the Chinese added substantial political strength to their existing economic predominance. The Tunku, who has always been considerably in advance of Malay opinion in his attitude to the problem of the future relationship of the Malays and the other races, has done his best to allay Malay suspicions about the increase in Chinese influence that will eventually result from their increased voting potential by insisting on adequate constitutional safeguards for the special position of the Malays in trade and commerce and in public life. It is doubtful, however, whether any such paper safeguards will in practice be able effectively to counterbalance Chinese surge and drive. All this, combined with difficulties over language and educational policy, will probably have the effect in the post-independence years of heightening rather than reducing the latent tension between the two communites.

6.   The Tunku in fact faces a painful dilemma. If he were to ensure for the Chinese equal opportunities with the Malays in all walks of life, he would be playing right into Chinese hands. But if he tried to maintain them in a permanently second-class political condition they would almost certainly be compelled to look more and more to Communist China for backing in their claim to a proper share of political power. The Tunku has clearly made up his mind that while the Chinese must be given reasonable opportunities, he cannot afford to ignore the Malay demand for the best

place in the sun. Present indications are that, if the present Alliance leadership does not move towards a more extreme position in support of purely Malay demands, it might very well fall from power and be replaced by more extreme Malay leaders.

7. Through all these conflicting considerations, Tunku Abdul Rahman has hitherto been guided by one principle which he has done his best to maintain, i.e. to ensure the present political predominance of the Malays while retaining the co-operation of the other communities and their contribution to the general welfare. He has stated his view that Malaya must, if it is to survive, choose between the protection of the United Kingdom and that of China; and since the protection of China, in whatever form it were given, would mean the end of Malay dominance, he is determined that the Federation should look in the main to the United Kingdom for support. In furtherance of this policy he has accepted the idea that the Federation should remain within the Commonwealth after independence, has agreed to conclude a Defence Agreement with the United Kingdom and has decided that the Federation should remain a member of the sterling area and abide by its rules of self-denial in dollar expenditure. Although he has made no direct statement on foreign policy, there is every reason to hope that he will wish, as far as possible, to keep in line with the Commonwealth and co-operate with the United Kingdom, except perhaps on those issues where Asian and Muslim sentiment may have a particular appeal. He has certainly made it clear that his policy will be strongly anti-Communist. Within Malaya, he has taken a very realistic line about the Emergency and present indications are that he intends to continue to do so, to the extent of having already agreed in principle to seek assistance, after independence, from overseas Commonwealth forces. He has also recognised the importance for the general well-being of the country of an orderly transfer of power and has tried to ensure this by offering reasonable terms to retain as large a number as possible of the expatriate civil servants who have hitherto been largely responsible for running the country.

8. He has thus already to a very large extent committed himself to retain the closest of links with the United Kingdom and the Commonwealth. This is in part due to the fact that in Malaya the transfer of power is being effected without bloodshed and in an atmosphere of remarkable goodwill; but it is of course in the main due to the deeply held conviction of the Tunku that the only alternative to an especially close relationship with the United Kingdom is to risk falling under Chinese, and eventually, Communist, domination.

9. The extent to which the Tunku has already felt able to commit himself in this way has been largely due to the support of his ample following in the country. This has so far ensured that, apart from the Communists, the (left-wing) Labour Party and some of the more extreme Malay nationalists, there has been remarkably little overt opposition to the Tunku, though there has been much grumbling in private and some criticism in public of his allegedly too pro-British attitude. The unity of the Alliance and even of UMNO has not, however, as yet been seriously tested and so it is difficult at present to assess to what extent its policies will continue unchanged after the post-independence strains begin to show themselves.

10. At the moment, however, the Tunku seems to be firmly in the saddle and there is very little doubt that, if elections were held immediately after Merdeka, i.e. before the register of newly enfranchised non-Malays has been compiled, he would be returned to power with a majority not far short of that which he at present enjoys.

The only parties which, since political power is mainly in Malay hands, present any serious opposition are, first, the extreme nationalist Pan-Malayan Islamic Party (PMIP), and second, the left-wing Party Ra'ayat, which is groping for a means of attracting support on a [non]-communal basis. As the astute leader of PMIP, Dr. Burhanuddin, sees it, neither has as yet an organisation sufficiently powerful seriously to rival the Alliance, even if they could win a much larger measure of support than at present. Dr. Burhanuddin realises clearly that for the next few years the Malays are likely to be attracted by a strongly communal policy and that the need to compromise between Malay and Chinese feeling is the greatest weakness in the Tunku's political position. He also, however, maintains contact with supporters of the Malayan Communist Party and those elements in the Federation which follow the policies of the Singapore People's Action Party. Perhaps the main hope of the opposition is that the present moderate leadership of the Alliance can be overthrown, that in the ensuing trouble the Alliance will disintegrate, and that the opposition Malay parties will benefit from the destruction of UMNO. Such a development would clearly be a most serious threat to the maintenance of stable government after independence, and it is clear that the opposition Malay leaders see their opportunity after Merdeka rather than before. The Pan-Malayan Islamic Party, which regards Western Imperialism as a greater danger than Communism, has recently declared its determination to secure the repeal of the Emergency Regulations, to foster co-existence with the Malayan Communist Party, to secure the withdrawal of all the Commonwealth military forces in Malaya and to opose [sic] military pacts with the West. This group may, if the Emergency continues, extend its influence and it is, of course, an ideal target for penetration by MCP sympathisers. Although their immediate prospects of ousting the Tunku are slight, as time goes on a left-wing group of this kind might in the end prove strong enough to displace the Alliance, which is in essence strongly conservative.

11. Time is thus not on the side of the Tunku. He has a number of serious difficulties immediately ahead, his success in handling which may well decide, when elections eventually take place in 1959 or 1960, whether or not he will remain in power. These difficulties include the possibility of administrative decay, communalism, terrorism, subversion, and perhaps an economic slump. Of these, administrative decay, though the latest obviously threatening, may prove to be in Malaya, as it has proved to be elsewhere, e.g. in Indonesia, the most serious; and the Tunku's insistence that he fears corruption, even at the very highest level, as much as any other danger, shows that he too is well aware of the seriousness of this problem. The number of expatriate officers retiring under the compensation scheme is still increasing and it is already clear that some departments will soon be operating under very serious handicaps. It may be that if, as is expected, the present government remains firmly in control after Merdeka, expatriate officers will settle down, and the rate of retirement will fall off. If they do not, it is unquestionable that the efficiency of the Government will be dangerously impaired. In any event, it is already clear that in the early years at least, because of a shortage of skilled administrators, the Government has little prospect of maintaining its development programme at the planned level; and any slowing down of the Government's extensive plans for social and economic development might well have damaging repercussions on the Alliance's chances of winning the next election.

12. An immediately obvious danger facing the Alliance Government is the

handling of the various problems that arise from the continuance of the Emergency.* The Tunku remains firmly opposed to any kind of deal with the Malayan Communist Party and is determined to prosecute the campaign against the terrorists on much the present lines, with the assistance [of] United Kingdom and Commonwealth military forces. It has, however, long been argued in many quarters in the Federation that the fight against the terrorists is not worth its cost in money and effort which would otherwise be available for social services and economic development. Moreover, [the] Emergency Regulations, or the action taken under them, have inevitably been unpopular. If they are continued, and if in addition, British troops remain employed in large numbers on Emergency duties, the pressure on the Tunku to end the Emergency, if necessary by renewed negotiations with Chin Peng, will undoubtedly increase. Vocal opposition to the continuance of the Emergency comes largely from the extreme Malay nationalists; and if their hold on the Malay voter increases, this pressure might well prove most embarrassing, especially as it would undoubtedly be supported by large sections of the population who are at present inarticulate. Some Malay elements, notably Dr. Burhanuddin, may go so far as to ally themselves with the M.C.P. in order to destroy Western influence in Malaya. Some such paradoxical coalition seems to represent the main—if not the only—chance of the M.C.P. extending its influence among the Malays, whose religion and loyalty to the Rulers could otherwise be expected to arm them against the blandishments of the Communists, who remain predominantly Chinese. At the Baling talks in December, 1955, the M.C.P. revealed its anxiety to transfer its main effort from the armed struggle to the political arena, even to the extent of foregoing its demand for legalisation of the Party provided that individuals were allowed to return to civil life with the cloak of apparent respectibility [sic].

13. In an attempt to win support from the people, the M.C.P. has dropped the indiscriminate terrorism of the early days of the Emergency. Railways are no longer sabotaged; the murder of individuals with pronounced anti-Communist sympathies has virtually ceased, and except where the situation has been particularly favourable to them, the terrorists are avoiding contact with the security forces. They presumably hope to maintain the present state of affairs indefinitely. At the same time, Party sympathisers outside the jungle are doing their best to engage in "legal work" in the various political, social, educational and trades unions organisations, with the object of building up popular pressure on the Government to negotiate for peace on terms favourable to the M.C.P.

14. The present intention of the Alliance Government seems to be to continue to resist a deal with the Communists: they appear to believe, or to profess to believe, that the remaining terrorists are now a nuisance rather than a serious threat, and to be hoping to make a progressive reduction both in Emergency expenditure and restrictions. But herein lies a new danger which they must take into account: a sudden ending of the Emergency would present the Government with the formidable task of re-settling the large number of young Malays now happily employed in the Security forces. Were they simply thrown out of employment they would certainly present a serious social, political and economic problem for the Government, which would then have on its hands large numbers of young Malays trained to the use of

* A separate paper has been prepared on the Emergency in Malaya after Independence; see Sec.Min(57)659—for circulation.

arms against Chinese, with no occupation, little hope and a strong sense of grievance. To train them for agriculture and settle them on the land would not only be costly but would not necessarily succeed in its object since experience has shown that such men, during their service, enjoy a standard of life and acquire tastes which cannot be satisfied in the Kampongs; many of them are therefore likely to end up in the towns, a dangerous reinforcement of extreme Malay nationalism.

15.   Although the difficulties of the Emergency are in themselves serious enough the real danger lies in the "legal" campaign of subversion arising from it. Although the capabilities of the M.C.P. itself are limited in this respect, their efforts will be immeasurably assisted by spontaneous left wing activities in the Chinese schools (possibly directed from Singapore) and by the support of the varied ranks of the Tunku's opponents who are not too particular about the company they keep. These groups are most likely to find common ground in a programme of

(a) ending the Emergency
(b) throwing out the British
(c) devoting defence and emergency funds to social and economic development.

This ill-assorted Popular Front opposition will, in our view, develop sufficient strength to compel the Tunku and his Alliance Government to make significant concessions to its views. Moreover, the Alliance, in order to preserve its own multi-racial characteristics, will be increasingly inhibited from destroying the centres of subversive activity in the Chinese schools since such action will be misrepresented as an attack on Chinese culture.

16.   Any examination of the economic problem is mainly outside the scope of this paper. It is perhaps enough to say here that the whole Malayan economy is so tied to the price of rubber and tin that a serious fall could lead to a significant reduction in Malay support for UMNO. Indeed, it would not be surprising to see the UMNO members in the Legislative Council withdrawing their support from the Government were it to get into serious difficulties on this question. And again, it is one on which the Western Powers, and in particular Britain and America, could incur a great deal of odium.

17.   There are also important economic implications for Malaya in the Defence Agreement. Whatever its merits or demerits, the Tunku has always recognised the value of the Defence Agreement for Malaya not merely as a potential stabilising factor but also as a means of providing for the external defence of Malaya on the cheap. It is a particularly important consideration of the Alliance Government since, even if the present price of rubber should be maintained, they will find it increasingly difficult to raise the money needed for the new educational programme which they regard as vital to the development of a Malayan national consciousness and for the economic and social development which is necessary to maintain standards of living in the face of the rapid rate of population increase.

18.   In addition to these problems, to which the Tunku has fallen heir, he has in a sense through the Defence Agreement which he has concluded with the United Kingdom Government and the pro-Commonwealth attitude which inspired it, created for himself some new difficulties. Although the Defence Agreement has been carefully drafted to take account of the susceptibilities of the newly independent Government, its very existence is an irritant to more extreme nationalist opinion which the Communists and other opponents of the Alliance are only too ready to

exploit. A good deal will depend on the way the agreement works in practice, but experience always suggests that, however tactfully it may be implemented, it will always be liable to rouse political feeling; and the Tunku, as its chief architect, might in time be forced, even against his better judgement, to seek revision of its terms.

19. The Defence Agreement will come under increasing criticism should the Federation decide to join SEATO. This is a question which, although it has not been formally put to or considered by the Government, has already divided Malayan opinion even within the Alliance. The Tunku has stated privately that he thinks it inevitable that Malays [Malaya] should join, but if he does move in that direction he can expect to encounter stiff opposition from Malay nationalists, the left-wing fringe and even from some of his own followers, many of whom will doubtless be influenced by the attitude of Indonesia and India, who can be expected to try to push Malaya towards the Afro-Asian bloc and away from too close an alignment with the West. On balance, it is unlikely that Malaya will join SEATO soon after Merdeka and the chances of her doing so will decrease as time passes.

20. The preceding paragraphs have emphasised and perhaps exaggerated the difficulties which will confront the Tunku after independence. The many solid counter-balancing advantages which he possesses should not be over-looked. First, he is regarded throughout the country as the architect of Malayan independence and, like Mr. Nehru and to a lesser extent U Nu,[1] may be able to retain popular support even outside the Party for some years to come, although, like both them, he may as time goes on, and the enthusiasm for Merdeka disappears, lose ground to other elements. There are many pitfalls ahead and much will depend on the Tunku's own ability. Although he possesses a considerable political flair and the air of authority which sits so easily on the best kind of Malay Raja, his intellectual powers are not great. However, his Alliance is still the only political organisation which embraces, however loosely, three major communities in Malaya. The efforts of the M.C.P. and their sympathisers during 1956 to weld together a united opposition front have been a failure. The Alliance controls all but one of the elected seats on the Legislative Council; they play a dominant role in the State Councils, and even in the local elections last year, in which they suffered some defeats, especially in Penang and Malacca, they nevertheless were still able to win over two-thirds of the seats.

21. In addition, whatever its potential political drawbacks, there are positive advantages for the Tunku and the Malays in general, in the presence of UK and Commonwealth troops in the Federation both as a guarantee of its external defence and as a discouragement to internal subversion. The benefits of membership of the Commonwealth and the sterling area too, ought as time goes on, to become increasingly recognised by Malayan public opinion as they have been in India, Pakistan and Ceylon.

22. Taking account of all this the Alliance Government should be able to hold itself together and maintain itself in power until at any rate the election of 1959. In order to do so it will, despite its own convictions, feel itself compelled to make concessions to its left wing opponents which will be reflected in a more critical attitude to British defence and foreign policy.

---

[1] See 336, note 2.

455   PREM 11/1926   6–9 June 1957

'Malaya': minutes by Lord Home (no 49/57) and Mr Macmillan on
suitable gifts from Britain to Malaya to mark independence

Prime Minister

We are now getting close to the date (August 31st) of Malayan Independence. I
should, therefore, like your early authority to explore with others of our colleagues
concerned the kinds of gift which could most appropriately be given to the
Government and Legislature of the independent Federation.

2. As regards the *Gift from the Queen*, I understand that the Colonial Secretary
has it in mind to suggest that the G.C.V.O. be conferred on the Yang di Pertuan
Agong (Head of State). In addition we both think that Her Majesty should be advised
to present some more tangible gift to the Head of State—some small token the form
of which can be decided on later.

3. As to a *Government to Government Gift*, the Colonial Secretary and I agree
that a suitable and imaginative gesture would be a Post Graduate Scholarship, to be
awarded to a suitably selected locally born resident of the Federation, and to be
tenable for a two-year period at a leading University in this country. The annual cost
of such an award, excluding travel charges, would not be higher than £700 per
annum. We would, of course, have to pay the scholars' fares to and from the United
Kingdom as well and this would involve an additional sum every two years. The total
cost over whatever period the scholarship would run for—and I think it is
unnecessary to specify this in advance—would, no doubt, be higher than for the
plaque or piece of statuary which we have offered (at a cost of some £2,500) to Dr.
Nkrumah.[1] But we shall not be repeating in Malaya the air display, costing some
£35,000, which was authorised at the time of Ghana's Independence.[2] Should the
proposal for a Scholarship meet with approval, we shall, of course, have to seek the
views of the Federation Government on the title and other details of the award.

4. As regards the *Gift from Parliament to the Federation Legislature*, the Chief
Minister has already said that a Speaker's Chair would prove most acceptable. This
would follow what we have done for Ghana, and the cost here would be of the order of
£1,000. Subject to your agreement on this point, I would propose taking the advice
of the Lord Privy Seal as to the procedure to be followed.

5. I am sending copies of this minute to the Lord Chancellor, the Lord Privy Seal,
the Chancellor of the Exchequer; to the Colonial Secretary (who agrees generally
with its terms) and to the Minister of Works.

H.
6.6.57

2 and 4 are clearly right.

I rather like the scholarship idea. But I think you might put it to the Cabinet. It is
the sort of thing Cabinets delight in.[3]

H.M.
9.6.57

---

[1] Prime minister of the Gold Coast, 1952–1957, and of Ghana, 1957–1960; president of Ghana, 1960–1966.
[2] See BDEEP, Series B, vol 1, R Rathbone, ed, *Ghana*, part II, 281.
[3] A joint memorandum by Home and Lennox-Boyd proposing a gift of a post-graduate scholarship to the
value of £600 pa over ten years was approved by the Cabinet on 11 July (see CAB 129/88, C(57)163, 10 July
1957, and CAB 128/31/2, CC 51(57)8, 11 July 1957).

456   DO 35/6280, no 6E   13 June 1957

'Federation of Malaya'; letter from N K Hutton[1] to Sir K Roberts-Wray on the draft Malayan Independence Bill

[The purpose of legislation was to enable Her Majesty to enter an agreement with Their Highnesses the Rulers to establish an independent Federation of Malaya. The Bill was introduced in the House of Commons in early July; it had its second reading on 12 July and its third reading on 19 July. It passed through the Lords in all its stages on 29 July and received the royal assent on 31 July. On 5 Aug, the Federation of Malaya Agreement was signed by MacGillivray, on behalf of Her Majesty, and by the Rulers. It was a brief document of seven clauses but appended to it were some 150 pages of schedules, including the constitutions of the Federation of Malaya, the state of Penang and the state of Malacca. On 15 Aug the federal legislative council passed the Federal Constitution Ordinance, 1957, to give the force of law to the agreement and the three constitutions contained in it, while each of the states passed similar enactments ratifying the federal constitution. In London the Federation of Malaya Independence Order in Council was issued on 23 Aug and laid before parliament on 29 Aug. Its purpose was to give the force of law to the new constitutions and to revoke previous Federation of Malaya Orders in Council.]

1. In enclose copies[2] of what is in fact a draft Bill. I have however left off the formal parts at the beginning so that it can, if you think fit, be shown to selected people in Malaya without embarrassment.

2. Clause 1 you have seen already, and the only difference is that I have made it clear that the button to start the rest of the Bill operating is pressed by the Order in Council and not by the Agreement. This insures against the theoretical possibility that an Agreement might be reached, but not approved by the local Legislatures, in which case no Order in Council could be made.

3. Clause 2 is of course the main clause, and I have found it most infernally difficult; for although the ingredients of the mixture are not themselves unfamiliar, I think we have never yet had to do so many contradictory things simultaneously. Within the last ten years we have seen a part of Her Majesty's dominions turned into a foreign country without frills (Burma); a part of those dominions converted into two separate Dominions, and subsequently recognized as independent Republics within the Commonwealth (India and Pakistan); a colony converted into a Dominion without frills (Ceylon); an association of a colony, a protectorate and a trust territory converted into a Dominion, in this case involving an element of annexation (Gold Coast); a colony and two protectorates federated without annexation (Rhodesia); and other operations in respect of Southern Ireland and Palestine. In the present case we are running together the operations of federating two colonies and nine protected states, ceding sovereignty over the colonies and jurisdiction over the States, and treating the end product simultaneously as an independent sovereign country and as a self-governing Dominion. The question is what in these circumstances has to be done with the existing law of the United Kingdom (as contrasted with the existing law of the Federation, including United Kingdom Acts and Orders in Council which now extend to the Federation as part of its law); and speaking for myself I find it infernally difficult to remember which ball one is supposed to be keeping the eye on at each moment.

---

[1] N K Hutton (later Sir Noel), first parliamentary counsel to the Treasury, 1956–1968.
[2] Not printed.

4.   As I understand it, however, having discussed the instructions in conference with Johnston and Steel,[3] the general lines of the policy on this are clear. So far as the law of the United Kingdom is concerned, all existing enactments, etc. are, generally speaking, to continue to apply exactly as before—i.e. the Federation, though now an independent (I suppose one must not say foreign) country, is to rank for all purposes of existing law as if there had been no change. Provisions which already relate to the colonies (not in the sense of extending to them as part of their law but as relating to things done in them and so forth) will continue to apply to the Settlements as States of the new Federation; and provisions relating in the same way to protected states will similarly continue to apply to the existing Malay States as units of the new Federation.

5.   So far, the general idea is similar to that followed in the case of India, Pakistan and Southern Ireland: but if the matter were left there the new Federation (as opposed to its constituent parts) would remain almost unrecognized by the existing law. It is therefore necessary to qualify the general proposition by a further limited proposition under which existing enactments which relate specially (in the sense already mentioned) to the self-governing Dominions and to India, Pakistan and Southern Ireland, are extended so as to relate in the same way to the new Federation as a whole. This qualification is in turn analogous to what was done for Ceylon and the Gold Coast, but with the subtle difference that the unit for which the operation is performed is not a part of Her Majesty's dominions but is a country to which existing enactments apply as if its constituent parts were colonies or protected states (as the case may be). I have assumed for this purpose that the Ceylon and Ghana Acts can be taken as a guide to what needs to be done. At all events I have had no chance to conduct a separate investigation of the Statute book for the purpose.

6.   There is of course another quite different question, namely how far existing enactments which relate in one way or another to the Settlements or the Malay States should be sorted out as between the Federation on the one hand and the constituent units on the other—by the sort of operation performed by s.13 of the Federation of Rhodesia and Nyasaland (Constitution) Order in Council, 1953. We agreed at our conference that even if there is a question of this kind in relation to the Federation (which is not clear) it would certainly be impossible to solve it by detailed amendments in the Bill. If at all, it should be dealt with under the power to make consequential adaptations by Order in Council.

7.   Accordingly the general proposition detailed in paragraph 4 above will be found in sub-section (1) of clause 2; and the qualification (described in paragraph 5) appears in paragraph (a) of the proviso, coupled with the First Schedule. There are certain differences of detail between the First Schedule and the relevant provisions of the Ghana Independence Act, 1957, to which I shall come in a moment, but I thought I should begin by attempting to account for the general structure of the present clause.

8.   Clause 3, again you have seen. This clause seems to me to be potentially inconsistent with the general proposition mentioned above, namely that all existing law in the United Kingdom continues exactly as before, and accordingly I have added a further paragraph to the proviso to subsection (1) of clause 2 making it clear that we do not purport to continue any right of appeal to Her Majesty in Council.

---

[3] H Steel was legal assistant, CO, 1955, senior legal assistant, 1960.

9. I now come to the First Schedule, on which I have the following detailed observations:—

Paragraph 1. In the Ceylon Act of 1947 the question of nationality (then of course quite a different question) was dealt with in the Schedule—i.e. by an amendment not extending to Ceylon as part of its law. In the Ghana Act, on the other hand, the question is dealt with a separate section which does not expressly disclaim operation in Ghana. I have followed the former precedent here (see paragraph (d) of the proviso to clause 2 (1)) because it seems to me that whatever contradictory results we may have to secure in this Bill, the one thing we can't do is to purport to legislate for the Federation after Merdeka Day. (I think this principle has more important results in relation to the Army Act than in relation to nationality).

The words in square brackets in this paragraph raise the question whether we need some provision similar to the proviso to s.2 of the Ghana Independence Act, 1957. On the face of it, it appears to me that such words are in fact unnecessary, because all the people who are British protected persons by virtue of their connection with the Malay States are already citizens of the existing Federation under the 1948 Agreement, and will automatically become citizens of the new Federation under the new Constitu tion. I cannot however be sure of this from my own knowledge, and the point requires your expert eye. Even if you come to the same conclusion on the facts, however, there is still the theoretical question whether the words in square brackets should not be retained, for this Bill does not know what is in the Constitution.

Paragraph 2. This follows subsection (2) of s.4 of the Ghana Independence Act, 1957. It is at this point that I become uneasy, in so far as we are amending a number of sections of the Army Act which undoubtedly do extend to the different units of the Federation by leaving [sic] out of the definitions of "colony" and "territory under Her Majesty's protection". If therefore the Army Act is included in the existing law which is continued in force by the Malay legislation, and no corresponding amendment made, there may be strange results, at least in theory. I doubt however if this matters in practice.

For reasons already discussed it appears to be unnecessary to reproduce subsection (3) of s.4 of the Ghana Act. In so far as the Army Act continues to apply as part of the law of the Federation, it will do so because that law says so. Subsection (1) of clause 2 merely prevents it from taking on a different meaning, in its application elsewhere than in the Federation, as the result of Independence. If and when the Army Act is renewed the renewal will not make it part of the law of the Federation unless the Federation's law has produced that situation for itself. I imagine that the Service Departments will want to see a Visiting Forces Act in the Federation. No doubt however the Ministry of Defence will be among those to whom you will circulate the draft, and no doubt they will make their own comment.

In sub-paragraph (2) I have referred to the existing Naval Discipline Act. It will unfortunately be necessary to leave it like that until the current Naval Discipline Bill is through, and then amend this Bill at the last moment. I only hope we remember between us to do so.

Paragraphs 3 to 7. These paragraphs come straight out of the Second Schedule to the Ghana Independence Act, 1957, and I am not aware of any point on them. I should however add that I have copied them more or less blind, and I hope they will be seen by the departments concerned.

Paragraph 8. I hope this gives effect to the requirements outlined in the telegrams attached to my instructions. The paragraph differs slightly from the corresponding paragraph in the Second Schedule to the Ghana Independence Act because (as I understand it) any Bill which is passed by the Federal Parliament must be submitted for Assent so the normal system would be impracticable. Rowe is very much troubled about this particular provision, which he says ought to be cleared with the Malay Government as soon as possible to give time for them to pass the necessary legislation. I think myself that the paragraph will do the trick, but am not too confident about it. No doubt the Treasury will tell us.

Paragraphs 9 to 13. These paragraphs are again taken straight from the Second Schedule to the Ghana Independence Act without modification. They look odd in relation to a country which is not part of the dominions, but as I understand it, the effect of what we say about nationality is that ships of the Federation will be "British ships" within the meaning of existing laws, quite apart from subsection (1) of clause (2) of the Bill. In this case, I hope we shall have the views of the Ministry of Transport and Civil Aviation.

Paragraph 14. The position here is, I think, greatly simplified by the fact that the Copyright Act, 1956, has now been brought into force. This, coupled with the facts:—

(a) that the Copyright Act, 1911, applied only to the two Settlements as colonies, and to some but not all of the Malay States as foreign countries; and

(b) that copyright is a federal subject in the new Constitutional List,

may make it necessary to go into the elaborations of paragraph 12 of the Second Schedule to the Ghana Independence Act. On the other hand I am inclined to think, on reflection, that it was rash to hope that it could come down to anything as brief as my paragraph 14. Perhaps the Board of Trade can help us on this one?

There is nothing in the Schedule about Colonial Development and Welfare or about the Colonial Development Corporation.[4] Steel told me at an early stage that we could remain silent about those, but as that was before we had discussed the instructions in conference I am not sure if it is still true having regard to clause 2 (1). As regards your talk with Fiennes[5] this week, it is just worth recording that with the House coming back on Tuesday, 25th June, we can't send in notice of presentation before that day, so that First reading cannot be before 26th June, with publication, at earliest on the afternoon of that day. If we have trouble at Legislation Committee we might be a day late or even two, but I sincerely hope not. Time is unbearably short already. There is also nothing specific in the Schedule about Teachers' Superannuation. I hope clause 2 (1) covers that point as it stands, but I will take this up with Dale[6] direct.

---

[4] Clause 3(4) of the Ghana Bill, which excluded the Colonial Development Corporation from undertaking new projects in Ghana after independence, encountered considerable criticism in the Commons and Lords. See BDEEP, series B, vol 1, R Rathbone, ed, *Ghana*, part II, 273, 283, 285 and 286. In the event references to Colonial Development and Welfare and to the Colonial Development Corporation were omitted from the Malayan legislation.

[5] J S W Twistleton-Wykeham-Fiennes, second parliamentary counsel, Treasury, 1956–1968; parliamentary counsel, Malaya, 1962–1963; succeeded Hutton as first parliamentary counsel, 1968.

[6] Before his appointment as legal adviser, Ministry of Education, 1954–1961, W L Dale had had several years as deputy legal adviser in the CO.

457   CO 1030/437, no 13   4 July 1957

'Malaya': minutes PMM(57)10 of a meeting of Commonwealth prime ministers on Malaya's prospective membership

[Amongst those who attended this meeting, which was chaired by Macmillan, were the following ministers and prime ministers: Selwyn Lloyd, Home, Lennox-Boyd (UK); J Diefenbaker and G R Pearkes (Canada); R G Menzies and H E Holt (Australia); T L MacDonald (NZ); E H Louw (S Africa); J Nehru and V K Krishna Menon (India); H S Suhrawardy and Malik Feroze Khan Noon (Pakistan); M W H de Silva (Ceylon); and K Nkrumah (Ghana).]

Mr. Macmillan said that last year the Commonwealth Prime Ministers had settled by correspondence the admission of Ghana to membership of the Commonwealth. They now had an opportunity to consider the admission of Malaya, which was due to achieve independence on the 31st August. Outlining the progress of Malaya towards self-Government, he said that a United Kingdom–Malaya Conference had agreed in 1956 to take steps to prepare for an independent Malaya in August, 1957. In May of this year, a further conference accepted, subject to certain amendments, the recommendations for the new Constitution of Malaya which had been made by the Constitutional Commission under Lord Reid. The final text for the Constitution would be submitted to the Rulers and would thereafter be debated in the Federal and State Legislatures in Malaya. A Bill would be introduced into the United Kingdom Parliament providing for Malayan independence on 31st August.

The Federation had expressed the hope that, on achieving her independence, she would be recognised as a member of the Commonwealth. Commonwealth membership, which carried the right to be represented at meetings of Commonwealth Prime Ministers and to take part in the day-to-day consultation and exchange of information on international affairs, could only be granted with the agreement of the existing members. Before the Meeting considered whether to accept Malaya as a member of the Commonwealth, it would wish to be assured that she satisfied the usual criteria of membership. In fact, the Federation was in every sense viable; and her economy was stable. The Government had a firm majority, and terrorism was under control. Finally, the Chief Minister of Malaya had made it clear that his country wished to link her future with the Commonwealth.

In discussion, there was general agreement in principle that Malaya should be accepted as a member of the Commonwealth if, on achieving independence, she applied for membership.

Mr. Diefenbaker said that this was a matter of congratulation not only to Malaya but also to the United Kingdom as regards the way in which she continued to lead her dependent peoples towards self-government.

Mr. Menzies said that, although no one would wish to refuse Malaya Commonwealth membership, it would be improper to mention the Meeting's decision in the final communiqué in advance of the notification from Malaya, on achieving her independence, that she wished to be recognised as a full member of the Commonwealth.

In general discussion of this point, the following points were made:—

(a) Malayan independence lay only a few weeks ahead, and it was clearly convenient to discuss her prospective membership of the Commonwealth at the present Meeting in order to ensure that, when her formal application arrived, it could be dealt with expeditiously, in the knowledge of the views of the other members.

(b) Public opinion was expecting some mention of Malayan independence in the final communiqué, and there was some risk that the absence of any reference to Malayan membership of the Commonwealth would be interpreted in Malaya as a rebuff to her legitimate aspirations.

(c) On the other hand, although it was highly unlikely that, in the case of Malaya, her attainment of her independence and Commonwealth membership would suffer any setback at the eleventh hour, it might be undesirable to establish a precedent by publicly welcoming the prospect of the admission of a dependent territory to Commonwealth membership before it was formally competent, as a result of actually achieving independence, to apply for membership.

(d) Moreover the decision of Parliament in respect of Malayan independence should not be anticipated.

(e) Any indication in the final communiqué that the Commonwealth representatives had agreed that Malaya should be granted membership of the Commonwealth on the attainment of independence might be held to be an attempt by the member countries to influence the free choice in this matter which the Malayan Government would be entitled, on attaining independence, to exercise.

Mr. Macmillan said that while any reference to this question in the final communiqué would clearly need to be worded with care, it would be foolish to risk offending Malayan opinion by too slavish an observance of constitutional niceties. The communiqué, amplified by guidance to the Press, should therefore be so worded as to imply, without any infringement of propriety, that there was a reasonable expectation of Malaya's achieving membership of the Commonwealth in the near future.

458   DO 35/6281, no 30   10 July 1957
[Commonwealth membership]: letter from A W Snelling[1] to R C C Hunt[2] on the Commonwealth prime ministers' meeting, 4–5 July

As I was present at the session of the Prime Ministers' Meeting when the question of the admission of Malaya to membership of the Commonwealth was discussed I think you may like to have from me an account of what happened.

To start before the Meeting, we prepared a brief for the Prime Minister, a copy of which I enclose.[3] As you will see from it, we had reason to think that Mr. Louw, on behalf of South Africa, might use the opportunity of the Malayan item to air a pet grievance of his and Mr. Strijdom's to the effect that we are in practice bouncing Commonwealth Prime Ministers over the admission of new members because, before

---

[1] Deputy British high commissioner in South Africa, 1953–1955; assistant secretary, CRO, 1956–1959; British high commissioner, Ghana, 1959–1961.
[2] CRO representative attached to the office of high commissioner, Malaya, 1956–1957; British deputy high commissioner, Malaya, 1957–1959.
[3] Not printed.

the stage is reached at which the proposal to admit a new member is submitted to all Commonwealth Prime Ministers, we agree off our own bat to grant the emerging territory "independence within the Commonwealth". The argument which we were led to expect that Mr. Louw would put forward was all the more tiresome because it had a measure of logic in it, but it was not a point which on political grounds we could possibly concede. However, in the event it was not Mr. Louw but Mr. Menzies who proved awkward.

I enclose the minutes of the discussion in the Prime Ministers Meeting.[4] There was a full attendance except for Welensky[5] who, as his country is not a member, does not take part in discussions about admission. As you will see, Mr. Macmillan spoke to the brief and all was going well until Mr. Menzies raised the lawyer's point that it would not be proper to mention in the communiqué the decision of the Commonwealth Prime Ministers on the question of the admission of Malaya whilst that question remained hypothetical because of the number of constitutional steps both in Malaya and in the U.K. which had still to be taken before independence became actual. The ensuing discussion was extraordinarily confused, and the minutes are a brilliant example of the art of the Cabinet Office in making sense of the chaotic. In the end, the Prime Minister came down firmly on the right side of the fence, by saying that it would be foolish to risk offending Malayan opinion by too slavish an observance of constitutional niceties.

Late that night we had the usual meeting of U.K. and Commonwealth officials under Brook's chairmanship to produce one of the many drafts of the communiqué and Brook took the opportunity to state very firmly to the Australians that their Prime Minister was on the wrong tack, and that Prime Ministers had agreed on a number of occasions to reach decisions on questions which, according to Mr. Menzies' criteria, would be hypothetical. Thus, the Prime Ministers had settled by correspondence before the date of Ghana's independence the question of her admission to the Commonwealth;[6] and decisions had been taken in regard to both Pakistan and Ceylon that if and when they decided to adopt a republican form of government their membership of the Commonwealth would not be affected. Presumably this homily had some effect, because when the final session of the Prime Ministers' Meeting took place[7] at which the communiqué was blessed, there was no argument about the form of words which had been drafted by Brook. Consequently the communiqué contained the following final paragraph:—

> "The Commonwealth Ministers noted that the Federation of Malaya was on the eve of attaining independence. They extended to the Federation their warm good wishes for its future, and they looked forward to being able to welcome an independent Malaya as a member of the Commonwealth on the completion of the necessary constitutional processes."

The result therefore is not such a muddle as we feared at one stage might emerge. We have not yet had time to consider just what if any further steps about the admission of Malaya to membership of the Commonwealth will need to be taken at or

---

[4] See 457.   [5] Sir Roy Welensky, prime minister of the Central African Federation, 1956–1963.
[6] See 444, notes 2–4.   [7] On 5 July.

about the time of independence. No doubt we shall be preparing something further on this in due course.[8]

---

[8] On 12 Aug, when the legal process of Malayan independence was virtually complete (see 456, note), Lord Home informed Macmillan that the time had come to ask other Commonwealth prime ministers formally to recognise Malaya as a member (see CO 1030/437, no E/24).

459 CO 1030/443, no 1   15 July 1957

'First governors of Penang and Malacca': minute by J B Johnston to E Melville and Sir J Martin

As you know the final agreement on this subject was that the first Governors should be nominated jointly by the Queen and the Conference of Rulers and then appointed on Merdeka Day by the Yang di-Pertuan Agong.

2. I had a discussion with the High Commissioner when I was in Malaya about these Governorships. He proposes and the Tunku agrees that Raja Sir Uda should be asked to be the first Governor of Malacca. This seems a very sensible choice. They have sounded Raja Sir Uda and he would accept.

3. The real problem arises over Penang. In my view it is absolutely essential if race relations in the Federation are not going to get off to an extremely bad start for a Chinese to be appointed as the first Governor of Penang. If a Malay was put in the Chinese everywhere (and opinion in this country) will point to this as an indication that all their fears of Malay dominance and disregard of Chinese interests were justified and I doubt very much whether the Secretary of State ought to or could advise the Queen to agree to a Malay appointment in Penang.

4. Nevertheless the practical difficulties are formidable. The High Commissioner had a candidate whom he thought he could get accepted and whom he mentioned to the Secretary of State, but he has since died. There seem no eminent Chinese in Penang who are not mixed up in politics or who have not some slightly shady back-history of secret societies and the like. The Tunku is being very difficult. While I was there he told the High Commissioner that he thought Sir Cheng Lock Tan was the only Chinese he could get the Penang Malays to accept and he suggested that he should be appointed as the first Governor for a temporary period of six months. Cheng Lock Tan is now so senile, the High Commissioner says, that he could scarcely read a speech if it were typed out and put into his hand, and I suggested that the device of appointing him for six months would be so transparent a gesture and so clearly designed to get round the obligation of a joint nomination for the first Governorship that it would be derided in the Federation and certainly could not be accepted here. When I left the High Commissioner was very uncertain on this subject and at a loss to know where to find a Chinese or how to withstand the Tunku's pressure for a Malay. The one thing we were agreed on was that we must hold the matter up until after the debates in the Federation and here so that the appointments to these offices did not become a subject of Parliamentary controversy at either end. The time is rapidly approaching when we should have to reach decisions and I greatly fear that unless there is some stiffening from here we may get a recommendation from the High Commissioner that a Malay should be appointed in Penang simply because he has not felt able to take a tough enough line with the Tunku.

5. I would therefore propose that we send a personal telegram to the High Commissioner from the Secretary of State as in the attached draft,[1] and follow it up if he agrees with a telegram in the non-personal series which he could show to the Tunku. If the latter is in sufficiently uncompromising terms it might just turn the scale in the local argument.

---

[1] Not printed.

460   CO 1030/443, no 6   1 Aug 1957
[Governors of Penang and Malacca]: inward telegram no 224 from Sir D MacGillivray to Mr Lennox-Boyd on nominations

My telegram Personal No. 212.

Appointment of Governors.

Chief Minister had various talks with leaders of Malay community in Penang over last week-end and subsequently with M.C.A. leaders in Penang. As you know the (corrupt group ?present) Mayor of Georgetown is a Chinese. The view of the Malays is that they could accept a Chinese as Governor if these other two posts of supreme authority were not also held by Chinese. This view is held especially strongly in Province Wellesley.

2. I have discussed with the Tunku the possibility of getting the Alliance councillors in Penang to accept a Malay M.C.S. officer as first Chief Minister. There is no Malay among the Elected Members in Penang who will both be suitable and willing to undertake the duties of this post. You are aware that (group omitted ?Penang) has a majority of Elected Members both in Settlement Council and in Executive Council and the Tunku considers (and I agree) that it will be impossible to get them to agree to appointment of a Nominated Member or an Official as first Chief Minister. It seems clear then that first Chief Minister will have to be appointed from among the Chinese Elected Members and I understand that the Alliance will nominate Lim Cheong Eu (the present Alliance leader in Penang and the Settlements' [sic] representative in the Federal Legislative Council).

3. If therefore posts of Mayor and Chief Minister are to be held by Chinese there is something to be said for appointment of a Malay as Governor. The Resident Commissioner and the Tunku have now quite independently recommended to me that Raja Sir Uda should be appointed Governor of Penang. I think that from personal point of view he would be acceptable to most people in Penang. There would be criticism however from some Chinese that despite the fact that both Chief Minister and Mayor are to be Chinese, the Governor should also be a Chinese and from others that the Governor should be a local man. If Lim Cheong Eu is to be Chief Minister the appointment of Uda would have advantages from the point of view that it is very desirable that there should be a Governor:—

(a) with personality and character who could keep an eye on and control Cheong Eu's tendency to pander to those who undertake non-Malayan pro-Chinese activities; and

(b) with long administrative experience who would be used behind the scenes to guide the new largely elected inexperienced executive.

4.   You will have learnt from Johnston that I had Uda in mind for Malacca. Tunku had already agreed to this. I had informally sounded Uda who has expressed willingness to serve there for two years and I have already put forward his name to the Rulers for their consideration. The intention was that Uda would appoint a Malay M.C.S. officer as Chief Minister since there is no one among the Elected or Unofficial Nominated Members in the least qualified to fill the duties of this onerous new executive position. The Tunku agreed to this also. This was an ideal solution for Malacca and I am sure that Uda's appointment would have been well received there.

5.   I have now told the Tunku that if Uda is to be appointed to Penang instead, it will be necessary to find a Chinese for Malacca with a senior Malay M.C.S. officer as Chief Minister. (Fortunately one such officer is readily available in the person of Osman bin Talib, Deputy Mentri Besar Perak, who expected to be appointed as Mentri Besar in succession to Buki[t] Gantang and who is now mortified that the Perak Executive Council should have invited His Highness to appoint the Malay leader of the Elected Members and that His Highness has accepted this advice.) The Tunku reverted to Tan Siew Sin (Cheng Lock's son). I made it very clear that I could not agree to either. Tan Siew Sin might be alright as a Minister (and I know that the Tunku had it in mind to bring him into the Cabinet after Merdeka) but he has not got the qualities required for Governor. The Tunku then said that he could not persuade the Malays in Malacca to accept a Chinese unless it should be a Chinese who had prominently identified himself with the Alliance and the cause of independence. I think this is probably true. He suggested Leong Yew Koh (now Minister for Health). There are points in favour of Yew Koh. More than any other Chinese leader he is strongly anti-Communist and has played a courageous part in the Emergency effort, constantly visiting the worst villages in Perak (his home), and exhorting the villagers to give up support of the terrorists. He is a Catholic and has given much support to the Church. Portuguese and other Catholics in Malacca would no doubt welcome his appointment. His wife is active in welfare matters, speaks good English, and is a pleasant person. One daughter is undergoing training as a nurse in England now. He is 69. For further particulars see my savingram No. 995/55 of 15th August, 1955. On the other hand he has a reputation for being impecunious and not too scrupulous in financial matters, and he deemed it necessary to use loud pedal when playing anti-Colonial notes in some of his election speeches of two years ago. My main objection to his appointment as Governor is that he is a politician and it would be said that the appointment had been made for political reasons. Some of the rulers are likely to voice objection on the same grounds. On the other hand I cannot think of a better solution for the problems of Penang and Malacca taken together, objectionable though a political appointment to Malacca may be regarded.

6.   Having regard to the influence of Cheng Lock Tan and his son it would certainly be desirable to obtain their acceptance of Yew Koh's appointment. The Tunku is now trying to get hold of Tan Siew Sin to speak to him about this.

7.   I have asked the Rulers to come by themselves and have a quiet informal discussion with me about this at mid-day on Saturday. If you could let me have your reactions to these proposals before I see them I shall be very grateful.

8.   In paragraph 3 of my telegram Personal No. 212, I suggest the possibility of Abdoolcader[1] for Penang. (The word "only" in the first sentence in that telegram

---

[1] Sir Husein Hasanally Abdoolcader was a Penang lawyer; Indian member, Penang Municipal Commission,

should have read "probably".) Enquiries I have made reveal that he would be quite unsuitable. Gujerati is the language of his household and he is invariably spoken of with tolerant contempt by his fellow practitioners at the Bar.

9. I should have added to paragraph 7 of my telegram Personal No. 212 that it would probably prove impossible to obtain a Chinese from Singapore with the necessary qualification of Federal citizenship.[2]

1925–1941, and Straits Settlements Legislative Council, 1928–1941; member, the Governor's Advisory Council, Malayan Union; member, Indian Immigration Committee, 1925–1953.

[2] On reflection the CO accepted MacGillivray's proposal and, on independence day, Raja Uda and Leong Yew Koh became governors of Penang and Malacca respectively.

461   PREM 11/1928, ff 14–15   8 Aug 1957
'Internal security after Merdeka': inward telegram no 237 from Sir D MacGillivray to Mr Lennox-Boyd on the role of British forces

Your telegrams Personal No. 242 and No. 243.

Internal Security after Merdeka.

The G.O.C. Federation Army and Commissioner of Police have been giving consideration to the internal security situation in the immediately post-independence period with particular reference to the possibility of inter-racial trouble. There is no overt evidence that such trouble will occur, but there are continued and wide-spread rumours which have caused distinct uneasiness in both the major communities. The situation is such that a minor outbreak could spark country-wide disturbances. The extent to which these could develop is wide and unpredictable although it is clear that the Alliance Government will do all in its power to nip them in the bud.

2. I am confident that in normal circumstances the police, supported by the Federation Army, could cope with any eventuality of this nature, but the present deployment of Federation forces for emergency duties leaves certain areas very thinly covered, while in Johore there are no Federation Army units at all. The celebrations commitments are a further complication. It would be impossible to make any special precautionary moves now without (a) causing alarm and thereby increasing the risk of an outbreak and (b) seriously curtailing current operations against the terrorists.

3. There are, I suggest, two ways in which H.M.G. might be able to give valuable assistance to the Federation Government in such a way as to cause the least embarrassment to both Governments. First, in the event of disturbances occuring on or before 30th August, it would be perfectly correct for British forces (as opposed to other Commonwealth forces) to be committed for the restoration of law and order. If the disturbances should continue after 30th August, would H.M.G. agree that such forces should continue to act either until law and order are restored or until relieved by Federation forces? In the worst case I think you will agree that troops could not be expected at midnight on 30th August to leave a town at the mercy of rioters. Legal cover for their continued action would be provided by the cancellation of certain Sections of the criminal Procedure Codes referred to in my despatch No. 1380/57 (which follows by bag). Secondly, in the event of disturbances occurring shortly after independence, you will appreciate that, if they are to be dealt with solely by the Police

and Federation Army, everything will depend on the speed with which such forces can be re-deployed. Would H.M.G. therefore agree to all or any of the following?

(a) That R.A.F. transport aircraft, light communication aircraft and helicopters
(b) R.N. ships and other military craft and
(c) British Army transport with drivers may be used to move Police, troops and stores; and
(d) that helicopters and voice aircraft may be used for observation, crowd control and announcements.

5. With reference to paragraph 4 above, it would not be the intention that any British Service officer or Other Rank should be directly engaged in suppressing disorder. All movements therefore would be so arranged that none of the aircraft or ships disembarked troops in the immediate vicinity of the disturbances. The same would apply to Military transport, but there would be some risk of such transport running into disturbance inadvertently. Even in that case, I am advised that no legal cover would be required as drivers would have an automatic right of private defence for themselves and their vehicles (they would in fact be well escorted).

6. Lacking both an Air Force and a Navy, and having only a limited amount of Military transport, this assistance could be vital and might well prevent a situation arising where a request for British troops to restore law and order, would have to be made. You will appreciate that the mobilisation of local civilian resources as the only alternative to the assistance in paragraph 4 would be inefficient and slow and, as far as the air is concerned, very limited.

7. I should be grateful for your views so that early consideration can be given here to the manner in which the problem should be presented to Ministers with a view to a formal request being made before independence for such assistance, or at least an indication being given to them that, if such a request was made at short notice, it would be immediately met by the Commanders O.C.F. at least, during the first three months after independence after which the situation can be further reviewed.

462   CO 1030/833, no 364   12 Aug 1957

[Anglo-Malayan defence agreement]: minute no PM(57)39 from Mr Profumo[1] to Mr Macmillan. *Appendix A:* 'Note on the Malayan defence agreement'

Prime Minister
At the Federation of Malaya Constitutional Conference held in January and February, 1956, it was agreed that when the Federation attained independence within the Commonwealth at the end of this month, the Government of the Federation would enter into an agreement on external defence and mutual assistance with H.M.G. in

---

[1] John Profumo, Conservative MP, 1940–1945 and 1950–1963; joint parliamentary secretary, Ministry of Transport and Civil Aviation, Nov 1952–Jan 1957; parliamentary under-secretary of state, CO, 1957–1958, and FO, Nov 1958–Jan 1959; minister of state, FO, 1959–1960; secretary of state for War, July 1960–June 1963.

the U.K. A joint U.K./Malayan Working Party, attended by observers from Australia and New Zealand, was set up under the chairmanship of the Commissioner-General for the United Kingdom in South East Asia to prepare such an agreement, and the text drafted by them was subsequently approved by the United Kingdom Ministers concerned at the end of last year during the visit of the Chief Minister of the Federation to this country, when agreement was also reached on a number of matters which had not been resolved in the Working Party.[2] Since then, a number of minor technical and drafting points have been resolved. On the U.K. side, all interested departments and the Chiefs of Staff have been closely consulted at all stages in the negotiations, and the text of the Agreement, which is attached as Appendix B[3] to this minute, is also agreed with the Government of the Federation, with the exception of a technical point on Section 4(3) of Annex 2, concerning the extent of H.M.G.'s responsibility to indemnify in the event of accidents to explosives, and this should be cleared within the next day or so.

2. I also attach at Appendix A a brief note on the main provisions of the Agreement.

3. The Australian and New Zealand Governments have indicated that on their deciding formally to approve the terms of the agreement they will wish to associate themselves with it to the extent that its provisions concern their forces by means of an exchange of letters with the Government of the Federation. We are now waiting to hear from them that they do so formally endorse it and have asked them to inform us of this as soon as possible as we should wish to leave this information before we tell the Federation Government formally that we accept it.

4. The Agreement will enter into force as soon as it is signed, which will be upon independence or as soon as possible thereafter, when it will be published both in the Federation of Malaya and in this country, and will be presented to Parliament as a White Paper. It is intended, however, that before independence, the two Governments should formally confirm to each other that the Agreement as now drafted (subject to the satisfactory resolution of the outstanding point on Annex 2, Section 4(3)), is acceptable to them and should undertake to bring it forward for signature upon independence. It is proposed that this be done by means of an exchange of letters between the Colonial Secretary, as the Minister at present responsible for the Federation, and the Chief Minister of the Federation. The texts of such an exchange are attached at Appendix C, and I now seek your formal authority to initiate that exchange on behalf of Her Majesty's Government.

5. I have sent copies of this minute to the Minister of Defence, the Secretary of State for Foreign Affairs, the Chancellor of the Exchequer, the Secretary of State for Commonwealth Relations, the Secretary of State for War, the Secretary of State for Air and the First Lord of the Admiralty.[4]

---

[2] See 431, 432 and 441.   [3] Appendices B and C not printed.

[4] Macmillan approved this course of action on 21 Aug and Lennox-Boyd accordingly prepared for a preliminary exchange of notes with Tunku Abdul Rahman. The British intention was for the defence agreement to be signed on independence day or within forty-eight hours after it. On 24 Aug, however, the Tunku informed MacGillivray that he had overlooked a promise he had made some months earlier to UMNO's general assembly that the agreement would be debated by the federal legislature before it was concluded and that, since he must honour his word, the ceremony would have to be postponed until Oct. Meanwhile, a more serious threat to the speedy completion of the defence arrangements had arisen. On 20 Aug the minister of defence (Duncan Sandys) told a press conference in Canberra that the UK force in the

Appendix A to 462

Under the Agreement, the Federation of Malaya undertakes to provide bases and facilities for the U.K. forces and a Commonwealth Strategic Reserve, which are to be stationed in the Federation after independence to assist in its external defence and for the fulfilment of Commonwealth and international obligations. The agreement also contains four annexes dealing with:—

(i)   the assistance which H.M.G. undertake to give on repayment for the training and development of the Armed Forces of the Federation (this assistance is distinct from the financial aid which was negotiated with the delegation from the Federation in January of this year);

(ii) the bases and training, and other facilities, which U.K. forces are to have in the Federation;

(iii) provisions governing the status of the U.K. forces;

(iv) matters of land tenure and disposal.

2.   The vital provisions of the Agreement are to be found in Articles VI, VII and VIII, which set out the circumstances and conditions under which we may take military action from bases in the Federation. The emergence of the Federation as an independent nation means that, if we are not to derogate from her sovereignty, we have to accept some restriction on the complete discretion we have hitherto possessed while the Federation was constitutionally dependent on us; we have, nevertheless, retained for ourselves a very considerable degree of freedom. Under Article VII, we have the right to react automatically to any attack on the Federation or on our own territories in the Far East; moreover, under Article VIII we have complete freedom to withdraw our forces from the Federation in order to commit them to act if we become involved in hostilities elsewhere from which the Federation wishes to steer clear. Under Article VI, if the Federation or our own territories in the Far East are threatened with an attack, or if there is any other threat to the

---

SEATO area would in due course include an element of nuclear power and mentioned that Canberra bombers (which formed the major part of Britain's air strike force in Malaya) were equipped to carry atomic weapons. Although Sandys did not specifically say that nuclear warheads would be stored in Malaya, it was with that interpretation that his remarks were reported by the Malayan press. Worried lest public agitation in Malaya might jeopardise the agreement or force them to give an undertaking not to use nuclear weapons, the British authorities debated whether or not to assure the Tunku and his Cabinet that Malayans would have a veto over any British proposal to deploy nuclear weapons in the region. The CO official, John Hennings, subsequently stated the case for such as assurance as follows: 'we recognised that we were not surrendering a discretion which we might otherwise possess but were doing no more than admit the political consequences implicit in the Federation's becoming a sovereign state. We had insisted on the Americans giving us similar undertakings in relation to their bases in this country, and felt that we could not expect the Malayans to be content with less.' Despite the objections of Robert Scott and the still-absent Sandys, MacGillivray and G W Tory (British high commissioner designate) were authorised by Macmillan (who was in charge of the ministry of defence during Sandys' absence) to make overtures on these lines, although they were delayed by the independence celebrations (see 'Nuclear weapons in Malaya' by John Hennings, 20 Sept 1957, CO 1030/836, nos 85 and 86). The defence agreement was presented to the British parliament in Sept (see *Proposed Agreement on External Defence and Mutual Assistance between the Government of the United Kingdom of Great Britain and Northern Ireland and the Government of the Federation of Malaya*, Cmnd 263) and signed by Tunku Abdul Rahman and G W Tory (UK high commissioner in Kuala Lumpur) on 12 Oct 1957. The Australian and New Zealand governments associated themselves with the agreement by exchange of letters with the Federation government.

preservation of peace in the Far East (including an actual attack on any other country in the area), we can take action to counter it after consulting the Federation Government. This means that in certain circumstances our ability to act in support of ANZAM or SEATO would be dependent on Malayan consent. We hope that in due time the Federation will decide to join SEATO, but even if she remained outside that Organisation, we would hope that in pursuance of her pledge of full cooperation under Article VI, she would not raise any difficulty at the time to any action we might wish to take in support of SEATO. These articles which were negotiated after the fullest consultation with the U.K. ministers concerned, with the Chiefs of Staff and with the Australian and New Zealand Governments give us as much as we could reasonably hope to obtain, and the Malayans had an unanswerable case in insisting that they should have the right to be consulted on any action we might want to take under Article VI if their sovereignty was to be respected and they were to be treated as independent and equal partners with us.

4. Another point of difficulty concerned Annex 3, Section 3(a)(ii). We were most anxious to ensure that in accordance with present day international practice between independent nations the Service authorities should possess the primary right of jurisdiction over offences arising out of any act or omission done in the performance of official duty. In the Federation at the present time, as a consequence of the country's constitutional dependence on the United Kingdom, the civil courts commonly try certain types and classes of such offences, and the Malayans argued strongly that any departure from these arrangements would be unacceptable to local public opinion. In the end a compromise was reached under which the Malayans agreed that we should have the primary right of jurisdiction in these cases, while we (as set out in published letters attached to the Agreement (letters (3) and (4)) agreed to make administrative arrangements under which existing practice would continue. We were able to accept this in the knowledge that the Federation's intention to permit appeals to continue to be made to the Privy Council here would safeguard the standard of the administration of justice in the Federation, and because we retain the right to approach the Federation for their agreement to an individual case's being remitted to a service tribunal where we considered there to be urgent reasons for this.

5. The Agreement contains no provision for duration or review, and can therefore stand perpetually. We recognise, however, that it will in fact endure only so long as both Governments wish this, and we have therefore provided in a published exchange of letters (letters (1) and (2) attached to the Agreement) that is will be open to either party to request a review at any time. For internal political reasons, the Malayans were most anxious that they should not appear in an agreement negotiated before independence to commit the Federation to a permanent military dependence upon the United Kingdom, although Tunku Abdul Rahman and his colleagues regard such a dependence as an essential guarantee to the continued existence of the Federation as an independent nation in the free world.

6. A number of understandings have also been reached with the Federation Government in pursuance of the provisions of the Agreement. Most of these are clarificatory of its provisions, but a few represent matters to which, for reasons of security, we do not wish to give publicity. These are:—

(a) under Article III, we have undertaken that in the normal conditions of peacetime and in the absence of our invoking Articles VI, VII or VIII, our forces in the Federation (including the Commonwealth Strategic Reserve) will not exceed one and one-third divisions and eight operational squadrons of aircraft, together with their appropriate supporting units;

(b) under Article IV, the locations of the bases and training areas which will be made available to our forces will be set out in schedules attached to these letters;

(c) under Article IX we have undertaken that, when the emergency is ended, we shall first obtain the agreement of the Federation Government before introducing into the Federation forces other than from the United Kingdom, Australia, New Zealand, Borneo, Fiji or Sarawak or Gurkhas.

463 PREM 11/1927   15 Aug 1957
[Independence celebrations]: letter from P de Zulueta[1] to Miss J M D Ward[2] about the prime minister's broadcast

[On 6 Mar following the 9 pm news, Macmillan had given a five-minute radio broadcast in the Home and Overseas Services of the BBC to welcome independent Ghana to the Commonwealth. On 18 July he had agreed to make a similar broadcast on the occasion of Malayan independence.]

As we agreed on the telephone, I am writing to explain that the Prime Minister has now decided that he would rather not make a radio and television broadcast on the B.B.C. to celebrate the independence of Malaya. The Prime Minister is, however, still prepared to make his recording for the broadcast by Commonwealth Prime Ministers in the Federation itself.

As you know, Lord Home originally proposed this broadcast in his minute of July 18, but at that time there was no suggestion that the Prime Minister should record a message for use on the Malayan services. The Prime Minister feels that his obligations to Malaya will be fulfilled by making the recording and that other reasons make it undesirable for him to appear on the air in the United Kingdom on this subject. These considerations are that, since he became Prime Minister, Mr. Macmillan has only made three major appearances on sound and television. The first was when he assumed office, the second was on the occasion of Ghana's Independence and the third concerned the Commonwealth Conference. The first broadcast went well but the last two are not thought to have been particularly successful, mainly because the public were not interested in the subjects which were of their nature somewhat uninspiring. The Prime Minister also feels a certain unwillingness to appear twice on the air in order to celebrate what many people may think to be a weakening of the United Kingdom. There is the further point that recorded broadcasts never look so well on television and, as you know, the audience for purely sound broadcasts is now comparatively small.

For all these reasons the Prime Minister has decided that it would be better not to make the proposed broadcast and we have told the B.B.C. that he will not be doing so.

---

[1] Private secretary to successive prime ministers, 1955–1964.
[2] Assistant private secretary to Lord Home, 1956–1958.

I am sending a copy of this letter to Moreton[3] in the Colonial Office so that he will be aware that the Prime Minister has changed his mind about this.

---

[3] J O Moreton, private secretary to Lennox-Boyd, 1955–1959.

464　DEFE 4/99, COS 66(57)2, confidential annex　[15 Aug 1957][1]
'Directive to commanders of overseas Commonwealth forces in Malaya after independence': COS Committee minutes of a meeting on 15 Aug
[Extract]

The Committee considered a minute from the Secretary covering a draft Colonial Office reply to a telegram[2] from the High Commissioner, Federation of Malaya. A telegram giving the comments of the British Defence Co-ordination Committee (Far East) on a draft Directive approved by the Committee at a previous meeting[3] was also relevant to their discussion.

A.　*Draft Colonial Office telegram*
Sir William Oliver[4] said that he thought the telegram from the High Commissioner posed the worst situation that could arise and was not necessarily a forecast of what would happen. The telegram raised three distinct problems:—

(i)　The use of British troops to restore law and order during the delicate days of transition from British rule to independence.
(ii)　The use of British transport (sea, land and air) in support of the Federation Army and Police on internal security duties during the three or four months immediately after independence.
(iii)　The question of providing the British Military authorities on the spot with precise instructions as to their responsibilities in various eventualities.

On the first problem it had already been established that after independence the Federation Government became entirely responsible for I.S. matters and that only in a grave emergency could British troops be used. The High Commissioner's telegram appeared to seek some relaxation of this principle and the draft reply quite rightly started by reiterating it. The Malayan Government would be well aware of the dangers to themselves of asking for assistance from British troops. While, therefore, he agreed with the line taken by the Colonial Office on this problem, in their draft reply, he felt perhaps that this point of principle could be made more concisely.

The whole of our future position in Malaya would be dependent on goodwill. If the Malayans were to ask for British troops during the two or three days transition period, a long delay in acceding to the request might prove fatal to that goodwill. Although therefore a request for the use of British troops in this period must if possible be referred to London for Ministerial approval, the High Commissioner

---

[1] The meeting was held on 15 Aug; the minutes are dated 17 Aug.　　　　　　[2] See 461.
[3] This directive set out responsibilities for internal security and the lives of Commonwealth nationals in Malaya after independence. See DEFE 4/99, COS 63(57)1, 1 Aug 1955.
[4] Vice-chief, imperial general staff, 1955–1957.

must be given latitude to act on his own authority if time did not permit reference to London.

With regard to the use of British transport in support of the Federal forces, refusal to assist in this respect would have a most lamentable effect on the Federal Government and on local opinion. He considered that the High Commissioner should be authorised to agree to the provision of transport on request, but only on the strict understanding that such transport was kept outside the area in which riots were in progress. To do otherwise would damage our reputation for goodwill and co-operation on which our position in Malaya largely rested.

The answer to be sent to the High Commissioner on both these problems would require Ministerial approval. Once this had been obtained the Chiefs of Staff would be able to give the necessary parallel instructions to the Service Commanders in Malaya.

Mr. Johnston (Colonial Office) said that the draft reply which had been tabled represented the Colonial Office point of view very fully. His department was particularly concerned that the telegram from the High Commissioner, which represented the views of the G.O.C. Federation Army and the Commissioner of Police as well, appeared to disregard the principle with regard to the use of British troops which the Vice Chief of the Imperial General Staff had stated and with which he fully agreed.

Mr. Snelling (Commonwealth Relations Office) said that his department agreed with the general line of the draft reply and with the views of the Vice Chief of the Imperial General Staff. He agreed that more precise instructions needed to be given to the High Commissioner with regard to the transition period. It was also necessary to find out whether the situation described in the High Commissioners' [sic] telegram was likely to arise or whether the High Commissioner was only preparing for the worst that could happen. If the former then the question of the forthcoming visit of royalty to the Independence ceremonies would have to be reconsidered. If the Federal Government really thought that a situation beyond their control was likely to arise they would be well advised to ask in advance for assistance so that the matter could be put to Ministers and also to the Australian and New Zealand Governments. No firm promise to help could be given until the matter had been put to Ministers.

Mr. Way[5] (Ministry of Defence) said he fully agreed with what the previous speakers had said. He particularly wished to emphasise the principle that British troops were not available for internal security duties after independence and also the point that more precise instructions must be sent to the High Commissioner to cover the transition period. The High Commissioner should be instructed to tell the Federation Government that they must make preparations to deal with internal security troubles throughout the period of transition. It was quite wrong for the Federation authorities, for example, not to have the necessary internal security forces in Johore. Unless they made plans for all eventualities they might be forced into asking for British assistance unnecessarily. He thought that there were distinct political dangers in the use of British transport and that it should be made clear that it could only be used when all other resources had failed.

Sir Caspar John[6] said that there appeared to be some doubt as to whether the Royal Malayan Navy would be available to the Federation Government at the time of

---

[5] R G K Way, deputy secretary, Ministry of Defence, 1957–1958.   [6] Vice-chief of naval staff, 1957–1960.

independence. Up till now it had been under the control of the Singapore Government and he understood that negotiations to transfer it to the Malayan Government were in progress. If these negotiations had not been completed by Independence Day there might be difficulty if the Federation Government wished to use it in connection with internal disturbances. He undertook to find out the latest situation from the Commander-in-Chief, Far East Station, and to inform the Committee and the Colonial Office when he had done so.

In discussion *The Committee* agreed:—

(a) That the draft Colonial Office telegram should be revised in the light of their discussion, and submitted to Ministers for approval.

(b) That, in view of the urgency of the matter, an interim personal telegram should be sent to Sir Donald MacGillivray, explaining the views that had been agreed in discussion, and asking for clarification of his views as to whether the situation described in his telegram was likely to arise.

(c) That, after the revised draft telegram had been approved by Ministers, appropriate instructions should be sent to the Commanders of overseas Commonwealth Forces in Malaya to cover the period of transition.

(d) That further information should be obtained with regard to the status of the Royal Malayan Navy, as the Vice Chief of Naval Staff had suggested.

465   PREM 11/1928, ff 7–8, 10–13   16 Aug 1957
[Internal security after Merdeka]: minutes by Mr Profumo (no PM(57)40) and C O I Ramsden[1] to Mr Macmillan. *Annex:* draft outward telegram (reply) from Mr Lennox–Boyd to Sir D MacGillivray

Prime Minister

I attach a copy of a telegram from the High Commissioner in Malaya,[2] together with the draft of a proposed reply.

The problem raised in the High Commissioner's telegram has been considered by the Vice Chiefs of Staff, the Ministry of Defence, the Commonwealth Relations Office and the Colonial Office, and the reply, which is self-explanatory, represents their agreed view.[3] I accordingly seek your authority for its despatch. I have separately asked the High Commissioner for an assurance that the situation which has prompted these precautionary enquiries is not sufficiently serious to warrant any reconsideration of the desirability of the Duke and Duchess of Gloucester's visit.

Prime Minister

I have made enquiries about these papers. My first impressions, as perhaps yours will have been, were that:—

(a) a new and potentially very tiresome little crisis was about to arise.

(b) all this ought to have been thought of months ago.

I am, however, assured by the Colonial Office that neither they nor the Chiefs of Staff

---

[1] One of Macmillan's private secretaries.   [2] See 461.   [3] See 464.

believe that there is any serious danger of trouble. Had there been any, the authorities in Malaya would already be making the necessary troop movements. In fact, Sir D. MacGillivray is simply trying to take out an insurance policy (this, of course, reinforces point 'b' above).

I asked the Colonial Office what urgency there was about this. Could it not wait for the Colonial Secretary's return on Monday? (Mr. Lennox-Boyd has finally decided to submit to his operation as planned). I am told that it cannot wait since the last meeting of the Executive Council before Independence Day is to take place on Tuesday morning. The Colonial Office reply seems to be on the right lines. They have already pointed out to the High Commissioner that if there is really danger of trouble, Her Majesty's Government would have to consider whether it would be right for the Duke and Duchess of Gloucester to go for the ceremony.[4] There has been no reply yet to this telegram but I will, of course, let you know as soon as one is received.

Annex to 465

Your telegram Personal No. 237.

Internal Security after Merdeka.

While sympathising with anxieties underlying your telegram we regard it as fundamental that after independence Federation Government must meet internal security responsibilities from their own resources and only turn to us for help in situation of extreme emergency threatening collapse of organised Government. All public pronouncements have been on this assumption (see for example reply to Bromley-Davenport's P.Q. (my telegram 442 and your telegram 400 of 1st July) and the proposed White Paper on emergency operations).

2. Any departure from this policy would invite accusations of having granted independence in form and not in substance and would lay Tunku open to charge that he is British creature. Such departure would be propaganda gift to Communists generally.

3. We cannot therefore agree as seems suggested in your paragraph 7 that any encouragement should be given to Malayan Ministers to regard British assistance during first three months of independence as being on call and all plans should be laid and British and Federation forces disposed now on assumption that any internal security troubles after 30th August will have to be met from Federation resources.

4. We nevertheless recognise special difficulties of period immediately before and after 30th August since there must clearly be continuity in any precautionary plans that are made.

5. First objective of such plans should therefore be to ensure that Federation forces are available in any area where they may be required for internal security purposes. If necessary it should be emphasised to Ministers that it is their responsibility to deal with situation after midnight on 30th August and that they can only hope to do this if their plans are laid now. Any necessary redeployment should be carried out before 30th August during which period maximum help should be given on lines of your paragraph 4.

---

[4] See 467, note.

6. British troops should accordingly only be used for internal security purposes during period before independence if any local situation is beyond control of Malayan police and Federation army. If British troops were committed during this period Tunku should be advised, unless you are satisfied that disturbances will be ended before independence, to make immediate request to U.K. Government that their use be allowed to continue after independence date. It is in interests of both Tunku and ourselves that no post-independence help on the lines of your paragraph 5 should be necessary, and if necessary dispositions are made before independence these potential embarrassments should be avoided. All experience elsewhere is that precautionary moves diminish rather than increase risk of disturbances.

7. If however after independence situation developed in which Federation had to ask for help with transport, etc. on lines of your paragraph 4 (a) (b) (c), such help may be given but only to extent that it is possible to defend it as part of general redeployment as between British and Federation forces engaged in emergency operations consequent on diversion of Federation forces to internal security task.[5]

---

[5] Macmillan authorised this telegram, which was despatched by the CO at 22.30 hrs on 16 Aug, but, in so doing, he complained to Profumo: 'I do not understand why all this arose so suddenly. It seems to me very wrong that we should not have been warned.'

466   PREM 11/1928, f 6   16 Aug 1957

'Internal security after Merdeka': inward telegram no 253 from Sir D MacGillivray to Mr Lennox-Boyd. *Minute* by C O I Ramsden

[Docs 461, 464 and 465, together with this reassuring telegram and Ramsden's comment on it, reveal the nervousness beneath the apparent calm of Anglo-Malayan relations on the eve of transfer of power.]

My telegram Personal No.237[1] may not have brought out clearly enough that issues which it discussed had been raised by G.O.C. Federation Army and Commissioner of Police in precautionary planning of measures to meet worst foreseeable eventualities. To avoid any possible misunderstanding, I now wish to say that danger of outbreaks of kind envisaged is not great and has tended to recede during last few weeks, more particularly since recent public announcements of new constitutional arrangements and discussion thereon (e.g. appointment of Governors and Chief Ministers of Settlements) have created atmosphere of great goodwill. The need for taking precautions should certainly not be interpreted as indicating a degree of danger such as, for example, would raise any doubts about desirability of Duke and Duchess of Gloucester's visit or itinerary.

Minute on 464

Prime Minister
The attached telegram has just arrived about possible Malayan trouble. From it you

---

[1] See 461.

will see that it is not in fact Sir D. MacGillivray who is getting worried but the local authorities who would be responsible in the event of trouble. It also looks as though trouble was in fact very unlikely.

C.O.I.R.
16.8.57

467 PREM 11/1927, f 2   24 Aug 1957

[Independence day]: personal letter from Mr Macmillan to Tunku Abdul Rahman on Malaya's achievement of independence

[The Duke of Gloucester represented the Queen at the independence day ceremony in Kuala Lumpur on 31 Aug. The British government sent a delegation which, since Lennox-Boyd was due in hospital for an operation, was led by Lord Kilmuir, the lord chancellor, and included Lord Perth (CO) and C J M Alport, parliamentary under-secretary, CRO. Creech Jones attended on behalf of the Commonwealth Parliamentary Association. In an expansive mood, and until Sir Norman Brook reminded him of the principles governing the conduct of ministers, Macmillan had suggested that the public purse should cover the expenses of ministers' wives 'just as if they were the wives of tycoons' whose expenses would be set against profits. Kilmuir carried with him this personal message to the Tunku from Macmillan, who, in the opening sentence of the draft, had substituted the word 'glad' for 'happy'. Malay politicians had wished to invite representatives from Egypt, Syria and Saudi Arabia, but their presence at independence celebrations so soon after the Suez crisis would have embarrassed the British government which decided not ask them on the ground that they did not have diplomatic relations with these states. At the stroke of midnight on 30–31 Aug and before a large crowd, the union jack was lowered and simultaneously the flag of independent Malaya was hoisted on a mast on the *padang* between the old secretariat building and the Selangor Club. MacGillivray's term as high commissioner thus ended and (Sir) Geofroy Tory (assistant under-secretary at the CRO who had previously served in Canada, Ireland, Pakistan and Australia) became the first UK high commissioner to independent Malaya, 1957–1963. Late in the morning of 31 Aug at Merdeka Stadium and in the presence of Their Highnesses the Malay Rulers, the Duke of Gloucester presented the Tunku with the constitutional instruments providing for the withdrawal of British protection over the Malay states and of the Crown's sovereignty over Penang and Malacca. The Tunku then read out in Malay the Proclamation of Independence and his speech was greeted with cries of 'Merdeka!']

Dear Prime Minister

I am very glad to be able to send you, by the hand of the Lord Chancellor, who is leading the United Kingdom delegation, this message to welcome the Federation of Malaya on this historic occasion of its achievement of Independence and of Membership of the Commonwealth.

Lord Kilmuir brings you the warmest good wishes of the Government and people of the United Kingdom for the future happiness and prosperity of your country.

The emergence of the Federation of Malaya as an independent Member country of the Commonwealth is the culmination of the joint work of our two Governments over the past years. May the 31st August long be remembered in your history and in ours as a great and happy day in the continuing development of Malaya and of the Commonwealth of Nations.

Yours very sincerely,
Harold Macmillan

Biographical Notes: parts I–III

Abdul Aziz bin Ishak

Brother of Yusof bin Ishak, Singapore's first yang di-pertuan negara (head of state); Malay schools in Kuala Kurau and Taiping, Victoria Bridge School and Raffles Institution, Singapore; newspaper reporter in Singapore, 1934–1936; government service, FMS, 1936–1941; president of Gerakan Angkatan Pemuda Melayu (Malay Youth Action League), 1946–1948; editor of *Utusan Melayu*, 1948–1951; member of UMNO, 1948–1951; joined IMP, 1951 and was an unsuccessful IMP candidate in the KL municipal elections, 1952; re-joined UMNO, 1952 or 1953; member of Round Table Conference of UMNO-MCA Alliance, 1953; attended coronation of Queen Elizabeth II, 1953; elected to Federal Legislative Council, 1955; minister of agriculture and co-operatives, 1955–1962; one of three vice-presidents of UMNO, 1958–1962; dismissed as minister and expelled from UMNO, 1962; formed the National Convention Party, 1963; detained during 'confrontation' with Indonesia, 1965

Abdul Rahman Putra Al-Haj, Tunku (Tunku Abdul Rahman), 1903–1990

CH 1961; son of Sultan Abdul Hamid Halim Shah of Kedah; schools in Bangkok and Alor Star, Penang Free School, St Catharine's, Cambridge, and Inner Temple, London; entered Kedah government service, 1931; served as director of education (Kedah) and director of passive defence during Japanese occupation; returned to study law at Inner Temple, 1946, and called to the Bar; returned to Malaya, 1949, joined Kedah Legal Department and became chairman of UMNO, Kedah division; seconded to Federal Legal Department as deputy public prosecutor, 1949; president of UMNO, Aug 1951, and left government service; unofficial member of Federal Executive Council, 1952; leader of Alliance, 1952; led Alliance delegation to London, May 1954; launched boycott of government business, June 1954; reached agreement with MacGillivray, July 1954; elected to Federal Legislative Council, July 1955; became chief minister and minister of home affairs, Aug 1955; also acquired portfolio of minister for internal defence and security, 1956; held talks with Chin Peng at Baling, Kedah, Dec 1955; led Alliance delegation to London talks, Jan-Feb 1956, Dec 1956-Jan 1957 and May 1957; prime minister of Malaya, 1957–1963, of Malaysia 1963–1970; after retirement from politics he served as secretary-general of the Islamic Secretariat in Jeddah, 1970–1973, and wrote a weekly column in *The Star* newspaper, Penang.

Abdul Razak bin Hussein, Dato (later Tun Haji Abdul Razak), 1922–1976

Malay school, Pekan, and Malay College, Kuala Kangsar; joined Malay Administrative Service, 1939; further training at Raffles College, Singapore, 1940; captain in Wataniah and liaised with Force 136, 1945; ADO, Raub, 1945; Lincoln's Inn, 1947–1949; secretary of Malay Society of Great Britain, 1947–1948, president, 1948–1949; appointed to MCS and attached to state secretariat, Pahang, 1950; leader of UMNO Youth and a vice-president of UMNO, 1950; deputy president, UMNO, 1951; Federal Legislative Council, 1951; state secretary, Pahang, 1952; played a leading part in the Alliance Roundtable, 1953; joined Tunku Abdul Rahman in Alliance delegation to S of S, May 1954; mentri besar, Pahang, 1955; resigned government service to contest federal elections, June 1955; minister for education, 1955–1957; minister of defence, 1957–1960; deputy prime minister of Malaya, 1957–1963; deputy prime minister of Malaysia, 1963–1970; director of operations, 1969–1971; prime minister, 1970–1976

Abdul Wahab bin Toh Muda Abdul Aziz, Haji (Dato Panglima Bukit Gantang), 1905–1959
Malay school and Anderson School, Ipoh, and London University and Inner Temple; hon sec (later president), Malay Students' Association (England), 1927–1930; government service, FMS, 1931; left government service for private legal practice, 1932; succeeded grandfather as Dato Panglima Bukit Gantang (one of the eight principal chiefs of Perak), 1936; member of the Perak State Council, 1937–1941; leader of the Persatuan Melayu Perak (Perak Malay Union), 1939–1940 (?); acted as judge during the Japanese occupation; president of the Perikatan Melayu Perak (Perak Malay League), 1946–1947; secretary-general of UMNO, 1946–1947; mentri besar (chief minister) of Perak, 1948–1957; member of the Federal Legislative Council, 1948; member of the Communities Liaison Committee, 1949–1950; expelled from UMNO and formed the short-lived National Association of Perak, 1953; leader of the Malay rulers' delegation to the London constitutional conferences, 1956–1957; resumed private legal practice, 1957

Ahmad Boestamam (real name Abdullah Sani bin Raja Kechil), 1920–1983
Malay school and Anderson School, Ipoh; founder-member of Kesatuan Melayu Muda (Union of Malay Youth), 1938; detained by the British, 1941; leader of Japanese-sponsored youth group and worked in propaganda department in Ipoh; started newspaper, *Suara Raayat*, after Japanese surrender; founder-member of Malay Nationalist Party, 1945; founder-president of API (Angkatan Pemuda Insaf), 1946; tried for sedition on account of *Testament Politik Api*, 1947; detained, 1948–1955; founded Partai Raayat, 1956; led Socialist Front in Federal Parliament, 1959; detained during 'confrontation' with Indonesia

Attlee, Clement Richard (1st Earl cr 1955) 1883–1967
MP (Lab) 1922–1955; parliamentary private secretary to leader of Opposition, 1922–1924; parliamentary under-secretary of state for War, 1924; chancellor of the Duchy of Lancaster, 1930–1931; postmaster general, 1931; member of the Indian Statutory Commission, 1927; deputy leader of the Labour Party in House of Commons, 1931–1935; leader of the Opposition, 1935–1940; lord privy seal, 1940–1942; S of S for Dominion Affairs, 1942–1943; lord president of the Council, 1943–1945; deputy prime minister 1942–1945; prime minister, 1945–1951 and minister of defence, 1945–1946; leader of the Opposition, 1951–1955

Bennett, John Cecil Sterndale, 1895–1969
KCMG 1950; King Edward VII School, Sheffield, and St Catharine's, Cambridge; entered the Diplomatic Service, 1920; head of Far East Department, FO, 1940–1942 and 1944–1946; British representative (later minister), Bulgaria, 1947–1949; senior civilian member on staff of the Imperial Defence College, 1949–1950; deputy commissioner-general SE Asia, 1950–1953; head of British Middle East Office, 1953–1955

Boestamam, see Ahmad Boestamam

Bourdillon, Henry Townsend, 1913–1991
CMG 1952; Rugby and Corpus Christi, Oxford; entered CO, 1937; seconded to DO, 1939, to FO, 1942, to Cabinet Office, 1943 and to Ministry of Production, 1944; returned to CO, 1944; assistant secretary, 1947; head of Eastern Department CO, 1947–1948; assistant under-secretary of state, 1954; deputy UK commissioner, Singapore, 1959; returned to CO, 1961; under-secretary of state, Ministry of Education, 1962; assistant under-secretary of state, Department of Education and Science 1964–1973

Briggs, Harold Rawdon, 1894–1952
KCIE 1947; Bedford School and Royal Military College, Sandhurst; Indian Army from 1914; served in Eritrea, Western Desert, Iraq and Burma, 1940–1944;

GOC-in-C, Burma Command, 1946–1948; lieutenant-general; director of operations, Malaya, 1950–1951

Brook, Norman Craven (1st Baron Normanbrook cr 1963), 1902–1967
KCB 1946; Wolverhampton School and Wadham, Oxford; entered Home Office, 1925; deputy secretary (civil) to War Cabinet, 1942; permanent secretary Ministry of Reconstruction, 1943–1945; additional secretary to Cabinet, 1945–1946; secretary to Cabinet, 1947–1962; joint secretary of Treasury and head of Home Civil Service, 1956–1962

Burhanuddin Al-Helmy, Dr (Dr Burhanuddin bin Mohamad Noor), 1911–1969
Malay school, Kota Bahru, Islamic school, Padang Pajang (Sumatra), Madrasah Al-Mashoor Aslamiyah, Penang, and Aligarh University (India) where he obtained a degree in homeopathic medicine; returned to Malaya and worked as a journalist, 1937; detained briefly by the British; taught Arabic at Madrasah Aljunied (Muslim secondary school), Singapore, 1937–1940; founder-member of Kesatuan Melayu Muda (Union of Malay Youth), 1938; detained by the British, 1941; adviser on Malay customs and culture at the headquarters of Japanese military administration, Taiping (Perak); deputy president, Malay Nationalist Party, 1945, and president, 1946–1947; detained in connection with Hertogh riots (Singapore), 1950–1951; president of the PMIP (Pan Malayan Islamic Party, later Partai Islam Se Malaysia), 1956–1964; elected to house of representatives, 1960; led PMIP in opposition to the formation of Malaysia, 1962; disqualified from 1964 elections; detained during 'confrontation' with Indonesia, 1964–1966

Caine, Sydney, 1902–1991
KCMG 1947; Harrow County School and London School of Economics; assistant inspector of taxes, 1923–1926; entered CO, 1926; assistant secretary, 1940; member Anglo-American Caribbean Commission, 1942; financial adviser to S of S, 1944; deputy under-secretary of state, 1947; transferred to Treasury, 1948; head

of UK Treasury and Supply Delegation, Washington, 1949–1951; led World Bank Mission to Ceylon, 1951; vice chancellor, University of Malaya, 1952–1956; director, London School of Economics, 1957–1967

Chin Peng (real name Ong Boon Hua)
during the Japanese occupation was member of central executive committee MCP and secretary MCP in Perak, and member central military committee and leader fifth regiment MPAJA; liaised with Force 136; secretary general MCP, 1947; leader of MRLA (later MNLA and Malayan People's Army), 1948; attended Baling talks, Dec 1955; abandoned armed struggle, 1989

Churchill, Winston Leonard Spencer, 1874–1965
KG 1953; MP (Conservative) 1900–1904, (Liberal) 1904–1918, (Coalition Liberal) 1918–1922, (Constitutionalist) 1924–1931, (Conservative) 1931–1964; under-secretary of state, CO, 1906–1908; president of Board of Trade, 1908–1910; S of S for Home Affairs, 1910–1911; first lord of the Admiralty, 1911–1915; chancellor of the Duchy of Lancaster, 1915; minister of Munitions, 1917; S of S for War and Air, 1919, for Air and Colonies, 1921 and for Colonies, 1922; chancellor of the Exchequer, 1924–1929; first lord of the Admiralty, 1939; prime minister and minister of Defence, 1940–1945; leader of the Opposition, 1945–1951; prime minister, 1951–1955, and minister of Defence, 1951–1952

Cranborne, Viscount, see Salisbury, 5th Marquess of

Creech Jones, Arthur, 1891–1964
MP (Labour) 1935–1950 and 1954–1964; executive member, Fabian Society; member, CO Education Advisory Committee, 1936–1945; chairman, Fabian Colonial Bureau and Labour Party Imperial Advisory Committee; vice-chairman, Higher Education Commission to West Africa, 1943–1944; parliamentary private secretary to minister of Labour and National Service (E Bevin), 1940–1945; parliamentary under-secretary of state for colonies, 1945–1946; S of S for colonies, 1946–1950

Del Tufo, Morobe Vincenzo, 1901–1961
KBE 1952; Royal College, Colombo, and Trinity, Cambridge; MCS from 1923; interned by Japanese, 1942–1945; superintendent of census, Malaya, 1946–1948; deputy commissioner for labour, 1948; deputy chief secretary, 1949, and chief secretary, Federation of Malaya, 1950–1952; officer administering government, Oct 1951 – Feb 1952; Malayan delegate on International Tin Council, 1956

Dening, Maberly Esler, 1897–1977
KCMG 1950; entered consular service, 1920; appointed to FO, 1938; chief political adviser to SACSEA, 1943–1946; assistant under-secretary of state, 1946–1950; special mission to Asia, 1950–1951; UK political representative in Japan, 1951–1952; ambassador to Japan, 1952–1957

Eden, Robert Anthony (1st Earl of Avon cr 1961) 1897–1977
KG 1954; MP (Conservative) 1923–1957; parliamentary private secretary to S of S for foreign affairs, 1926–1929; parliamentary under-secretary of state for foreign affairs, 1931–1933; lord privy seal, 1934–1935; minister without portfolio for League of Nations affairs, 1935; S of S for foreign affairs, 1935–1938, for dominion affairs, 1939–1940, for war, 1940, for foreign affairs, 1940–1945; leader of House of Commons, 1942–1945; deputy leader of the Opposition, 1945–1951; S of S for foreign affairs and deputy prime minister, 1951–1955; prime minister, 1955–1957.

Gater, George Henry, 1886–1963
Kt 1936; Winchester and New College, Oxford; local government from 1912; CO permanent under-secretary of state, 1939–1947 (seconded to Ministry of Home Security and Ministry of Supply, 1940–1942)

Gent, Gerard Edward James, 1895–1948
KCMG 1946; King's School, Canterbury and Trinity College, Oxford; CO since 1920; assistant secretary to Indian Round Table Conference, 1930; assistant secretary and head of Eastern Department, CO, 1939–1942; assistant under-secretary of state and supervising Eastern Depart-

ment, 1942–1946; gov of Malayan Union, 1946–1948; high commissioner of Federation of Malaya, 1948; killed in air crash.

Gray, William Nicol, 1908–1988
Trinity College, Glenalmond; Royal Marines, 1939–1946; inspector-general, Palestine police, 1946–1948; commissioner of police, Federation of Malaya, 1948–1952; agent to the Jockey Club, Newmarket, 1953–1964.

Griffiths, James, 1890–1975
MP (Labour) from 1936; minister of national insurance, 1945–1950; S of S for colonies, 1950–1951; deputy leader and vice-chairman of the parliamentary Labour party, 1956–1959; S of S for Wales, 1964–1966

Gurney, Henry Lovell Goldsworthy, 1898–1951
Kt 1947; Winchester and University College, Oxford; served in Kenya, 1921–1935; Jamaica, 1935; CO 1935; East Africa, 1936–1944; colonial secretary, Gold Coast, 1944–1946; chief secretary, Palestine, 1946–1948; high commissioner, Federation of Malaya, 1948–1951; assassinated by Malayan communists

Hall, George Henry (1st Viscount cr 1946) 1881–1965
MP (Labour) 1922–1946; civil lord of Admiralty, 1929–1931; parliamentary under-secretary of state, CO, 1940–1942; financial secretary to Admiralty. 1942–1943; parliamentary under-secretary of state, FO, 1943–1945; S of S for the colonies, 1945–1946; first lord of Admiralty, 1946–1951; deputy leader, House of Lords, 1947–1951

Higham, John Drew, b 1914
Manchester Grammar School and Gonville and Caius, Cambridge; served in Admiralty, 1936–1946; transferred to CO, 1946; assistant secretary, 1948; head of Eastern (later SE Asian) Department, 1948–1953; seconded to Singapore as under-secretary, 1953–1955, and director of personnel, 1955–1957 (acted on various occasions as chief secretary); transferred to ministry of housing and local government, 1965; head of Development Control Division,

Department of the Environment, 1970–1974

Hogan, Michael Joseph Patrick, 1908–1986
Kt 1958; Belvedere, Stonyhurst and Trinity College, Dublin; solicitor and advocate, supreme court of Ireland; barrister-at-law, King's Inn, Dublin, and Inner Temple; chief magistrate, Palestine, 1936; crown counsel, 1937; attorney-general, Aden; 1945; solicitor-general, Palestine, 1947; attached to FO, 1949; solicitor-general, Malaya, 1950; attorney-general, Malaya, 1950–1955; acting high commissioner, Malaya, 1951; acting chief secretary, Malaya, 1954; chief justice, Hong Kong, 1955–1970, and Brunei, 1964–1970; member, Courts of Appeal of the Bahamas, Bermuda and Belize, 1970–1975, and Gibraltar, 1970–1984; president, Courts of Appeal of Brunei, 1970–1973, the Bahamas, 1975–1978, Bermuda and Belize, 1975–1979, and Seychelles, 1977–1984.

Home, Alexander Frederick Douglas – (Baron Home of Hirsel, life peer, cr 1974) b 1903
14th Earl of Home 1951–1963; Sir Alec Douglas Home 1963–1974; Eton and Christ Church, Oxford; MP (Conservative) 1931–1945, 1950–1951 and 1963–1974; parliamentary private secretary to prime minister, 1937–1940; joint parliamentary under-secretary of state, FO, 1945; minister of state, Scottish Office, 1951–1955; S of S for Commonwealth relations, 1955–1960; leader of House of Lords, 1957–1960; lord president of the Council, 1957 and 1959–1960; S of S for foreign affairs, 1960–1963; prime minister, 1963–1964; S of S for foreign and Commonwealth affairs, 1970–1974

Hone, Herbert Ralph, 1896–1992
KBE 1946; Varndean Grammar School, Brighton, and London University; barrister-at-law; legal service in E Africa, 1923–1933, and Gibraltar, 1933–1937; attorney-general, Uganda, 1937–1943; adviser, political branch of GHQ, Middle East, 1942–1943; major-general, 1942–1946; head of Malayan Planning Unit, 1943–1945; chief civil affairs officer,

Malaya, 1945–1946; secretary-general to gov gen, Malaya, 1946–1948; deputy commissioner general, SE Asia, 1948–1949; gov, North Borneo, 1949–1954; head of legal division, CRO, 1954–1961; resumed practice at the bar, 1961; constitutional adviser to various British dependencies in 1960s

Ishak bin Haji Mohamed, 1910–1991
Malay and English schools, Pahang, and Kuala Kangsar Malay College; Malay Administrative Service: Malay novelist; journalist on *Warta Negara* and *Utusan Melayu* in 1930s; founder-member of Kesatuan Melayu Muda (union of Malay youth), 1938; leader of PUTERA, 1947–1948; president, MNP, 1947–1948; detained, 1948 1953; chairman, Labour Party of Malaya, 1957–1958; detained during 'confrontation' with Indonesia

Ismail bin Dato Abdul Rahman, Dr Dato (later Tun), 1915–1973
Brother of Suleiman bin Dato Abdul Rahman; English College, Johore Bahru, and University of Melbourne; private medical practice in Johore Bahru, 1947–1953; member of Johore State Council, 1948–1954, and Johore Executive Council from 1954; member of Federal Legislative Council; member in Federal Executive Council for lands, mines and communications, 1953, and member for natural resources, 1954–1955; minister for natural resources, 1955; minister for commerce and industry, 1956–1957; minister plenipotentiary (without portfolio), delegate to UN and ambassador to Washington, 1957; minister for home affairs and deputy prime minister to Abdul Razak, 1970–1973

Johnston, John Baines, b 1918
KCMG 1966; Banbury Grammar School and Queen's College, Oxford; entered CO, 1947; assistant secretary, West African Council, Accra, 1950–1951; UK liaison officer, Commission for Technical Co-operation in Africa South of the Sahara, 1952; principal private secretary to S of S for the colonies, 1953–1956; assistant secretary and head of Far Eastern Department, CO, 1956; transferred to CRO,

1957; deputy high commissioner, South Africa, 1959–1961; British high commissioner, Sierra Leone, 1961–1963, Federation of Rhodesia and Nyasaland, 1963, Rhodesia, 1964–1965; assistant (later deputy) under-secretary of state, FCO, 1968–1971; British high commissioner, Malaysia, 1971–1974, and Canada, 1974–1978

Jones, Arthur Creech, see Creech Jones

Killearn, 1st Baron cr 1943 (Miles Wedderburn Lampson) 1880–1964
Eton; FO from 1903; first secretary, Peking, 1916; acting British high commissioner, Siberia, 1920; British minister, China, 1926–1933; high commissioner, Egypt and the Sudan, 1936–1946; special commissioner, SE Asia, 1946–1948

Lee, Henry Hau-Shik, Colonel (Colonel H S Lee, later Colonel Tun Sir Henry), 1901–1988
KBE 1957; Queen's College, Hong Kong, and St John's, Cambridge; tin mining since 1924; sole proprietor of H S Lee Tin Mines; chairman, China press Ltd; member, FMS Chamber of Mines Council, 1929–1955; president, Selangor Chinese Chamber of Commerce, 1946–1955; Miners Association of Negri Sembilan, Selangor and Pahang, 1938–1955; All-Malaya Chinese Mining Association, 1949–1956; Associated Chinese Chambers of Commerce, 1947–1955; Malayan delegate, international tin meetings, 1946–1960; Kuomintang leader in Selangor during 1930s; chief of Passive Defence Forces, KL, 1941; escaped to India in 1942 and became liaison officer between British and Chinese governments with the rank of colonel in the Chinese army; member, Selangor State Council and Malayan Union Advisory Council, 1946–1947; MU (later federal) finance committee, 1946–1956, chairman, 1956–1959; Federal Legislative and Executive Councils, 1948–1957; member, director of operations committee, 1948–1956; president, Selangor MCA, 1949–1956; co-founder of Alliance, 1952; member, Alliance executive committee and national council, 1953–1959; member for transport, 1953–

1955; minister of transport, 1955; minister of finance, 1956–1959; member of Alliance delegation to constitutional conference, 1956, and financial talks, 1957

Lennox-Boyd, Alan Tindal (1st Viscount Boyd of Merton cr 1960) 1904–1983
MP (Conservative) 1931–1960; parliamentary secretary, Ministry of Labour, 1938–1939, Ministry of Home Security, 1939, Ministry of Aircraft Production, 1943–1945; minister of state, CO, 1951–1952; minister of transport and civil aviation, 1952–1954; S of S for colonies, 1954–1959

Leong Yew Koh (later Tun Leong Yew Koh)
Anglo-Chinese School, Ipoh, St Xavier's Institute, Penang, and University of London; tin-mining business and legal practice in Ipoh (Perak); a leader of Chinese Chambers of Commerce and active in Kuomintang, Malaya; returned to China where he served as an administrator in Yunan, 1932–1942; served in Chinese 25th army with rank of major-general, 1942–1945; after Second World War he resumed his legal practice in Ipoh; member of the Consultative Committee on Constitutional Proposals for Malaya (Cheeseman Committee), 1947; member, Federal Legislative Council, 1948–1957; founder member and first secretary-general of MCA, 1949; escaped assassination attempt; member, Alliance Round-table and the special committee of the Alliance National Convention, 1953; minister for health, 1955–1957; gov of Malacca, 1957

Lloyd, Thomas Ingram Kynaston, 1896–1968
KCMG 1947; Rossall and Gonville and Caius, Cambridge; CO from 1921 (from Ministry of Health); secretary, Palestine Commission, 1929–1930; secretary, West India Royal Commission, 1938–1939; CO assistant secretary from 1939; assistant under-secretary of state from 1943; head of Eastern Department, 1946–1947; permanent under-secretary of state, 1947–1956

Lyttelton, Oliver (1st Viscount Chandos cr 1954) 1893–1972
KG 1954; company director; MP (Con-

servative) 1940–1954; president of Board of Trade, 1940–1941; minister of state in War Cabinet, 1941–1942; minister of production, 1942–1945; president of Board of Trade and minister of production, 1945; chairman, Associated Electrical Industries Ltd, 1945–1951; S of S for colonies, 1951–1954; chairman, AEI Ltd, 1954–1963

MacDonald, Malcolm John, 1901–1981
OM 1969; son of James Ramsay MacDonald, prime minister, 1924, 1929–1931 and 1931–1935; MP (Labour) 1929–1931, (National Labour) 1931–1935, (National Government) 1936–1945; parliamentary under-secretary of state for dominions, 1931–1935; S of S for dominions, 1935–1938 and 1938–1939; S of S for colonies, 1935 and 1938–1940; minister of health, 1940; high commissioner, Canada, 1941–1946; gov-gen, Malaya, 1946–1948; commissioner-general, SE Asia, 1948–1955; chancellor, University of Malaya, 1949–1961; high commissioner, India, 1955–1960; co-chairman, International Conference on Laos, 1961–1963; gov, Kenya, 1963; gov gen, Kenya, 1963–1964; British high commissioner, Kenya, 1964–1965; British special representative in East and Central Africa, 1963–1966; special envoy to Sudan and Somalia, 1967

MacGillivray, Donald Charles, 1906–1966
KCMG 1953; Sherborne and Queen's, Oxford; entered Colonial Administrative Service, 1928; served in Tanganyika, 1929–1938, and Palestine, 1938–1947; colonial secretary, Jamaica, 1947–1952; deputy high commissioner, Malaya, 1952–1954; high commissioner, Malaya, 1954–1957; retired to Kenya; vice chairman, commission on the Federation of Rhodesia and Nyasaland (Monckton Commission), 1960

MacKintosh, Angus MacKay, 1915–1986
Fettes, Edinburgh University and University College, Oxford; CO from 1946; principal private secretary to S of S, 1950–1952; assistant secretary, 1952; head of SE Asian Department, 1953–1956; seconded to FO as deputy commissioner general, SE Asia, 1956–1960; seconded to Cabinet Office, 1960–1963; high commissioner, Brunei, 1963–1964; transferred to Minis-

try of Defence; assistant under-secretary of state 1965–1966; senior civilian instructor, Imperial Defence College, 1966–1968; assistant under-secretary of state, FCO, 1968–1969; high commissioner, Ceylon/Sri Lanka, 1969–1973

MacMichael, Harold Alfred, 1882–1969
KCMG 1932; King's Lynn and Bedford Schools and Magdalene, Cambridge; Sudan Civil Service from 1905; civil secretary and periodically acting gov gen, 1926–1933; gov, Tanganyika, 1933–1937; high commissioner, Palestine and Trans-Jordan, 1938–1944; special representative of HMG, Malaya, 1945; constitutional commissioner, Malta, 1946

Macmillan, Maurice Harold (1st Earl of Stockton cr 1984) 1894–1986
MP (Conservative) 1924–1929, 1931–1964; parliamentary secretary, Ministry of Supply, 1940–1942; parliamentary under-secretary of state for colonies, 1942; minister resident, Allied HQ in NW Africa, 1942–1945; secretary for air, 1945; minister of housing and local government, 1951–1954; minister of defence, 1954–1955; S of S for foreign affairs, 1955; chancellor of the Exchequer, 1955–1957; prime minister, 1957–1963

Macpherson, John Stuart, 1898–1971
KCMG 1945; Watson's College, Edinburgh, and Edinburgh University; Malayan Civil Service, 1921–1937; seconded to CO, 1933–1935; Nigeria, 1937–1939; chief secretary, Palestine, 1939–1943; head of British colonies supply mission in Washington and member of Anglo-American Caribbean Commission, 1943–1945; comptroller for development and welfare in West Indies and British co-chairman of Caribbean Commission, 1945–1948; gov, Nigeria, 1948–1954; gov-gen, Federation of Nigeria, 1954–1955; chairman, UN visiting mission to trust territories in Pacific; permanent under-secretary of state, CO, 1956–1959

Martin, John Miller, 1904–1991
KCMG 1952; Edinburgh Academy and Corpus, Oxford; entered DO, 1927; seconded to MCS, 1931–1934; secretary,

Palestine Royal Commission, 1936; private secretary to prime minister, 1940–1945 (principal private secretary, 1941–1945); assistant under-secretary of state, 1945, supervising Far Eastern Department, CO, 1954–1956; deputy under-secretary of state, 1956–1965; high commissioner, Malta, 1965–1967

Monson, William Bonnar Leslie, 1912–1993
KCMG, 1965; Edinburgh Academy and Hertford, Oxford; entered DO, 1935; transferred to CO, 1939; principal, Eastern Department, 1939–1944; assistant secretary, 1944; seconded as chief secretary to West African Council, 1947–1951; assistant under-secretary of state, CO, 1951; high commissioner, Zambia, 1964–1966; deputy under-secretary Commonwealth (later Foreign and Commonwealth) Office, 1967–1972

Mountbatten, Louis Francis Albert Victor Nicholas (Lord Louis, 1st Viscount of Burma cr 1946, 1st Earl of Burma cr 1947) 1900–1979
Royal Navy since 1916; chief of combined operations, 1942; supreme allied commander in SE Asia, 1943–1946; viceroy of India, 1947; gov-gen, India, 1947–1948; returned to active naval service, 1948; first sea lord and chief of Naval Staff, 1955–1959; admiral of the fleet, 1956; chief of Defence Staff and chairman of Chiefs of Staff Committee, 1959–1965; assassinated by Provisional IRA

Mustapha Albakri, Haji (later Dato)
Anderson School, Ipoh, and Malay College, Kuala Kangsar; joined Malay Administrative Service, 1924; served in different parts of FMS in various capacities but mostly as magistrate; promoted to MCS, 1935; DO in Lower Perak during Japanese occupation; administrator in Kinta district (Perak) during BMA; seconded to Perak police to organise recruitment of special constabulary; state secretary (later acting mentri besar), Perak, 1949–1951; keeper of rulers' seal and secretary to conference of rulers, 1951; Federal Legislative Council, 1952; member for industrial and social relations, 1953; promoted to staff A rank in MCS, the highest rank

yet achieved by any Asian official, 1954; re-appointed keeper of rulers' seal, 1956; represented rulers at the defence treaty talks in KL and London, 1956–1957; after retirement in Aug 1957 he was appointed chairman, Elections Commission

Newboult, Alexander Theodore, 1896–1964
KBE 1948; Oakham and Kingswood Schools and Exeter, Oxford; MCS since 1920; under secretary, FMS, 1940; colonial secretary, Fiji, 1942; officer administering government, Fiji, 1943; Malayan Planning Unit, 1943–1945; deputy chief civil affairs officer (with rank of brigadier), Malaya, 1945–1946; accompanied MacMichael on mission to Malay rulers, 1945; chief secretary, Malayan Union, 1945–1946; chief secretary, Federation of Malaya, 1948–1950; officer administering government, Malaya, July-Oct 1948

Nik Ahmed Kamil bin Nik Mahmood, Dato (Dato Stia Raja Kelantan, later Tan Sri) 1909–1977
Majlis Ugama School, Kota Bahru, Malay College, Kuala Kangsar, University of Bristol and Lincoln's Inn, London; entered service of Kelantan government, 1931; state secretary, 1934; deputy mentri besar, 1938; was the mainstay of state administration during the Japanese/Thai occupation and the Allies' principal contact in Kelantan; witnessed his sultan's signature to the MacMichael treaty, 1945; founder-member of UMNO, 1946; rulers' representative on the Constitutional Working Committee, 1946–1947; deputy resident commissioner, Kelantan, 1947–1948; mentri besar, Kelantan, 1948–53; member of Federal Legislative Council, 1948–55; member for lands, mines and communications, 1953; member for local government, housing and town planning, 1953–1955; stood as Party Negara candidate in federal elections, 1955; one of the rulers' representatives at the London constitutional talks, 1956; Malayan high commissioner in Australia, 1956–1957, and UK, 1957–1958; ambassador to Washington, 1959; speaker of Dewan Raayat, 1974; a prominent Malaysian businessman

Ong Yoke Lin (later Tan Sri Omar Ong Yoke Lin)

Victoria Institute, KL; businessman; leading member of MCA, Selangor and instrumental in forming electoral pact with UMNO, Feb 1952; secretary-general, MCA; member of the Alliance Roundtable and special committee of the Alliance National Convention, 1953; minister of posts and telecommunications, 1955; minister for transport, 1955–1957; president of MCA Selangor; 1956; minister of labour and social welfare, 1957

Onn bin Jaafar, Dato, 1895–1962

KBE 1953; grandfather, father and two elder brothers were mentri besar of Johore; adopted son of Sultan Ibrahim; Malay school, Johore Bahru, Aldeburgh Lodge, Suffolk, and Malay College, Kuala Kangsar; entered service of Johore government; fell out with Sultan Ibrahim and exiled to Singapore where he edited *Warta Malaya*, 1930–1933, *Lembaga Malaya*, 1934–1936, and *Lembaga*; reconciled with sultan and became unofficial member of Johore Council of State, 1936–1941, and of Johore Executive Council; private secretary to regent of Johore, 1938; information and publicity officer, Johore, during Malayan campaign, 1941–1942; during Japanese occupation he was food controller and later DO, Batu Pahat; mentri besar, Johore, 1946–1950; founder-president of Pergerakan Melayu Semanjong Johore (Johore movement of peninsular Malays), 1946, and of UMNO, 1946; member of the Constitutional Working Committee, 1946–1947; Federal Legislative Council, 1948–1955; Federal Executive Council, 1948–1955, and member for home affairs; member of the Communities Liaison Committee, 1949–1950; chairman of RIDA, 1950; left UMNO to form the IMP, 1951; formed Party Negara, 1954; elected to federal parliament as sole Party Negara member, 1959

Paskin, Jesse John, 1892–1972

KCMG 1954; King Edward's, Stourbridge, and St John's, Cambridge; transferred from Ministry of Transport to CO, 1921; assistant secretary, 1939; principal private secretary to S of S for colonies, 1939–1940; head of Eastern Department, CO, 1942–1947; assistant under-secretary of state supervising Eastern/SE Asian Department, CO, 1948–54

Poynton, Arthur Hilton, b 1905

KCMG 1949; Marlborough and Brasenose, Oxford; CO from 1929; private secretary to minister of supply (Lord Beaverbrook) and minister of production (Oliver Lyttelton), 1941–1943; reverted to CO, 1943; deputy under-secretary of state, 1948–1959; permanent under-secretary of state, CO, 1959–1966

Purcell, Victor William Williams Saunders, 1896–1965

Bancroft's School and Trinity, Cambridge; MCS from 1921; protector of Chinese and director-general of information, 1940; lectured in USA for Ministry of Information, 1941; Malayan Planning Unit; principal adviser on Chinese Affairs, BMA, with rank of colonel, 1945–1946; consultant, ECAFE, 1947; university lecturer in Far Eastern History, Cambridge, 1949

Raja Uda, see Uda bin Raja Muhammad

Rees-Williams, David Rees (1st Baron Ogmore cr 1950) 1903–1976

Member, Straits Settlements Bar, 1930–1934; practised law in Cardiff, 1934–1939; MP (Labour) 1945 1950; member, government mission to Sarawak, 1946; chairman, Burma Frontier Areas Committee of Inquiry, 1947; parliamentary under-secretary of state, CO, 1947–1950; parliamentary under-secretary of state, CRO, 1950–1951; minister of civil aviation, June–Oct 1951

Reid, Baron (life peer) cr 1948 (James Scott Cumberland Reid) 1890–1975

Admitted to Scots Bar, 1914; MP (Conservative) 1931–1935 and 1937–1948; solicitor-general for Scotland, 1936–1941; lord advocate, 1941–1945; lord of appeal in ordinary, 1948–1975; chairman, Federation of Malaya Constitutional Commission, 1956–1957

Roberts-Wray, Kenneth Owen, 1899–1983
KCMG 1949; Royal Military Academy, Woolwich, and Merton, Oxford; called to the Bar, 1924; professional legal clerk, Ministry of Health, 1926; assistant chief clerk, 1929; second assistant legal adviser, DO and CO, 1931; assistant legal adviser, CO, 1943; legal adviser, CO, 1945–1960

Salisbury, 5th Marquess of, 1947 (Robert Arthur James Gascoyne Cecil) 1893–1972
Viscount Cranborne 1942; MP (Conservative) 1929–1941; parliamentary under-secretary of state, FO, 1935–1938; paymaster general, 1940; S of S for dominion affairs, 1940–1942 and 1943–1945; S of S for colonies, 1942; lord privy seal, 1942–1943; leader of House of Lords, 1942–1945 and 1957; S of S for Commonwealth relations, 1952; lord president of the Council, 1952–1957; resigned over Conservative colonial policy

Sambanthan, V T (later Tun Sambanthan)
Clifford School, Kuala Kangsar, and Annamalai University, S India; took up planting; president of MIC, 1954–1973; elected to Federal Legislative Council, 1955; minister for labour, 1955–1957; member of Alliance delegation to London constitutional talks, 1956; at various times after independence held the posts of minister of works, posts and telecommunications, minister of labour and minister of health

Sardon bin Haji Jubir (later Tun)
Malay school, Raffles Institution, Singapore, and London, 1937–1941; practised law in Malaya and Singapore; attended inaugural conference of the Malay Nationalist Party, Nov 1945; president, Kesatuan Melayu Singapura, 1947–1951; elected member of Singapore Legislative Council, 1948–1951; president, UMNO Youth, 1951, later a vice-president of UMNO; Johore State Council, 1952; Federal Legislative Council from 1954; minister for works, 1955–1957; acting president of UMNO during the absence of Tunku Abdul Rahman at London talks, Jan–Feb 1956; minister of works, posts and telecommunications, 1957, and member of Alliance government until 1972; later was appointed gov of Penang

Scott, Robert Heatlie, 1905–1982
KCMG 1954; Queen's Royal College, Trinidad, and New College, Oxford; entered consular service in China, 1927; served in Peking, Shanghai, Canton, Hong Kong, Singapore; Ministry of Information and member of governor's War Council, Singapore, 1941–1942; interned by the Japanese, 1942–1945; on staff of the UK special commissioner SE Asia (Lord Killearn), 1946; entered FO, 1948 (attached to the Imperial Defence College); head of SE Asia Department, 1948; assistant under-secretary with responsibility for Far Eastern affairs, 1950; minister, Washington Embassy, 1953; commissioner-general SE Asia, 1955–1959; commandant, Imperial Defence College, 1960; permanent secretary, Ministry of Defence, 1961–1963

Spencer, Oscar Alan, 1913–1993
Mayfield College, Sussex, and London School of Economics; Colonial Service from 1945; economic adviser and development commissioner, British Guiana, 1945–1950; economic secretary, Malaya, 1950; member for economic affairs, Malaya, 1951; minister for economic affairs, Malaya, 1955; economic adviser and head of Economic Secretariat, Malaya, 1956–1960; chairman, Central Electricity Board, Malaya, 1952–1960; adviser to Malayan delegation, London constitutional and financial conferences, 1956 and 1957; joined UN Technical Assistance Service, 1960, and advised the governments of Sudan, Ethiopia, and Seychelles; retired 1983

Stanley, Oliver Frederick George, 1896–1950
MP (Conservative) 1924–1950; parliamentary under-secretary of state, Home Office, 1931–1933; minister of transport, 1933–1934; minister of labour, 1934–1935; president of Board of Education, 1935–1937; president of Board of Trade, 1937–1940; S of S for war, 1940; S of S for the colonies, 1942–1945

Sterndale Bennett, Sir John, see Bennett

Strachey, Evelyn John St Loe, 1901–1963
MP (Labour) 1929–1931; resigned from

the parliamentary Labour Party, 1931; MP (Labour) 1945–1963; parliamentary under-secretary of state for air, 1945–1946; minister of food, 1946–1950; S of S for war, 1950–1951

Suleiman bin Dato Abdul Rahman, Dato
Brother of Ismail bin Abdul Rahman; Bukit Zaharah English School, Johore Bahru, Johore English College, Raffles Institute, Singapore, and Queens', Cambridge; joined Johore legal service, 1939; registrar, Johore, during Japanese occupation; magistrate, Batu Pahat, 1945–1947; private legal practice, 1947; Johore State Council from 1949; joined UMNO, 1951; elected to Federal Legislative Council, 1955; minister for local government, housing and town planning, 1955; acting chief minister during Tunku Abdul Rahman's absence in London for constitutional talks; minister of interior and justice, 1957

Tan Cheng Lock (Dato Sir Cheng-lock Tan, later Tun Dato Tan Cheng Lock), 1883–1960
KBE 1952; father of Tan Siew Sin; Malacca High School and Raffles Institution; built up large proprietary rubber business; from c.1915 was a leading member of the Straits Born Chinese Association; served in the Legislative and Executive Councils of the Straits Settlements, 1920s and 1930s; spent the period of the Japanese occupation in India where he formed the Overseas Chinese Association; leader of the AMCJA movement against the federation, 1946–1948; founder-member and president of MCA, 1949–1958; member, Communities Liaison Committee, 1949–1950; founder-member, IMP, 1951; active in formation of Alliance from 1952

Tan Siew Sin (later Tun Tan Siew Sin)
Malacca High School and Raffles College, Singapore; businessman particularly in rubber; spent Japanese occupation in India; Federal Legislative Council from 1948 and member of its standing committee on finance, 1949–1955; member of MCA and played leading part in formation of MCA-UMNO Alliance from 1952; member of the federal elections committee, 1954; minister of commerce and industry, subse-quently finance, 1957–1974; president of MCA, 1961

Tan Tong Hye (T H Tan, later Tan Sri T H Tan)
St Joseph's Institute and Raffles College, Singapore; journalist with successively *Malaya Tribune, Straits Times*, 1936, and *Singapore Standard*, 1952; founder-member of MCA, 1949, and chief executive secretary, 1952; secretary-general, Alliance from 1953; accompanied Tunku Abdul Rahman on mission to London, 1954; co-secretary to the federal delegation to London constitutional talks, 1956; president, Associated Chinese Chambers of Commerce

Templer, Gerald Walter Robert, 1898–1979
KBE 1949; Wellington and Royal Military College, Sandhurst; joined the Royal Irish Fusiliers, 1916; active military service in First World War, Middle East in interwar years, and Second World War; director, Military Government 21 Army Group (Germany), 1945–1946; director, Military Intelligence, War Office, 1946–1948; vice-chief, Imperial General Staff, 1948–1951; GOC-in-C, Eastern Command, 1950–1952; high commissioner and director of operations, Malaya, 1952–1954; CIGS, 1955–1958; field-marshal, 1956

Thuraisingham, Ernest Emmanuel Clough, Dato (Dato Sir Clough Thuraisingham)
Thomas College, Colombo, and Selwyn, Cambridge; practised law in Singapore; 1927–1934; managed family rubber estates in Johore and Perak, 1934–1941; founder-member of Malayan Estates Owners Association; member of Malayan Union Advisory Council, 1946, also of Selangor State Council and Selangor Executive Council; Federal Legislative Council from 1948; president of the Ceylon Federation of Malaya; Communities Liaison Committee, 1949–1950; member for education, 1951–1955; founder-member of IMP, 1951, and Party Negara, 1954; retired from politics, 1955

Uda bin Raja Muhammad, Raja (Raja Uda, later Raja Tun Uda)
KBE 1953; Malay College, Kuala Kangsar;

joined government service, 1910; Malay Administrative Service, 1914; promoted to MCS, 1924; secretary to the British Resident, Selangor, 1939 (the first Malay to hold such an appointment); Selangor State Council and Federal Council before Japanese occupation; state secretary, Selangor, 1948; mentri besar, Selangor, 1949–1953; commissioner for Malaya in UK, 1953–1954; mentri besar, Selangor, 1954–1955; speaker of Federal Legislative Council, 1955–1957; gov of Penang, 1957

Watherston, David Charles, 1907–1977
KBE 1956; Westminster and Christ Church, Oxford; entered MCS, 1930; seconded to CO, 1939–1944; member, MPU, 1944–1945; British Military Administration, Malaya, 1945–1946; secretary of constitutional working committee which negotiated the Federation of Malaya Agreement, 1946–1948; secretary for defence and internal security, Malaya, 1948; chief secretary, 1952–1957, and administered the government of Malaya on occasions; special counsellor, Malayan High Commission in the UK, 1957–1959; member, Commission of Enquiry, North Borneo and Sarawak (Cobbold Commission), 1962

Willan, Harold Curwen, 1896–1971
Kt 1947; Kendal School and Jesus, Oxford; entered MCS, 1920; deputy legal adviser, FMS, 1934; solicitor-general, Kenya, 1937; attorney-general, Zanzibar, 1940; legal adviser, Civil Affairs, East Africa Command, and acting chief political officer, 1941; president of the high court, Ethiopia, 1942; member of the MPU, 1943–1945; deputy chief civil affairs officer, Malay peninsula, with rank of brigadier, 1945–1946; chief justice, Malayan Union, 1946–1948, and Federation of Malaya, 1948–1950; chief justice, UK Territories in S Africa, 1952–1956

Bibliography 1: Public Record Office sources searched

The documents reproduced in this collection constitute only a minute proportion of the official records which relate to Malaya in the period 1942-1957. The following classes were searched in arriving at the preceding selection. It should not be assumed that all files in the runs listed below are actually available for consultation.

1. *Cabinet*

   (i) *Cabinet committees*
      War Cabinet Committees
         Far East: CAB 96/1–6 (1940–1945)
         Malaya and Borneo: CAB 98/41 (1944–1945)
      General series from 1945:
         Malayan operations: CAB 130/65 (1950–1951)
         Committee on Malaya: CAB 130/74 (1952)
         South East Asia: CAB 130/101 (1954)
         Commissioner-General: CAB 130/109 (1955)
         Committee on Eastern Asia: CAB 130/118 (1956)
         Expenditure in Eastern Asia: CAB 130/122 (1957)
         Malaya Committee: CAB 134/497 (1950–1951)
         Development in S & SE Asia: CAB 134/866 (1952)
         Far East (Official) Committee: CAB 134/897–898 (1952–1953)
         Mutual Aid (Official) Committee: CAB 134/1051 (1955)
         Colonial Policy Committee: CAB 134/1201–1203 (1955–1956)

  (ii) *Cabinet Office*
      War Cabinet conclusions (minutes): CAB 65/17–67 (1941–1945)
      War Cabinet memoranda: CAB 66/14–67 (1941–1945)
      Cabinet conclusions from 1945: CAB 128/1–31 (to 1957)
      Cabinet memoranda from 1945: CAB 129/1–88 (to 1957)
      Cabinet Office registered files: CAB 21/1369, 1681, 1682, 1714, 1954, 1955, 1957, 1958, 2510, 2559, 2883
      Official histories: CAB 101/69

2. *Chiefs of Staff Committee*

The following papers shed light on the strategic defence aspects of ending British rule in Malaya:

DEFE 4/99, 100 (1957)
DEFE 5/78 (1957)
DEFE 7/493–496, 501 (1955–1957)

3. Colonial Office

(i)   *CO original correspondence, 1942–1957: geographical classes*
Straits Settlements: CO 273/669–680 (1942–1946)
Federated Malay States: CO 717/149–204 (1946–1951)
Eastern: CO 825/35–90 (1942–1951)
South-East Asia: CO 1022/1–494 (1951–1953)
Far East: CO 1030/1–411 (1954–1956)
          CO 1030/412–851 (1957)

(ii) *CO original correspondence, etc, 1942–1957: subject classes*
Colonies supplementary ['secret']: CO 537
This is the most important subject class for the period 1946–1951. The CO
537 lists are arranged in years and by country and by subject but, since
the indexes are not comprehensive, a thorough search is recommended.
The most important files in this series of SE Asia are as follows:
CO 537/1526–1670 for 1946
CO 537/2138–2210 for 1947
CO 537/3655–4253 for 1948
CO 537/4740–4873 for 1949
CO 537/5955–6103 for 1950
CO 537/7245–7353 for 1951

(iii) Federation of Malaya Constitutional Commission, 1956: CO 889/1–9

(iv) Minutes of the Working Party on the Constitution of the Federation of
Malaya, 1957: CO 941/85

(v)   Other relevant subject classes are CO 852 (Economic); CO 865 (Far Eastern
Reconstruction); CO 875 (Public relations); CO 877 (Personnel); CO 967
(Private Office); CO 968 (Defence); CO 1032 (Colonies general).

4. Commonwealth Relations Office

DO original correspondence: DO 35
This extensive series becomes useful as Malaya advances towards independence and Commonwealth membership. The file runs for the period 1953–
1957 are DO 35/6258–6300.

5. *Foreign Office*

FO general correspondence, political: FO 371
The papers specifically consulted in this extensive and important series were those of the Far Eastern and (from 1951 onwards) SE Asian departments, notably:
FO 375/69695 (1948)
FO 371/77570 (1948–1949)
FO 371/76049 (1949)
FO 371/84478 (1950)
FO 371/93005–93119 (1951)
FO 371/101223–101231 (1952)
FO 371/106950–107015 (1953)
FO 371/111852–111861, 111915–111919 (1954)
FO 371/116913–116915, 116939–116945, 116962 116971 (1955)
FO 371/123210–123213, 123254–123264 (1956)
FO 371/129336–129344, 129362, 129366 (1957)

6. *Prime Minister's Office*

Correspondence and papers, 1945–1957: PREM 8/189, 459, 1126, 1171, 1406, 1407
Correspondence and papers, 1951–1957: PREM 11/121, 122, 404, 639, 645, 647, 649–651, 873–875, 878, 1302, 1726F, 1925–1930, 2298

7. *Treasury*

The most relevant runs of files on Malaya are to be found in T 220 (Imperial and foreign division), especially T220/52, 85–87, 134, 160, 186, 233, 234, 281–285, 493.

8. *War Office*

Three series have a particularly significant bearing on Malayan affairs: WO 203 (War of 1939 to 1945: military headquarters papers, Far East [SEAC]); WO 216 (Chief of the imperial general staff); and WO 220 (Directorate of civil affairs papers).

Note: the holdings of the Arkib Negara Malaysia (National Archives of Malaysia), which include papers of the British Military Administration (1945–1946), Malayan Union Secretariat (1946–1948) and the Federal Secretariat (from 1948), have not been searched for the purposes of this collection.

Bibliography 2: Official publications, unpublished private papers, published documents and secondary sources

1. *Official publications*

   (a) *United Kingdom*
   Parliamentary Debates (Hansard), 1942–1957
   Malayan Union and Singapore: Statement of Policy on Future Constitution Cmd 6724, 1946
   Report on a Mission to Malaya by Sir Harold MacMichael GCMG, DSO October 1945–January 1946, Col 194, 1946
   Malayan Union and Singaore: Summary of Proposed Constitutional Arrangements Cmd 6749, 1946
   Federation of Malaya: Summary of Revised Constitutional Proposals Cmd 7171, 1947
   British Dependencies in the Far East: 1945–1949 Cmd 7709, 1949
   Report of the Federation of Malaya Constitutional Conference held in London in January and February 1956 Cmd 9714, 1956
   Report of the Federation of Malaya Constitutional Commission (chairman, Lord Reid) Col 330, 1957
   Constitutional Proposals for the Federation of Malaya Cmnd 210, 1957
   Proposed Agreement on External Defence and Mutual Assistance between the Government of the United Kingdom of Great Britain and Northern Ireland and the Government of the Federation of Malaya Cmnd 263, 1957

   (b) *Malaya*
   Report on the British Military Administration of Malaya, September 1945 to March 1946 (by Major-General H R Hone) 1946
   Malayan Union Advisory Council Proceedings, 1946–1948
   Constitutional Proposals for Malaya: Report of the Working Committee Appointed by a Conference of His Excellency the Governor of the Malayan Union, Their Highnesses the Rulers of the Malay States and Representatives of the United Malays National Organization, 1946
   Constitutional Proposals for Malaya: Report of the Consultative Committee Together with Proceedings of Six Public Meetings, a Summary of Representations Made and Letters and Memoranda Considered by the Committee (chairman, H R Cheeseman) 1947
   Constitutional Proposals for Malaya: Second Report of the Working Committee Appointed by a Conference of His Excellency the Governor of the Malayan Union, Their Highnesses the Rulers of the Malay States and Representatives

of the United Malays National Organization, 24 April 1947, 1947

Proceedings of the Federal Legislative Council, 1948–1957

Labour and Trade Union Organization in the Federation of Malaya and Singapore (by S S Awbery and F W Dalley) Col 234, 1948

Report of the Police Mission to Malaya (chairman, Sir Alexander Maxwell) 1950

Report of the Committee on Malay Education (chairman, L J Barnes) 1951

Chinese Schools and the Education of Chinese Malayans. The Report of a Mission Invited by the Federation Government to Study the Problem of the Education of the Chinese in Malaya (by W P Fenn and Wu Teh-yao) 1951

Establishment Organization and Supervision of Local Authorities in the Federation of Malaya (by H Bedale) 1953

Report of the Committee Appointed to Examine the Question of Elections to the Federal Legislative Council (chairman, M J Hogan) 1954

Report of the Committee on the Malayanization of the Government Service (chairman, D C Watherston) 1954

Educational Policy: Statement of Federal Government on the Report of the Special Committee on the Implementation of Educational Policy Together with the Report of that Committee, 1954

Report of the Constituency Delineation Commission (chairman, Lord Merthyr) 1954

Report of the Mission of Enquiry into the Rubber Industry of Malaya (chairman, Sir Francis Mudie) 1954

Report of the First Election of Members to the Legislative Council of the Federation of Malaya (by T E Smith) 1955

2.   *Unpublished collections of private papers in the UK*

(a) *Institute of Commonwealth Studies, London*
Sir Ivor Jennings

(b) *National Army Museum, London*
Sir Gerald Templer

(c) *Royal Commonwealth Society, Cambridge*
British Association of Malaysia

(d) *Rhodes House Library, Oxford*
R Heussler   Mss Brit Emp S 480
Sir Ralph Hone   Mss Ind Ocn S 271
Sir Harold MacMichael Mss Brit Emp S 421

(e) *University of Durham*
M MacDonald

The Arkib Negara Malaysia (National Archives of Malaysia) and the Institute of South East Asian Studies, Singapore, hold important collections, notably: Tan Cheng Lock (ANM and ISEAS) and the United Malays National Organisation (ANM).

3. *Published selections of documents*

J de V Allen, A J Stockwell & L R Wright, eds, *A collection of treaties and other documents affecting the states of Malaysia 1761–1963* 2 volumes (London, Rome, New York, 1981)

D Goldsworthy, ed, BDEEP series A, vol 3, *The Conservative government and the end of empire 1951–1957* in 3 parts (London, 1994)

R Hyam, ed, BDEEP series A, vol 2, *The Labour government and the end of empire 1945–1951* in 4 parts (London, 1992)

A N Porter & A J Stockwell, eds, *British imperial policy and decolonization, 1938–64* vol I *1938–51*, vol II *1951–64* (London, 1987 & 1989)

R Rathbone, ed, BDEEP series B, vol 1, *Ghana*, in 2 parts (London, 1992)

4. *Select list of published books*

Tunku Abdul Rahman, *Looking back, Monday musings and memories* (Kuala Lumpur, 1977)

J de V Allen, *The Malayan Union* (New Haven, Conn, 1967)

R Ampalavanar, *The Indian minority and political change in Malaya 1945–1957* (Kuala Lumpur, 1981)

D Anderson & D Killingray, eds, *Policing and decolonization: politics, nationalism and the police* (Manchester, 1992)

A Boestamam (translated by W R Roff), *Carving the path to the summit* (Athens, Ohio, 1979)

Lord Chandos (Oliver Lyttelton), *The memoirs of Lord Chandos* (London, 1962)

Cheah Boon Kheng, *Red star over Malaya: resistance and social conflict during and after the Japanese occupation, 1941–1946* (Singapore, 1983)

Chin Kee Onn, *Malaya upside down* (Singapore, 1946)

Chin Kin Wah, *The defence of Malaysia and Singapore: the transformation of a security system, 1957–1971* (Cambridge, 1983)

J Cloake, *Templer tiger of Malaya: the life of Field Marshal Sir Gerald Templer* (London, 1985)

C Cruickshank, *SOE in the Far East* (Oxford, 1983)

P Darby, *British defence policy east of Suez, 1947–1968* (London, 1973)

J Darwin, *Britain and decolonisation: the retreat from empire in the post-war world* (London, 1988)

P Dennis, *Troubled days of peace: Mountbatten and South East Asia Command, 1945–46* (Manchester, 1987)

F S V Donnison, *British military administration in the Far East* (London, 1956)

N J Funston, *Malay politics in Malaysia: a study of the United Malays National Organisation and Party Islam* (Kuala Lumpur, 1980)

D Goldsworthy, *Colonial issues in British politics, 1945–1961* (Oxford, 1971)

Heng Pek Koon, *Chinese politics in Malaysia: a history of the Malaysian Chinese Association* (Singapore, 1988)

R Heussler, *Completing a stewardship: the Malayan Civil Service, 1942–1957* (Westport, Conn, 1983)

R F Holland, *European decolonization, 1918–1981* (London, 1985)

R F Holland, ed, *Emergencies and disorder in the European empires after 1945* (London, 1994)

A Lau, *The Malayan Union controversy 1942–1948* (Singapore, 1991)

J M Lee, *Colonial development and good government: a study of the ideas expressed by the British official classes in planning decolonization, 1939–1964* (Oxford, 1967)

J M Lee & M E Petter, *The Colonial Office, war and development policy: organization and the planning of a metropolitan initiative* (London, 1982)

W R Louis, *Imperialism at bay 1941–1946: the United States and the decolonization of the British empire* (Oxford, 1977)

A McCoy, ed, *Southeast Asia under Japanese occupation. Transition and transformation* (New Haven, Conn, 1980)

G Means, *Malaysian politics* (London, 1970)

H Miller, *Menace in Malaya* (London, 1954)

H Miller, *Prince and premier: a biography of Tunku Abdul Rahman Putra al-Haj first prime minister of the Federation of Malaya* (London, 1959)

A Milner, *The invention of politics in colonial Malaya* (Cambridge, 1995)

T R Mockaitis, *British counterinsurgency, 1919–60* (London, 1990)

Mohamed Noordin Sopiee, *From Malayan Union to Singapore separation* (Kuala Lumpur, 1957)

J V Morais, *The leaders of Malaya and who's who, 1957–1958* (Kuala Lumpur, nd [1958])

D J Morgan, *The official history of colonial development* 5 vols (London, 1980)

V Purcell, *Malaya: communist or free?* (London, 1954)

K J Ratnam, *Communalism and the political process in Malaya* (Kuala Lumpur, 1965)

W R Roff, *The origins of Malay nationalism* (New Haven, Conn, 1967)

W Shaw, *Tun Razak: his life and times* (Kuala Lumpur, 1976)

A Short, *The communist insurrection in Malaya 1948–1960* (London, 1975)

R B Smith & A J Stockwell, eds, *British policy and the transfer of power in Asia: documentary perspectives* (London, 1988)

M R Stenson, *Industrial conflict in Malaya: prelude to the communist revolt of 1948* (Kuala Lumpur, 1948)

A J Stockwell, *British policy and Malay politics during the Malayan Union experiment 1942–1948* (Kuala Lumpur, 1979)

R Stubbs, *Hearts and minds in guerrilla warfare: the Malayan emergency 1948–1960* (Singapore, 1989)

Tan Sri Mohamed Suffian bin Hashim, *An introduction to the constitution of Malaysia* (Kuala Lumpur, 1972)

C Thorne, *Allies of a kind: the United States, Britain and the war against Japan, 1941–1945* (Oxford, 1978)

R K Vasil, *Politics in a plural society: a study of non-communal political parties in West Malaysia* (Kuala Lumpur, 1971)

5. *Select list of published articles*

S R Ashton, 'The India office and the Malayan Union: the problem of the Indian princes and its possible relevance towards the Malay rulers, 1943–1946' in R B Smith & A J Stockwell, eds, *British policy and the transfer of power in Asia* (London, 1988), pp 126–143

M Caldwell, 'From "emergency" to "independence", 1948–57' in Mohamed Amin

& M Caldwell, eds, *Malaya: the making of neo-colony* (Nottingham, 1977), pp 216–265

J Darwin, 'British decolonization since 1945: a pattern or a puzzle?' *Journal of Imperial and Commonwealth History* vol 12 (1984) pp 187–209

D Goldsworthy, 'Keeping change within bounds: aspects of colonial policy during the Churchill and Eden governments, 1951–1957' *Journal of Imperial and Commonwealth History* vol 18 (1990) pp 81–108

T N Harper, 'The politics of disease and disorder in post-war Malaya' *Journal of Southeast Asian Studies* vol 21 (1990) pp 88–113

Ishak bin Tadin, 'Dato Onn and Malay nationalism, 1946–1951' *Journal of Southeast Asian History* vol 1 (1960) pp 56–88

P Kratoska, 'The post 1945 food shortage in British Malaya' *Journal of Southeast Asian Studies* vol 19 (1988) pp 27–47

A K H Lau, 'The Colonial Office and the emergence of the Malayan Union policy 1942–1943' in R B Smith & A J Stockwell, eds, *British policy and the transfer of power in Asia* (London, 1988) pp 95–125

Lee Kam Hing, 'Malaya: new state and old elites' in Robin Jeffrey, ed, *Asia: the winning of independence* (London, 1981) pp 213–257

Mohamed Noordin Sopiee, 'The Penang secession movement 1948–51' *Journal of Southeast Asia Studies* vol 4 (1973) pp 52–71

M Rudner, 'Rubber strategy for post-war Malaya, 1945–8' *Journal of Southeast Asian Studies* vol 1 (1970) pp 23–36

M Rudner, 'The draft development plan for the Federation of Malaya 1950–55' *Journal of Southeast Asian Studies* vol 3 (1972) pp 63–96

M Rudner, 'Financial policies in post-war Malaya: the fiscal and monetary measures of liberation and reconstruction' *Journal of Imperial and Commonwealth History* vol 3 (1975) pp 323–348

M Rudner, 'Malayan rubber policy: development and anti-development during the 1950s' *Journal of Southeast Asian Studies* vol 7 (1976) pp 235–259

C R Schenk, 'The origins of a central bank in Malaya and the transition to independence, 1954–59' *Journal of Imperial and Commonwealth History* vol 21 (1993) pp 409–431

R B Smith, 'Some contrasts between Burma and Malaya in British policy in South-East Asia, 1942–1946' in R B Smith & A J Stockwell, eds, *British policy and the transfer of power in Asia* (London, 1988), pp 126–143

S C Smith, 'The rise, decline and survival of the Malay rulers during the colonial period, 1874–1957' *Journal of Imperial and Commonwealth History* vol 22 (1994) pp 84–108

Soh Eng Lim, 'Tan Cheng Lock. His leadership of the Malayan Chinese' *Journal of Southeast Asian History* vol 1 (1960) pp 29–55

A J Stockwell, 'Colonial planning during World War II: the case of Malaya' *Journal of Imperial and Commonwealth History* vol 2 (1974) pp 333–351

A J Stockwell, 'British imperial policy and decolonization in Malaya' *Journal of Imperial and Commonwealth History* vol 13 (1984) pp 68–87

A J Stockwell, 'The approach to a possible "transfer of power" series on Malaysia and Singapore' in R B Smith & A J Stockwell, eds, *British policy and the transfer of power in Asia* (London, 1988) pp 77–94

A J Stockwell, 'Counterinsurgency and colonial defence' in A Gorst, L Johnman

& W S Lucas, eds, *Post-war Britain, 1945–64: themes and perspectives* (London, 1989) pp 135–154

A J Stockwell, 'Policing during the Malayan emergency, 1948–60: communism, communalism and decolonisation' in D Anderson & D Killingray, eds, *Policing and decolonisation. Politics, nationalism and the police, 1917–65* (Manchester, 1992) pp 105–126

A J Stockwell, ' "A widespread and long-concocted plot to overthrow government in Malaya"? The origins of the Malayan emergency' in R Holland, ed, *Emergencies and disorder in the European empires after 1945* (London, 1994) pp 66–88

N Tarling, ' "Some rather nebulous capacity": Lord Killearn's appointment in Southeast Asia' *Modern Asian Studies* vol 20 (1986) pp 559–600

K G Tregonning 'Tan Cheng Lock: a Malayan nationalist' *Journal of Southeast Asian Studies* vol 10 (1979) pp 25–76

C M Turnbull, 'British planning for post-war Malaya' *Journal of Southeast Asian Studies* vol 5 (1974) pp 239–254

N J White, 'Government and business divided: Malaya, 1945–57' *Journal of Imperial and Commonwealth History* vol 22 (1994) pp 251–274

Index of Main Subjects and Persons: Parts I–III

This is a consolidated index for all three parts of the volume. It is not a comprehensive index, but a simplified and straightforward index to document numbers, together with page references to the Introduction in part I, the latter being given at the beginning of the entry in lower case roman numerals. The index is designed to be used in conjunction with the summary lists of the preliminary pages to each part of the volume. A preceding asterisk indicates inclusion in the Biographical Notes at the end of Part III. Where necessary (eg particularly in long documents), and if possible, paragraph or section numbers are given inside round brackets. In the case of a British official or minister (such as Lennox-Boyd, Malcolm MacDonald and Templer), who appears prominently in the volume, the index indicates the first and last documents of his period of office. Further references to his contribution can be identified from the summary lists.

The following abbreviations are used:

A — appendix or annex (thus 257 A I = first appendix to document 257)
E — enclosure
N — editor's link note (before main text of document)
n — footnote.

Documents are divided between the three parts of the volume as follows:

nos   1–138   part I
nos 139–303   part II
nos 304–467   part III.

450